AF576586

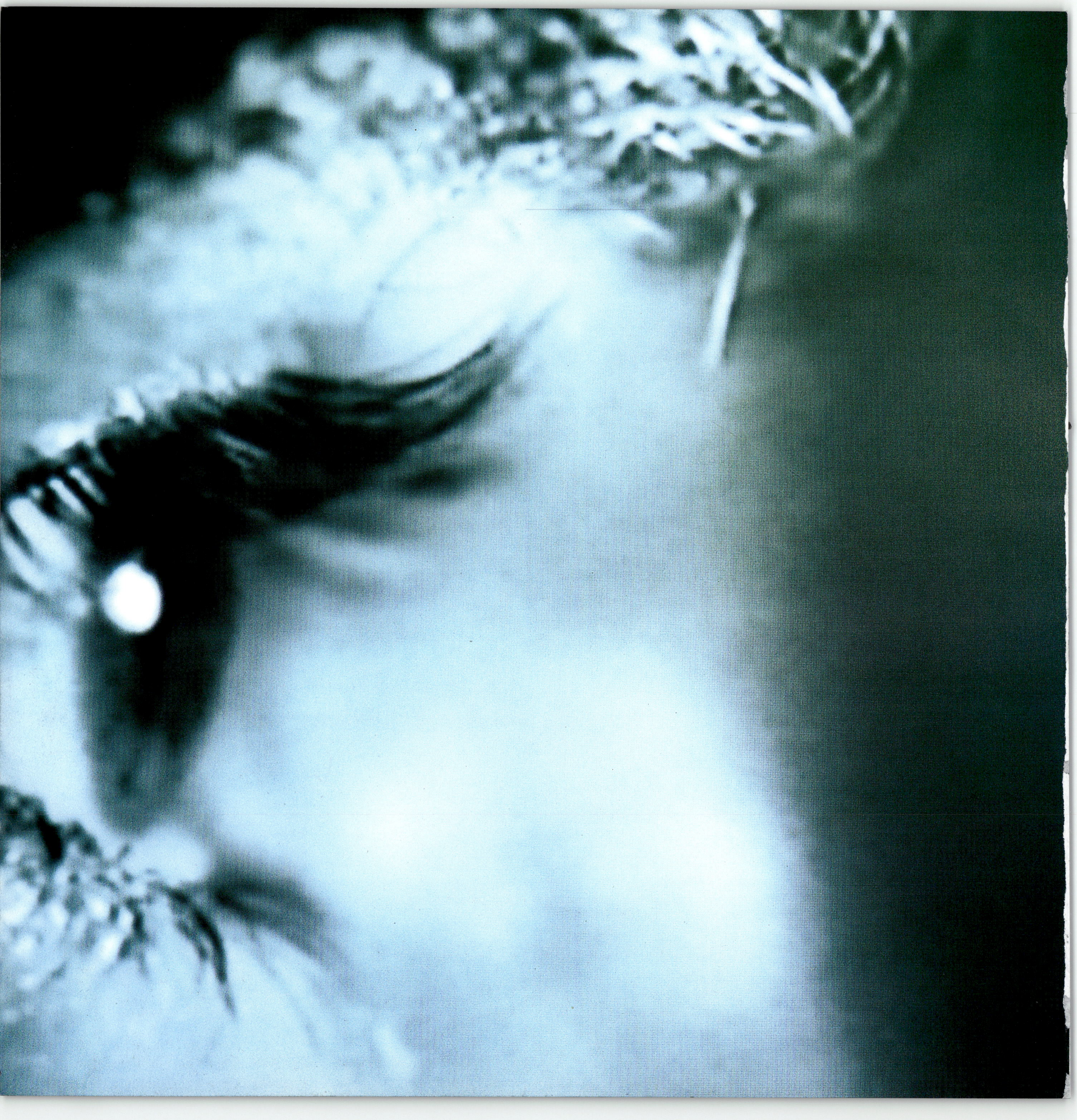

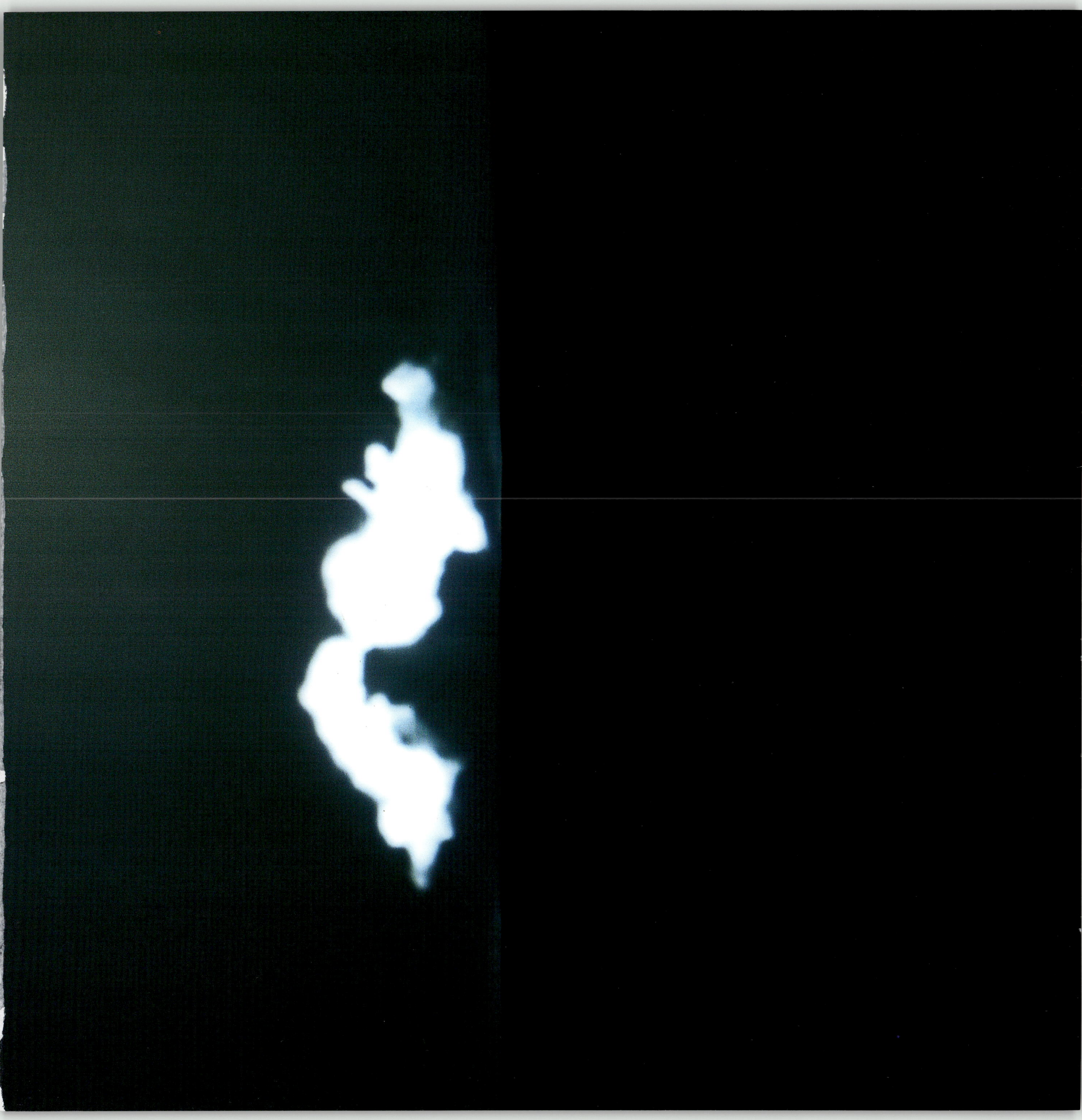

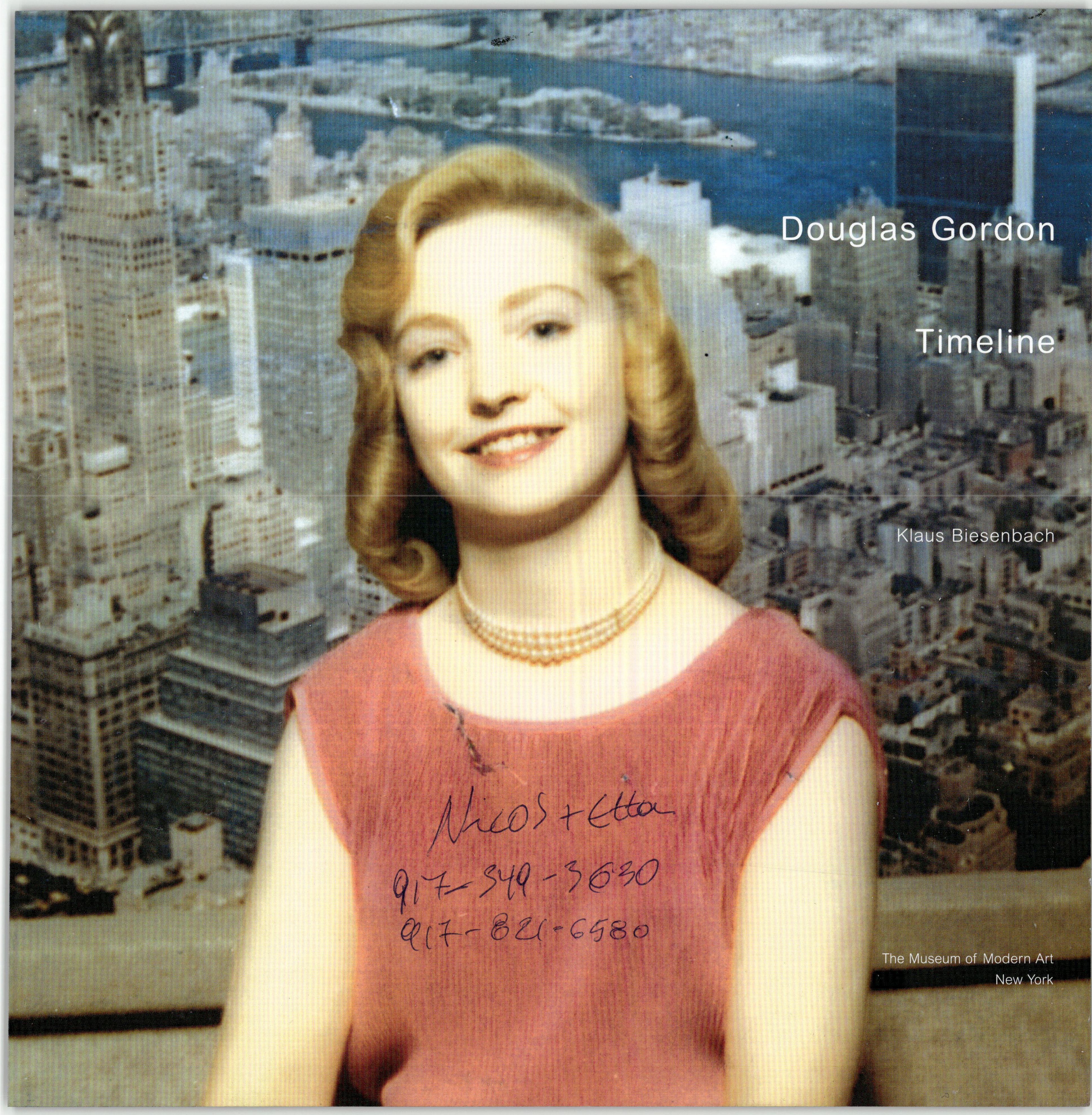

Douglas Gordon

Timeline

Klaus Biesenbach

The Museum of Modern Art
New York

Letter (Number 9). 1992
Letter and wall text in Bembo typeface, dimensions variable
Goetz Collection, Munich

I remember more than you know.

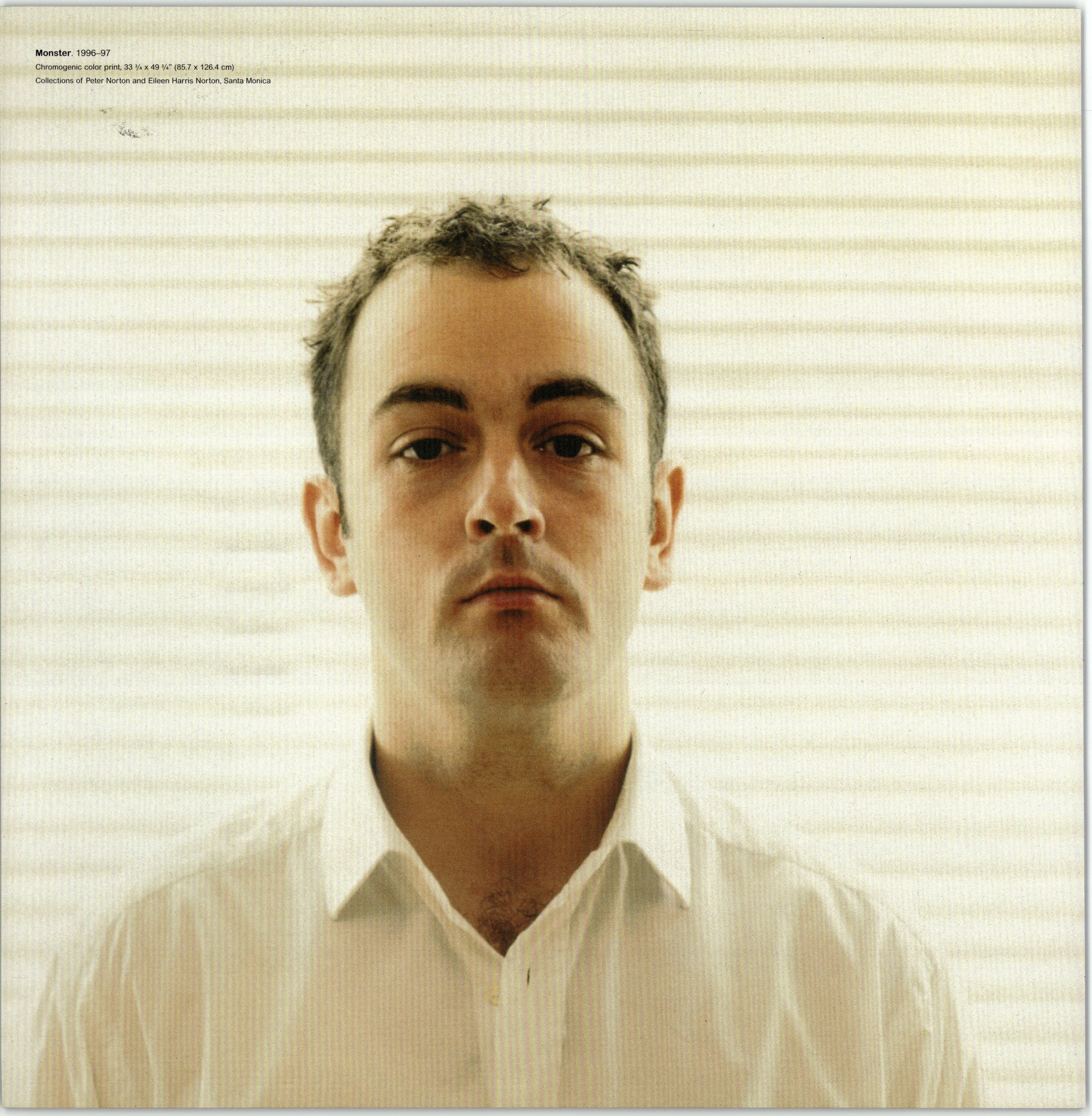

Monster. 1996–97
Chromogenic color print, 33 ¾ x 49 ¾" (85.7 x 126.4 cm)
Collections of Peter Norton and Eileen Harris Norton, Santa Monica

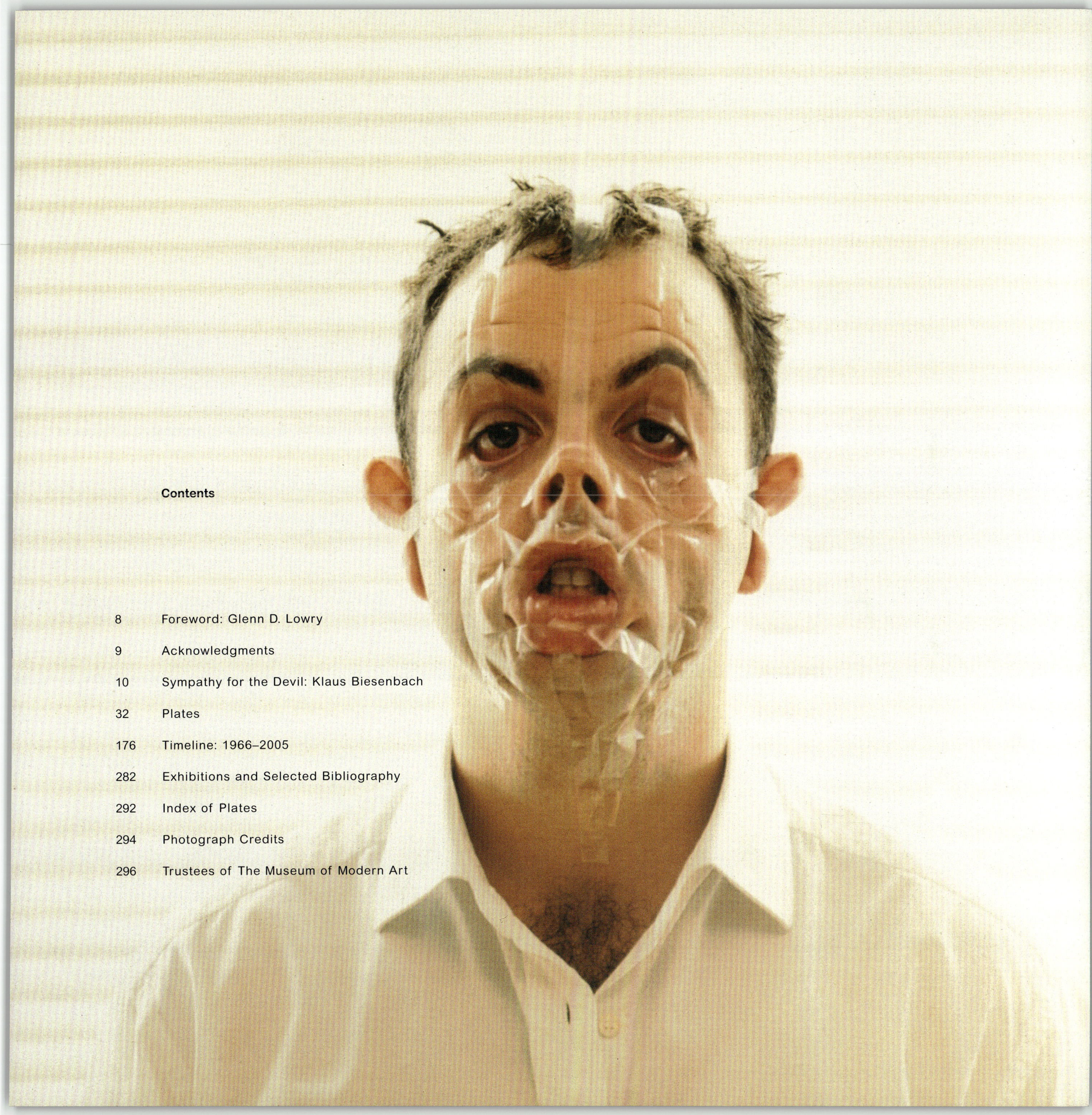

Contents

Foreword

The exhibition *Douglas Gordon: Timeline* was initiated with the great enthusiasm of Mary Lea Bandy, Chief Curator in the Department of Film and Media. Douglas Gordon's intelligent and innovative art and practice have earned him international acclaim, and it is a great pleasure to present his mid-career retrospective. The Department of Film and Media at The Museum of Modern Art has gracefully undertaken the challenge of acknowledging the important role of new approaches in artistic practice and, in focusing on Douglas Gordon, has selected one of the foremost artists of this genre in the world.

This exhibition emphasizes the growing role of moving pictures in contemporary art production. The nature of Gordon's monumental works requires the commitment of a significant amount of gallery space, and his work experimentally and poetically connects the subject and matter of his work—movies and film—with the contemplative experience of being a museum visitor.

I would like to express my gratitude to The Contemporary Arts Council of The Museum of Modern Art for their generosity in making this publication possible. I am thankful as well for the generosity of Richard J. Massey, Celeste and Adam Bartos, Sid Bass, Drue Heinz, Marlene Heiss, and Michael Ovitz, whose generous donations have enabled the Museum to acquire Gordon's work for our collection.

I wish to thank Klaus Biesenbach, Curator in the Department of Film and Media, who worked closely with the artist on the organization of the exhibition and publication. The exhibition is accompanied by a catalogue, the result of a collaboration between the artist and the Museum's team, that thoughtfully balances an insightful discussion of Douglas Gordon's art, a suite of stunning images of the artist's work, and a timeline of historic images derived from the forty years of Gordon's lifetime and representing a form of collective memory.

Finally, we are most grateful to Douglas Gordon for this exciting exhibition and publication; his enthusiasm and generosity have been integral to the success of this project.

Glenn D. Lowry
Director
The Museum of Modern Art

Acknowledgments

It has been a great pleasure to work with the excellent and committed people at The Museum of Modern Art who have contributed tremendously to this exhibition and publication. I would like to extend my sincere gratitude to Glenn D. Lowry, Director, for his exceptional guidance and support of this project.

This exhibition has provided the opportunity to work closely with several esteemed colleagues in the Department of Film and Media. I would like to thank Mary Lea Bandy, Chief Curator, for her integral and inspirational role in this exhibition from its inception. Without her strong enthusiasm and initiative this exhibition would have not been possible. I would also like to acknowledge and thank Steven Higgins, Interim Chief Curator; Larry Kardish, Senior Curator; Jytte Jensen, Curator; Barbara London, Associate Curator; Sally Berger, Assistant Curator; Anne Morra, Assistant Curator; Josh Siegel, Assistant Curator; Natalie Hirniak, Department Manager; Jenny He, Research Assistant; and Leigh Goldstein, Executive Assistant, for all of their support. I also appreciate the extraordinary efforts of Cara Starke, Curatorial Assistant, who made significant contributions to the organization of the exhibition and catalogue, and the skillful research of Jenny Schlenzka.

The organization of this exhibition would not have been possible without the contributions of a team of committed individuals. Very warm thanks to Jennifer Russell, Senior Deputy Director for Exhibitions, Collections, and Programs, for her decisiveness and open-minded guidance; Peter Reed, Senior Deputy Director for Curatorial Affairs, for his generous help; and Mike Margitich, Senior Deputy Director of External Affairs, for directing the efforts to build a strong group of supporters for this exhibition. The success of this exhibition was greatly dependent on the talents of James Gara, Chief Operating Officer; Katy McDonald, Director of Government and Community Relations; Jay Levenson, International Program Director; Ramona Bannayan, Director of Collection Management and Exhibition Registration; Sydney Briggs, Associate Registrar; and Randolph Black, Associate Coordinator of Exhibitions. It has also been a great pleasure to work with David Little, Director of Adult and Academic Programs; Ruth Kaplan, Deputy Director of Marketing and Communications; Kim Mitchell, Director of Communications; Todd Bishop, Director of Exhibition Funding; Mary Hannah, Assistant Director of Exhibition Funding; Paul Power, Senior Film and Media Publicist; Bonnie Ralston, Senior Graphic Designer; and Claire Corey, Production Manager of Graphic Design. For their thoughtfulness and sophisticated guidance, special thanks to Stephen Clark, Deputy General Counsel, and Nancy Adelson, Associate General Counsel. I am also grateful to Jerry Neuner, Director of Exhibition Design and Production; David Hollely, Production Manager; and Charlie Kalinowski, Media Services Manager, for their excellence in helping to realize the design and installation of the exhibition.

In the Department of Publications, Christopher Hudson, Publisher, has generously provided his thoughtful direction and support for this exhibition catalogue. My gratitude extends to David Frankel, Managing Editor; Emily Hall, Associate Editor; and Krystyna Kobylinski, Intern, for their meticulous editorial skills and enthusiasm for the project, as well as to Marc Sapir, Production Director, for his attention to detail and supervision of this catalogue's production, and to Pascale Willi for her creative design. I would also like to thank The Contemporary Arts Council of The Museum of Modern Art for their support of this publication.

Outside of the museum, I would like to thank Ealan Wingate, Kara Vander Weg, Bert Ross, and Gary Rough for their contributions to the exhibition, and P.S.1 Director Alanna Heiss, who supported me as a colleague in my decision-making. It also has been a great pleasure to have the generous support of Getty Images for this exhibition catalogue, and I would like to thank Eileen Flanagan, Director of Archive Sales, for her enthusiasm for the artist's vision and passion for the project.

Douglas Gordon's work has been the basis of exceptionally fruitful discourse among curators, so my acknowledgments also go to fellow curators Charles Esche, Hans Ulrich Obrist, Nancy Spector, and Philip Monk. It is truly rewarding to have the opportunity to collaborate with Douglas Gordon, and I would like to offer my most sincere thanks and gratitude for his ideas, time, and generosity of spirit. This book is dedicated to the artist's son, James Gray Gaskell Gordon.

Klaus Biesenbach
Curator
Department of Film and Media

Klaus Biesenbach

Sympathy for the Devil

In the mid-1960s, Marshall McLuhan predicted that the first generation to grow up with the mass media would change the world.[1] Perhaps it is true that the children who grew up with an overdose of news, television, pop music, and movies mimicked what they were immersed in; certainly media images have long since become reality's mirror—the images that make people do what they do, eat what they eat, wear what they wear. The iPod provides every situation with a variety of sound tracks; cellular phones, particularly those with integrated digital cameras, make everyone a potential live reporter. Photographic pictures can be made anytime and anywhere and can be distributed almost simultaneously. The pace of video games caters to short attention spans, and the digital video recorder TiVo frees us from the television schedule. The Internet has changed how we search for potential partners, objects to buy, and information that would traditionally be found in libraries and archives. To me, the digital animation of an Xbox 360 looks as real as the image on a high-definition television looks artificial.

Because the insurmountable multiplicity of media—magazines, movies, television channels, and news—leads to an overload of information, there are only a few songs, people, and events that can possibly be internalized by the public. These images and narratives become a unifying experience shared among contemporaries. Not just the content but the form of media images has an effect on how we see the world and move in it; everyday life is now lived, shaped, and recorded as though it were a movie, music video, or song. It seems more than appropriate that the artists who grew up in the generation that McLuhan anticipated use music, television, and film as the materials and object of their artistic practice.

This catalogue, published on the occasion of the exhibition *Douglas Gordon: Timeline* at The Museum of Modern Art in 2006, contains two different timelines describing the last forty years. The first is a biographical timeline of Gordon as a person and an artist, and as mid-career retrospectives do, features a selection of works created from the beginning of his career to the present. The second timeline is a chronological collage of images, of both individuals and events, that have played a memorable part in the visual mass media world of the last forty years, which also happens to be Gordon's present lifetime. These images have been seen all over the world, collapsing time and space, here and now, everywhere, anytime, blending seduction and influence, imagination and memory, fiction and document. Showing these images, no matter how grim, must be understood as a responsibility.

Together the timelines form a collection of single pictures and image sequences dealing with the idea of visual memory. In Gordon's oeuvre, our visual memories are informed by both real and fictional events, by the interwoven texture of imagined and recollected plots, and by what we remember contrasted with what actually happened. Gordon's work takes as its point of departure how we perceive, or used to perceive, different media as well as memories, and makes of perception's oppositions—memory and imagination, interpretation and description, wishful thinking and denial, experience and ignorance—a complex picture of the world as a collection of images that are private and historical and personal and collective in their origin. Many of his works draw on the discrepancy between viewers' immediate perception of the works in the exhibition space and the associations, memories, and ideas that the work triggers in their minds; within this framework, Gordon sculpts time into a physical experience.[2]

1. For a lengthy explanation of McLuhan's ideas about the impact of new media on the TV generation see "Marshall McLuhan: A Candid Conversation with the High Priest of Popcult and Metaphysician of Media," in *Essential McLuhan*, ed. Eric McLuhan and Frank Zingrone (New York: Basic Books, 1996), 233–69.

2. Russell Ferguson, describing this relationship between Gordon and our memories of real and fictional events, writes, "Gordon succeeds in entrapping his audience in the space between his own life and the work of art. He is able to use an unambiguously autobiographical strategy that at the same time taps into a widely shared set of cultural references. The all but inevitable associations that his audience has . . . become integral to the reception of the piece, creating a shared frame of reference that is at the same time intimately specific to Gordon himself." Russell Ferguson,"Trust Me," in *Douglas Gordon* (Cambridge, Mass.: The MIT Press, 2001), 21.

The average life expectancy in Western nations is nearly eighty years.[3] The age of forty, which Gordon will reach in 2006, could therefore be an axis on a timeline, an occasion for a person to look back over the first half of his life, from the earliest oceanic feelings in utero to the clearer memories of his impressionable childhood years and adolescence, and think about what has influenced his view of the world. He could ask himself what he remembers from those forty years and do some research into what actually happened and into those events he cannot remember. The results may tend toward bad news—images of assassinations, catastrophes, wars, earthquakes, floods, airplane crashes—or toward high-profile cultural events, such as sports and media sensations, or personal memories, or significant pop songs. The memories of people in a certain age group would almost certainly contain the faces of Mother Teresa, Nelson Mandela, and Michael Jackson; the images from Bhopal, Chernobyl, and the Asian tsunami of 2004 will not be forgotten by those who were alive when those catastrophes happened. (But are the memories accurate? Or, compared to "real" images, are they modified, faded, idealized, exaggerated?) Then there would be the private and crucial experiences of the first day of school, the summer holidays, the illnesses and deaths of family members, the first kiss, and the loss, finally, of virginity. What would be recalled is a collage of the personal and the historical.

Something between my mouth and your ear (1994), one of Gordon's early works, features a playlist of the songs that his mother was likely to have heard while she was pregnant with him. Scientific research has proven that a fetus reacts to the sounds it is exposed to through the womb's protective barrier, so it could be true that Gordon would have absorbed these works if his mother had happened to hear them.[4] But for this person delving into his memories, trying to recall his very first one, it would be difficult to know whether he was remembering an actual experience, a reconstructed fragment, or the memory of trying to remember something at some point in the past.

1966

Sometime during the holiday season of 1965, Douglas Gordon was conceived by Mary and James Gordon in Glasgow, Scotland. The mid-1960s was a period during which the paradigms of contemporary art and culture were shifting, but these shifts did not much concern Mary. She had traveled to New York the year before her son's birth, and although the Jehovah's Witnesses Watchtower in Brooklyn was visible from downtown Manhattan, she was not interested in that either. Not yet, at least. There is a photograph of Mary at the Empire State Building, taken during that trip (p. 3). The year before, Andy Warhol had shot *Empire* (1964), an eight-hour 16mm film about that building, at the time the tallest structure in the city; Warhol described his film as "an eight-hour hard-on. It's so beautiful. The lights come on and the stars come out . . ."[5]

Several significant events from his childhood are included in a short biography of the artist written by "a friend" and published in the catalogue for a 2000 exhibition.[6] Douglas Gordon was born on September 20, 1966, at Redlands Hospital in Glasgow. He was the first of four children. Although he was born on the 20th of September, his mother went into labor on the 19th; Douglas was born after an excruciating twenty-four-hour labor, during which his mother actually died for a short period of time and was resuscitated by doctors. Six years later, Mary experienced another type of rebirth when she left the Protestant Church of Scotland to become a Jehovah's Witness, a sect that believes Satan is everywhere, tempting us to sin, but faith in God and adherence to strict religious practices will bring salvation. As a child, Douglas accompanied his mother preaching door to door and gave Bible readings at her congregation.

The text continues, telling us that as a teenager Douglas develops a fondness for art. He is interested in stuffed birds, as was the character of Norman Bates in *Psycho* (1960), but depicts them only in drawings rather than engaging in taxidermy. He also likes to draw rotting vegetables. In 1983 and 1984, he works the late shift in a supermarket. After work he returns home, where everyone is already asleep, and turns the television to Channel 4, the only station broadcasting at that time of night. It is then, watching Channel 4, that Douglas

3. See the Organisation for Economic Co-operation and Development, http://www.oecd.org.

4. See B. S. Kisilevsky et al., "Maturation of fetal responses to music," in ***Developmental Science*** 7, no. 5 (November 2004): 550–59.

5. Victor Bockris, ***Warhol: The Biography, 75th Anniversary Edition*** (Cambridge, Mass.: Da Capo Press, 2003), 207.

6. "A Short Biography—by a friend," in ***Douglas Gordon • black spot***; ed. Mark Francis (London: Tate Publishing, 2000), 361–68.

is first exposed to filmmakers like Jean-Luc Godard, François Truffaut, and Eric Rohmer, as well as B movies and films noir by Nicholas Ray, Rudolph Maté, and Otto Preminger. His high school English teacher recommends art school instead of university, but Douglas is not convinced—he thinks he might like to be a writer, or an architect. His art teachers promise to bring him books about artists who might interest him but who are not included in the curriculum of his conservative high school.

The biography recounts the events of a particular night, which begins with Douglas at his supermarket job, stacking Coke cans and juice cartons. On this particular night, as he walks home with six others, a stranger calls out, asking the score of that evening's football match between the Rangers and the Celtics. Before he goes to bed, Douglas listens to the radio, hoping to hear some information about a Smiths concert he wants to attend. Instead, the radio reports that "some trouble" occurred after the evening's football match; two fans of one team threw a supporter of the opposing team out of a train window. The next morning at school, everyone is talking about the incident, and everyone knows who was involved. Douglas goes straight to his art class; the room is silent until the door opens and a staff member asks someone in the class to go to the headmaster's office, where the police are waiting. It's one of the boys responsible for "some trouble." The art teacher, upset by these events, walks over to Douglas and hands him the two promised books, which are about Marcel Duchamp and Warhol.

Douglas attends art school in Glasgow from 1984 to 1988 and has his first solo show in 1986. He then moves to London and studies at the Slade School of Art from 1988 to 1990. After London, he returns to Glasgow and becomes involved in the artist-run Transmission Gallery, where local artists and internationally known artists such as Lawrence Weiner exhibit their work and discuss art and art-making.

Simultaneities

I am sixty-four days older than Douglas Gordon, so we share similar timelines. When I was a child, the German colloquialism for television was *Flimmerkiste*, or "flicker box." The adults worried about how close we sat to that box, and that we might eventually crawl right into it. They warned us that sitting so close to the television set would harm our eyesight or give us cancer.

In Germany in the 1960s, '70s, and '80s, the topic of history, and in particular German history, was a taboo subject. For many adolescents, television became a source of information, unearthing the darkened past in small doses; by accumulating these details, we began to understand what it meant to come from a country that had committed the worst possible crimes against humanity, crimes that were evil and should never happen again. Children begin to consider the question of evil when they reach a certain maturity and independence of thought, when they start to question their parents' and society's religious beliefs and ethics. It is a question, however, that German-born individuals of my era could not consider; it seemed not a question but a truth that we were evil. The omniscient media, showing us images from our own past, confirmed our roles in history.

But history continued. The bloc system, which divided capitalist from socialist, West from East, was one of the dichotomies that most strongly imprinted on those of us who grew up in the 1980s. Germany was literally divided by this duality; it was built in concrete in the Berlin Wall. People in the former East Germany and East Berlin did not have access to the advances of technology; there wasn't even a real phone network, since the telephone was considered an uncontrollable means of communication in that thoroughly spied-upon country. The first portable telecommunication device—the car satellite phone, with its hardware stored in the trunk of a car (it needed that much room) and a "handy" headset in the front of the car—was unaffordable; those phones, also available in a suitcase, cost about $5,000. When a landline network was finally established in the early 1990s and faxes became a viable option, handwritten letters quickly became anachronistic. Within a very short time, mobile phones became more affordable and the Internet introduced an easy way to relay messages and text, but because I had moved to East Berlin in the winter of 1989–90, undergoing a temporary disconnection from the rest of the world, these developments seemed very abrupt indeed.

When in 1992 I first received Gordon's strange and alienating text pieces, which he sent through the mail, they seemed to me to be especially appropriate: disturbing, intriguing, ephemeral. But since I thought that the disturbance—the communicated information and not the actual object—was the art, I threw the letters away. One letter delivered the instructions "Close your eyes, open your mouth" (p. 114); it seemed to describe the tension between devotion and aggression, between a spiritual expectation and the arrival of some effect, either sensorial, physical, or symbolic. Like many of Gordon's textual works, the meaning varies depending on the reader's imagination and predisposition. It could be a sadistic command, the initiation of a more or less benevolent torture; it could, on the other hand, be preparation for gentle lovemaking. It could be a passionate plea to stop passively observing and speak out, or the leap of faith made by the recipient of Holy Communion or of recreational drugs.

The other letter I received, which read, "From the moment you read these words until you meet someone with green eyes," contains its own deadline: one reads the sentence and projects into the future a span of time, a moment of conscious recognition, and a final relief, completing the cycle set into motion by the text. It seems, like so much media, to be an instruction delivered from above.

13

Douglas Gordon lives on the thirteenth floor of a New York apartment building, but his apartment number is 14D because the thirteenth floor is routinely eliminated from the world of numbers in apartment buildings and hotels. The elimination of the thirteenth floor could come as something of a relief to a person who finds numbers too powerful or threatening, who thinks they bring good or bad fortune or have some meaning beyond whatever it is that's being counted: three musketeers, seven deadly sins, seven samurai, twelve people on a jury, twelve monkeys. This person may take airplanes only on certain days or shop in seemingly meaningful units, buying three or five or seven yogurts or apples rather than four or six or eight (seven frequently seems to be a lucky number). This person may turn the key in the lock three times before leaving his house—as effective a tool for good fortune as picking the right combination of numbers in the lottery. This belief in the ill will of some higher force blends reality and fantasy, caution and phobia, reason and insanity. Psychological "explanations" can certainly be found to describe such behaviors: perhaps a certain degree of paranoia mitigated by complete obedience to self-imposed rules and rituals, or else a sacrifice, the price you pay for still being alive, unlike those who have been taken out of the race—the schoolmates who died too early, the victims of accidents that could have just as easily happened to you.

1993

Gordon was born in Glasgow in 1966; he will be thirty-nine years old when his exhibition at The Museum of Modern Art opens and forty when it closes. Thirteen years ago, the twenty-six-year-old Gordon showed *24 Hour Psycho* (1993; pp. 34–83) at Tramway in Glasgow and in Berlin at Kunst-Werke (KW), where I was the director. I had never met Gordon, and when I picked him up, along with curator Charles Esche, at the train station at Friedrichstrasse, I was surprised that he didn't look exactly as I had imagined him. Real life, however, is not a casting call. Apart from bagpipe players and men wearing kilts, the only Scots I could name were Sean Connery and Christopher Lambert from *Highlander* (1986), who I later heard was not really Scottish anyway. I had never been to Scotland, and my knowledge of the northern tip of the United Kingdom consisted primarily of picturesque landscapes, Loch Ness, castles, and other fairy tales and movies.

KW at that time was not much more than an abandoned East German factory complex with some decrepit courtyards, garages, and a small, completely ruined Baroque mansion adjacent to it. On the third floor there was a rather big and undivided loftlike space that we used for our larger exhibitions. There we set up a VCR equipped with a jog/shuttle control to allow it to play in extreme slow motion. Gordon and Esche had brought a ten-by-fourteen-foot translucent screen that we leaned against one of the pillars for support. Before he arrived, Gordon had asked me to buy an ordinary copy of *Psycho* from a video store. Hollywood movies distributed in Germany are dubbed into German, but that didn't matter, since the installation would be silent. We placed a single-lens video projector on the floor next to the VCR, and Gordon manually adjusted its speed so that the projection of the film, which normally took less than two hours, would be slowed to the twenty-four hours indicated by the work's title. Next to the third-floor gallery was a room that used to be the factory's cafeteria and canteen. When we started KW, we left everything there as we had found it, including tables, chairs, buzzing neon lights, and a cooking area with a gas stove and dishwashers.

The day of the opening, about seventy people squeezed into that post-socialistic ambience to hear Gordon lecture about duration in painting and bodily resonance in sculpture. The talk dealt with the intricate connections between biographical and historical events, and the discrepancy between what you remember and what you know, imagine, see, fear, and desire. Gordon described to the audience the time it took to physically walk by a Barnett Newman painting he had seen in a museum. The concept of a painting being felt and experienced as a variety of durations rather than a single static moment had many possible applications for his audience, who would return to the video installation after the lecture. There was the time it took to enter the room, and the time it took to reach the image oscillating on the leaning screen. There was the time passing in the movie's narrative—both the memory of its intended pace and the pace imposed by the artist. The viewer's impatience tended to lead to attempts to fast-forward mentally through the film's plot, which was more or less futile; such attempts were thwarted by imperfect recall of the details and logic of the plot and by the near-impossibility of recognizing in the projected image—almost standing still, but slowly moving—an exact moment in a scene. The viewer could see the film's original orientation and could walk around the piece and see a flipped image through the translucent screen. Sometimes a viewer would stand between the projector and the projection surface, temporarily marking the work by casting a shadow on the screen. The images seemed to tremble; Gordon had explained in his lecture that this was the result of the projection oscillating between even and odd frames.

In this early exhibition, the art center stayed open around the clock for the first twenty-four hours in order to provide, for those who wanted it, the full viewing experience. One person stayed in the space for eleven hours, convinced that his perception would adjust to the slowness of the work. At some point, he thought, he would simply be able to follow the story. A local radio station sent a reporter to KW; he, too, remained for some time, even though he could barely understand why what he was seeing was art. He was fascinated by it nonetheless and reported the experience on the air, advising people to come to KW in the middle of the night or in the early morning, when he predicted the memorable scenes on the staircase or in the shower would occur.

Gordon had used the well-known thriller *Psycho* because it was a classic piece of film history and a household word. Even people in the former and isolated East Germany would both know the film in detail and have memories of the first time they saw it. And, as they spent time with *24 Hour Psycho*, they would try to compare their memories of the film to the insufferably slow unfolding narrative that so explicitly alludes to the idea of life as a storyboard, containing suspense and unexpected turns that occur according to the commonly understood logic of the psychoanalyzed human being. *24 Hour Psycho* perfectly evokes this commonality, the shared knowledge of movie plots and media images that have replaced history and religion to become the source of contemporary civilization's leading narratives.

Television series such as *Roots* (1977) and *Holocaust* (1978) and movies such as *Schindler's List* (1993) provide viewers with images they can remember without having been contemporaries or eyewitnesses of the events they depict, and these images are so persistent that they allude to the strength and incomparable impact of firsthand memories. In a television series, this is achieved partly by the weekly or daily interruption of the story, which extends the narration time and makes the show a longer, more relevant part of viewers' lives. The similarity between a narrative elongated in this manner and the slow projection of a familiar film is evinced in the viewer's urge, in both cases, to invent or imagine a number of possible continuations and endings. The audience is creatively engaged in constructing a future narrative and comparing it with the work's actual ending. The interruption of the story allows for such reflection and for the creation of a public space in which to discuss what has been seen; indeed, one of the successes of these works was that they brought about a critical awareness of important historical events that must never recur. Series that could, in many aspects, be described as extremely long movies, such as Edgar Reitz's *Heimat—Eine deutsche Chronik* (1984) and Rainer Werner Fassbinder's *Berlin Alexanderplatz* (1980), through their sequential duration make viewers such intimate witnesses of nearly real-time experiences that their images may become as detailed as memories of viewers' own lives. (By contrast, extreme duration creates momentum and increasing energy and involvement for spectators of a seven-hour Wagner opera, which might not work if each chapter was seen in a weekly dose.)

The French philosopher Henri Bergson made a distinction between physical time and duration. The former can be measured with a watch or the movement of the sun; the latter, in his definition, unfolds in the unconscious and is independent of surrounding space, so that a movie may have two completely different durations for two people—one who finds it boring and endless, the other for whom it passes in the blink of an eye.[7] The more detailed the memory of a certain time, the longer that time seems to have been; a past summer could seem short or long depending upon one's memories of it. A single second can be etched in memory—the moment in which you understood that an accident was about to happen, that you were going to walk through a glass door, that you would break your arm falling on slippery ground, that your car was about to crash. Duration is immeasurable; it has its own inner rhythm. Cinema at its best makes the flow of duration perceptible, and *24 Hour Psycho* intensifies this quality, utterly exposing *Psycho*'s subliminal, nearly imperceptible moments.[8]

In a 1970 work called *Rotating Glass Walls*, Bruce Nauman projected four films, each showing a rotating piece of glass, onto the walls of a gallery. One of the installation's effects was to blur or (more precisely) make impossible the viewer's clear perception of the space. In *24 Hour Psycho*, the perception of time seems similarly affected. In this radically slow work, theatrical elements such as suspense, climax, turning point, and conclusion become quite abstract. The magic of the single frame is revealed; the composition of each one can be dissected. Scale and size matter. The close-up of a face on the monumental screen is akin to a divine appearance. Today most classic movies are seen at home on television rather than in movie theaters; Gordon rescales such films close to their original presentation size, generally exhibiting them on ten-by-twelve-foot screens, and by showing them in museums and galleries, he puts the act of viewing back into the public sphere. In the very specific setting of *24 Hour Psycho*, the viewer also has the opportunity to go behind and around the screen, to respond to the instinctive wish to see both sides of the image and make it a volumetric object of contemplation. The work's sculptural presence makes viewers aware of their bodies in the exhibition space; the temporal sluggishness not only accentuates the slowness or speed of things about to happen, but also creates an atmosphere of hypersensitivity in which viewers, alone with the silent movie, become aware of the rhythmic pace of their own breathing.

In the 1960s and '70s, the body's relationship to space and time was frequently investigated by experimental filmmakers and also by artists using other media, in particular by performance artists, who took the question into galleries, art centers, and museums. The duration of these works frequently made viewers compare their own lives with the time consciously spent watching the performer. This experience, spending an excess of time somewhere with something that doesn't pass quickly enough, can create moments of strong anxiety. It is a feeling of being held down or kept still, of losing the freedom to move. The presence of the performer, or a stilled Douglas Gordon image, turns this anxiety into an elongated and revealing moment of contact.

Waiting can be compared to pushing your finger across a table with your eyes closed: you know only what you're touching at the moment and what you've touched before, but you have no idea of what you might encounter next.[9] You don't know if the waiting will be over very soon, or if it will go on indefinitely, or whether or not your expectations will be fulfilled. The experience of *24 Hour Psycho* is different, however, because the memory of the film suggests plausible before-and-after images. It is an experience of "seeingly waiting," a combination of perception and anticipation. Suspense, essential to the movie's plot, is paralyzed and at the same time emphasized by the action's unbearable slowness. The work's motion falls somewhere between seeing, guessing, imagining, perceiving, and remembering.

7. Henri Bergson, ***Creative Evolution***, trans. Arthur Mitchell (New York: Henry Holt and Company, 1911), 1–87.

8. Hitchcock's ***Psycho*** falls under the category of what Deleuze calls the "movement-image" of classic cinema, but Gordon's ***24 Hour Psycho*** is the "time-image" of contemporary cinema. By slowing down the movement of Hitchcock's frames, Gordon disrupts the conventional narrative links between them and transforms ***Psycho*** into pure image, free of any narrative function; according to Deleuze, this is where time (or Bergson's duration) becomes perceptible in its heterogeneous flow. See Gilles Deleuze, ***Cinema 1: The Movement-Image***, trans. Hugh Tomlinson and Barbara Habberjam (Minneapolis: University of Minnesota Press,1986) and ***Cinema 2: The Time-Image***, trans. Hugo Tomlinson and Robert Galeta (Minneapolis: University of Minnesota Press, 1989).

9. Geert Lovink, "Der Daten-Dandy," in ***Zeitschrift für Semiotik*** 16, nos. 1–2 (1994): 89–91.

Many of the dominant themes of Gordon's works are present in *Psycho*'s plot. Norman Bates (Anthony Perkins) has a split personality; he acts as both himself and as his mother, and, in thrall to his psychiatric particularities, he's not really free or grown up. His victim Marion Crane (Janet Leigh) is guilty of stealing money. Stopped in her getaway by a heavy rainstorm, she decides to stay at a motel but cannot escape her guilt. She attempts to sidestep it by signing the hotel's register with an alias; she tries, like a modern Lady Macbeth, to wash it away, leading to her murder in the shower. In his book *Enjoy Your Symptom!,* Slavoj Žižek points out that Alfred Hitchcock once mentioned he always left bathrooms as clean as possible, without traces, and by doing so treated the bathroom as if it were a crime scene.[10] Žižek elaborates on the multilayered symbols of the bathroom apparatus in *Psycho*'s famous scene, and the theme of clean and dirty echoes the dualities of dark and light and good and evil found throughout Gordon's oeuvre: Marion is killed in the shower; her body ends up in the muddy swamp; the shower, cleaned after the murder, is indeed a crime scene; Marion's attractive body finds a wet grave in the mud; Norman Bates's mother dries out, a dusty mummy.

The diagnostic border between neurosis and psychosis occurs when the patient can no longer cover up his symptoms, when the inner voice or paranoid plot within him takes over and rules his daily behaviors.[11] These higher forces and voices, and the belief that such third parties direct all of one's actions and reactions, cause both pleasure and suffering, but the patient's only choice is to follow and obey. Norman Bates is the agent of a plot he cannot control, a captive typical of Gordon's oeuvre: a steered protagonist in a league of hysterics, spastics, and all manner of "unfree" characters who do not determine their own moves.

10. Slavoj Žižek, ***Enjoy Your Symptom! Jacques Lacan in Hollywood and Out*** (New York: Routledge, 2001), 232.

11. See Sigmund Freud, "The Loss of Reality in Neurosis and Psychosis," in ***The Standard Edition of the Complete Psychological Works of Sigmund Freud***, vol. 19 (London: Hogarth Press and the Institute of Psychoanalysis, 1961).

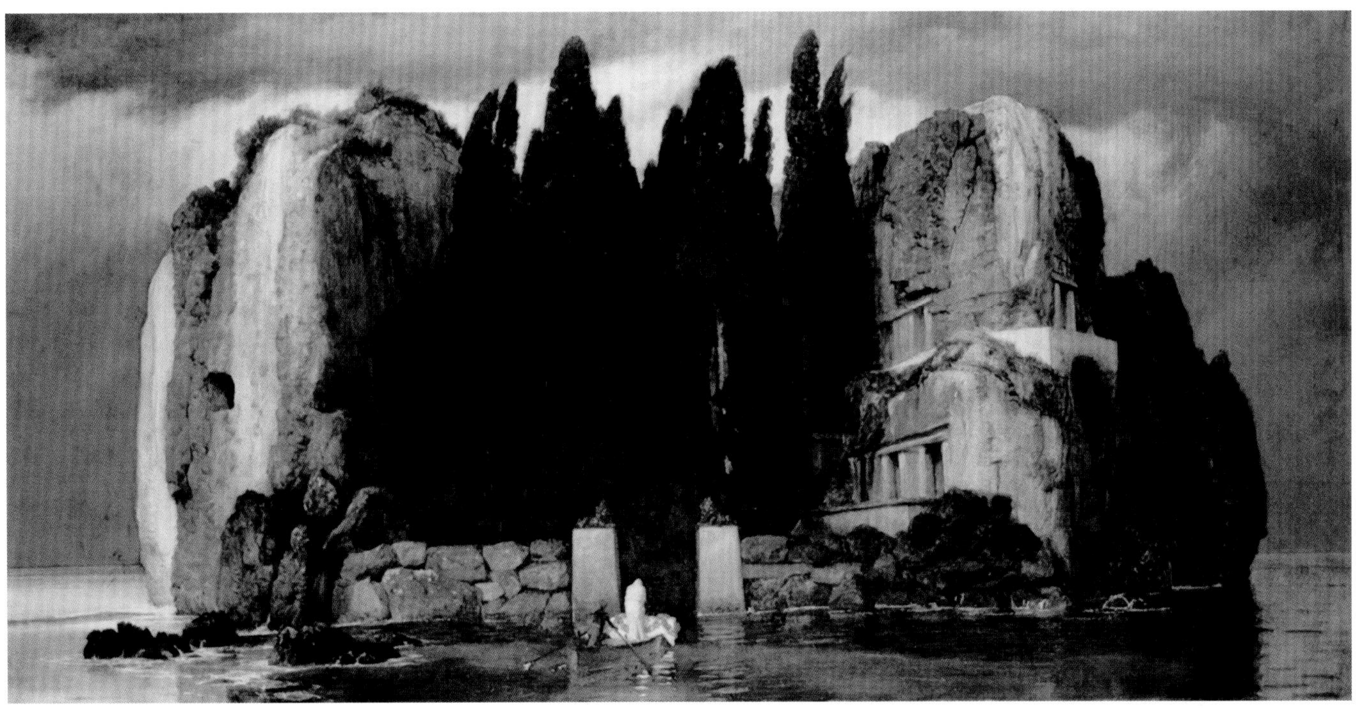

Arnold Böcklin (Swiss, 1827–1901)
Island of the Dead (Die Toteninsel). 1886
Oil on wood, 31 ½ x 58 ¹⁄₁₆" (80 x 150 cm)
Museum der bildenden Künste, Leipzig

Life and Death

In Arnold Böcklin's 1886 painting *Island of the Dead (Die Toteninsel)*, we see a little boat with two figures in it approaching a mysterious island. As in significant Romantic paintings, the viewer's gaze follows that of the people in the picture; our destination is their destination. Unlike those paintings, we are not looking at a mountain range, or into a mysterious clearing in a deep forest, or over the infinite wideness of the sea. We see instead a rocky island that, in the steepness of its topography, looks like two identical towers or a double tombstone with a gate in the middle. The trees between the gate and the mountains are nearly symmetrical; the shape of the island, with an axis through the middle and a mountain peak on each side, recalls a Rorschach test. The *Toteninsel*, a still image, claims the viewer's perspective for a whole narrative, from the literal (the intent and fate of the passengers on the barge) to the metaphorical (the journey of life with death as its inevitable ending point), and the Romantic desire for nature's sublimity is here connected with an uncanny longing for death. Gordon could be seen as an heir to the Romantic painters, with his slow, allusive works that examine the tension between death and fear, as well as hope, belief, and curiosity. In works incorporating the filmic universe and the experience of the movie theater—looking over somebody's shoulder to see what other people are looking at—he enacts the remove from and longing for the danger and love taking place on the screen.

Death is the final stage of life, something that during life we think about, prepare for, and even hope for. The moment of death is the final moment of truth, revealing either the images that religions traditionally create for this transition or else nothing; at death, all loose ends come together, and time collapses. Gordon creates moments containing, in various forms, revelations that are more modest and less final than death's, from the consciously achieved deadline of "From the moment you read these words" to the manifestation of a quality's symmetrical relationship with its opposite, a dualism the artist embodies in Rorschach-style works. These are often "aha" moments, what Walter Benjamin described as a "chock"—the instant of recognition that closes a cycle of imagining and remembering.[12] Death is also the moment when a human being is, despite all promises and preparation, alone. It is the epitome of the isolated nature of being. The death of Mary Gordon during the artist's birth was a literal (if brief) death, but it also could be seen as the metaphorical separation between mother and newborn. Was Douglas Gordon, already burdened with original sin, born guilty for having nearly cost his mother her life?

Real and Fake

When a viewer sits in a movie theater, the surrounding world vanishes into the darkness. The viewer's gaze and the light of the projector point in the same direction, so the image doesn't seem at all intrusive; it appears dreamlike, as though produced by the viewer instead of the projector. Benjamin was one of the first to hint at the parallels between the structures of film and of the unconscious, writing that "the camera introduces us to unconscious optics as does psychoanalysis to unconscious impulses."[13] Indeed, cinema gained wider recognition at more or less the same time that the understanding of psychoanalysis allowed individuals to see their lives as a narrative influenced by cause and effect and imprinted by extraordinary influences—coping, avoidance, imagination, and memory. Consciously and unconsciously, life unfolds like a screenplay; Hitchcock's *Psycho* and *Vertigo* (1958), two mainstream films, acknowledged the way psychoanalysis and its language had become household terms. The plots of both films, with their dependence on now-common ways of describing psychological states, fused the two histories; even their titles contained psychoanalytical terminology. Gordon exploits the parallel between film and psychoanalysis by using films that allow for a level of psychoanalytic meta-explanation—the split personality in *Psycho*, different kinds of possession in *The Exorcist* (1973) and *The Song of Bernadette* (1943), compulsive kleptomania in *Whirlpool* (1949)—and letting them unfold in a manner that follows the film's complex form and densely woven plot.

As a satellite project of the 1995 Venice Biennale, Gordon and I collaborated on an exhibition titled *Projected Images*. This exhibition, situated appropriately at the Teatro Fondamenta Nuove, a movie theater and stage for experimental works in Cannaregio, across

12. This is often translated as "shock" in English; see Walter Benjamin, "On Some Motifs in Baudelaire," in ***Illuminations***, ed. Hannah Arendt, trans. Harry Zohn (New York: Schocken Books, 1969).

13. Benjamin, "The Work of Art in the Age of Mechanical Reproduction," in ***Illuminations***, 237.

from the graveyard island San Michele, investigated the spatial and theatrical qualities of the moving picture and laid out the ways that film manipulates space and time. We included the seductive and libidinous close-ups found in Katharina Sieverding's *Transformer* (1973); the enthusiastic and enduring quality of a utopian dream, as shown in Robert Smithson's film *Spiral Jetty* (1970), about the construction of his famous earthwork; and the psychological bombardment of Tony Oursler's work *Phobic* (1992), which involves, all at once, thinking, listening, identifying, and staying distant.

The exhibition also included Gordon's *10ms*$^{-1}$ (1994; pp. 86–87), a work based on the early medical research movie clips that were used to study motion in general and the details of animals and human movement in particular, as well as medical phenomena such as hysteria, spastic paralysis, and other anomalies in late-nineteenth-century psychopathological studies. *10ms*$^{-1}$ shows a life-size figure trying to stand up; the film ends before he can do so and loops back to the beginning, creating a continuous and Sisyphean trap in which the figure keeps trying and trying and trying. The film's looped sequence echoes the repeatability of technologies such as records and movies: a favorite piece of music replayed often, pictures of terrible events shown again and again on the evening news. Video, as the song said, killed the radio star; music videos made pop music's audiovisual pleasures repeatable at home, outside of the concert environment.[14] This kind of loop became one of the dominant structural patterns in art and media culture in the 1990s (the sampling and mixing characteristic of DJs were later even further exaggerated by the auto-repeat functions of CD players and iPods); the quotation of an original work over and over again in seemingly endless repetition creates a cycle of information that resembles an inescapable Escher staircase. The perpetuation inherent to looping serves the ideas of endurance and endlessness: an ecstatic moment endlessly prolonged and made into an ongoing spectacle, as in Gordon's *Bootleg (Bigmouth)* (1996; p. 112), a silent looped work in which a pop singer writhes and shakes in never-ending ecstasy.

Over the course of the twentieth century, media and life grew inseparable. Life became a narrative with infinite options; the impressionable phases of early childhood, puberty, and adolescence created life's chapters, and love, longing, loss, and trauma tinted the storylines. The number of filmic narratives increased, as did cross-references between them. The categories of document and artistic creation became fuzzy, and the absolute difference between original and copy vanished.

Movies, however, very rarely portray everyday routine. They create suspense and empathy by telling the story of the single, fatal moment, the turning point of the extraordinary life, the falling in love or out of grace—as well as narratives informed by extremities of love, longing, fear, hope, guilt, pleasure, crime, and heroism. Why would anyone watch them otherwise? An adolescent raised on a steady stream of exceptional moments will naturally expect a life full of them. Contemporary lifestyles have adjusted to this misperception of life as a movie; people travel like crazy, participate in extreme sports, go to swinger clubs, and spend weeks in exotic sex hotels.

Moving images have replaced the mirror as a source of adjustment, correction, and identification; science fiction and reality seem to influence each other. In 1977 *Star Wars* was released and became one of the most-viewed movies ever. In 1983 former-actor-cum-presidential-phenomenon Ronald Reagan called the United States government's military space initiative "Star Wars." The movie *Armageddon* (1998) makes references to biblical prophecies; recent terrorist acts and wars have involved, at least in part, a religious motivation claimed by the perpetrators. The recent renaissance of documentaries hints at the reverse—that ordinary lives contain potential movies. Reality television shows seem to have taken quite literally Warhol's prediction about fifteen minutes of fame; the television series *America's Next Top Model*, *I Want a Famous Face*, and *Nip/Tuck* all feature people turning themselves into figures compatible with those in the media. Many people suspected that the massacre at Columbine High School was triggered by the brutality of video games and everyday media; news images of that tragedy may have inspired other such crimes. The question of life versus movie was raised rather violently when the footage of the September 11 attacks in 2001 reminded many people of scenes in the American blockbuster *Independence Day* (1996).

A young Georgian artist once described for me the experience of being in New York as one in which seeing the yellow cabs and hearing the sirens of ambulances and police cars made him feel as if he were in a movie. Many people who come to New York to visit or

14. "Video Killed the Radio Star," written by Trevor Horn, Geoff Downes, and Bruce Woolley, recorded by the Buggles (Horn and Downes), 1979.

to live are assailed by a similar feeling, a sense of déjà vu, a familiarity with the location because they have seen it so often on television and in movies. Nowadays it is nearly impossible to go anywhere without already having some memory of that place, without having been preceded by a television program or a feature in a glossy travel magazine, and the real experience is often disappointing if the destination is not as spectacular as its media representation. The series *Miami Vice* (1984–89) so condensed the experience of a diverse and sprawling city that a real visit could hardly be as vivid, as extreme, or as fast. Real and fictional events and tragedies are connected to certain musical themes as if they had sound tracks in the way Enya's song "Only Time" is identified with September 11 and its aftermath for me and for others who watched those television channels that repeatedly used the song with their coverage of the terrorist acts. The song became such an integral part of the coverage that it was almost like an advertising jingle; CNN used a similarly recognizable piece of music in its coverage of Hurricane Katrina in 2005. As cynical as it may sound to assign sound tracks to such tragic and seminal moments in history, it fits perfectly into our culture of consumer orientation and distraction; every store, elevator, and daily situation has a musical score in which the consumer is—inescapably, it seems—wrapped.

Romance: Self and Other

Two people attending a movie together sit next to each other in a dark theater, looking in the same direction, absorbing and experiencing the film with their eyes and ears, but also aware of each other. Their divided attention contributes to the setting's romance, leading to a slight, perhaps inadvertent touch with the knee, a hand reaching for a hand, a kiss.

The experience of seeing a movie is partly informed by this fragile in-between space occupied by the viewers and its potential romance. The kiss on-screen is an illusion; the kiss in the dark may or may not be a moment of truth. The motif of the kiss appears frequently in Gordon's work, as in a series of photographs in which the artist prepared his models' lips with different forms of truth serum, as though it were possible to find out whether or not a kiss is based on real emotions (pp. 90–91). In *Self-Portrait (Kissing with Scopolamine)* (1994), Gordon kissed himself in a mirror; this could be seen as narcissistic, an act of true devotion to himself or to a version of himself, but who is the mirrored artist? Is Jekyll in love with Hyde? Is Gordon mocking himself? Whatever the relationship, it must be doomed; love, in the end, will tear us apart, according to the Joy Division song that was ubiquitous in the mid-1980s, Gordon's high school years.[15]

In other works, Gordon seems to investigate the promises of romance and the implications of those promises with various tattoos. For *Tattoo (I)* and *Tattoo (II)* (both 1994; pp. 94–95), Gordon had the phrase "trust me" tattooed on his left arm. As he did with the kiss in the mirror, he created a dialogue with himself, here by showing the arm twice, each in its own photograph. By pluralizing a single body part, he emphasizes the possibility of different meanings for the words, which could be the promise of a lover or an ominous seduction into something regrettable.[16]

Janis Joplin's last album, *Pearl* (1971), featured a song titled "Trust Me"; the singer was found dead of a heroin overdose in a Hollywood hotel room before the record was released. Joplin had been instrumental in reintroducing tattoos into American pop culture after they had been almost completely banned in the United States in the early 1960s because of a hepatitis epidemic; because their instruments breach the blood system, tattoo parlors are fertile ground for the disease.[17] Jehovah's Witnesses, who strongly believe in isolating an individual's bodily fluids, specifically the circulatory system, avoid blood transfusions (even in dire medical circumstances) as well as tattoos.[18] Tattoos are a clear, deeply cutting statement—willingly applied scars, witnesses to something, pieces of evidence. The images become part of the wearers' identities over the course of their lives; once applied to the skin, the pictures of loved ones favored by sailors and soldiers travel with them forever. Tattoos can be used forensically to identify a corpse. They often specify ethnic, religious, or tribal backgrounds, and their designs can serve as a logolike symbol of social groups, as they do for Goths, neo-Romantics, and circuit boys. A tattoo can be proof of piety or a penal marking, as it was during fifth-century Japan.[19] In Gordon's *Tattoo (for Reflection)* (1997; p. 136), the word "guilty"

15. "Love Will Tear Us Apart," written and recorded by Joy Division (Bernard Sumner, Ian Curtis, Peter Hook, and Stephen Morris), 1980.

16. Michael Darling writes, "In Gordon's mesmerizing universe of polar opposites, the noble quest for romantic love is often the perfect foil for his explorations into the ignoble aspects of the human condition. The ambiguity of his references to relationships does not discount the importance of longing and desire to his overall project. Rather, the detection of such sentiment, however embedded, becomes the starting point for a fascinating complication of numerous artworks." Michael Darling, "Love Triangulations," ***Douglas Gordon***, 84.

17. New York City banned tattooing in 1961; see Terisa Green, "A Stamp of Approval," ***New York Times***, July 24, 2005, sec. 14LI, p. 13.

18.See Watchtower, the Official Web Site of Jehovah's Witnesses, http://www.watchtower.org.

19. Margo Demello, ***Bodies of Inscription: A Cultural History of the Modern Tattoo Community*** (Durham, N.C.: Duke University Press, 2000), 72.

was tattooed onto a friend's shoulder, but reversed. The word isn't easily readable for the wearer (he'd have to look over his shoulder in a mirror); nevertheless, considering its content, such a word must have a nearly religious omnipresence for the person who carries it on his body.

"I am aware of who you are & what you do" (p. 33), the text of another of Gordon's letters, can be interpreted as either a promise or a threat. So does another tattoo, this time on each of the artist's forearms: the word "forever" in white on the right arm and in black on the left, and shown in *Never, Never (white)* and *Never, Never (black)* (both 2000; pp. 158–59). If a tattoo means proof of love, Gordon's tattoos can be taken as a romantic connection to himself, the dark side of Douglas Gordon in love with the bright side, the romantic longing for the other satisfied in oneself.[20]

He frequently applies such dichotomies to himself, using his own body to act out the eternal longing for the other, no matter how guilty or evil the other may be; in the video work *A Divided Self I* (1996; p.111), he shaves one arm and lets it struggle with the other, hairy one. In the installation *30 seconds text* (1996; p. 116), viewers have thirty seconds to read a text describing the decapitation of a criminal in early-twentieth-century France as recounted by a doctor observing the execution as part of a medical experiment. One of the experiment's conclusions, which the work evokes, was that it took thirty seconds to go from life to death. The doctor discovered this by repeatedly calling out to the head after it had been separated from the body, and after half a minute, he determined that a reaction was no longer visible in the executed person's eyes. In Gordon's work, the text is applied to a black wall, and when the time is up, the light goes out, and viewers are left in complete darkness. As a result, they have the bodily experience of the timeline for that significant transition, standing in the installation and imagining the decapitated victim's body in fragments . . . a head separated from the rest of the body . . . the ears hearing . . . the eyes reacting . . . still seeing . . . not seeing anymore.

Gordon often singles out a specific body part and makes it an autonomous agent. The emancipation of body parts is most clearly expressed in *Feature Film* (1999; pp. 140–47), in which Gordon focuses on the hands of a conductor leading an orchestra. They look, in the large-scale projection, like active, separate entities, autonomous little beings. A hand is the sole protagonist of the film *Scratch Hither* (2001; p. 163), in which a pointing finger reaches out and pulls back, as if dragging or seducing the viewer into the picture; in *Blue* (1998; p. 137), the pointing finger penetrates a fist made by the other hand. *Croque-mort* (2000; pp. 154–55) features photographs of babies biting their feet (a traditional method of testing the reflexes of a newborn), a gesture that might be called a proof of life.

Gordon, in fact, began his career with performance work, with a group called the Puberty Institution, which he started with Craig Richardson and Euan Sutherland in 1987. Not much is known about this work—Gordon doesn't often talk about it—but it was inspired by the work of Belfast-based performance artist Alastair MacLennan and Japanese Butoh dance. The image of a performer moving his body or an object slowly through space, as is typical in Butoh, is not so different from an actor moving in the nearly still image created by slowing down a movie.

Using one's body as the site of exploration raises questions of truth and the duration of meaning. What is true for you cannot be assumed for others. The presumably eternal love that is the precondition for a tattoo may not last, no matter how ardently one believes in it. We expect that images will remain as we remember them, but they, like memories, tattoos, scars, and emotions, fade and change over time.

In German the different notions of time are expressed by two very clear, very simple words: *Zeitpunkt* and *Zeitspanne*. *Zeitpunkt* describes a point in time; *Zeitspanne* indicates a duration. A still picture is always a *Zeitpunkt*, whether or not the single point alludes to a narrative. Some artworks, like *24 Hour Psycho*, manage to be both at once, and in 1999 Gordon had a wax figure made of his body by the renowned Musée Grévin in Paris; with it he makes time move forward and stand still. As he ages, his doppelgänger will remain frozen in time, a three-dimensional reference. The artist plans to be photographed every year with the figure, which will function as an inverted version of Dorian Gray's portrait. The artist's ongoing conceptual investigation of his split and doubled self, of the multiplicity created out of a single individual, seems to culminate in the duplication or, better, replication of his body in wax.[21] In this

20. Various interpretations of the ideal Platonic "missing piece" are discussed in Žižek, *Symptom*, viii–ix.

21. Nancy Spector parses the difference between the two very precisely, writing, "Thematically, Gordon's art pivots on the semantic difference between splitting and doubling. While both words indicate a process of one becoming two, the former implies a rending in half, the latter a multiplication of form. In Gordon's metaphoric work, splitting may indicate the internal violence associated with psychic dissolution, which can in some circles be construed as liberating. And doubling may suggest the presence of supernatural forces on earth or at least the idea that the inexplicable is still plausible. It is within the indeterminate or liminal space between these two readings that the meaning of Gordon's art may be located." See "a.k.a.," in *Douglas Gordon*, 132–34.

way, his tattoos could also be seen as identifying elements that reconnect individual, separate, or separated parts to create a single narrative, a single performing body.

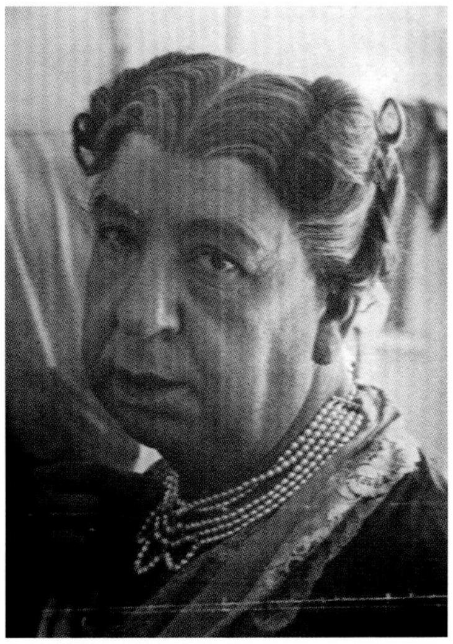

Alfred Hitchcock poses as a woman for a magazine article, c. 1964.

1996 / Split and Double and More

In 1996, in an exhibition I organized at the Kunstsammlungen zu Weimar, Gordon showed *Confessions of a Justified Sinner* (1995; pp. 100–1), a work consisting of two large-scale screens showing looped sequences excerpted from Rouben Mamoulian's *Dr. Jekyll and Mr. Hyde* (1932). The loops showed the transmutation from Jekyll into Hyde and back again, and each screen alternated between positive and negative prints of the film.

Later that year, Gordon won the Turner Prize, which is awarded annually by London's Tate Britain. For his official press photo, he created a self-portrait wearing a blond wig titled *Selfportrait as Kurt Cobain, as Andy Warhol, as Myra Hindley, as Marilyn Monroe* (1996; p. 115), a work that makes an obvious reference to self-portraits by such artists as Duchamp, who had himself photographed as Rrose Sélavy, or Warhol, who took Polaroids of himself wearing wigs other than the one he usually wore. In his self-portrait, Gordon created a collage of five people including himself, four of them dead, two of them female, and one a convicted murderer. The picture is an image of life and death unified; viewers bring to it their own associations with the famous and notorious lives gathered together by the artist. In this image, Gordon is an unshaven yet still oddly androgynous presence. The work's ambiguous sense of gender may be produced simply by the viewer connecting a portrait featuring a lot of blond hair with an image of Monroe or, given the obvious stubble, with a typical image of Seattle grunge icon Cobain. I remember that it was fashionable in the 1970s, which was also the era of Gordon's childhood, for women to create different looks with different wigs, and the artist's masquerade has echoes of a curious young boy trying on his mother's clothes. This kind of polymorphous experimentation certainly contributes to the alienation evinced by the self-portrait, but it is also the result of a montage of competing associations creating mixed messages.

The Turner exhibition also included the video of Gordon's two arms, one hairy and one shaven, struggling against each other, and a double portrait, *Monster* (1996–97; pp. 6–7), in which the artist temporarily disfigured himself with Scotch tape and juxtaposed the hideous result with a portrait of his natural face. A willing act of self-mutilation may sound outlandish and unlikely, until you think of the repeated and compulsive plastic surgery undergone by celebrities such as Michael Jackson, who appears to have subjected himself to a transgender and interracial transformation in which his face went from a recognizably African-American man's to a raceless and genderless sculpted version that to some looks uncannily like a two-dimensional Walt Disney cartoon character. The godlike wish to form and shape the human, pursued by figures from the fictional Dr. Frankenstein to today's plastic surgeons, could, in the end, create monsters.

In the last scene of *Psycho*, after Norman Bates claims that he wouldn't even harm the fly crawling across his hand, the image of his skeletal mother's face is superimposed on his own. Their faces blend, and they morph into one simultaneously living and dead creature. Warhol's emulation, with his platinum wig, of Marilyn Monroe's look is not comparable with Norman Bates's face merging with his mother's—the assimilation of the movie star by the artist isn't evil or fatal for anyone—it does make plain Warhol's desire to be a star himself. While Warhol, who spent so much of his life in a performance set, experimental movie studio, and quasi-nightclub (his silver-lined Factory) in the 1960s, must have been impressed by the artist Jack Smith, who scripted his entire life like a performance, complete with persona and costumes. But for Smith, there was no border between life and imagination. Onstage, Smith lounged around his elaborate sets in slow-motion works that viewers had to endure for hours, but his permanent residence in this in-between land caused him to do some startling and violent things offstage, such as attempting to strangle Katharina Sieverding in the back of a car driven by Sigmar Polke, and stabbing a life-sized doll, his alter ego, at a fellow artist's house in Amsterdam and leaving the "corpse" behind.[22]

22. See Edward Leffingwell, Carole Kismaric, and Marvin Heiferman, eds., ***Flaming Creature: Jack Smith, His Amazing Life and Time*** (London and Long Island City, N.Y.: Serpent's Tail and The Institute for Contemporary Art/P.S.1 Museum, 1997).

1997 / Between Spaces

In 1997, the German curator Kasper König invited Gordon to participate in *Sculpture Project*, a citywide exhibition in Münster. Because Gordon's conceptual practice tends to focus on sculpting time, information, messages, images, the meaning of words, and other, less graspable, matters, the making of a physical sculptural object is not the focal point of his work; indeed, he often points out that anyone who wants *24 Hour Psycho* can create it at home. So it's not surprising that for this sculptural task he made use of a situation rather than an object, engaging the city's pedestrian flow in what was essentially a negative space—an *Unterführung*, or underpass. These had been built in German cities to provide pedestrians with a safe way to cross busy intersections but had become places to avoid; they were ideal for muggings and were frequently misused as "public" toilets and for other obscure activities. Here, he installed a translucent projection screen and projected a movie onto each side.

This profane location was the first setting for *Between Darkness and Light (After William Blake)* (1997; pp. 118–33), which pairs a movie about divine revelation with another about satanic possession. The two images meet on the screen, where a dark area in one movie makes the other more visible, and two bright sequences nearly extinguish each other. When viewers walk into the path of the projections, they cast shadows on that side of the screen, revealing a clearer image of the other movie within it. Both movies—*The Exorcist*, directed by William Friedkin, and *The Song of Bernadette*, directed by Henry King—are about adolescent girls driven by external forces. In *The Exorcist*, Regan is possessed by the Devil; in *The Song of Bernadette*, the heroine's revelation leads her to steer her life toward God. Gordon played both movies at their actual speeds and with their original sound tracks; simply starting them at the same time and letting them run generated a constant variation in the image and sound level. The work has a nearly stroboscopic effect, given the number of images and the invasive sound created by the two simultaneous sound tracks.

In the Münster installation, *Between Darkness and Light* inhabited an in-between space in the city that echoed the thematic in-between space created by the meeting of the two movies. In an oscillating battle of images, a purgatorylike weighing of good and evil emerges. Neither heaven nor hell, neither Devil nor God, wins. The location in the city underpass made viewers aware of having to pass through the installation, of having to become part of it, of being unable to escape the overwhelming sound and the flickering of the images. In this installation, it is as impossible to watch one of the movies as it is to avoid the physical interference of the film on the other side.

Strong flickering light is notorious for triggering epileptic seizures; the scenes of Regan writhing in her bed are reminiscent of early medical studies of hysteria, especially the cataleptic and spastic phases. In the medical movies Gordon used for *Hysterical* (1994–95; pp. 88–89), the patient is often a woman treated by one or two doctors. In *The Exorcist*, the possessed adolescent girl is cared for by various doctors and then by two priests (interestingly, one of the priests is also a psychiatrist, unifying the areas of belief and knowledge). The "unfree" victim, the object of higher forces of religion or of physical or psychological compulsions, cannot differentiate between inner and outer voices; the doctors, psychoanalysts, and priests encourage these lost souls to speak freely, but as required by their professions—by the sacrament of confession or by doctor-patient confidentiality—they must keep secret what is divulged.

During the filming of *The Exorcist*, a spate of terrible events—the deaths of nine people, a fire that destroyed the set—led director William Friedkin to ask the film's technical advisor, the Reverend Thomas Bermingham, to exorcise the set. Bermingham eventually blessed the production, but would not exorcise it, for fear of creating additional dread. A sense of hysteria continued after *The Exorcist*'s release; according to media reports, the film made viewers rant and swoon in the theaters, and Christian evangelical minister Billy Graham denounced the film, saying the celluloid on which it was printed was evil.[23] The strong emotions provoked by such notorious movies, much like the aesthetic and erotic tensions of rock concerts, create an additional plot around the actual film; the interference of the movie plot by reality's "plot," whether in the public or private sphere, is a point of departure for the in-between spaces created by Gordon's work.

23. The Internet Movie Database, http://www.imdb.com/title/tt0070047/trivia.

Gordon tends to create these in-between spaces as a matter of course. The same year he created *Between Darkness and Light*, he had a show at the Kunstverein Hannover. He had been given a stipend by DAAD (Deutscher Akademischer Austausch Dienst), the German academic exchange program, to stay in Hannover for six months, and he was living in the space above the exhibition galleries. One of the peculiarities of working with Gordon is the difficulty of reaching him or pinpointing his physical location at any given time, and although the exhibition itself was proof that he had been present, he was technically unreachable for the duration of his stay—he had drilled a hole from his apartment into the exhibition space below and dangled his telephone receiver through it (p. 117). His mouth and ear, and the mouthpiece and earpiece of his phone, were clearly in the Kunstverein, but with the receiver off the hook, friends, curators, gallery owners, and press all received a busy signal when they attempted to call him.

1998

In 1998, Gordon was commissioned to create a new work for the first Berlin Biennale. The result was *Monument to X* (1998), a kind of remix of Warhol's *Kiss* (1963) and *Empire*: a real-time marathon kiss set in a park on Berlin's Sophienstrasse. He selected a couple and directed them to sit in the park and kiss for a whole day, as long as there was daylight. There they sat and kissed.

1999

In the installation *left is right and right is wrong and left is wrong and right is right* (1999; pp. 148–51), Gordon returns to several of his seminal themes—the driven protagonist, the mirroring of good and evil, and the potential revealed by splitting and doubling an original. For this work, the artist projects Otto Preminger's *Whirlpool* onto two adjacent screens; on the left screen in its original orientation and on the right in a mirrored version. It is tempting to describe the work according to the title's directions—the left one is the right one and the right one is the wrong one—but this superficial impression is incorrect. The title alludes to what Gordon did to the film, but does not explain it: he digitally separated the movie into even and odd frames and projected each set on one of the two screens, so that the linear sequence of the film is split in half. As a result, the images flicker with an intense stroboscopic rhythm, and the sound track appears to tremble. The film's dialogue seems intelligible, but everything has an unfamiliar staccato effect.

Whirlpool tells the story of Ann Sutton (Gene Tierney), the attractive wife of an already well-known and promising young psychoanalyst. Ann suffers from kleptomania and tries to hide it from her husband; hoping to find a cure for herself, she visits an obscure and manipulative hypnotist, who first tries to seduce her and then uses her for his own criminal purposes. Ann ends up a murder suspect, and only a detective, along with her husband, can get her out of her unfortunate predicament. In the end, the "good" forces of law and truth win out over the scheming and intrigue of the "evil" hypnotist; the rational, legal, scientific approach of the detective and the doctor foils the villain's devilish plot. (The hypnotist committed the murder, after a surgery for which he put himself under anesthesia and which gave him an alibi for the crime.) Ann, helplessly exposed both to her own thieving impulses and to the manipulation of the hypnotist, doesn't know why she does what she does, and so finds herself among Gordon's driven souls, a tool controlled by forces beyond her own free will, by strong outer and inner voices—in this case, both the hypnotist and her kleptomania.

Metaphorically, formally, and visually, the installation of *left is right and right is wrong* draws the viewer into the double picture. The mirror's axis—the space between the two large projected images—is an area of intense visual activity, an active rupture, a virtual in-between space created by doubling the image. Surprisingly kaleidoscopic shapes appear at this axis, for example when a car window's geometry is suddenly doubled into ornamental symmetry. Still, the viewer can follow the movie's narrative, since it is played at its original speed and has a vaguely understandable, if slightly alienating, sound track.

In the works Gordon made using *Psycho* and *The Searchers* (1956), with which he created the installation *5 Year Drive-By* (1995; pp. 98–99), slowing the projection speed deprived the films of their sound tracks; in *Feature Film,* the artist gave sound the leading narrative role. Here, Gordon asked conductor James Conlon to record Bernard Herrmann's original score for Hitchcock's *Vertigo* with the orchestra of the Paris National Opera. Most of *Vertigo*'s sound track is made up of Herrmann's score; only a relatively small part of the movie consists of dialogue and other nonmusical sounds. *Feature Film* shows Conlon conducting the orchestra, with the camera focused on different body parts—the conductor's eyes, hands, and face—as they move in and out of the frame. The work has been shown in two versions: one is, as the title says, a film that can be screened in a movie theater, and the other is an installation consisting of a large projection of Gordon's film with a muted version of *Vertigo* playing on a television monitor or in a smaller projection. Conlon's moves are completely in synch with the music, which maintains an absolute chronological congruency with the accompanying film. When the music stops, the viewer's attention shifts from the rather dark, larger image of *Feature Film* to the action in the smaller image of *Vertigo*. Because, for pacing purposes, there was a monitor playing *Vertigo* while Conlon and the orchestra recorded the music, the film's original soundtrack can be heard faintly in the film's background.

Here, Gordon ties together themes and elements of the original film and his own work, forming a complex connection between them. *Vertigo* opens with an extreme close-up of a face. The camera begins with the mouth and moves toward the eyes, then focuses on a single eye—like Conlon's eyes, like the elephant's eye in *Play Dead; Real Time* (2003; pp. 166–71), or a stilled frame of Norman Bates's voyeuristic eye in *24 Hour Psycho*—then zooms in, and a rotating spiral is superimposed on the iris and pupil. This spiral is repeated in the film's structure: two circles, two nearly identical narrative shapes connected by Detective John "Scottie" Ferguson (James Stewart) and his traumatic experiences of watching bodies fall from great heights. His mentally unstable situation is signaled throughout the movie with music, and the movie's repeating structure is also strongly guided by the musical score.

The camera's gaze often rests on the protagonists' faces and follows their wordless dreams and flashbacks, and these close-ups are tinted, as if the actors were standing in the strong-colored light of a projection room. Hitchcock reveals his poor, haunted characters' interior lives as if they were movies, forcing them to confront their memories and flashbacks and nightmares, montaging these images together with Hermann's music to make the movie flow, to make it entertaining and seductive. The score is nearly as important to the narrative as the dialogue is. In *Feature Film,* Gordon splits the movie into audio and visual components and gives the score a new visual identity. The camera, in Gordon's hands, focuses on the ears and eyes and hands of his star, the conductor, as he invests himself in the emotions and pace of the composition. The face of the conductor, however, is not as recognizable as those of *Vertigo*'s stars, Stewart and Kim Novak. Stewart as Scottie fails to recognize his former love when they meet early in the film's second half, but by gradually transforming her into the woman he once adored, he finally recognizes her; the circle closes, and the reassembled loved one dies for real. It is a nun—an innocent person whose deliverance from sin is assured—who ultimately drives Scottie's love to her suicidal/accidental fall; Scottie's misplaced desire leaves him stranded, like so many of Gordon's characters, in an in-between space created by salvation and damnation.

Absence and Presence

Most paintings in a gallery capture a viewer's attention for a certain period of time; this first encounter remains in the consciousness and long-term memory only if there is some epiphany or if the work has some special presence. A movie, any movie, asks for a different sort of attention span. The demands of duration are mitigated by the promise of entertainment, a captivating narrative; if it turns out not to be captivating, if the plot is not sufficiently absorbing, there is a tendency for viewers to drift away and sit in the dark theater in a strangely calm and isolated way, alone with their thoughts.

When, in the 1990s, many video-projection works began to appear in art galleries, the flirtation between filmmaking and art-making became what writer and curator Hans Ulrich Obrist has called one of the decade's most prominent "golden frames."[24] Many galleries included theater-style seating to allow visitors to follow the work as if they were in a movie theater. Group shows became a series of dark, isolated mini-cinemas. Although in many cases the creation of displays for moving pictures was simply a new form of contemporary art-making, Gordon's various strategies for dealing with the installation of moving pictures cut deeper, revealing a great deal about the use of film as the installation's source. In *5 Year Drive-By*, which uses John Ford's *The Searchers*, the screening time is expanded to match the duration of the film's narrated story: a five-year search becomes a five-year screening. At any given time, the viewer sees a single frame, which remains on the screen for more than a quarter of an hour; one second of the movie is extended to nearly seven hours (6.46 hours, to be precise). Gordon has proposed a screening of *5 Year Drive-By* that would take place outdoors, near the Monument Valley mountain range where several of the movie's scenes were filmed. *The Searchers*, slowed down in this manner, would be deprived of its original sound track but supplied with the natural sounds of the environment in which it was filmed. During the day, in the presence of the sun, the images on the screen would disappear; every evening at dusk, in the absence of the sunlight, the images would return. Of course, any attempt to follow the plot of this work is rendered hopeless. Who could possibly have the attention span and mental capacity to paste together images from a 43,824-hour screening, when even *24 Hour Psycho* seems too tough a challenge? (By contrast, it seems a reasonable length!) But this very impossibility has the effect of emancipating every single frame, turning each one into an independent image. After a short-lived and futile attempt to adjust their perception to match the work's pace, viewers would give up and, freed from the frustration, simply spend quality thinking-time with the work in its grandiose setting.

The speed of reality can be overwhelming; every day our schedules fill up with more and more options and obligations. Gordon, by contrast, offers a generous and luxurious notion of time with his installations' uncannily slow speeds. Experiencing a work in which time has become provisional, you are set free from time, no longer moving at a postmodern high speed toward death—an illusion of freedom that hits you with the force of revelation. Conceptual artistic practice often describes a pause in time and space, a bracket that allows a sudden and deeper understanding, an immeasurable moment in which you come to comprehend something more complex than can simply be described in words. Contemplation of works such as Felix Gonzalez-Torres's *Untitled (Placebo)* (1991) creates this kind of complex engagement that roots a viewer firmly in the present; in this work, sublime beauty and rigid form (an installation of foil-wrapped hard candies laid out precisely on the floor) are combined with an ephemeral and—considering the context and time in which it was created—unexpected generosity (viewers are encouraged to help themselves to a piece, a reversal of normal art-gallery behavior).

"Relational art" was a term coined to describe a practice, increasingly evident in the 1990s, that retranslated such elements as Minimalism, Situationist practices, and design utopias into works actively requiring the engagement of the artist with society and therefore with the audience.[25] The viewer was often an integral part of the final piece, be it a situation, a viewing room, a cooking-and-eating event, or a DJ performance. Rirkrit Tiravanija is perhaps the most visible of the many artists coping with these challenges and trying to put them into an aesthetic framework. From offering viewers home-cooked meals to setting up a radio station in a gallery, as he did for recent New York and London exhibitions, he changes the audience's perception of the art world by investigating social or societal behavior patterns rather, than by focusing on the creation of objects.

Tiravanija and Gordon collaborated on *Cinema Liberté Bar Lounge* (1996) at the FRAC Languedoc-Roussillon in Montpellier, France. The bar and the cinema were located on different floors but visually connected by a video monitor installed above the bar, which showed not just the film but all the activity in the cinema. Just as one could make an argument for Gordon as an artist who explores performance through new media, one could also argue that he is a relational artist, one who magnifies and distorts the behavior of people consuming culture; instead of sitting alone in a crowded theater or alone at home in front of the television, viewers of Gordon's installations act out their movie-watching behavior in a more conscious and public fashion. As he once said, "I make art so that I can go to the bar and talk about it."[26]

24. Hans Ulrich Obrist in conversation with Klaus Biesenbach during preparations for the first Berlin Biennale, which took place in 1996.

25. See Nicolas Bourriaud, ***Relational Aesthetics***, trans. Simon Pleasance and Fronza Woods with Mathieu Copeland (Dijon: Les presses du réel, 2002).

26. Hans Ulrich Obrist, ***Hans Ulrich Obrist: Interviews, Volume 1***, ed. Thomas Boutoux (Milan: Edizioni Charta, 2003), 323.

Local and Global

Visiting Tiravanija in his Bangkok setup, which includes the editorial offices of the magazine *oVER*, which he helped publish for many years, I understood how important a single artist can be for a local art scene. And once I was there, I realized that making strangers' lives pleasant—treating them generously, feeding them, giving them massages—is a common element of Thai street life. Tiravanija's work displaces and exaggerates these behavior patterns, making them more extreme, and in the situations that result, viewers are made to question the principles operating in the world outside Tiravanija's generous ethic. My ideas about the country before my visit were based on what I had put together from books, movies, and magazines, but there was certainly something integral missing from the image I had assembled, and much of my thinking about Tiravanija had been informed by a world that I had previously misunderstood. I had been asking to what extent his work could be seen as ironic, but Tiravanija's generosity is not ironic; it is only expressed more directly than we are accustomed to and uses an inventory of forms and habits informed by a daily life that is specifically Thai. His work has its origin in a humane daily practice, and both because of and in spite of this, it is globally understood.

Despite the nomadic life led in the 1990s by conceptual artists like Tiravanija, who was born in Argentina and currently lives in Berlin and New York, and despite the illusion of universal consumer culture, all practice seems local in its origin. Gordon, being Scottish, falls under the umbrella of the Anglo-American language and culture ruling the global market, although as a Scot he is set apart from it by a slight shift that allows him to perceive geographies in terms of centers and peripheries. This position gives him a slightly different perspective on film, for example, than the one he would have if he were from Los Angeles, the center of the industry's universe. The nomadic practices of the 1990s also contributed to a movement away from the centers of art production; cities such as Vancouver, Mexico City, and Glasgow, which were not traditionally considered influential, developed art scenes that produced many of the decade's seminal artists.

Nevertheless, American (and some British) pop songs, movies, advertising, and news dominate most of the world's media channels. A mudslide in California in early January 2005, which killed ten people, interrupted and briefly overshadowed news of the increasing death toll from the Asian tsunami that had happened a short time before.[27] Even the genocide in Rwanda, which resulted in the deaths of approximately eight hundred thousand people over three months, did not receive the critical mass of media coverage that a comparably smaller tragedy in an economically stronger country would have.[28] In culture, the global attention one pop star or actor receives relative to another can be informally measured by the number of hits each receives on Google's Web search engine: Madonna, the American pop icon, gets more than ninety million hits; Tom Cruise receives over twenty-two million hits, and Nicole Kidman receives nearly nine million.[29] Kidman is from Australia (another English-speaking culture), as is Mel Gibson, but what about the Chinese and Indian pop stars who are known by at least as many people internationally? Have countries like Japan and Germany, where former regimes are guilty of millions of casualties, produced no global stars at all?[30] A German-made or Japanese-made film in German or Japanese never would have worked on the same level that *Psycho* did, in large part because of the original work's universality.

The overflow of American and English movies and songs into non-English-speaking countries leads to constant translation errors and misunderstandings, and the in-between space of translation gives works in English an exotic aura and extra power to those consuming them abroad. In the United States and the United Kingdom, where she is understood perfectly, Madonna is considered an artist who adopts ideas early from the independent creative scene and then feeds them to the trendy larger audience. The songs on her album *American Life* (2003) were treated by serious German newspapers and critics—distanced from the work by imperfect understanding of the language—as if they were philosophical essays.[31]

How many people all over the world are singing or humming pop songs whose words they don't understand at all? Gordon, as a native English speaker, has direct access to the language, but as a Scot he has the distance to look at Hitchcock, Warhol, and Hollywood

27. See Associated Press, "U.S. Offers Aid in California after Mudslide," ***New York Times***, February 14, 2005, sec. A, p.17.

28. According to the United Nations Office on Drugs and Crime, in the April 1994 genocide in Rwanda, "roughly 800,000 Tutsis and moderate Hutus were killed." See http://www.unodc.org/kenya/en/country_profile_rwan.html.

29. Google results from February 14, 2006, 9:00 a.m. "Madonna" was searched without delimiters.

30. Klaus Biesenbach, "Es gab Marlene Dietrich, Fassbinder und Beuys. Warum kommen heute keine Weltstars mehr aus Deutschland?" in ***Frankfurter Allgemeine Sonntagszeitung***, October 10, 2004, p. 26.

31. See Ulf Poschardt, "Welcome in the Real World: Warum der Realismus weiterhin die einzig fortschrittliche Kunstform ist," in ***Kunstforum International*** 134 (May–September 1996): 119–31.

almost as if they were foreign cultures. The foreignness of the known and familiar, the alienation from something as intimate as the spoken or written word, the distance even from one's own image or parts of one's body—these seem to be recurrent elements in his visual repertoire.

2000 / Heaven and Hell

Scotland's two largest religious denominations are the Presbyterian Church of Scotland (the country's national church) and the Catholic Church. One important difference between the two is how each understands the concept of predestination: whether a tree grows apples because it is an apple tree or because it wants to and is free to do so; whether one must prove one's worth on earth or one's life unfolds according to a higher plan.

Religion's loss of stature in modern times has left the individual alone with questions of belief and knowledge and of doubt and decision. A person weighing the options of good or evil opens a space for freedom of choice and decision-making, a space in which to ask whether a terrible event is a punishment or a matter of chance. The cosmos of film noir that Gordon often draws upon is a world of clear-cut morality, an opposition of good and bad behavior that is part of his ongoing and obsessive dialectic of opposites. In Gordon's work, light never fails to produce dark, good is paired with evil, and the masculine is layered with the feminine. Since an act is unthinkable without its opposite, there is no innocence without guilt; everyone is, from some perspective, guilty. What one longs for and what one fears, as in Böcklin's painting, seem to blend into a single goal.

The past, in this universe of opposites, is unthinkable without an idea of the future. The approach of the year 2000 created a great deal of fin-de-siècle dread, fueled partly by the ongoing media commemoration of the high and low points of the soon-to-be-finished twentieth century (its achievements, two world wars, the Holocaust, atomic bombs, genocide, disease), but also by the emphasis the change of millennium put on a single date. It even had its own logo (2K) and its own disease (Y2K). What comes right after such a date provides a different perspective on all the anticipation of it—a turning point that makes both past and future palpable. Movies, through foreshadowing and repeated viewing, equip the viewer with similar movement back and forth in time, giving viewers the ability to see danger before the characters in the story do.

One film noir work appropriated by Gordon was the movie *D.O.A.* (1950), which he used in the large-scale installation *Déjà vu* (2000; pp. 156–57), and the year in which the installation was created—a year immersed in anxiety about movement through time—had everything to do with its meaning. The idea of a predetermined time span is embedded in *D.O.A.*'s plot: Frank Bigelow (Edmond O'Brien) has been poisoned by a dose of iridium and has only about twenty-four hours to live. Gordon, who often formally structures his works according or complementary to their original content, exploits *D.O.A.*'s deadline device and its questions of deserved and undeserved fates by projecting the movie at its normal film speed of twenty-four images per second in between two other projections of the film: a faster version, projected at twenty-five images per second, on the left, and a slower one, at twenty-three images per second, to the right. All three versions start at the same time, but when the version on the left is showing the film's final frames, after ninety-three minutes, the middle film still has four minutes to go, and the one on the right still has eight. Viewers, having seen the faster version, know what is about to happen in the slower version and are left powerless and disoriented in the present, watching a series of déjà vu images that could perhaps seduce them into thinking they might be able to help the murder victim escape his dramatic fate; in fact, viewers are in a similar position to Bigelow, who knows what will happen to him in the future but is unable to change it. Here Gordon splits the future and the memory of the past from the present; there is, as Gilles Deleuze wrote, "no present which is not haunted by a past and a future, by a past which is not reducible to a former present, by a future which does not consist of a present to come."[32]

D.O.A. also may be interpreted as a moral tale, in which Bigelow is punished for considering a walk on the wild side. He has left his monogamous fiancée, who is generous, beautiful, and devoted, and made a trip alone to the big city for a night of drinking,

32. Deleuze, ***The Time-Image***, 37. Philip Monk puts it a bit differently, noting that in a film, "the past is recalled or recounted in the ***present***, where it is simultaneously conflated: we are always in the present in film time." Philip Monk, ***Double-Cross: The Hollywood Films of Douglas Gordon*** (Toronto: Art Gallery of York University and The Power Plant, 2004), 190.

clubhopping, and flirting. Every time he is attracted to a woman, the sound track makes a silly sound, as if to emphasize his frequent arousal. The next morning, he wakes up feeling terrible and cannot remember what happened the night before. He feels hungover, guilty, and physically sick, and after consulting several doctors, he learns that what he has is not just a hangover—that the toxins in his system will soon kill him. (One doctor emphasizes his diagnosis by switching off the light and showing Bigelow a sample of the toxins glowing in the dark.)

During his night of carousing, Bigelow heard a man say that the wild music and nightlife were making people "flip." For centuries, people who led loose, promiscuous lifestyles were thought bound to earn the wages of sin. On a rational level, one could claim that Bigelow was murdered for signing and notarizing a certain document, but one cannot escape the implicit condemnation of loose lifestyles—that he dies for sex, drugs, and rock 'n' roll. From 1950, when *D.O.A.* was made, to now, the common sense of what is allowed and what is taboo has drastically shifted thanks to the sexual revolution, but *D.O.A.*'s morality is not as dated as it seems. The AIDS crisis in the 1980s and '90s revived the connection between promiscuity and danger, and social conservatives tended and still tend to connect the virus with evil, to describe the disease as "the gay plague" and a punishment from God.[33]

So Bigelow's life is on the fast track to death, but not in the sudden fashion of being hit by a trolley car or killed by a bullet; this is an announced death, death he must wait for—he is "seeingly waiting" for death. Like the sped-up films, he has jumped his own timeline, and the consequence is that he must live through hell before he dies. Anyone who has survived the pain of dying human tissue, such as in necrosis, knows that hell is part of life—a pain that cannot be looked upon in an unimpassioned manner or be put easily at a distance. For centuries before the invention of narcotics, painkillers, antibiotics, and simple surgical practices, physical pain led not only to short lives and suffering, but also to a feeling of hell on earth.

A simple dental infection or appendicitis can, without medication, lead to unimaginable and indescribable pain, but living with untreated mental pain—phobias, bipolar lows—can also be like living in hell. A sane person's morals and ethics could create hell through an unquiet, guilty conscience or the pain of being an unsaved soul with unresolved guilt. Hell on earth might be a situation in which one is trapped without escape or salvation, such as Scottie's guilt when he fails to save a second person from falling or Bigelow's awareness that he doesn't have long to live.

Marx described religion, which establishes serious conditions on earthly behavior in order to prepare for salvation and the afterlife, as the opiate of the masses, a way to assuage the pain of suffering on earth before the age of widely available prescriptions, tranquillizers, and mood enhancers. Gordon's works portray people in different states of ecstasy that have nothing to do with drugs, such as Bernadette's religious euphoria, which makes pain irrelevant, and Regan's rather ecstatic possession. In his essay "Rock My Religion," the artist Dan Graham describes the parallels Patti Smith made between the religious ecstasy of the Shakers in their circle dance and the secular ecstasy of teenagers at a pop music concert; he quotes her saying, "My belief in rock 'n' roll gave me a kind of strength that other religions couldn't come close to."[34]

Wet and Dry

Cast-in-stone ideas about gender shifted in the 1990s, as pointed out by writers like Deleuze and Félix Guattari, who proposed an all-inclusive attitude toward identity—not either/or but both/and.[35] This stance led artists to playful projects, with some temporarily leaving behind conventional identities and trying out different gender roles. Unlike in the 1960s and '70s, when new sexual roles had to be publicly defined and the political right to express them had to be defended, identity politics in the 1990s art world played out against a less serious, more ambiguous and playful background. Alix Lambert's *Male Pattern Baldness* (1994), in which the (female) artist, her head shaved like a balding man's—like Duchamp's in his self-portrait *Duchamp with Shaved Head* (1919)—adopts

33. See Susan Sontag, ***Illness As Metaphor and AIDS and Its Metaphors*** (New York: Picador, 2001), 150–53.

34. Dan Graham, ***Rock My Religion: Writings and Art Projects, 1965–1990***, ed. Brian Wallis (Cambridge, Mass.: The MIT Press, 1993), 85. Gordon cites Graham as an influence on the ecstatic loop of *Bootleg (Stoned)*.

35. Gilles Deleuze and Félix Guattari, ***Anti-Oedipus: Capitalism and Schizophrenia***, trans. Robert Hurley, Mark Seem, and Helen R. Lane (Minneapolis: University of Minnesota Press, 1983), 82.

the persona of a male basketball coach, was one of the first works to make me aware of that shift. In this climate, it was even considered politically correct to appropriate, also playfully, motifs informed by the politics of gender, such as Gordon kissing his mirror image or Pipilotti Rist kissing the video camera in *Good Morning (Kissing Mouth)* (1995).

In the early 1980s, images like these were still reserved for demonstrating serious narcissistic estrangement and a certain existential and tragic aura, the kind of drama that could come from loving the same rather than the other, from craving your own mirror image but being condemned, ultimately, to failure. It appears in Fassbinder's *Querelle* (1982), when the main character (Brad Davies) first kisses another man. At that moment, the screen goes blank and some text materializes, reading, "It seemed to him as if he were pushing his face against a mirror which reflected his own image, as if he were thrusting his tongue into the rigid interior of a granite head." Warhol used an image of a kiss in *Querelle*'s poster; the song "Each Man Kills the Thing He Loves" plays throughout the movie.[36] Because *Querelle* came out just before the global AIDS crisis, the song, in retrospect, seems to have been an uncanny premonition.

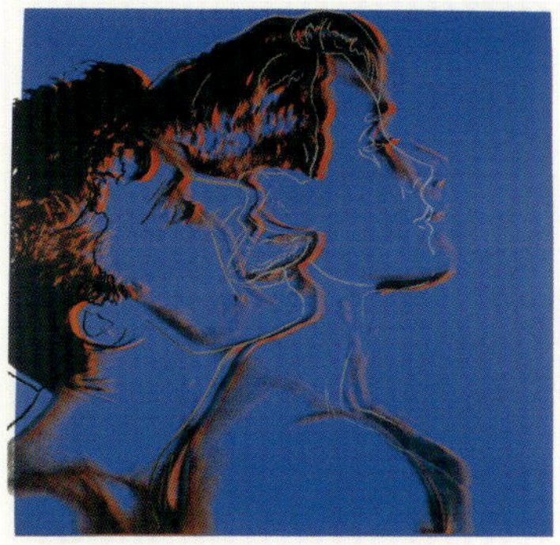

Andy Warhol (American, 1928–1987)
Querelle. 1982
Screenprint, 40 x 40" (101.6 x 101.6 cm)

Blood and sperm, the two liquids that cause the most HIV transferals, are wet, as are saliva, tears, sweat, and milk. Virtual reality is dry, and media images are dry. Here, wet and dry don't mix; the presence of liquid leads to short circuits in laptops and projectors. Basic activities such as eating and drinking connect the dry outer surfaces of the body with the wet insides, which is another suggestive resonance of "Close your eyes, open your mouth." During the international outbreak of SARS in 2003, the media showed images of whole cities of people covering their mouths, protecting the portal between inside and outside from infection. The phobic fear of the Ebola virus, mad cow disease, and global computer viruses happened at nearly the same time in history, and all three were based on a virulent predator being incorporated into a very complex, and therefore fragile, system. The more realistic threat was AIDS, which has killed more than twenty-five million people in the last twenty years.[37]

The fear of AIDS had an enormous influence on theoretical discourse in the 1990s, and the era's dominant artistic concerns included visualizing the dry and the wet, dealing with the phenomena of the inside and the outside of the body, and exploring different levels of concern and even hysteria.[38] The association of fluids with fear may have worked its way into as mainstream a vehicle as *Terminator 2: Judgment Day* (1991), one of the decade's most successful movies, in which the human-shaped robots assuming liquid form may have been an allusion to the wholesale digitization of the analog world.

In 1985, Rock Hudson died of AIDS. Memories of him in pajamas, flirting with Doris Day, contrasted starkly with the reality of his illness; for a whole generation of adolescents, his death signaled the end of the sexual revolution. Until the late 1990s, AIDS was a death sentence that without exception began from the moment the infection occurred and ended, generally, inside of a decade. The suggestion of a deadline in Gordon's text "From the moment you read these words . . ." was shockingly mirrored in the anamnestic reality of the AIDS epidemic. Gonzalez-Torres died in 1996, before the emergence of medication that could have saved his life.[39] His work *Untitled* (1989) is a photograph of a bed that still bears the imprints of the people who have just left it. In 1963 in upstate New York, Warhol watched John Giorno sleeping and decided to record it on 16mm film, creating the film *Sleep* (1963).

Liquids do not appear in Warhol's films, including *Blow Job* (1964) and *Kiss*, where you might expect to see them. Gordon's *Film Noir (Perspire)* (1995; pp. 106–7), which focuses on a sleeping face that is copiously sweating, seems like an updated and wet version of Warhol's *Sleep*, a translation between decades. The sleeper in Gordon's work, with wet, sweaty pearls on his forehead, has closed his eyes; the babies in *croque-mort* bite their toes, connecting the insides and outsides of their bodies, wet and dry uniting in proof of life.

2002

An elephant named Topsy killed three people, including a trainer, and was subsequently electrocuted at Coney Island in 1903.[40] The procedure was filmed by the Edison Manufacturing Company in a silent, minute-long black-and-white movie. The gruesome document,

36. "Each Man Kills the Thing He Loves," music by Peer Raben, 1982, with lyrics from a poem by Oscar Wilde.

37. See World Health Organization, "AIDS Epidemic Update: Special Report on HIV Prevention, December 2005," http://www.who.int/hiv/epi-update2005_en.pdf.

38. Arthur and Marilouise Kroker published a number of essays about these phenomena, such as "male hysteria"—men who are afraid of bodily fluids. See Arthur Kroker and Marilouise Kroker, eds., ***The Last Sex: Feminism and Outlaw Bodies*** (Gordonsville, Va.: Palgrave Macmillan,1993).

39. See John Hensel, "Attacking AIDS with a 'Cocktail' Therapy," in ***FDA Consumer*** 33, no. 4 (June–August, 1999), http://www.fda.gov/fac/features/1999/499_aids.html.

40. See Tom Vanderbilt, "City Lore: They Didn't Forget," in ***New York Times***, July 13, 2003, sec. 14, p. 3.

which showed the big, heavy animal crashing to the ground, became a traveling sensation. The movie replayed the spectacle at life size and its original speed.

In Wuppertal, close to where I grew up, an elephant named Tuffi fell at least forty-five feet out of the Schwebebahn, the city's suspension railway, into the river Wupper. As a child I used to imagine the heavy animal falling into the rather shallow riverbed. The elephant wasn't hurt, and afterward the local dairy factories were named for it. But that is just another memory.

In 2002, Gordon arranged for a circus elephant to be transported to the Gagosian Gallery in New York, where he filmed it playing dead and obeying other directions. As in so many of Gordon's works, *Play Dead; Real Time* features a protagonist whose actions are the result of an exterior force, in this case, Gordon's own commands. The artist focused the camera's gaze on the elephant's eye—but what does the creature see? What does it perceive? The animal's presumed incapacity for conscious thought creates a surface on which viewers may project anything they like, and the elephant becomes a caricature of the actor in general.

The elephant is an extremely large being, here ordered to lie down, play dead, and stand up; Gordon's *B-Movie* (1995; p. 103), *Film Noir (Fly)* (1995), and *Fuzzy Logic* (1995; pp. 108–9) all feature a fly, an extremely small being, lying on its back, unable to get up. Where the elephant seems emotionally engaging, the fly leaves viewers cold; whether it is playing dead or is dying for real doesn't seem to matter.[41] The existence of these beings is only a metaphor for life and death, the allegory of vanity embodied by the fragile being exposed to the artist's will. When body parts play the roles of beings, they are clearly separate and independent objects and subjects, such as the lovers' relationship implied by one hand fingering the other in *Blue*. This is Gordon's obsessively pluralistic universe at work (a multiplicity created out of a single individual); when there is a multiplicity of subjects, such as the public, he addresses it with his imperative text pieces.

Performance art, especially in its earlier days, was not always documented well or even sufficiently, so that some of those performances gained public notoriety, even achieving the status of modern legends, through word of mouth. Fact and fiction merged. In fifth-century Syria, St. Simeon Stylites stood on a sixty-foot-high pillar day and night for thirty years, until his death.[42] In *Play Dead; Real Time*, viewers enjoy the intimate sight of something rare and spectacularly different. Marina Abramovic's installation and performance *The House with the Ocean View* (2002) took place the same year, and visitors to the gallery could imagine that, as she sat quietly in her loftlike living units and looked longingly into space, she was seeing the view implied by the title. But what were the spectators looking at, and what were they expecting? For most of the history of civilization, only a small minority have claimed to be voyeurs and flâneurs; today it seems to be a general mindset, one identified with a certain impatient expectation of seeing something new and special, perhaps something titillating. The spectacle, good or evil, addresses the desires of the short attention span.

In a 1993 work set in an alternative gallery, Gordon removed the ceiling between two floors to make a single space with a high ceiling. He installed a tightrope halfway up, and hired someone to walk back and forth across it for the duration of the exhibition. The possibility of, even the surprising desire for, a spectacular fall, put the viewers in the position of discovering their sadistic sides, perhaps of uttering an evil wish. But Gordon called the work *Trust Me* (1993; p. 85). "Trust me," like something you'd say to calm an elephant in a gallery space or one about to be electrocuted. It's clear that the protagonists in the stories Gordon chooses have no real freedom of choice—they are all *fremdbestimmt* (controlled by something other than free will), from the spastic and the hysteric shaken and governed by their illnesses, to the girls in *The Exorcist* and *The Song of Bernadette* who are the tools of the Devil and God, to the artist's own body parts manipulated like puppets. The question is whether his audience is any freer.

2005

This essay is a montage of observations, descriptions, memories, and ideas; there is nothing original in it, nothing that hasn't been thought, told, said, written, quoted, misquoted, imagined, seen, witnessed, or lied about before. The allusions and references in Gordon's work

41. Jan Debbaut, however, was not left cold by this image. In an extensive interview with the artist, he asked, "Why was I more shocked by the dying fly than by these other images of human pathological disease? And why would I be more outraged if I thought that you actually made the image of the fly, rather than using it as a found image? . . . When you introduce doubt into the mind of the viewer as to the authorship of the images, you make the game even more sophisticated. Just when people thought that the work was readable and manageable, after initial difficulty, then you throw the whole thing up in the air again by introducing another factor. Real or unreal? The moral status is always changing." To which Gordon replied, "You have to look at the idea without the comfort, or cloud, of authority from the artist. You have to make up your own morals and ethics." ". . . in conversation: Jan Debbaut and Douglas Gordon," in ***Douglas Gordon: Kidnapping***, ed. Marente Bloemheuvel (Eindhoven: Stedelijk Van Abbemuseum, 1998), 53.

42. Simon Goldhill, ***Love, Sex, and Tragedy: How the Ancient World Shapes Our Lives*** (Chicago: The University of Chicago Press, 2004), 104.

constantly lead observers to seemingly unavoidable déjà vus, revelations, and conclusions, and these are all contained in a loop of anecdotes, oral history, and critical interpretation.

Re-enact, re-sample, re-assemble, re-create, re-do, and re-make: these were some of the key artistic strategies of the last fifteen years. Reaching back to the 1960s and '70s, a new generation of artists recontextualized artistic approaches in a framework of rapidly changing social, political, economic, and technological conditions. Gordon's frequent strategy is to use found footage appropriated from well-known feature films; in *New Color Empire* (2006; pp. 174–75), a new work created for the exhibition at The Museum of Modern Art, Gordon will follow a strategy often used in the movie industry by "remaking" an existing work, in this case paying homage to Warhol's *Empire* and, again, raising questions of memory and imagination.

Can *Empire* be remade today? And if so, what would it mean? When Warhol filmed the Empire State Building, he used a motion-picture camera to shoot a motionless object, and made an eight-hour movie in which the time it took the director to record it is the same length as the time it takes the projector to play it. When *Empire* was made, the Empire State Building was the tallest building in the city; it has now resumed that solitary and visible role. Yet it no longer looks as blunt and self-assuredly erect. A group of obsessed men flew two airplanes into the World Trade Center towers and changed how we look at the Manhattan skyline; our memories make the Empire State Building seem more fragile and at risk than it did before.

In the wake of this tragedy, which so vehemently shocked the world, the naming and listing of the victims has become an act of commemoration and respect. Gordon emphasizes the fragility of our daily life in *List of Names* (1990–present; endpapers, back), a poetic, gentle, and respectful gesture that requires him to perform the monumental task of trying to remember everyone he has ever encountered in his entire life. The results resemble the long lists of names you see at the end of a movie. In 1990, Gordon managed to come up with 1,440 names, recreating the world as it had existed for him up to that very point in time. In the Bible, naming is a powerful act; more profanely, calling someone by name is an act of power exercised over that person. So what does it mean, in this ongoing project, for the artist to forget important names? He becomes a bit like a child who thinks the world disappears when he closes his eyes.

"Close your eyes, open your mouth" could have been the pick-up line of the mysterious wanderer played by Terence Stamp in Pier Paolo Pasolini's *Teorema* (1968). One after the other, he seduces all the members of a prominent Italian family: the father, mother, son, daughter, and maid. And when he seduces them, he seduces them for life; when he leaves, they are devastated and shaken, a true pantheon of Douglas Gordon characters: the maid becomes a saint, the daughter goes crazy, the son becomes an artist, the mother turns into a nymphomaniac, the father gives his factories away and desperately wanders the world, searching for love. First praised as a successful metaphor for God's love, *Teorema* was later banned for being subversive, decadent, and scandalously blasphemous; what it seems to describe is the mystery of the relationship between ignorance and innocence, temptation and curiosity, expectation and fear. Ultimately, it expresses the unsettling freedom that comes with enlightenment: Close your eyes, open your mouth . . . trust me . . . from the moment you read these words . . . forever.

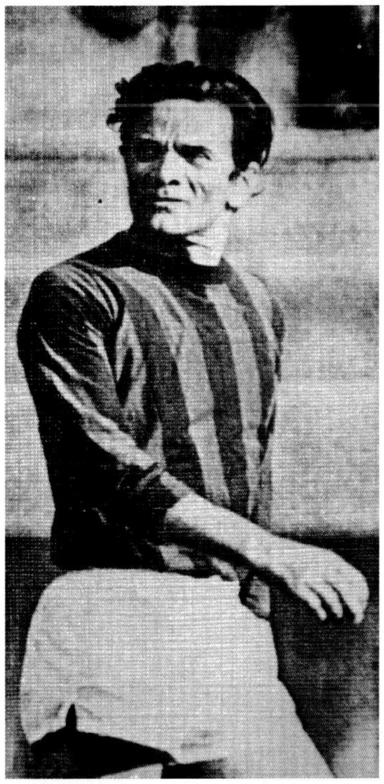

Pier Paolo Pasolini in the late 1960s.

Letter (Number 1). 1991
Letter and wall text in Bembo typeface, dimensions variable
Collection the artist

I am aware of who you are & what you do.

24 Hour Psycho, 1993
Video installation with screen and black-and-white video, 24 hr. loop, dimensions variable
Installation view at Kunst-Werke, Berlin, 1993
Private collection, Boston

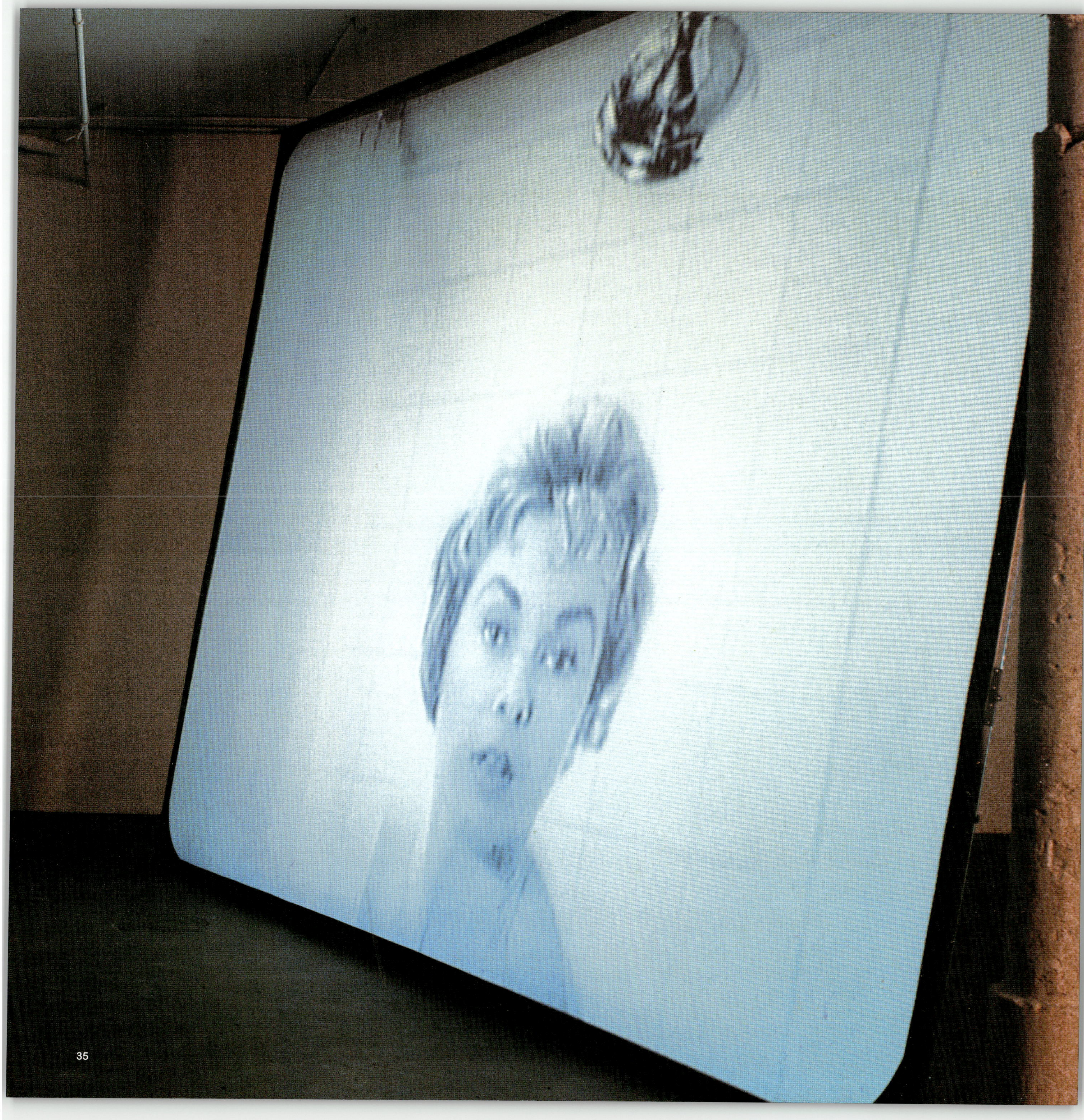

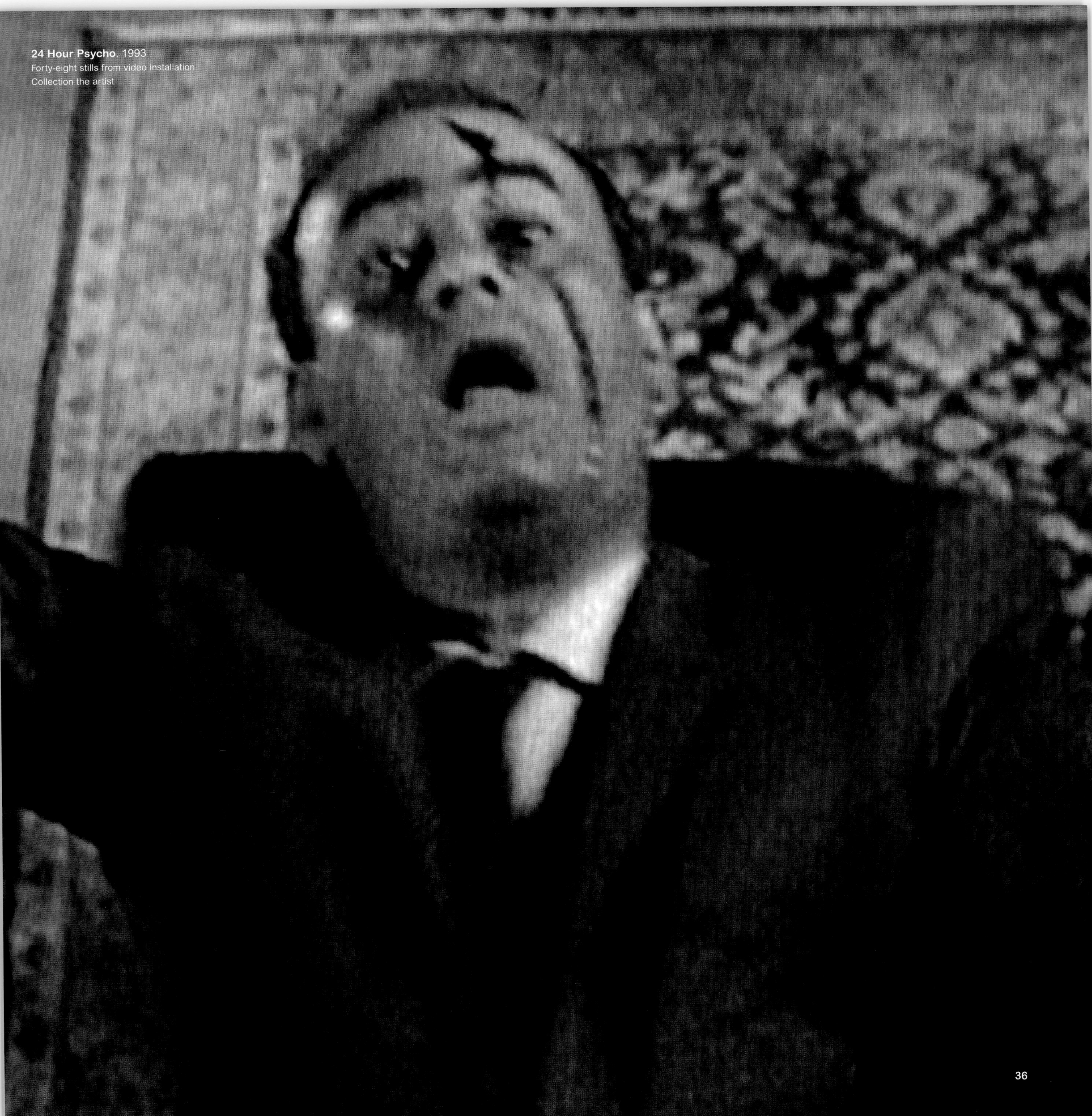

24 Hour Psycho. 1993
Forty-eight stills from video installation
Collection the artist

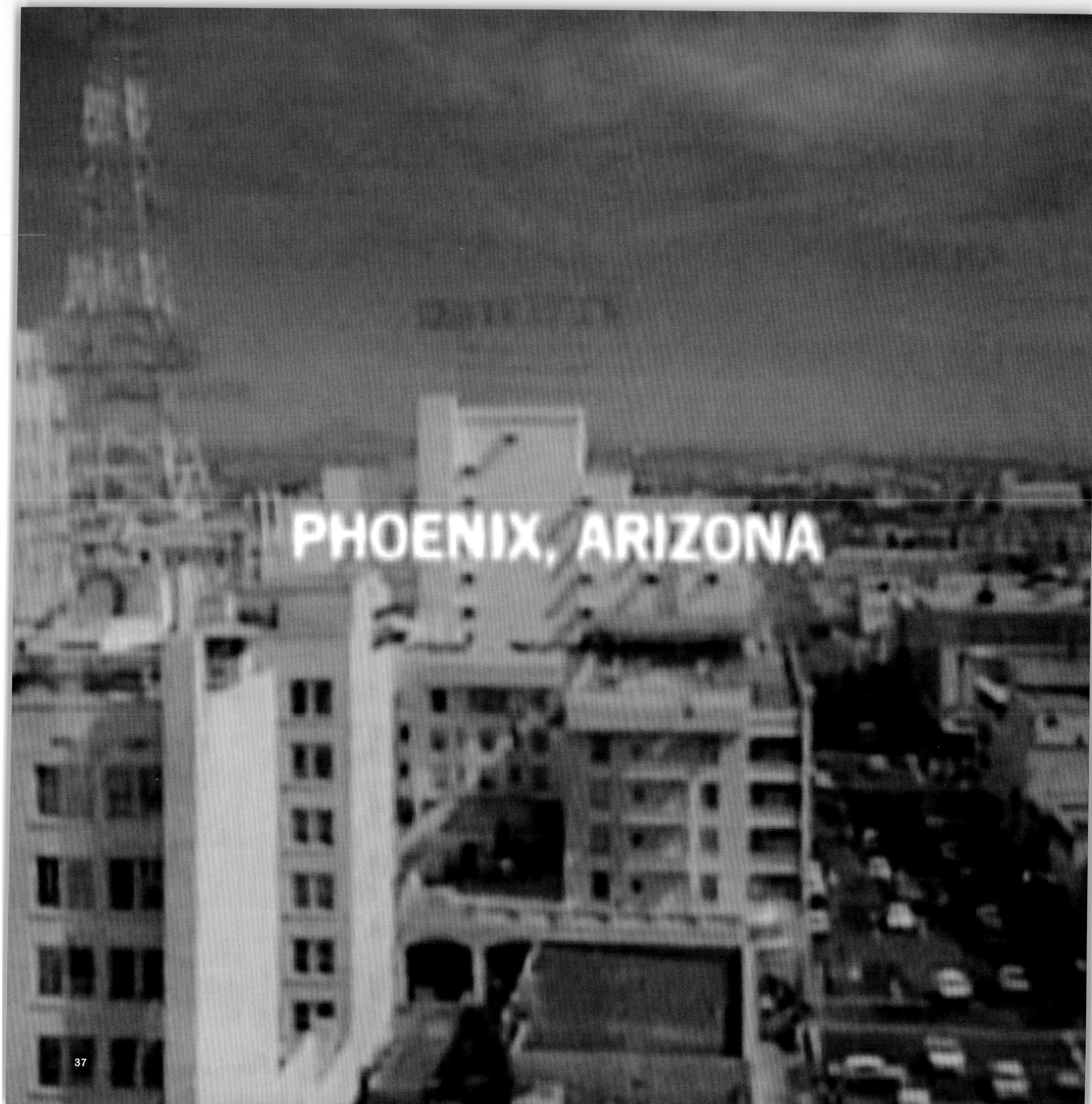
PHOENIX, ARIZONA

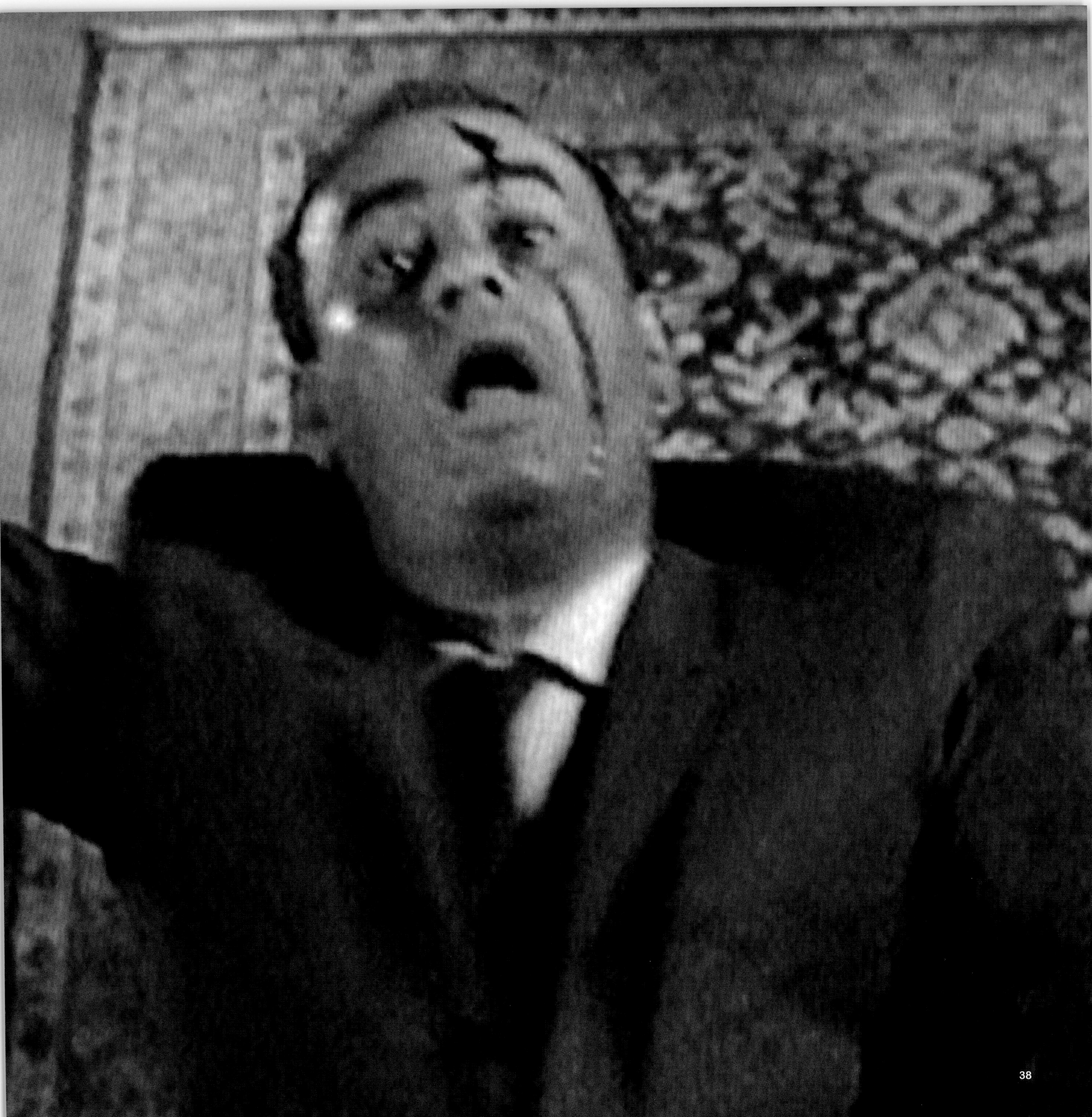

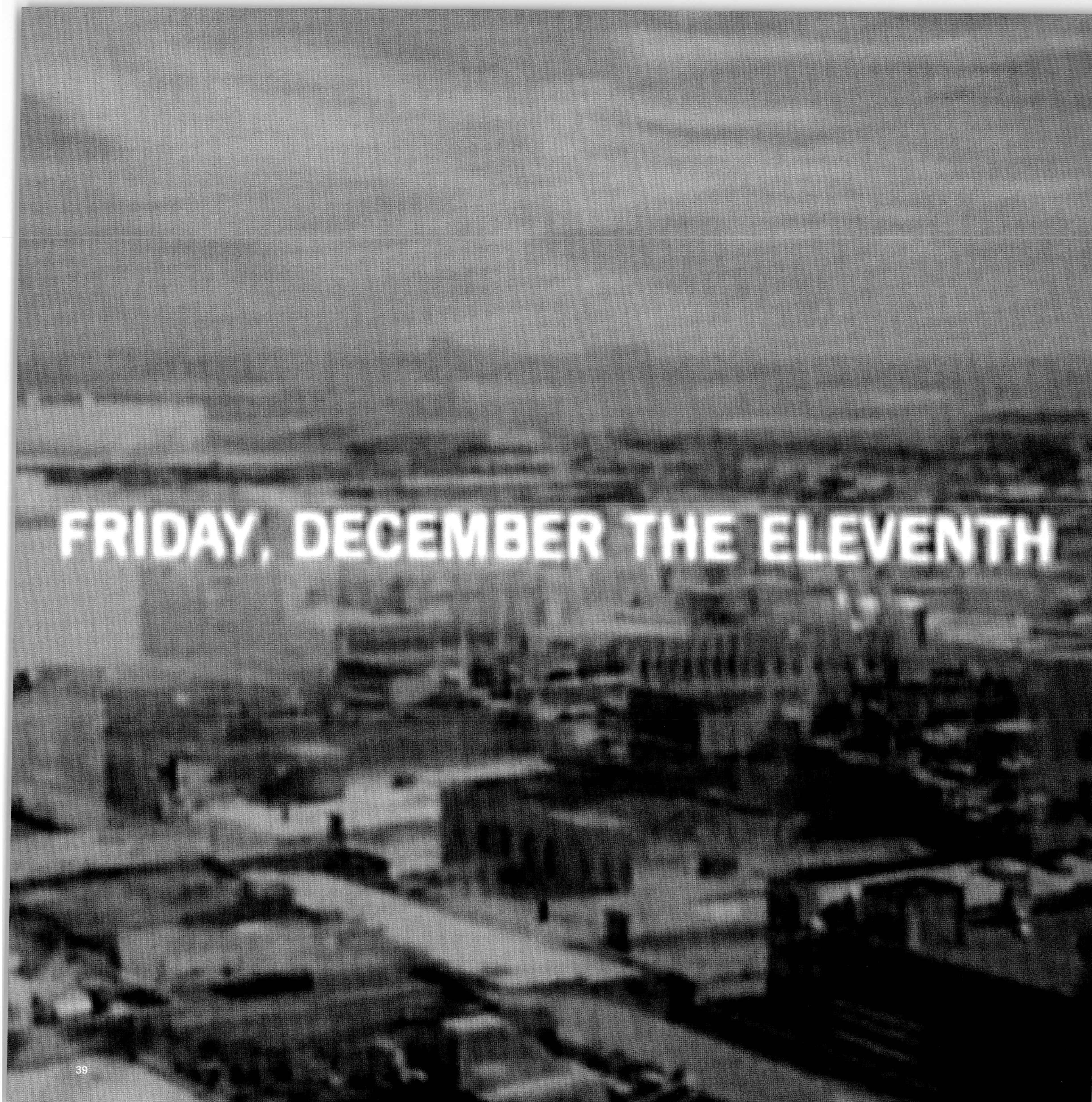
FRIDAY, DECEMBER THE ELEVENTH

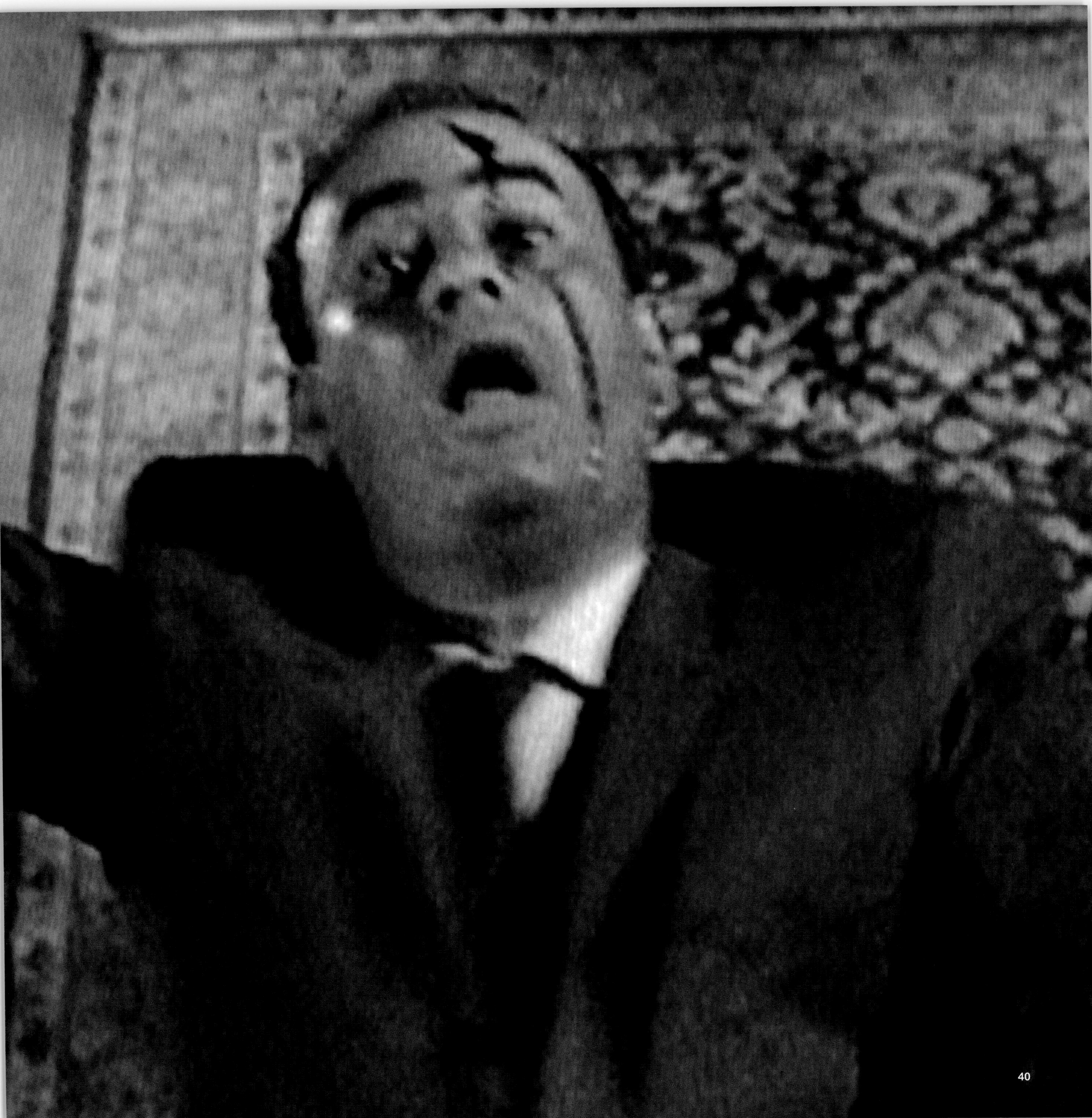

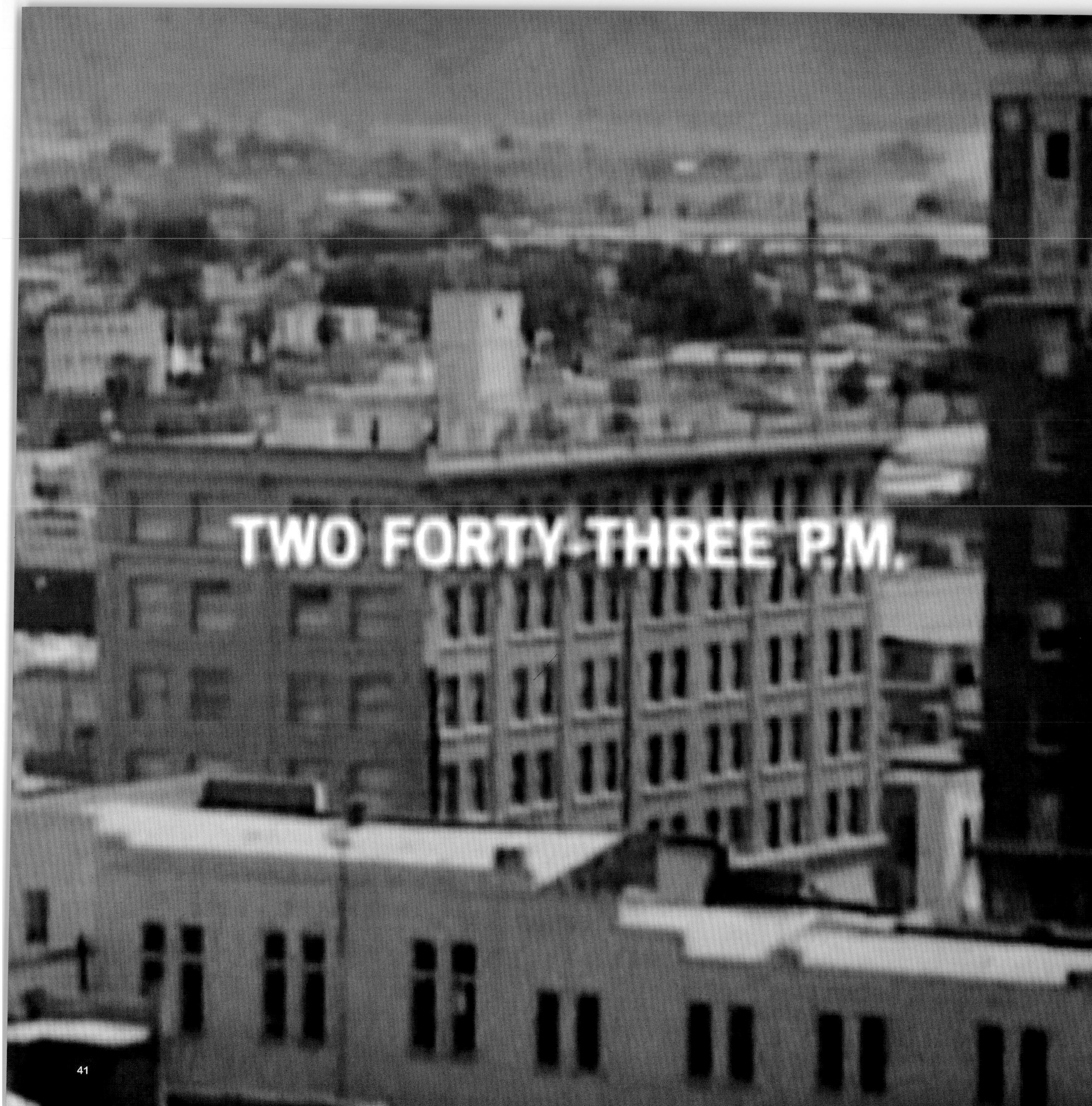
TWO FORTY-THREE P.M.

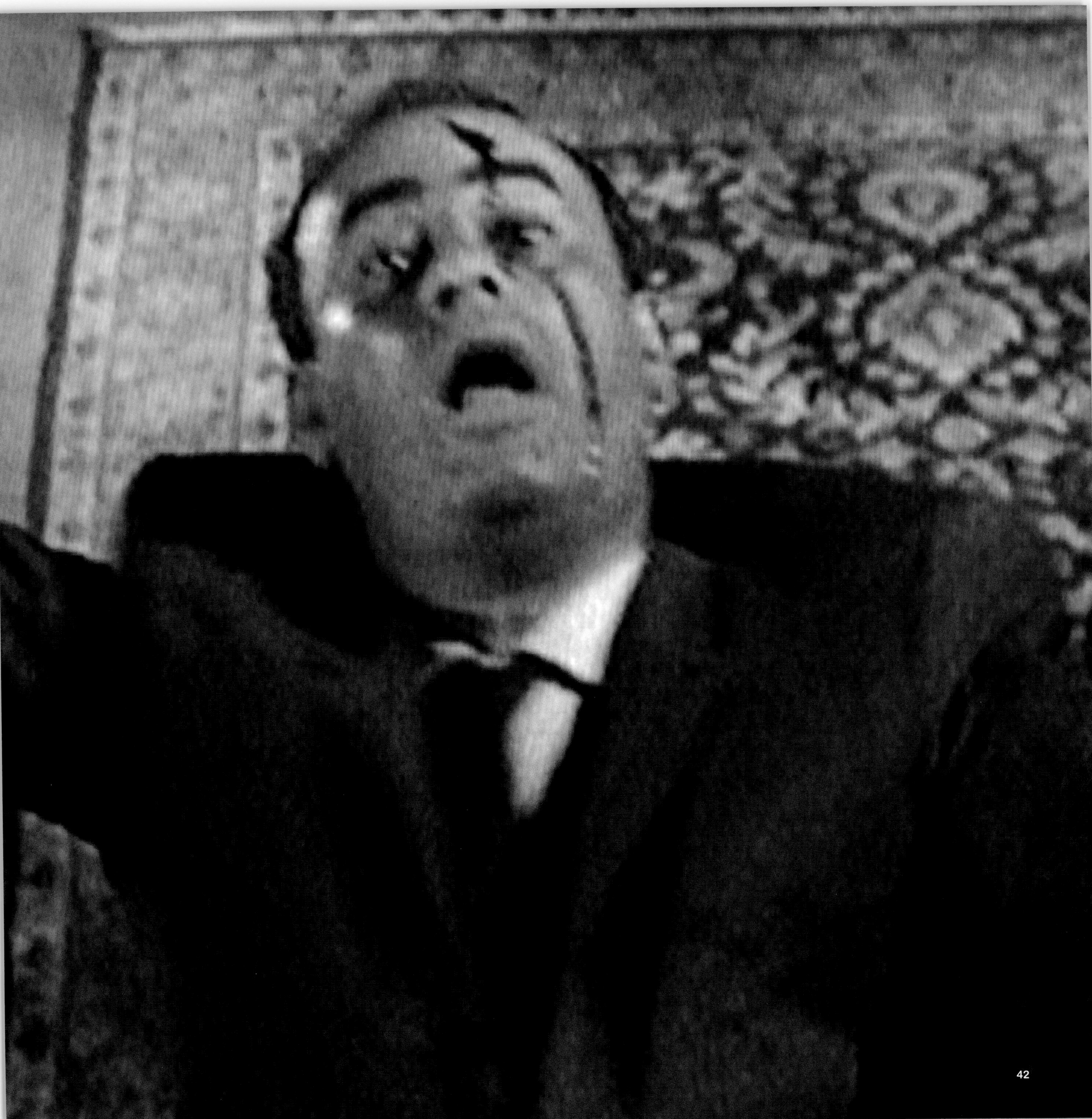

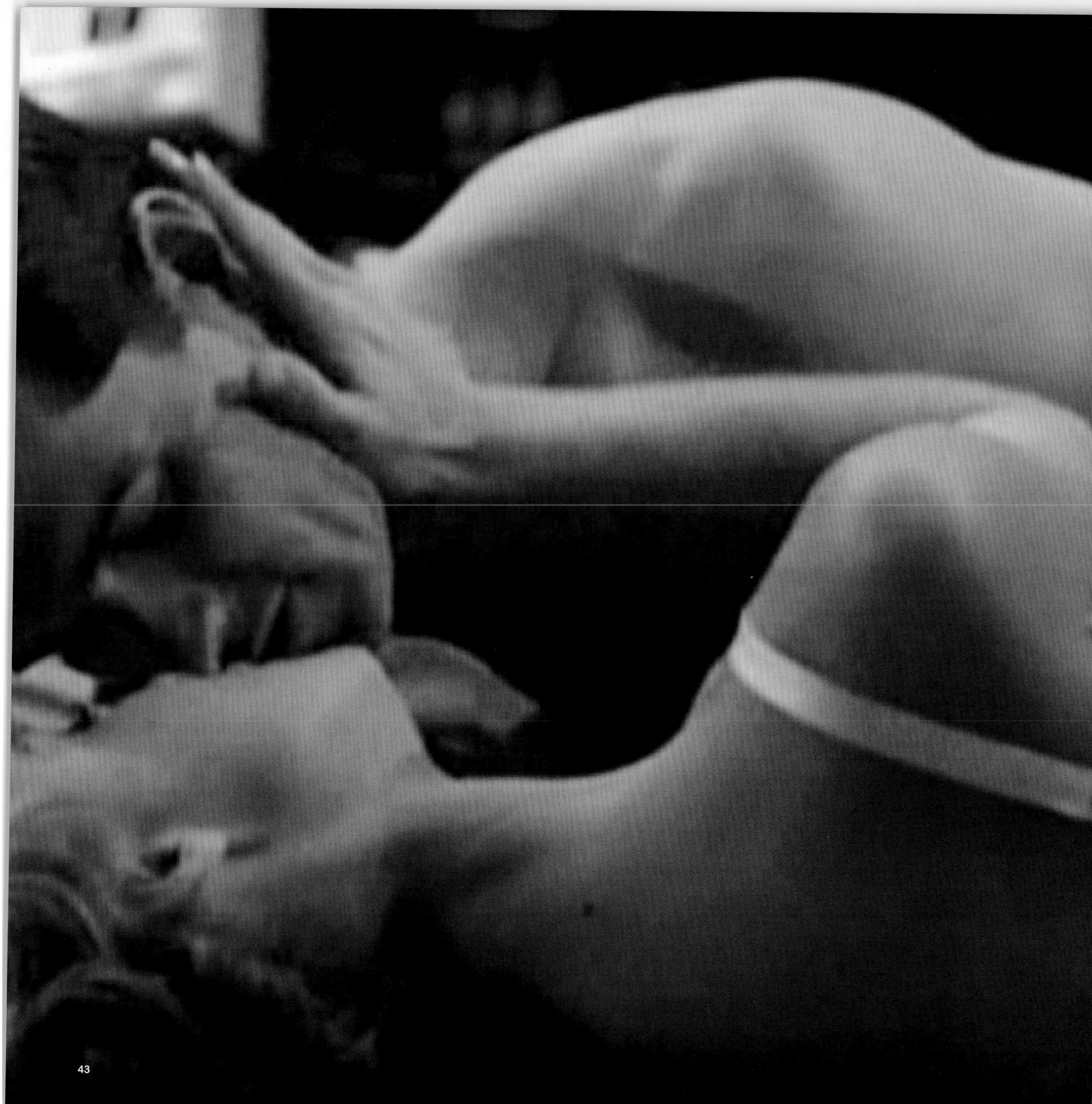

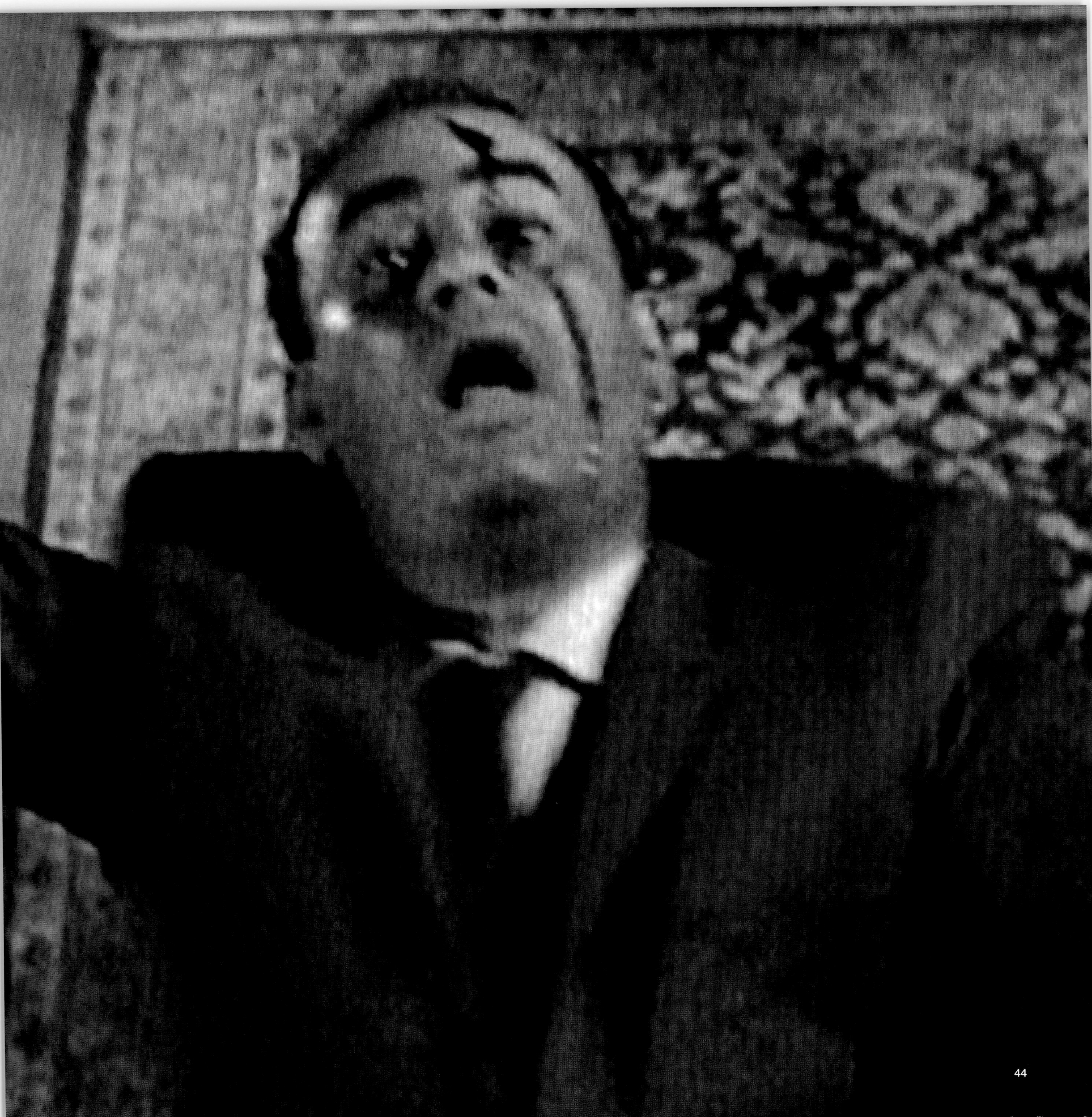

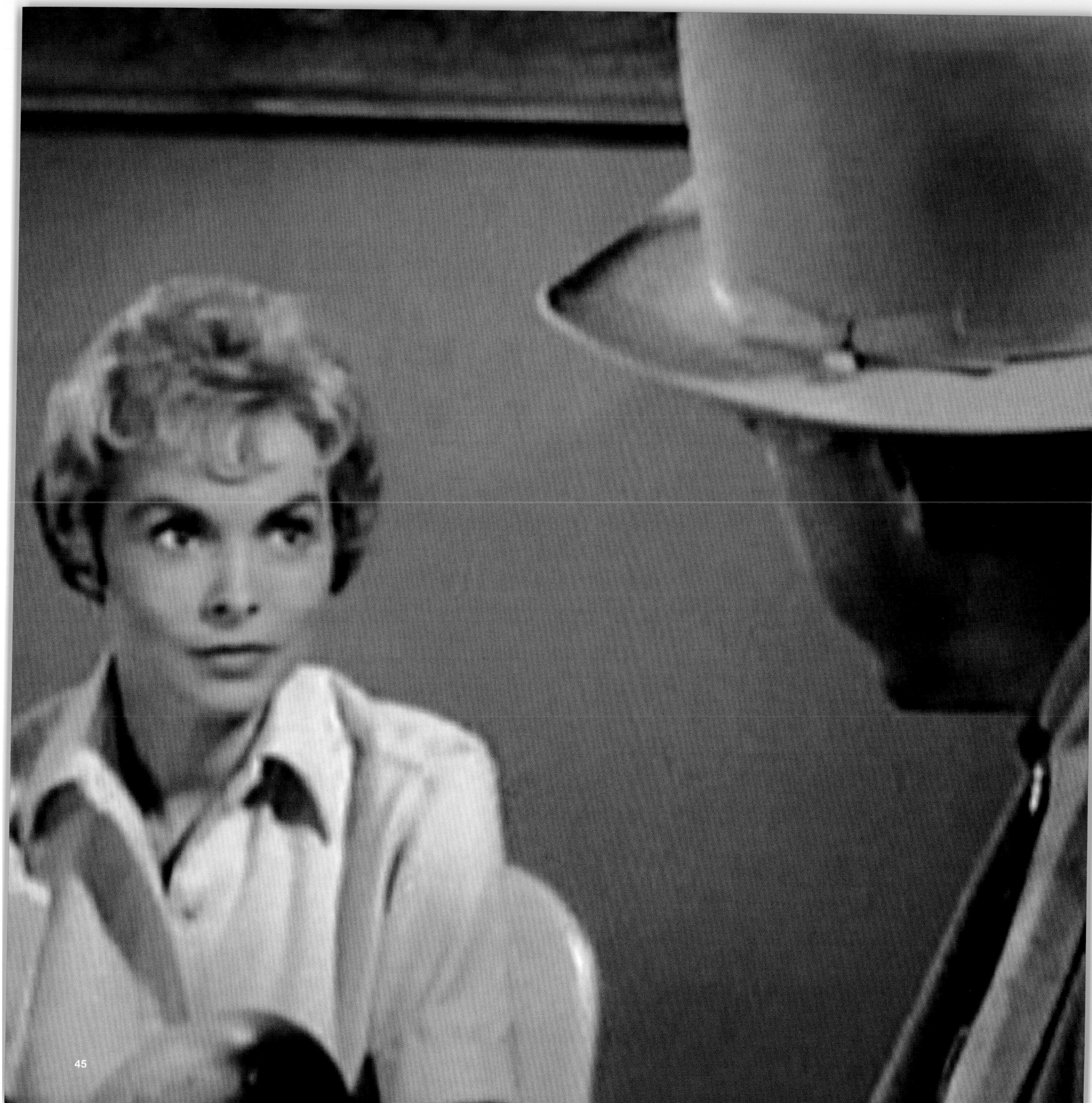

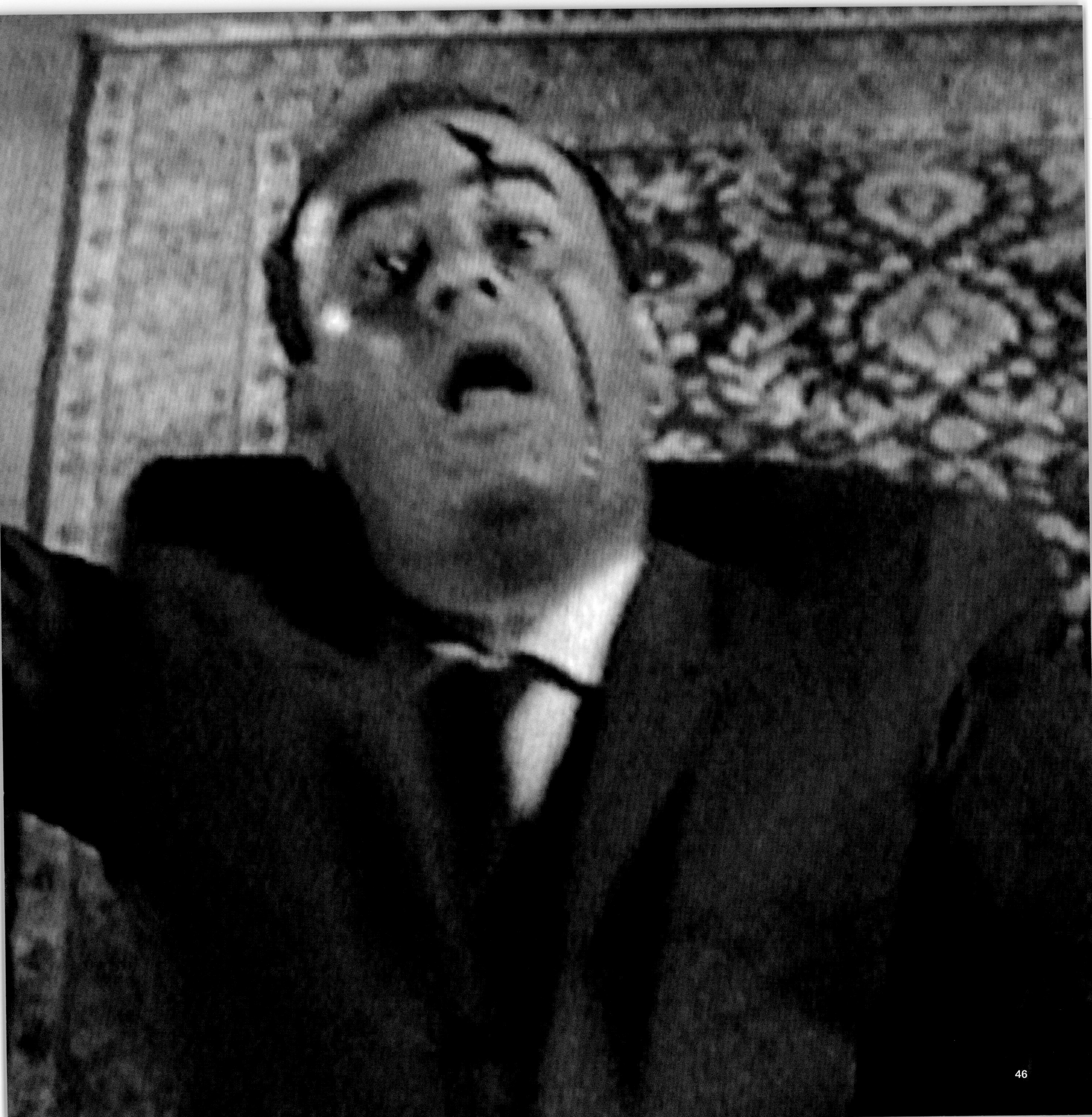

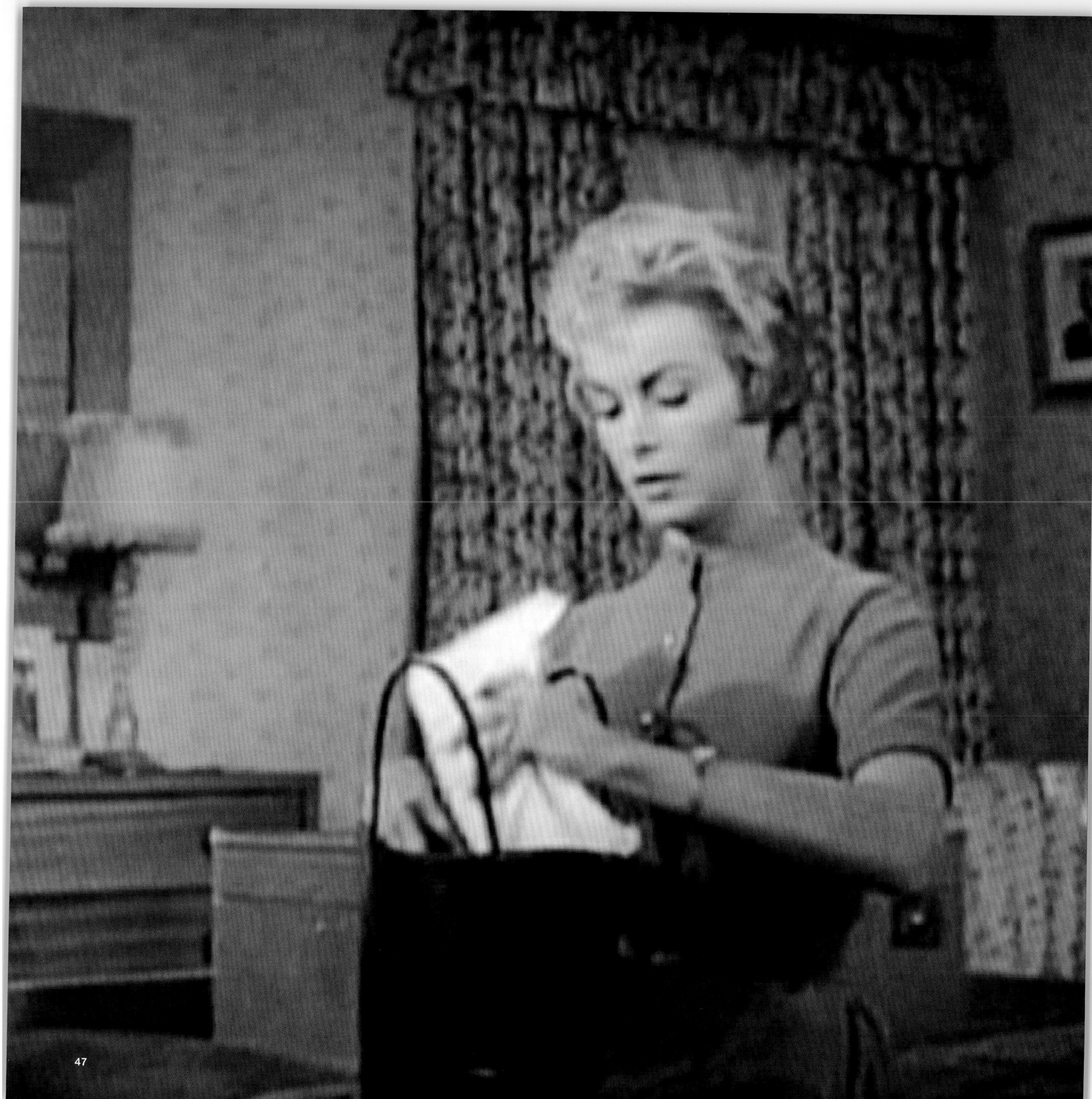

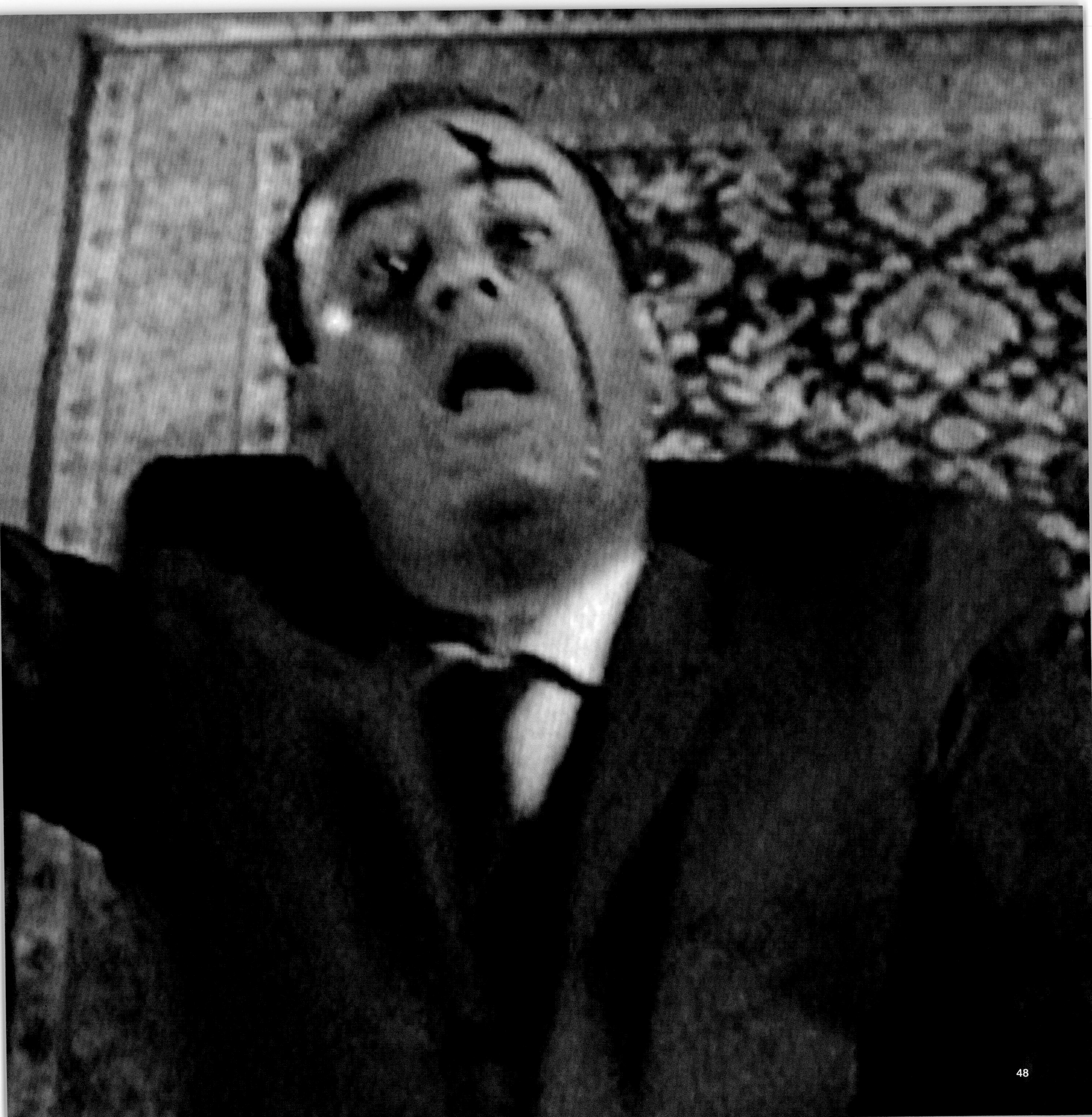

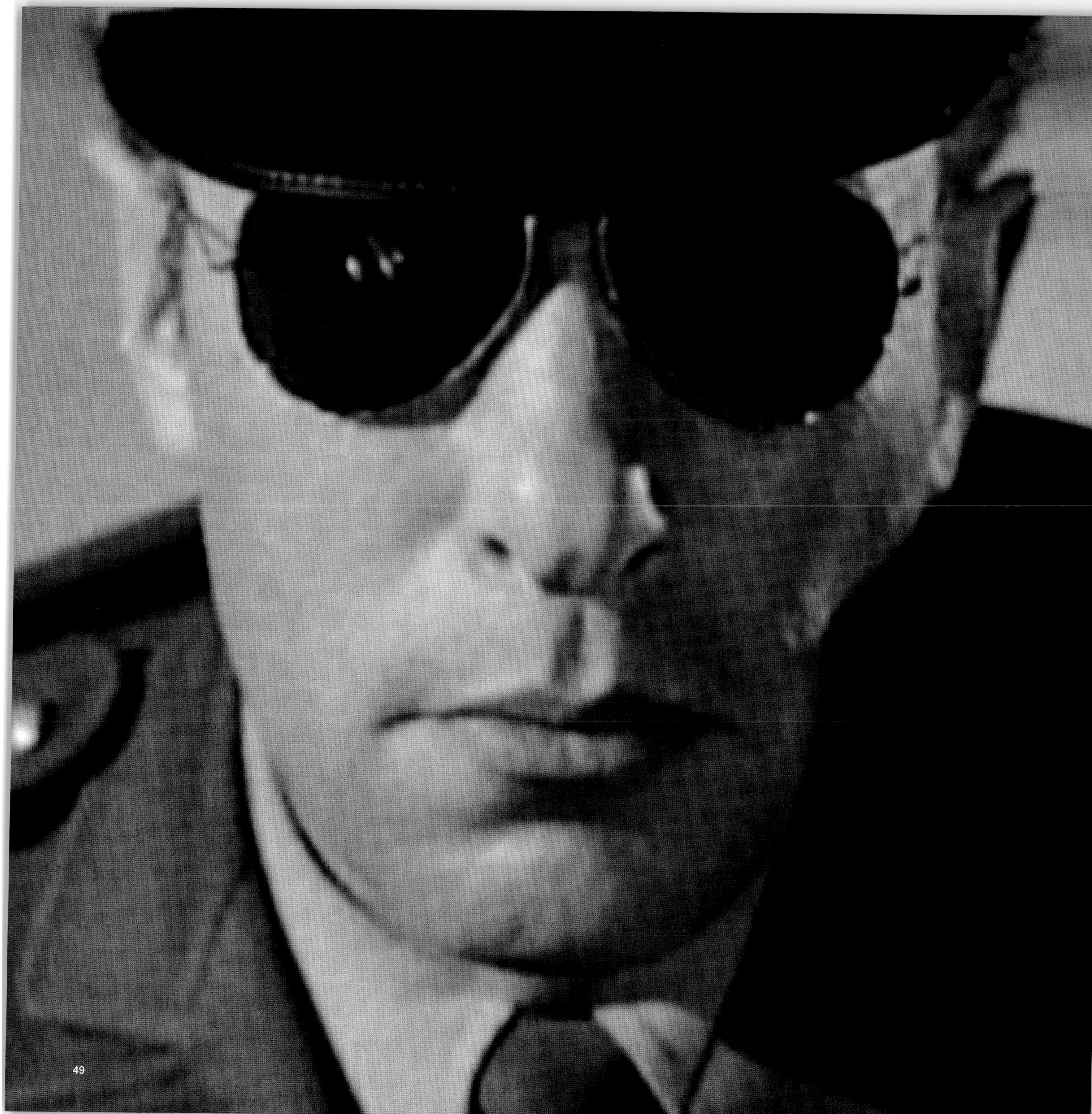

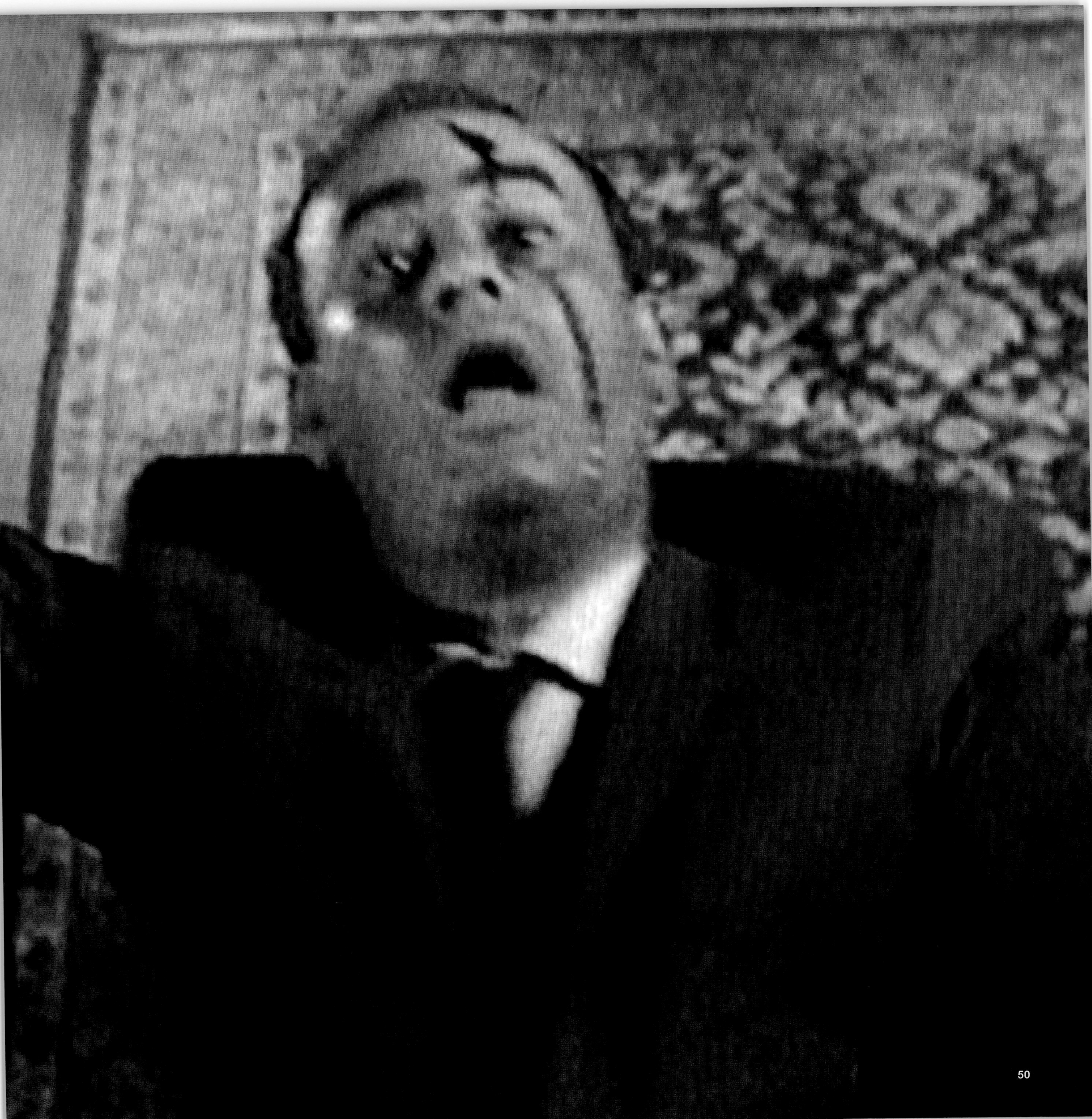

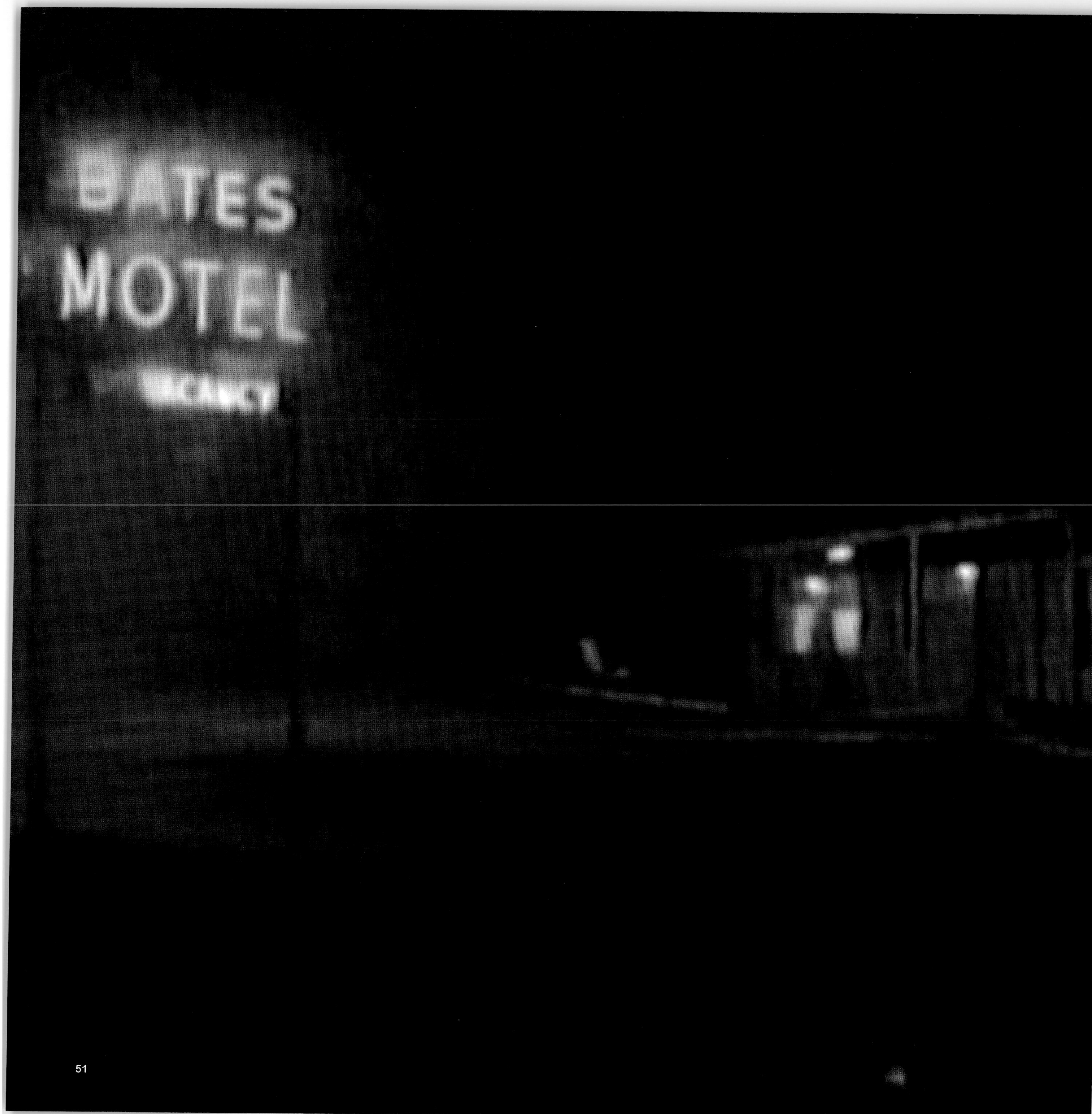
BATES
MOTEL
VACANCY

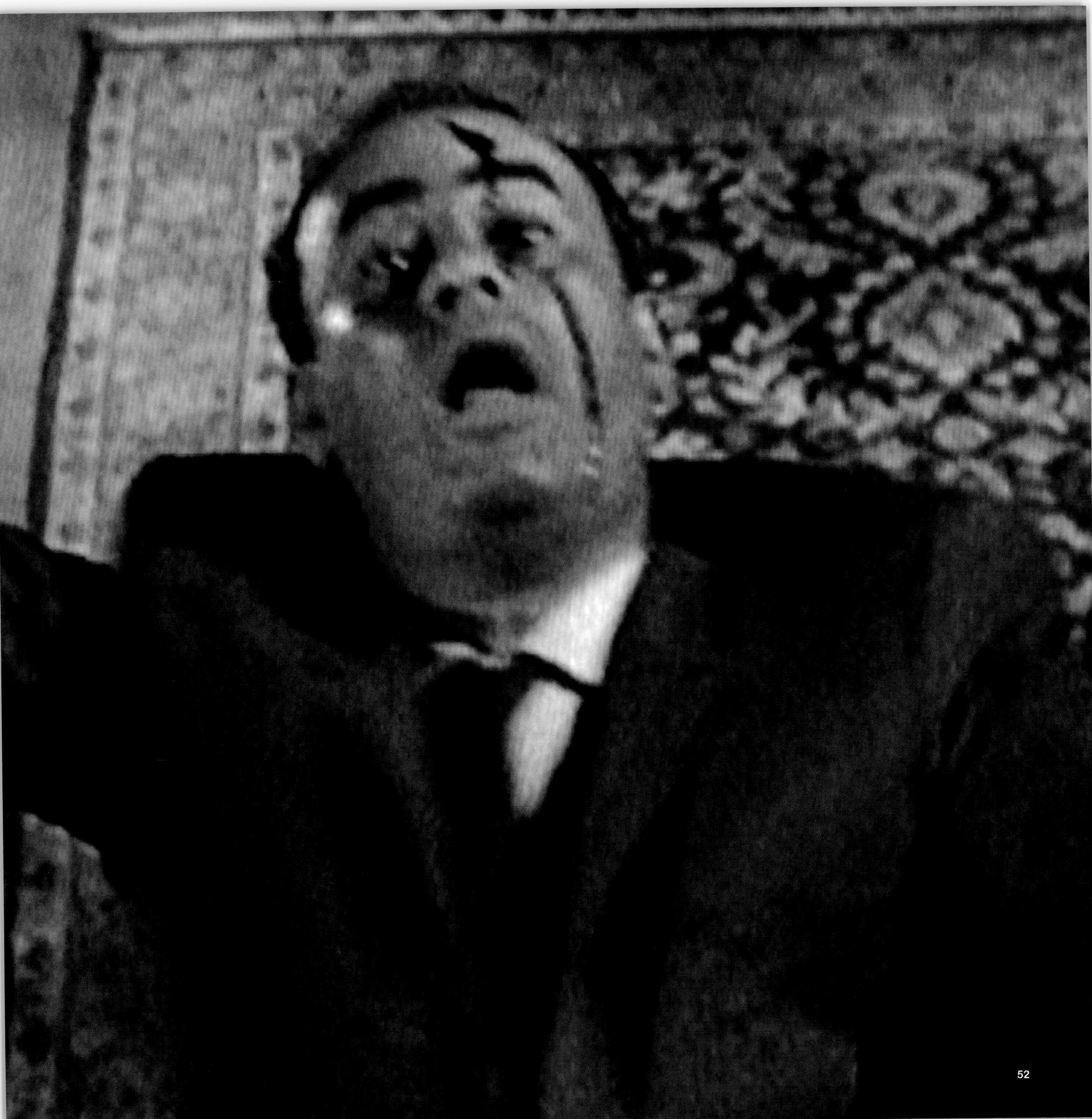

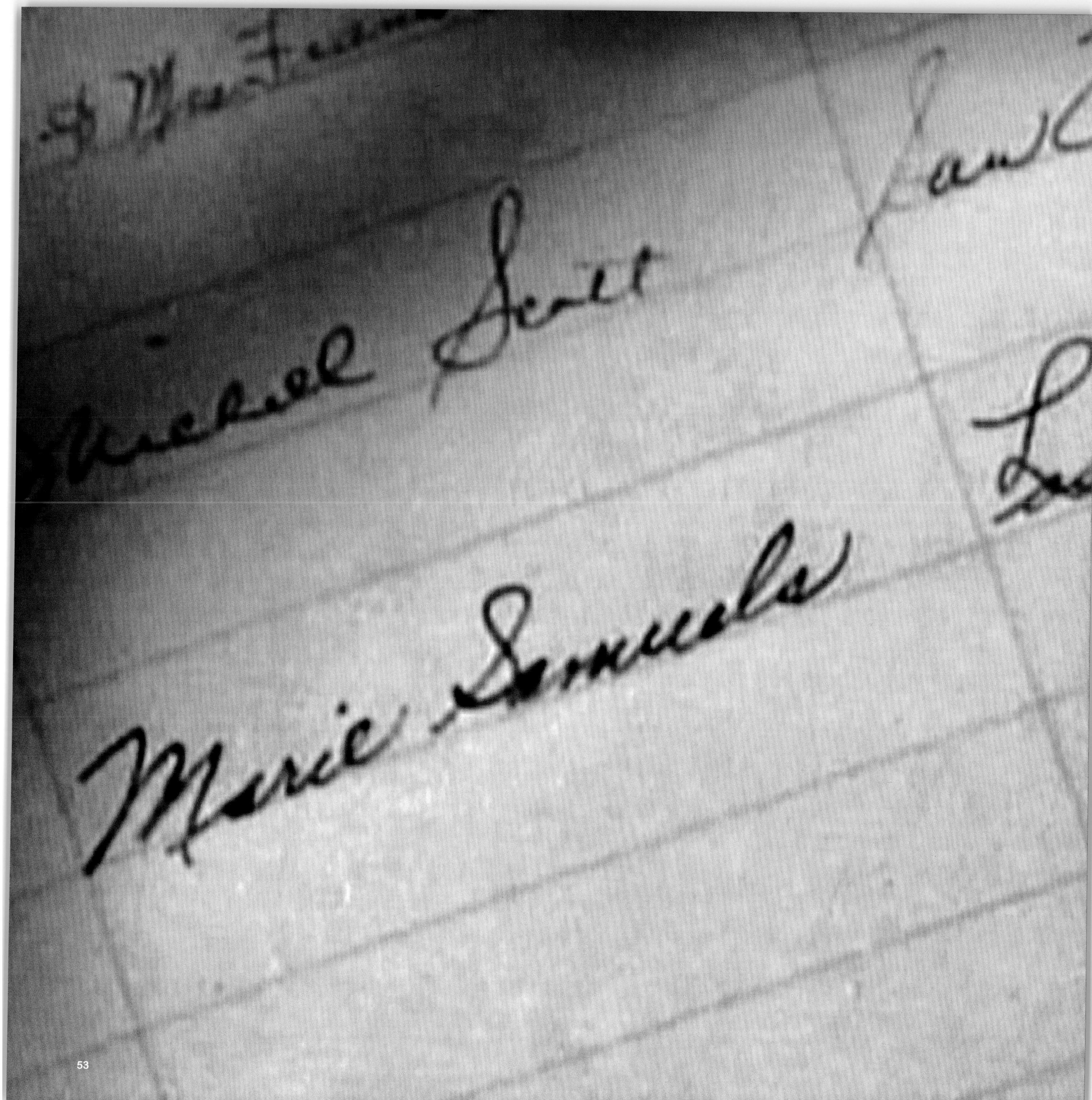

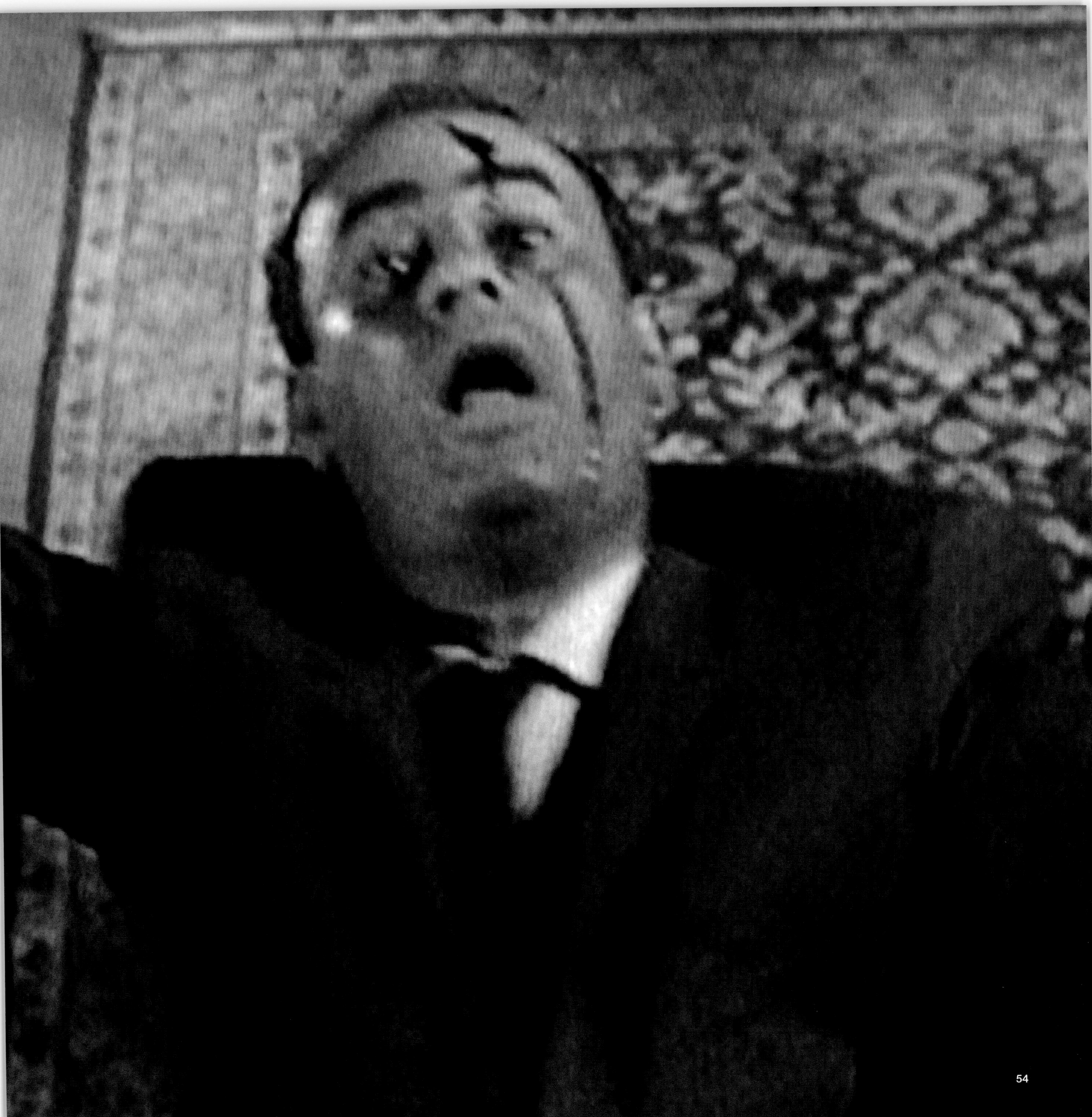

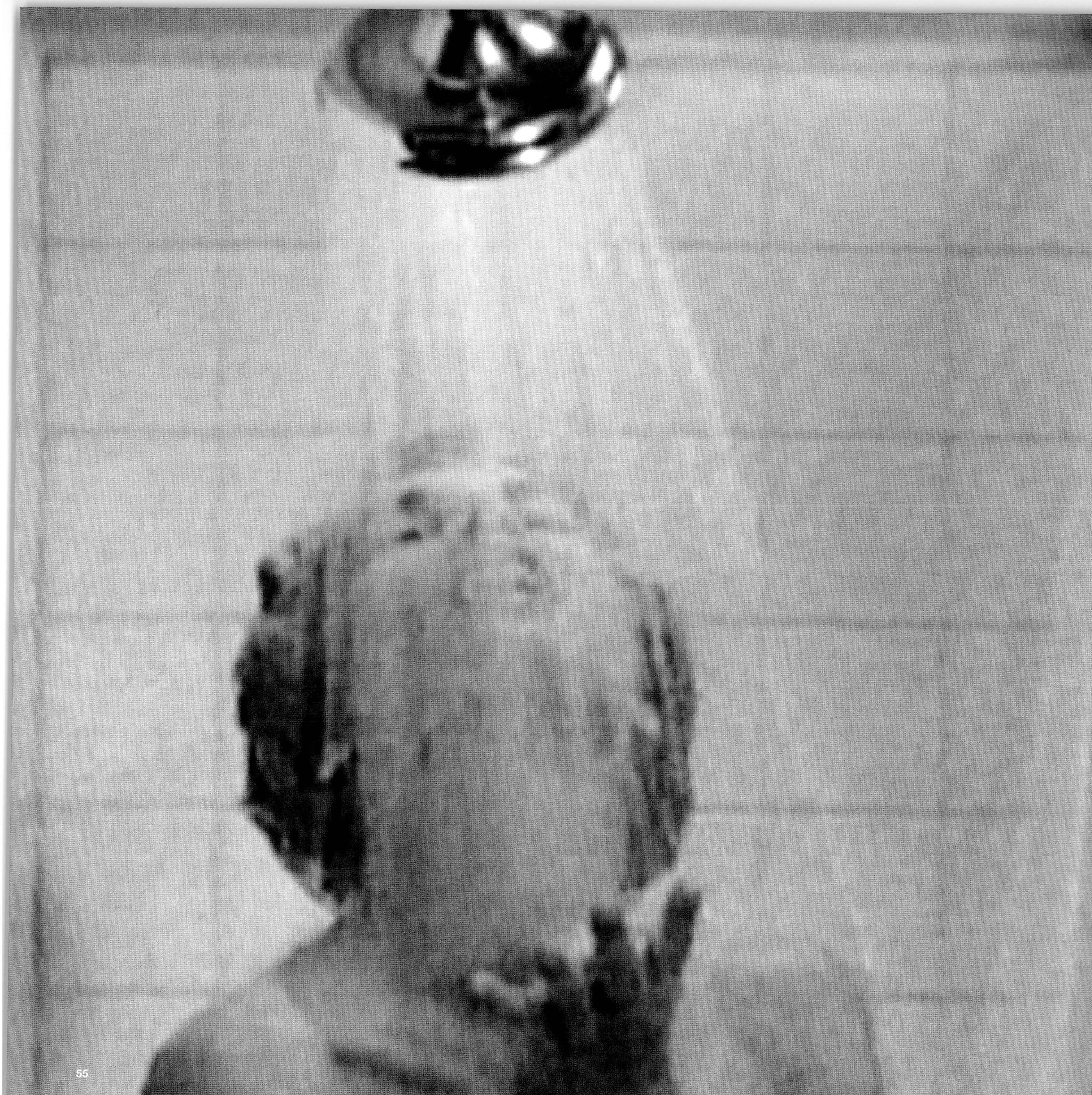

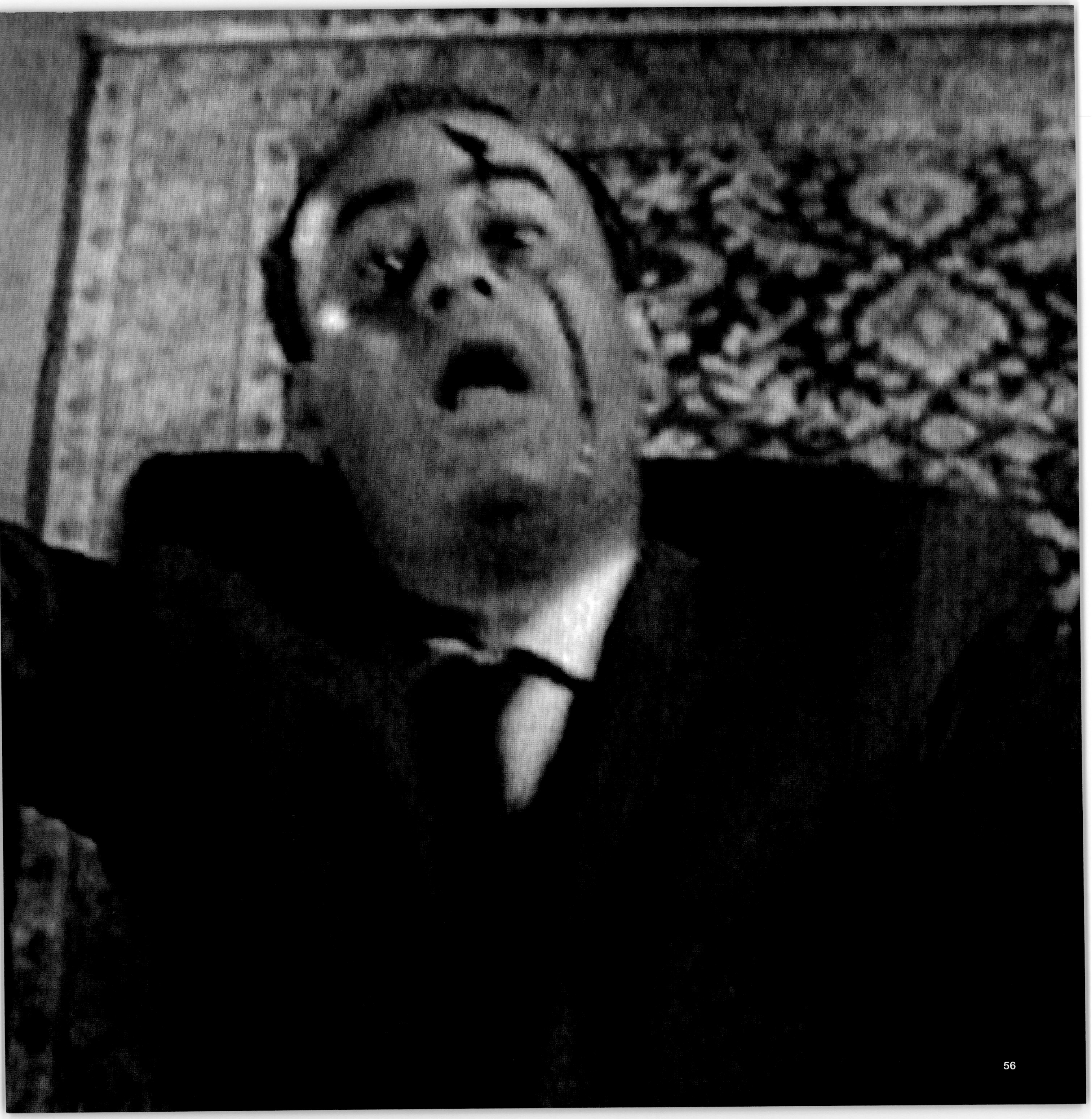

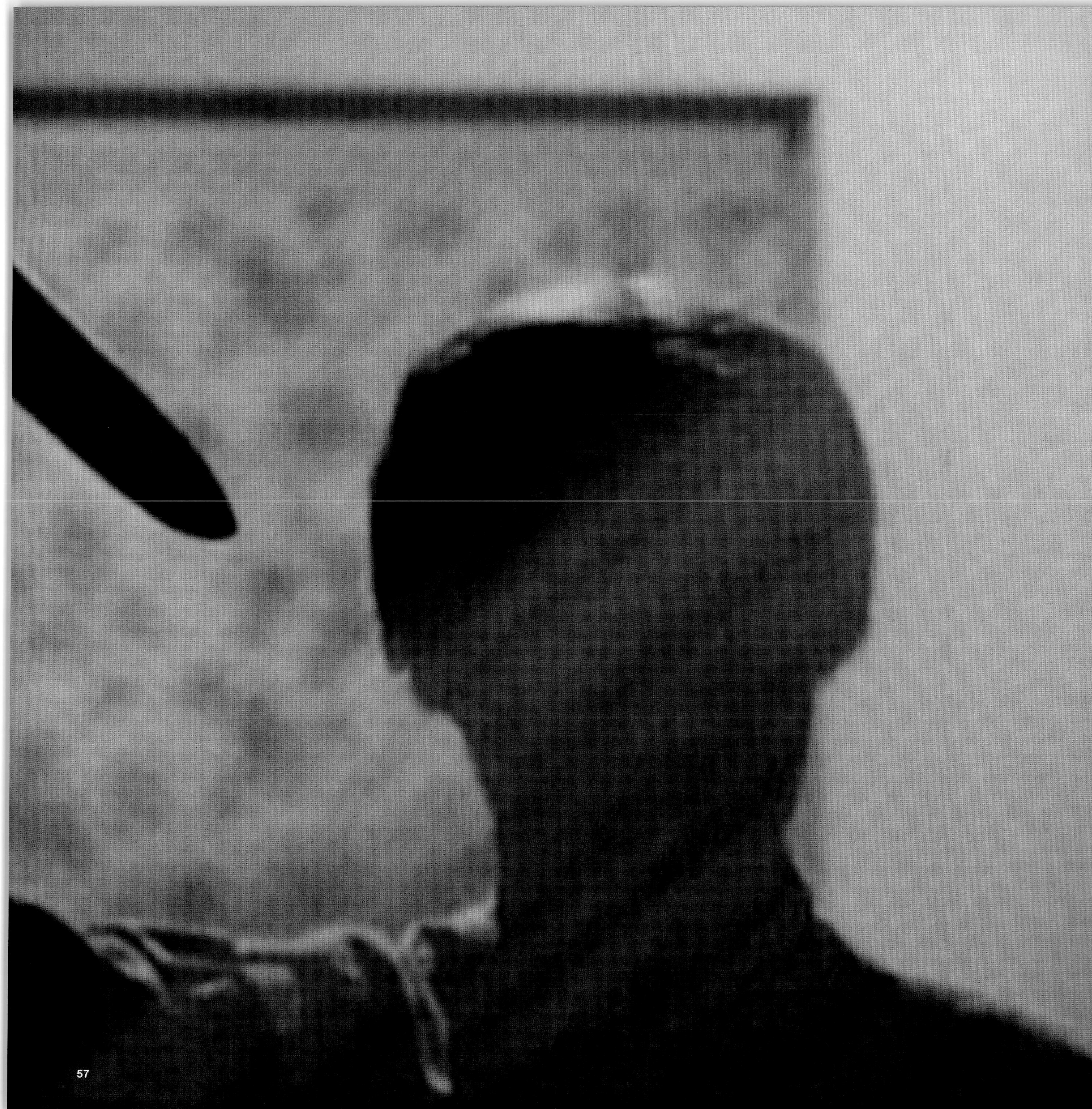

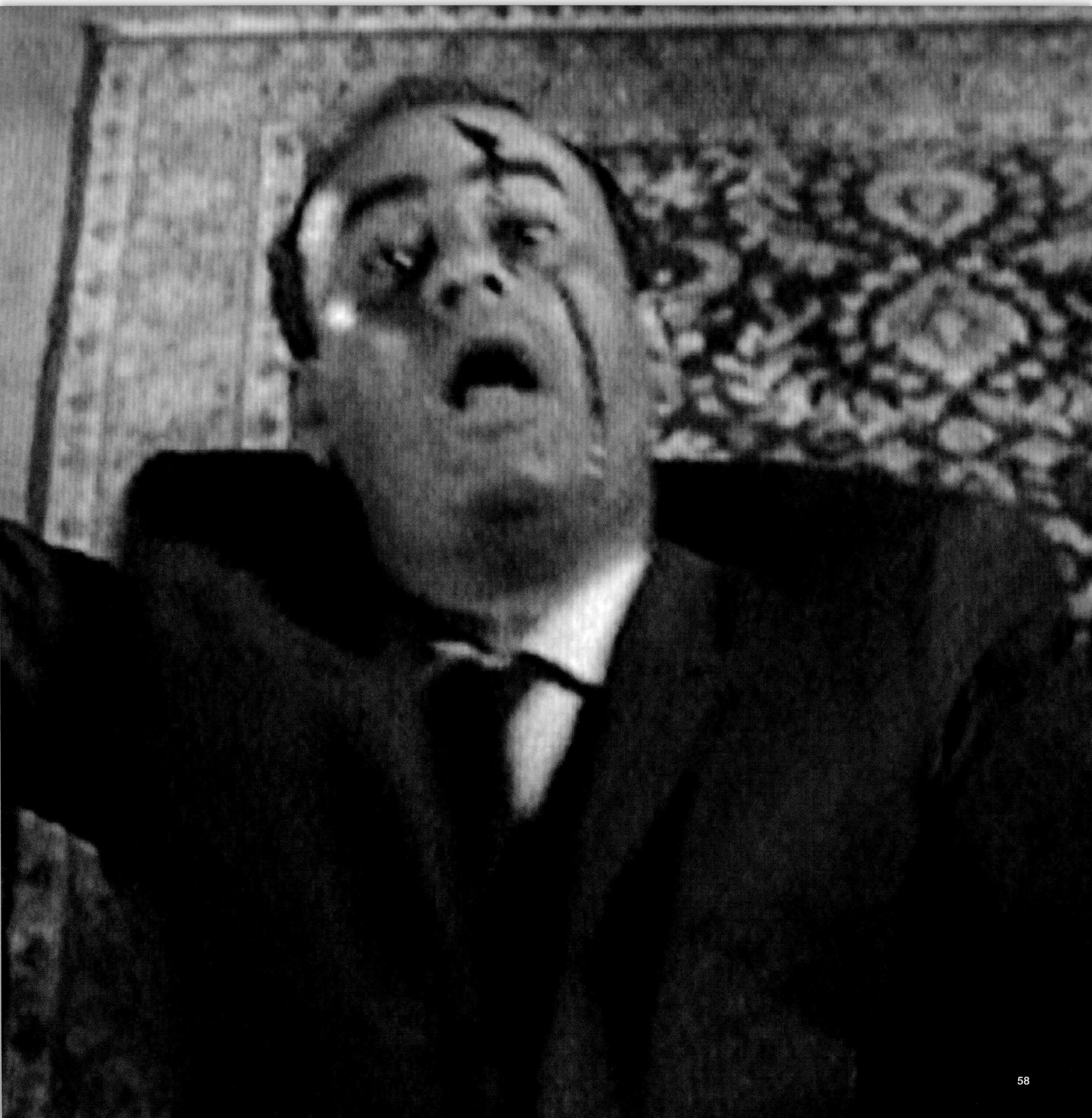

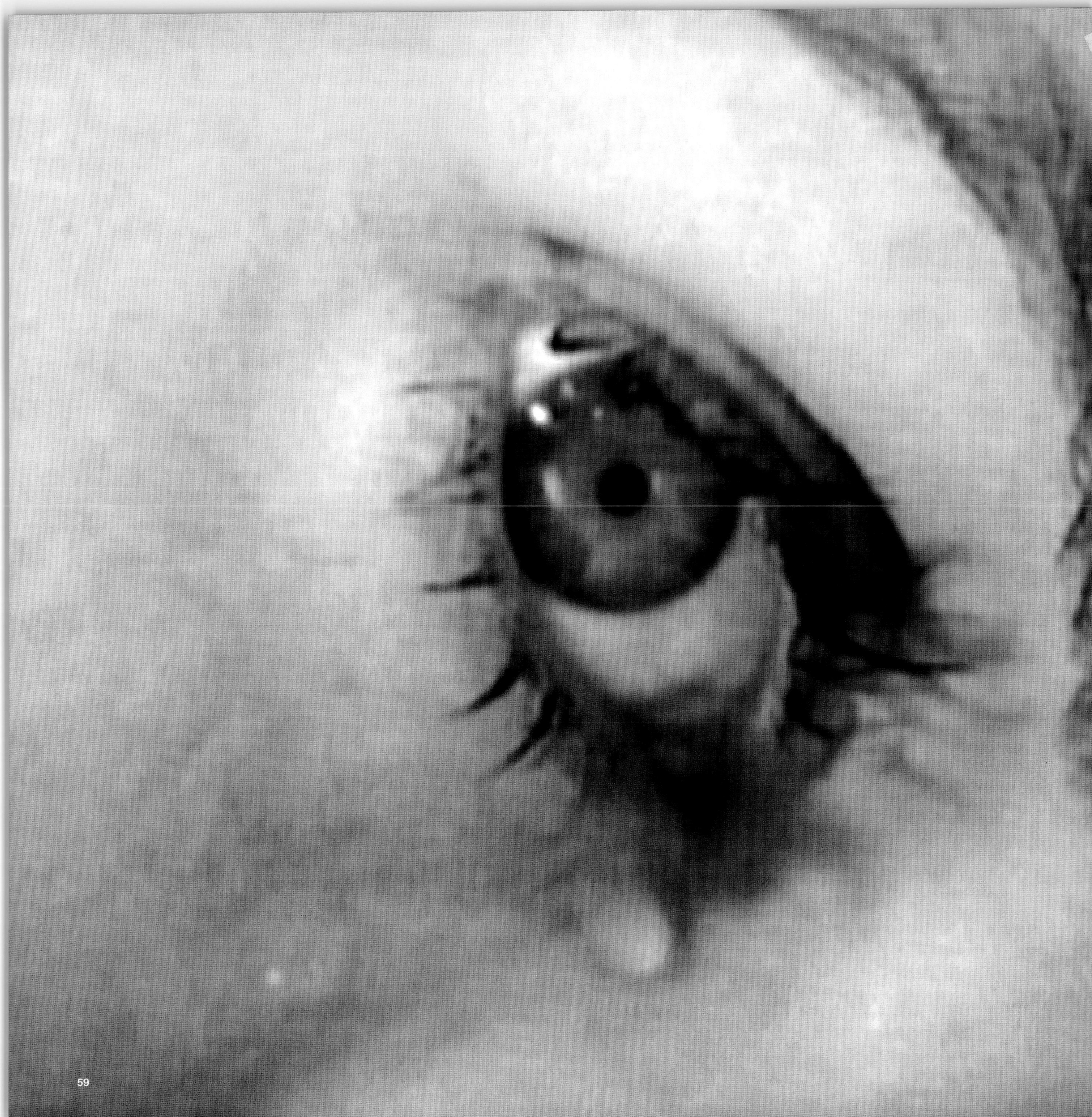

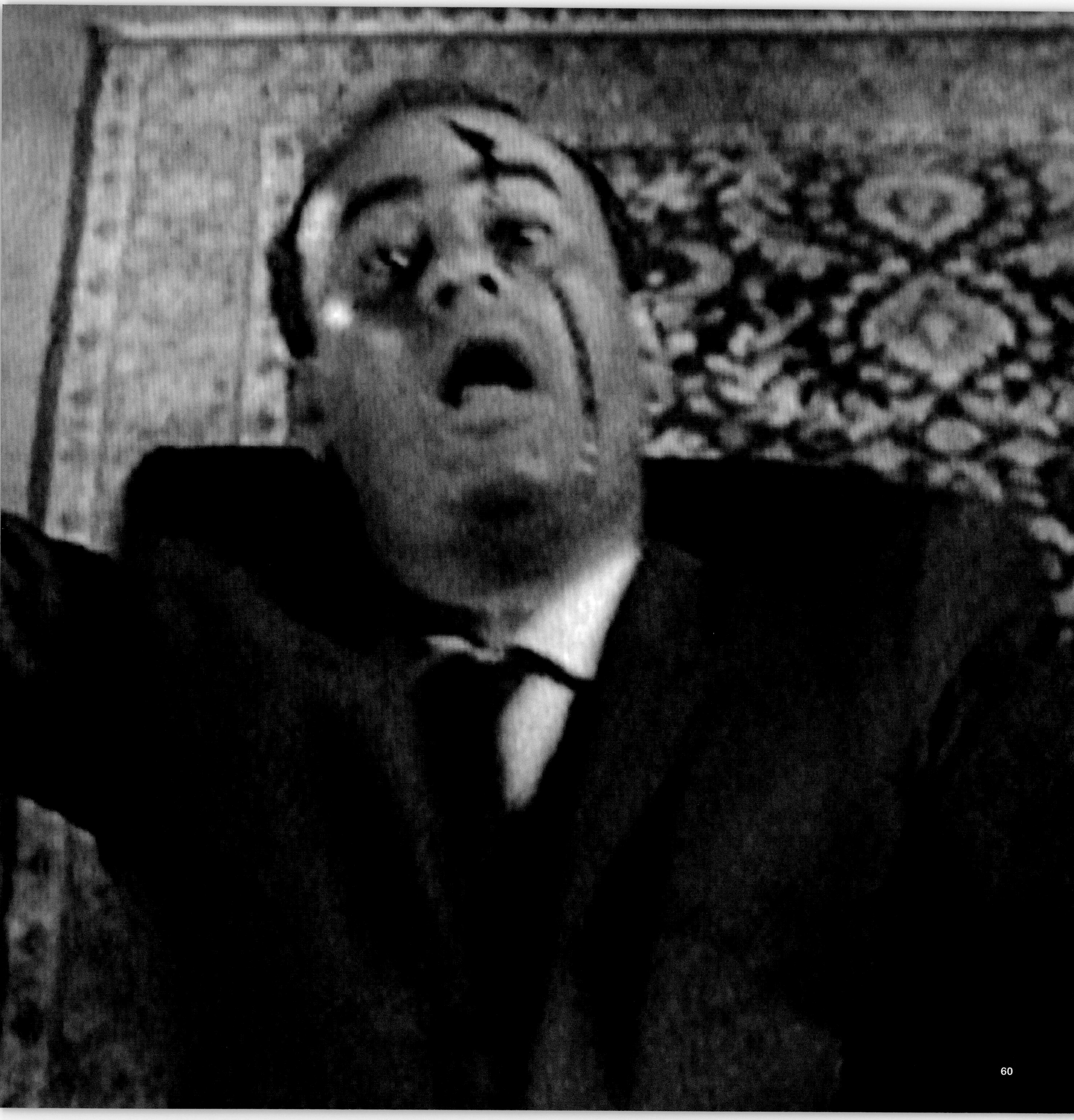

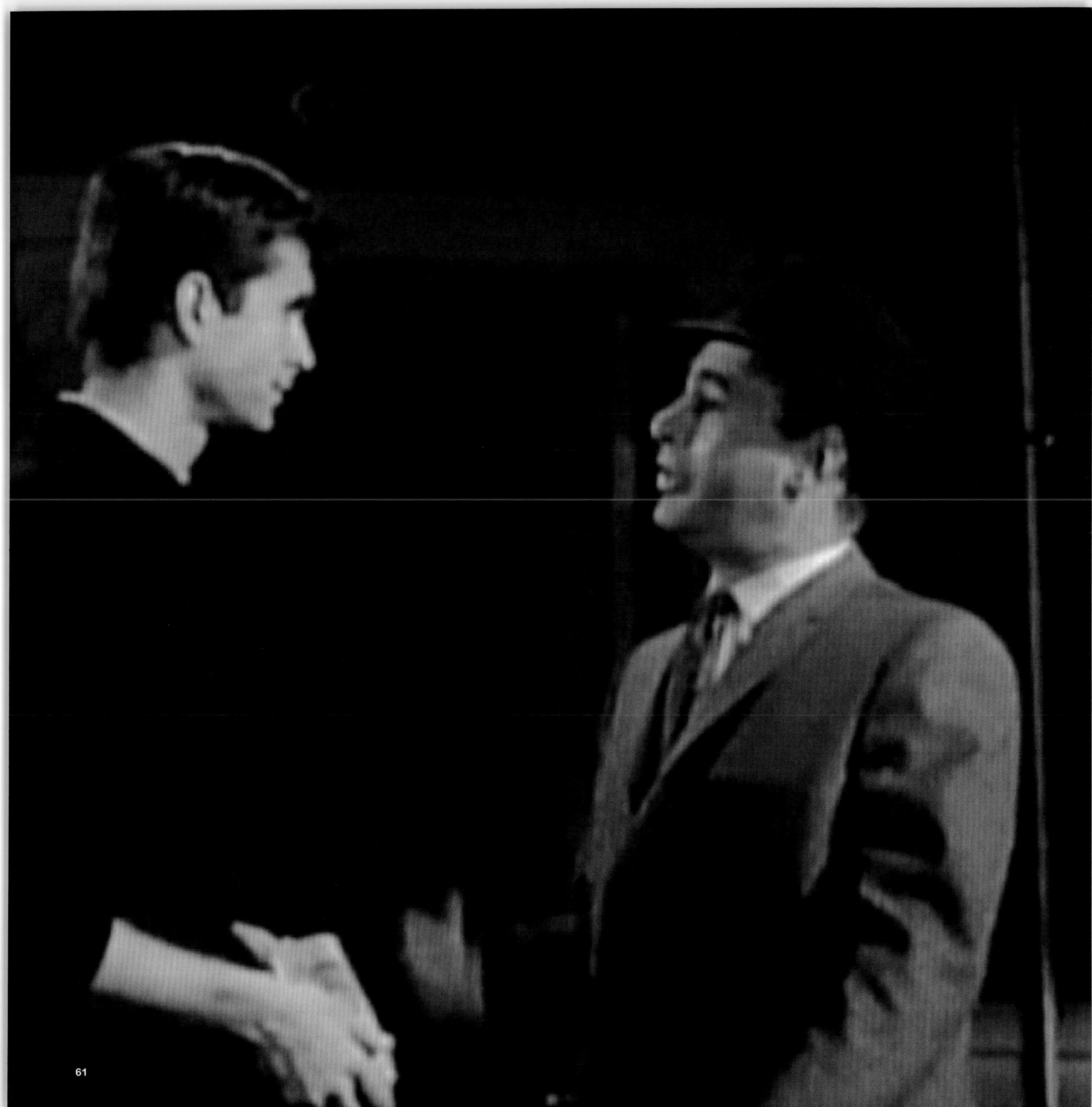

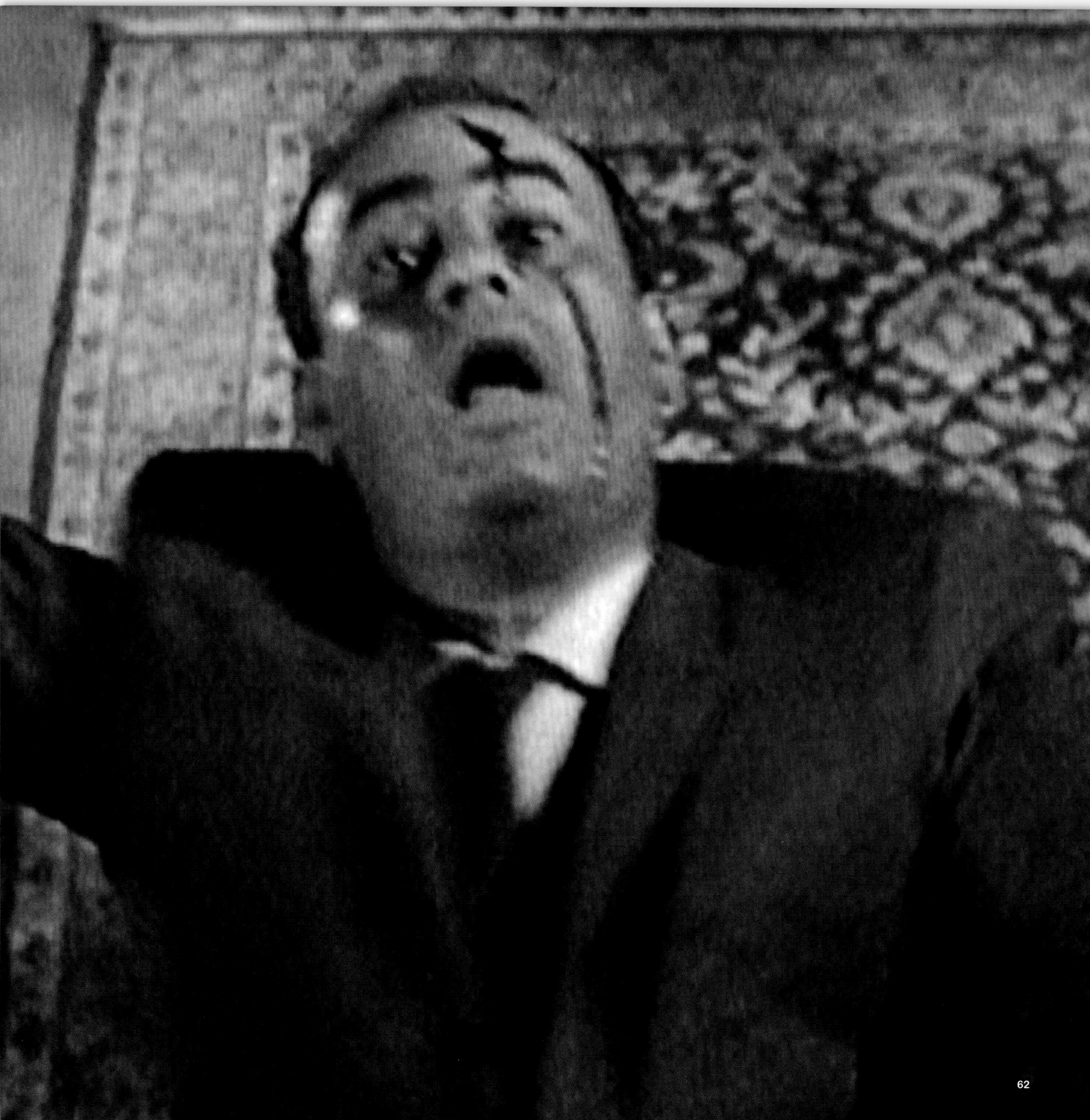

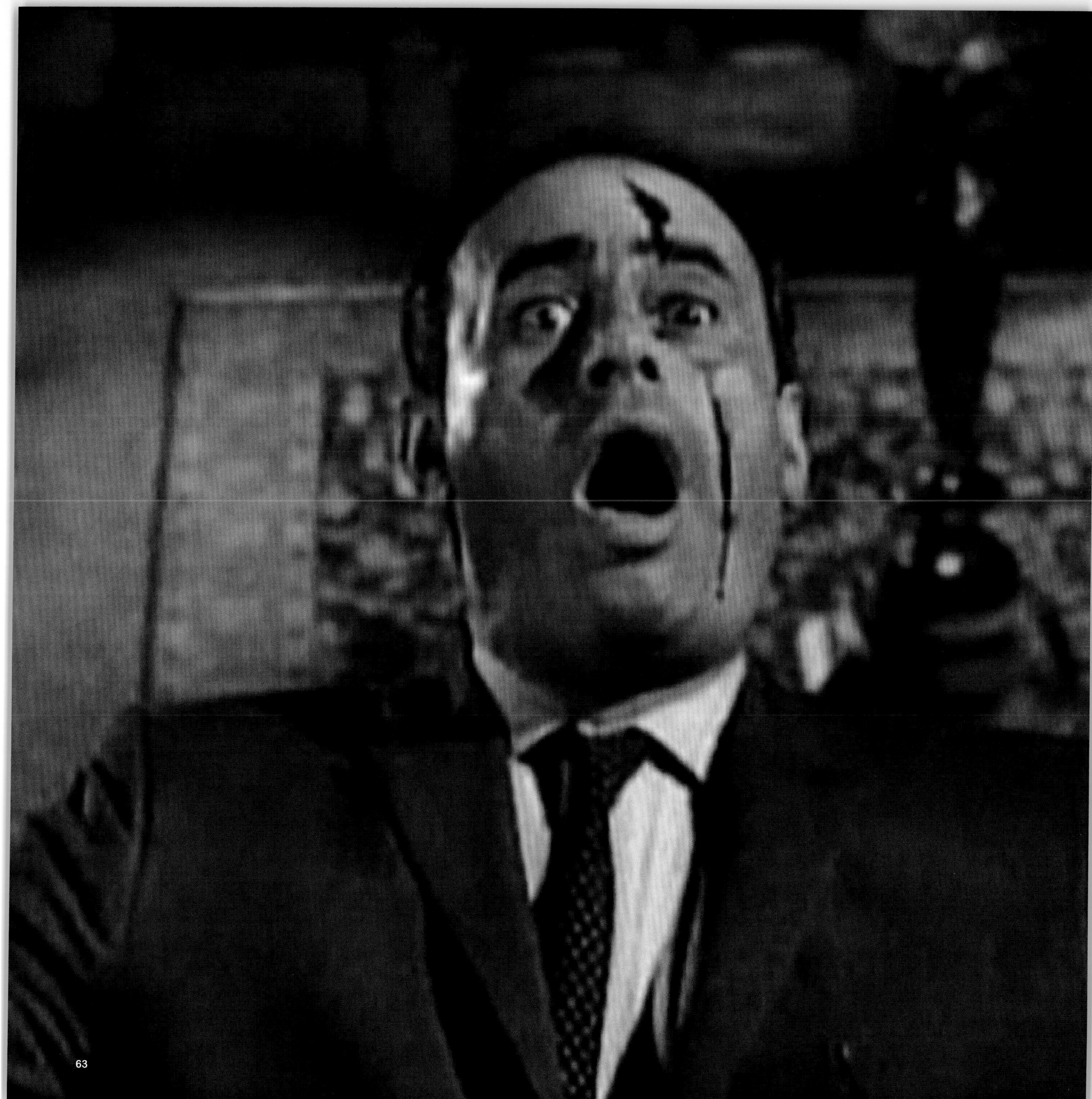

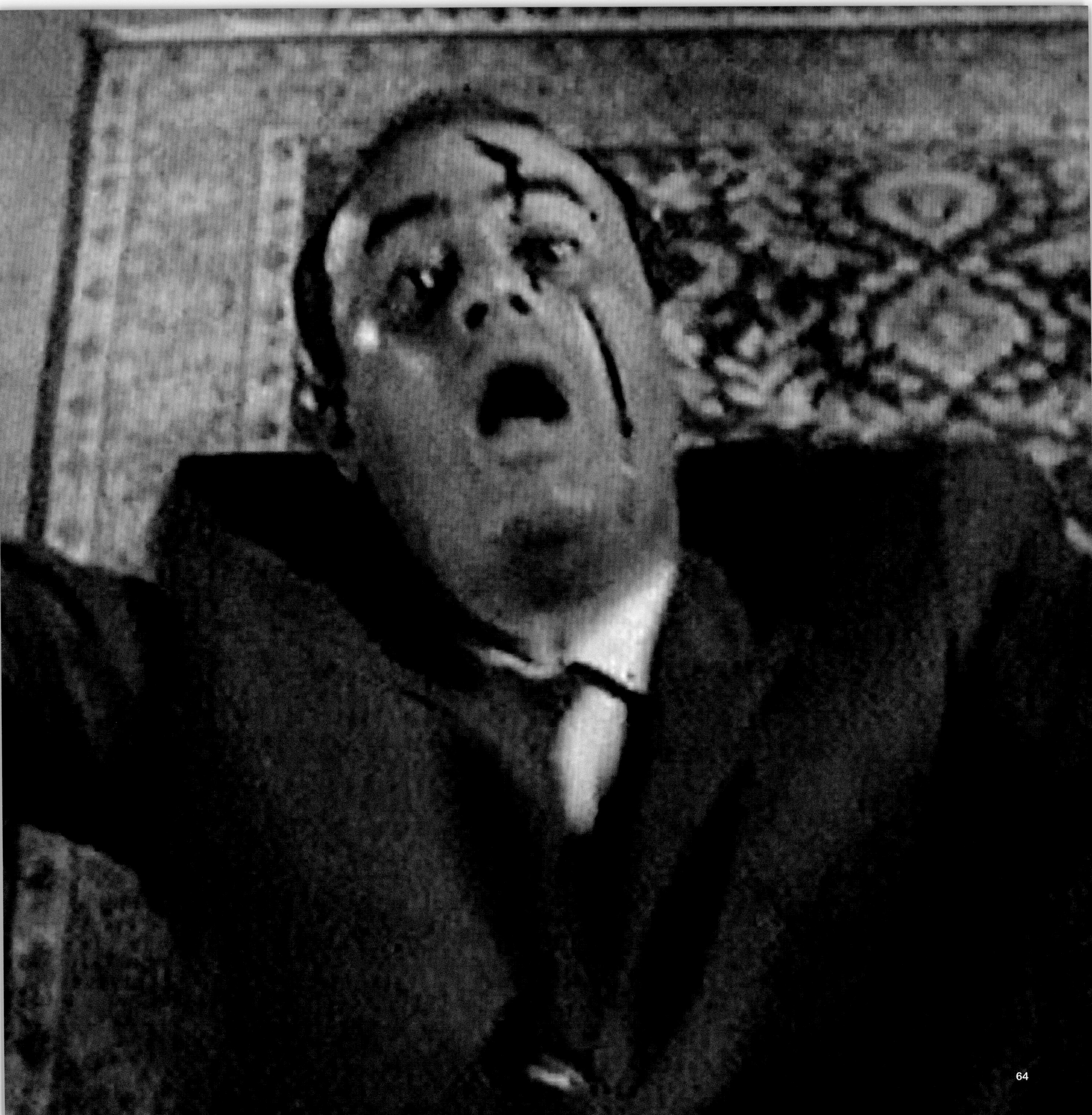

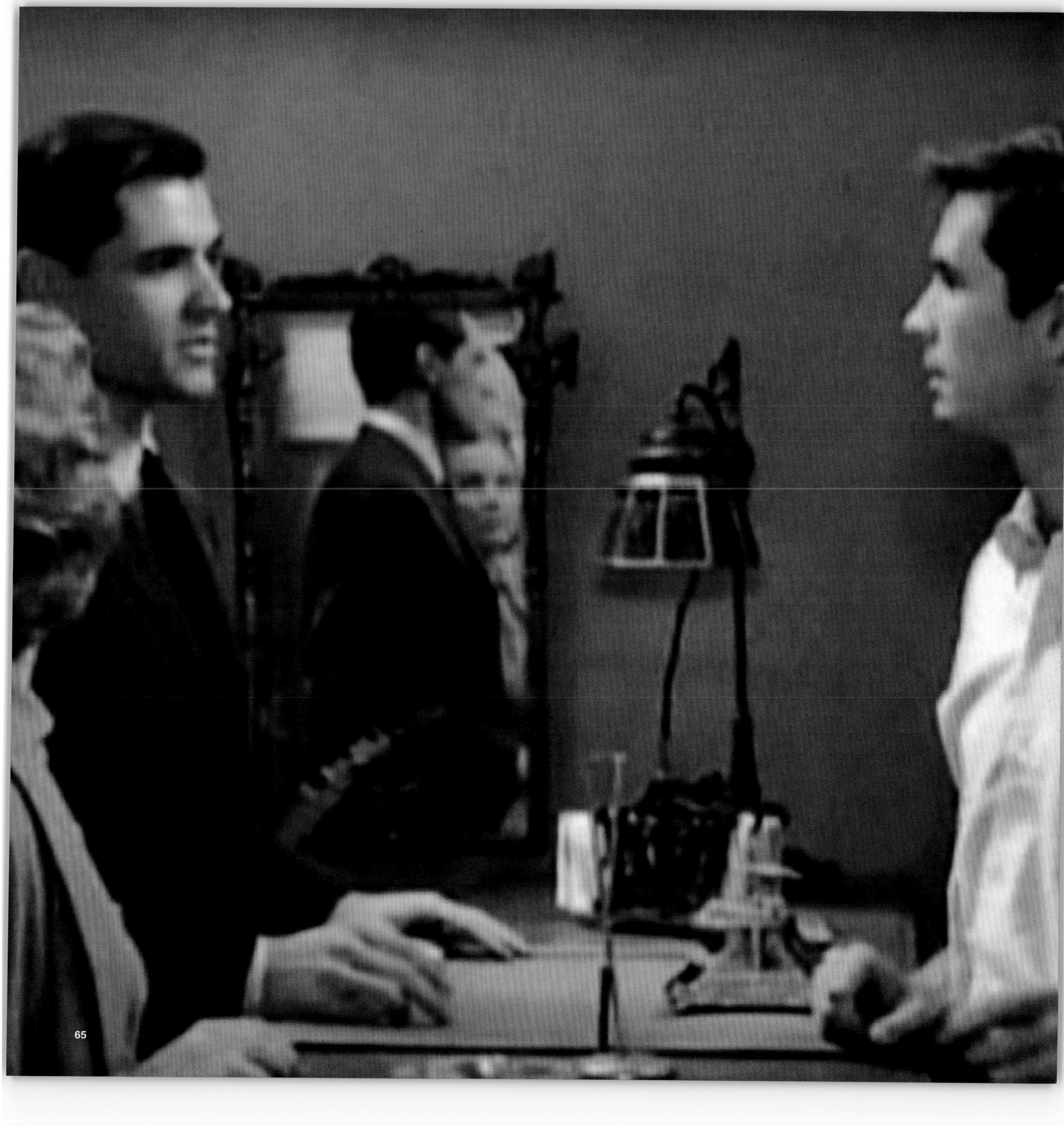

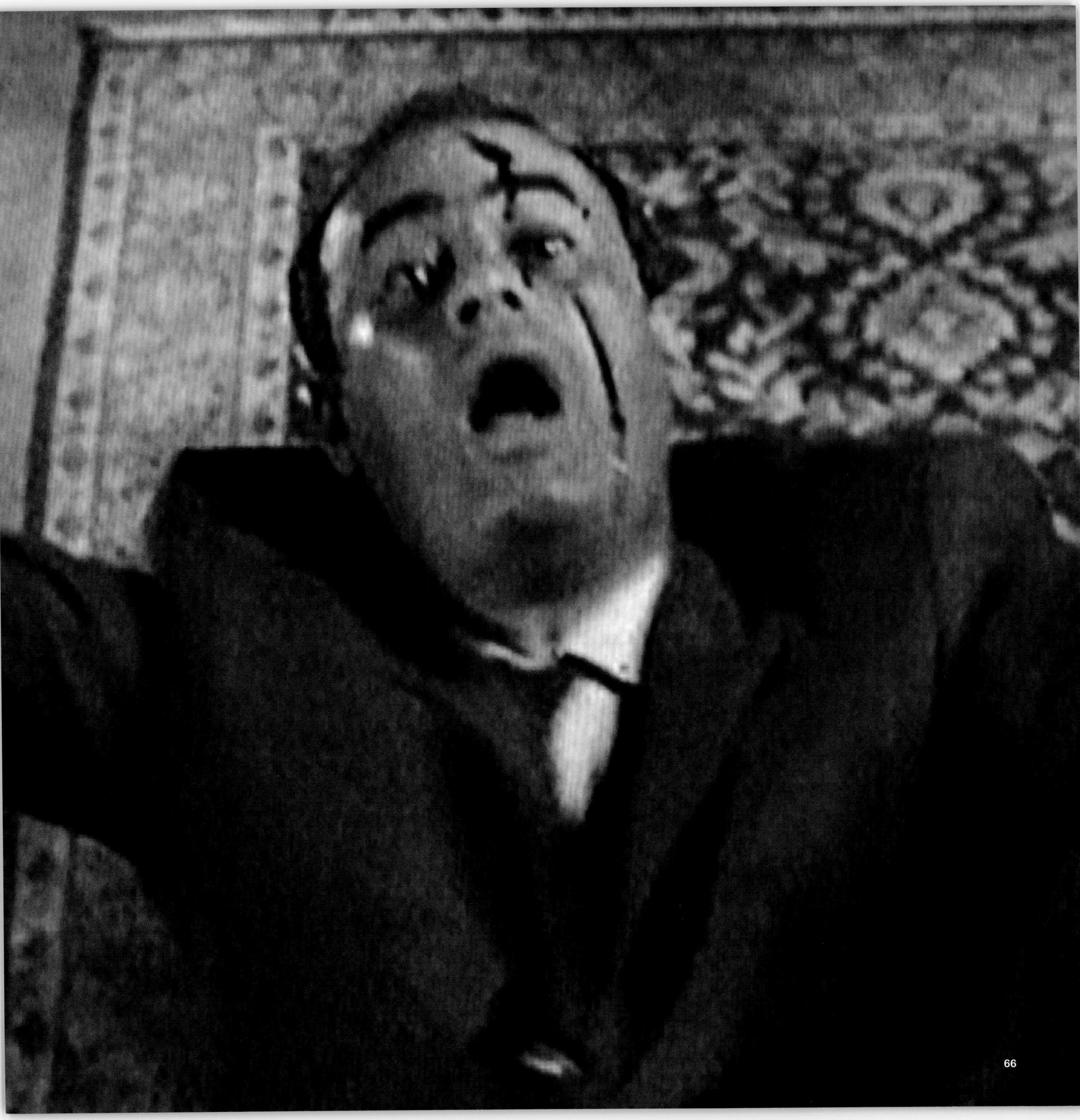

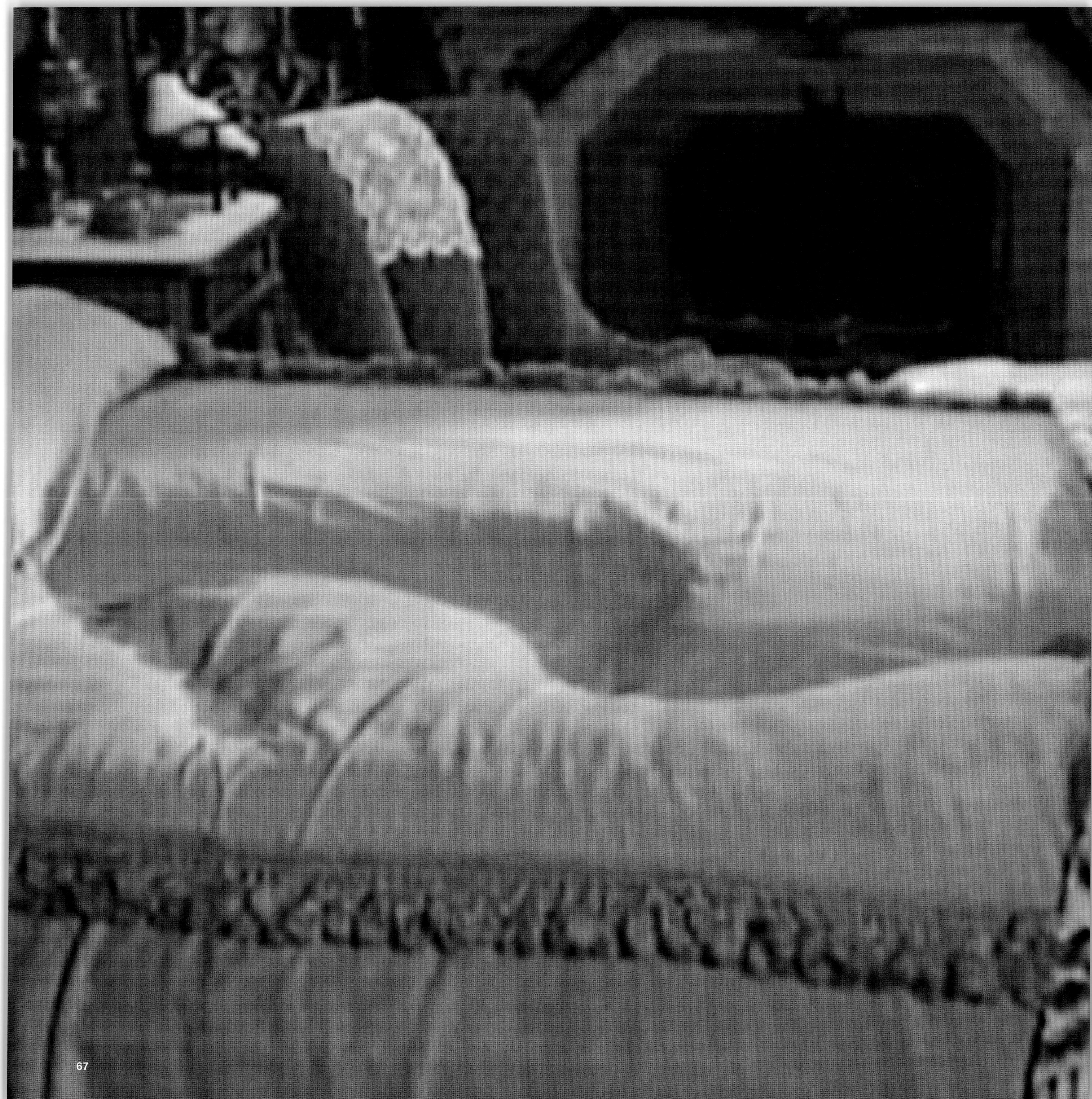

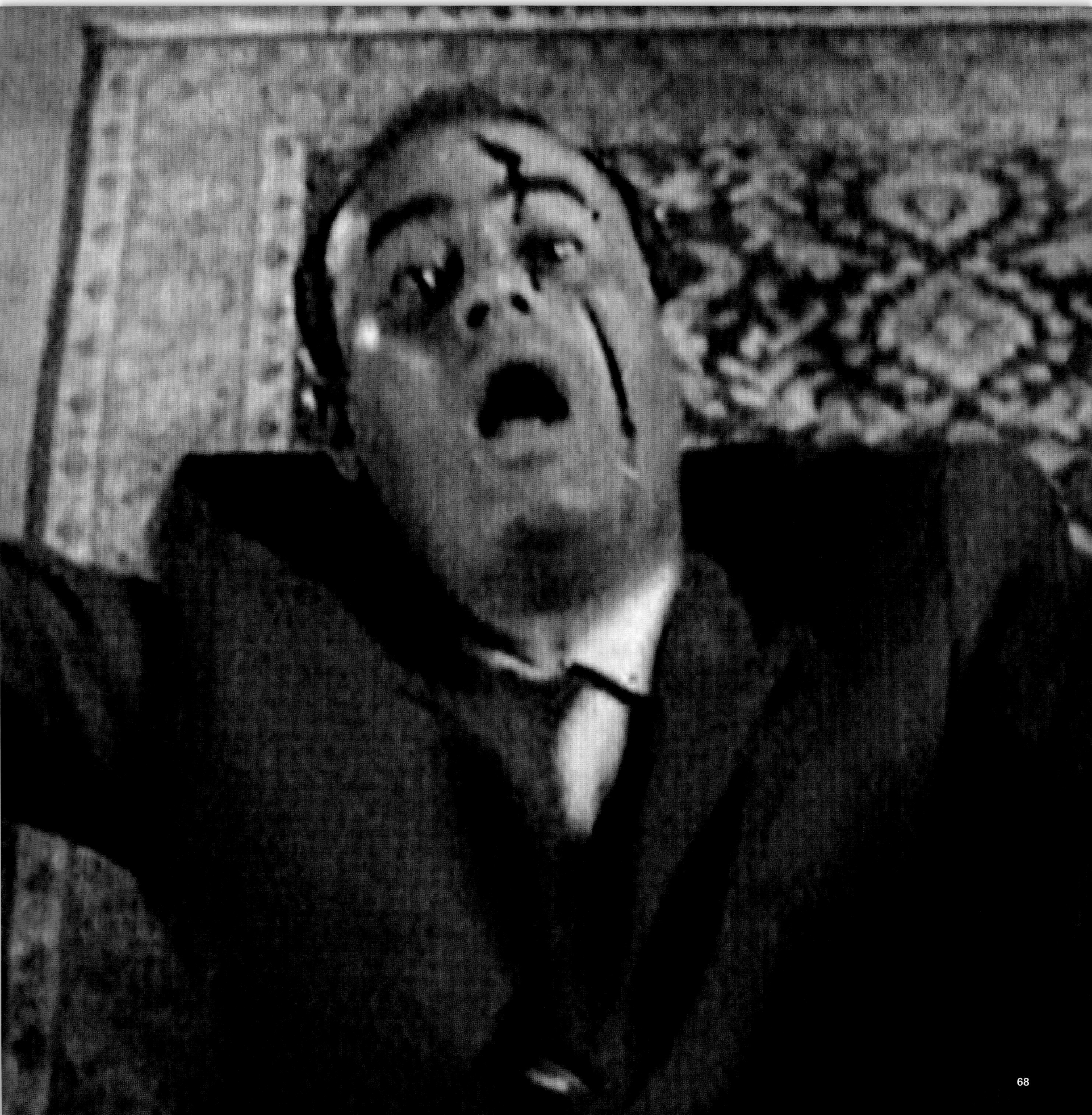

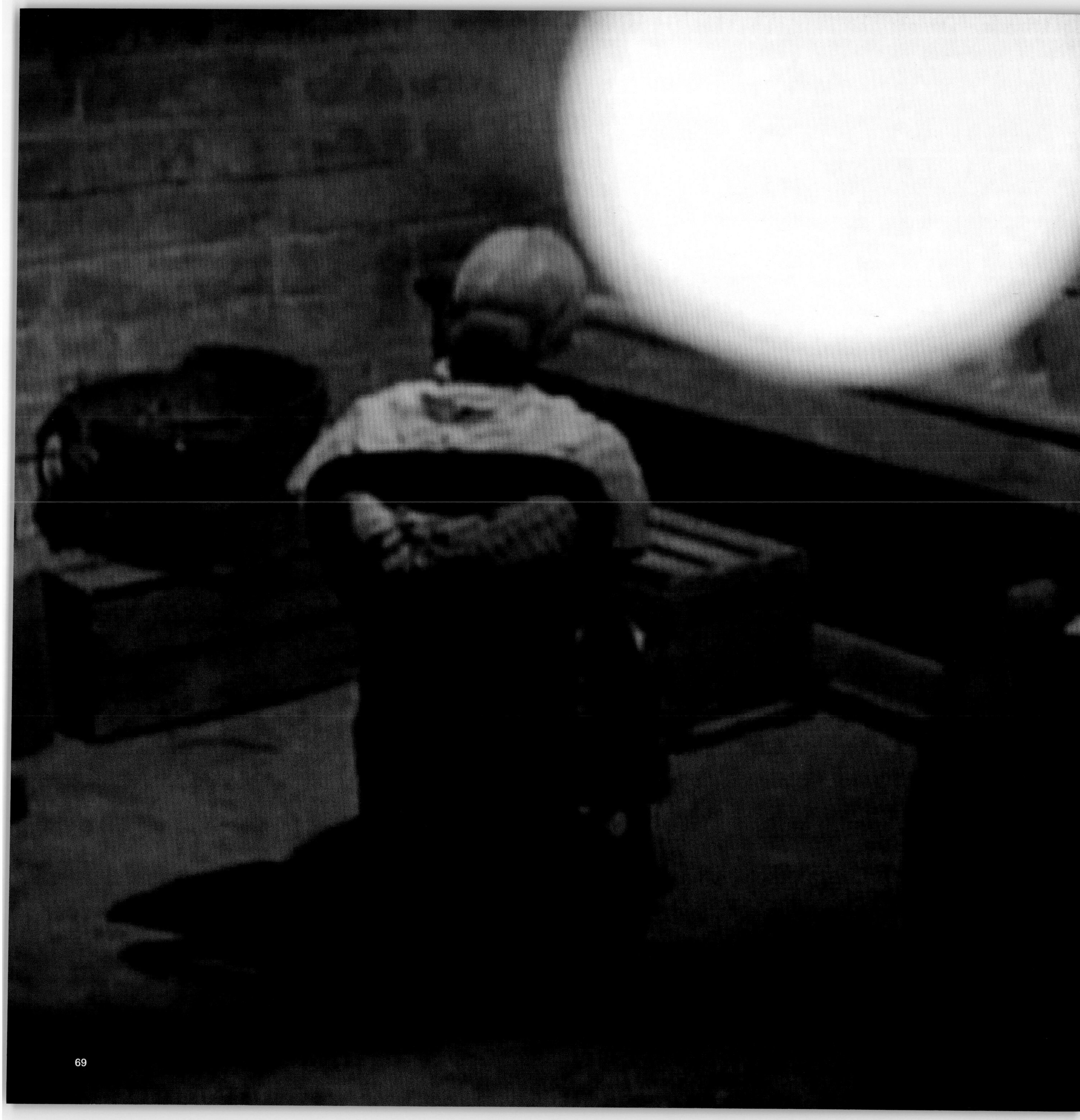

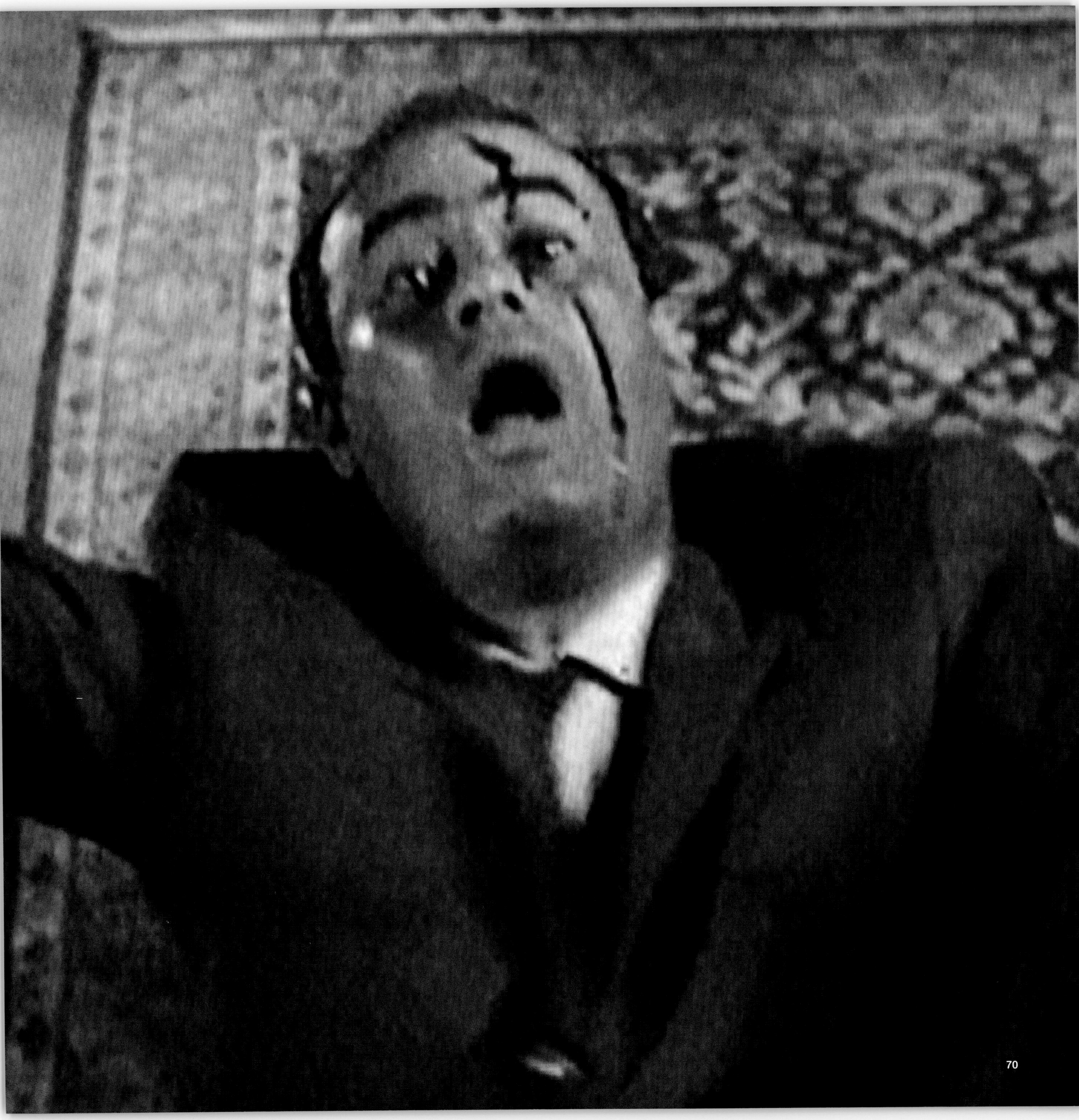

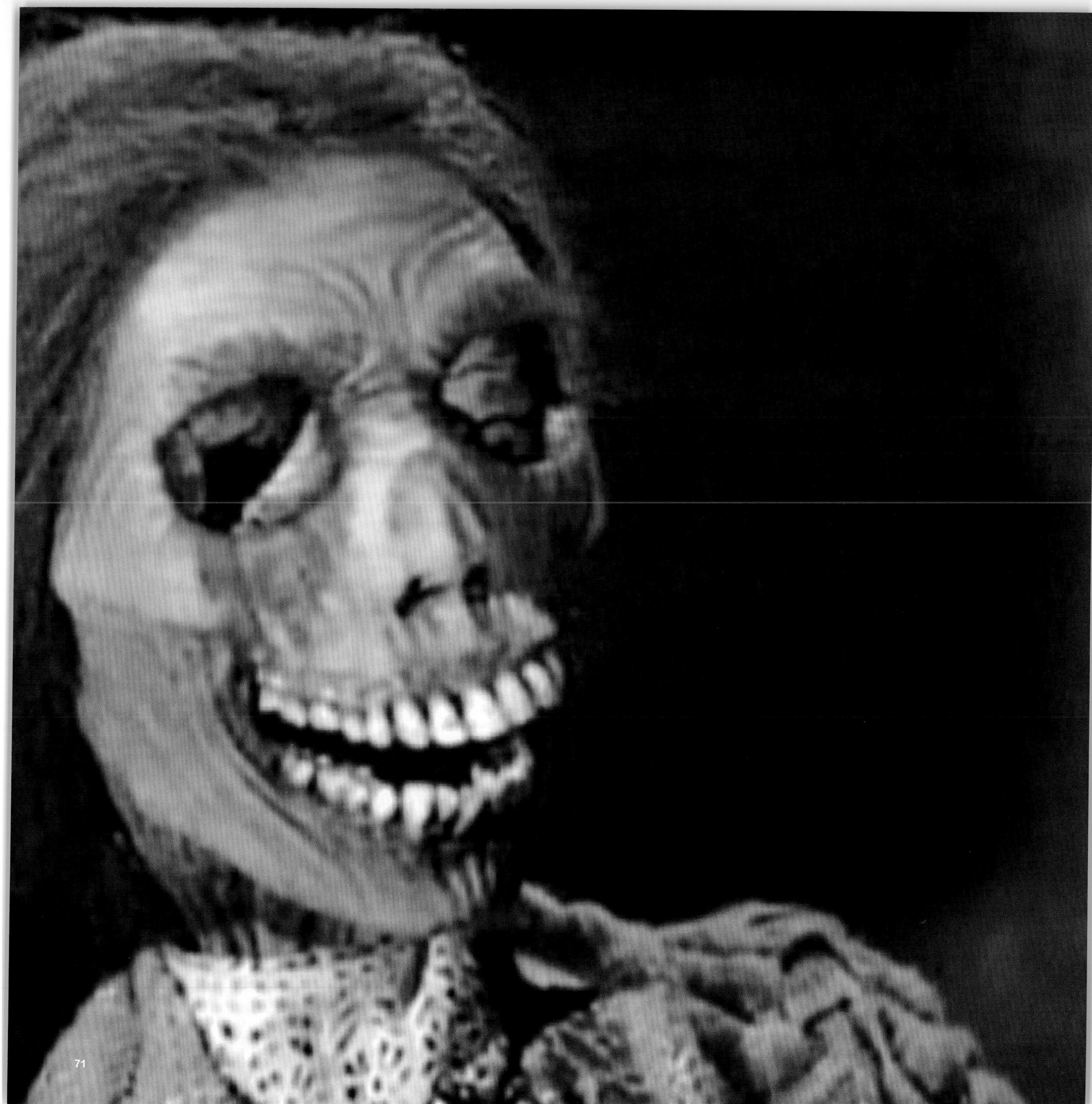

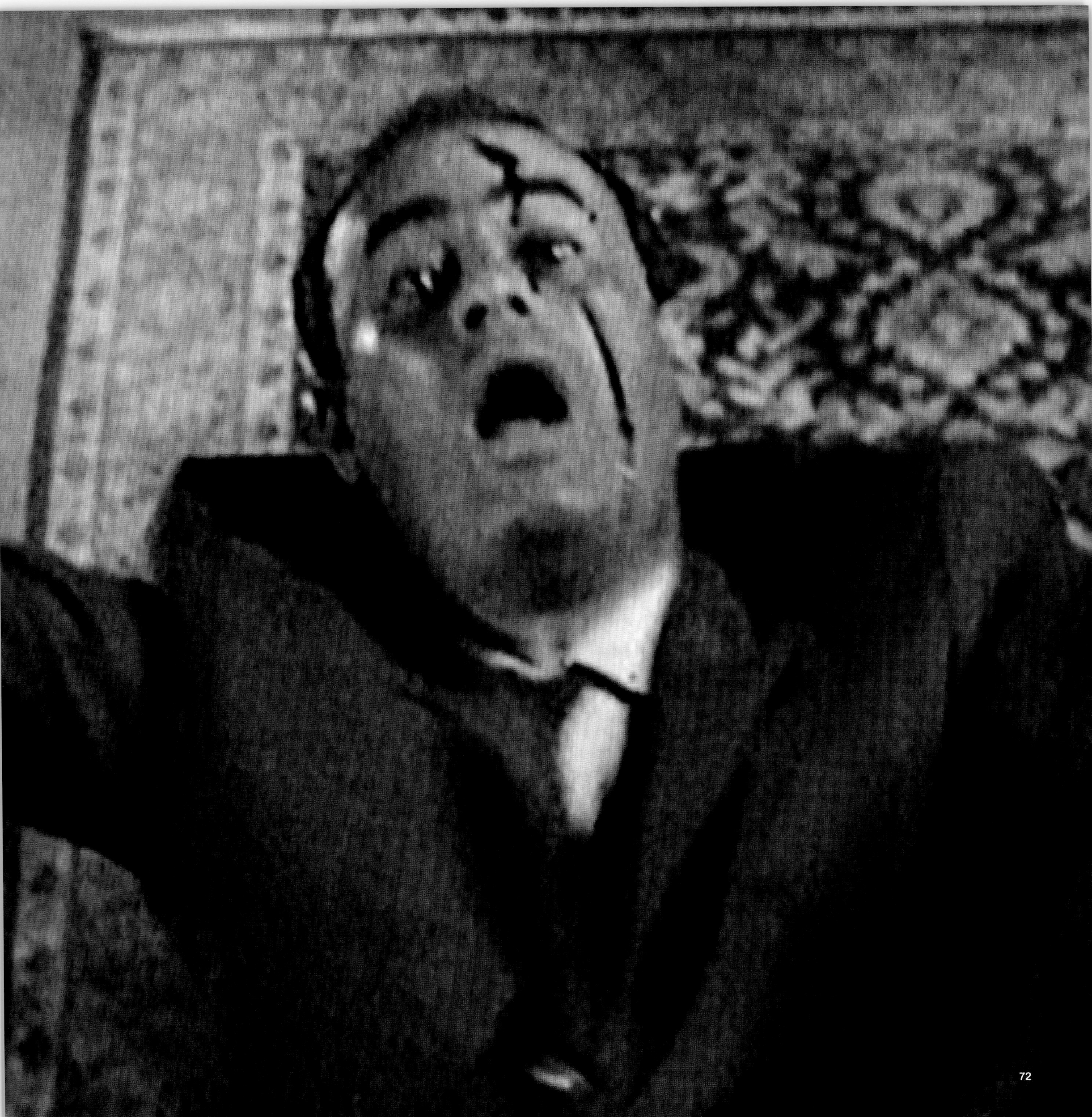

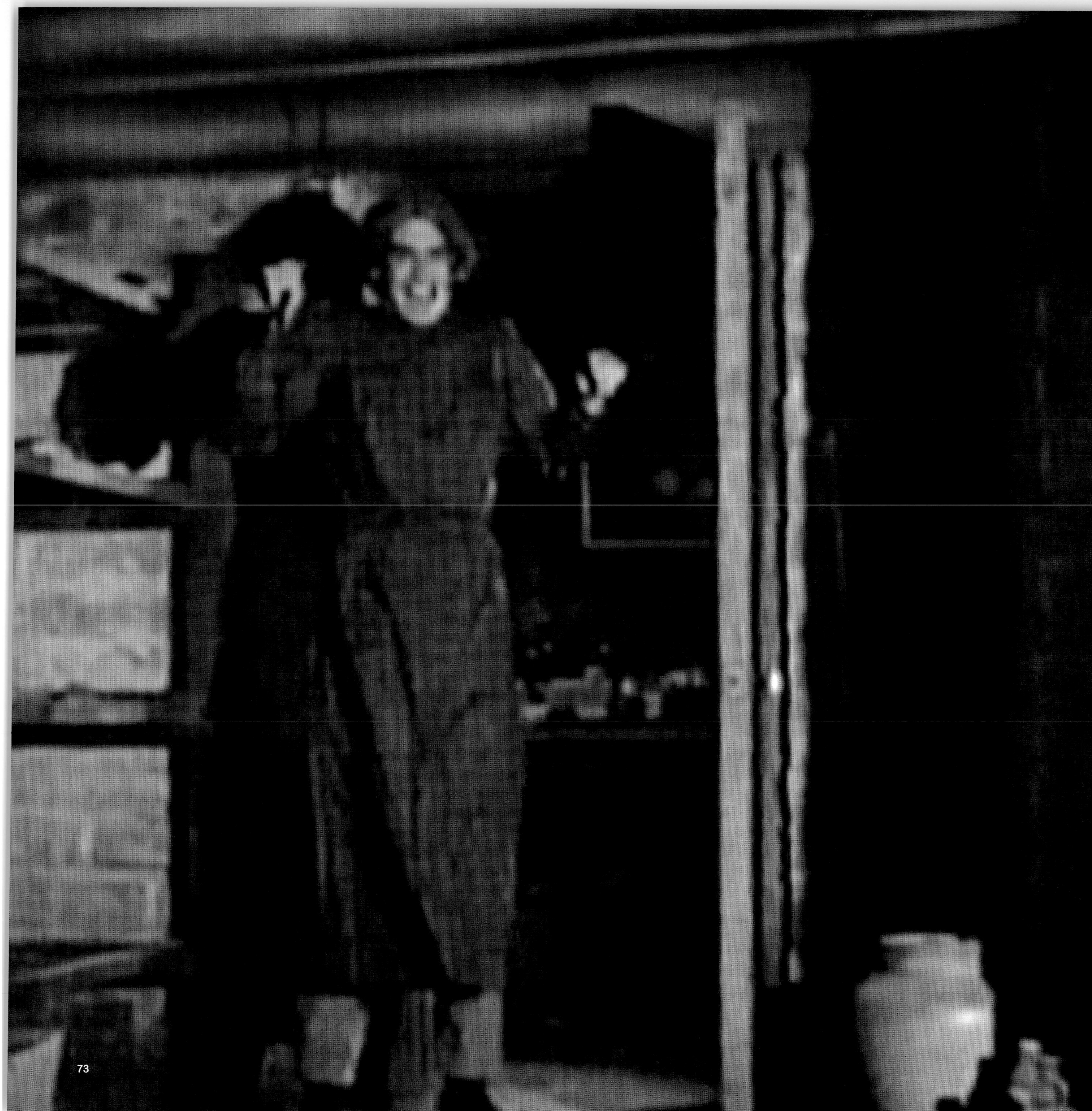

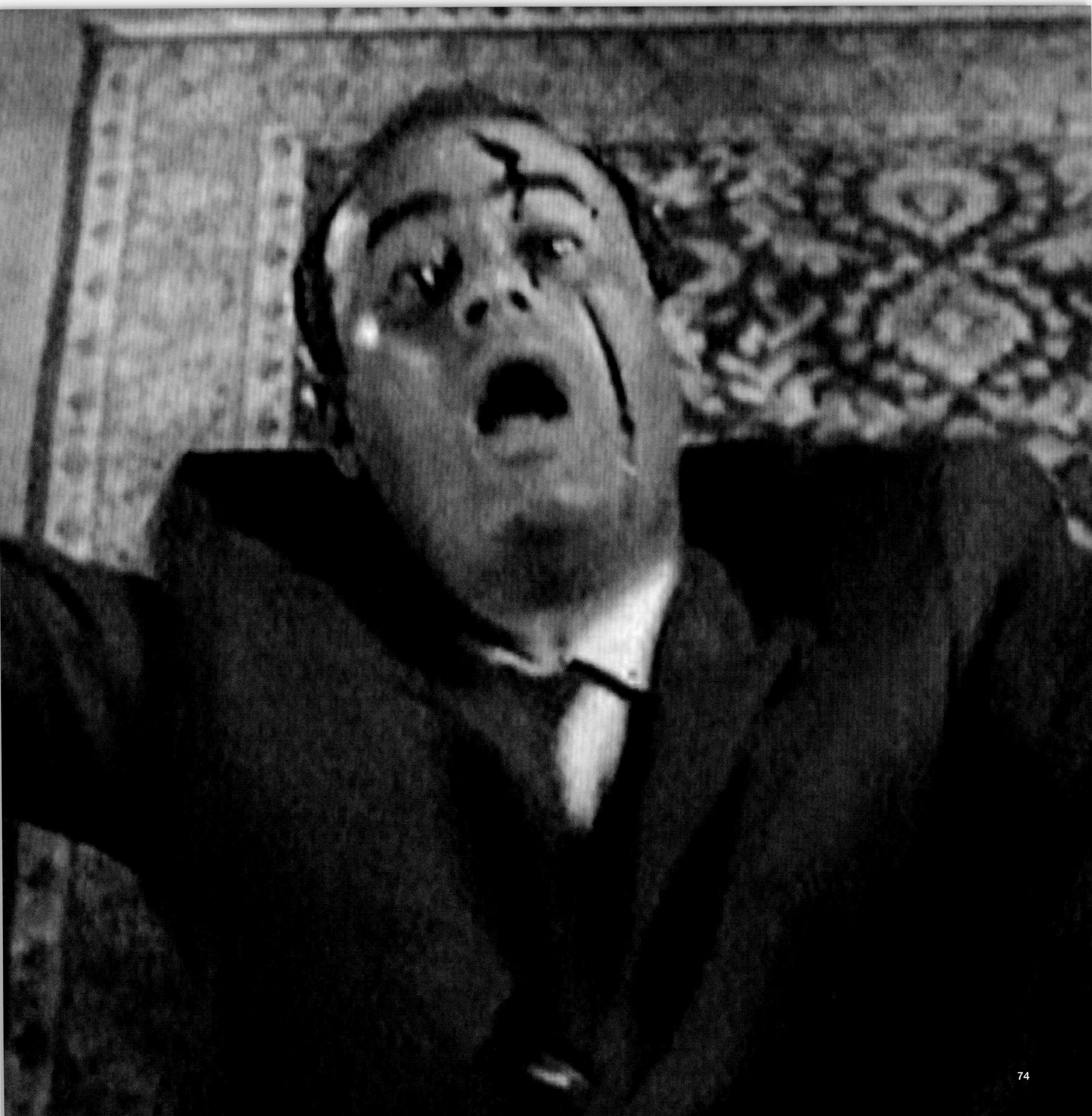

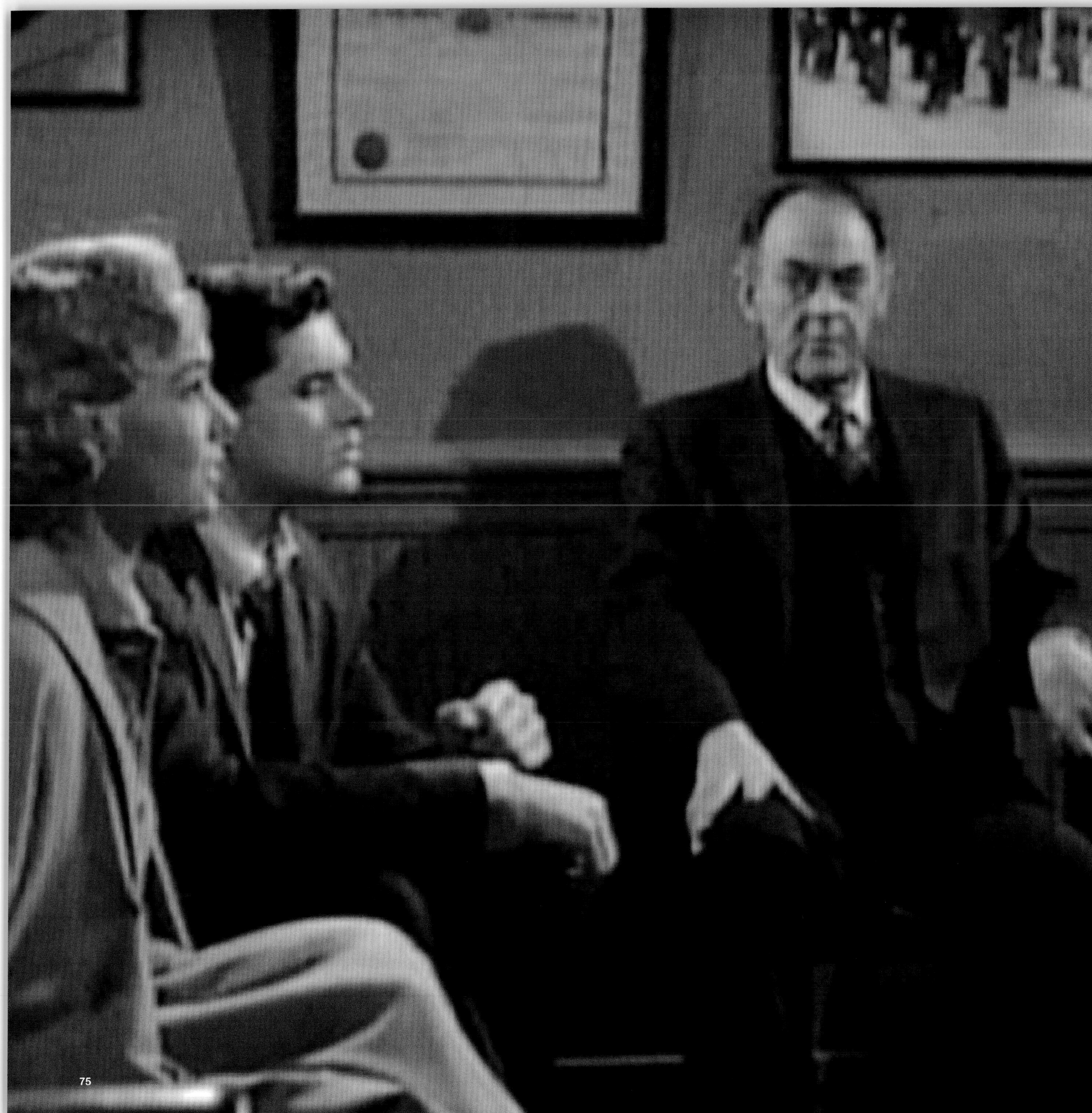

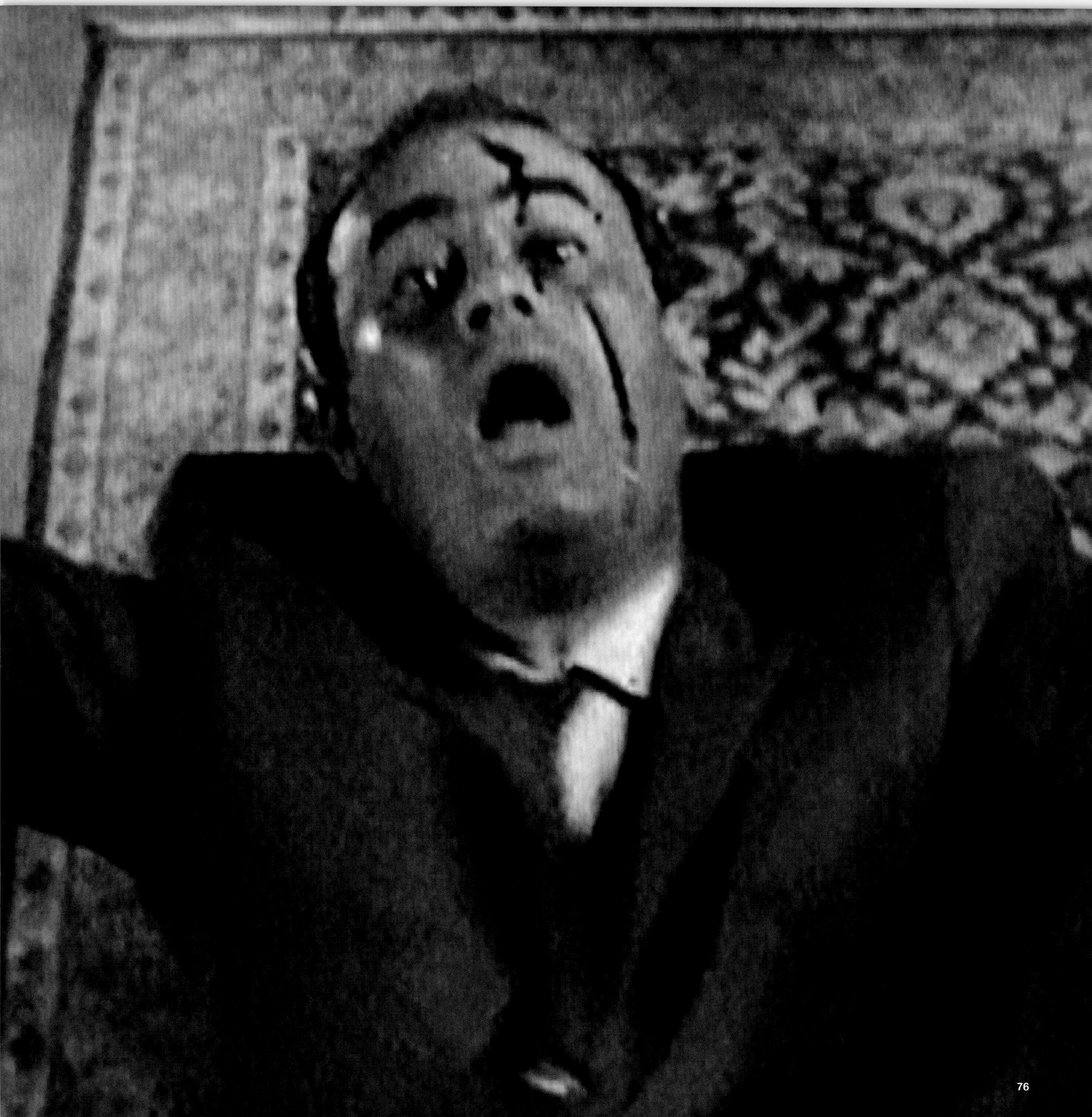

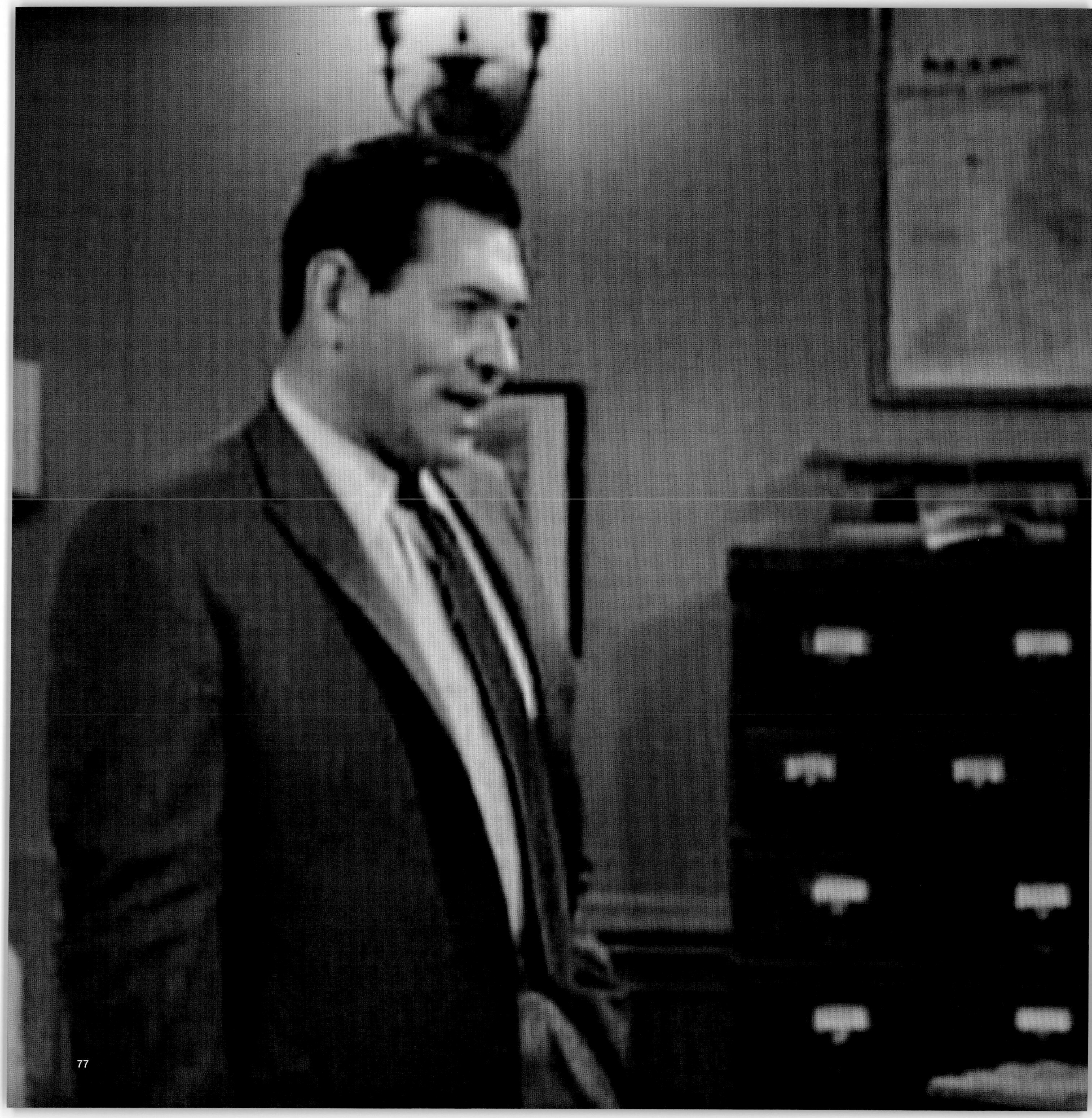

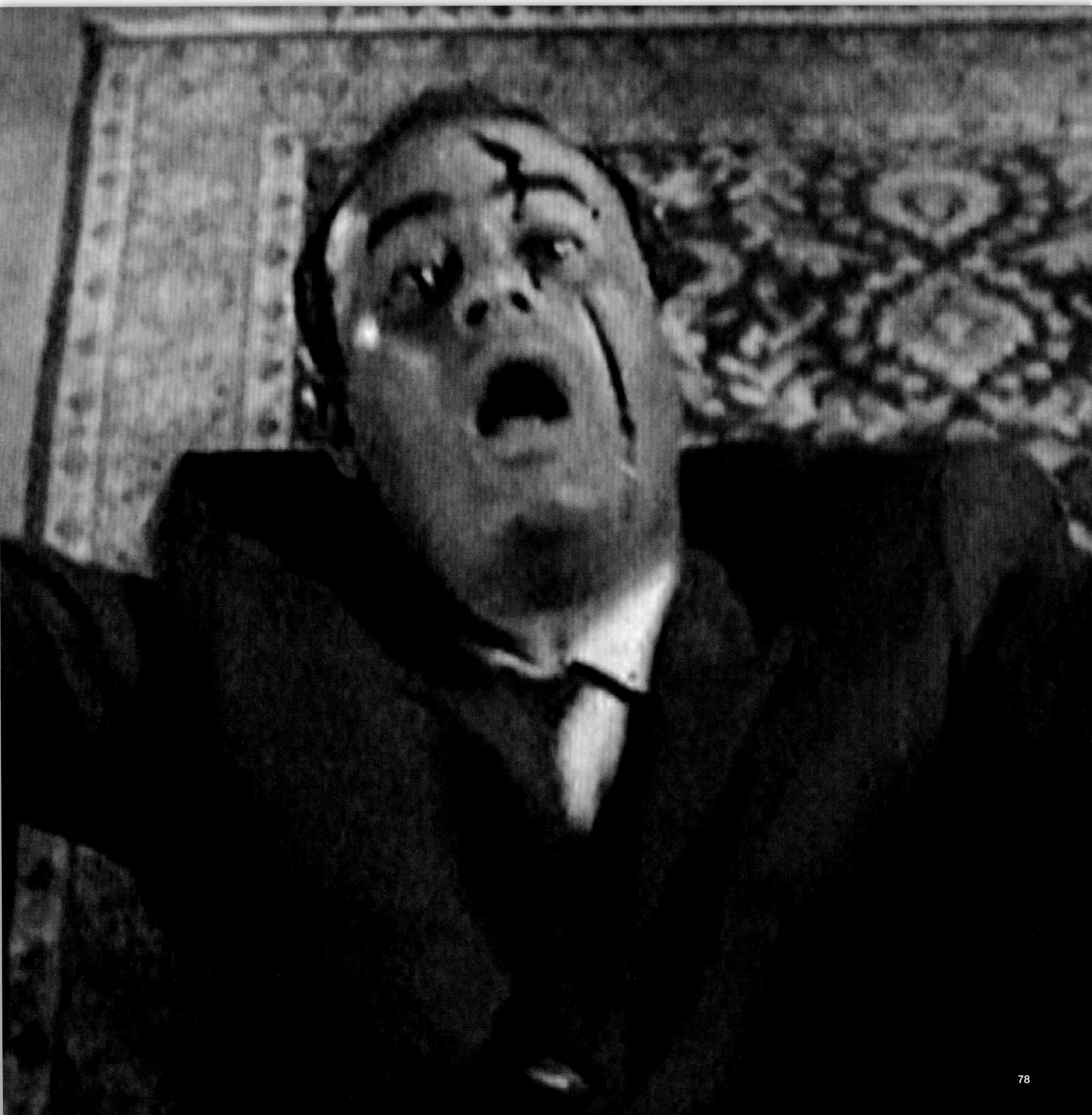

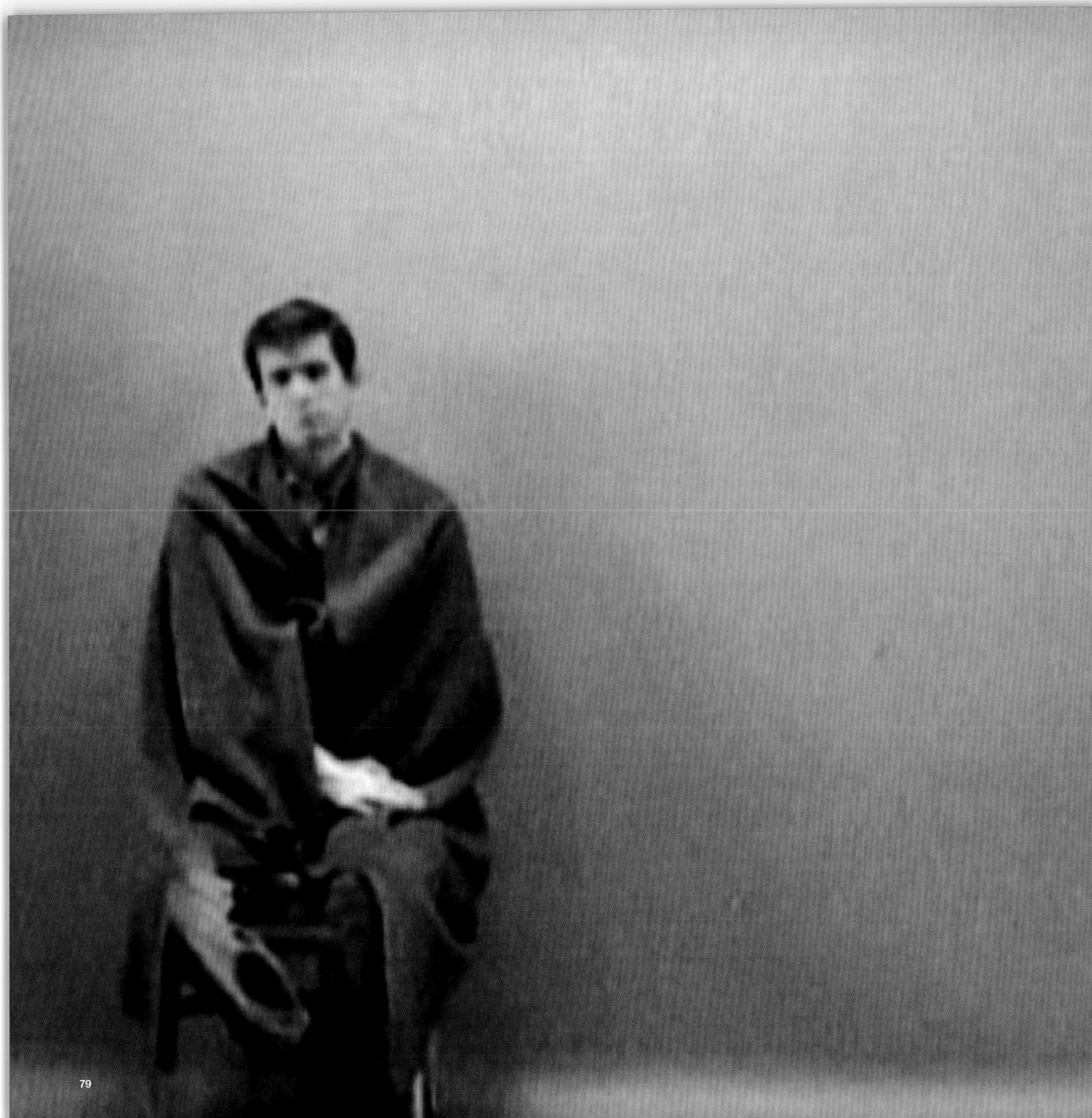

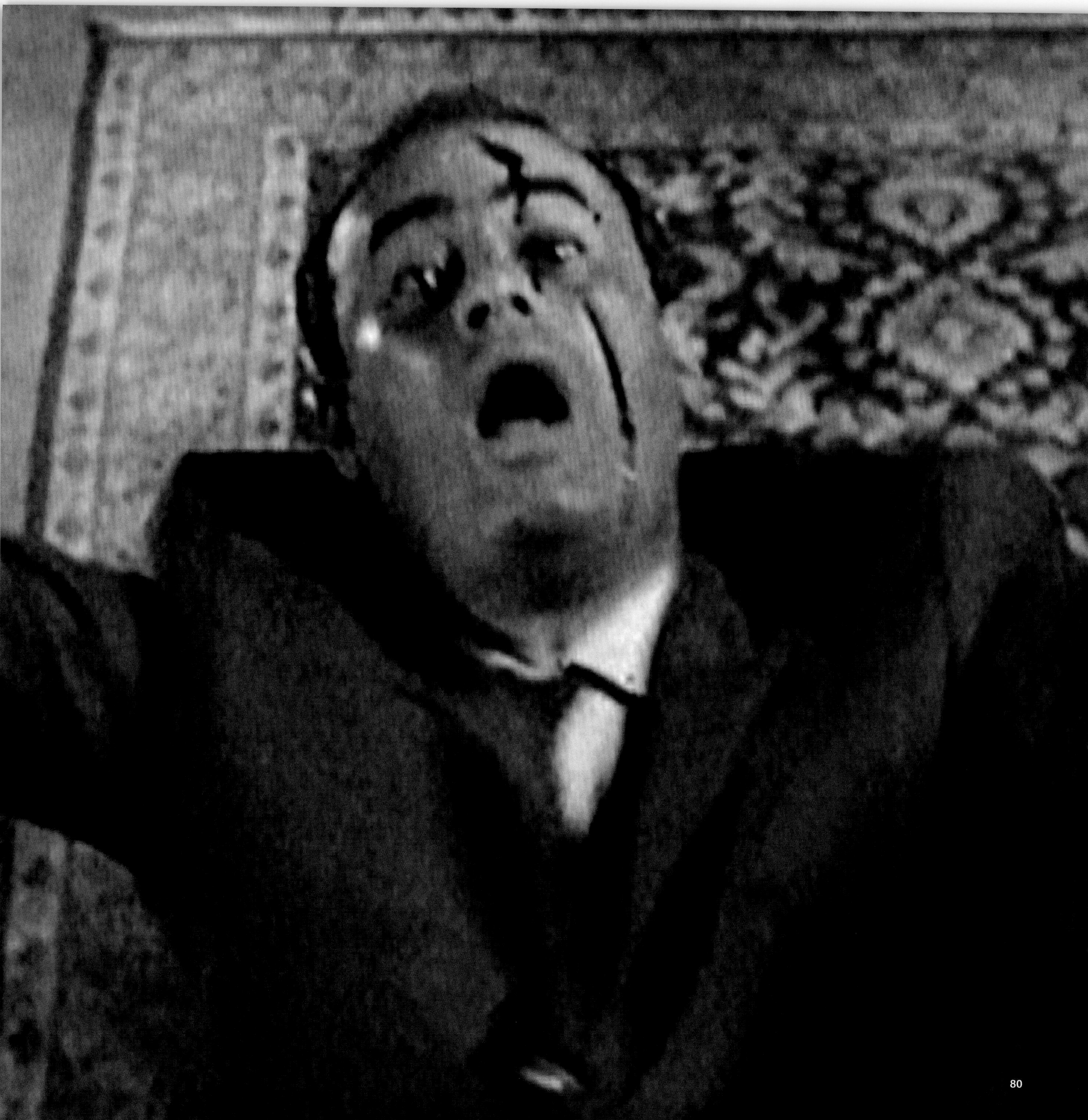

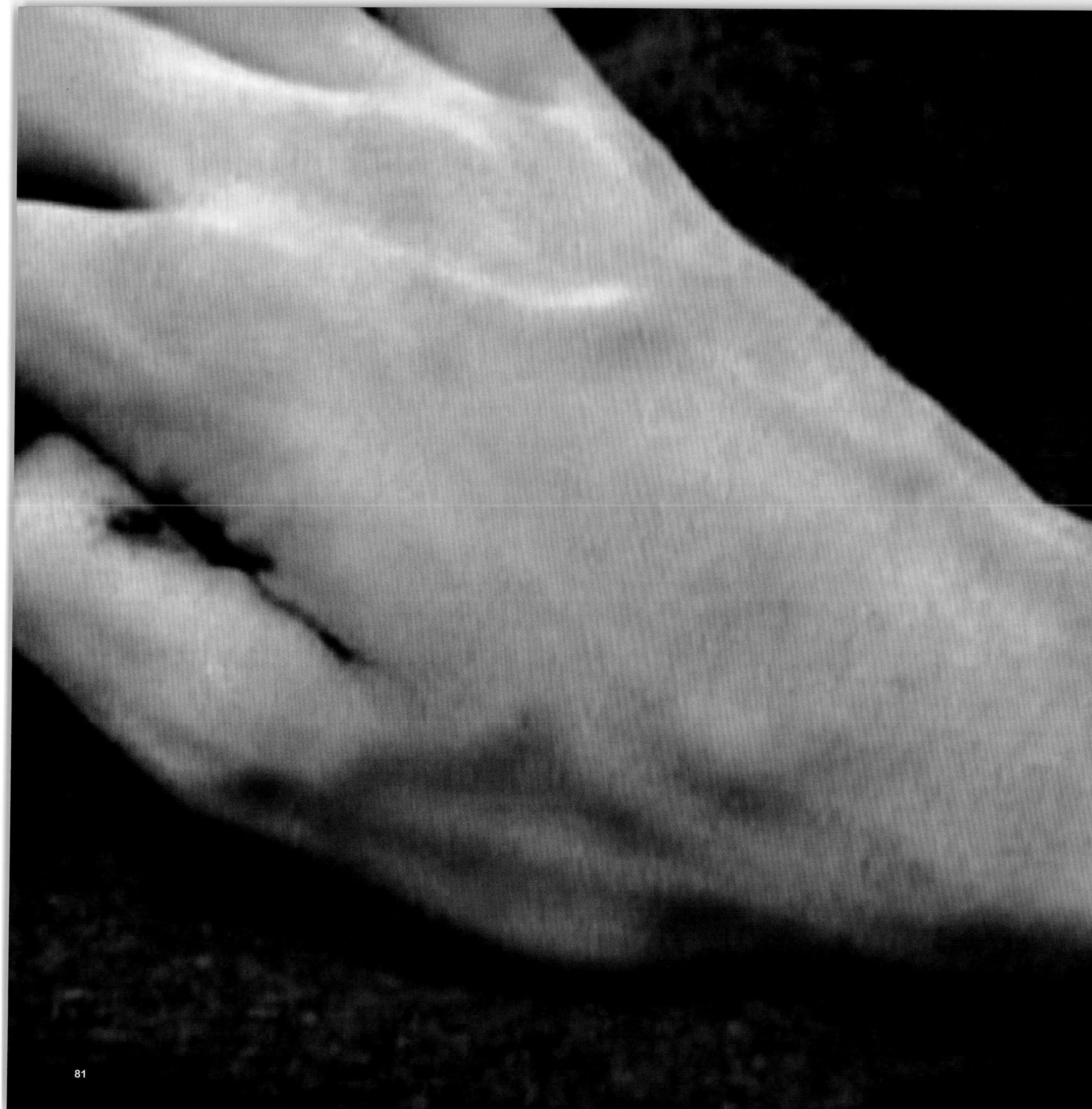

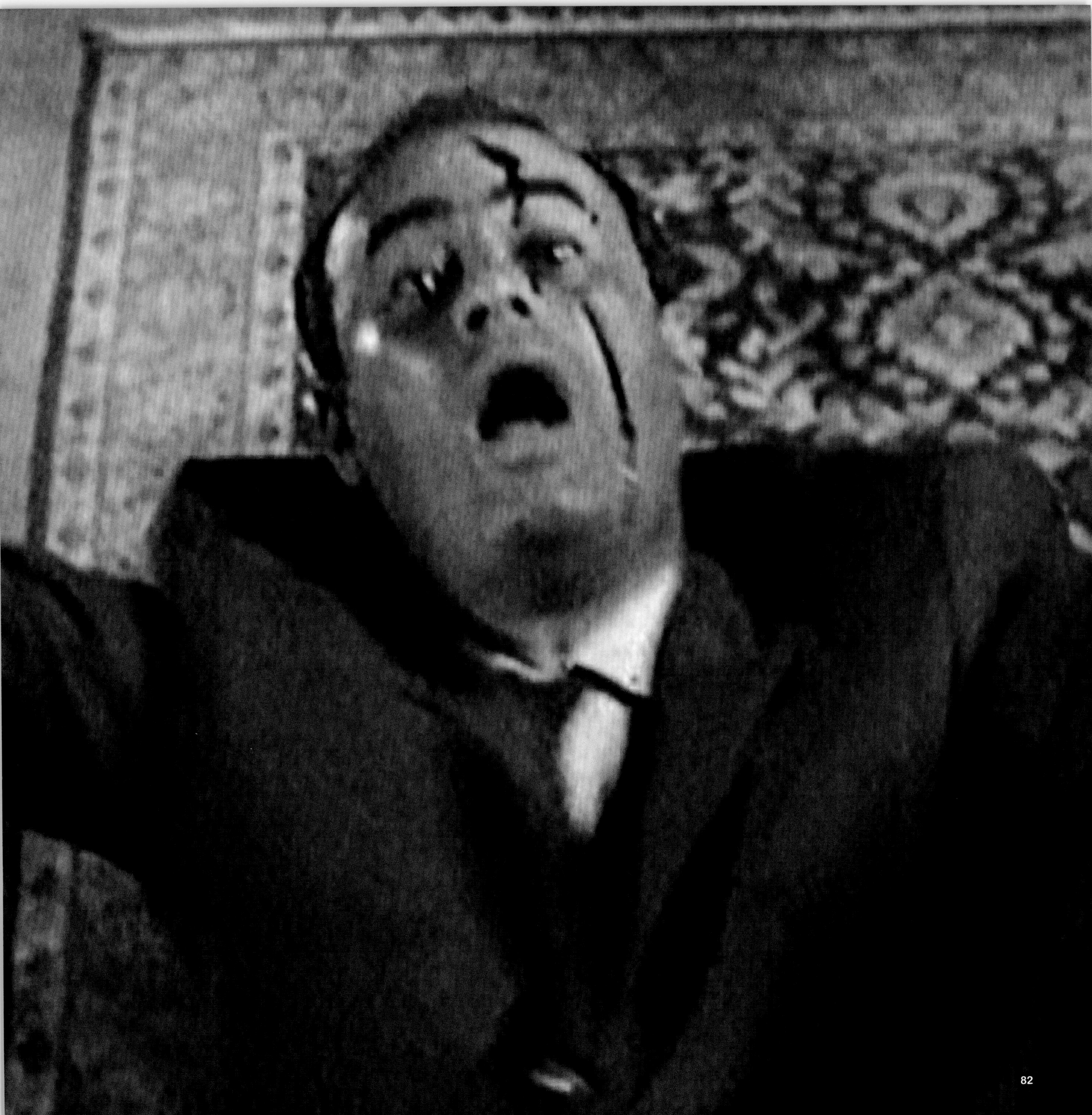

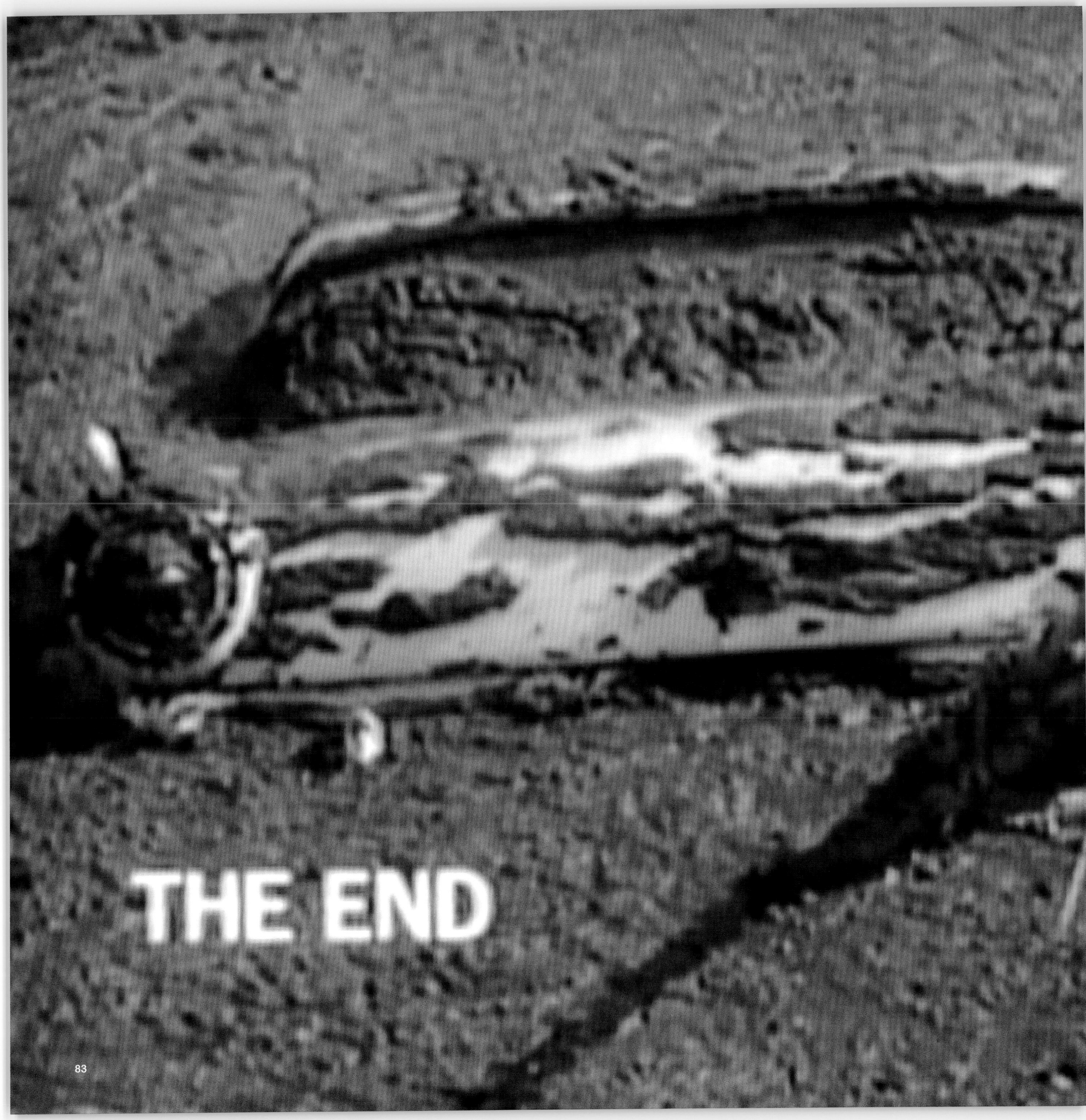
THE END

Psycho Hitchhiker. 1993
Black-and-white photograph, 18 ⅛ x 23 $^{7}/_{16}$" (46 x 59.5 cm)
Collection Sean and Mary Kelly, New York

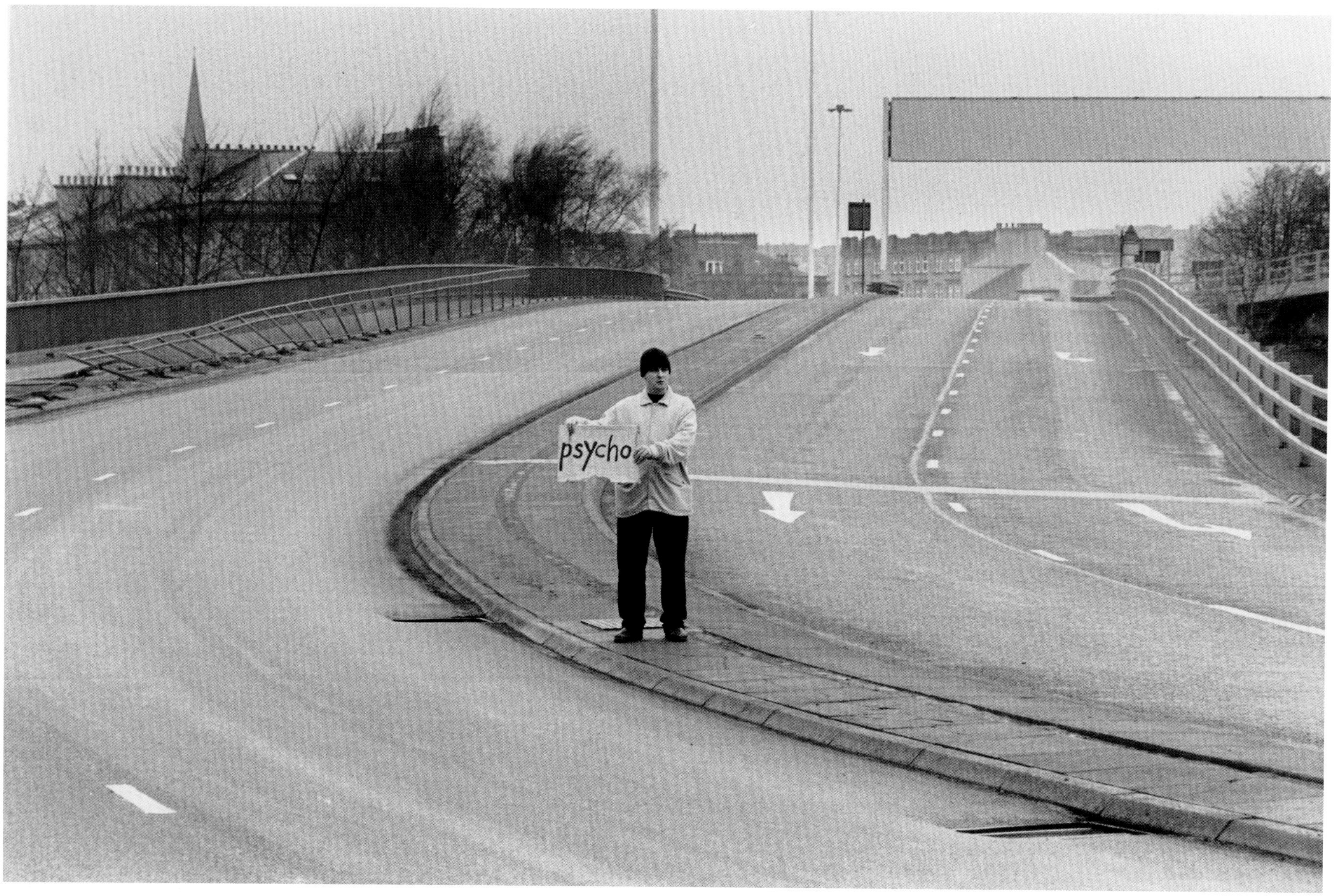

Trust Me. 1993
Performance and installation in the exhibition
Walter Benjamin's Briefcase, Porto, 1993
Collection the artist

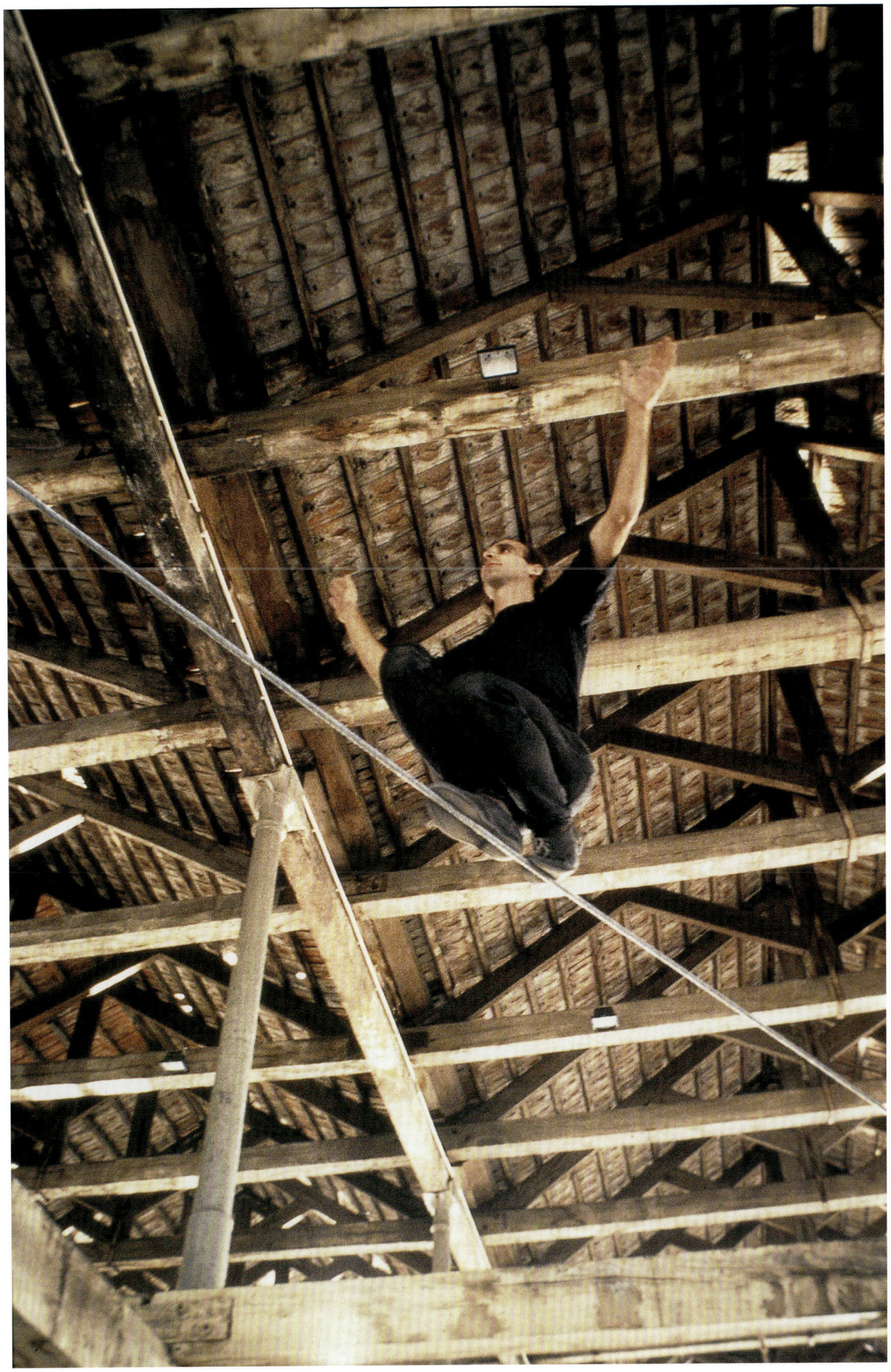

Trust Me was made in Porto for the exhibition *Walter Benjamin's Briefcase*, curated by Andrew Renton. The exhibition took place in a large, disused flourmill on the outskirts of the city. I proposed to remove the floor and ceiling between levels three and four of the building, creating one larger space out of two smaller areas. On the plane where the floor and ceiling had previously existed, I installed a circus tightrope from one corner of the room to the other. I also installed a single, short rope hanging from the rafters of the space down to the plane where the floor and ceiling had been. On entering the space, visitors could look up and into the upper level of the building. This upper level was occupied by a tight-rope walker, who was employed to be in the space for the duration of the exhibition.

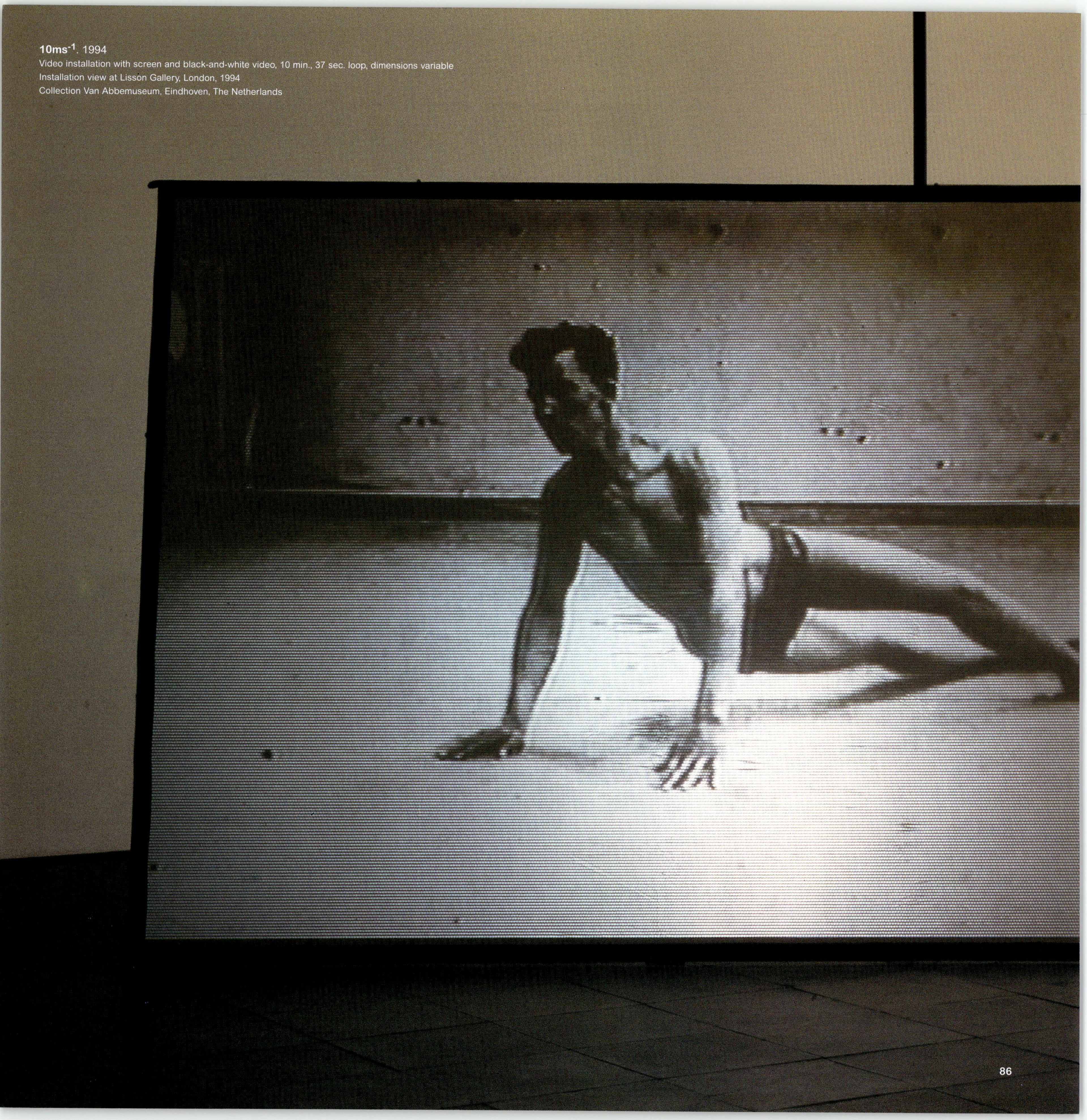

10ms^{-1}, 1994
Video installation with screen and black-and-white video, 10 min., 37 sec. loop, dimensions variable
Installation view at Lisson Gallery, London, 1994
Collection Van Abbemuseum, Eindhoven, The Netherlands

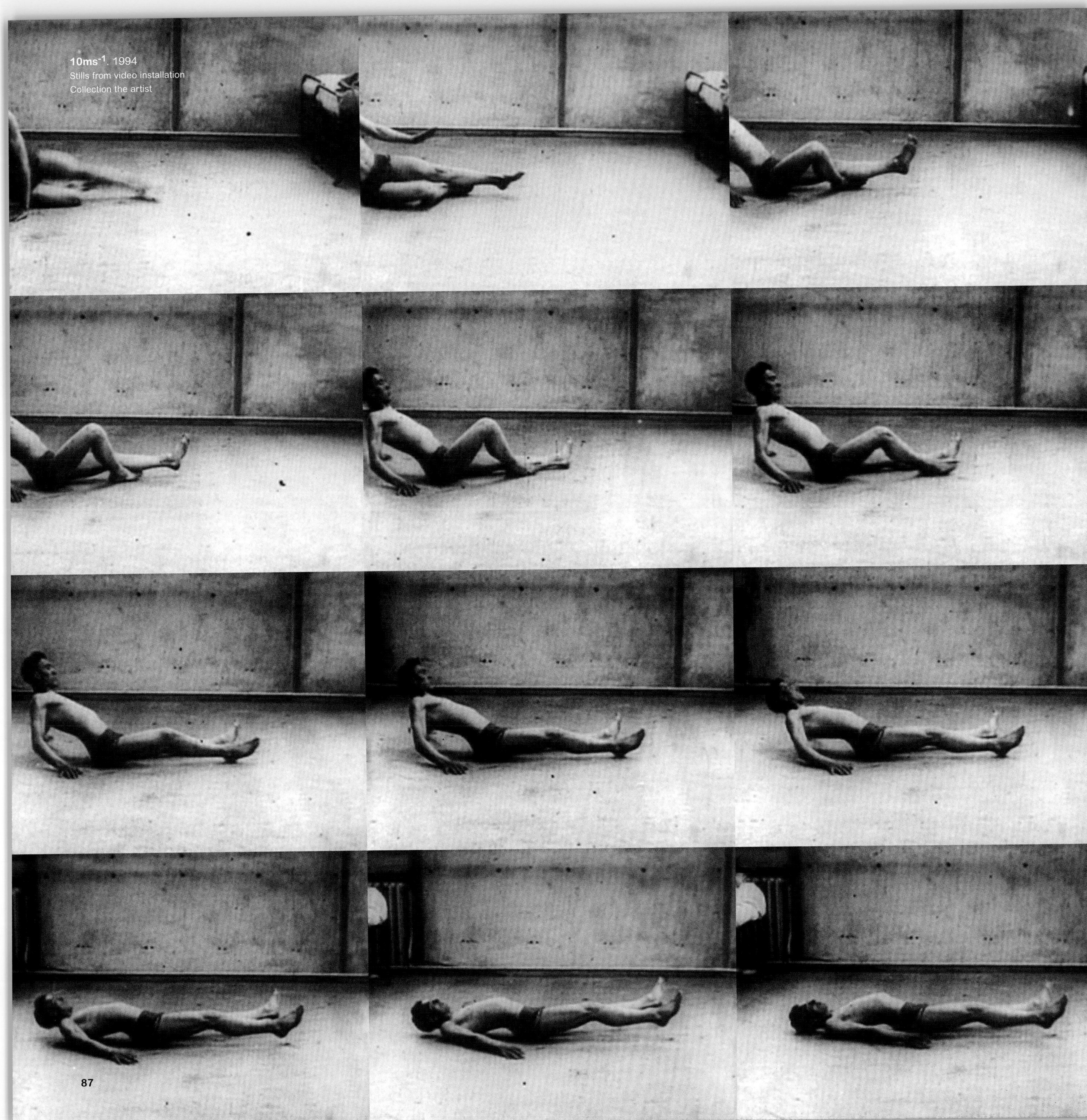

$10ms^{-1}$, 1994
Stills from video installation
Collection the artist

Hysterical. 1994–95
Video installation with two screens and black-and-white video,
29 min., 12 sec. loop and 29 min., 14 sec. loop, dimensions variable
Installation view in Turner Prize Exhibition, Tate Gallery, London, 1996
Southampton City Art Gallery

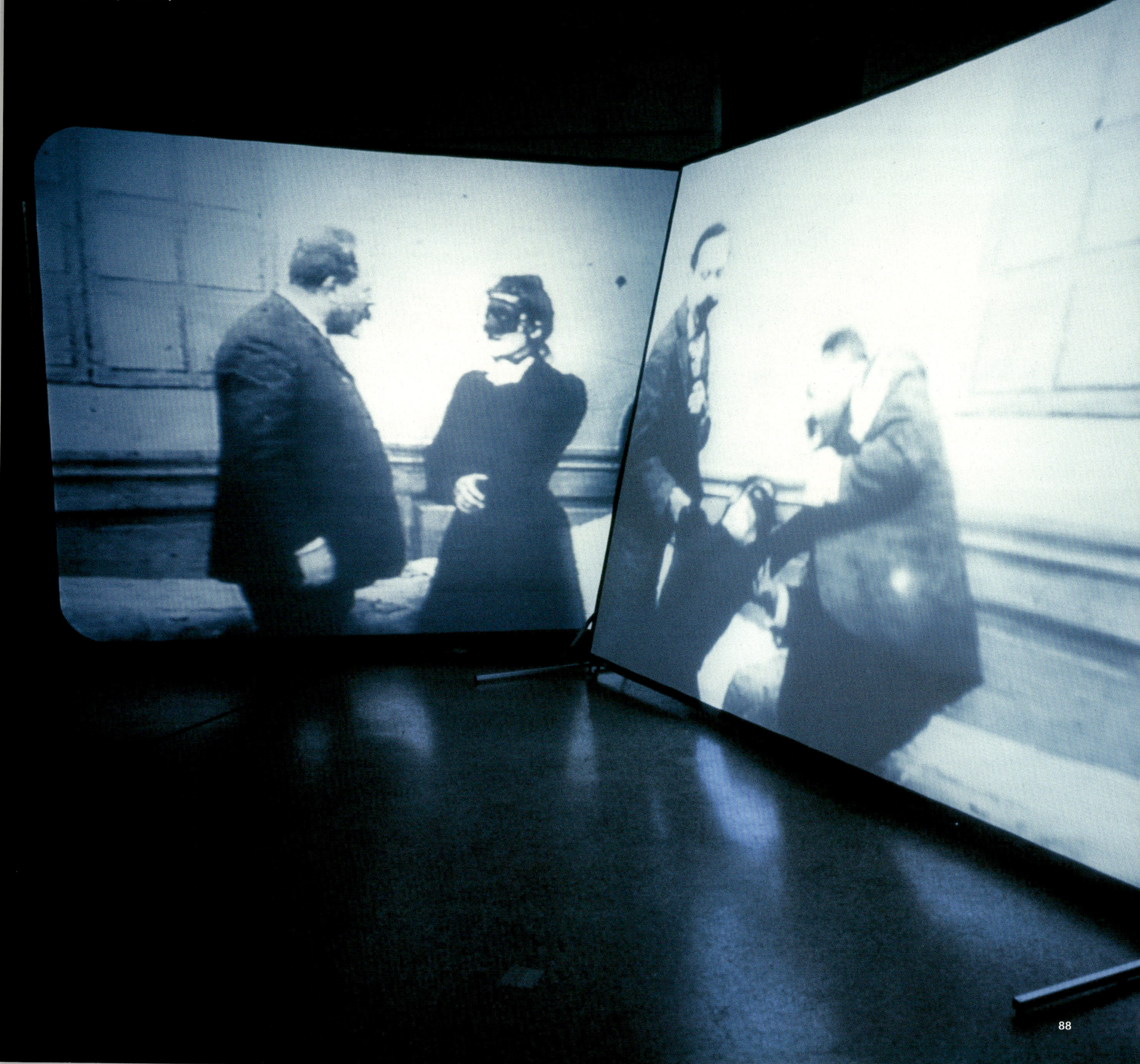

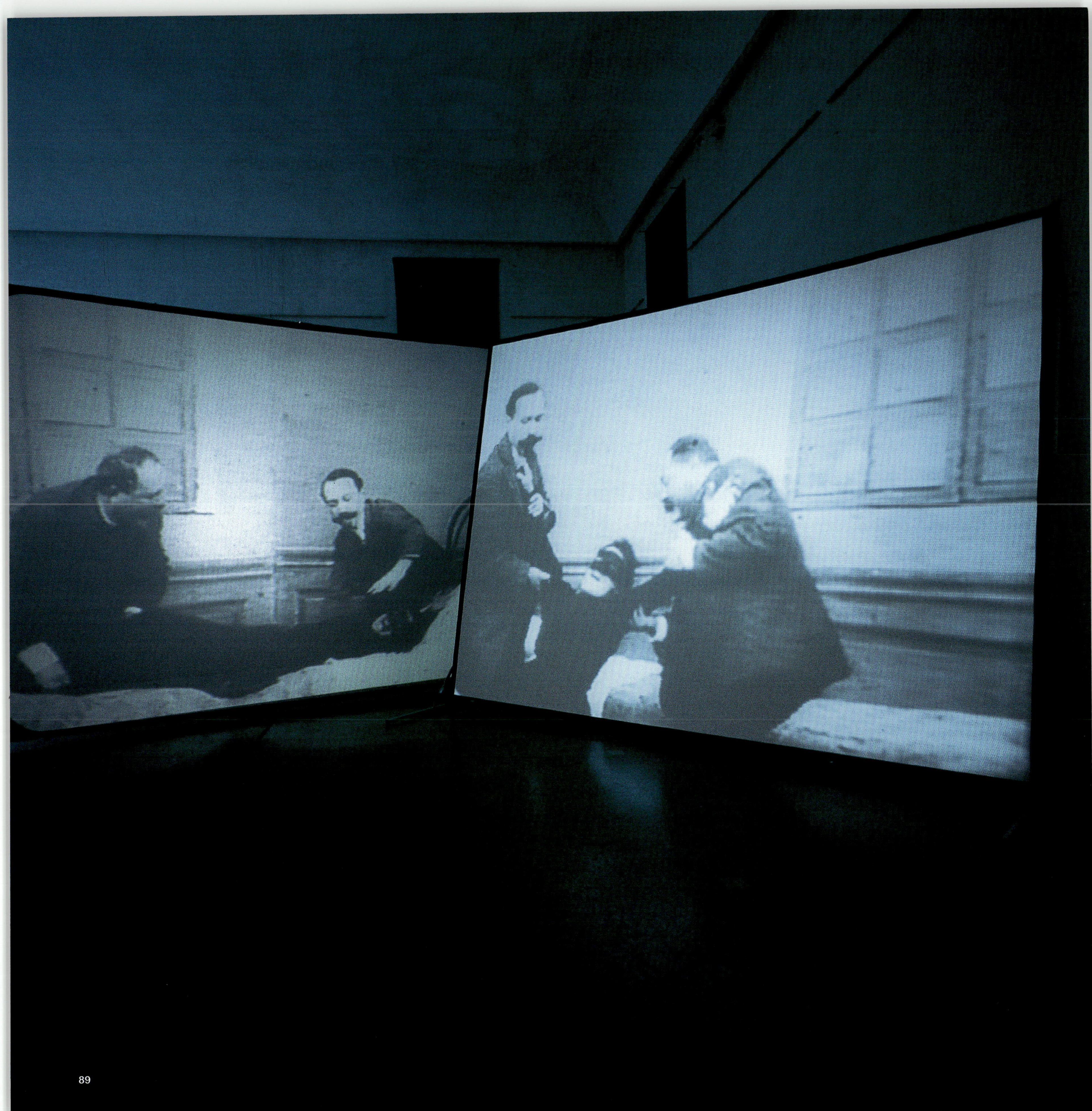

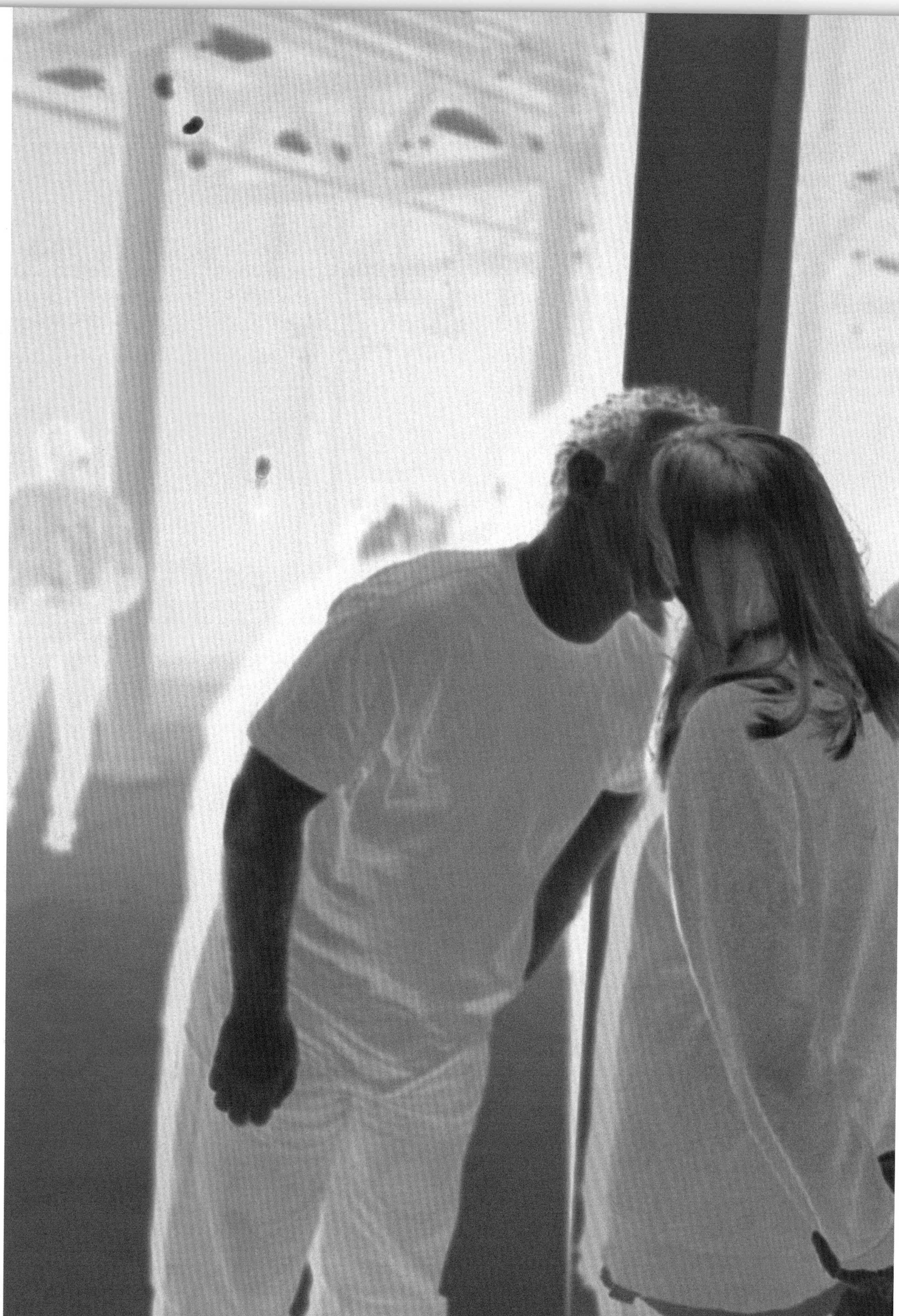

Kissing with Amobarbital. 1995
35mm slide projection, dimensions variable
Courtesy Galeria Estrany-de la Mota, Barcelona

Kissing with Sodium Pentothal. 1994
35mm slide projection, dimensions variable
Private collection, Boston

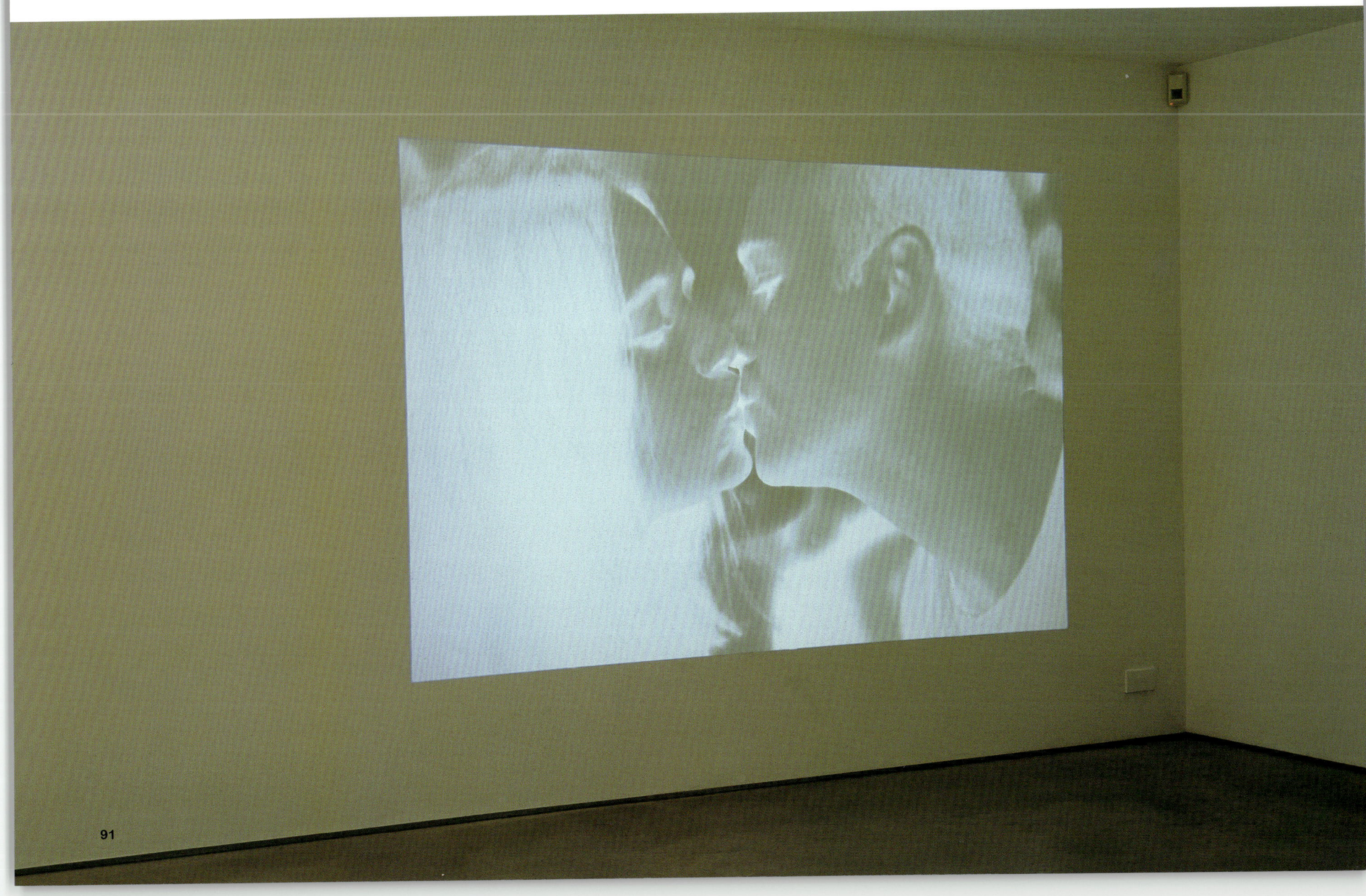

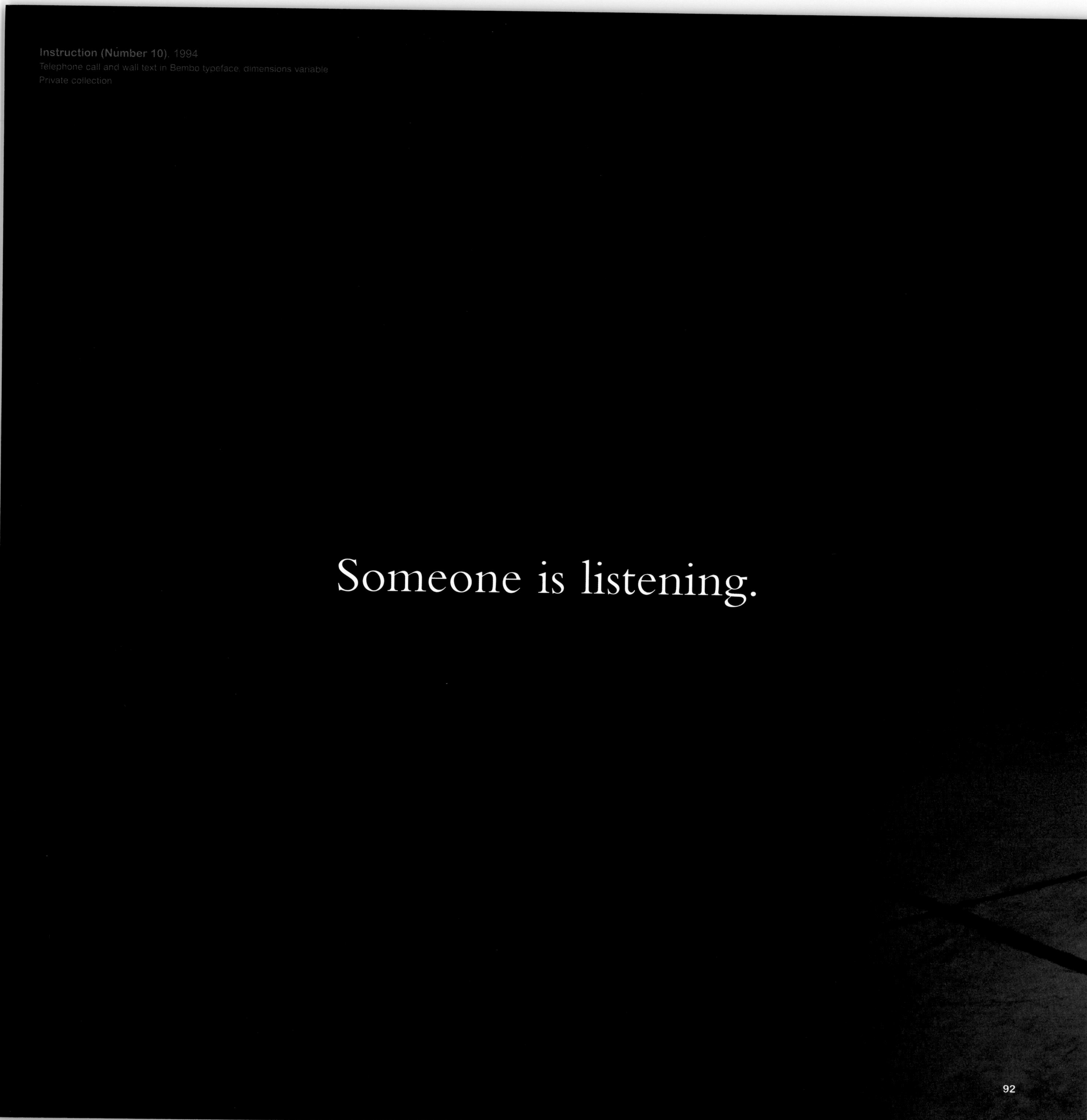

Instruction (Number 10), 1994
Telephone call and wall text in Bembo typeface, dimensions variable
Private collection

Letter (Number 16), 1994
Letter and wall text in Bembo typeface, dimensions variable
Carlotta and Edoardo Nesi, Prato

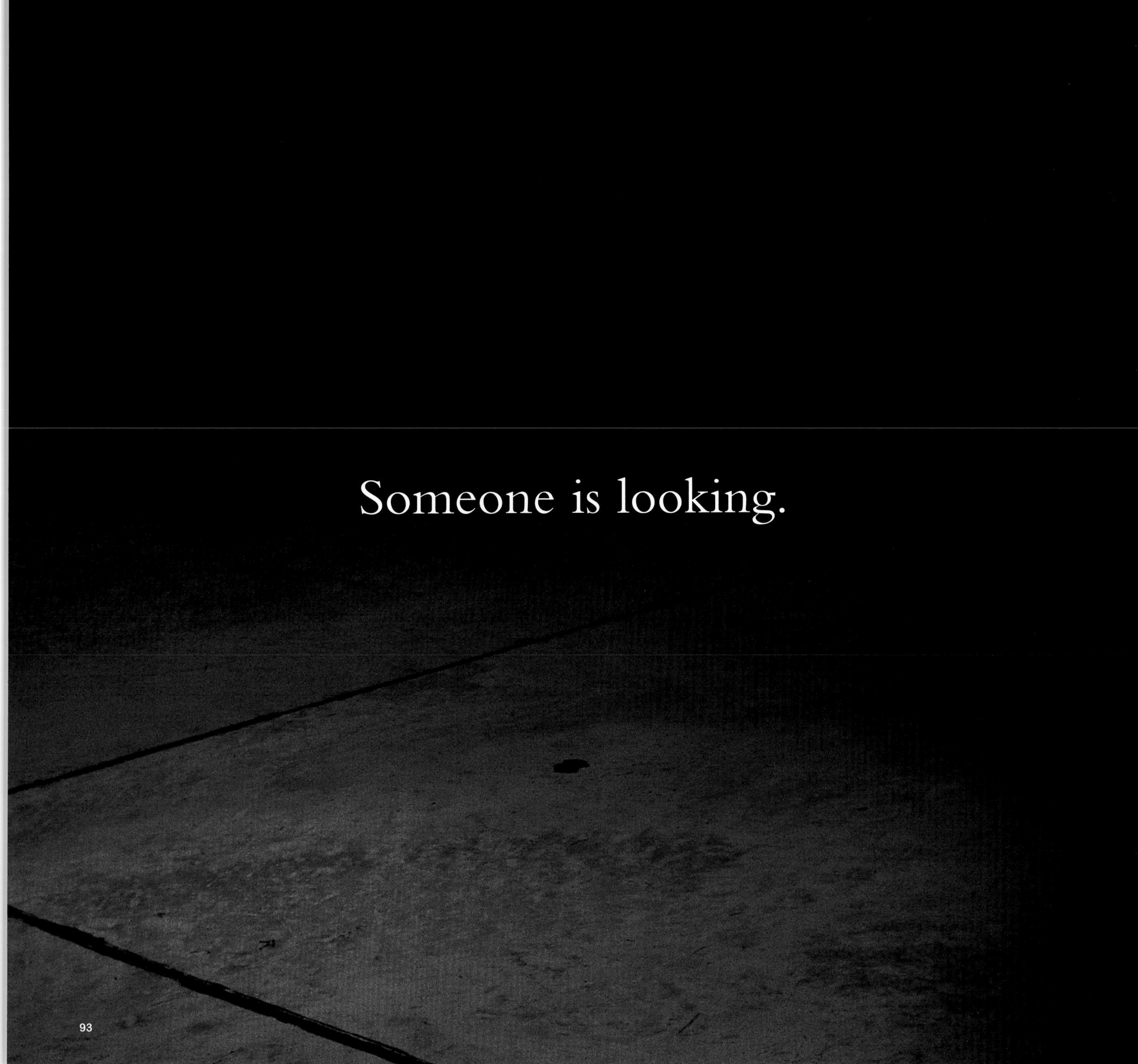

Tattoo (I). 1994
Black-and-white photograph, 53 x 34 ⅝" (134.6 x 88 cm)
Collection the artist

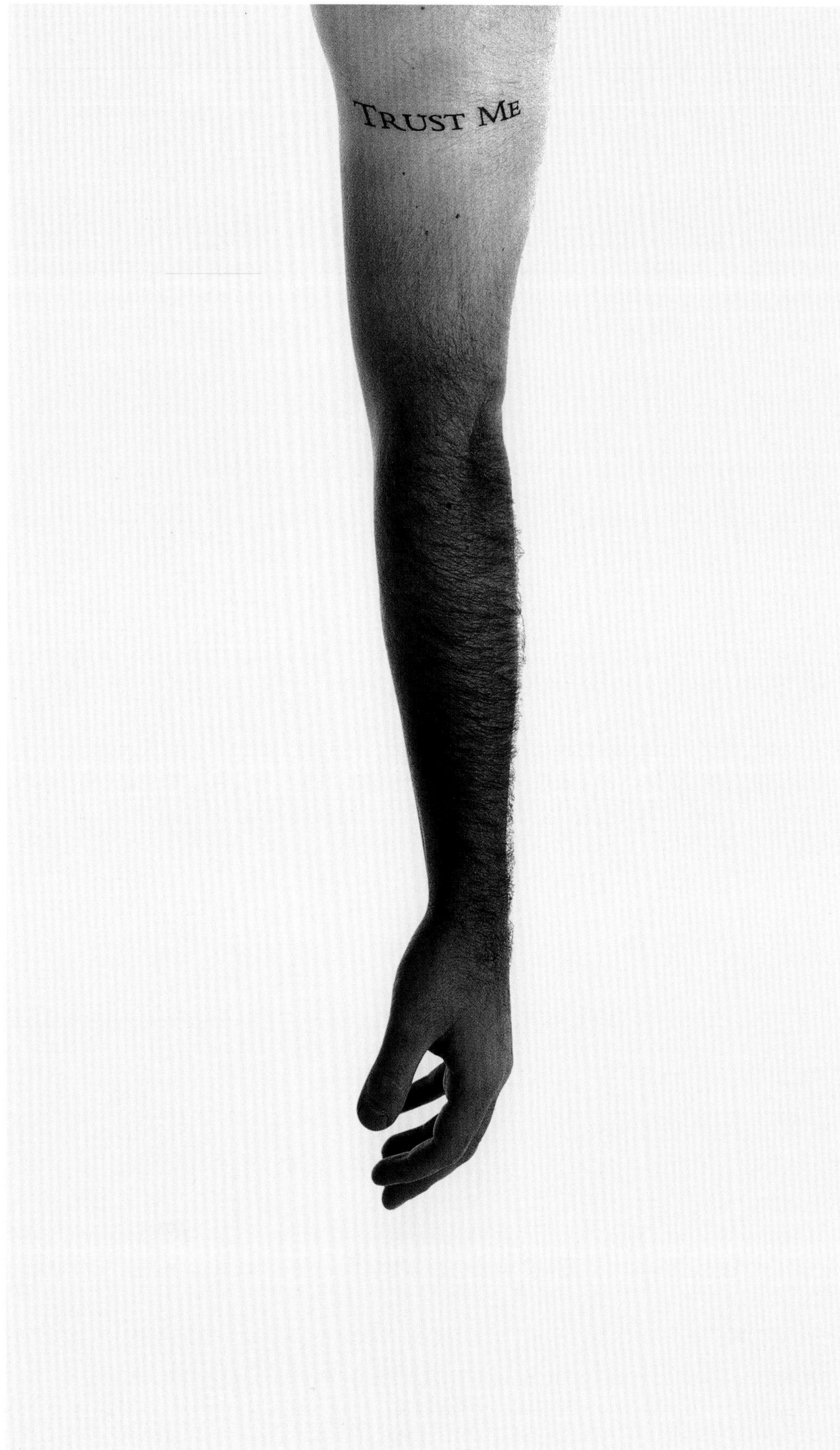

Tattoo (II). 1994
Black-and-white photograph, 53 x 34 $^{5}/_{8}$" (134.6 x 88 cm)
Collection the artist

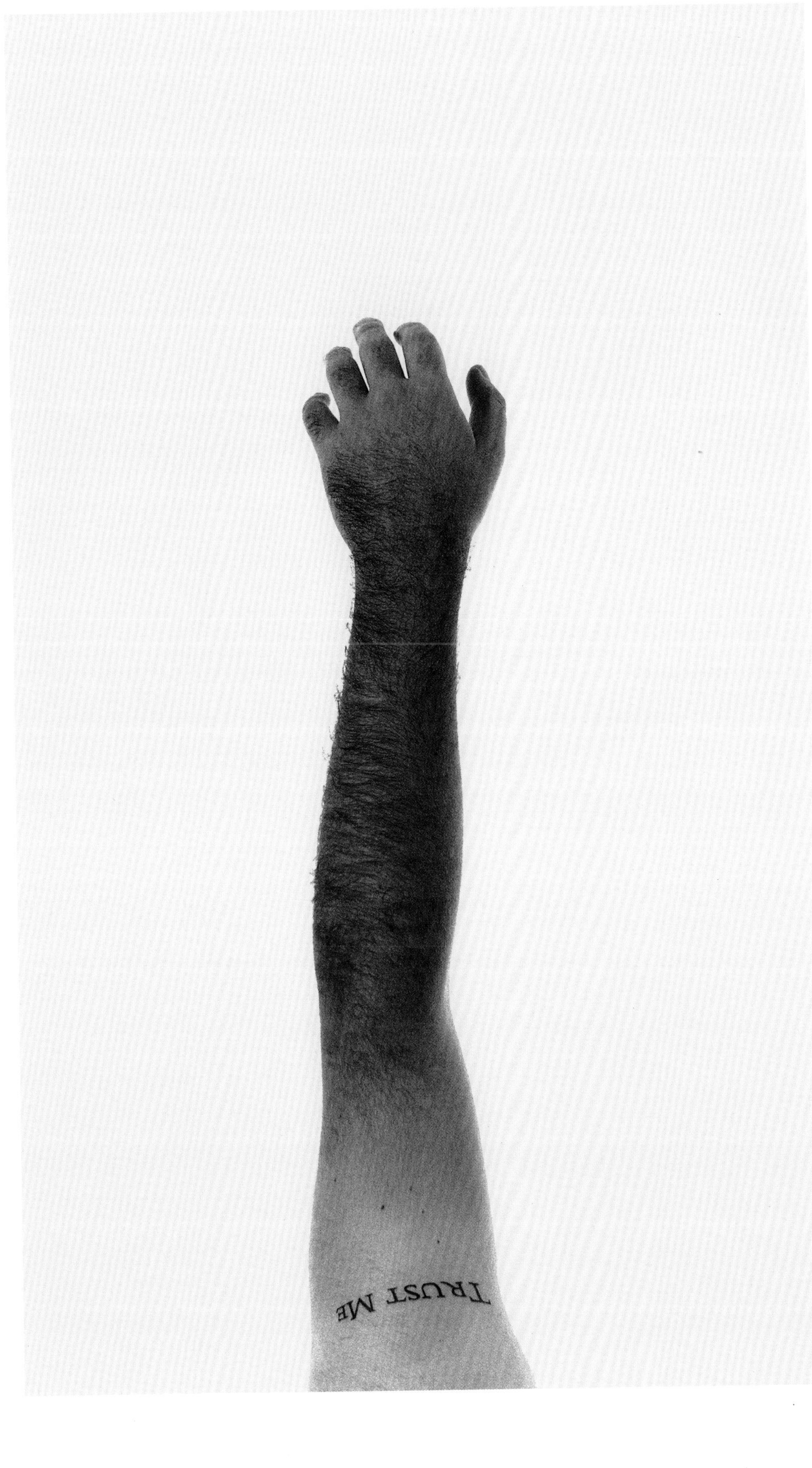

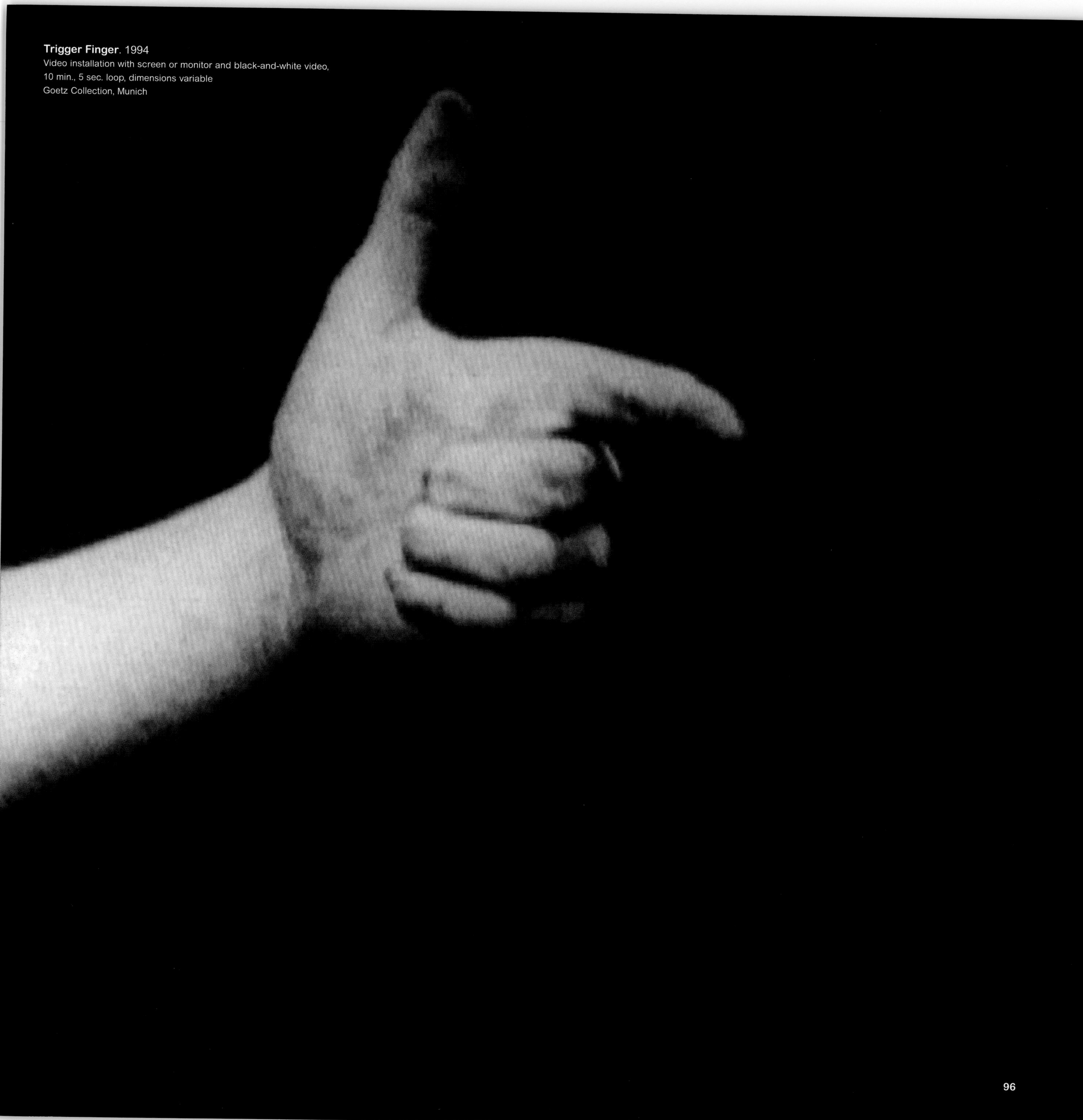

Trigger Finger. 1994
Video installation with screen or monitor and black-and-white video,
10 min., 5 sec. loop, dimensions variable
Goetz Collection, Munich

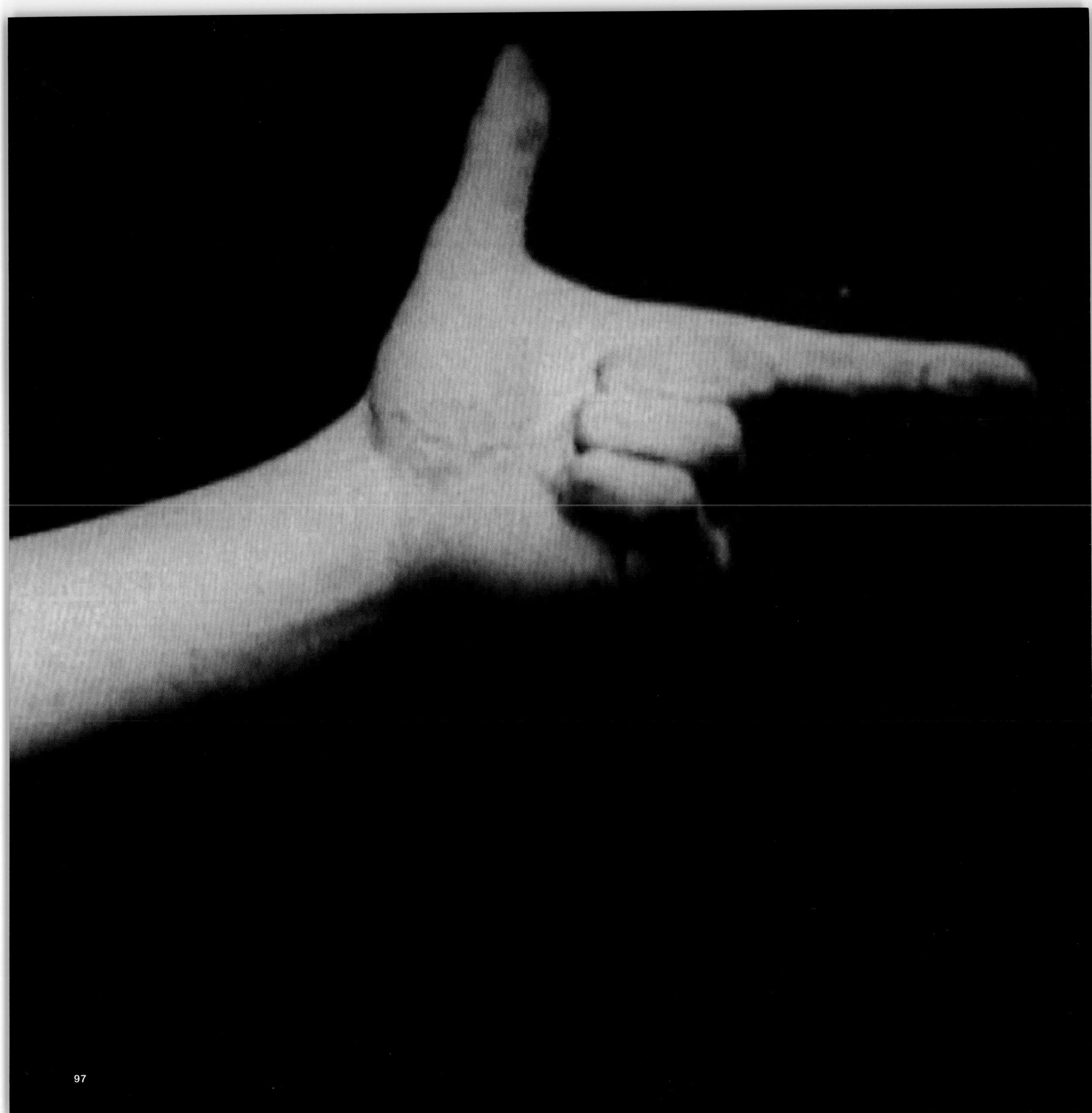

5 Year Drive-By. 1995
Video installation with screen and color video, 5 yr. loop, dimensions variable
Installation view at 29 Palms Inn, Twentynine Palms, California, 2001
Collection the artist

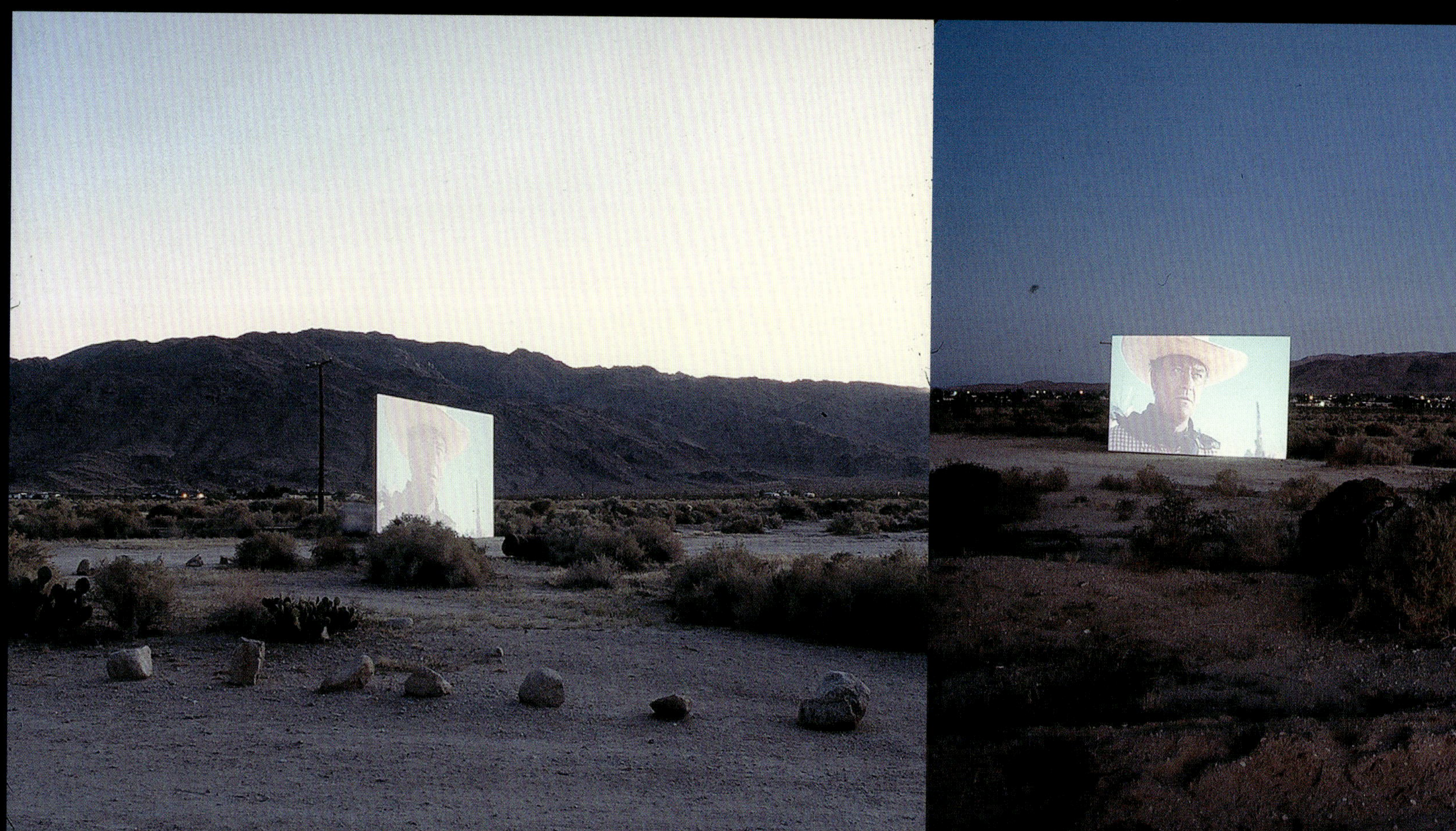

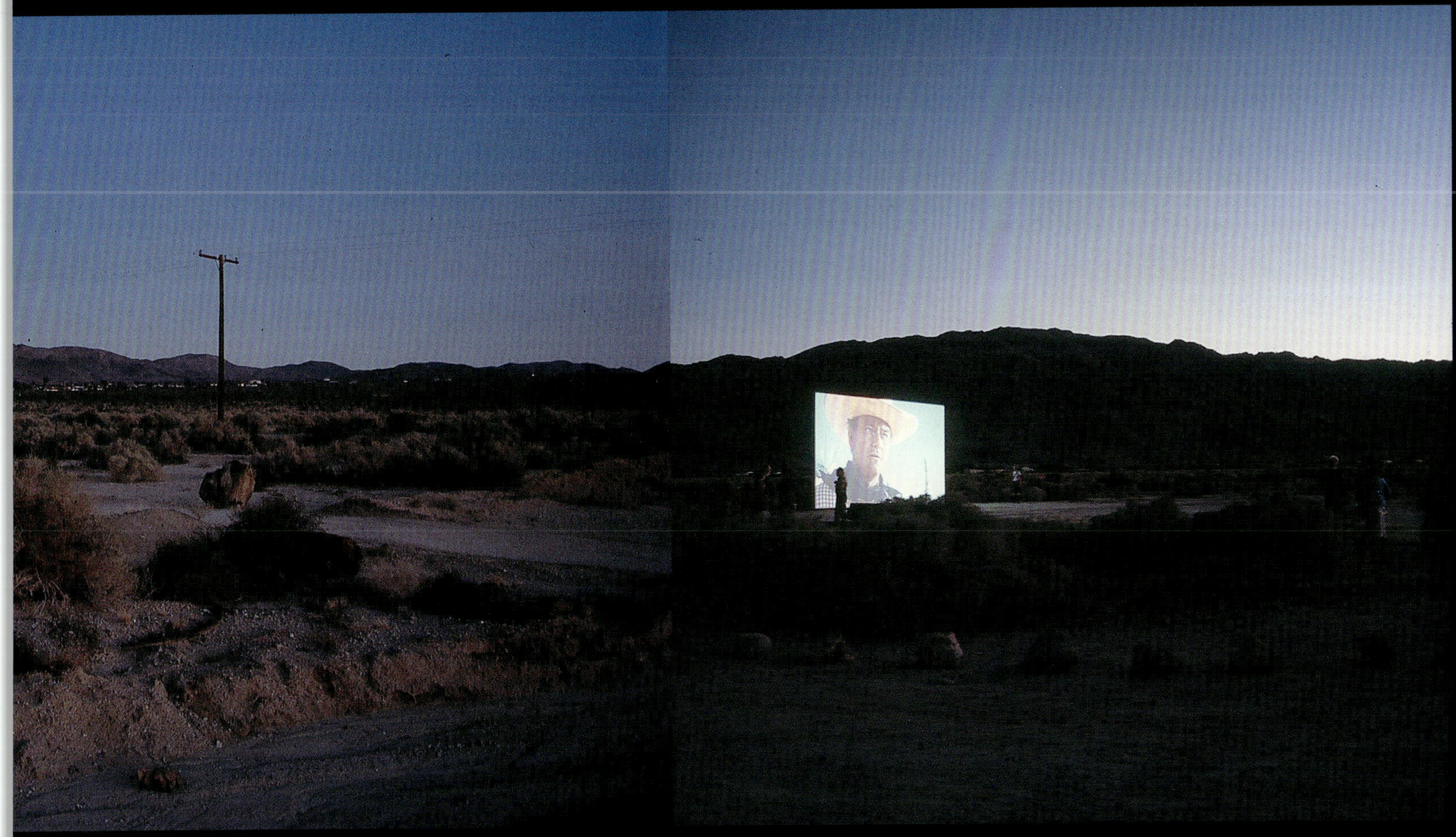

Confessions of a Justified Sinner. 1995
Stills from video installation
Collection the artist

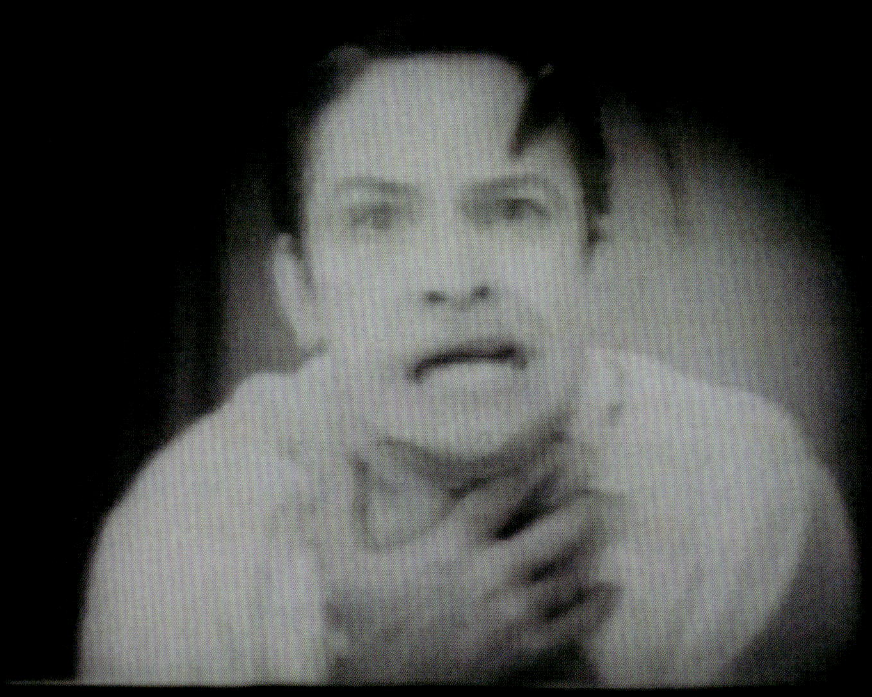

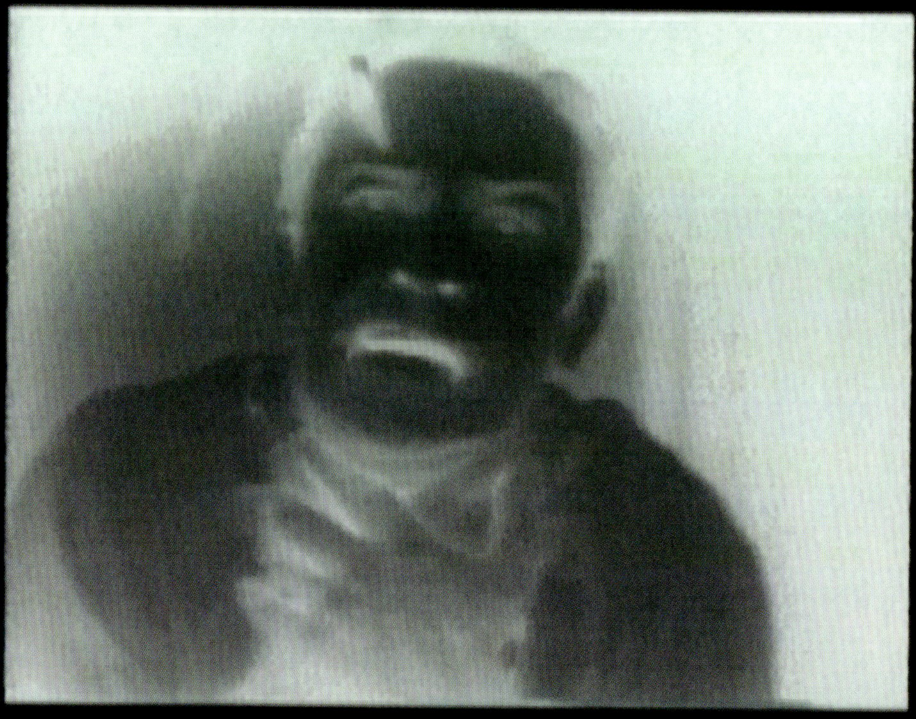

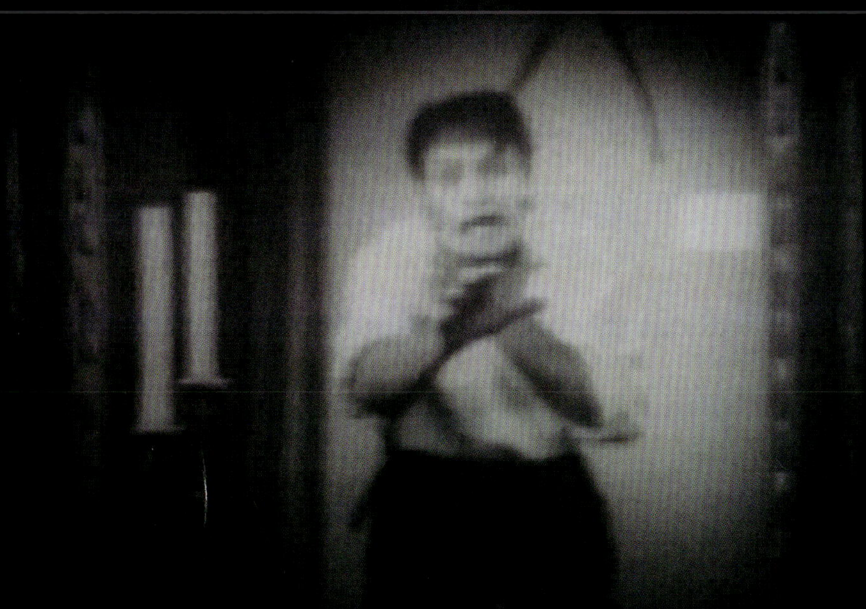

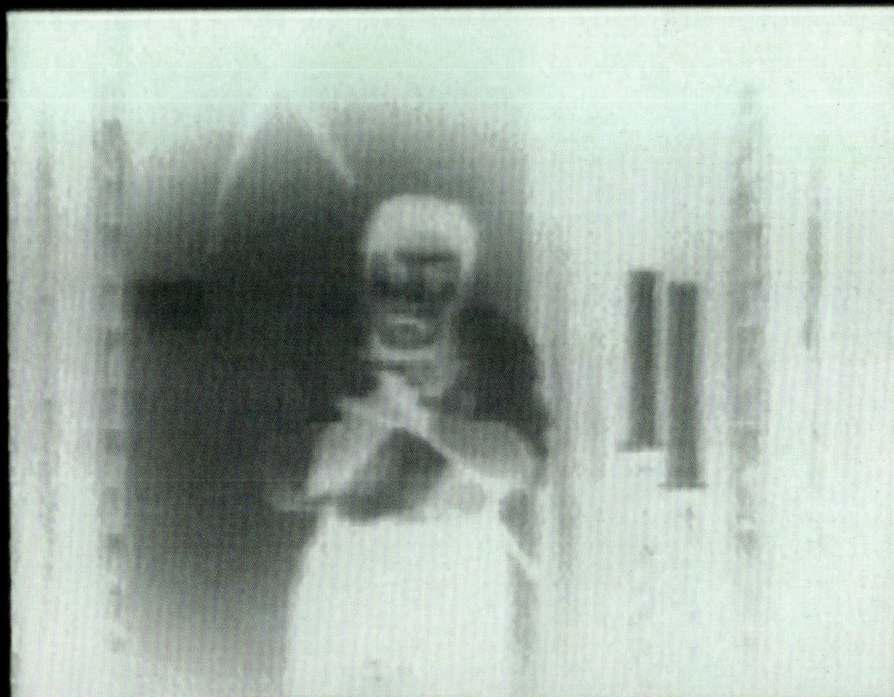

B-Movie. 1995
Video installation with screen and black-and-white video,
29 min., 50 sec. loop, dimensions variable
Goetz Collection, Munich

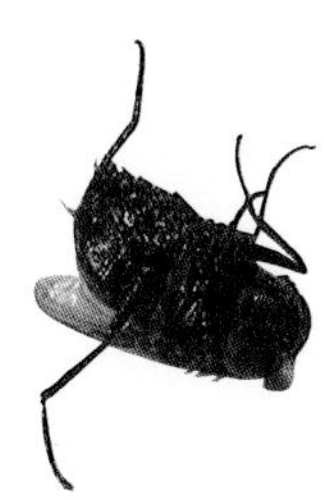

Film Noir videos. 1995
Installation view at Stedelijk Van Abbemuseum, Eindhoven, 1995

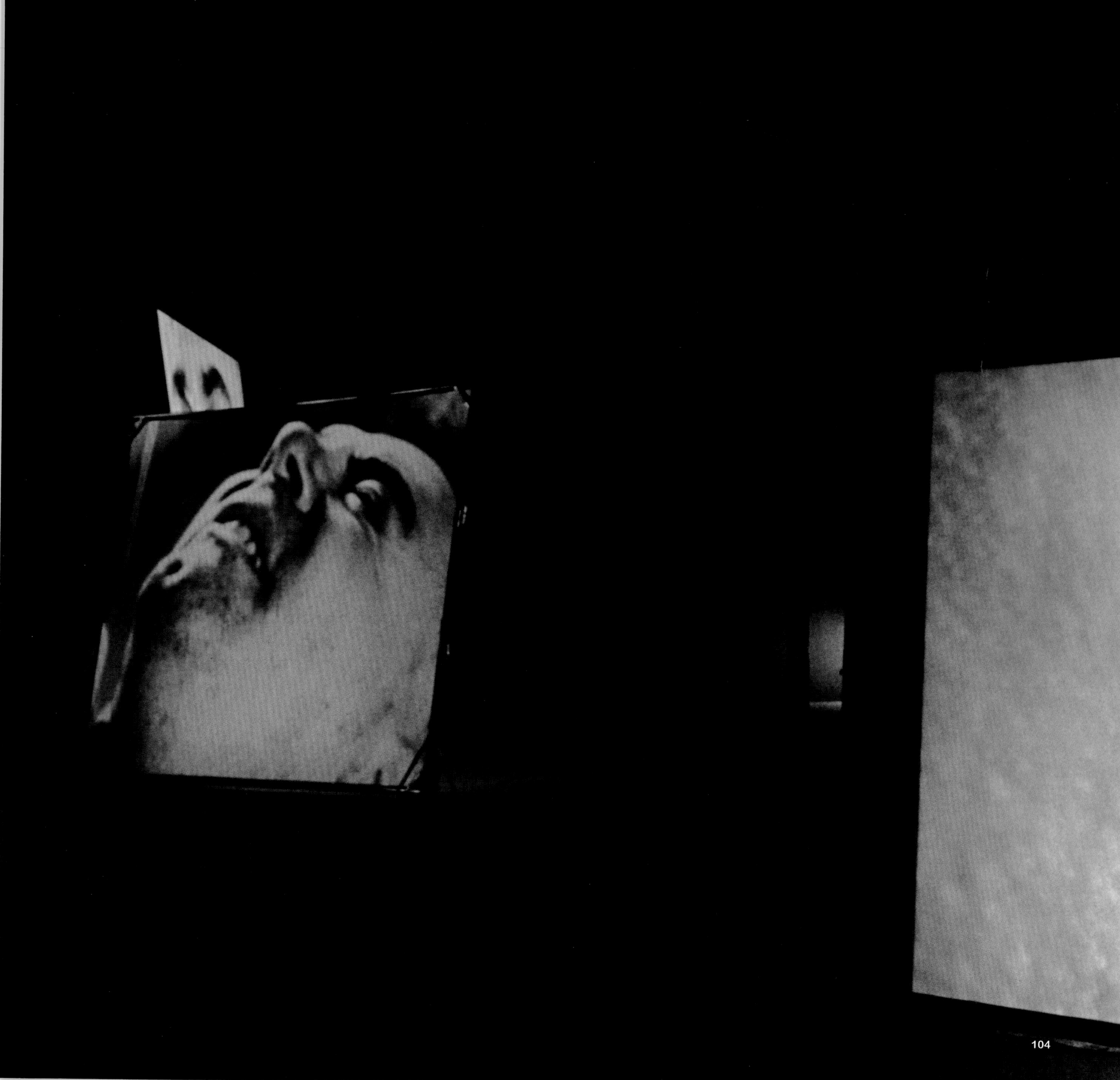

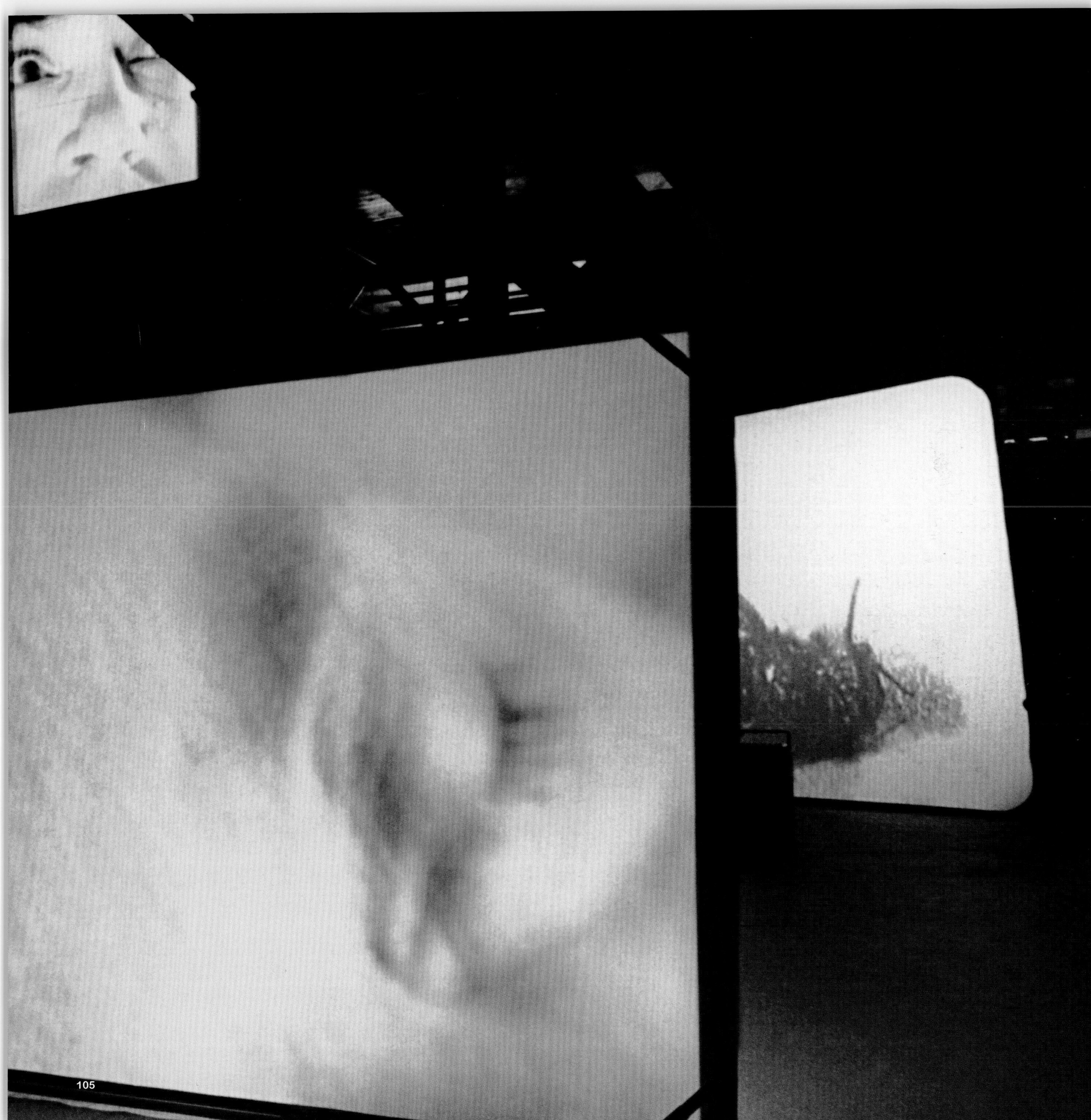

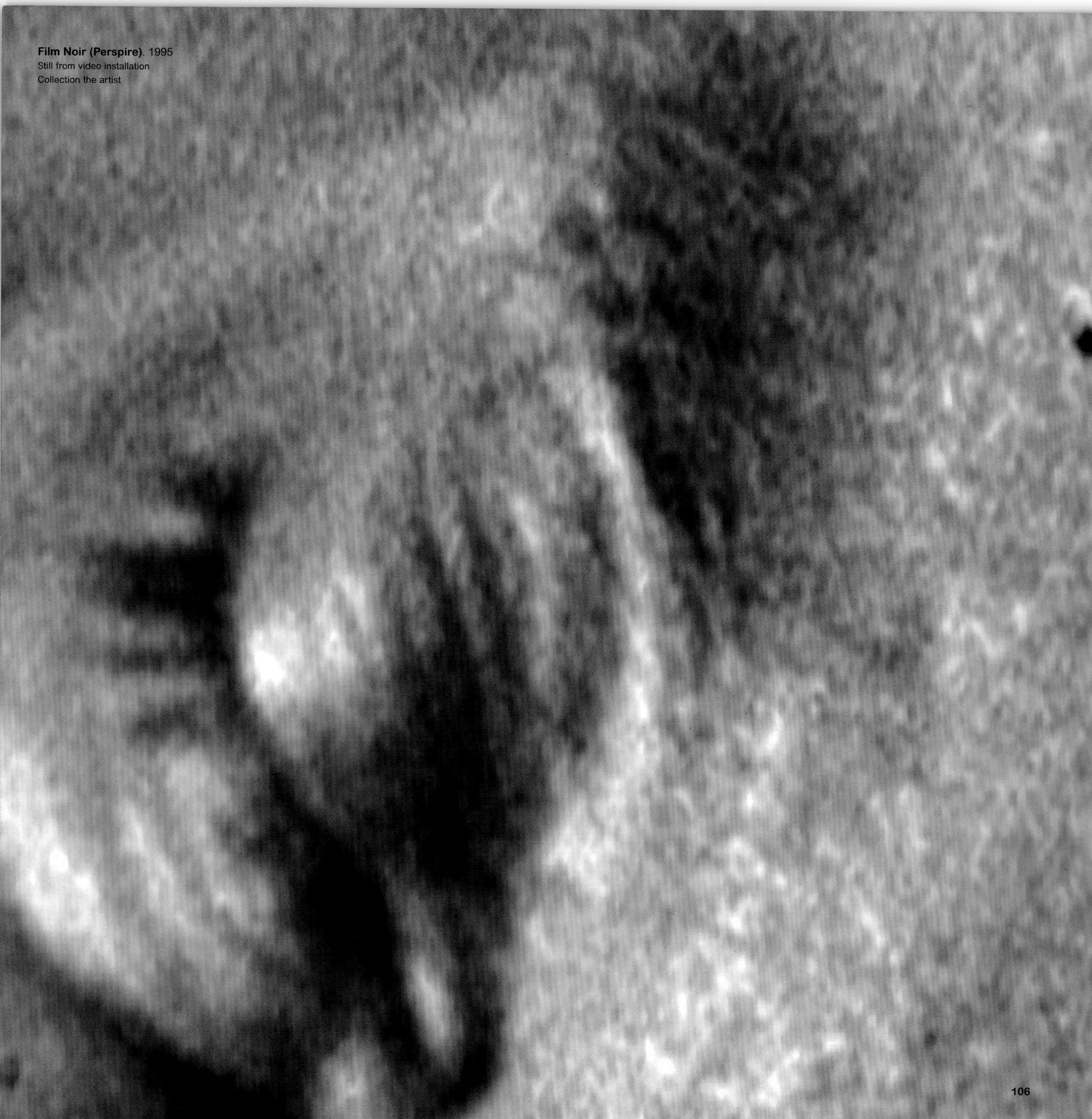

Film Noir (Perspire). 1995
Still from video installation
Collection the artist

Fuzzy Logic. 1995
Video installation with screens and black-and-white video,
51 min., 5 sec. loop, dimensions variable
Installation view at Centre national d'art et de culture Georges Pompidou, Paris, 1995
Collection the artist

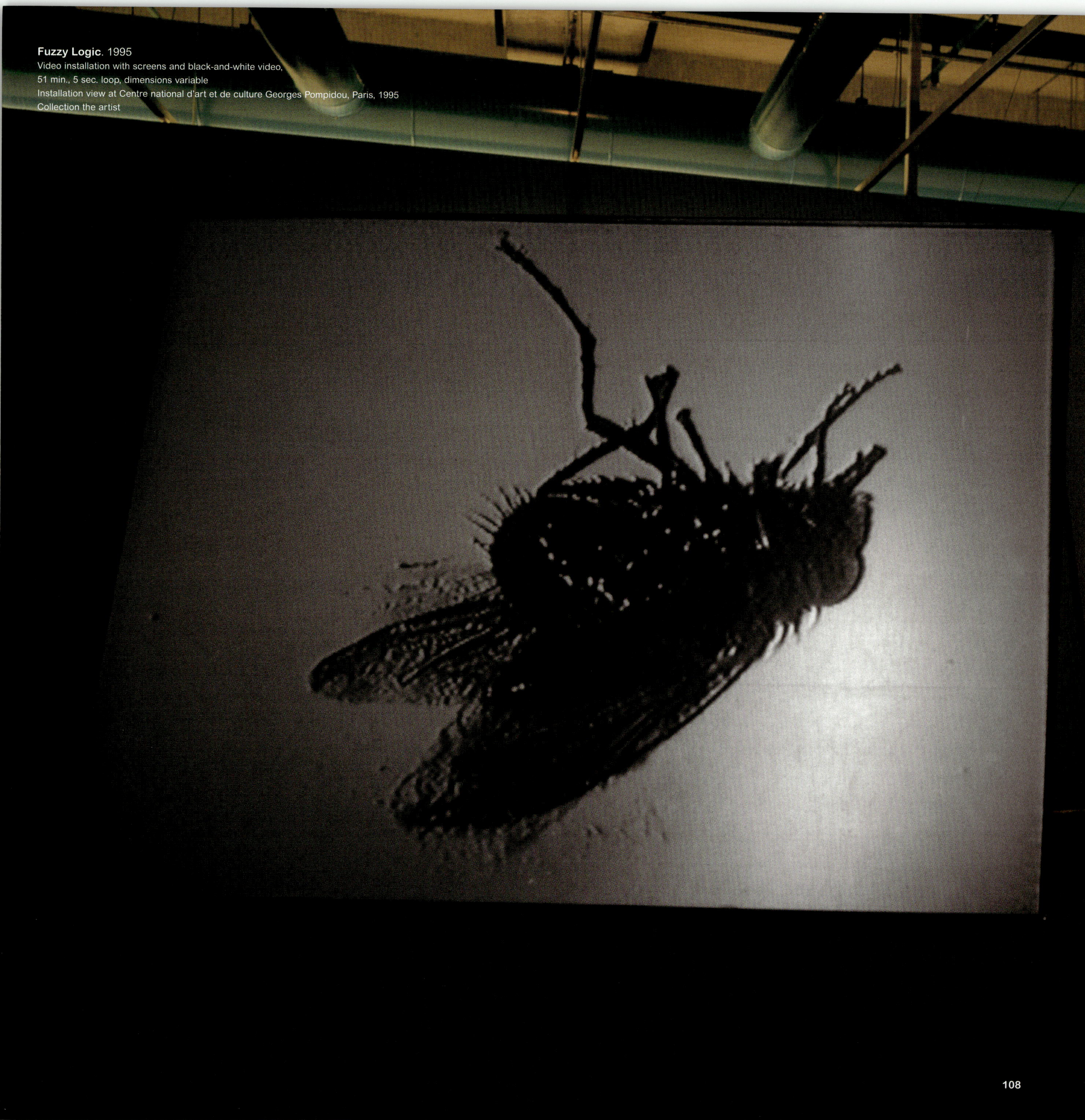

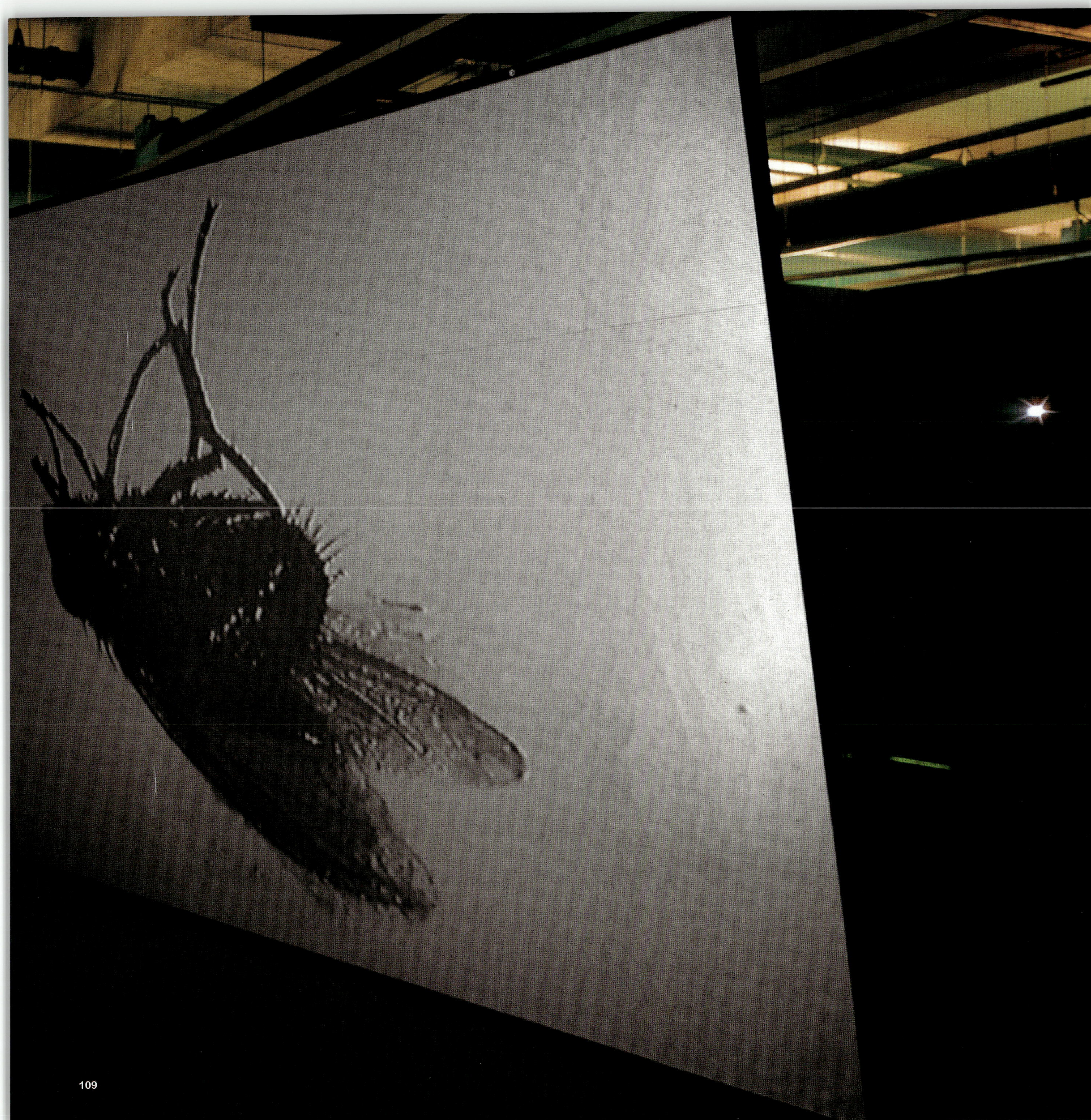

Hand and Foot (Right). 1995–96
Video installation with monitor or wall and color video,
32 min., 8 sec. loop, dimensions variable
Collection of Noah Garson and Ronald Schwartz

Hand and Foot (Left). 1995–96
Video installation with monitor or wall and color video,
30 min., 39 sec. loop, dimensions variable
Collection of Noah Garson and Ronald Schwartz

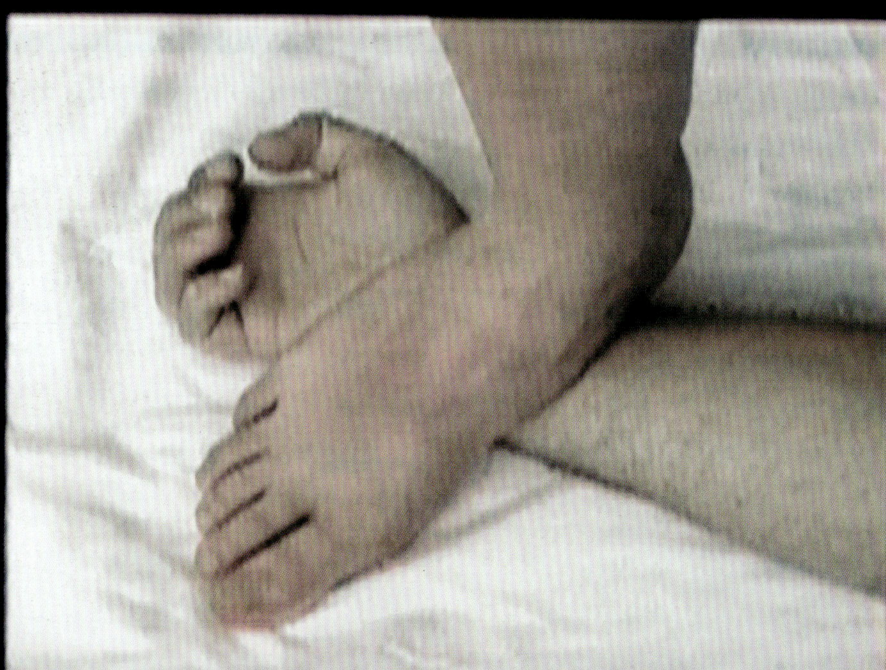

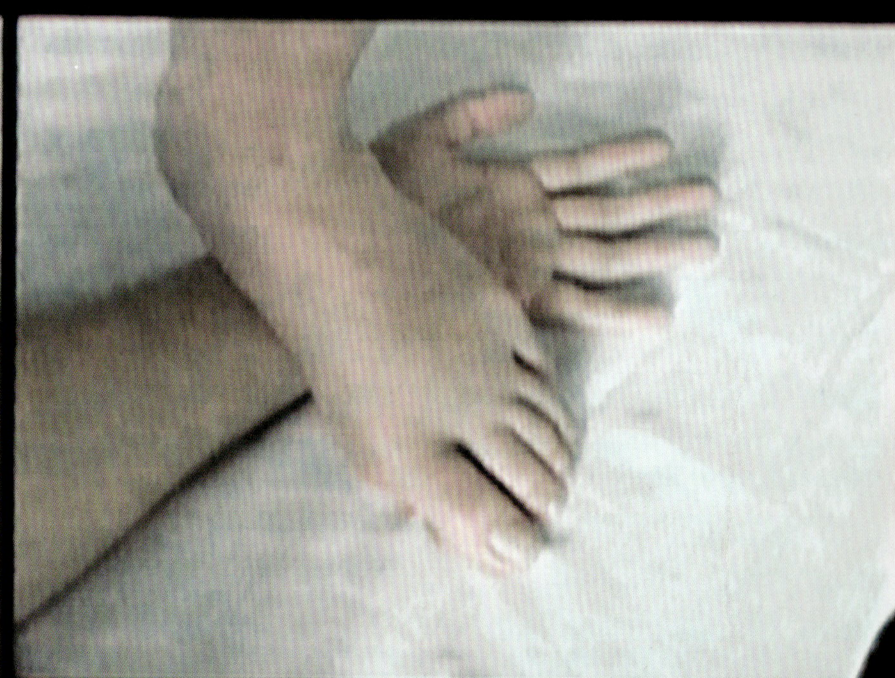

A Divided Self I. 1996
Stills from video installation
Collection the artist

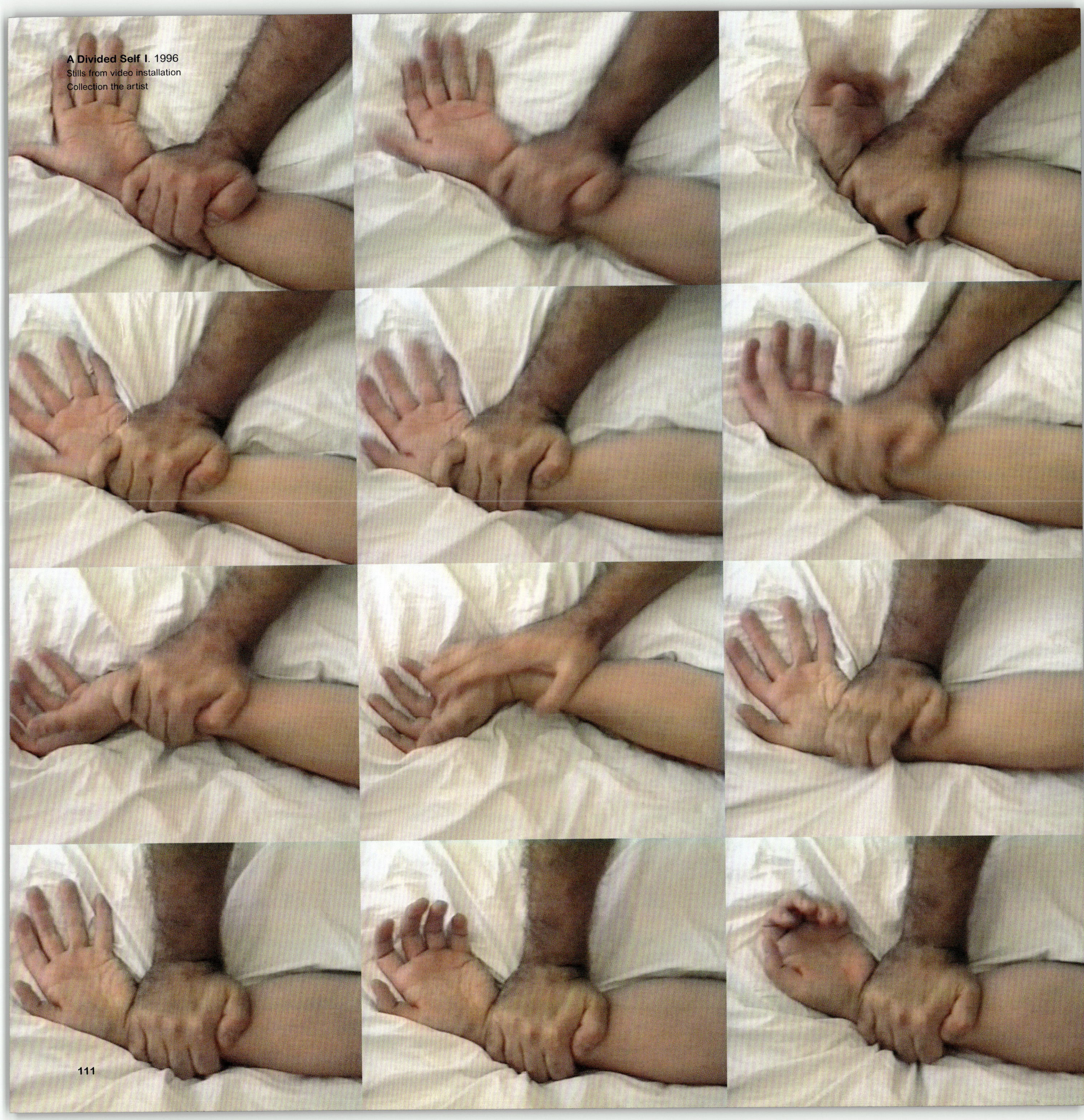

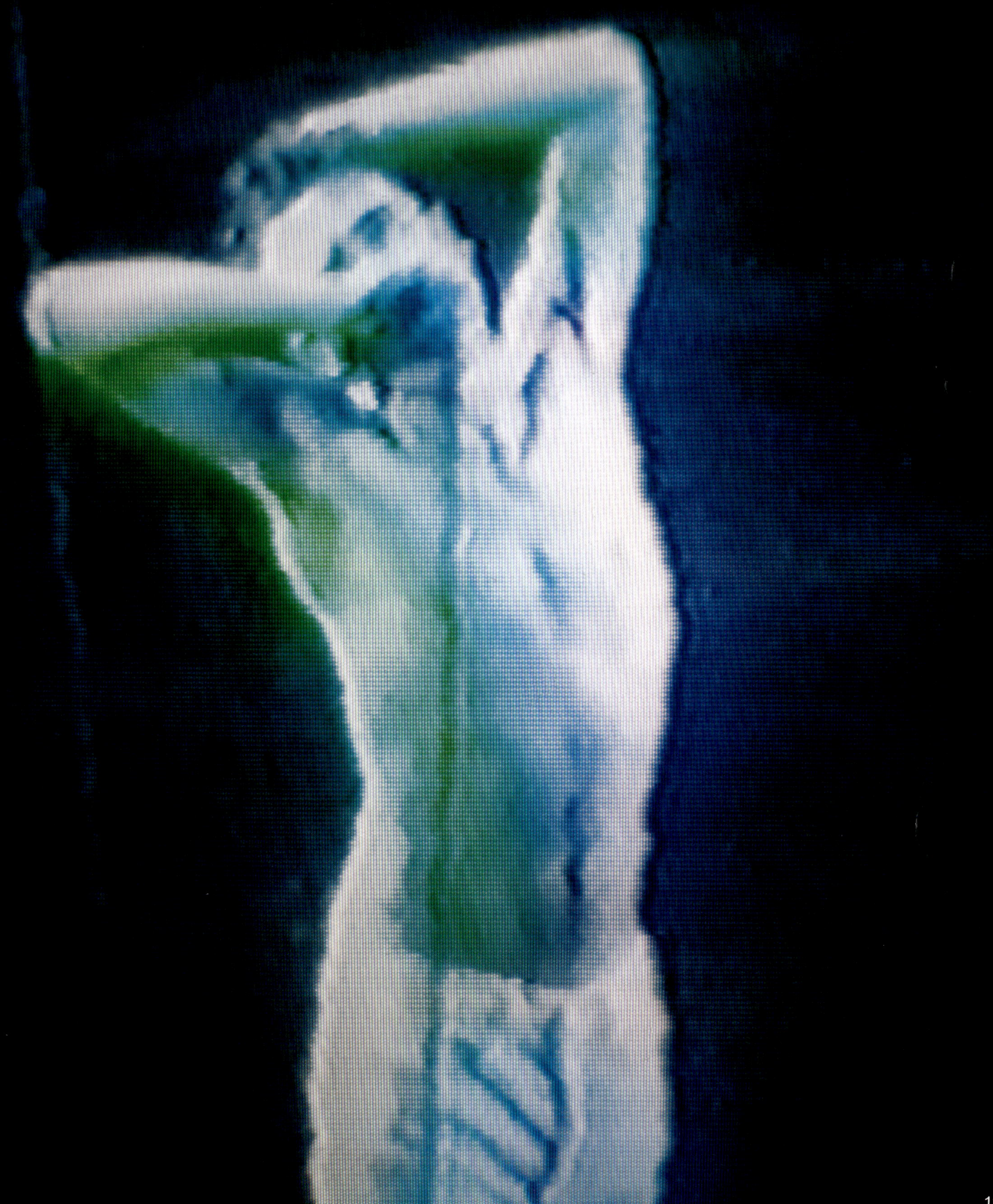

Bootleg (Bigmouth). 1996
Video installation with color video,
19 min., 44 sec. loop, dimensions variable
Sammlung migros museum für gegenwartskunst Zürich

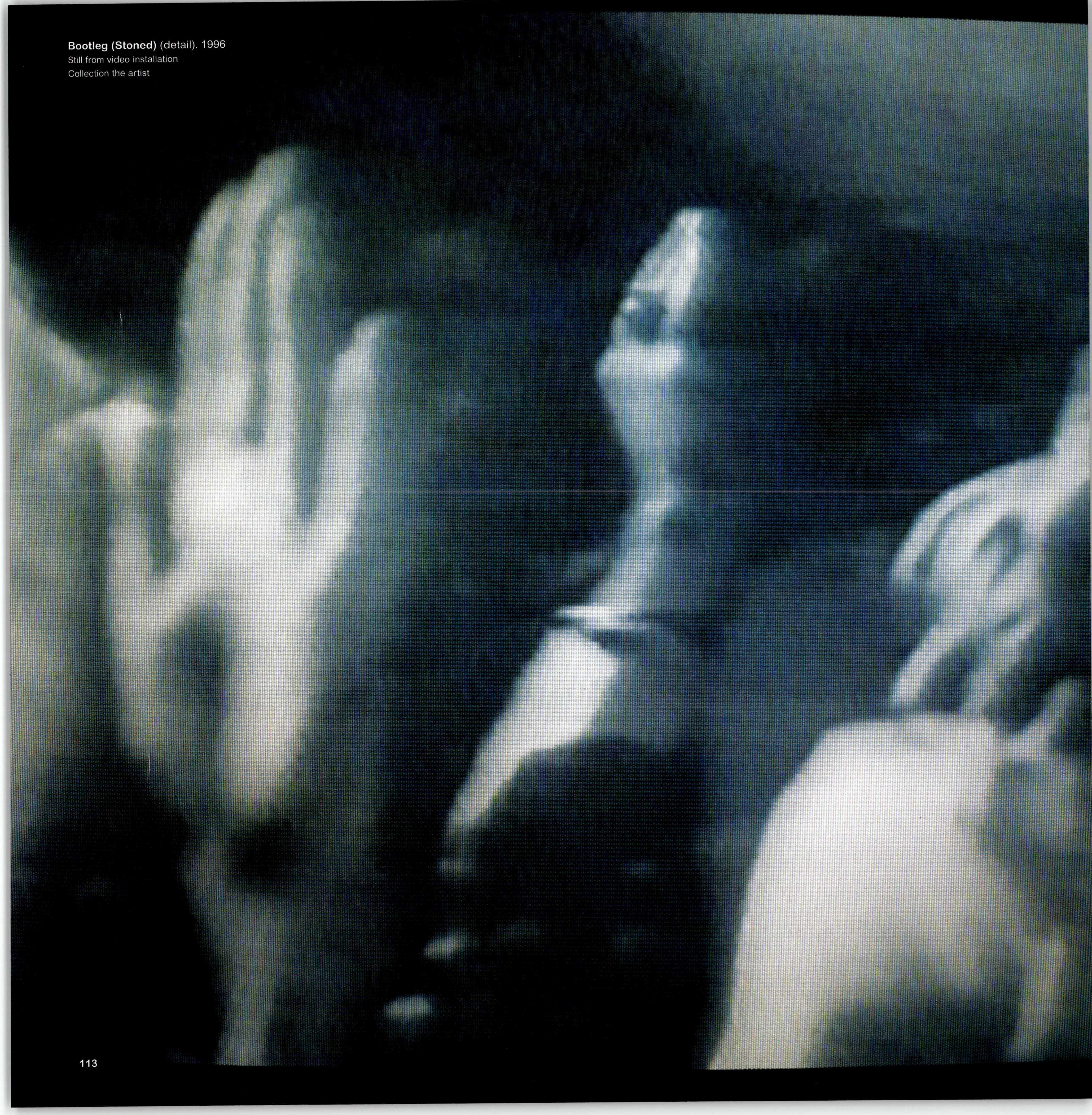

Bootleg (Stoned) (detail). 1996
Still from video installation
Collection the artist

A Few Words on the Nature of Relationships. 1996
Wall text in Bembo typeface, dimensions variable
Private collection

Close your eyes, open your mouth.

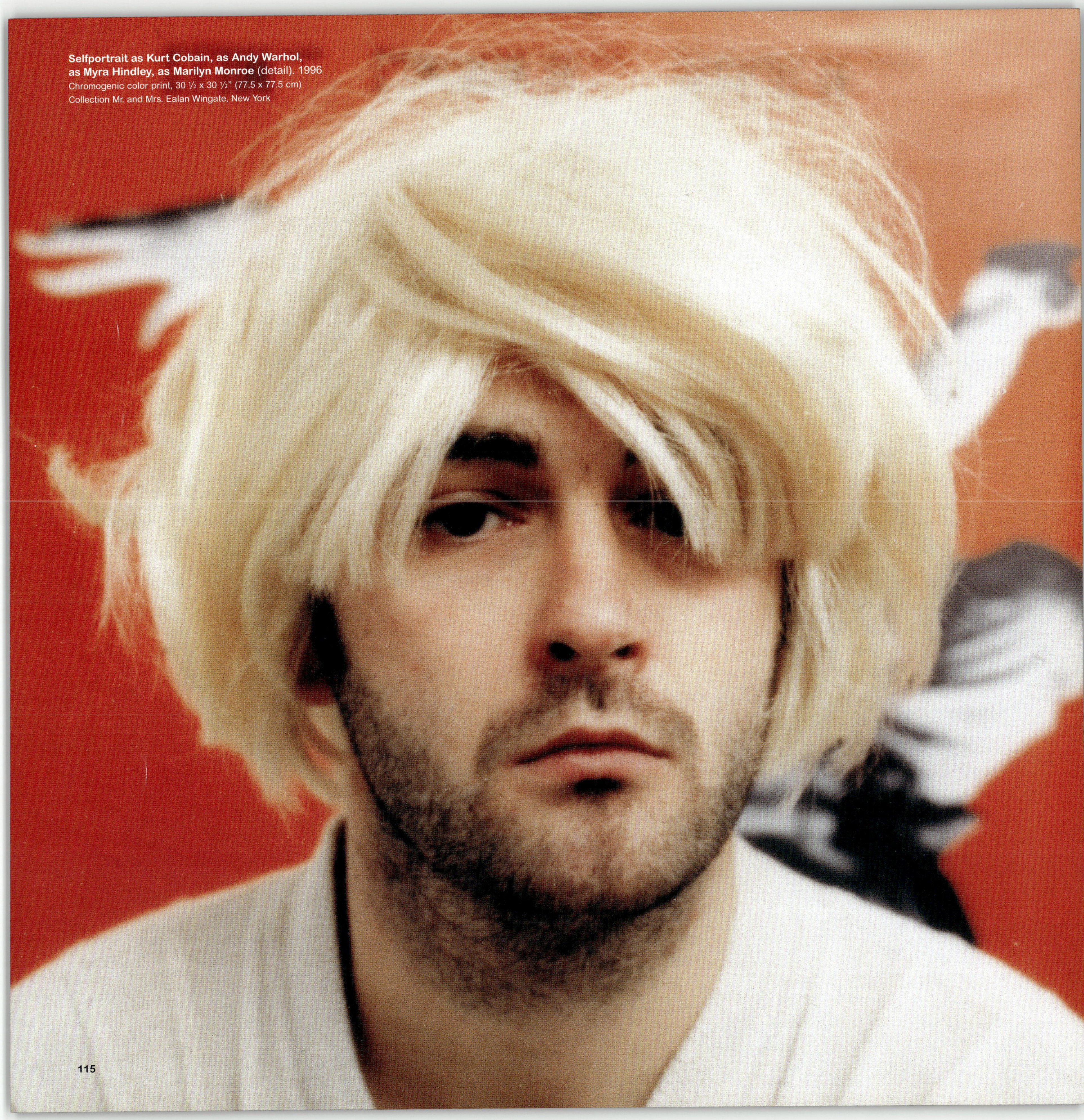

Selfportrait as Kurt Cobain, as Andy Warhol, as Myra Hindley, as Marilyn Monroe (detail). 1996
Chromogenic color print, 30 ½ x 30 ½" (77.5 x 77.5 cm)
Collection Mr. and Mrs. Ealan Wingate, New York

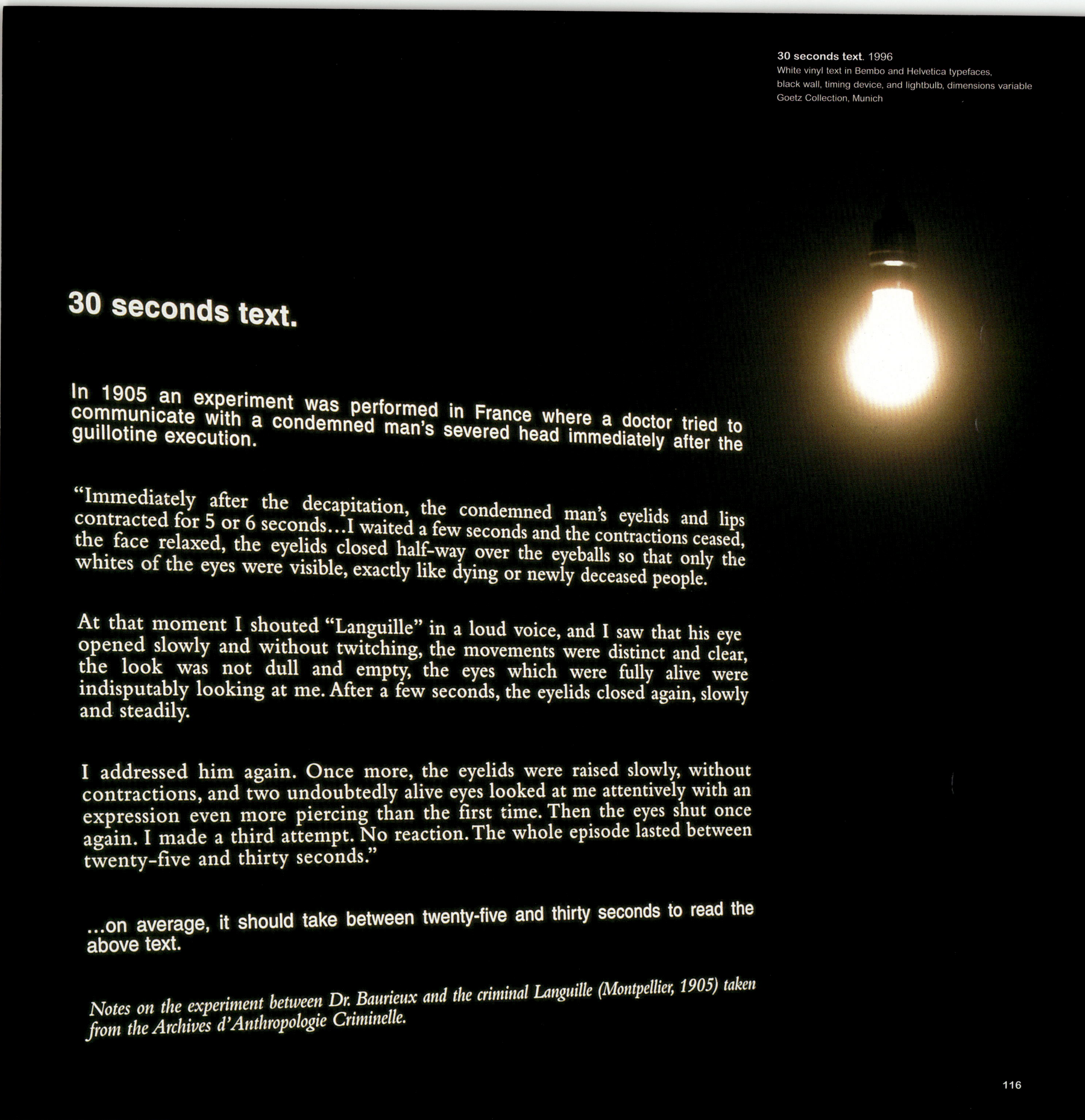

30 seconds text. 1996
White vinyl text in Bembo and Helvetica typefaces, black wall, timing device, and lightbulb, dimensions variable
Goetz Collection, Munich

Dead Line in Space. 1997
Time-based sculpture at Villa Minimo, Hannover, 1997
Collection the artist

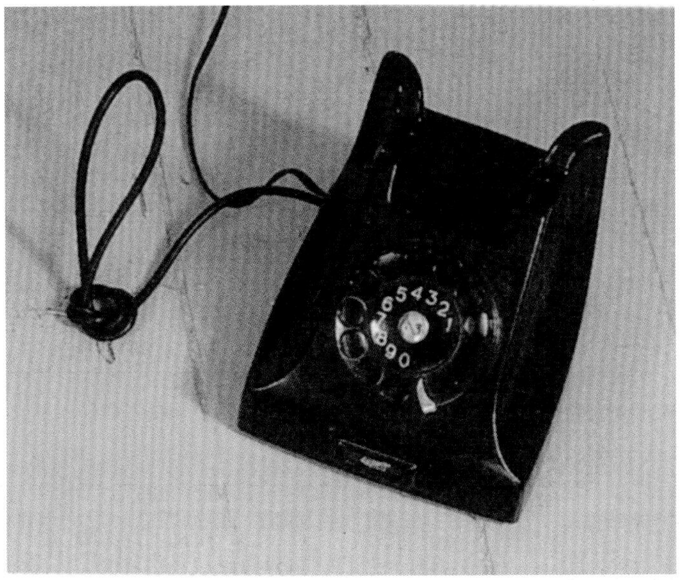

Dead Line in Space was made for an exhibition at Villa Minimo, Hannover, curated by the artist Hlynur Hallsson. The exhibition was to be installed in a room directly beneath my apartment. I drilled a hole through my bedroom floor and out through the ceiling of the apartment below. I took the handset of my telephone "off the hook" and installed it in the exhibition space below my apartment, the wire leading from the handset up through the ceiling into my bedroom and onto the main body of the telephone. The exhibition lasted four weeks. The telephone remained "off the hook" for this period, and there was no contact with me.

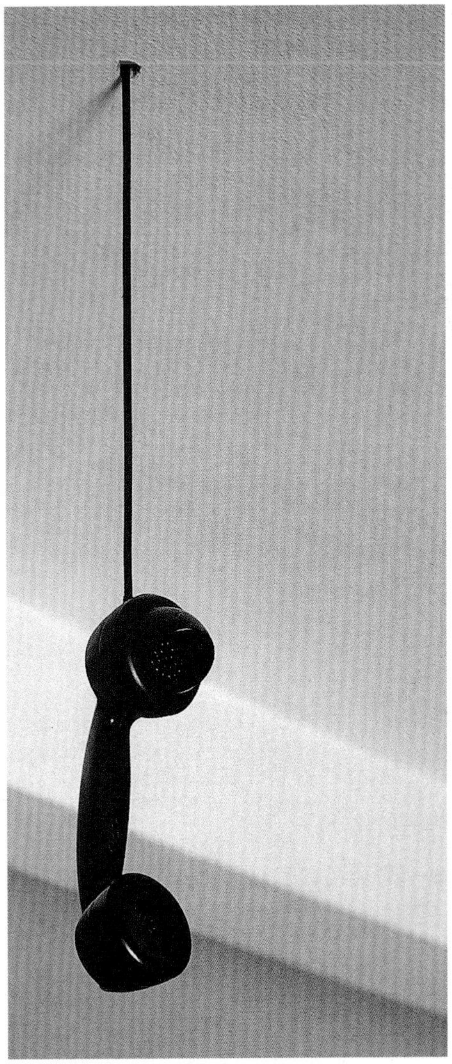

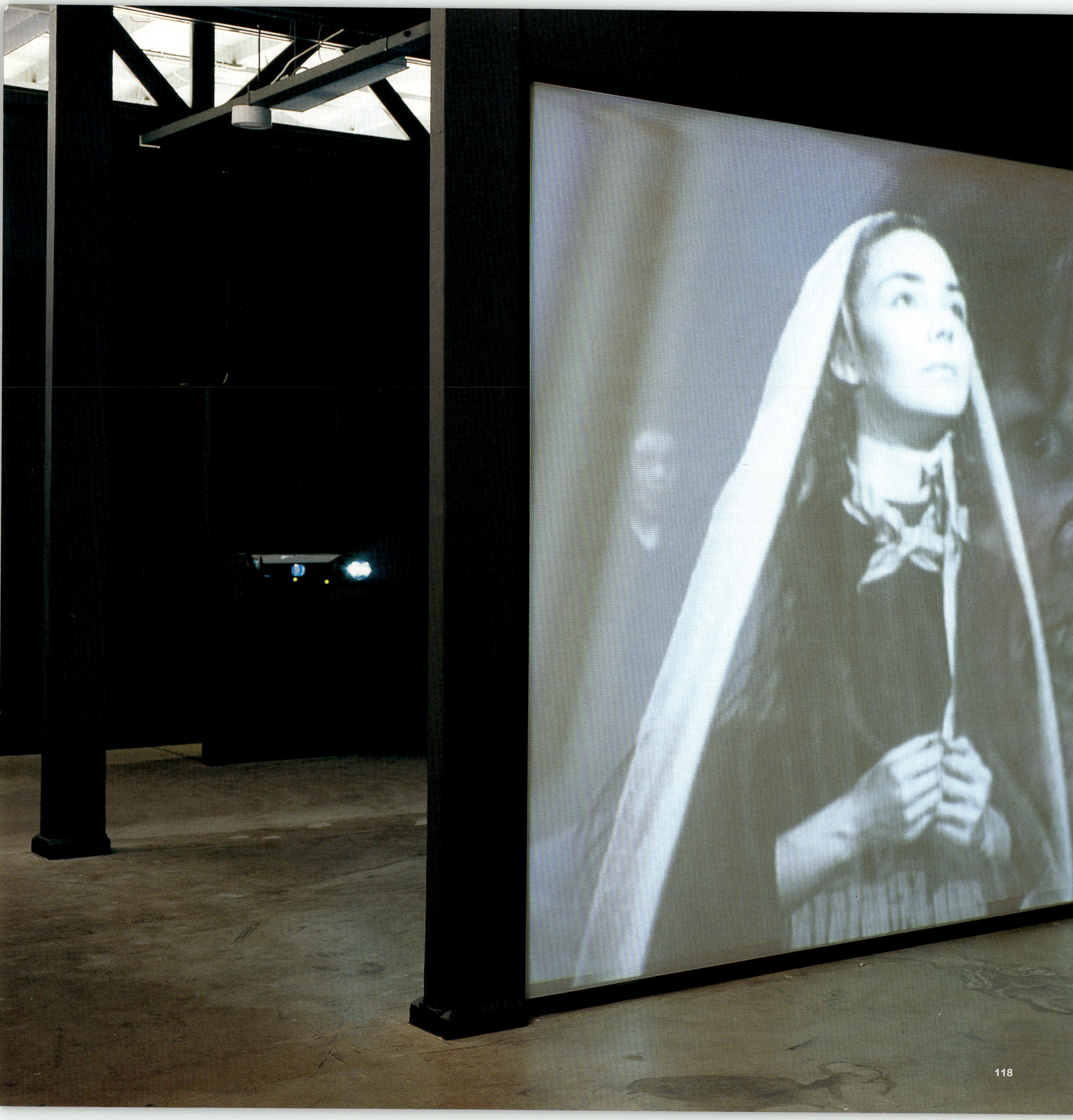

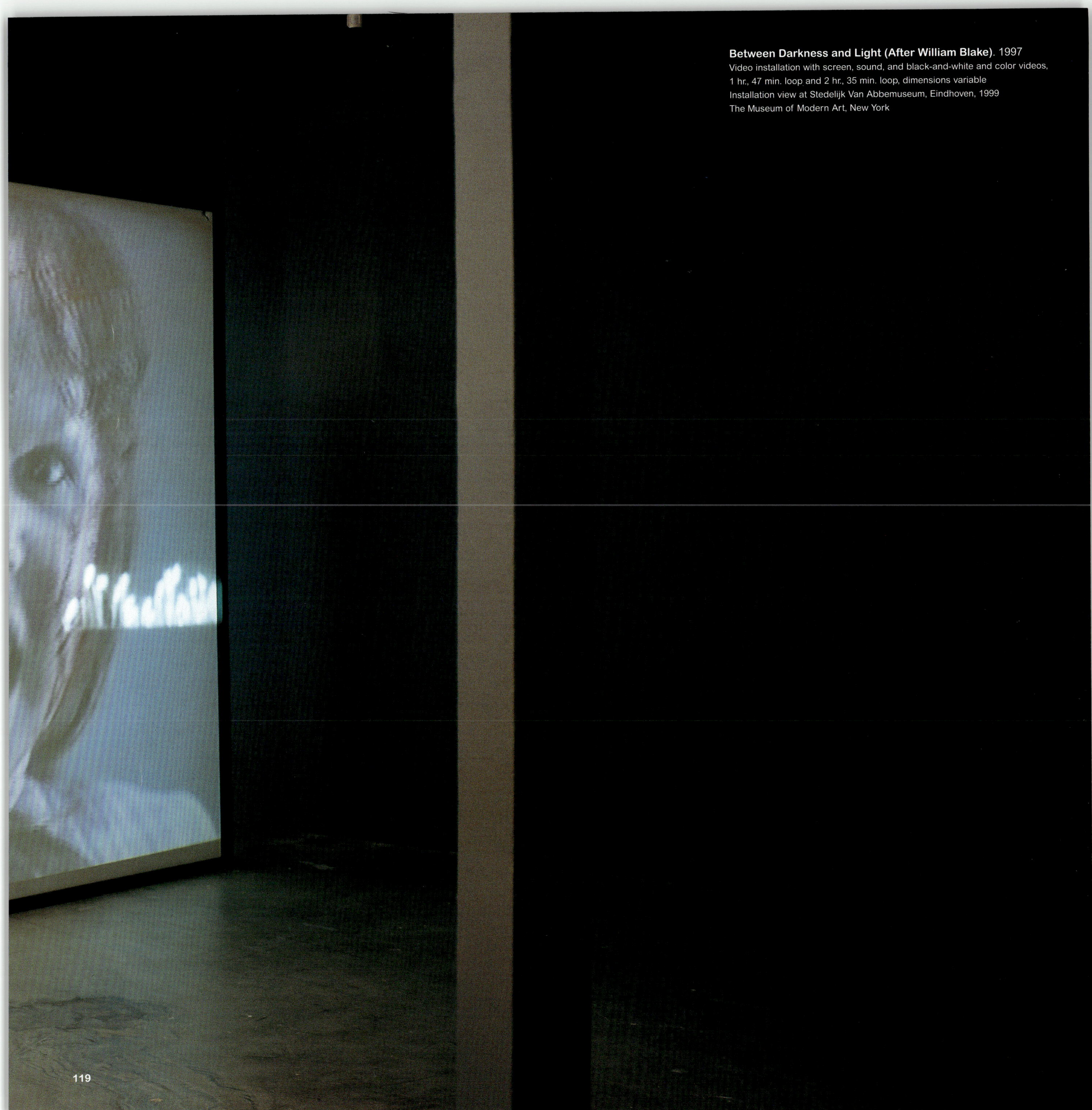

Between Darkness and Light (After William Blake). 1997
Video installation with screen, sound, and black-and-white and color videos, 1 hr., 47 min. loop and 2 hr., 35 min. loop, dimensions variable
Installation view at Stedelijk Van Abbemuseum, Eindhoven, 1999
The Museum of Modern Art, New York

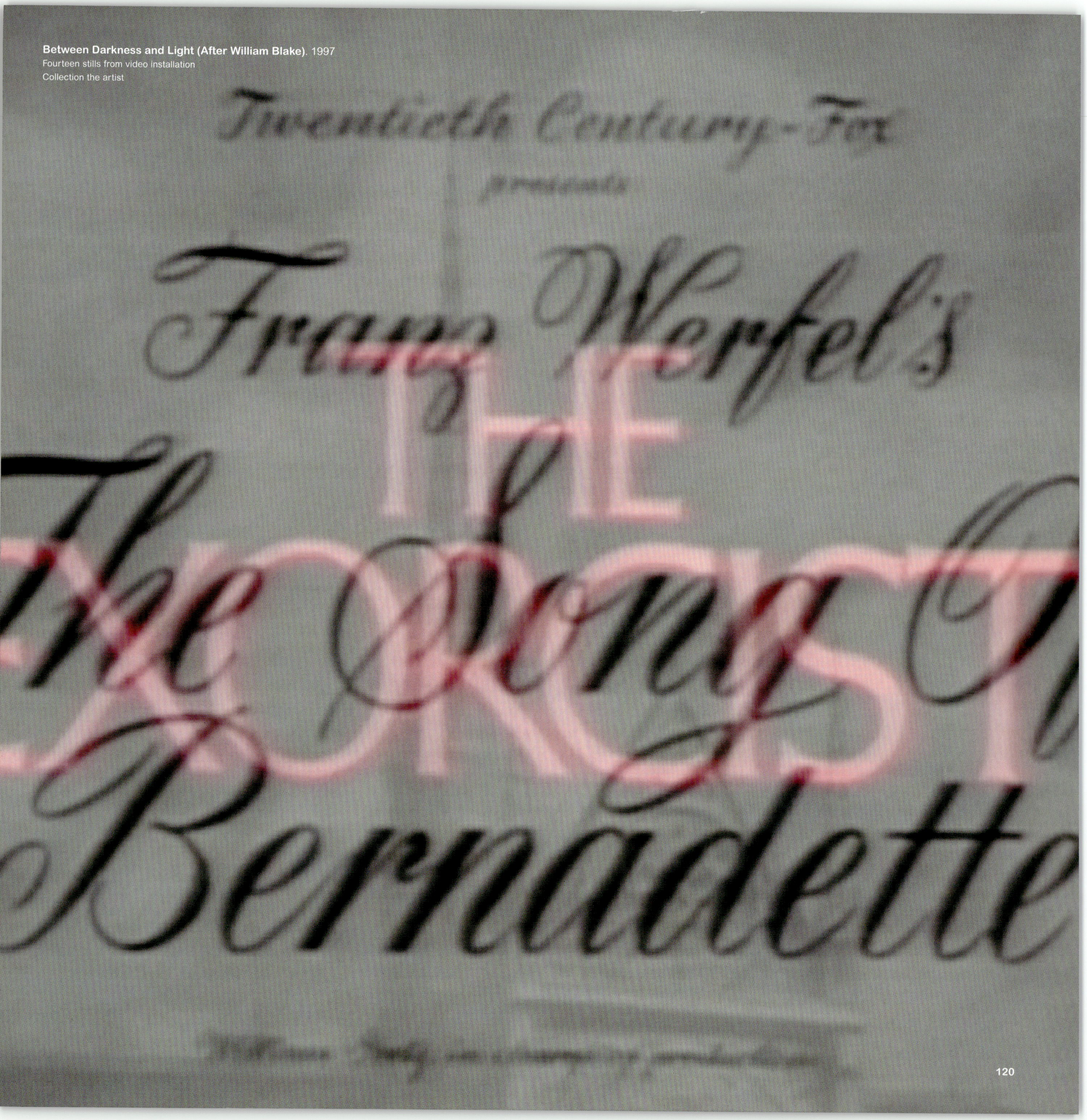

Between Darkness and Light (After William Blake), 1997
Fourteen stills from video installation
Collection the artist

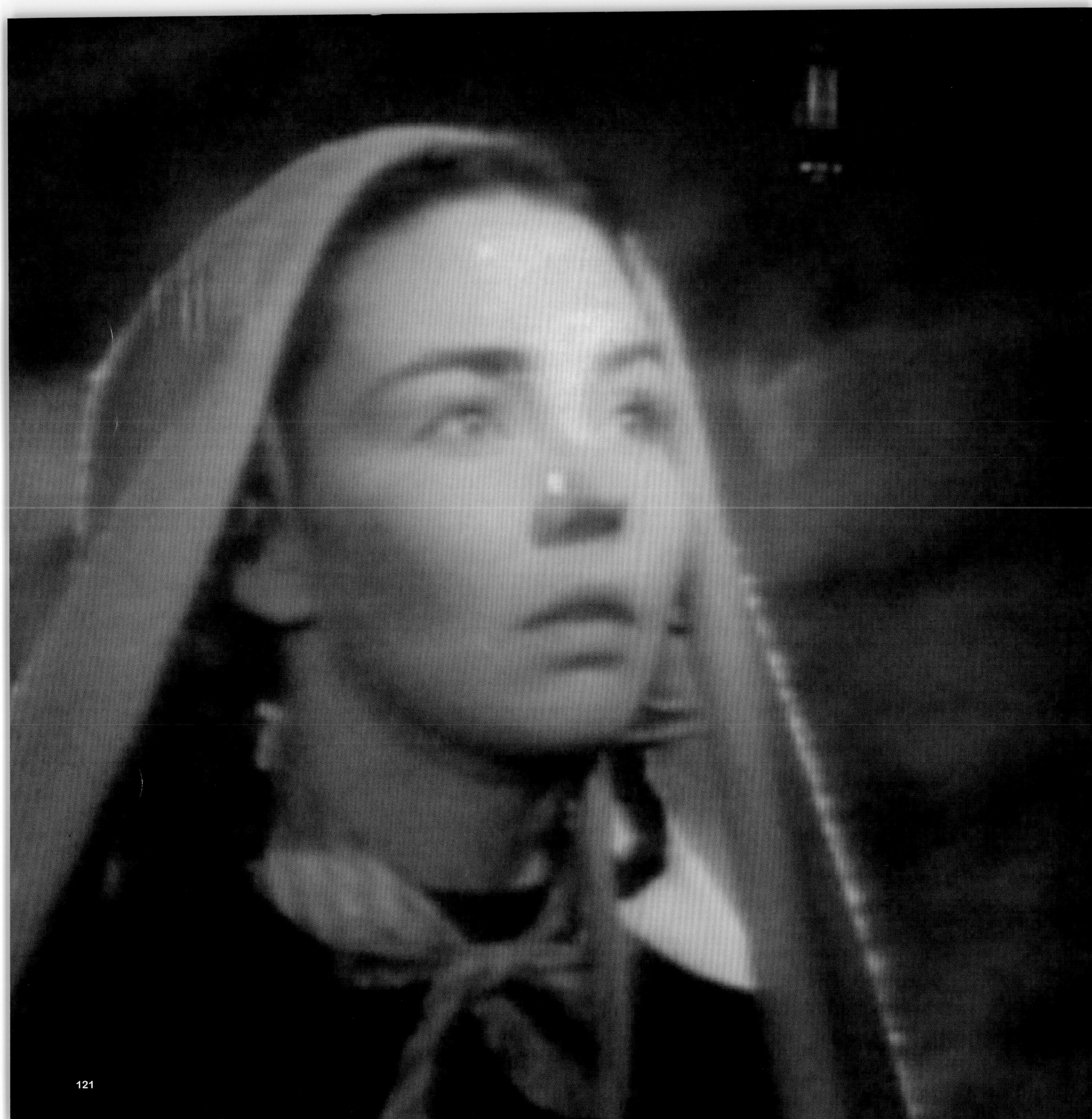

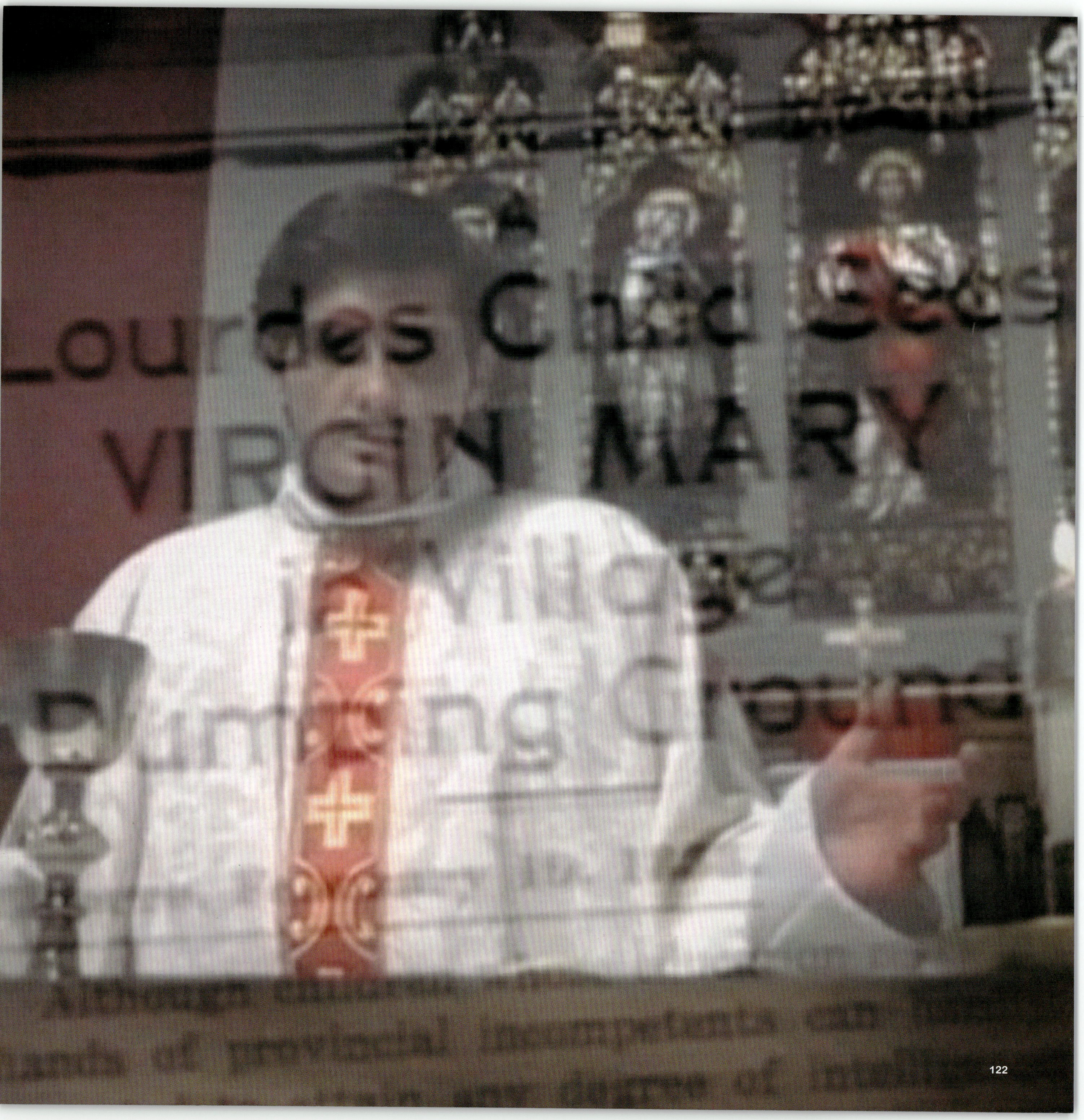
Lourdes
VIRGIN MARY
hands of provincial incompetents can

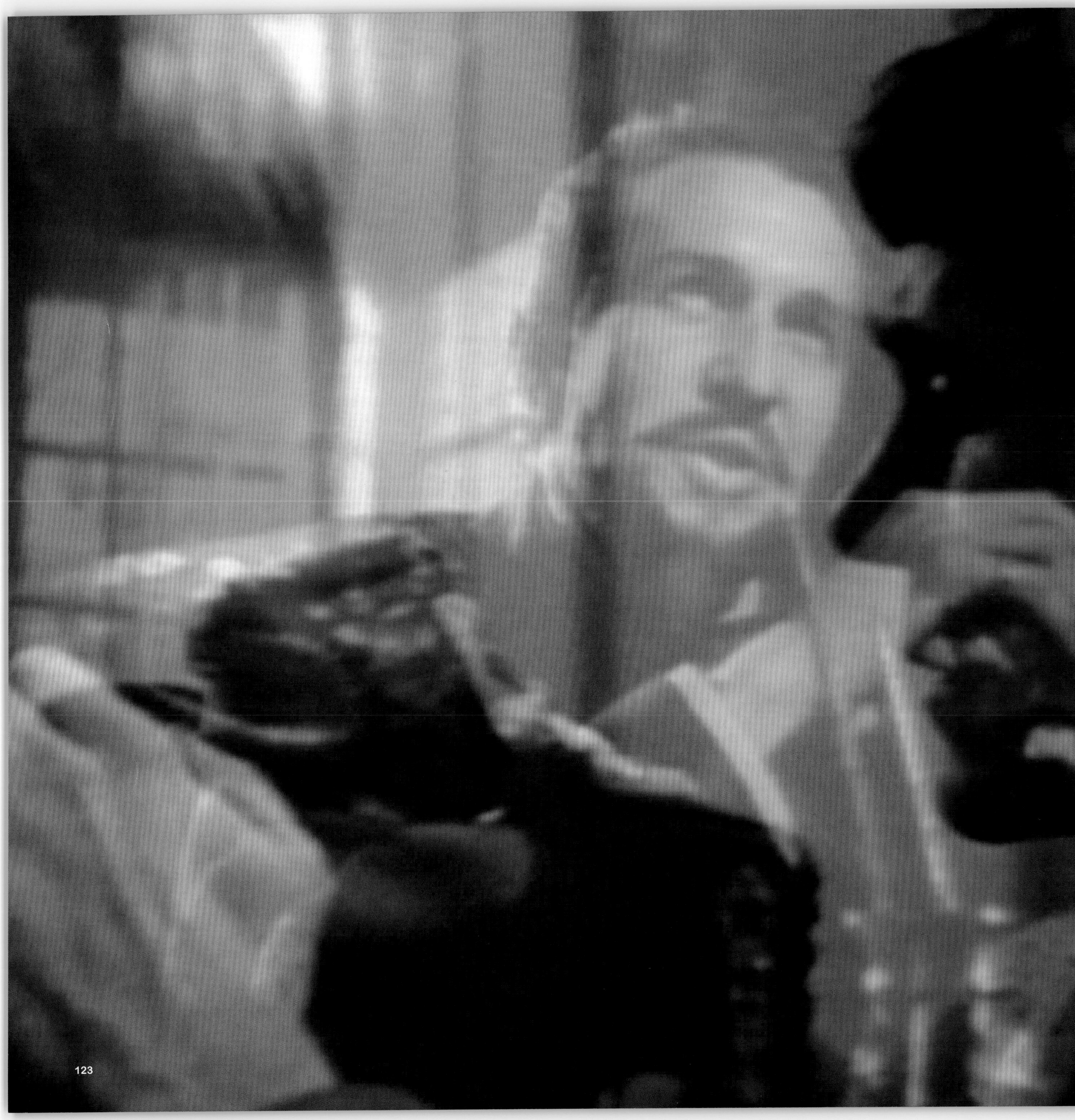

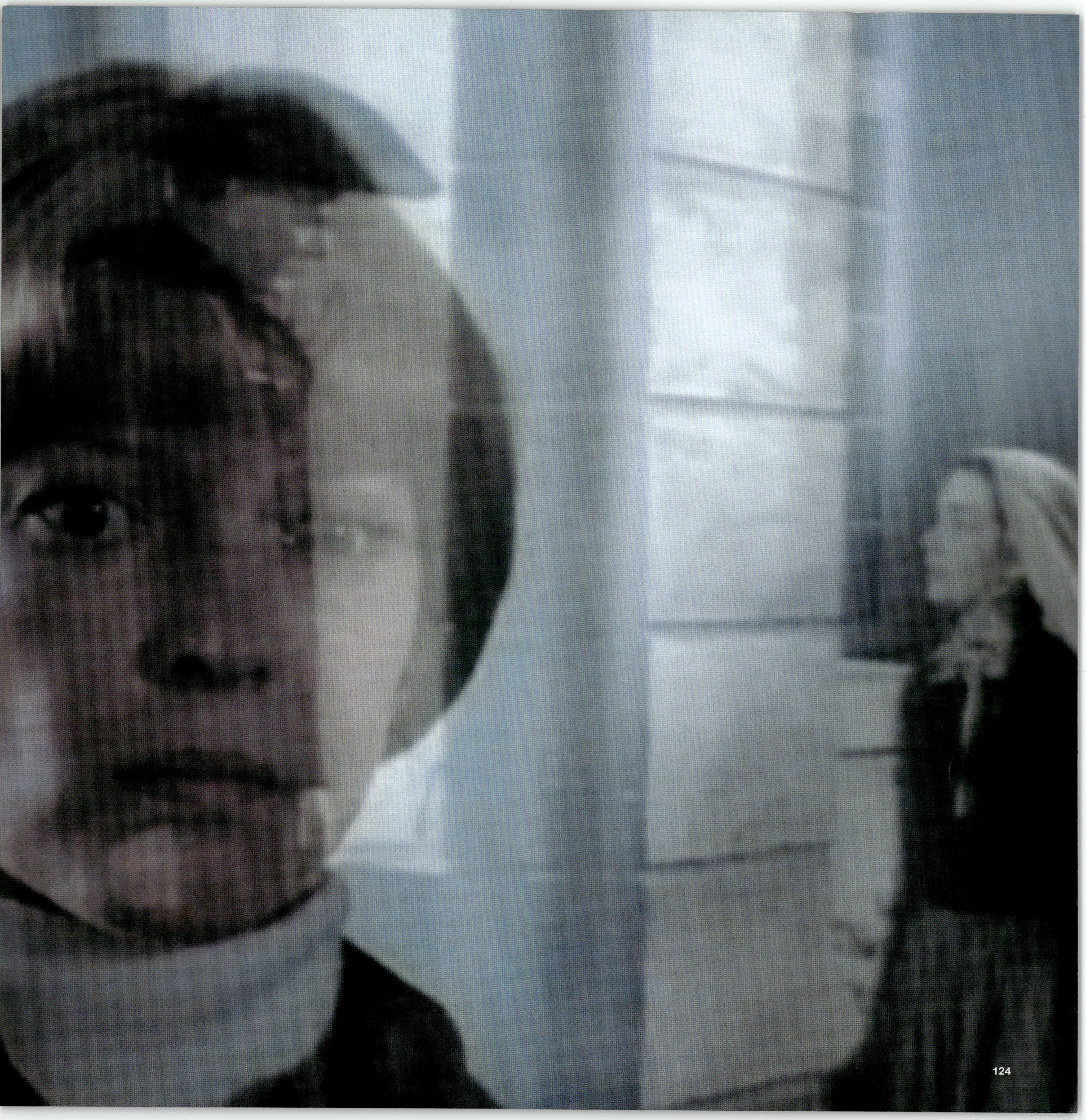

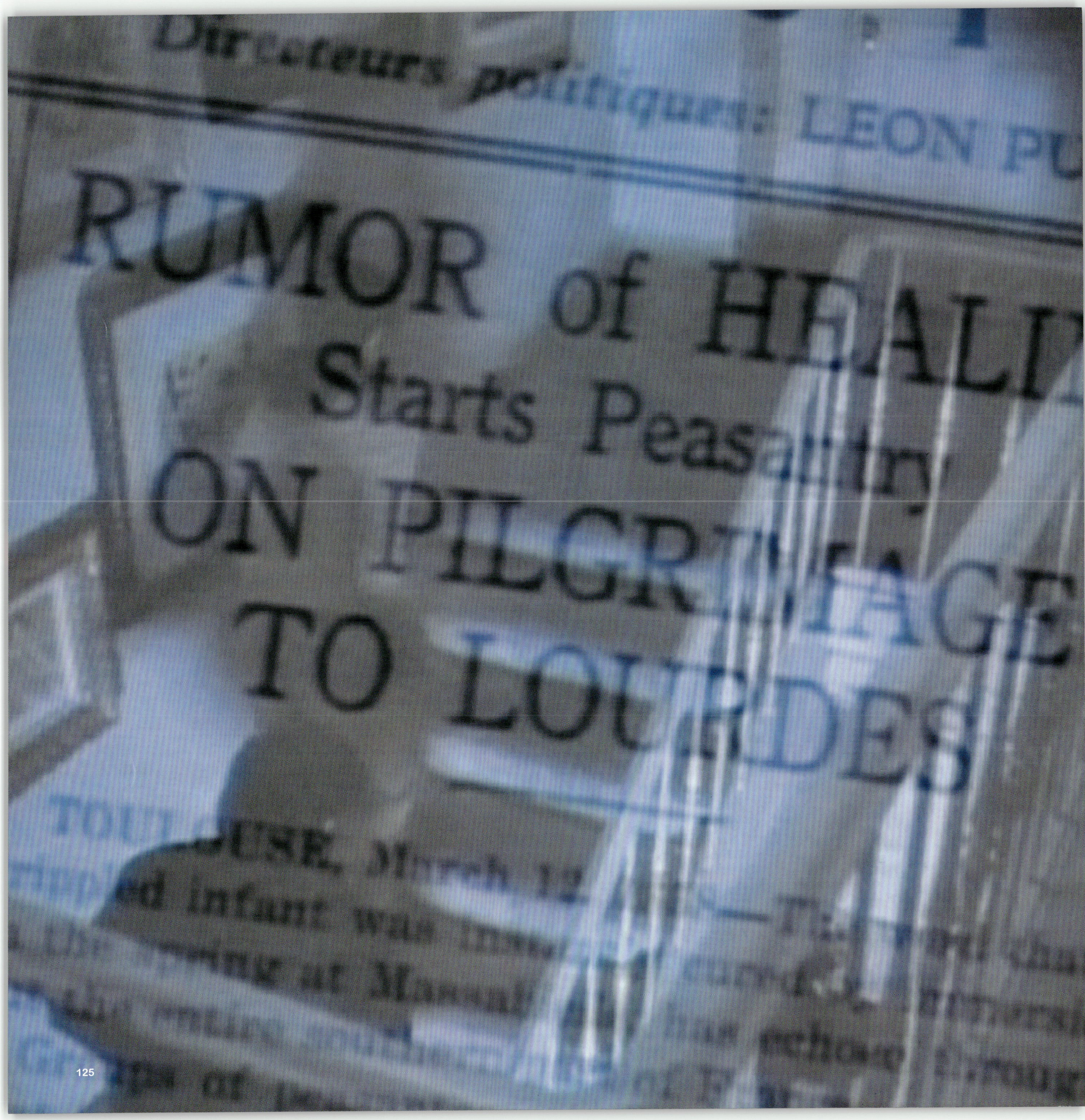
Directeurs politiques: LEON
RUMOR of
Starts Peas
ON PILGR
TO LOURDES
TOU
infant was
at Massa

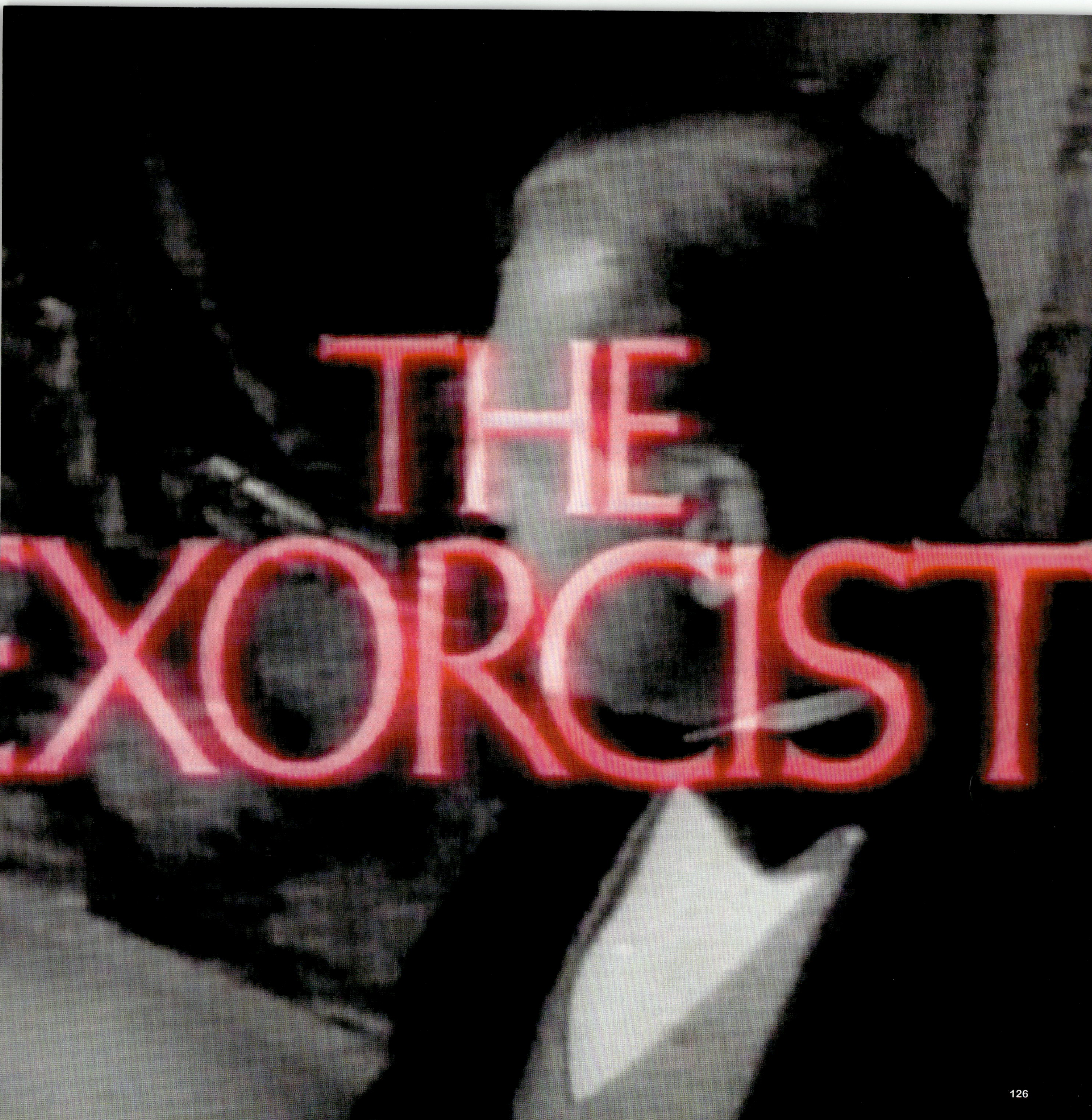
THE
EXORCIST

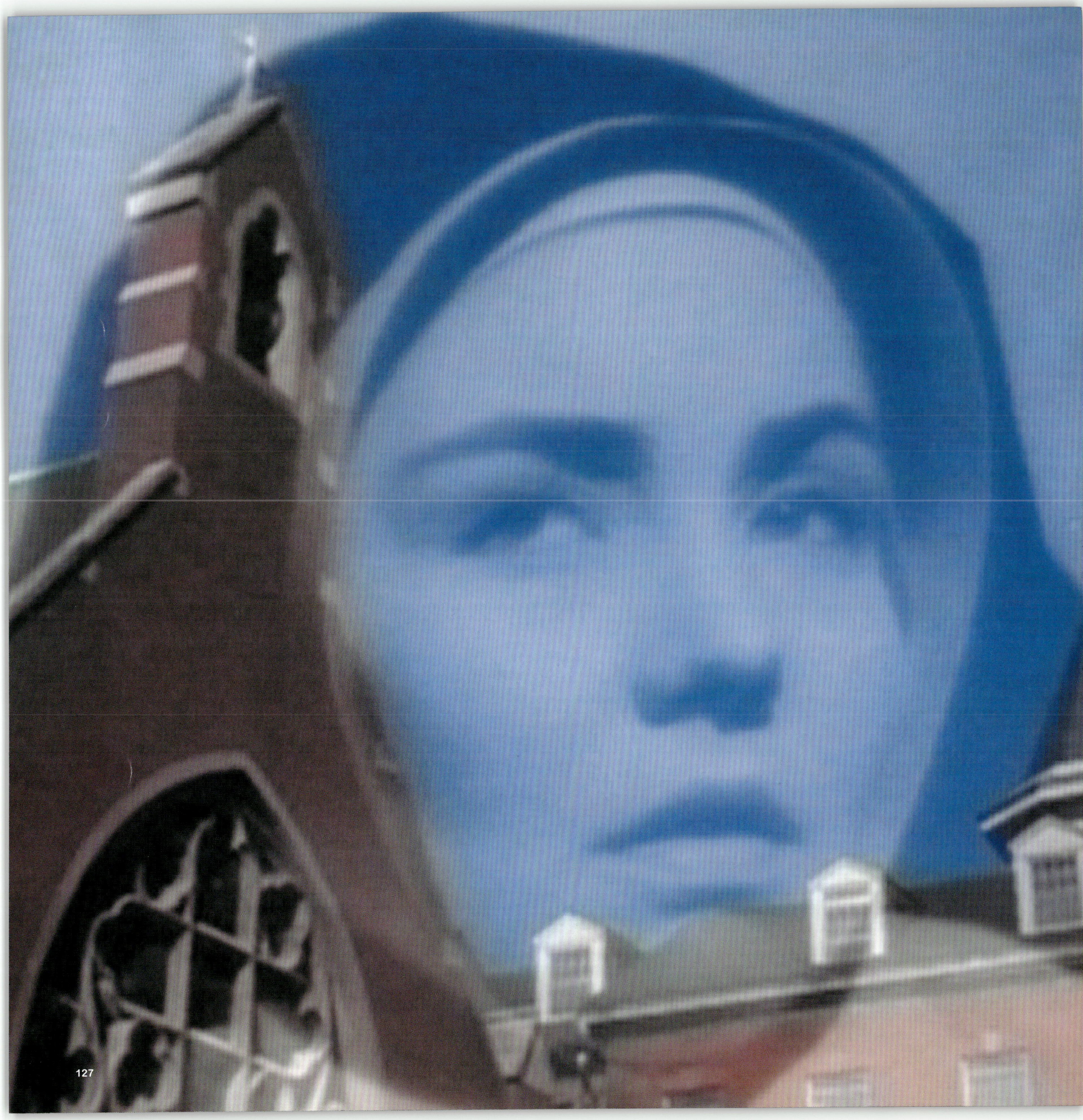

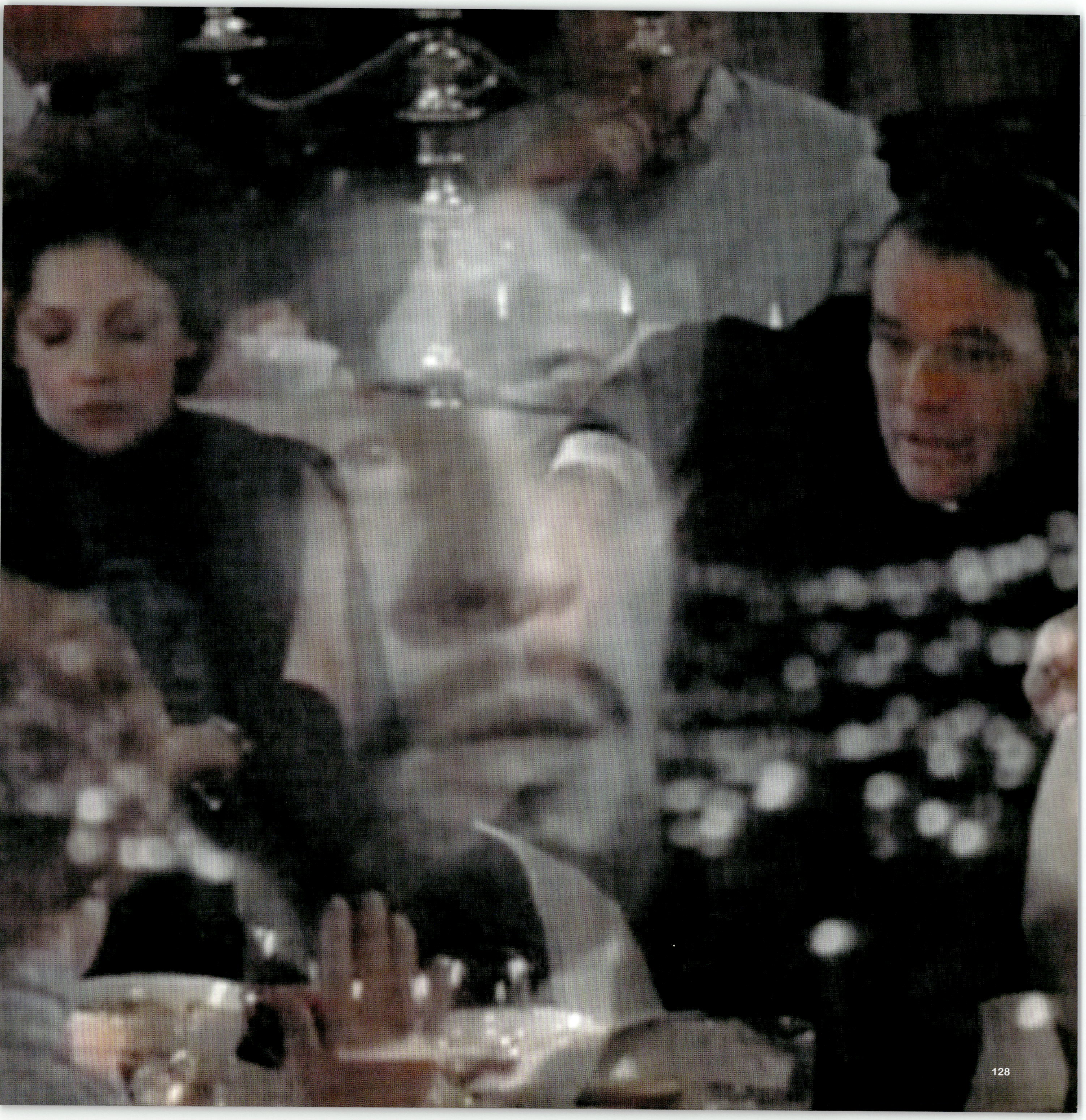

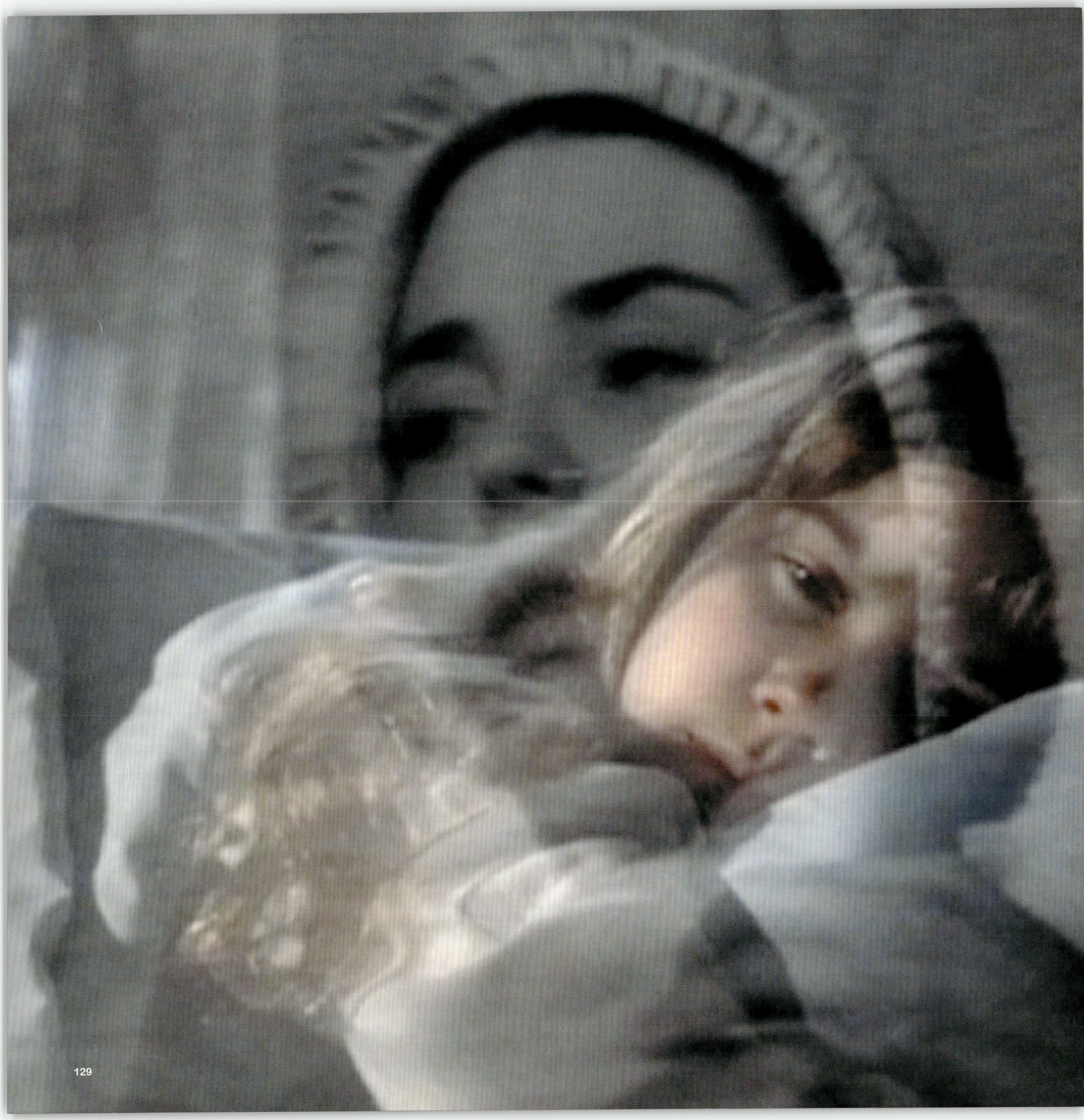

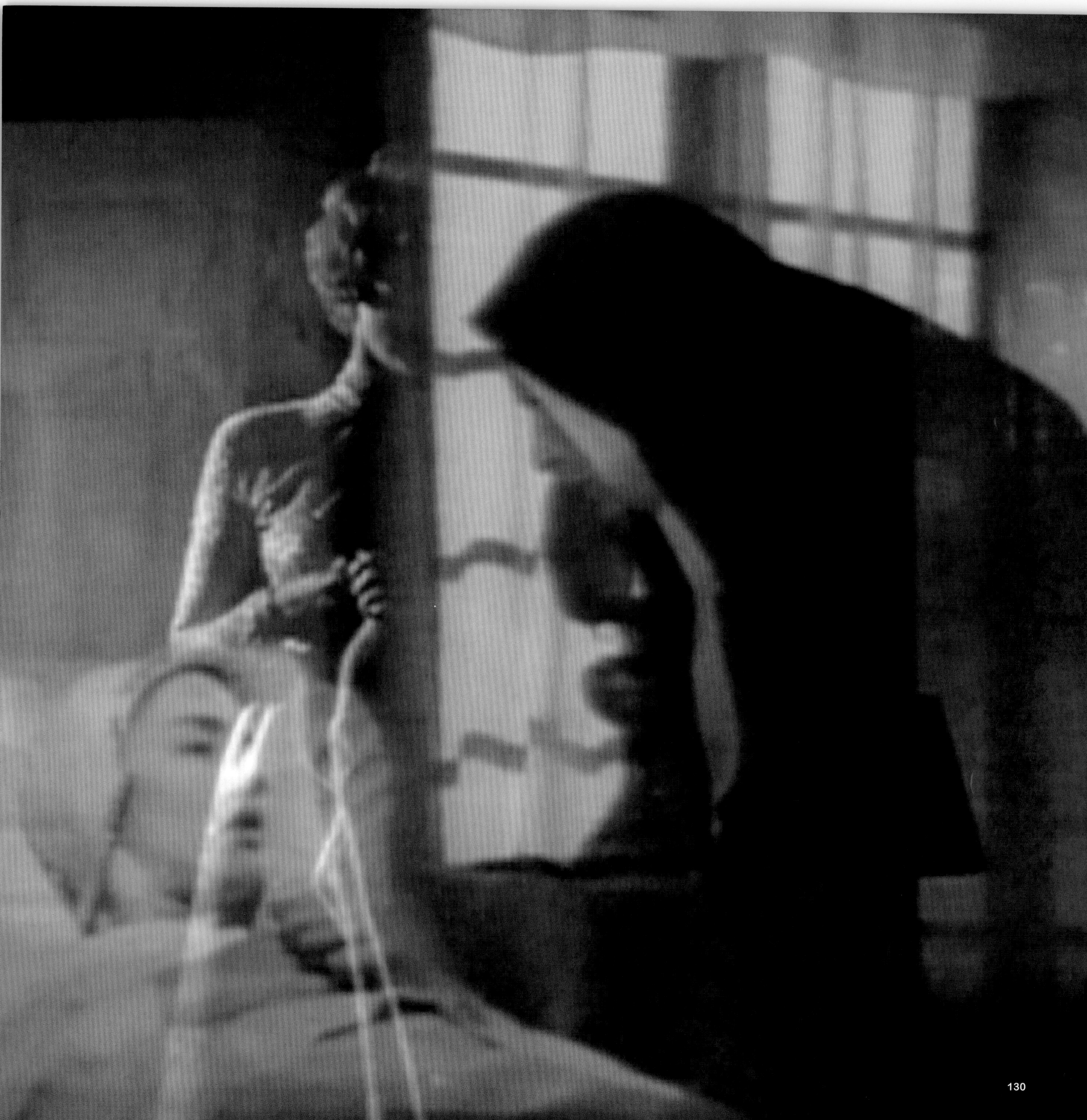

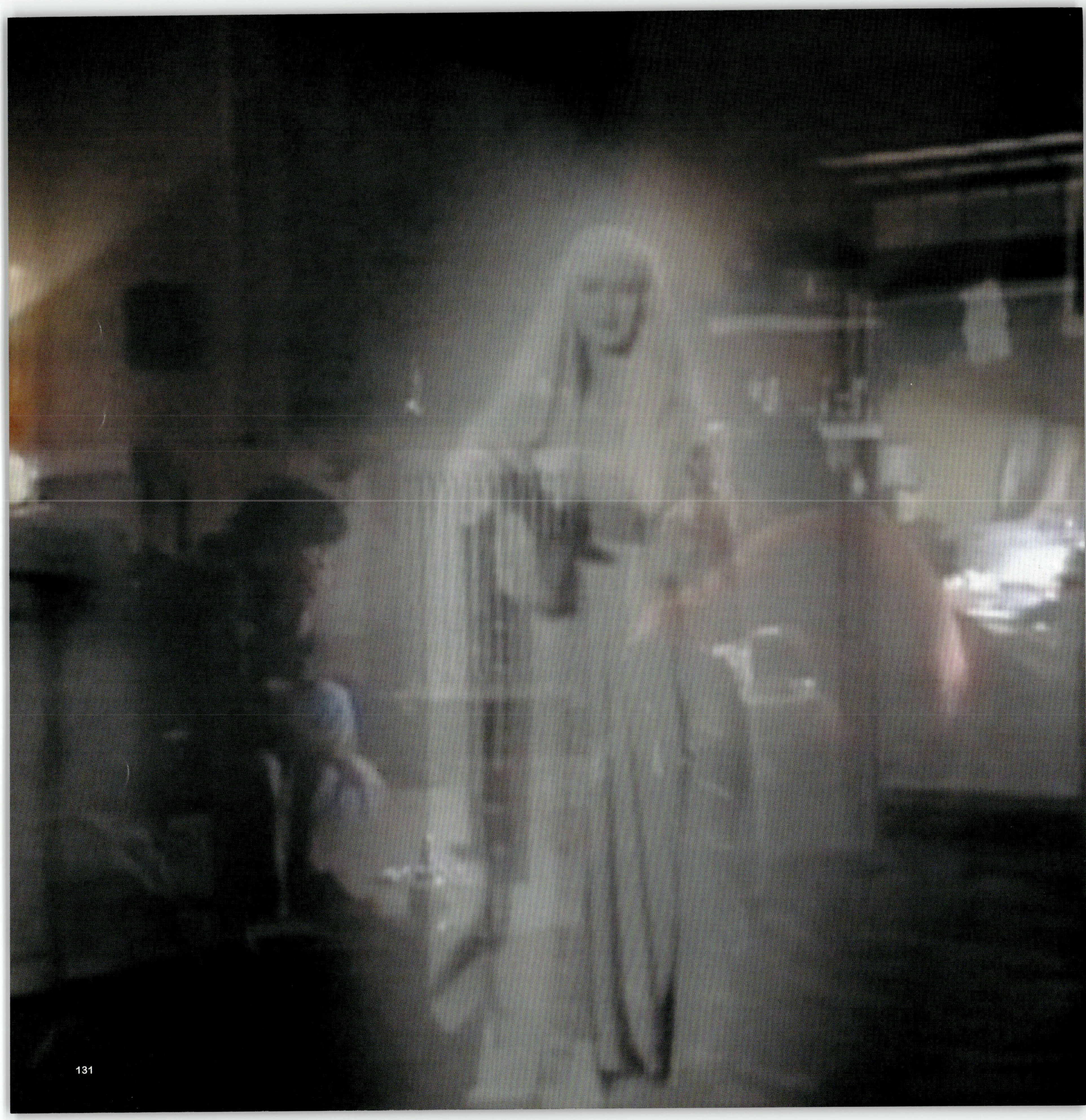

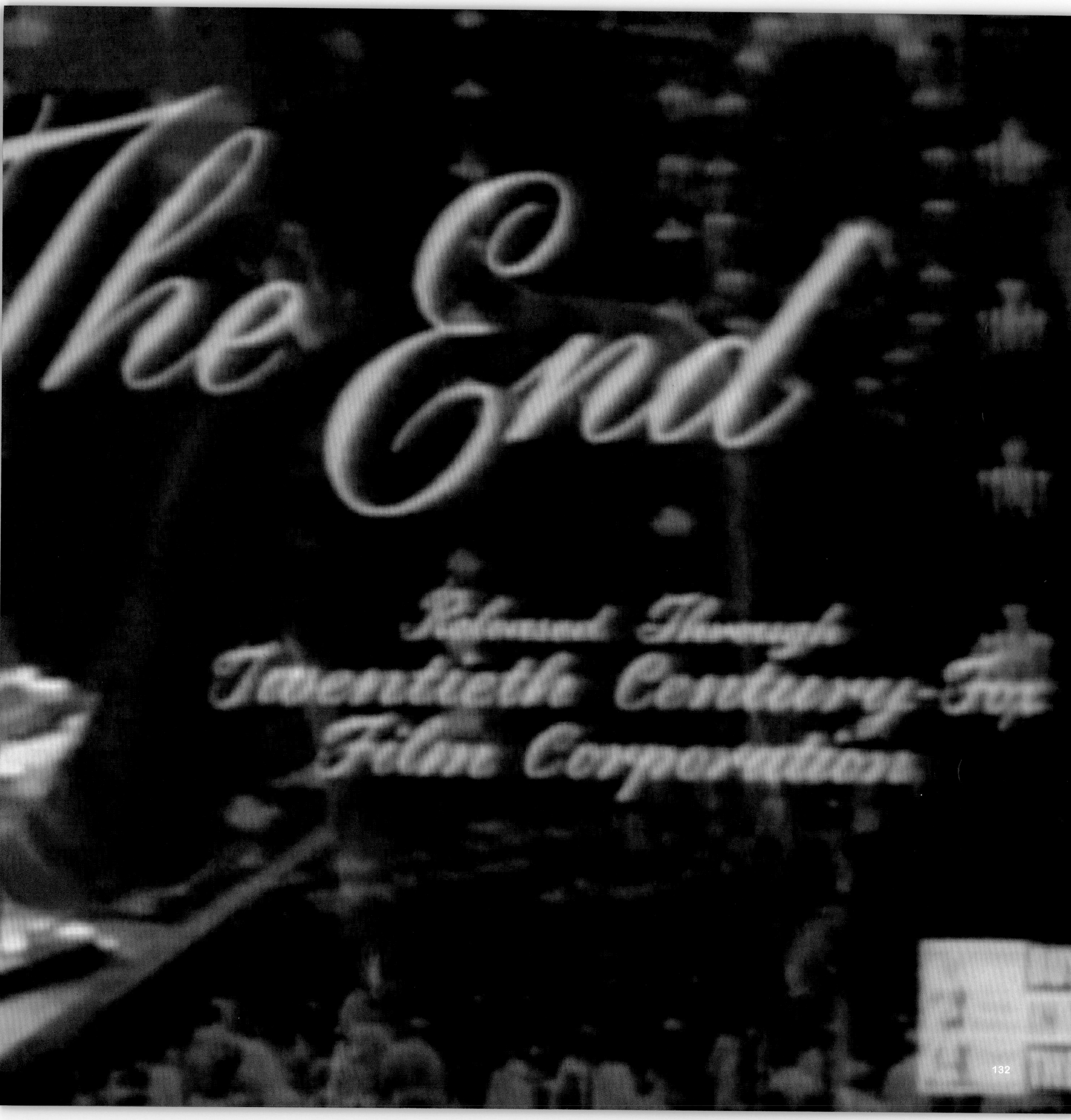
End
Twentieth Century-Fox
Film Corporation

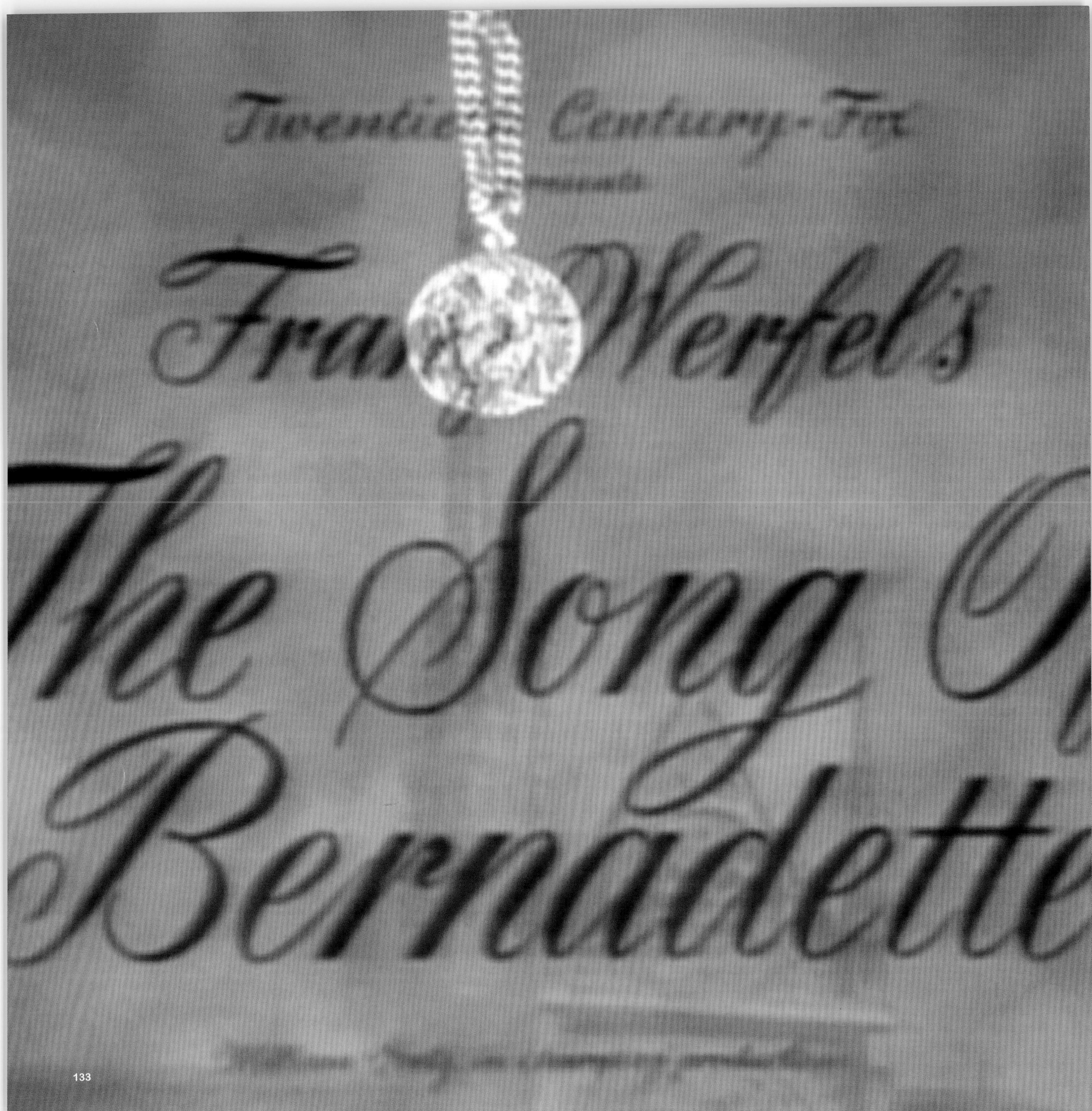
Century-Fox
Werfel's
Song
Bernadette

Three Inches (Black). 1997
Color photograph, 31 11/16 x 32 7/8" (80.5 x 83.5 cm)
Collection the artist and Yvon Lambert, Paris

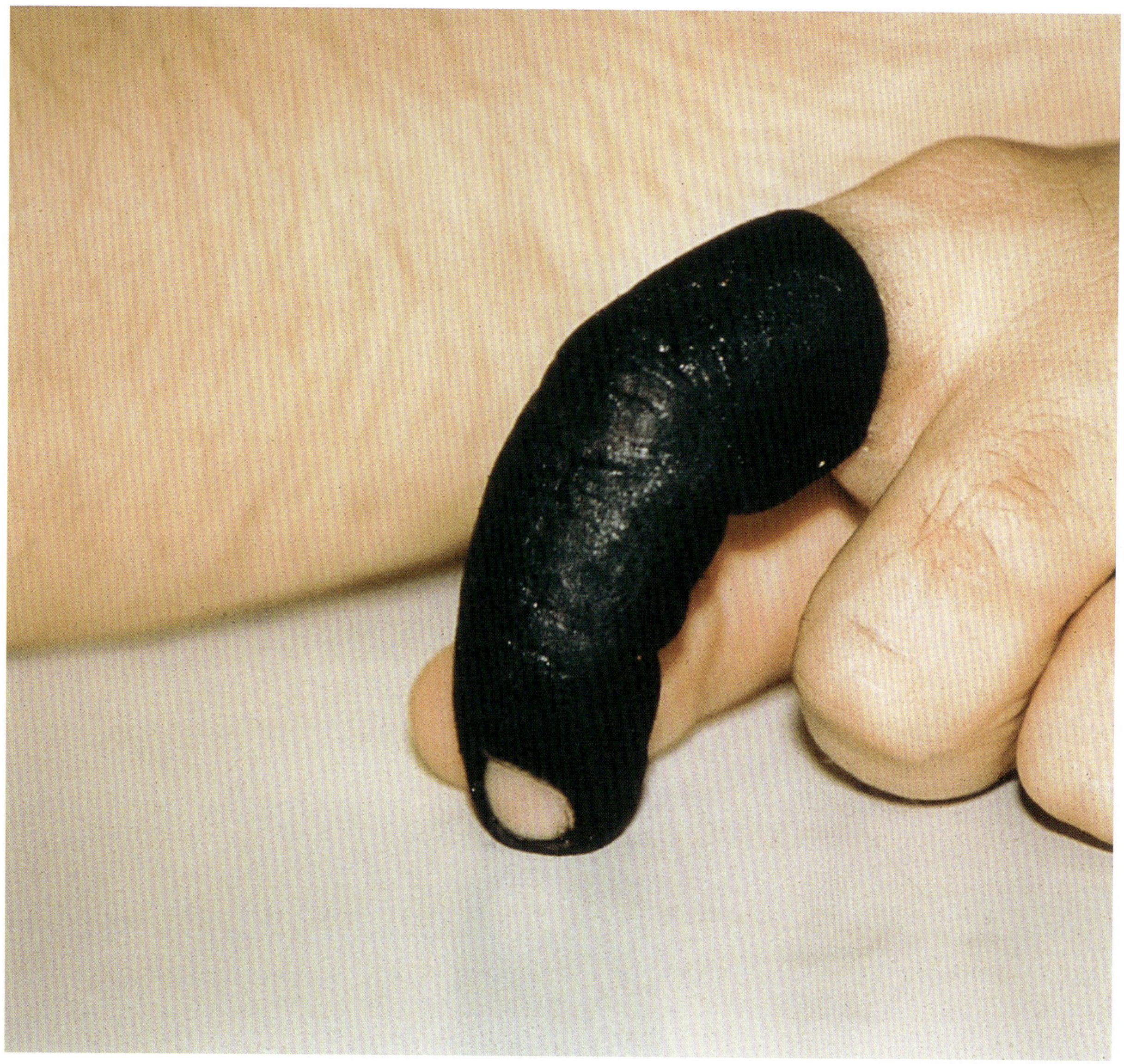

Three Inches (Black). 1997
Color photograph, 31 11/16 x 32 7/8" (80.5 x 83.5 cm)
Collection the artist and Yvon Lambert, Paris

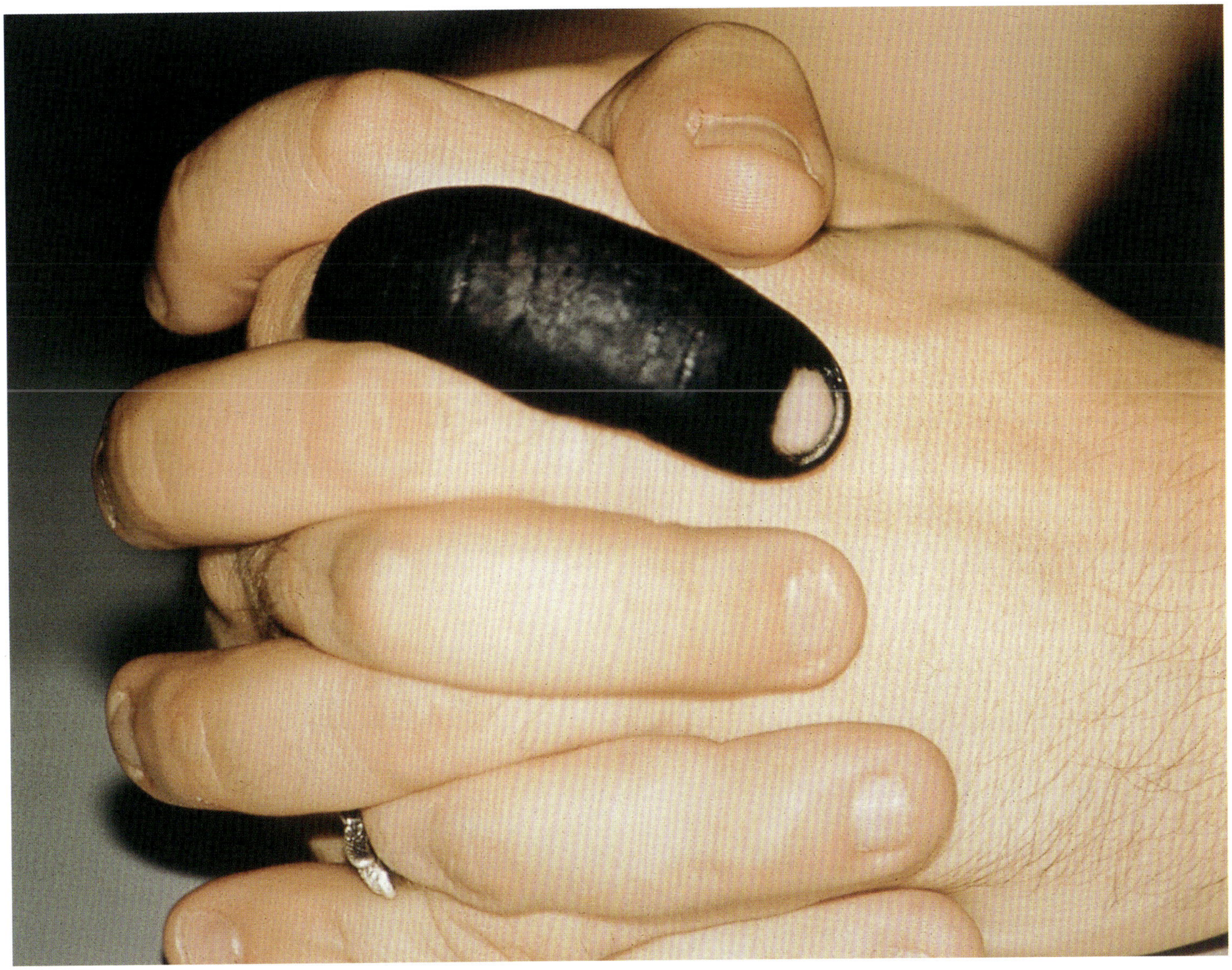

Tattoo (for Reflection). 1997
Chromogenic color print, 27 ¼ x 27 ¼" (69.2 x 69.2 cm)
Solomon R. Guggenheim Museum, New York
Purchased with funds contributed by the Photography Committee, 2002

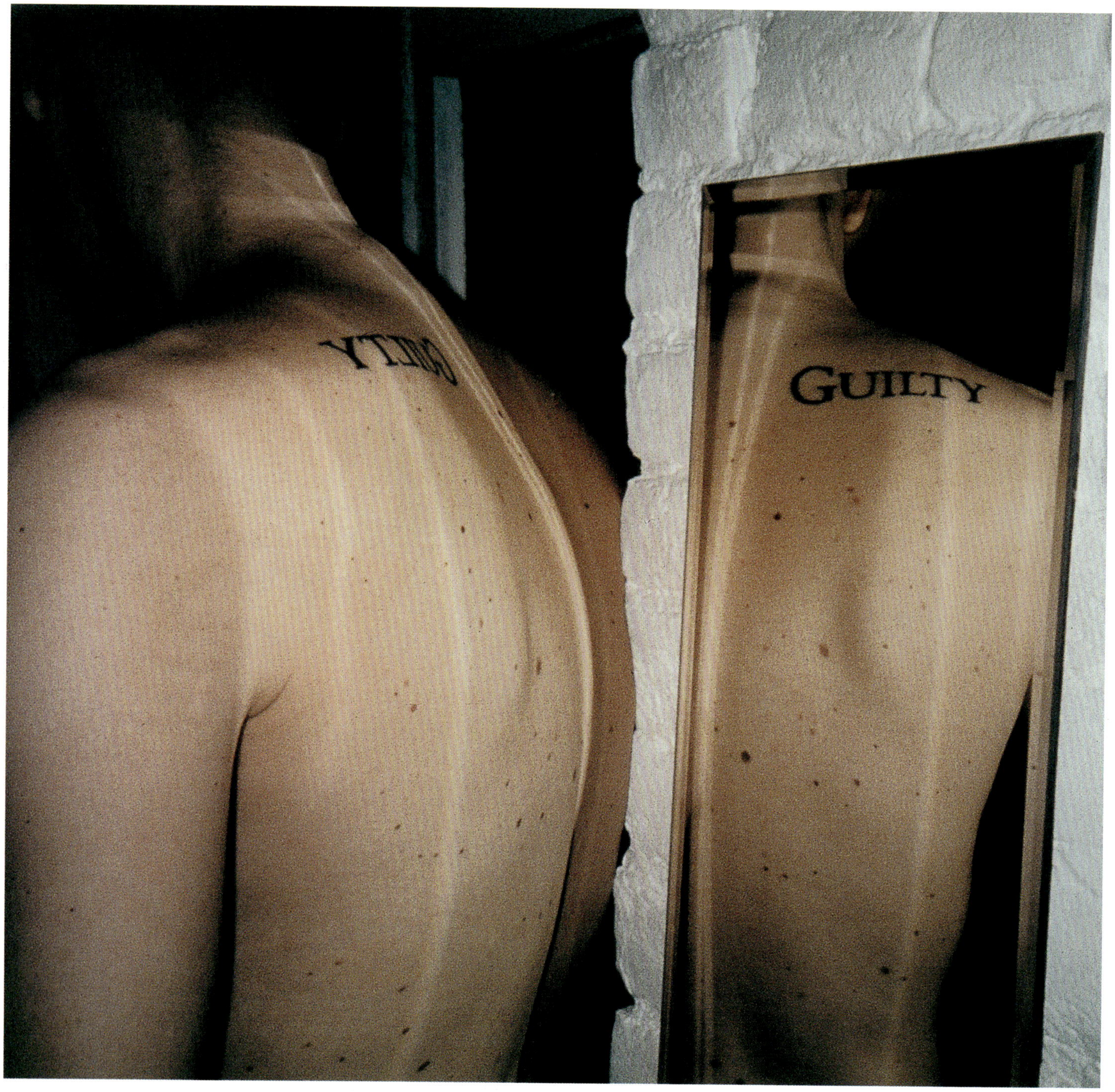

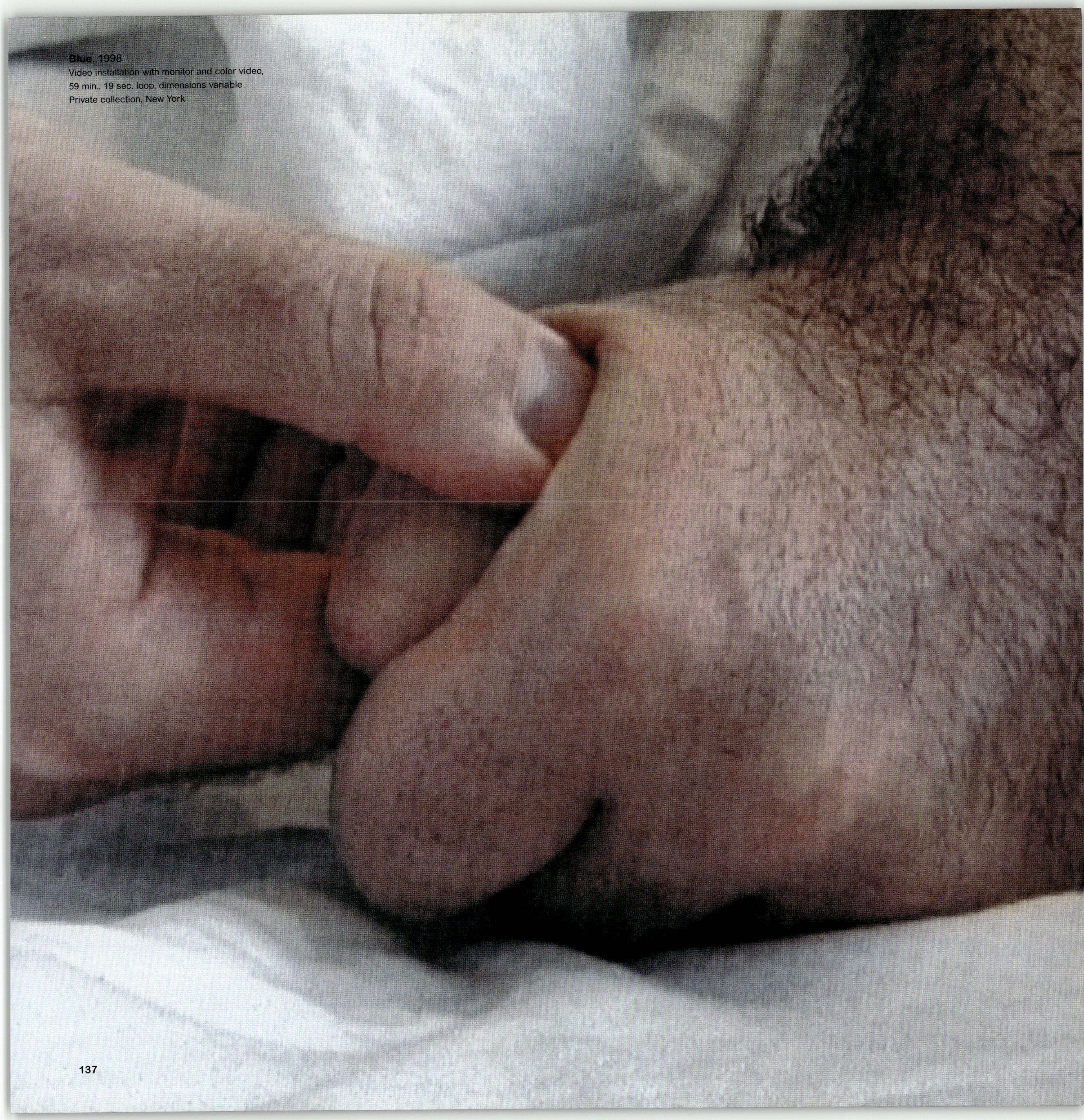

Blue. 1998
Video installation with monitor and color video, 59 min., 19 sec. loop, dimensions variable
Private collection, New York

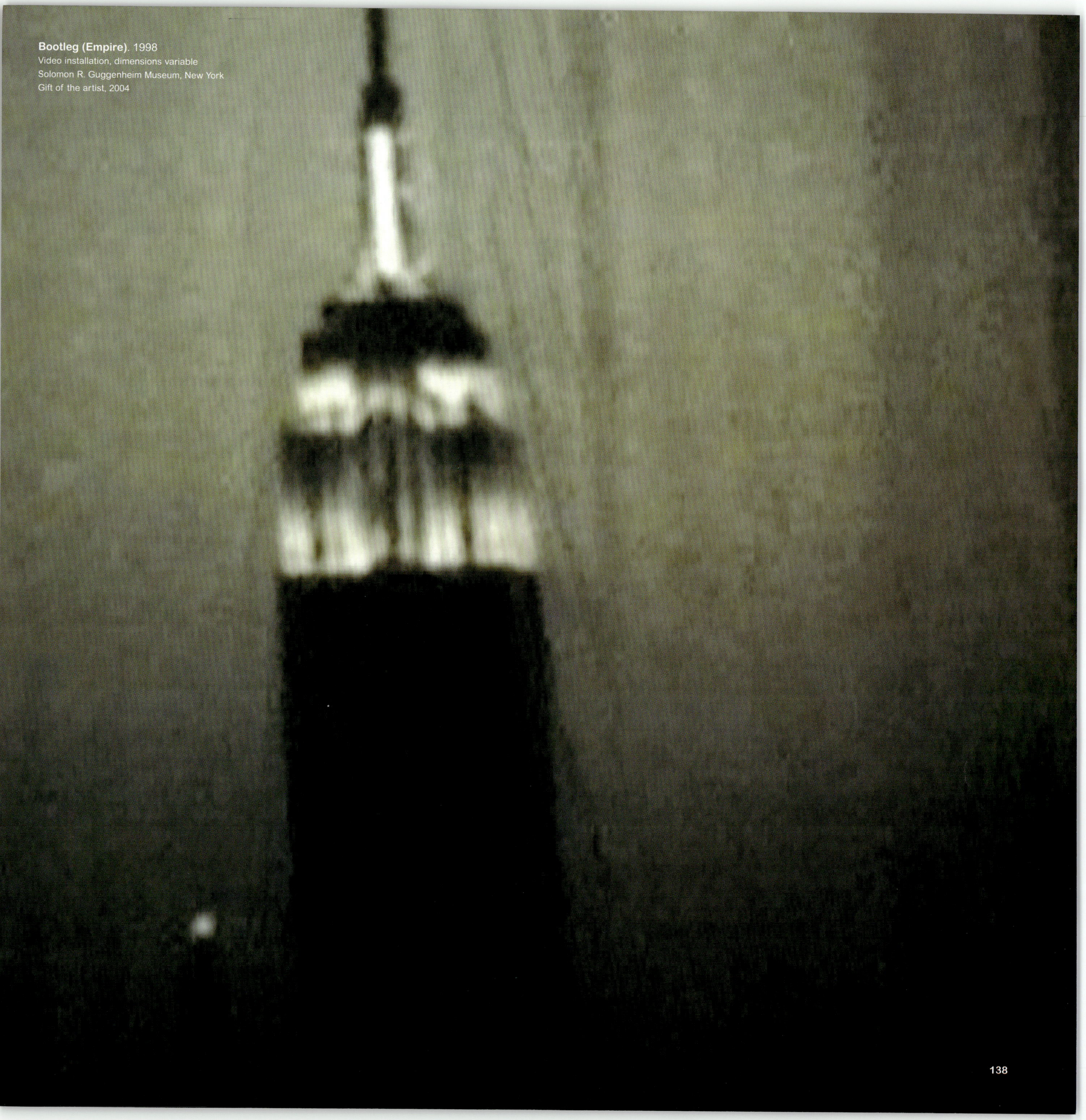

Bootleg (Empire). 1998
Video installation, dimensions variable
Solomon R. Guggenheim Museum, New York
Gift of the artist, 2004

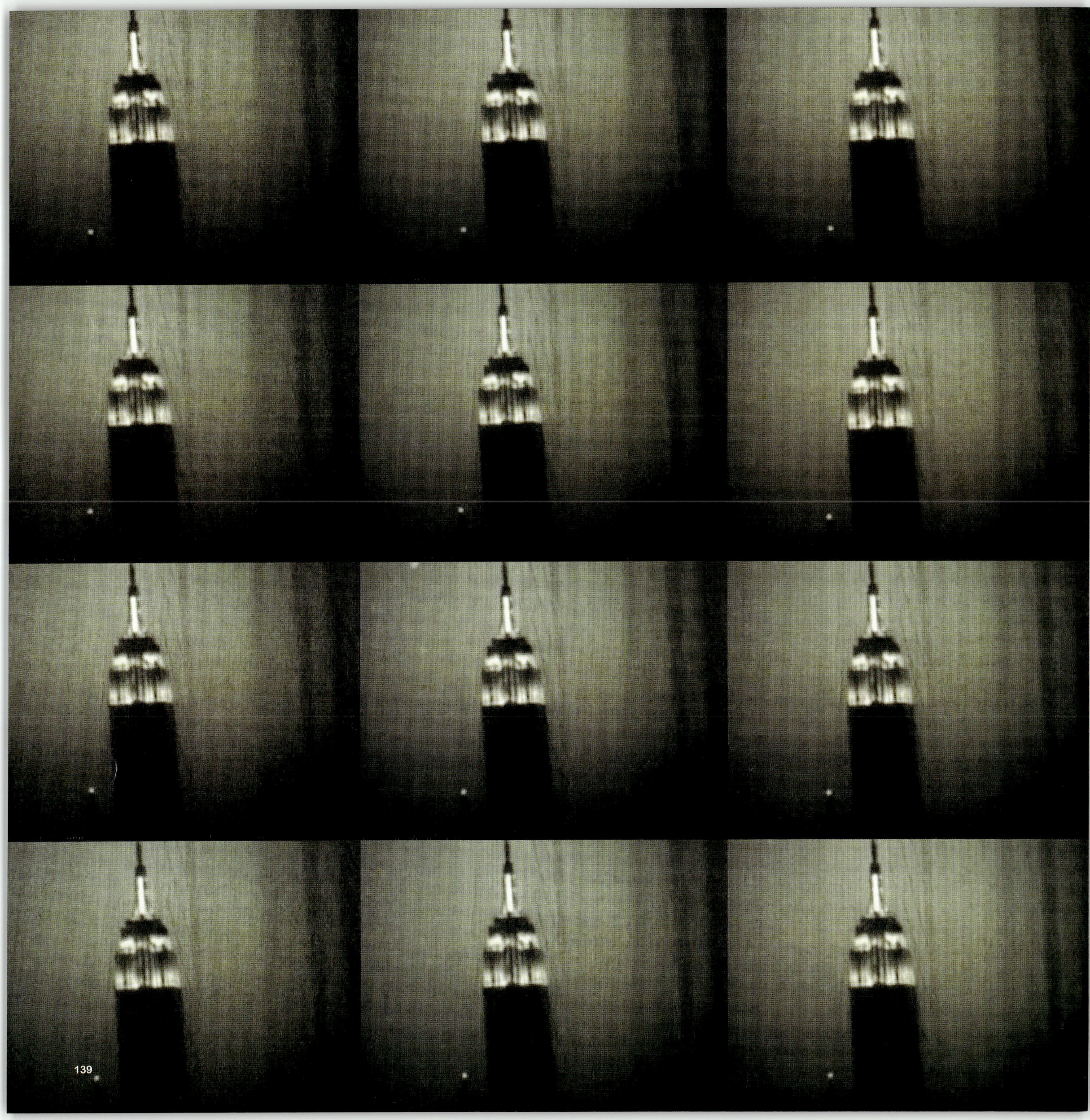

Feature Film. 1999
Video installation with two screens, monitor, sound, and color videos,
2 hr., 2 min. loop, dimensions variable
Installation view at Kölnischer Kunstverein, Cologne, 1999
Private collection, New York

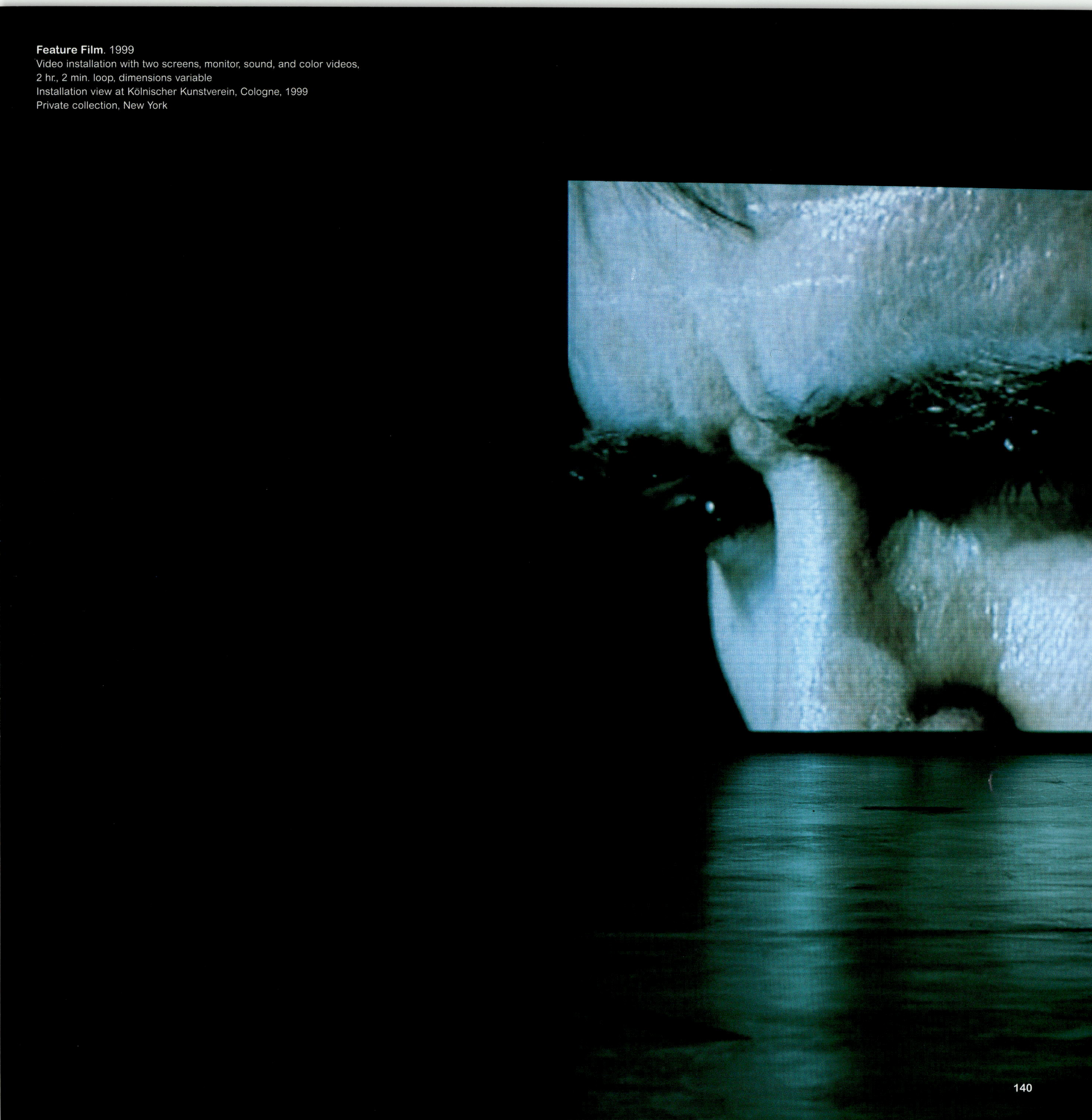

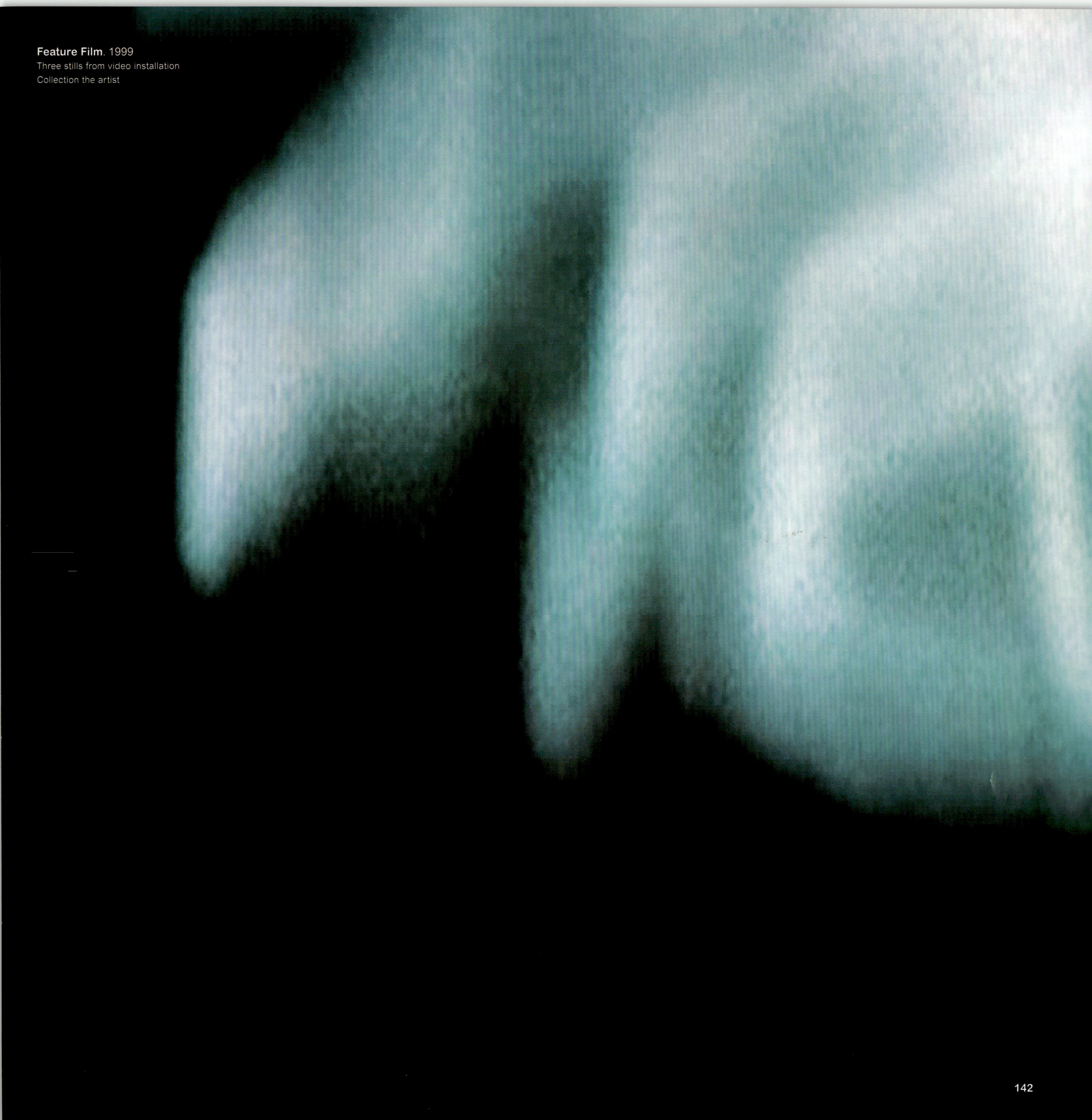

Feature Film. 1999
Three stills from video installation
Collection the artist

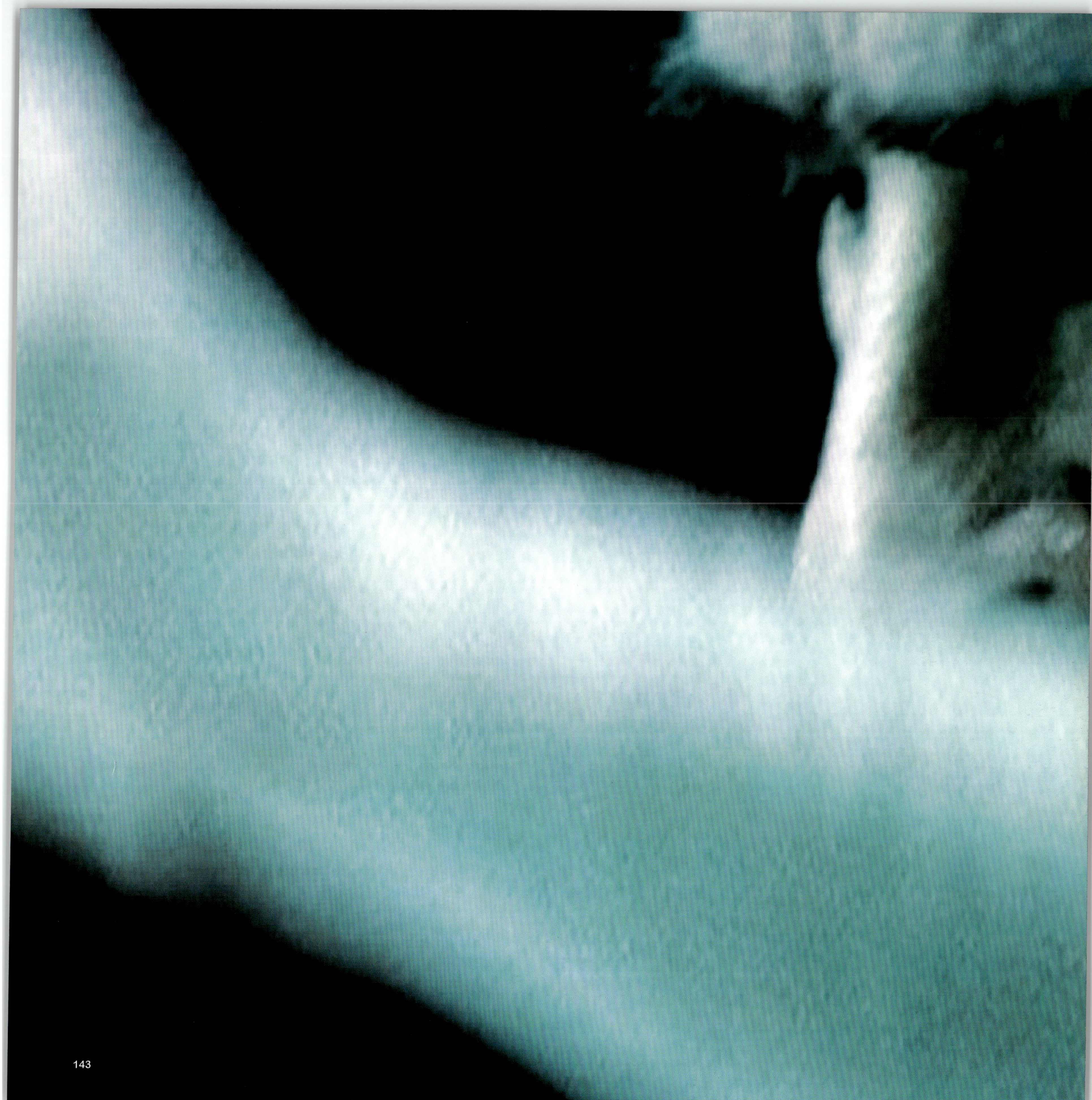

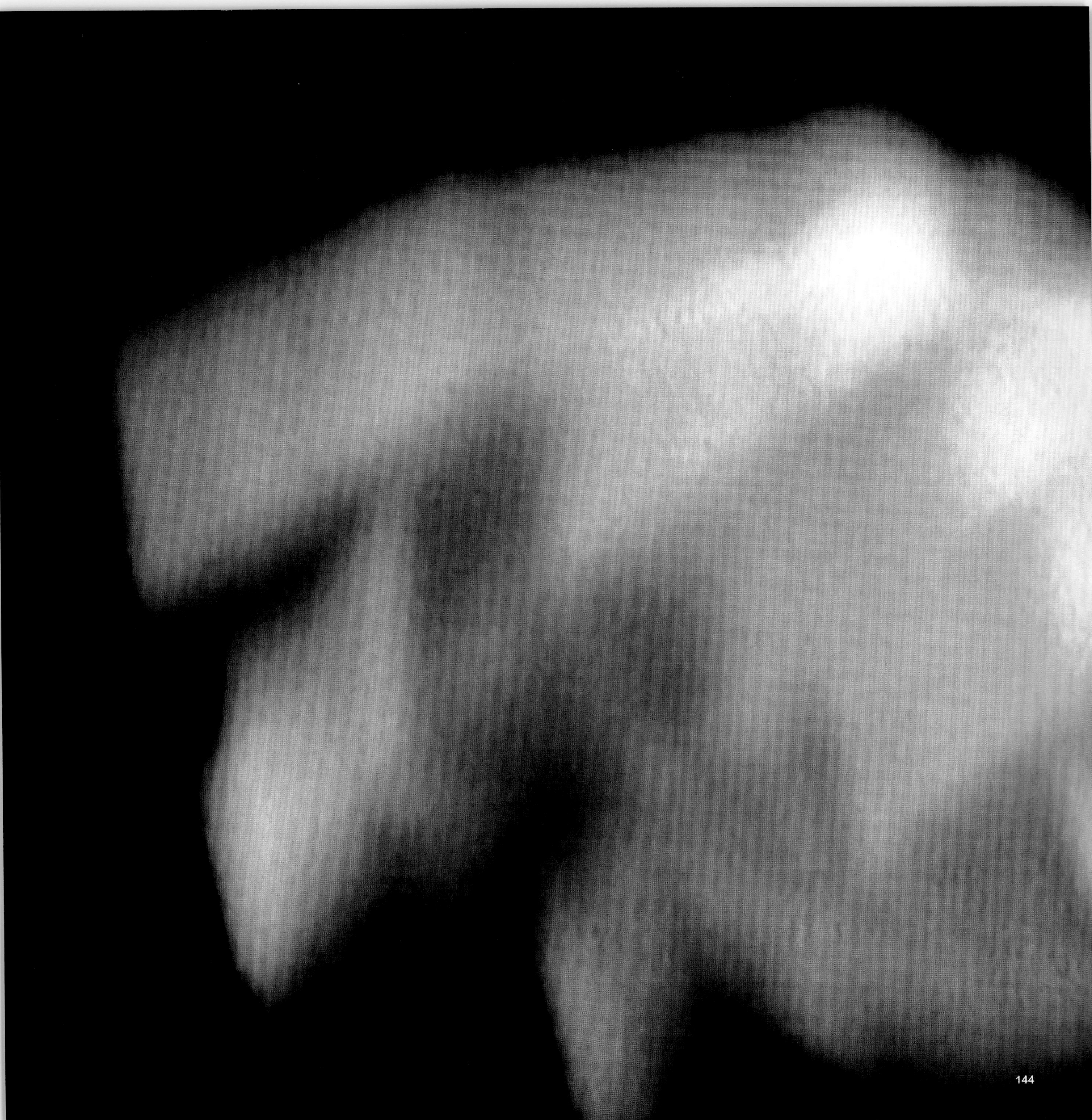

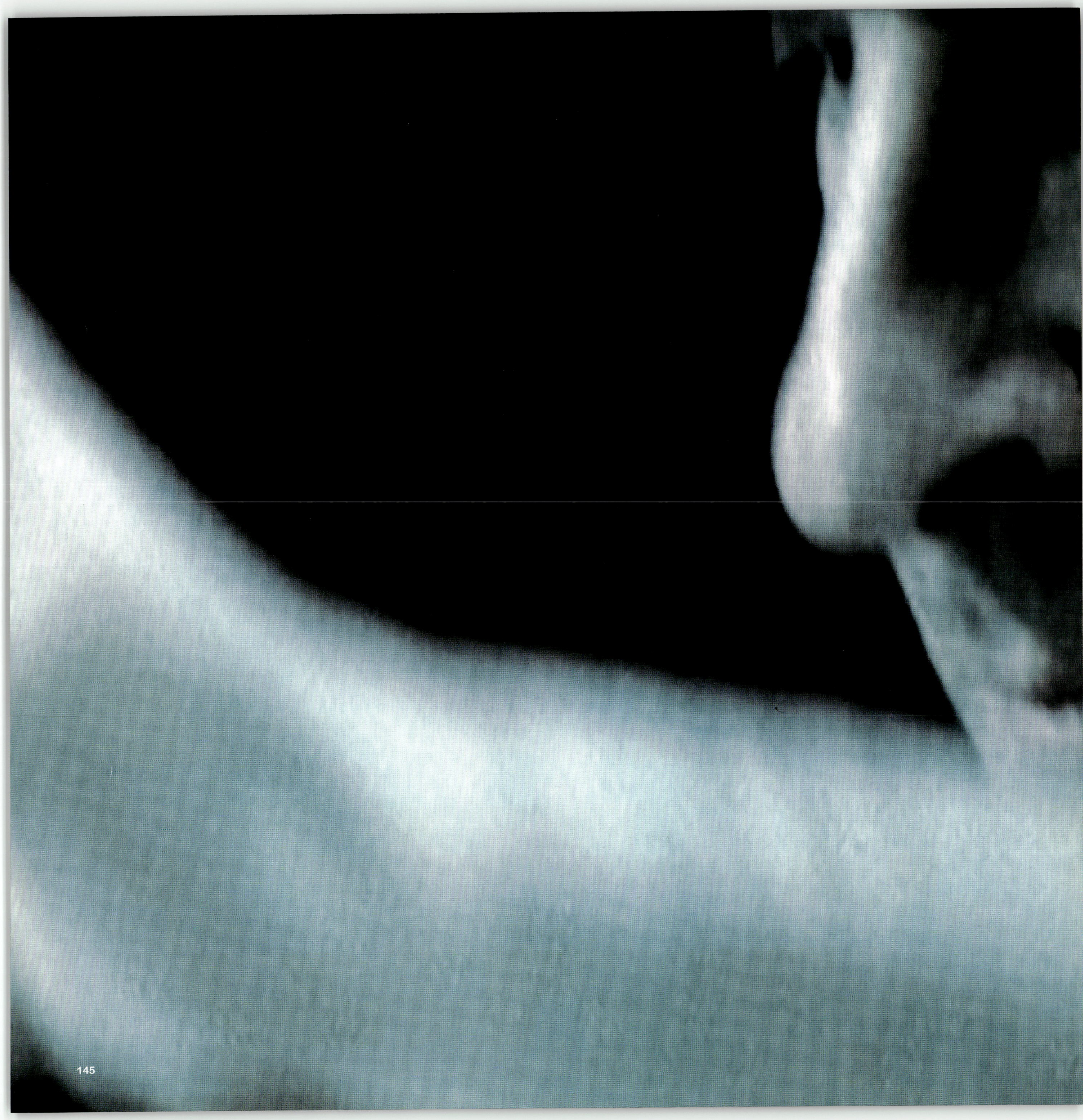

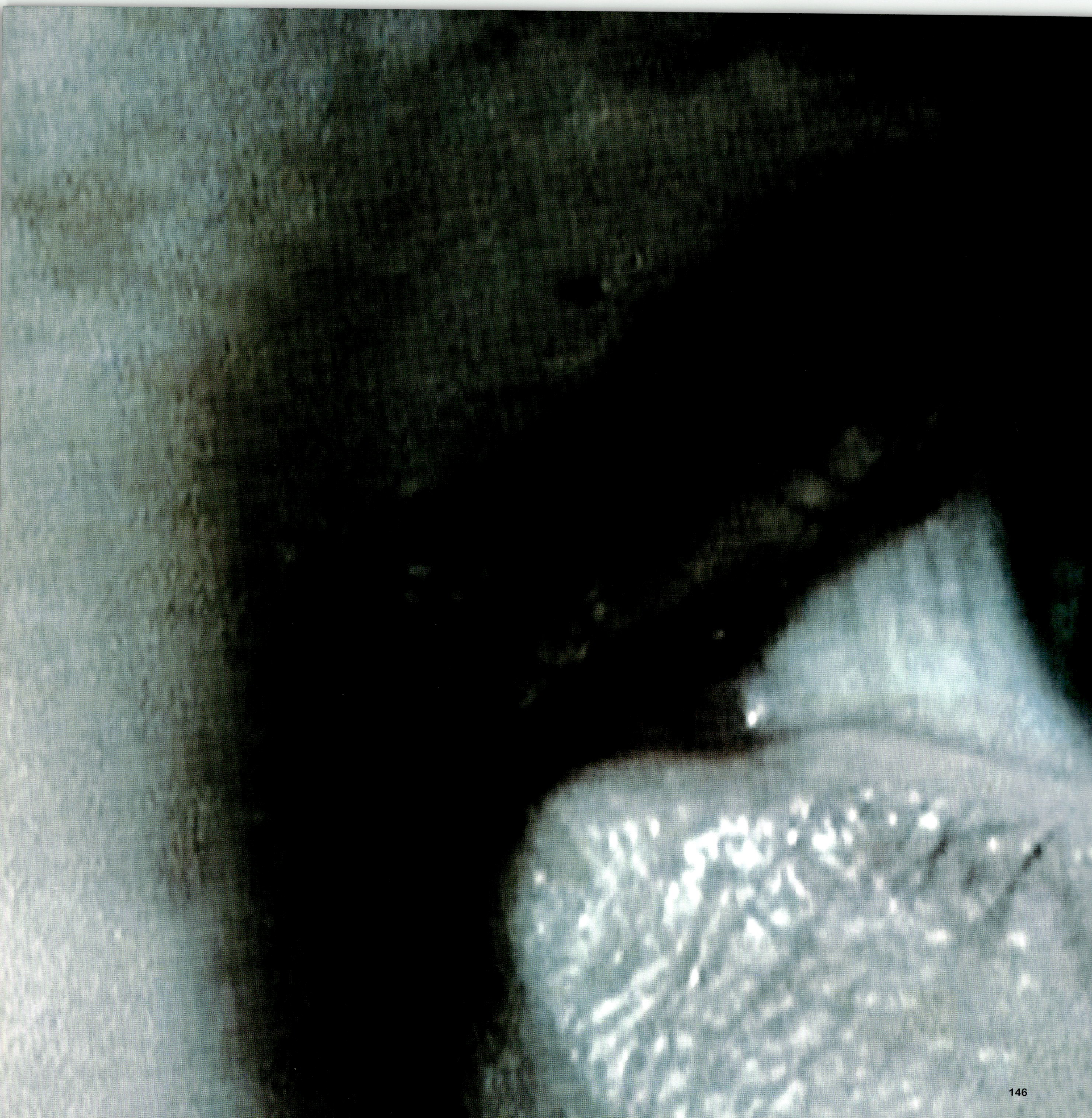

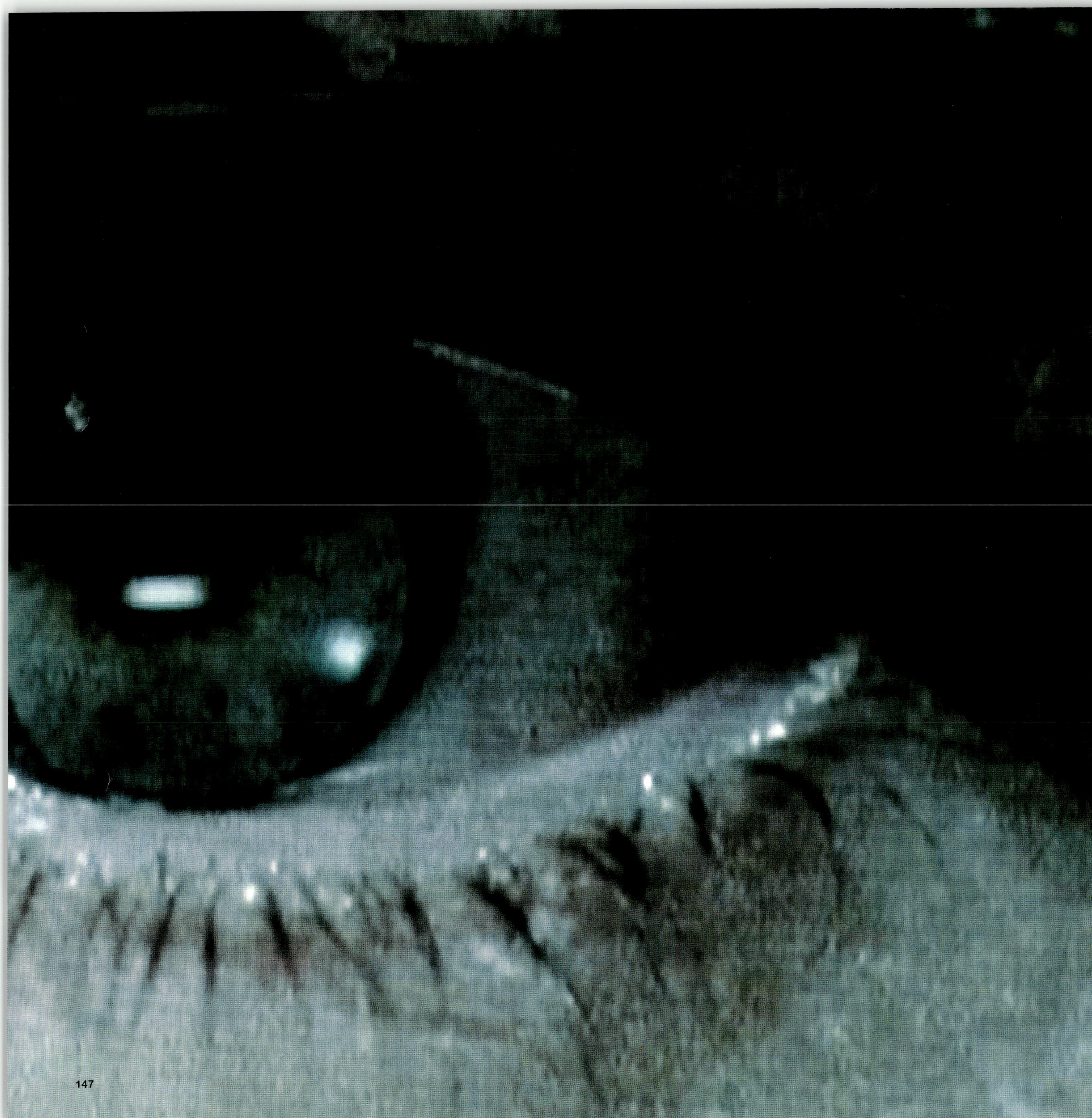

left is right and right is wrong and left is wrong and right is right. 1999
Video installation with two screens and black-and-white video, 97 min. loop, dimensions variable
Installation view at Dia Center for the Arts, New York, 2000
Collection Ydessa Hendeles

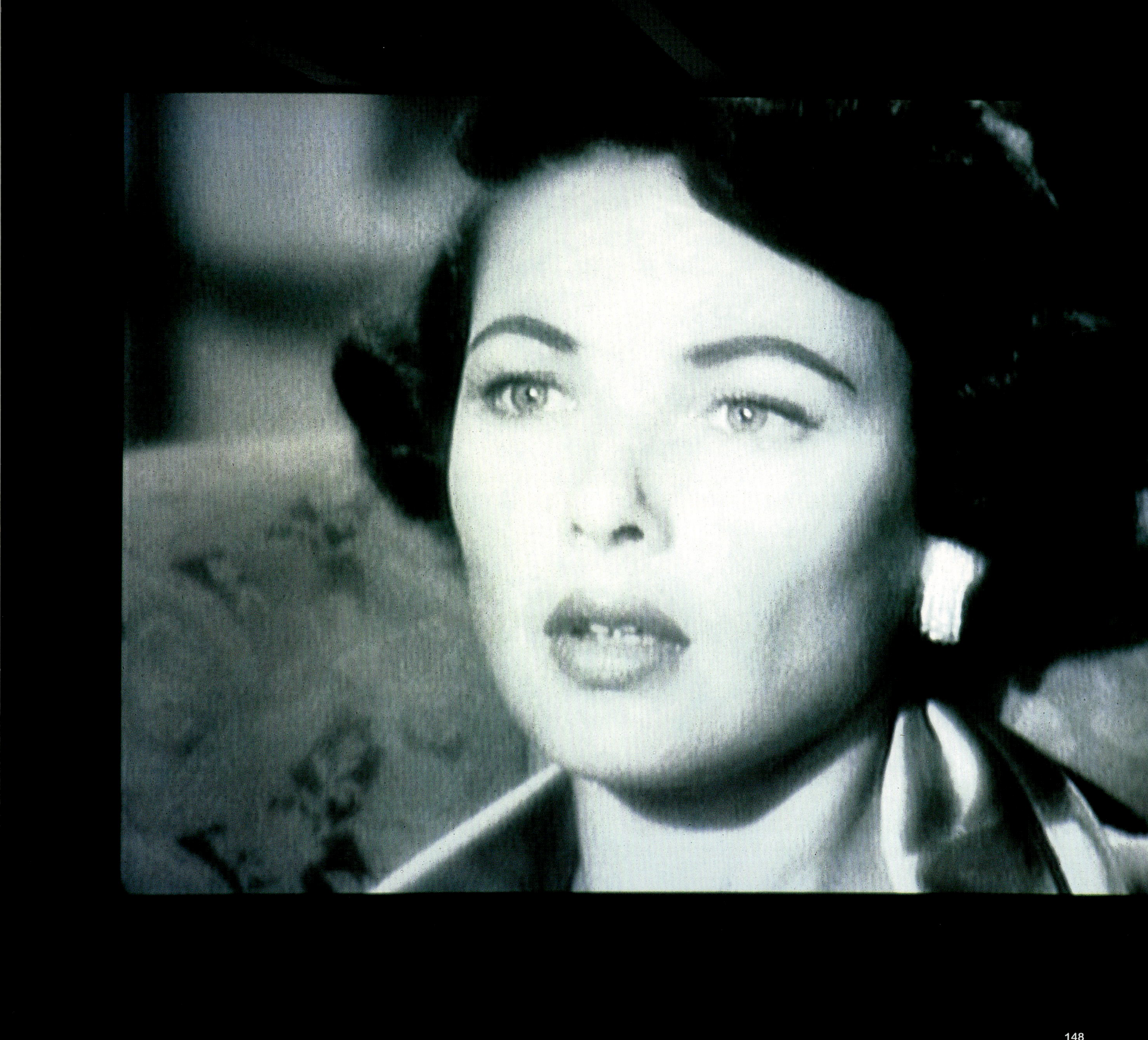

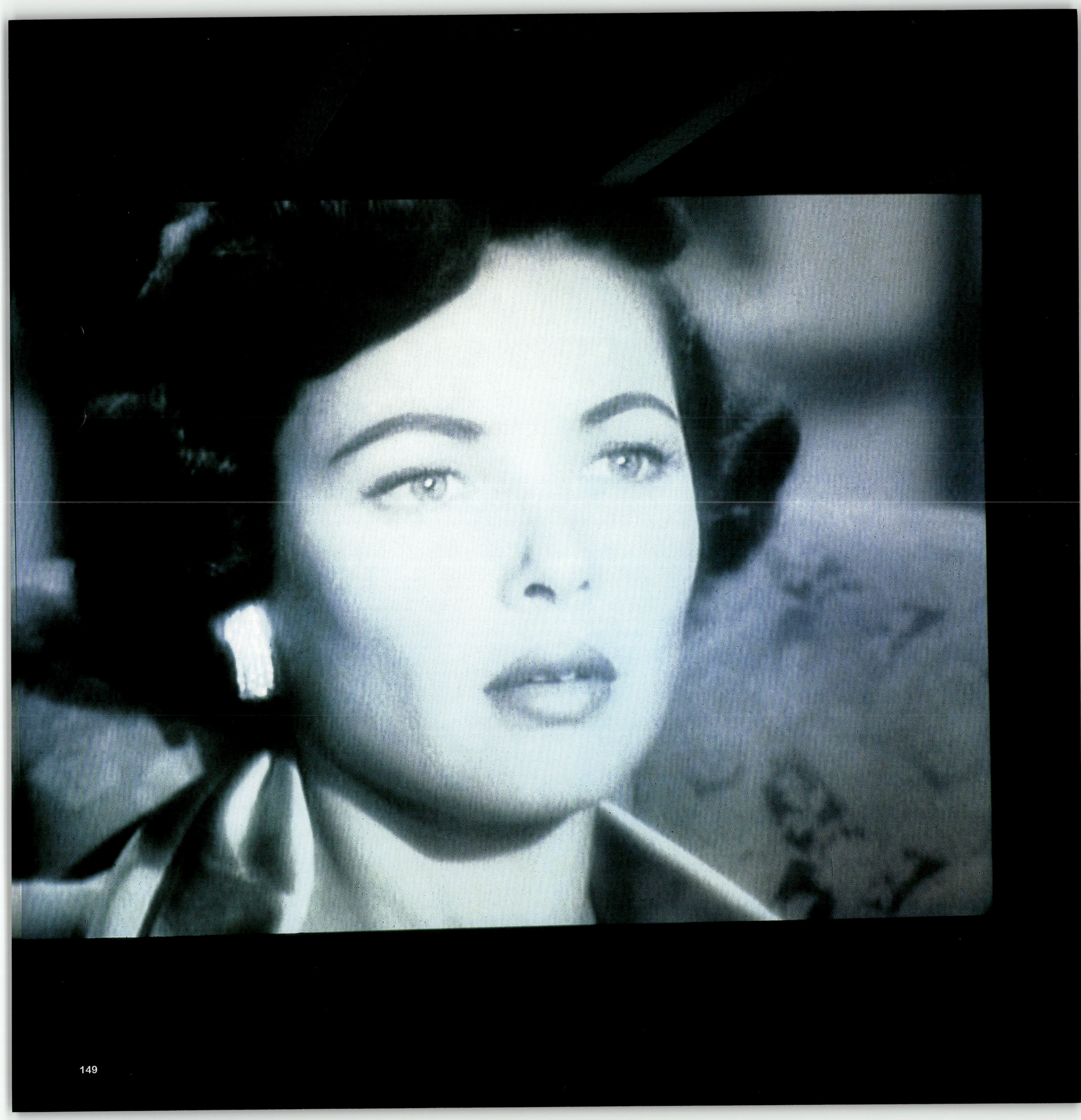

left is right and right is wrong and left is wrong and right is right. 1999
Video installation with two screens and black-and-white video, 97 min. loop, dimensions variable
Installation view at Dia Center for the Arts, New York, 2000
Collection Ydessa Hendeles

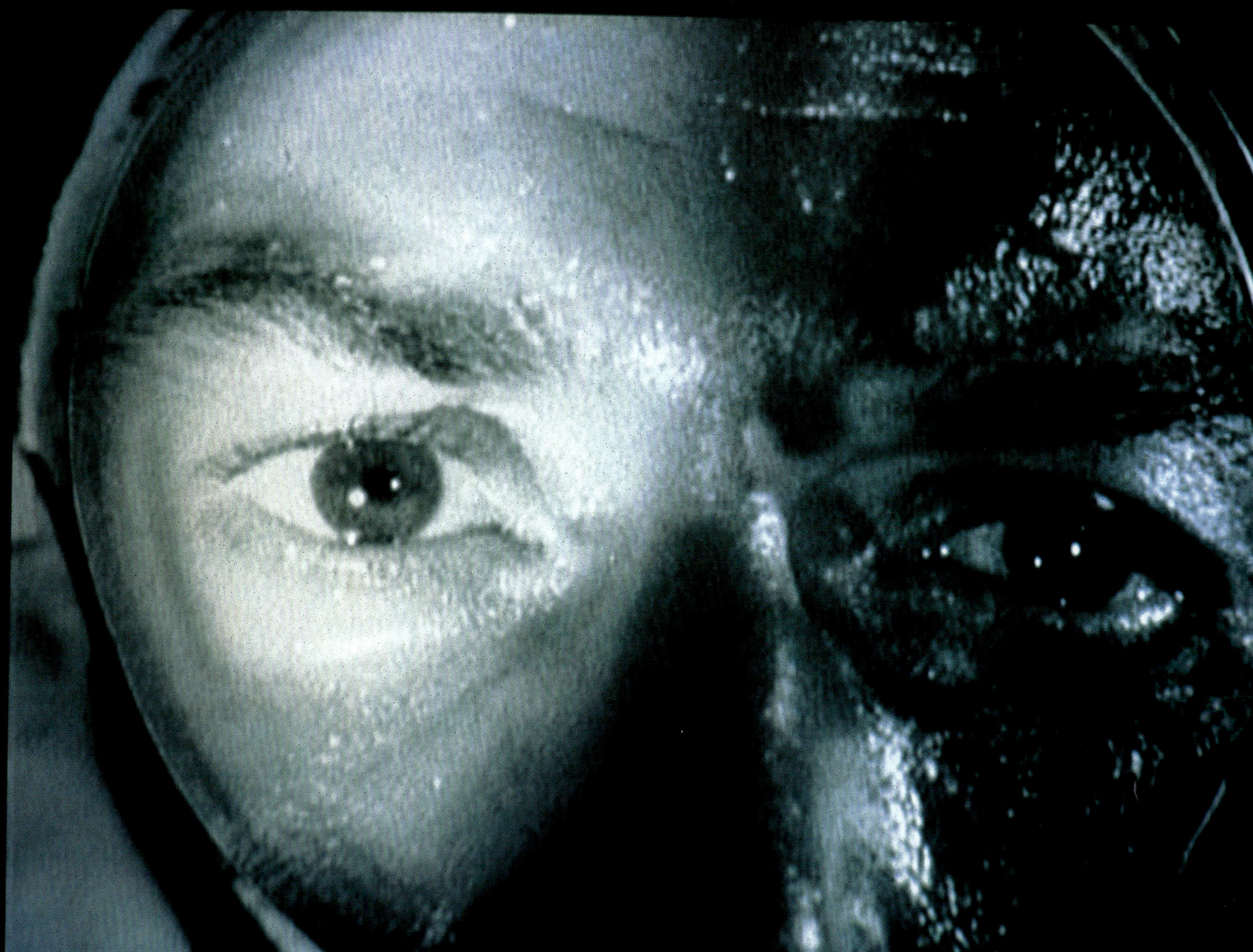

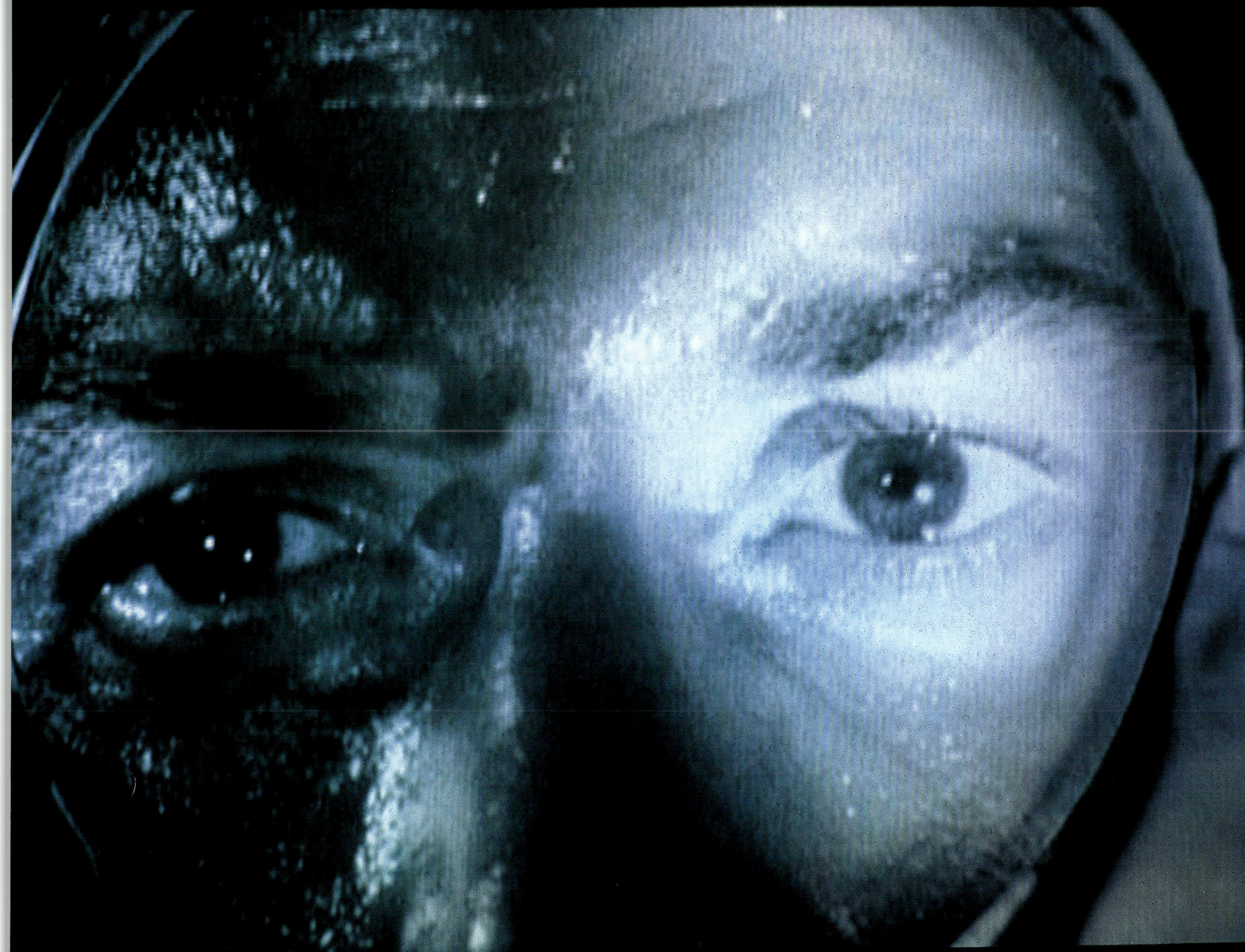

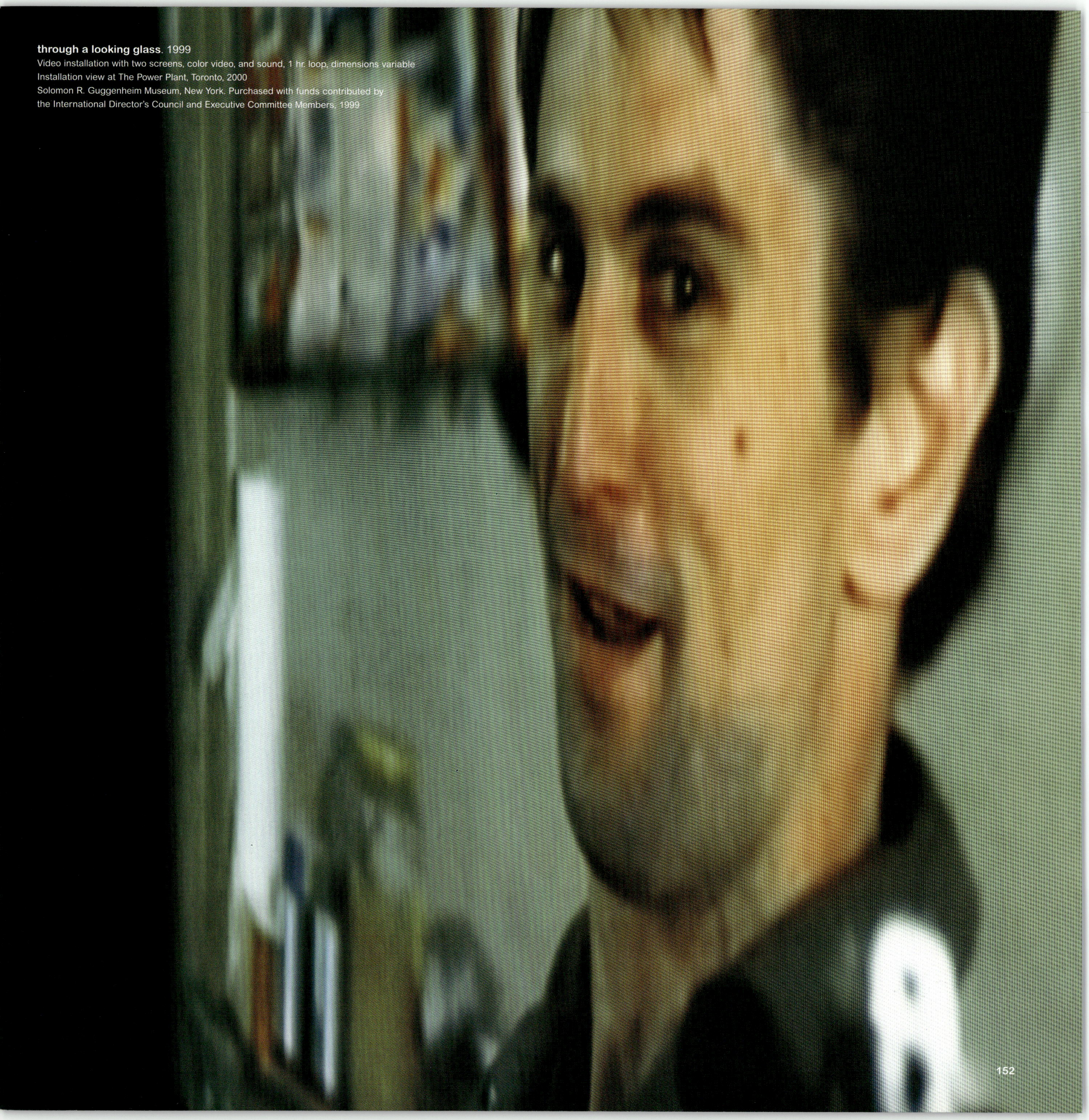

through a looking glass. 1999
Video installation with two screens, color video, and sound, 1 hr. loop, dimensions variable
Installation view at The Power Plant, Toronto, 2000
Solomon R. Guggenheim Museum, New York. Purchased with funds contributed by the International Director's Council and Executive Committee Members, 1999

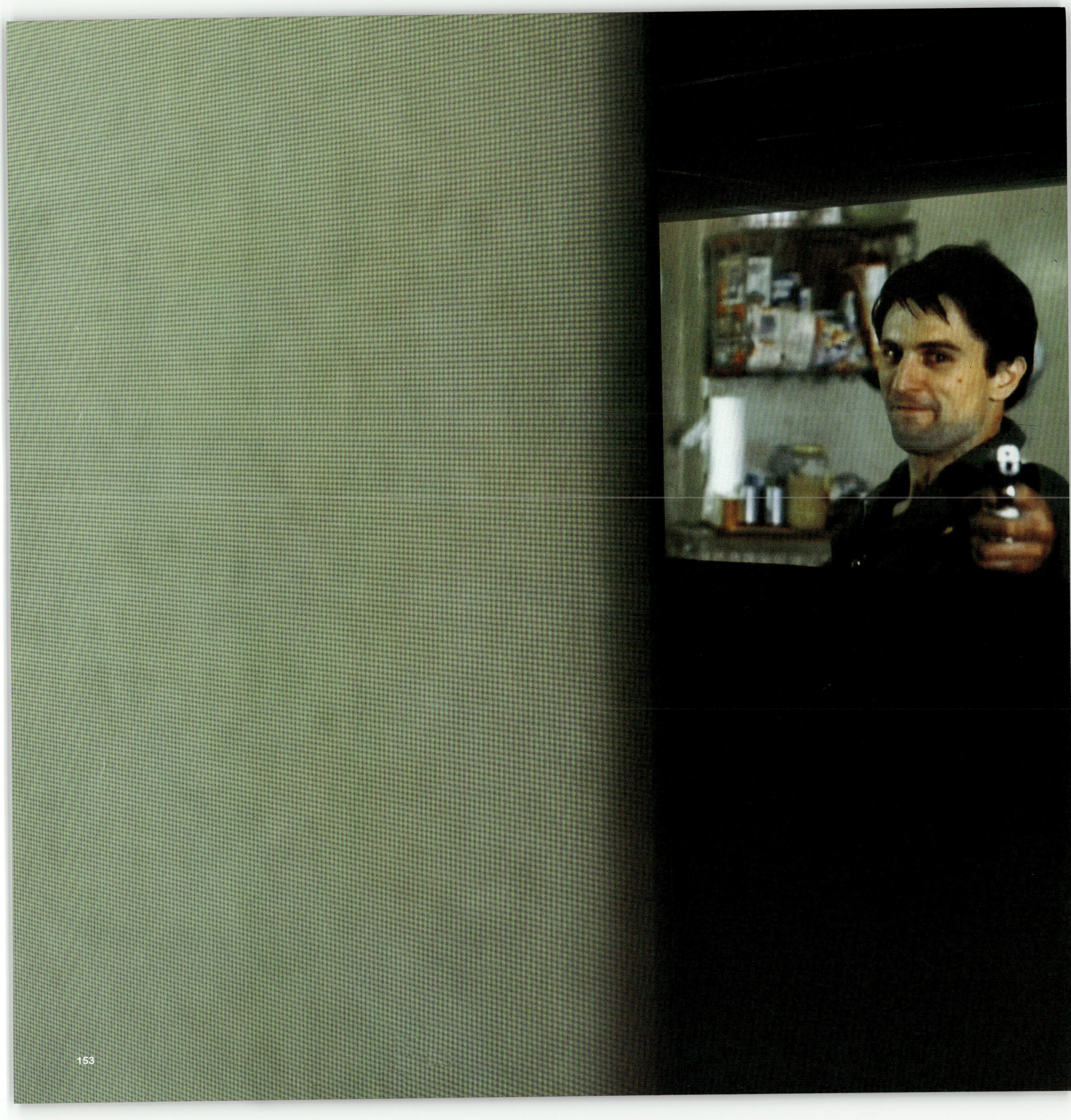

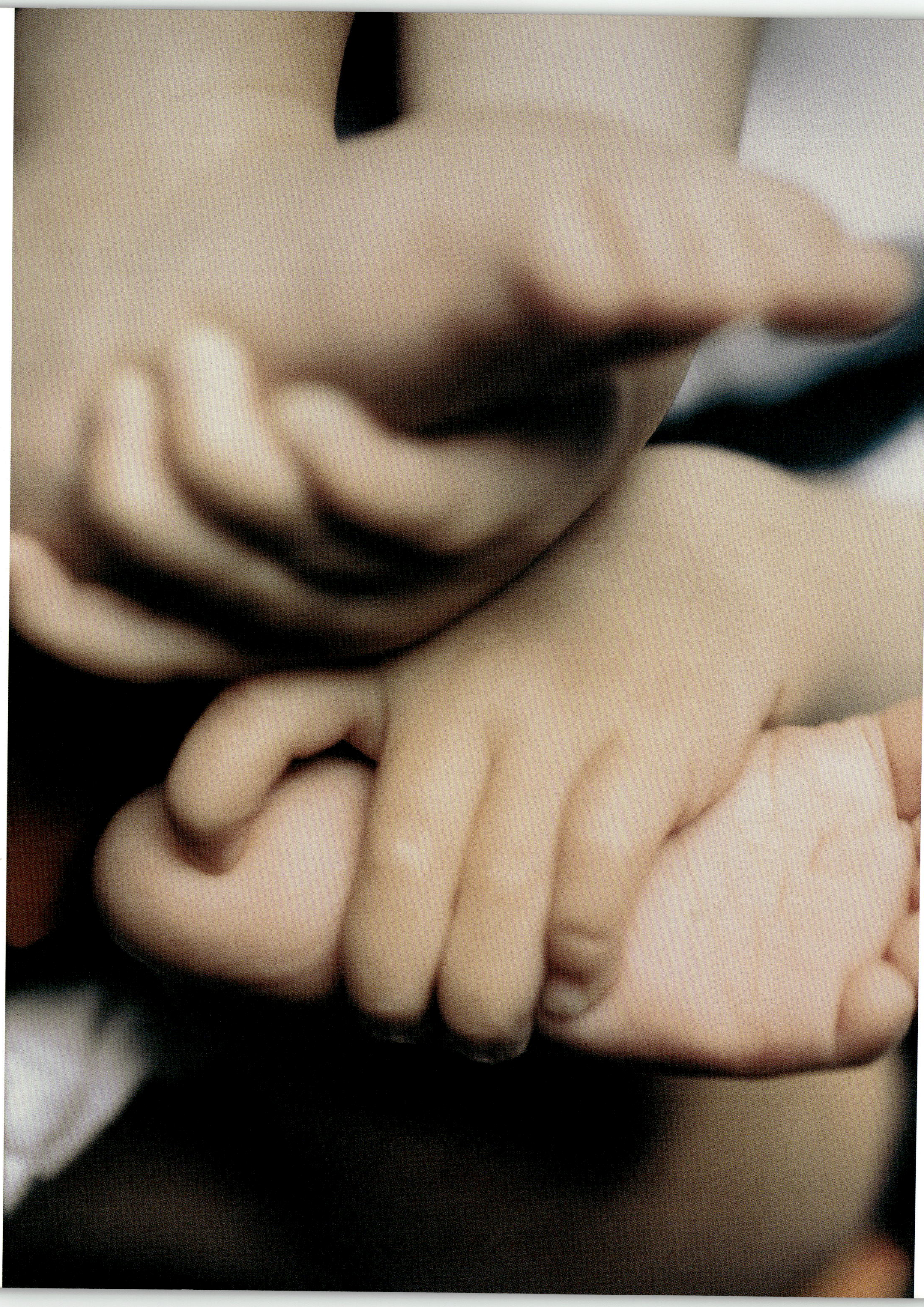

croque-mort. 2000
Chromogenic color print, 55 x 38 1/8" (139.7 x 96.8 cm)
Arts Council Collection, Hayward Gallery, London

croque-mort. 2000
Chromogenic color print, 38 1/8 x 55" (96.8 x 139.7 cm)
Arts Council Collection, Hayward Gallery, London

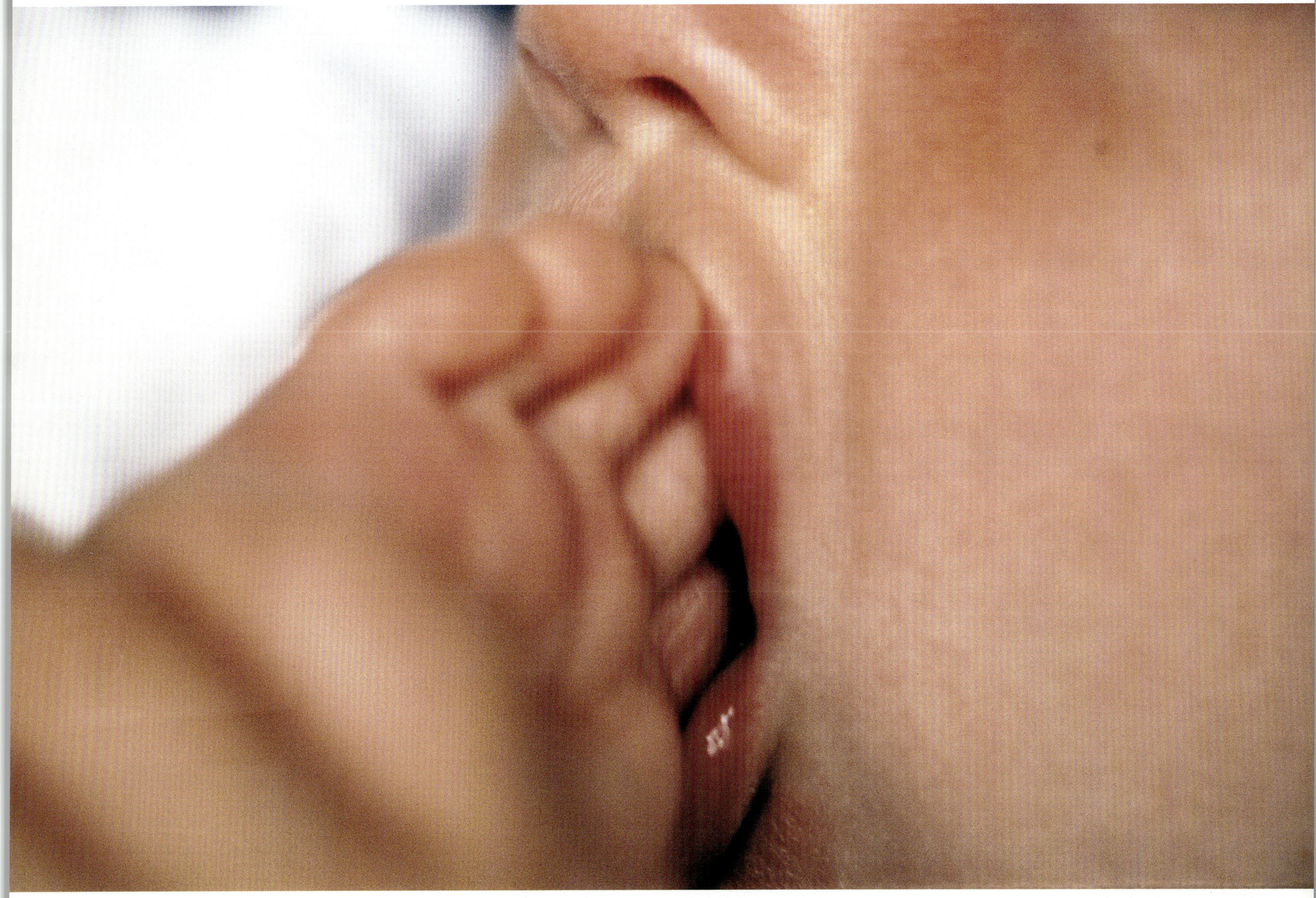

Déjà vu. 2000
Video installation with mirror, sound, and black-and-white video projected at 25, 24, and 23 frames per second, 1 hr., 37 min. loop, dimensions variable
Installation view at the Geffen Contemporary at the Museum of Contemporary Art, Los Angeles, 2002
Robin Vousden, London

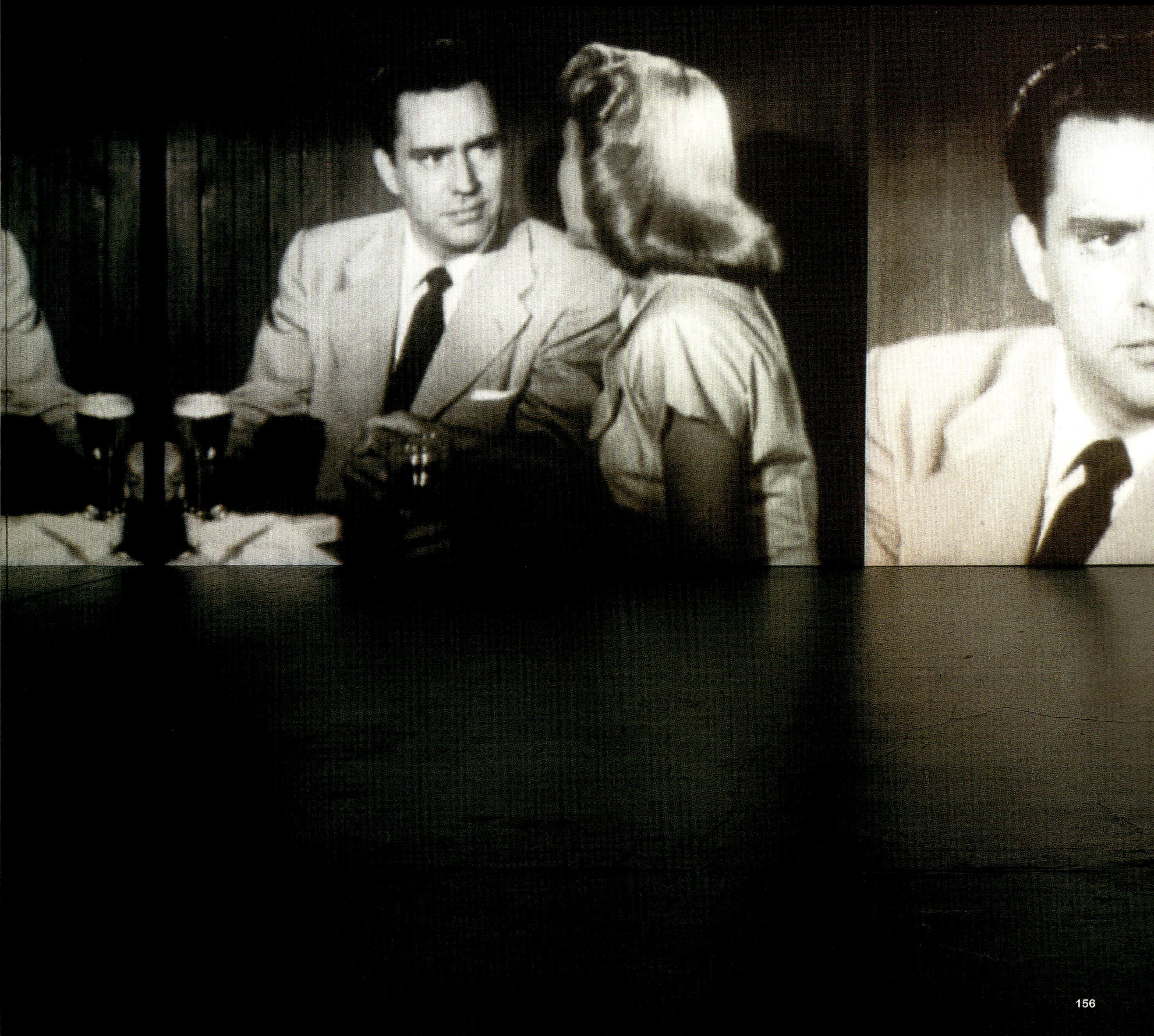

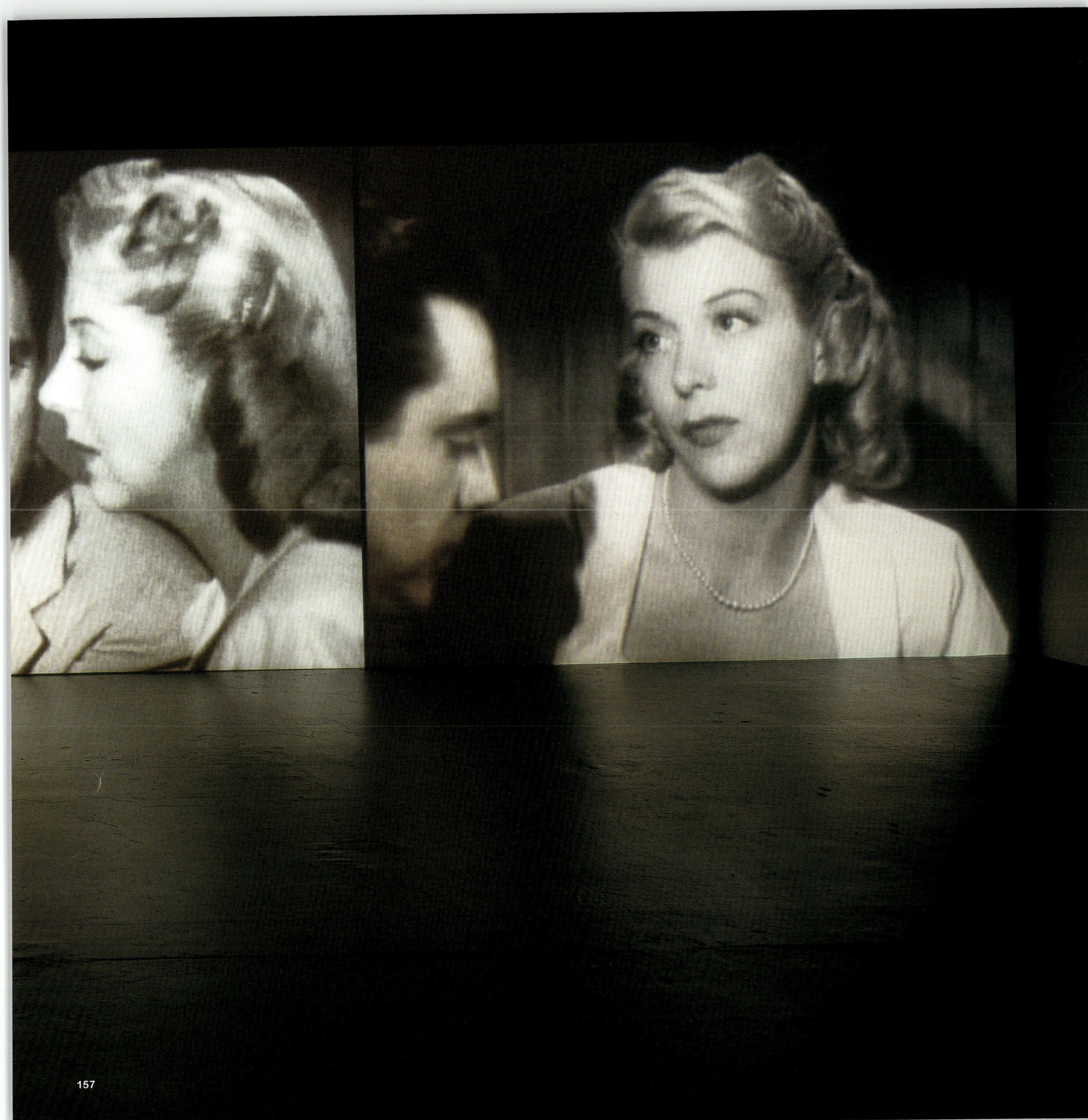

Never, Never (white). 2000
Chromogenic color print, 24 x 30" (61 x 76.2 cm)
Stefan Ratibor, London

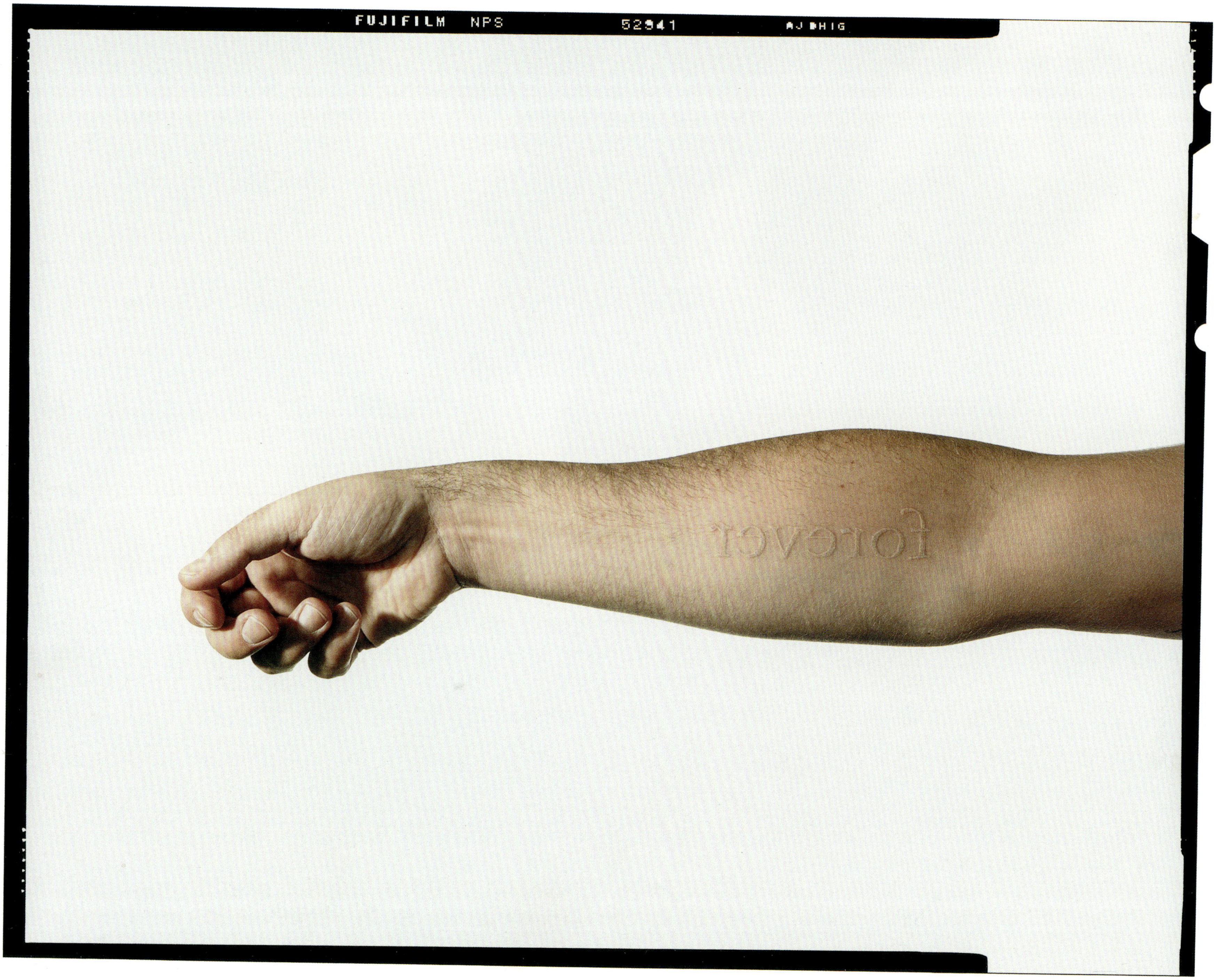

Never, Never (black). 2000
Chromogenic color print, 24 x 30" (61 x 76.2 cm)
Private collection

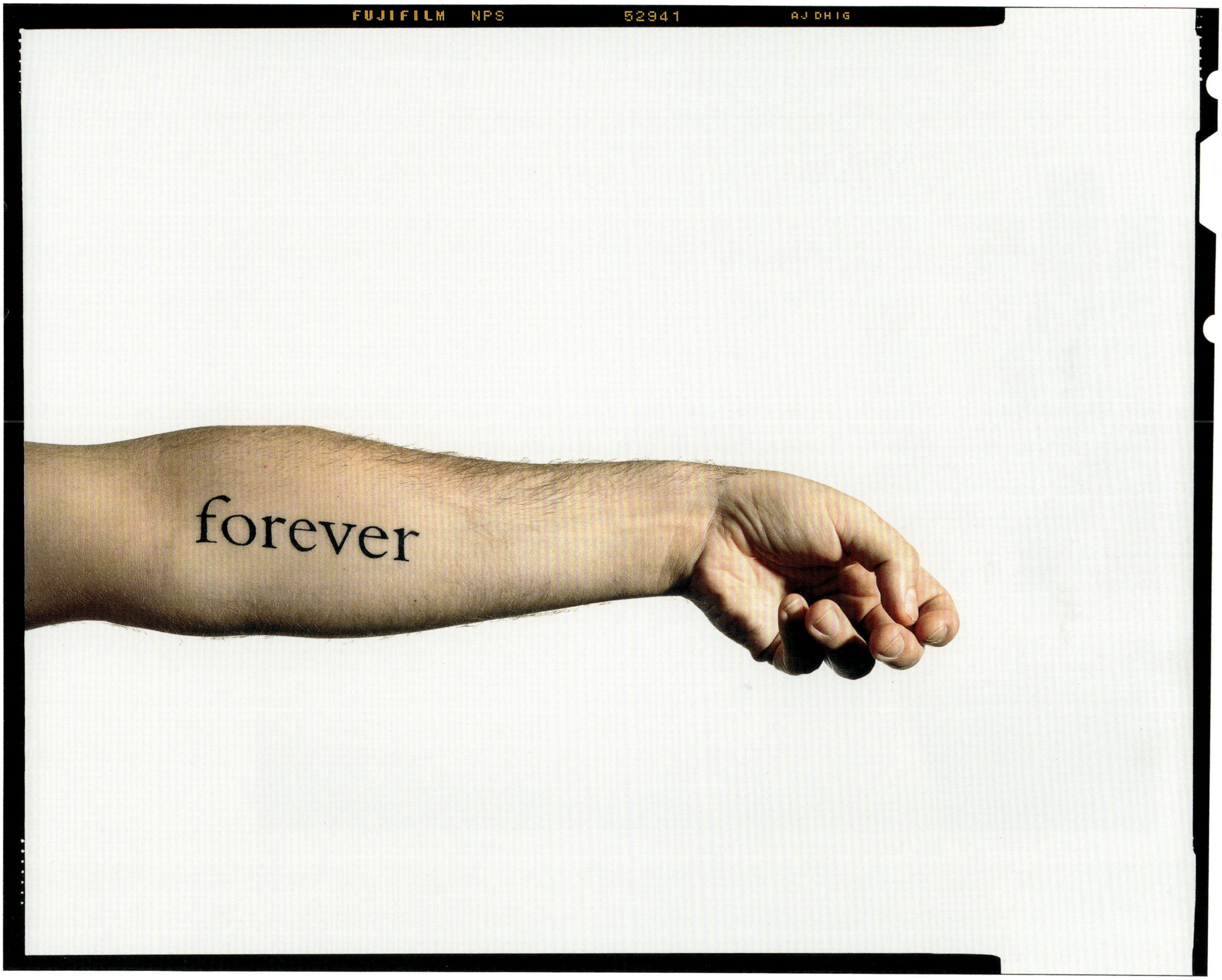

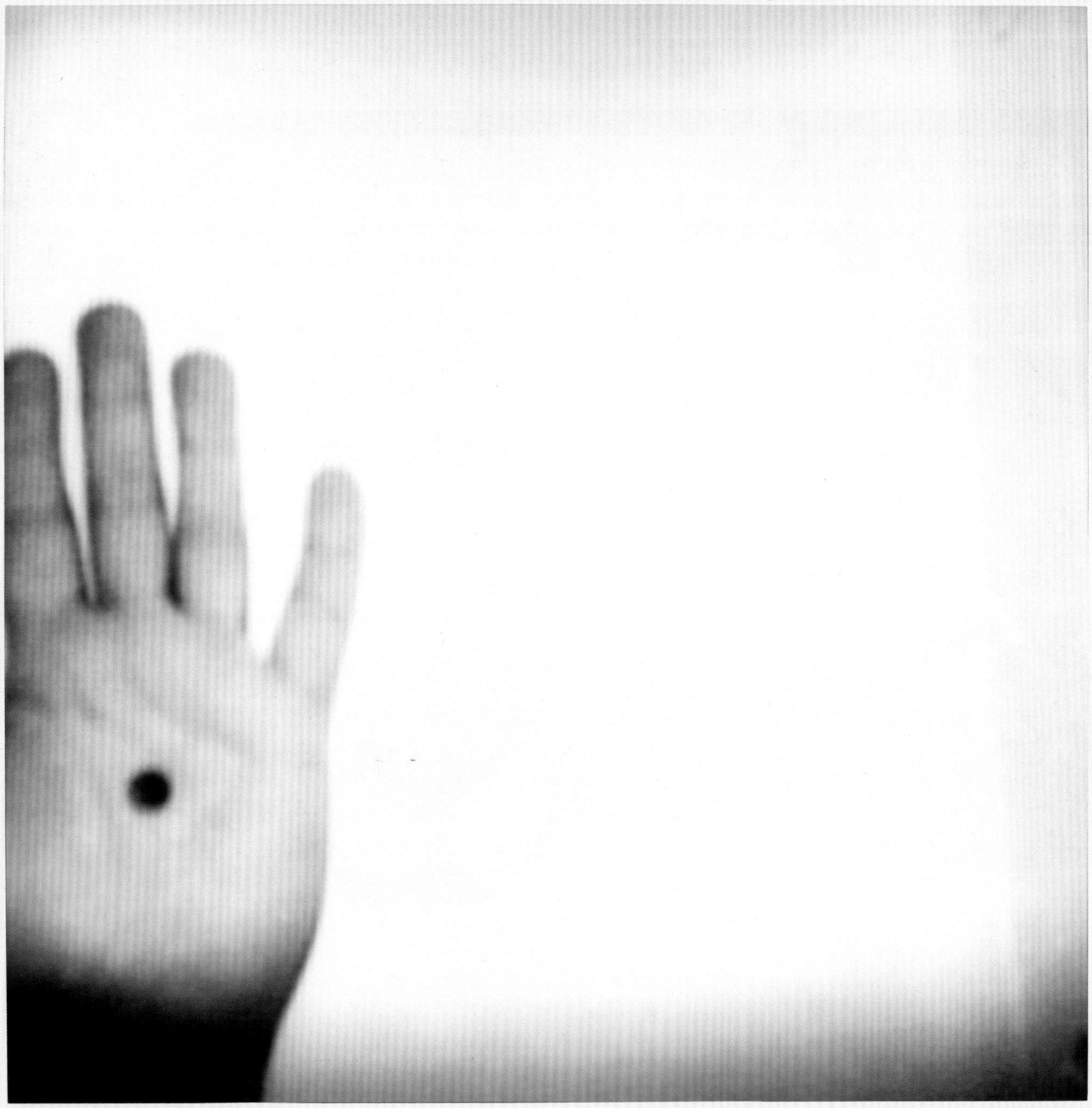

Hand with spot. 2001
Chromogenic color print,
57 ¾ x 48" (146.7 x 121.9 cm)
Courtesy Gagosian Gallery,
New York

Hand with spot. 2001
Chromogenic color print,
57 ¾ x 48" (146.7 x 121.9 cm)
Courtesy Gagosian Gallery,
New York

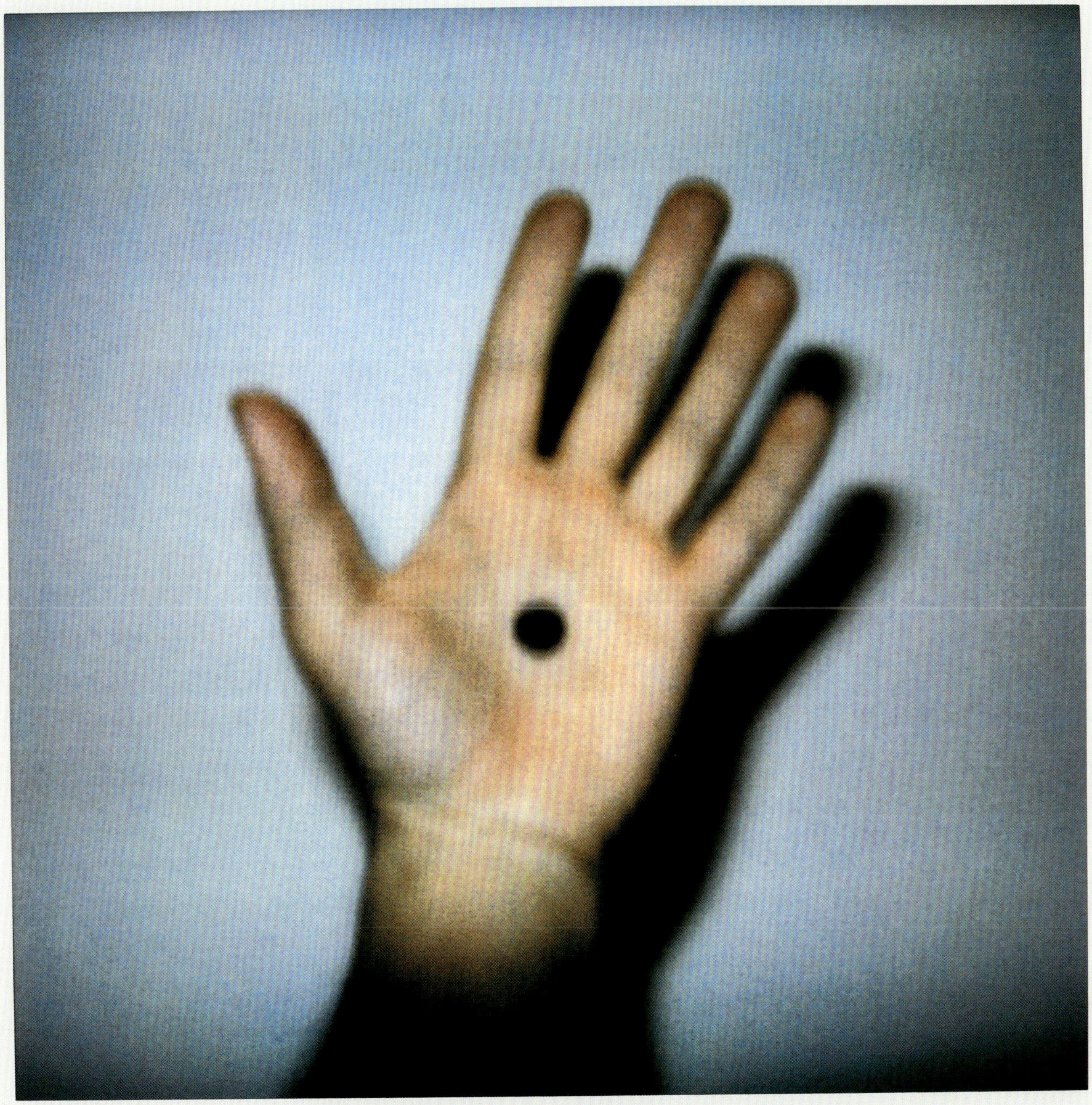

punishment exercise (in gothic) series: punishment exercise (in gothic). 2000
Ink-jet print, 10 ½ x 12 ½" (26.7 x 31.8 cm)
Stefan Ratibor, London

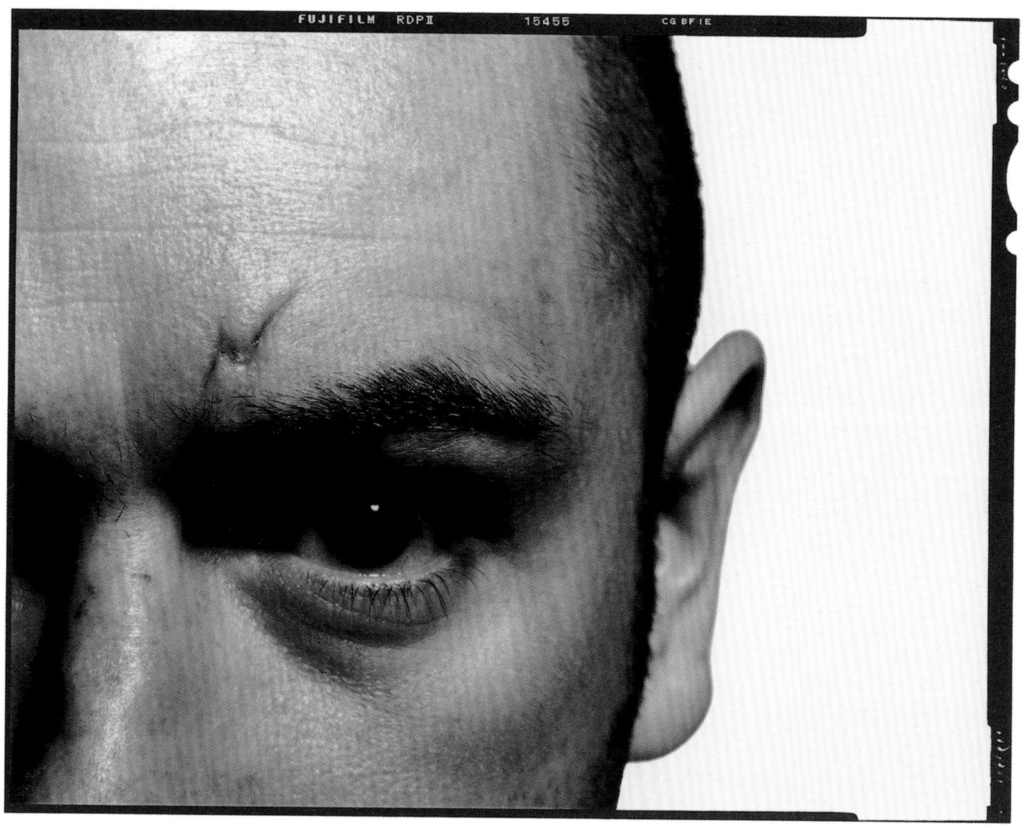

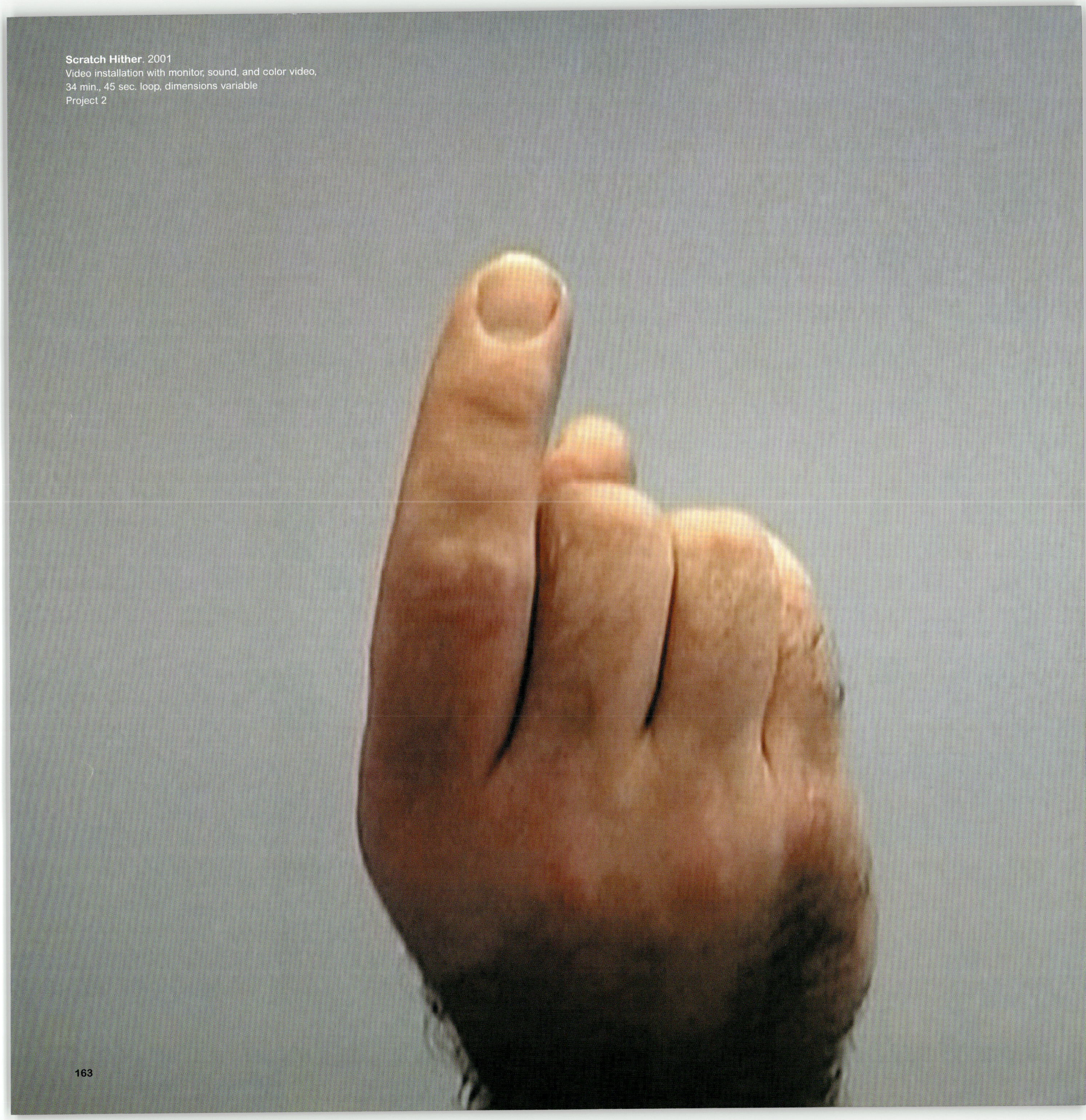

Scratch Hither. 2001
Video installation with monitor, sound, and color video,
34 min., 45 sec. loop, dimensions variable
Project 2

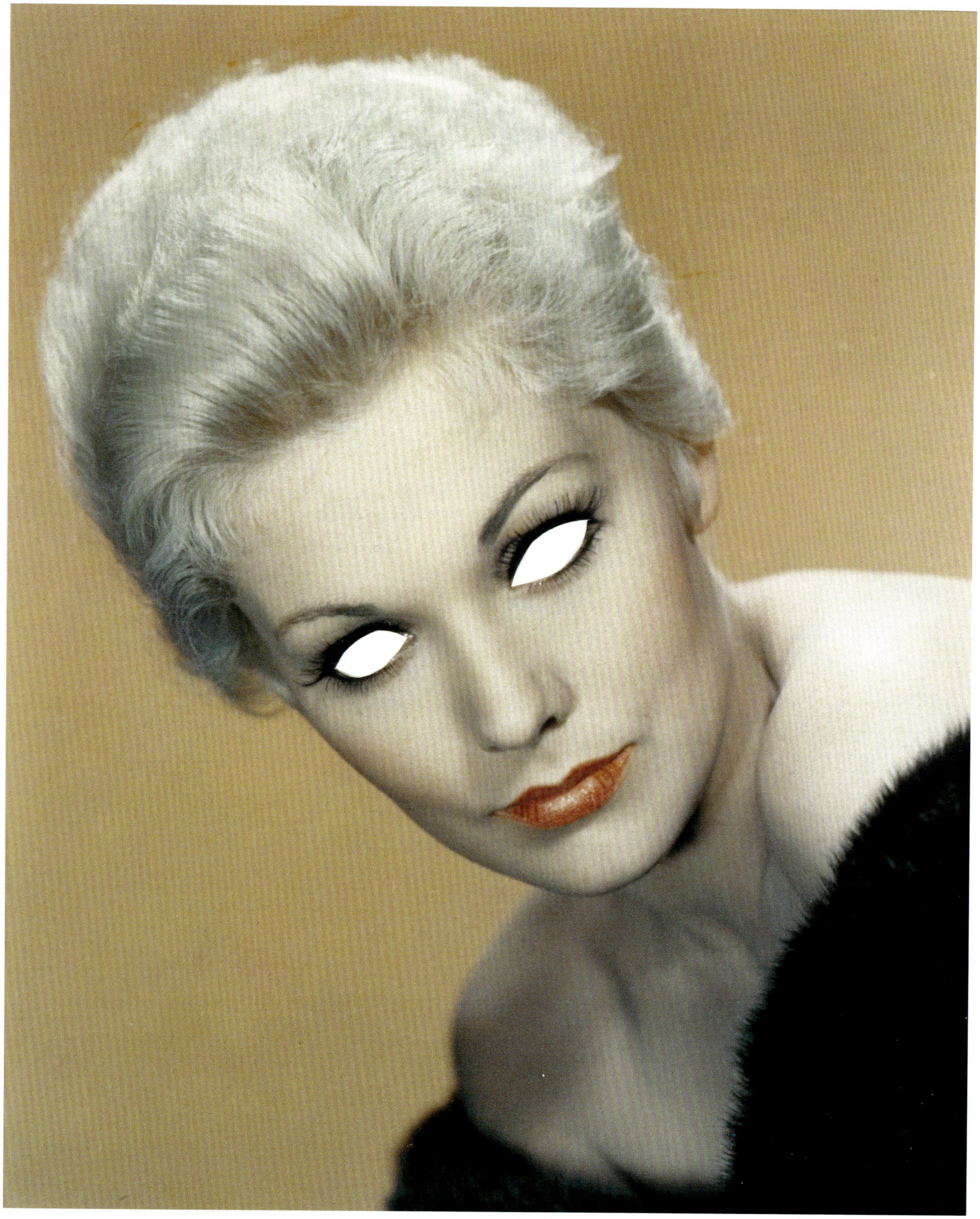

Blind Star series:
White Blind Kim. 2002
Photograph and archival board,
26 x 24" (66 x 61 cm)
Collection of Monica and Peder Lund

Blind Star series:
Mirror Blind Charles. 2002
Photograph and archival board,
26 x 24" (66 x 61 cm)
Collection of Deb and Rob Stone

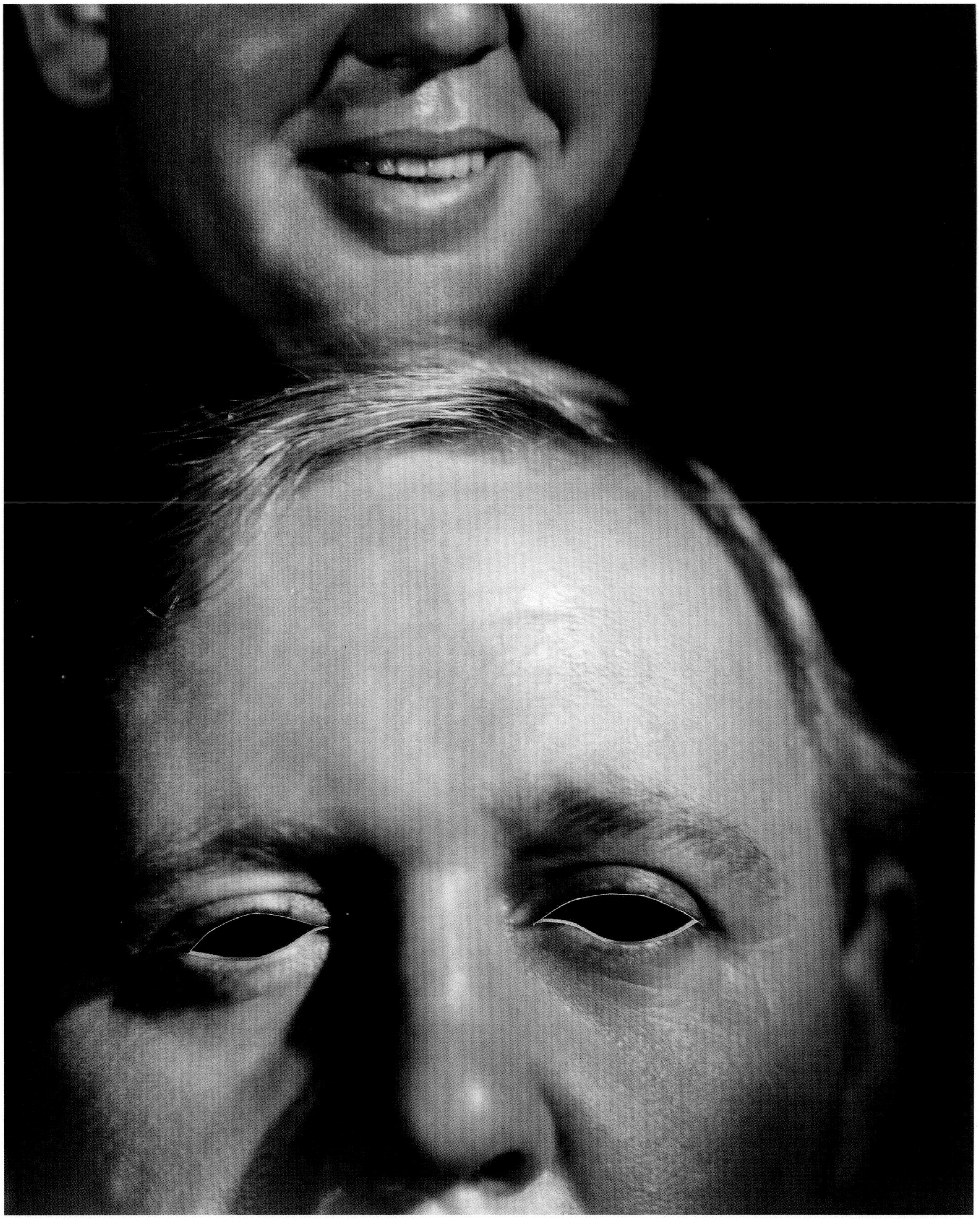

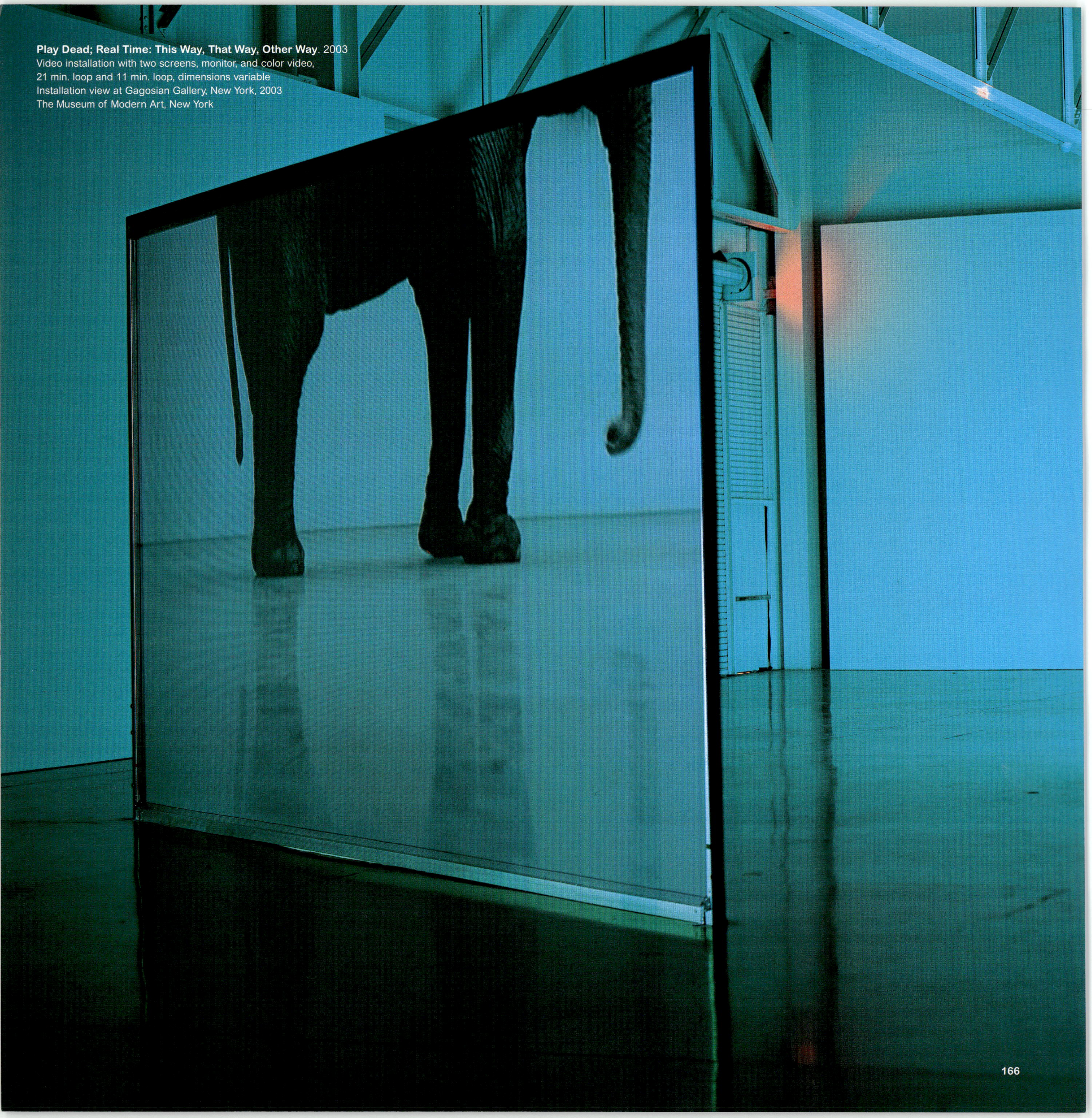

Play Dead; Real Time: This Way, That Way, Other Way. 2003
Video installation with two screens, monitor, and color video,
21 min. loop and 11 min. loop, dimensions variable
Installation view at Gagosian Gallery, New York, 2003
The Museum of Modern Art, New York

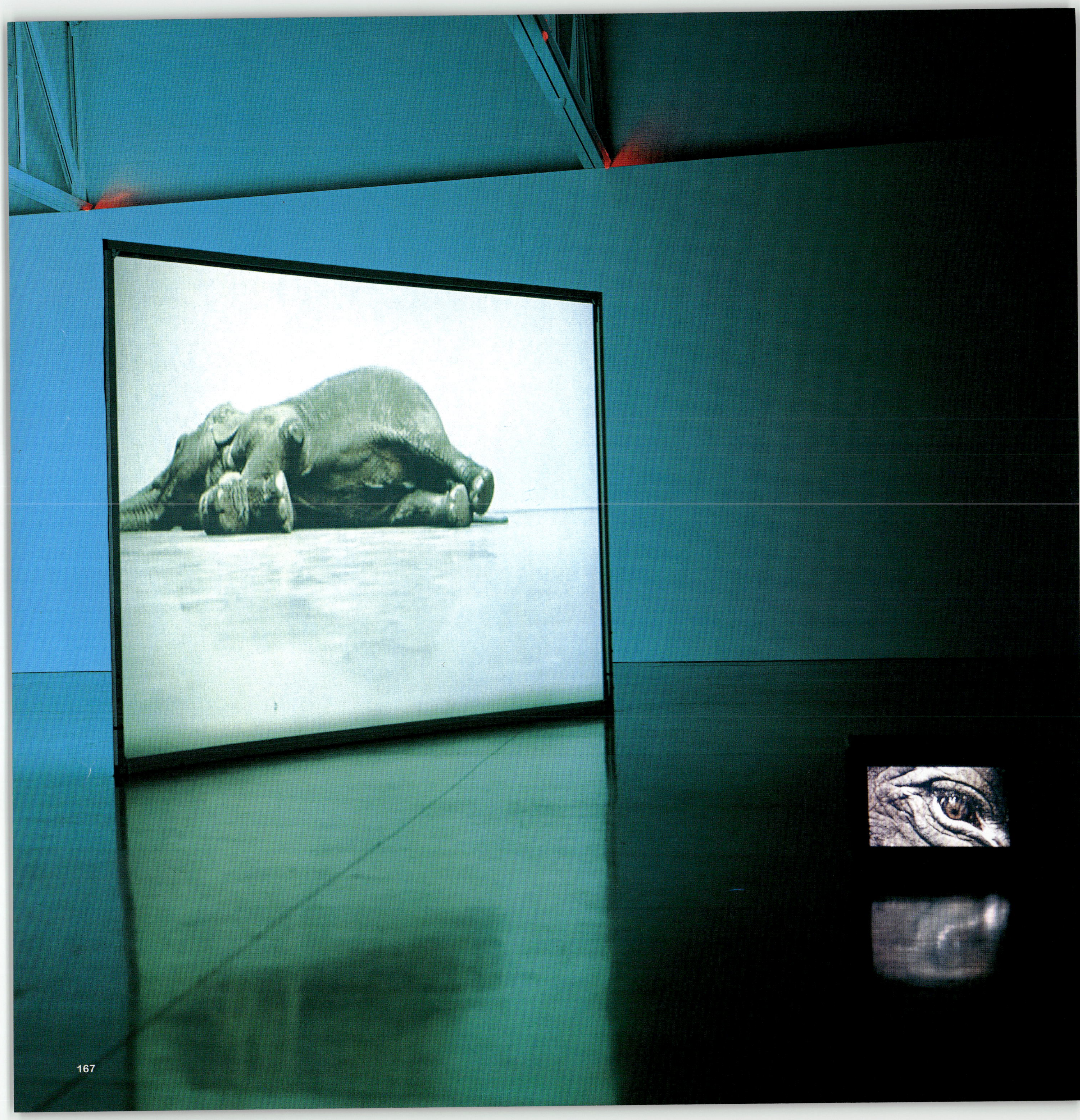

Play Dead; Real Time. 2003
Two stills from video installation
Collection the artist

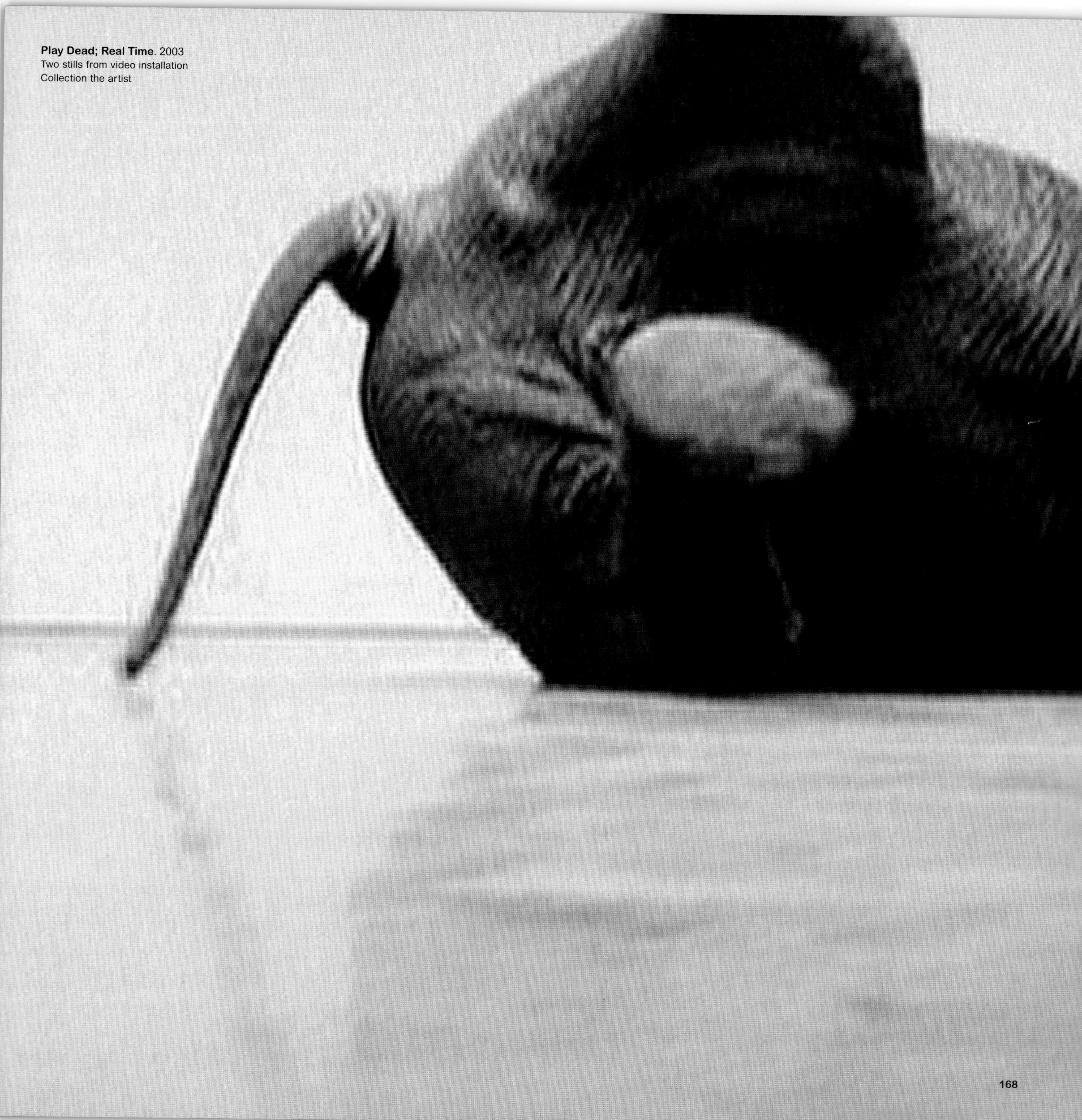

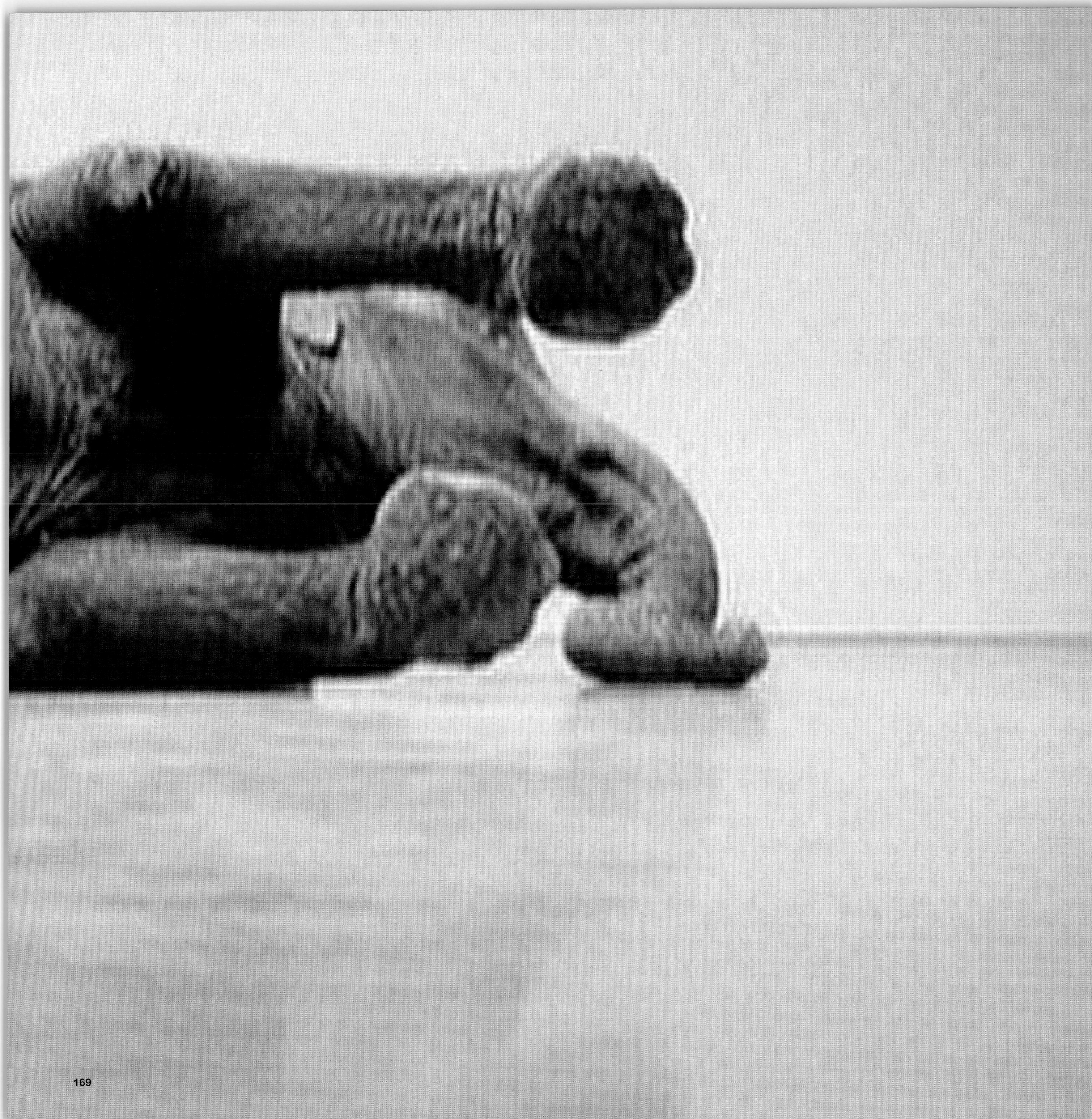

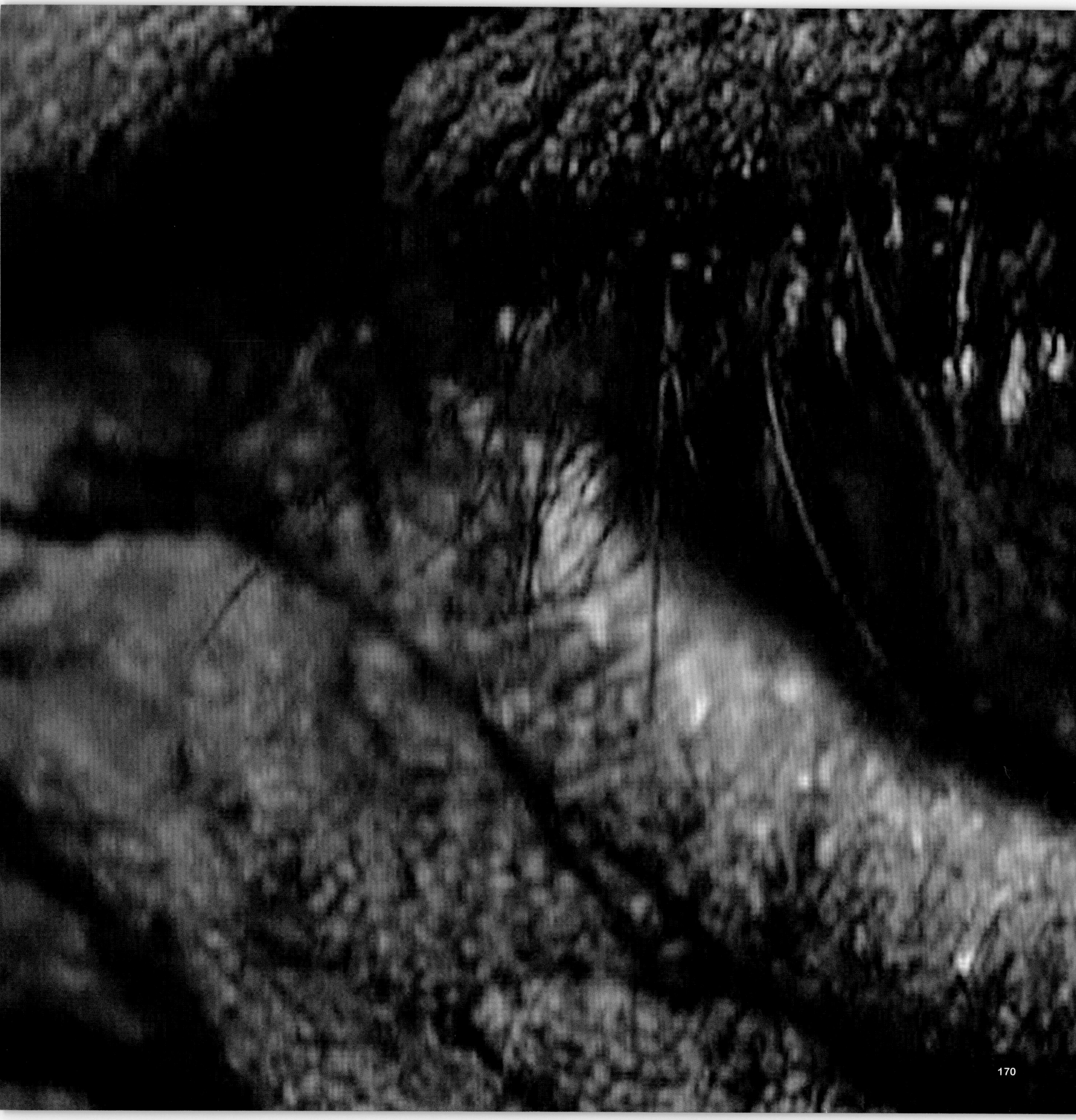

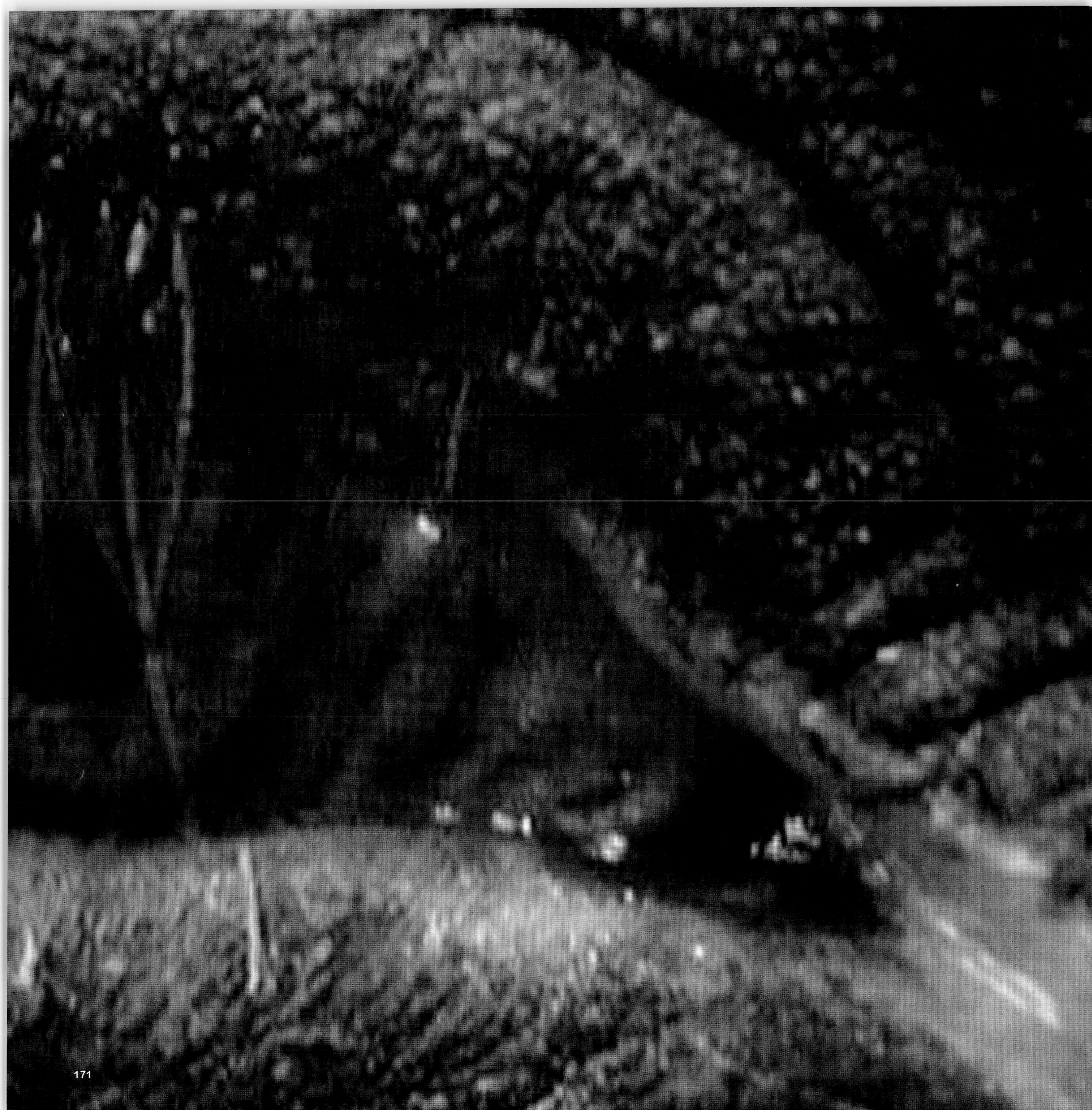

The Left Hand Can't See That the Right Hand Is Blind. 2004
Video installation with monitor and color video, 12 min., 18 sec. loop, dimensions variable
Linda and Harry Macklowe

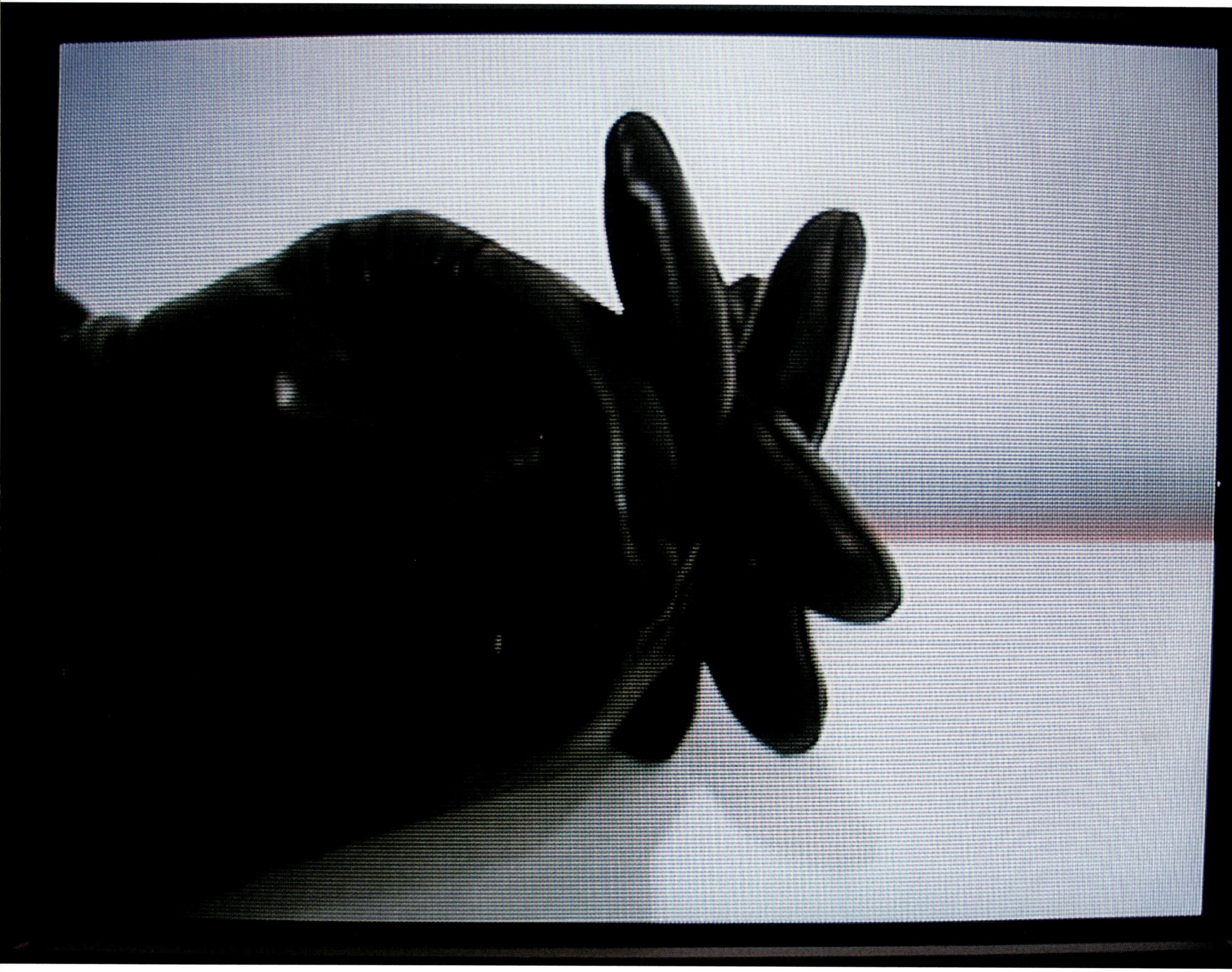

The Left Hand Doesn't Care What the Right Hand Isn't Doing. 2004
Video installation with monitor and color video, 24 min., 58 sec. loop, dimensions variable
Courtesy Gagosian Gallery, New York

The Right Hand Doesn't Care What the Left Hand Isn't Doing. 2004
Video installation with monitor and color video, 25 min., 55 sec. loop, dimensions variable
Courtesy Gagosian Gallery, New York

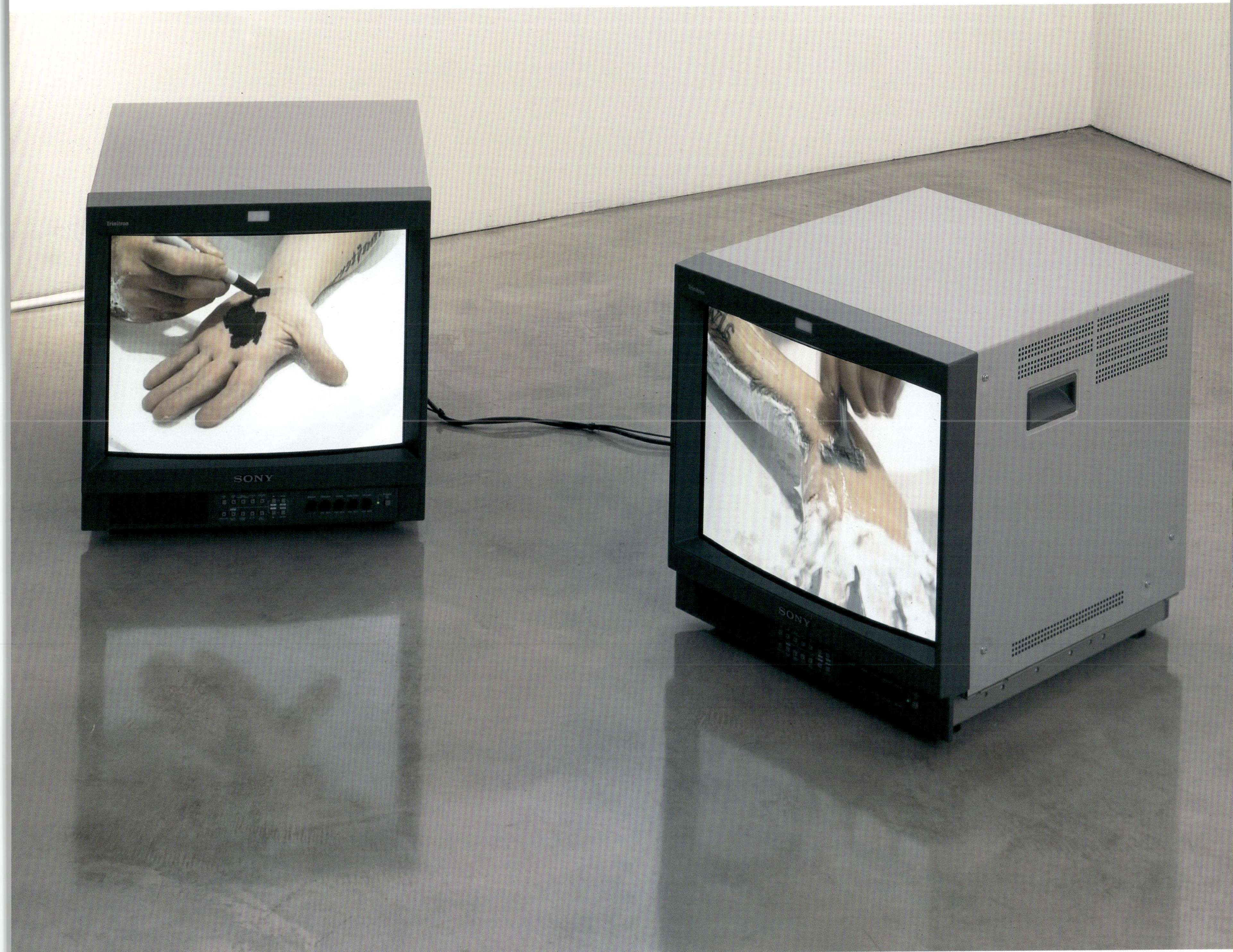

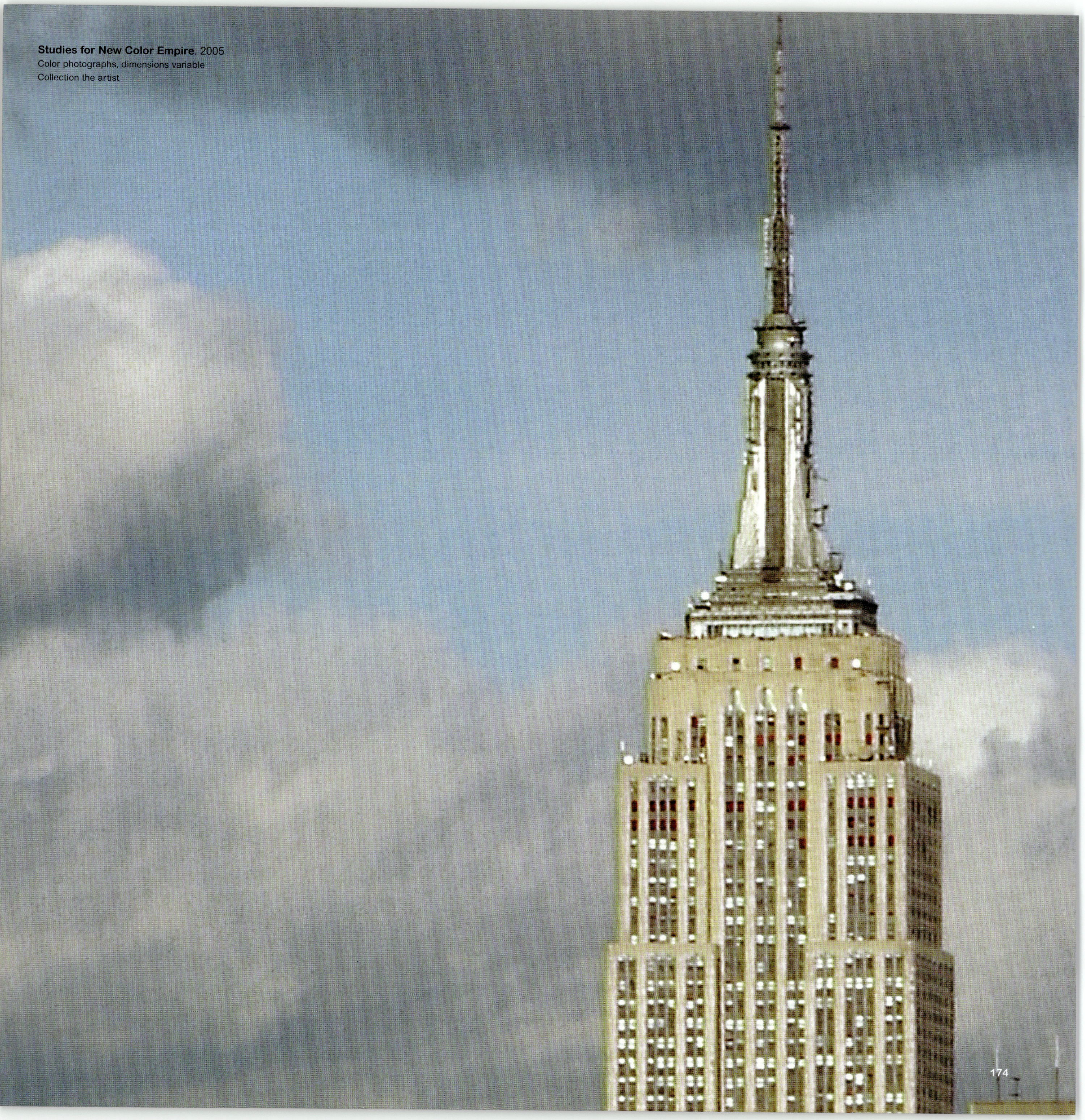

Studies for New Color Empire. 2005
Color photographs, dimensions variable
Collection the artist

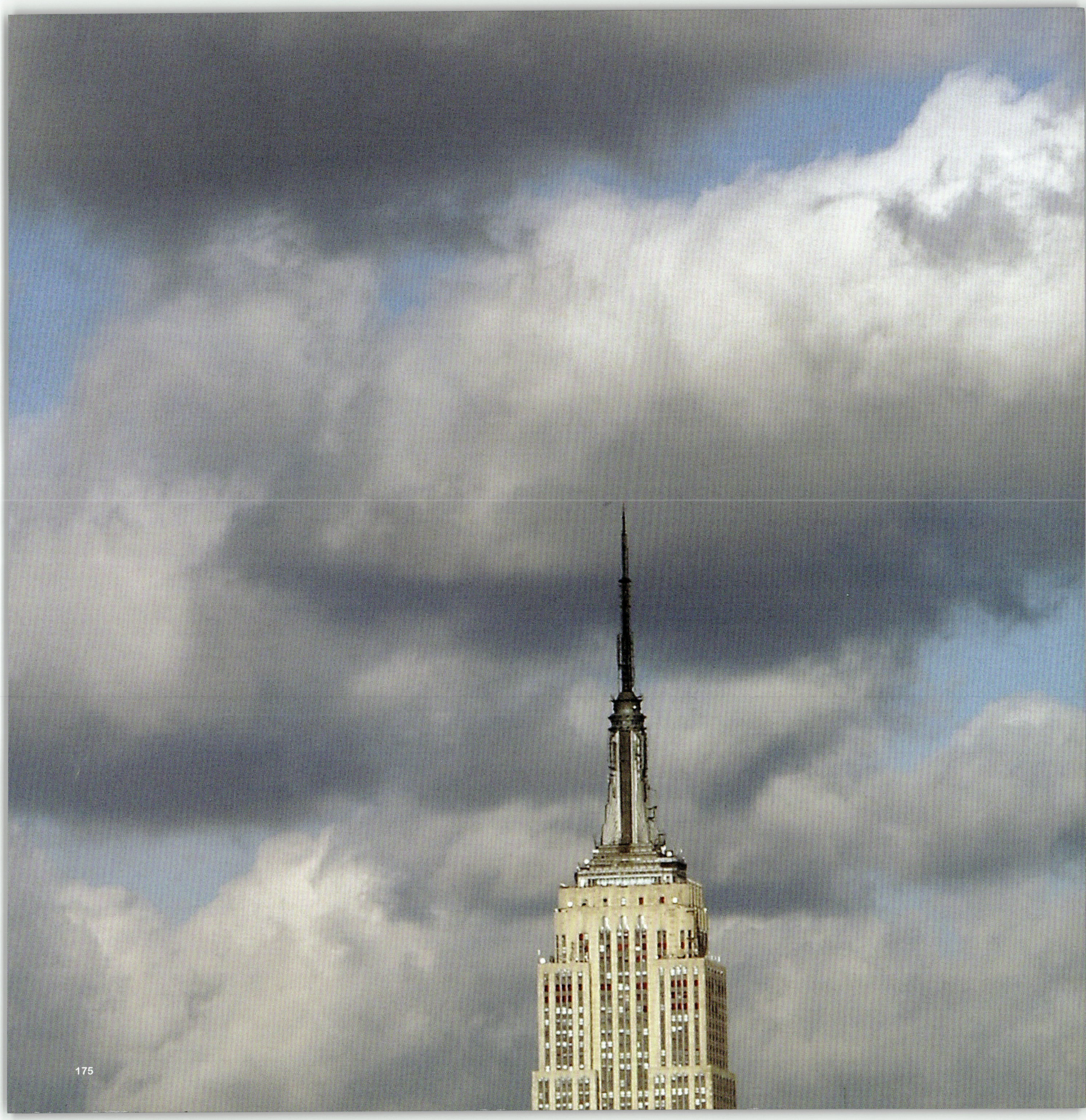

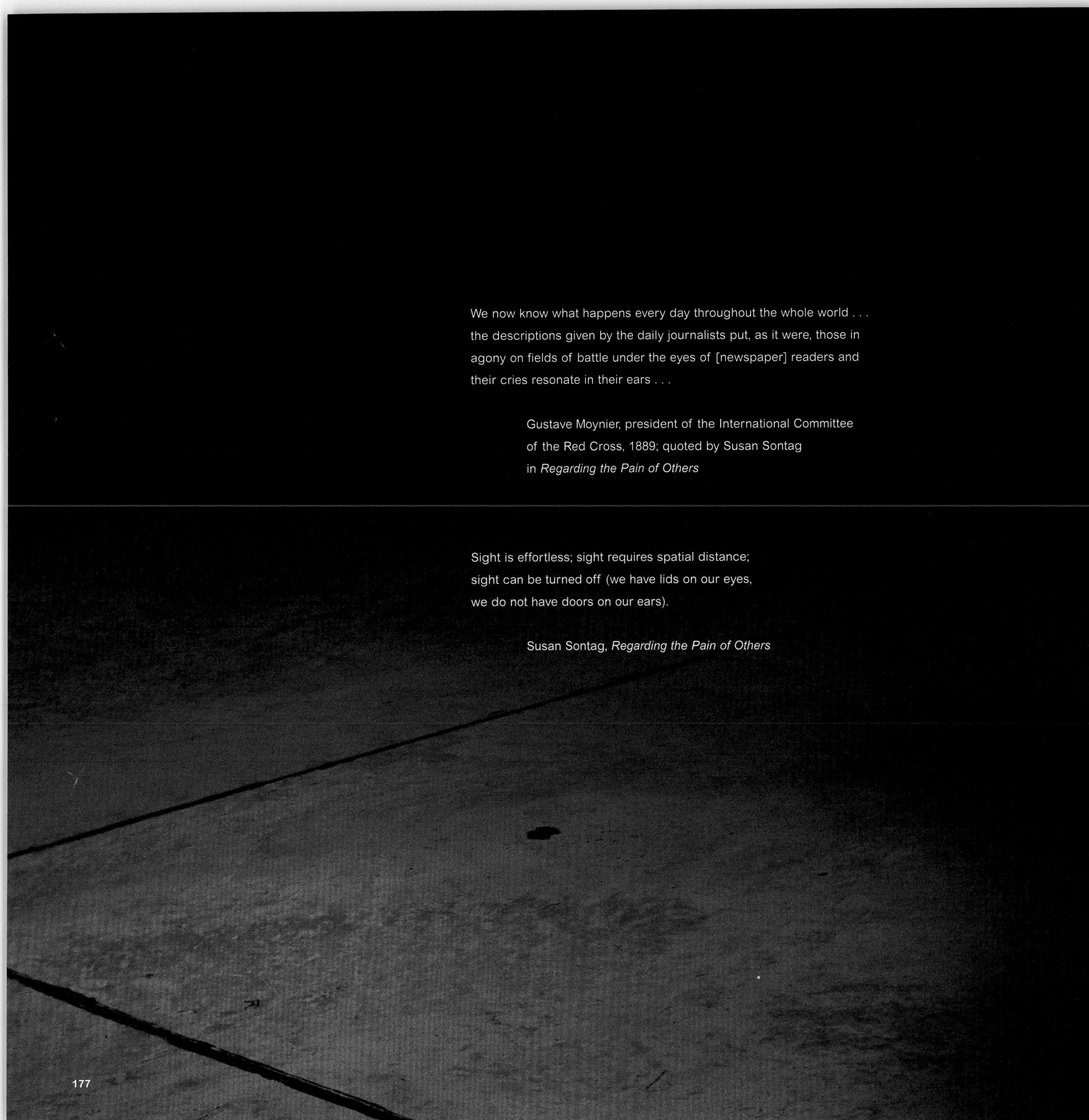

We now know what happens every day throughout the whole world . . . the descriptions given by the daily journalists put, as it were, those in agony on fields of battle under the eyes of [newspaper] readers and their cries resonate in their ears . . .

Gustave Moynier, president of the International Committee of the Red Cross, 1889; quoted by Susan Sontag in *Regarding the Pain of Others*

Sight is effortless; sight requires spatial distance; sight can be turned off (we have lids on our eyes, we do not have doors on our ears).

Susan Sontag, *Regarding the Pain of Others*

IN DEFENS

1966 - 1971

Extract of an entry in a REGISTER of

Registration of Births, Deaths and Marriages (Scotland)

District No **645-3**	Year **1966**	E

BIRTH Registered in the District of ....

in the **Burgh** .... of ....

(1) Name(s) and Surname	**Douglas**	
	Lamont	
	Gordon	
(3) When Born } Date / Time	19 **66** ...... **September**	(4) W
	Twentieth	B
	4h. 30m. P.M.	
(5) Father's Name(s) Surname and Occupation	**James Gordon**	
	Patternmaker	
Mother's Name(s) Surname and	**Mary Clements Gordon**	

1703829CE

IRTHS

1965

No.	1369	Record Linkage

Glasgow

Glasgow

	(2) Sex
	M.

re	Redlands Hospital
	Glasgow

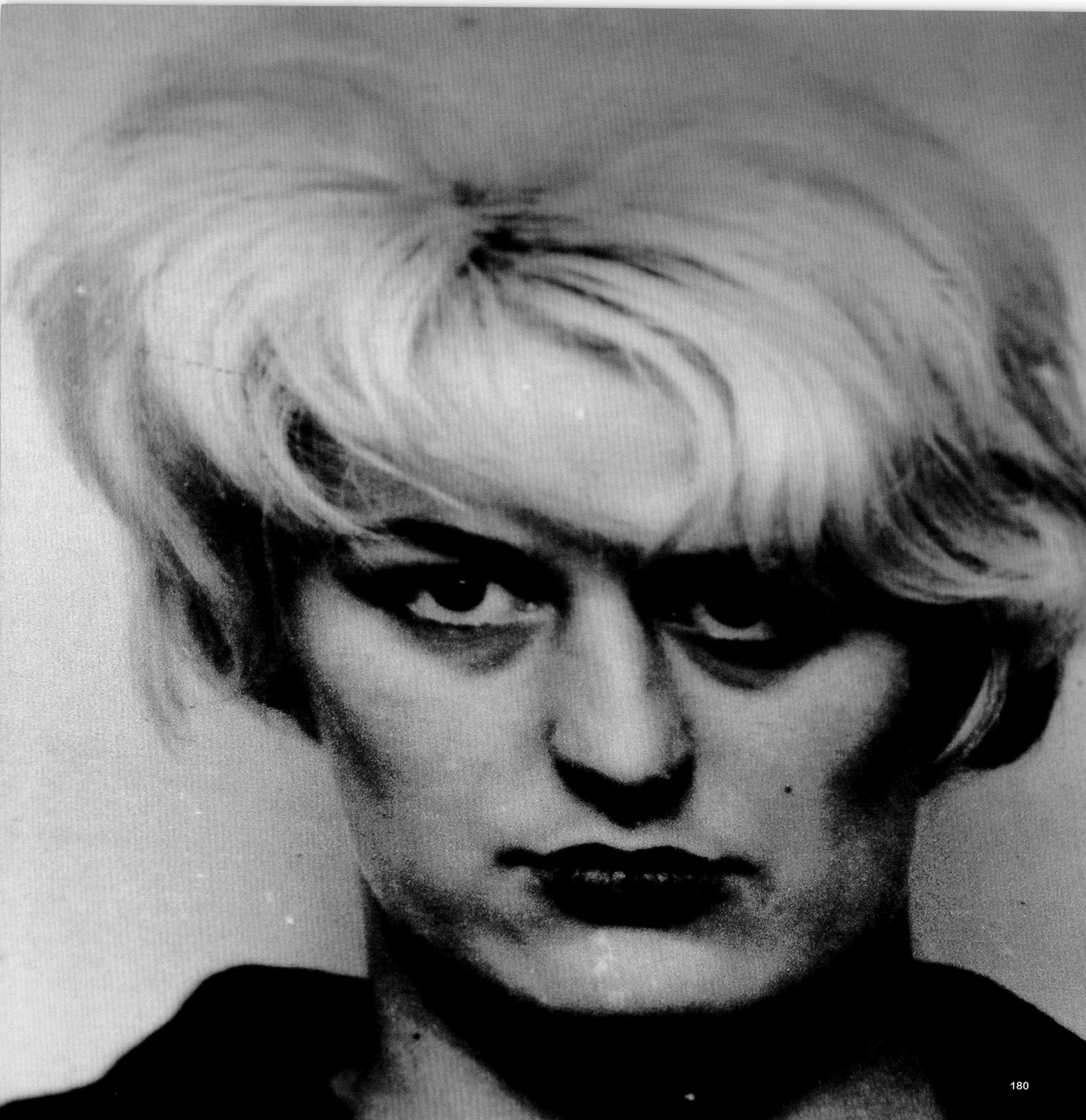

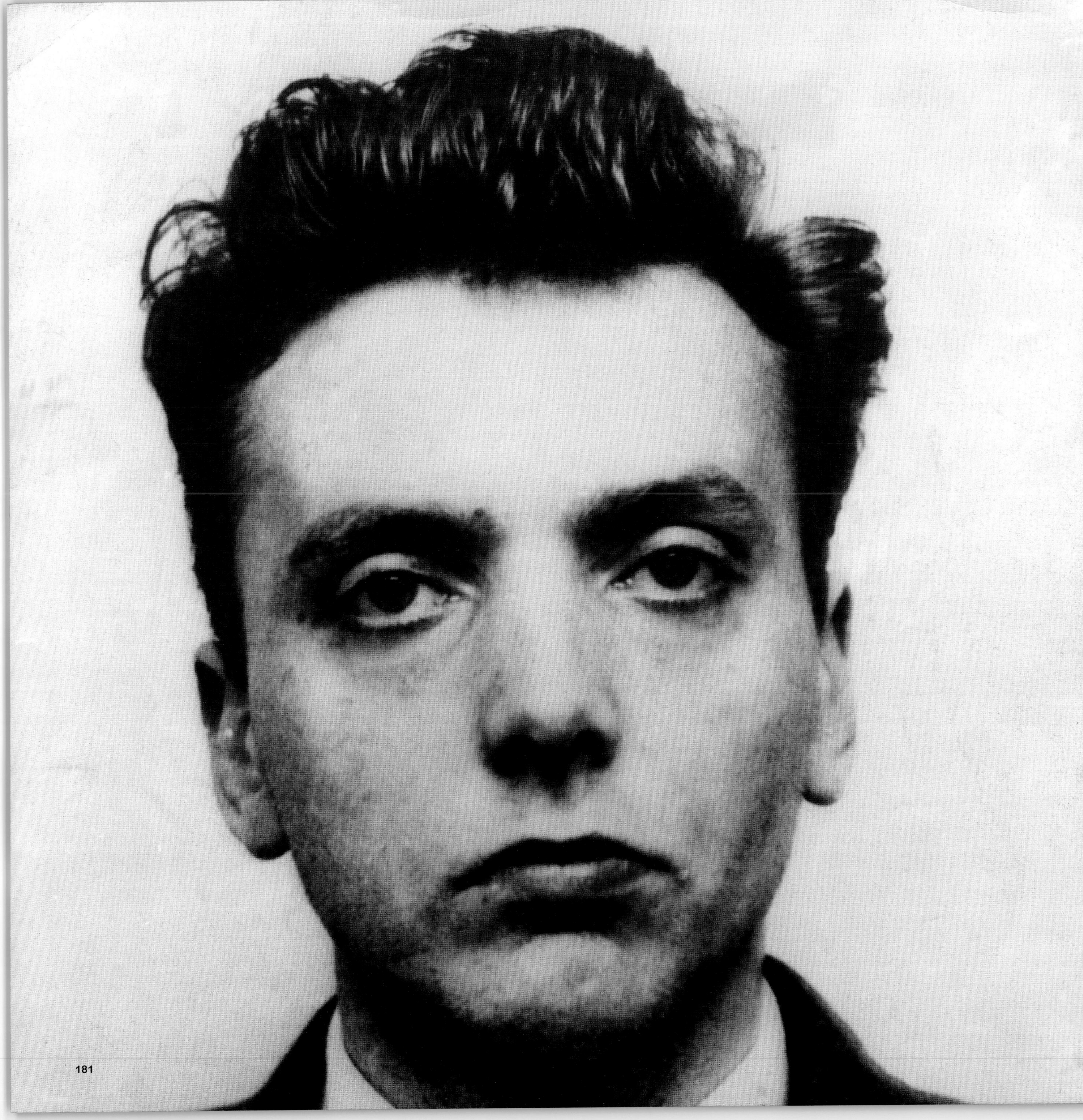

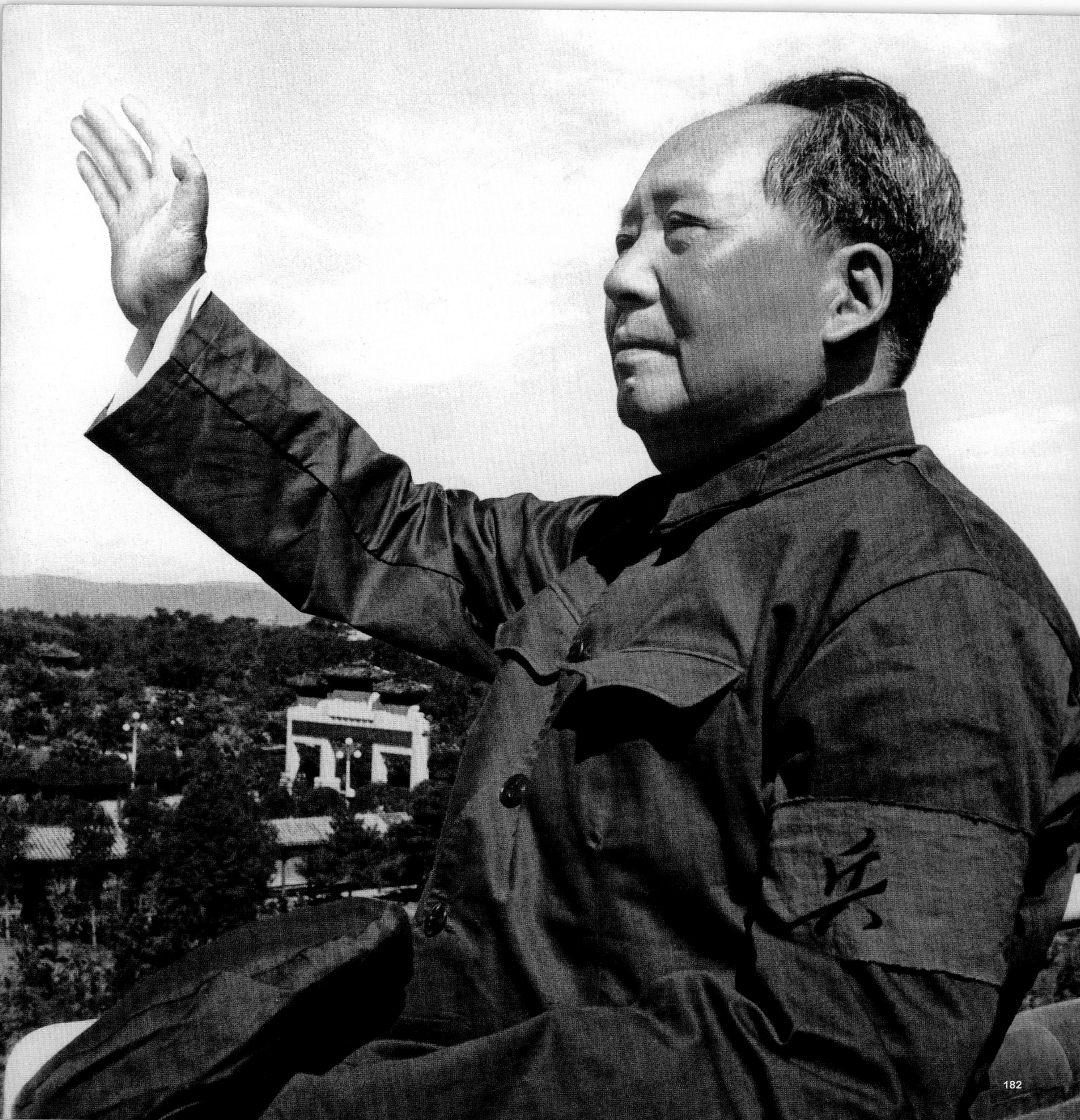
兵

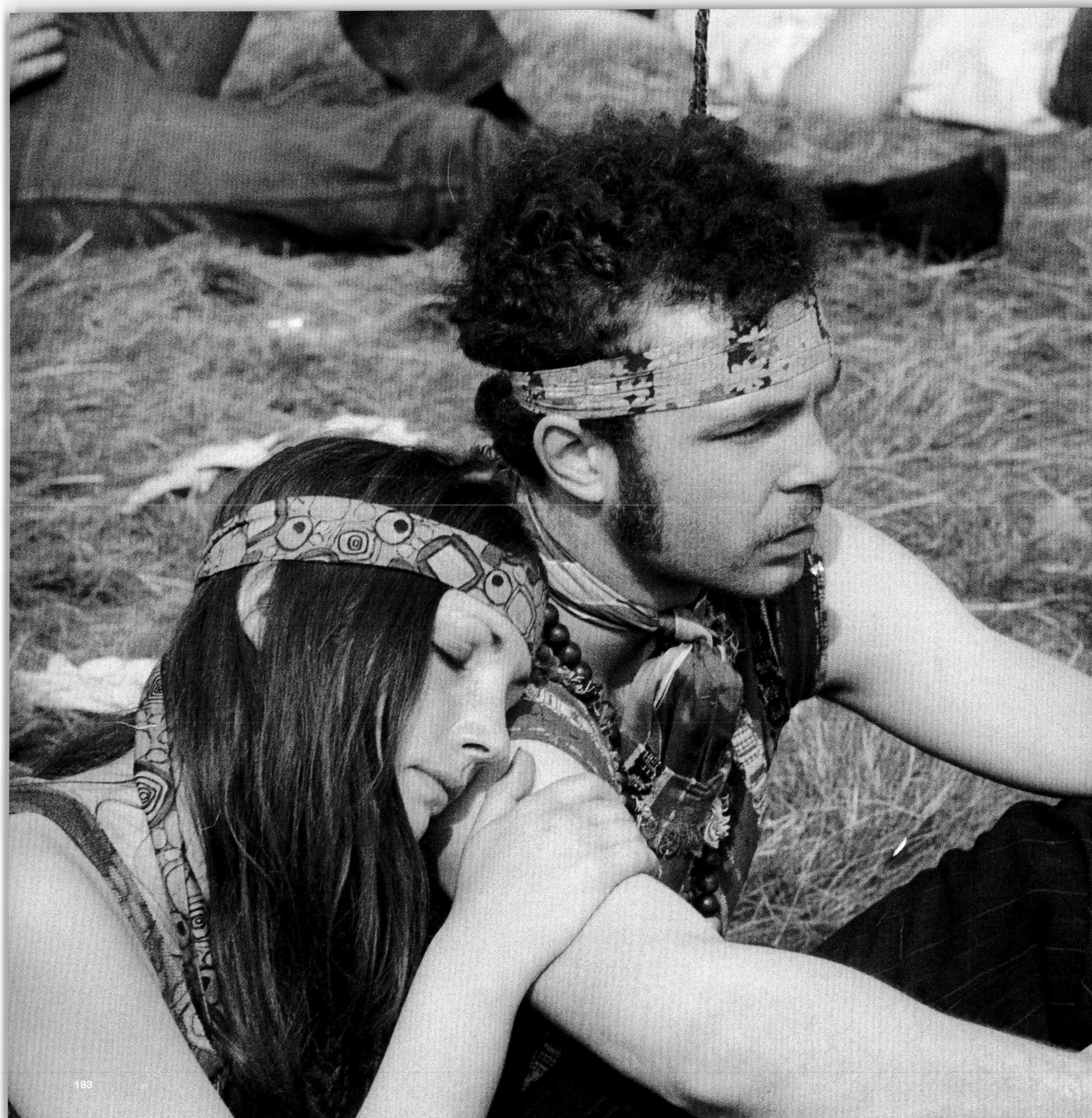

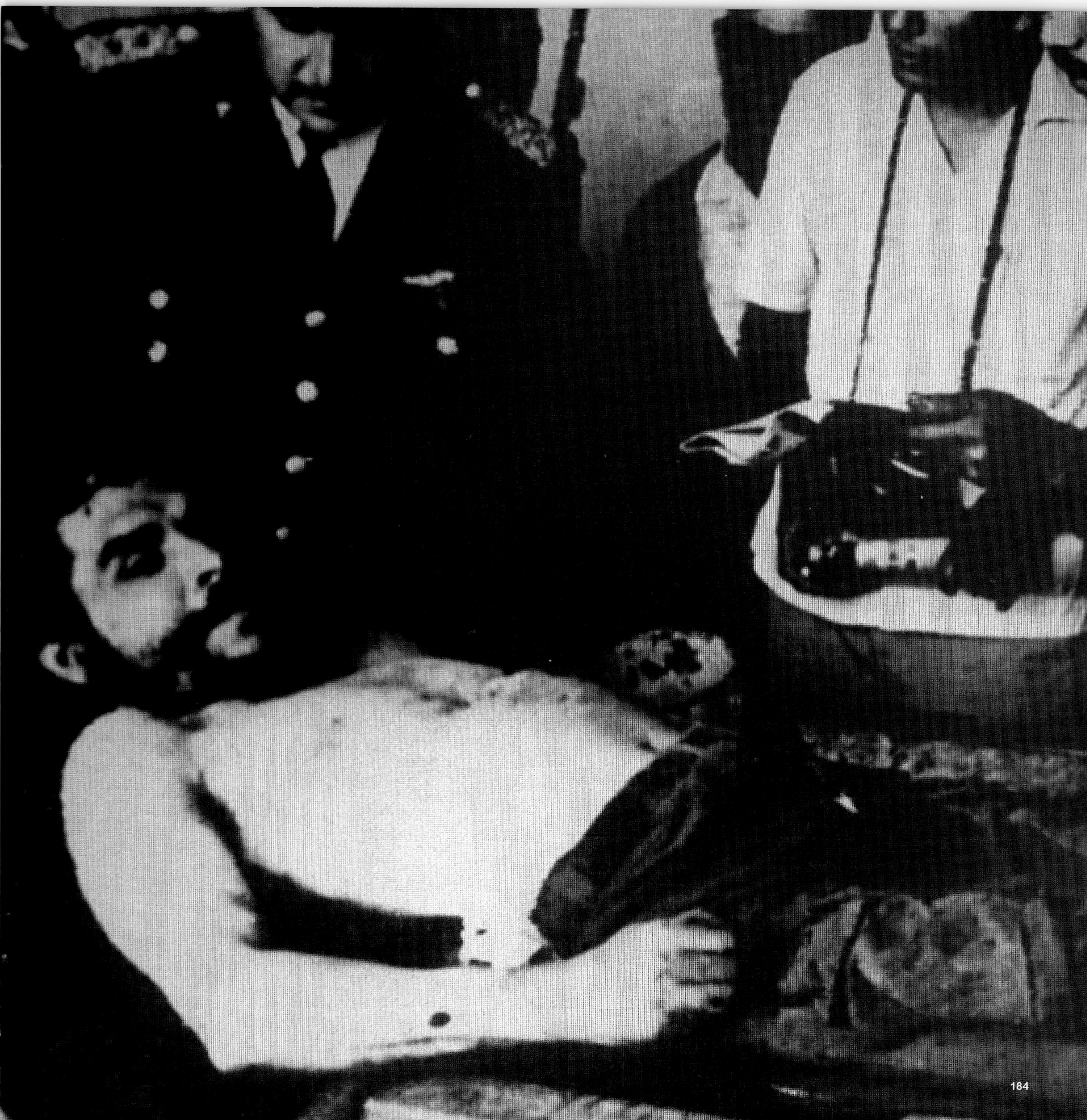

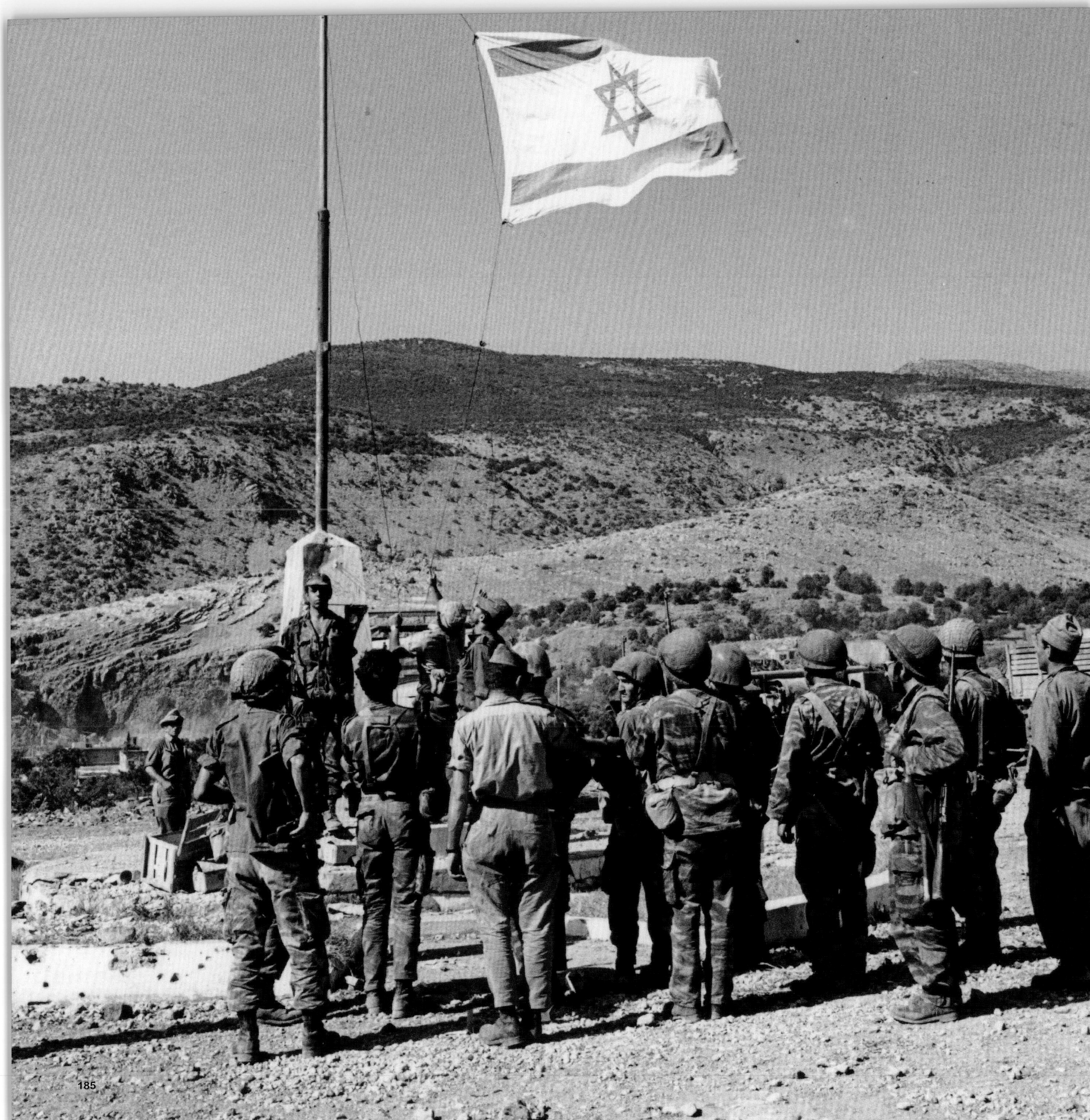

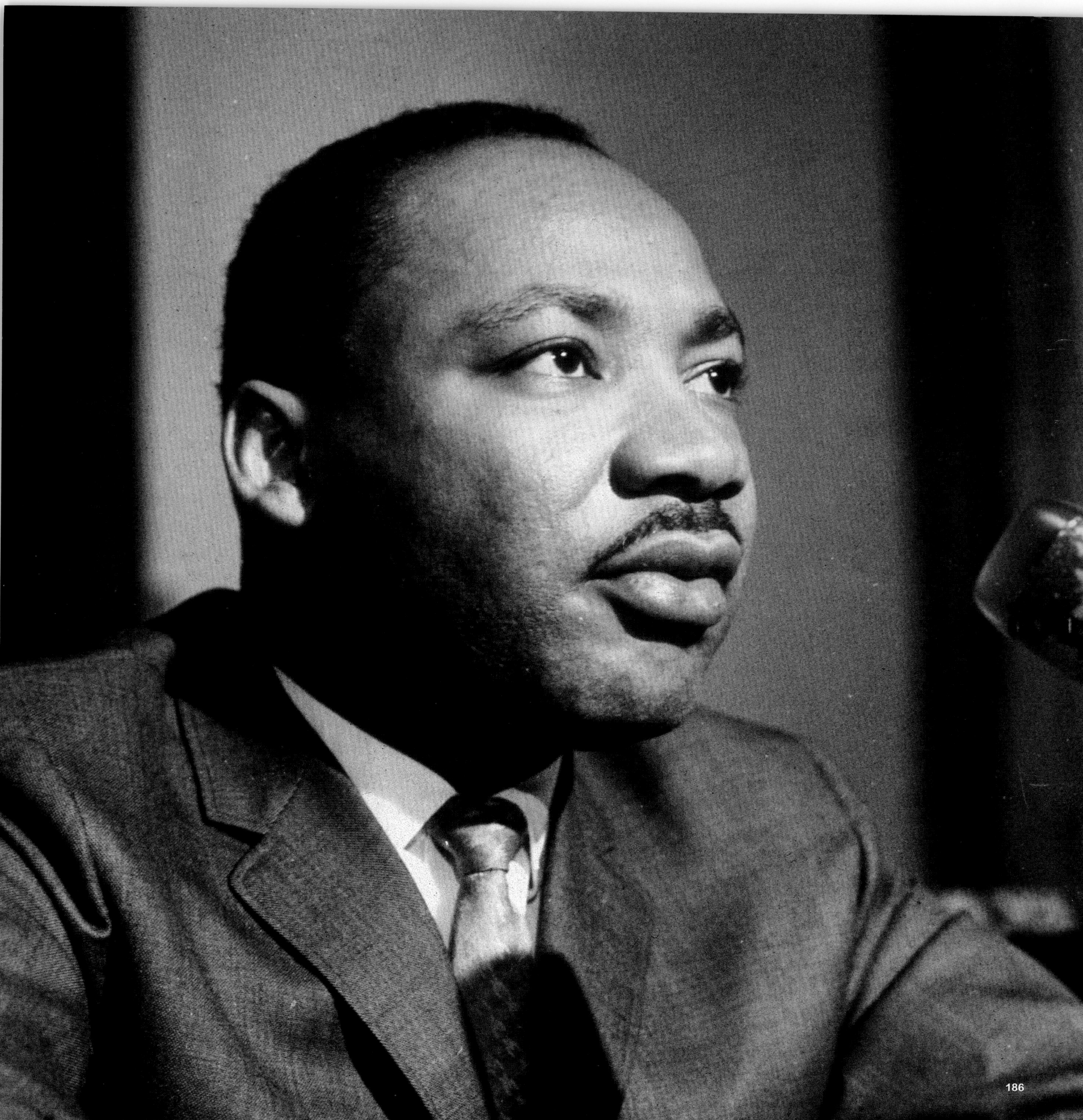

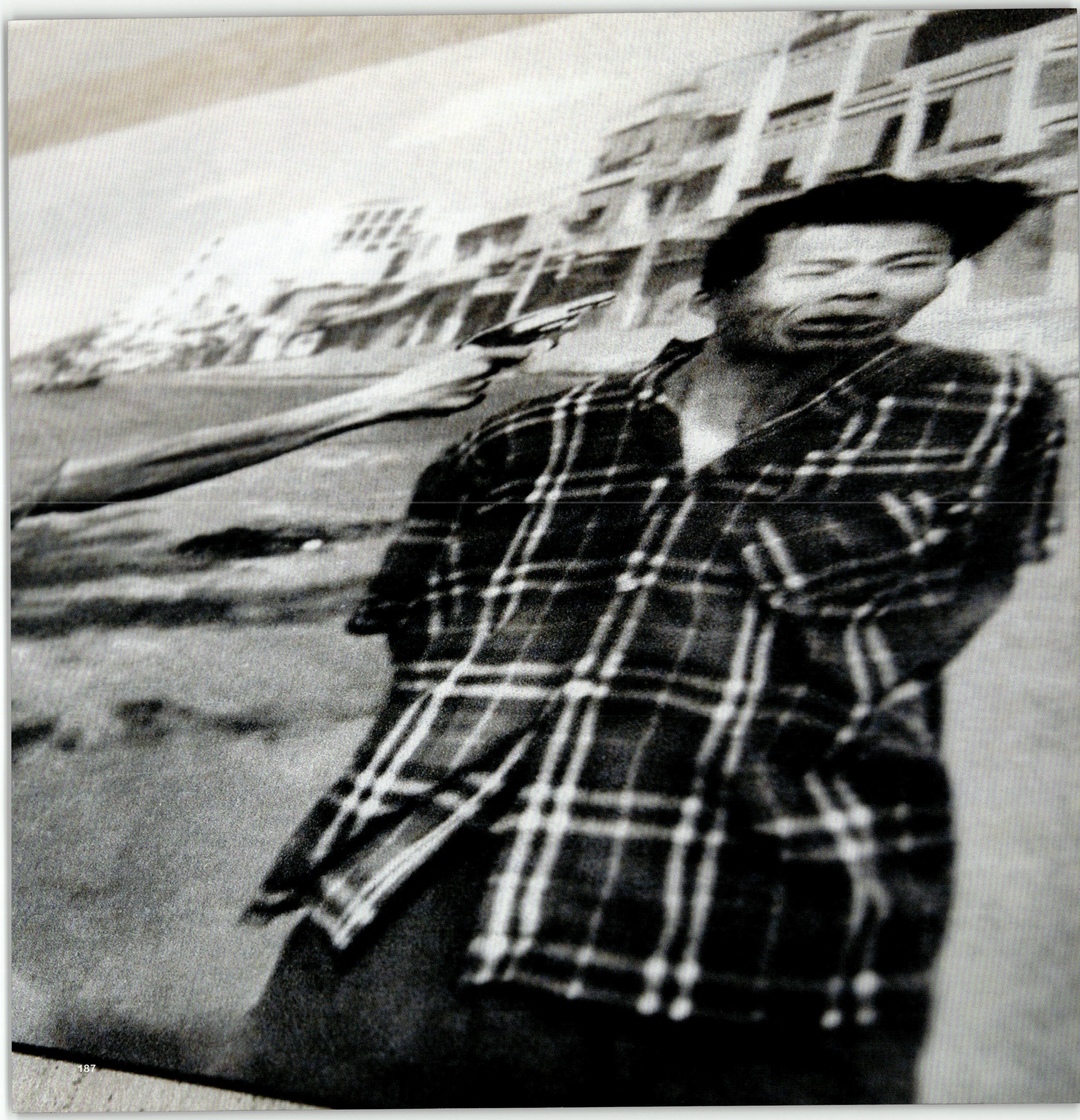

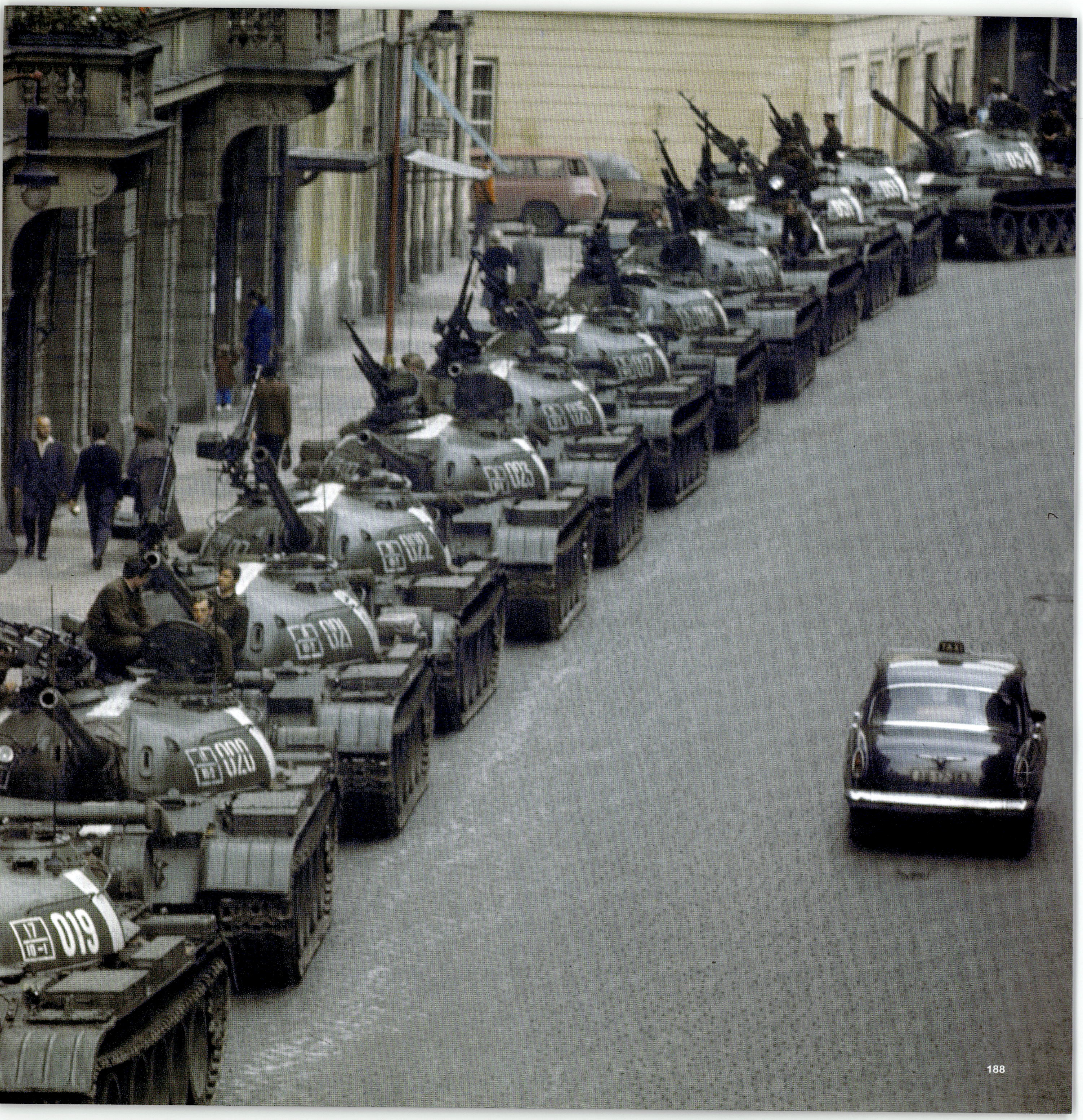

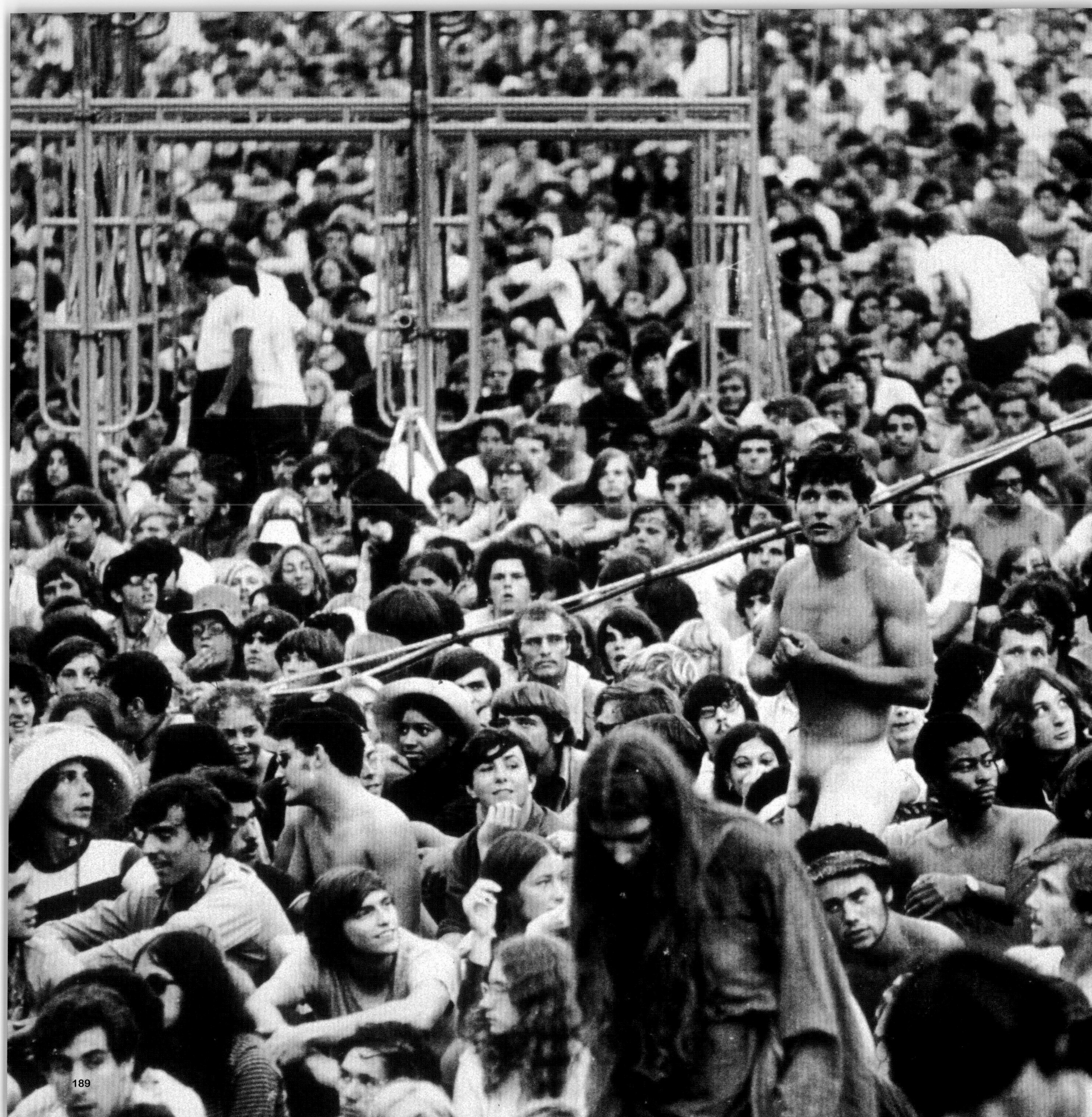

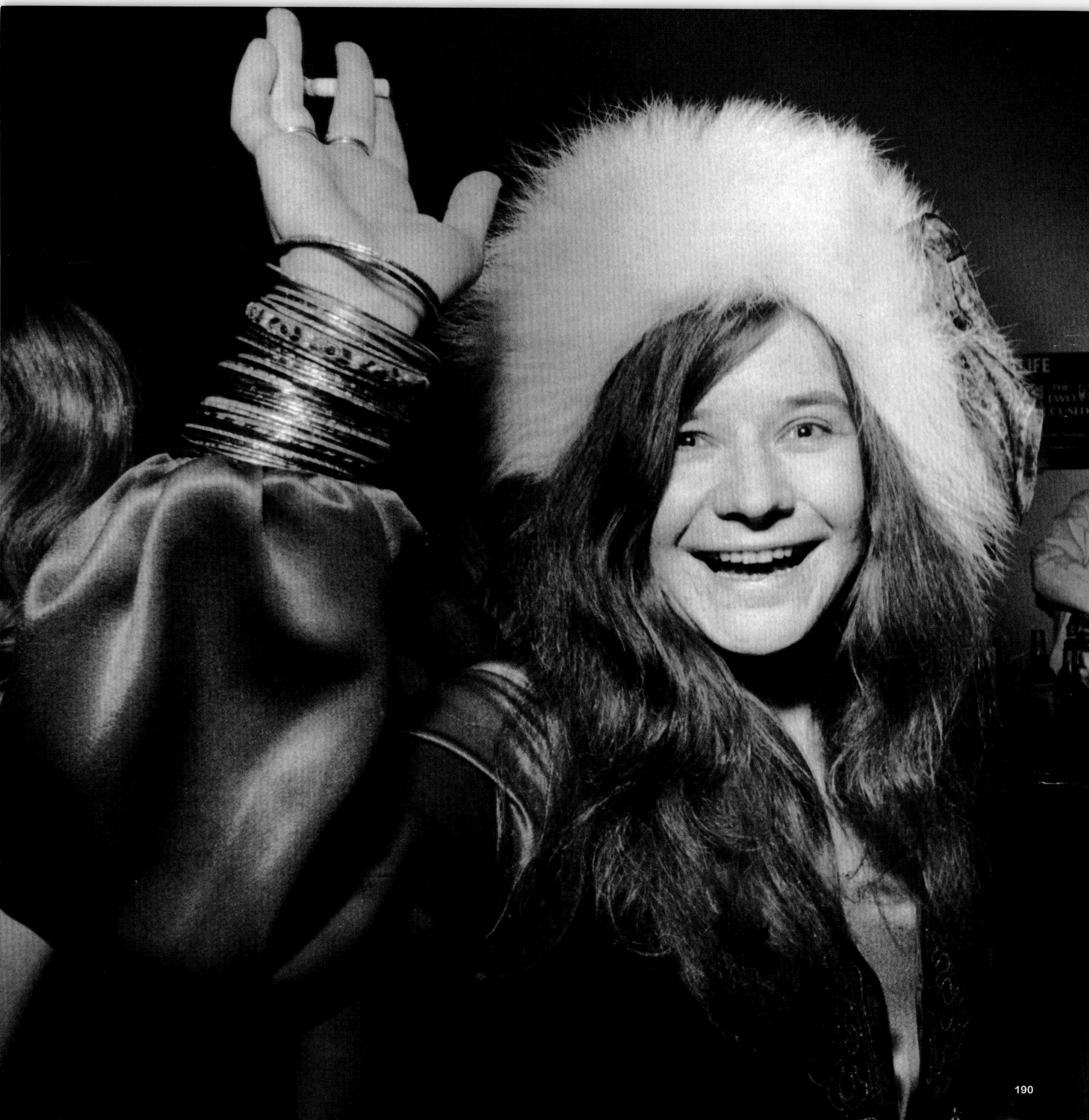

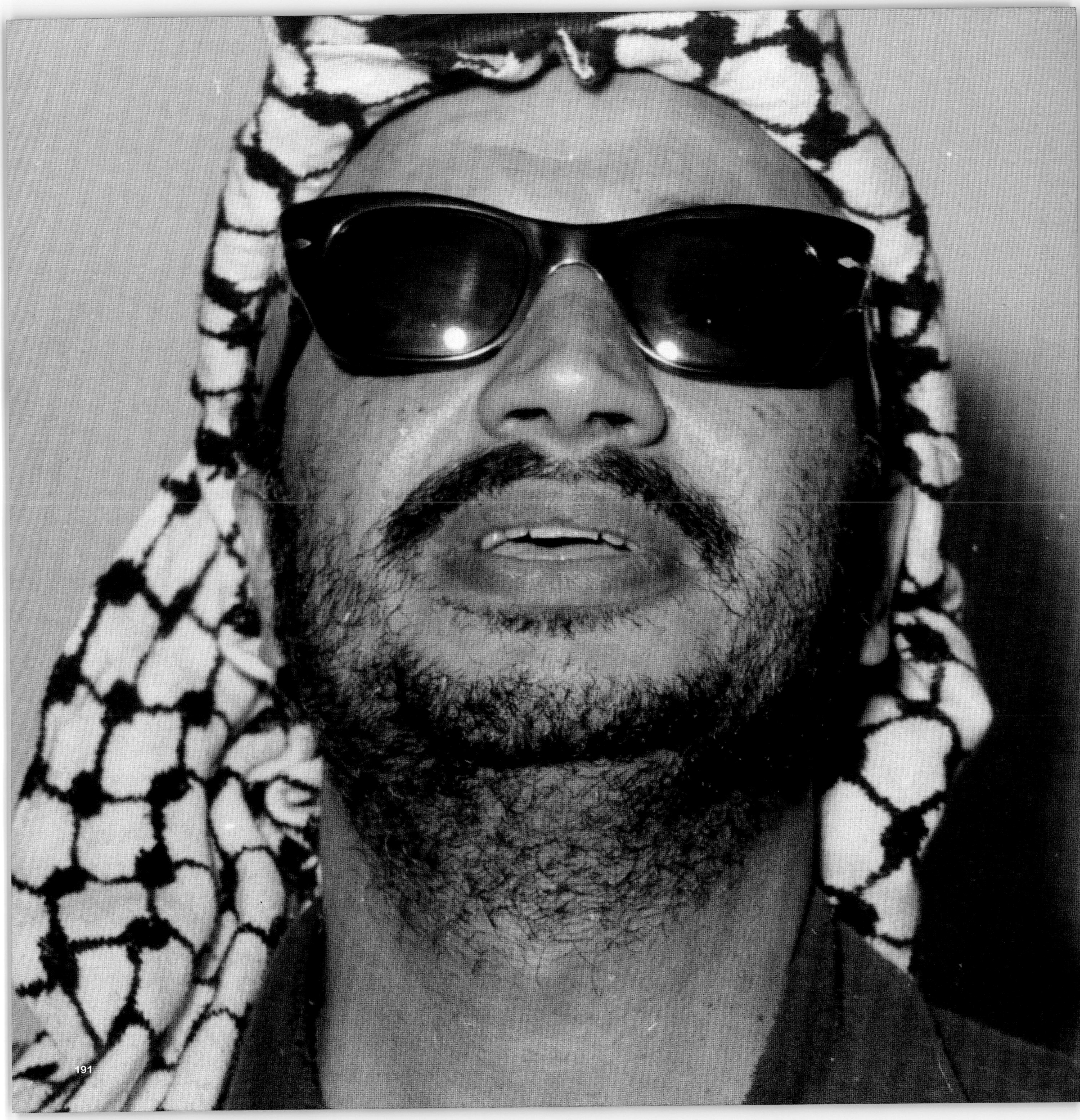

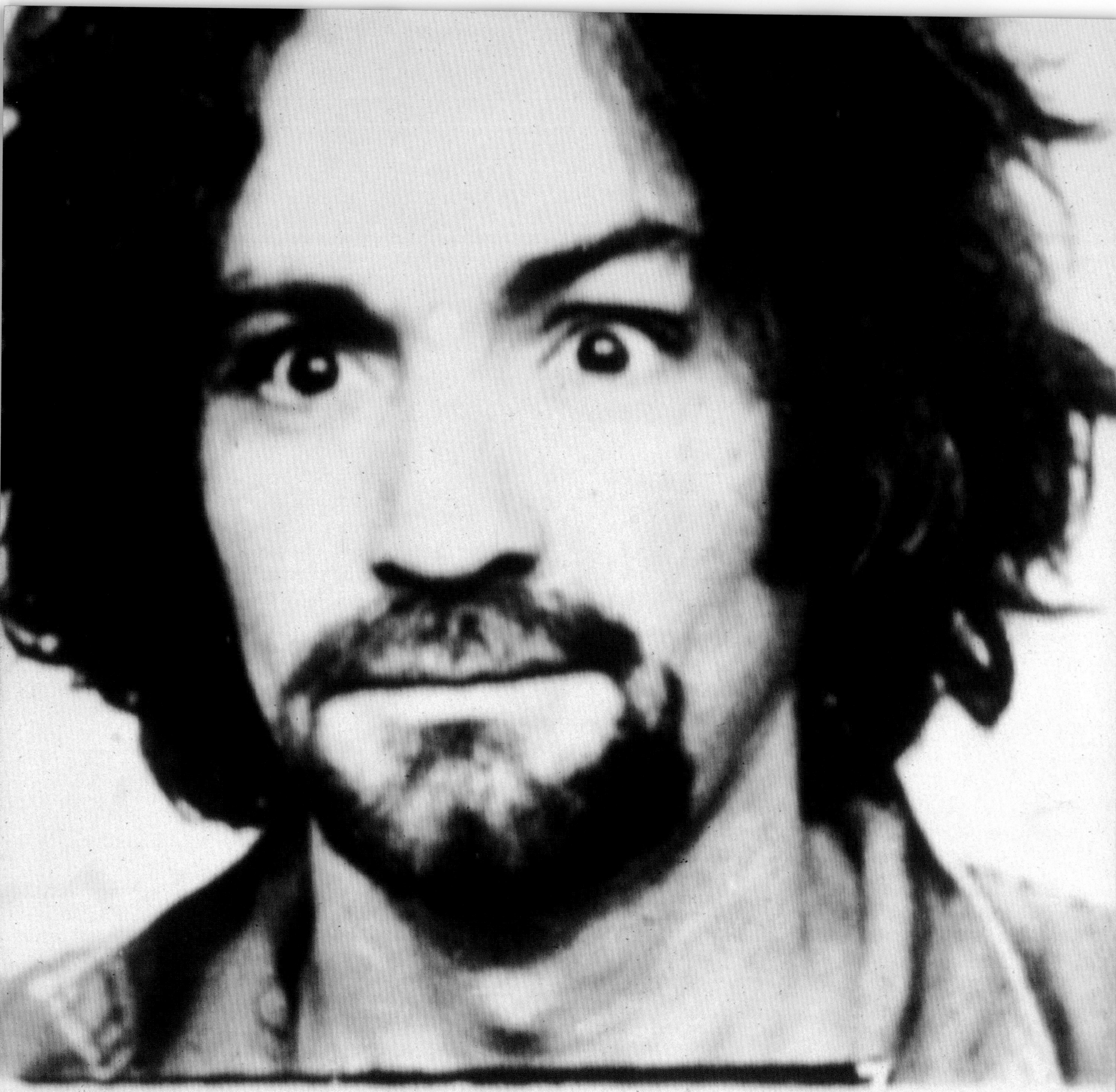

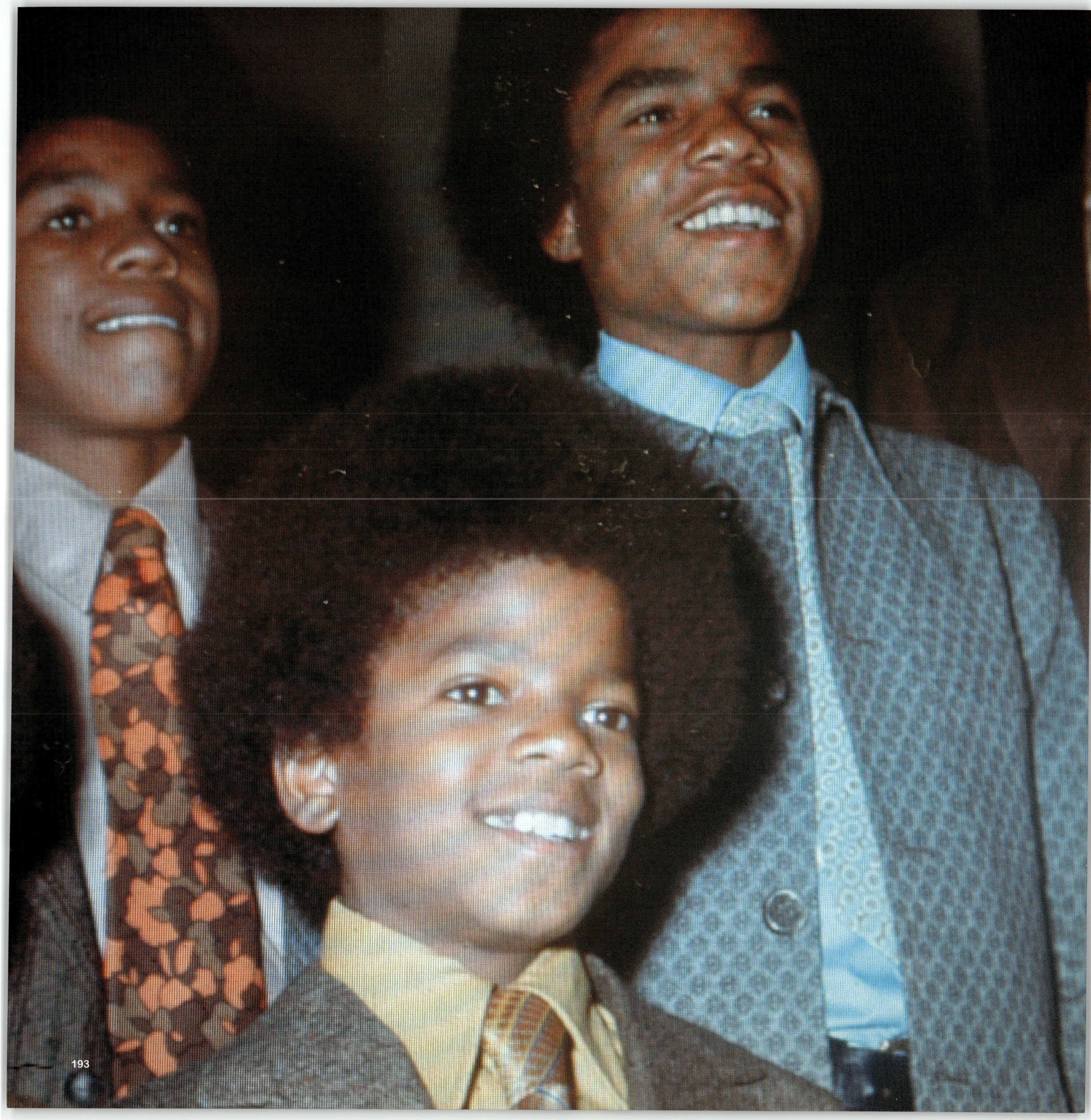

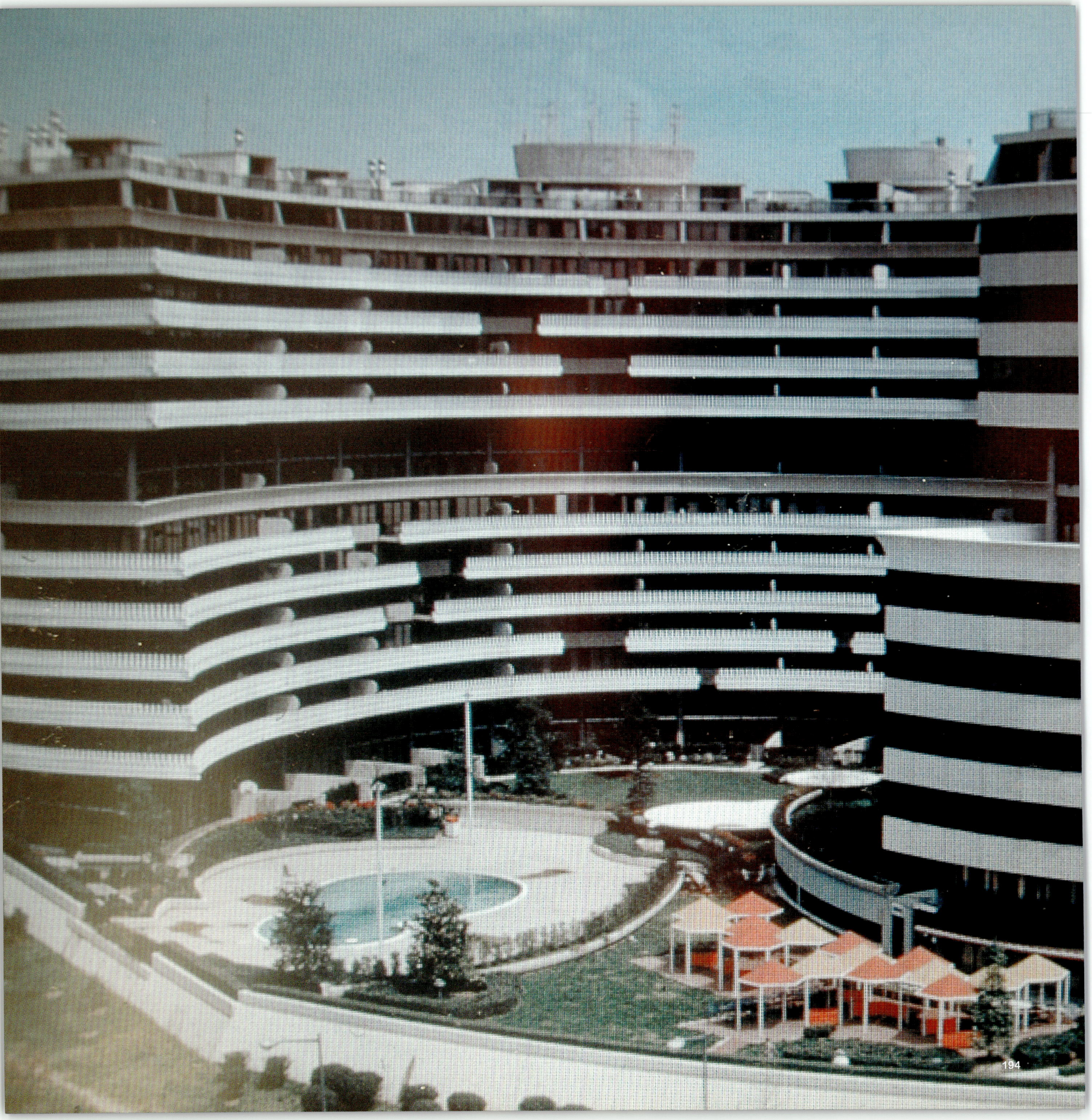

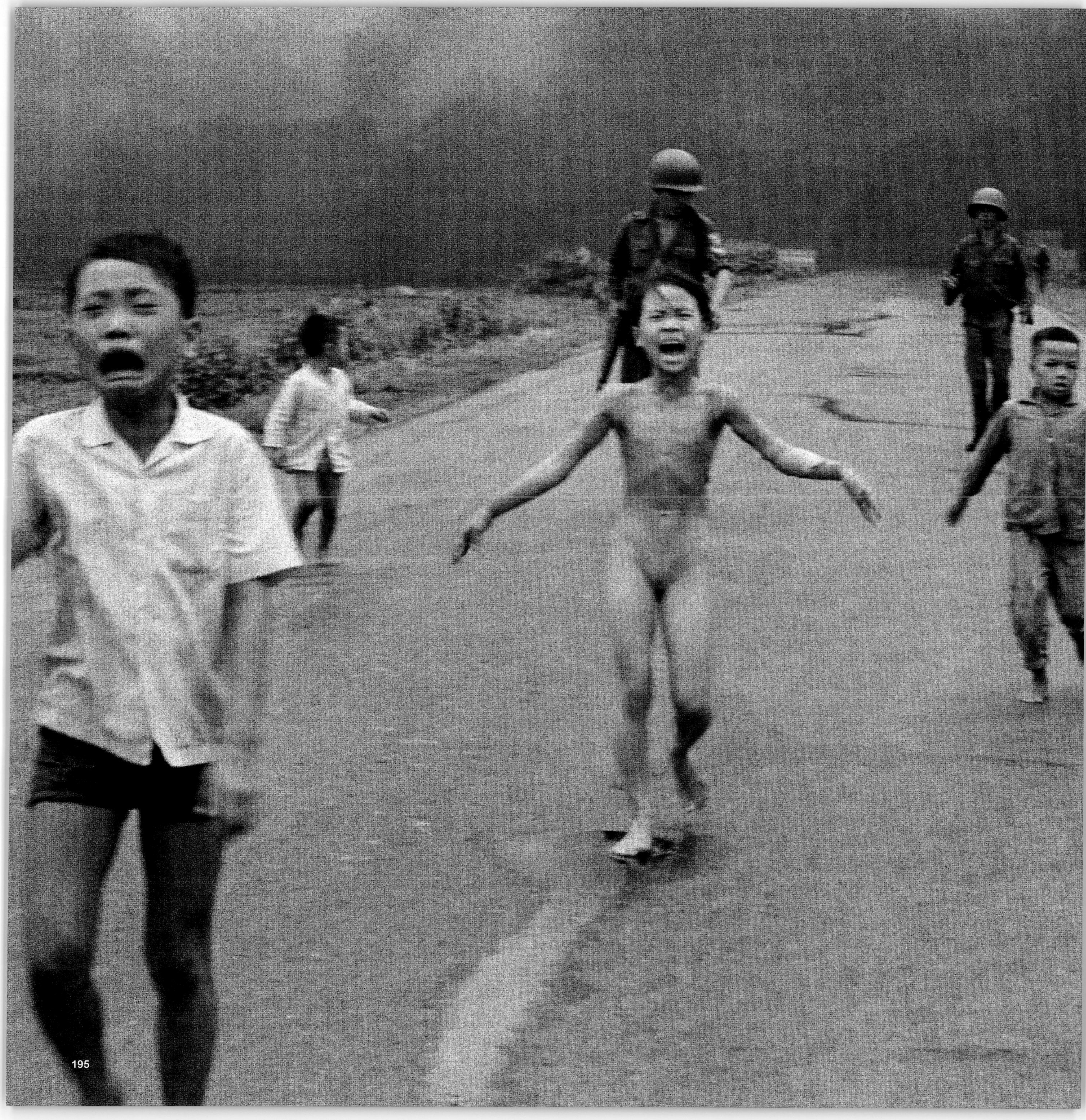

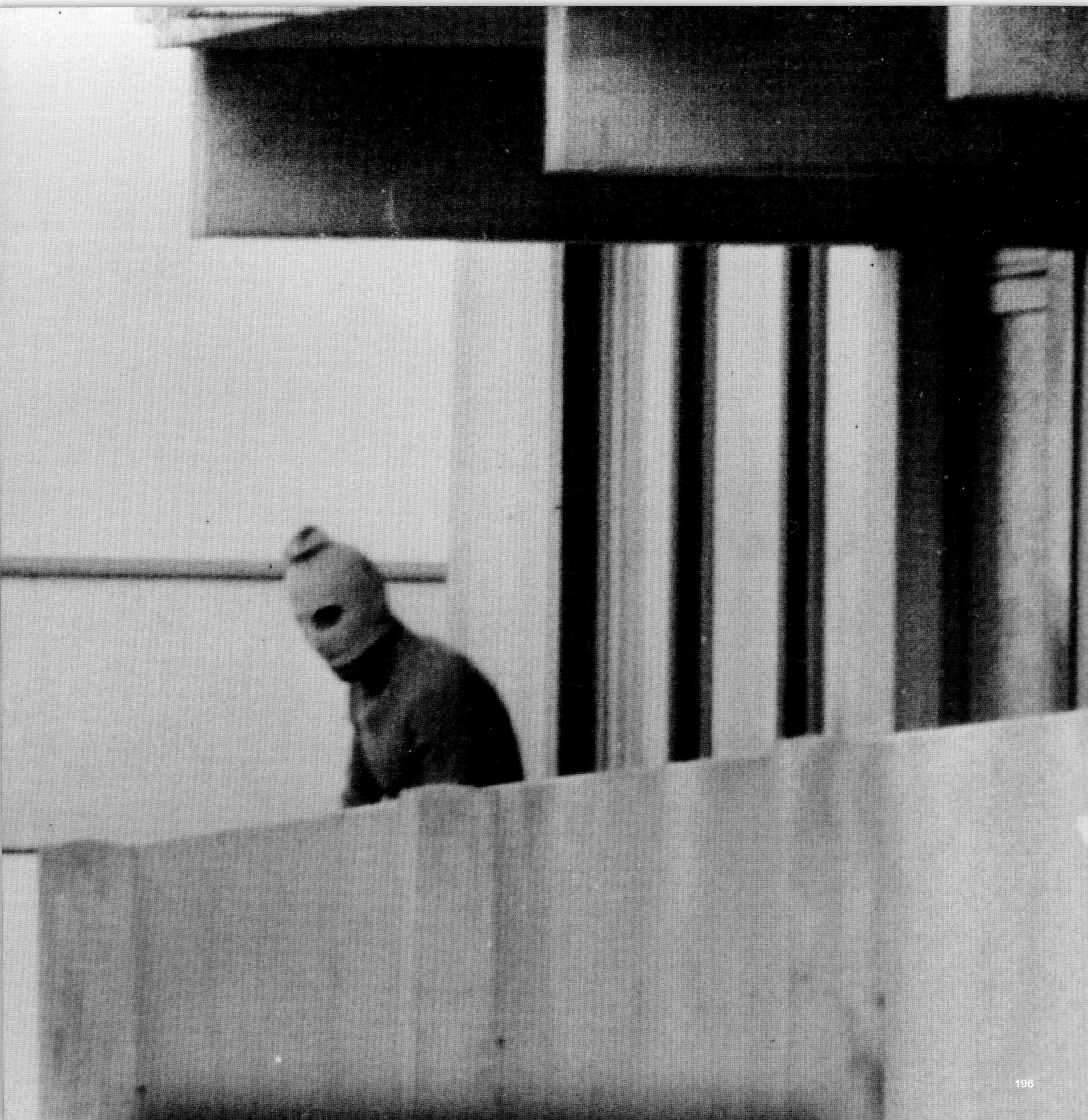

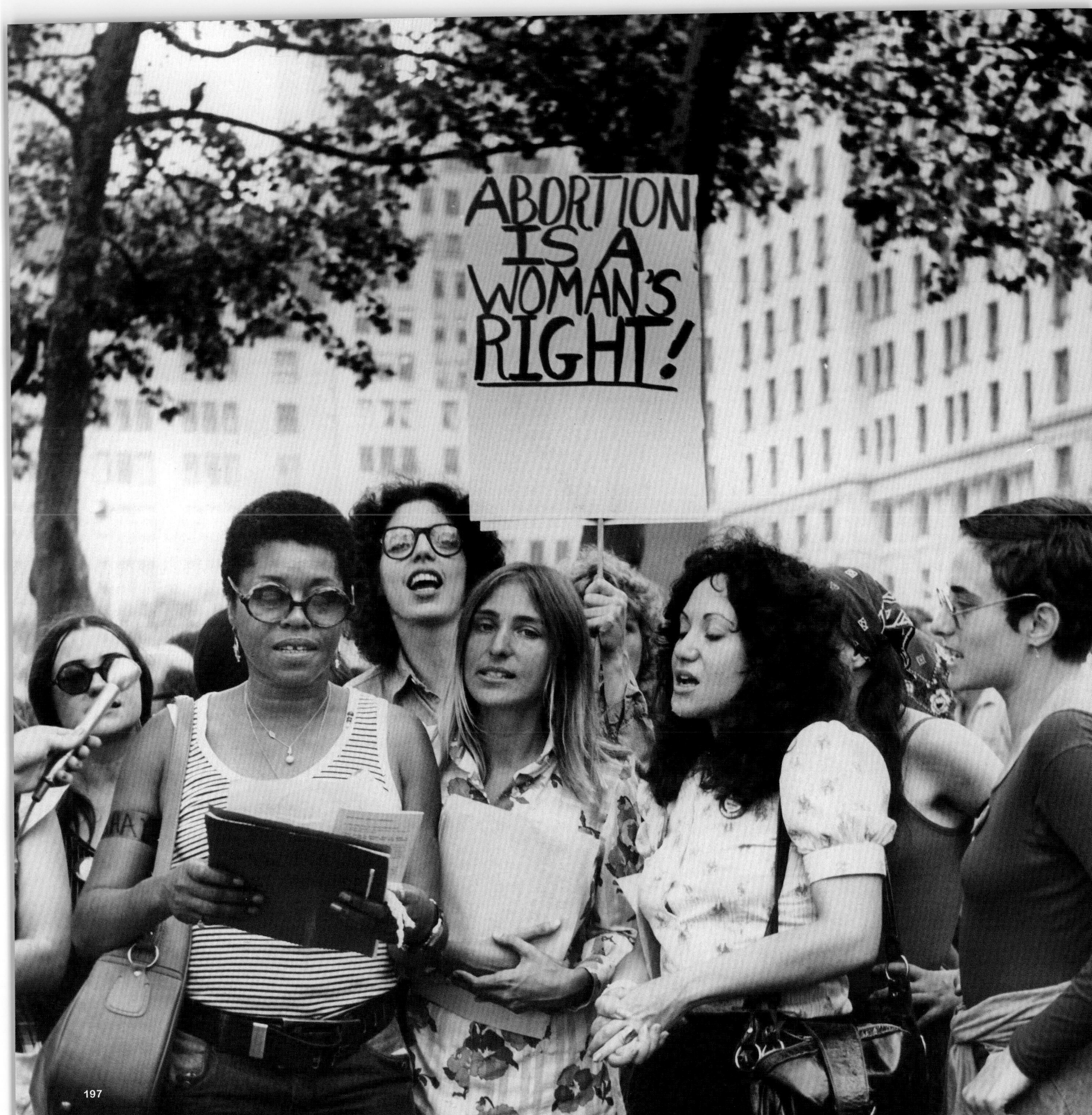
ABORTION
IS A
WOMAN'S
RIGHT!

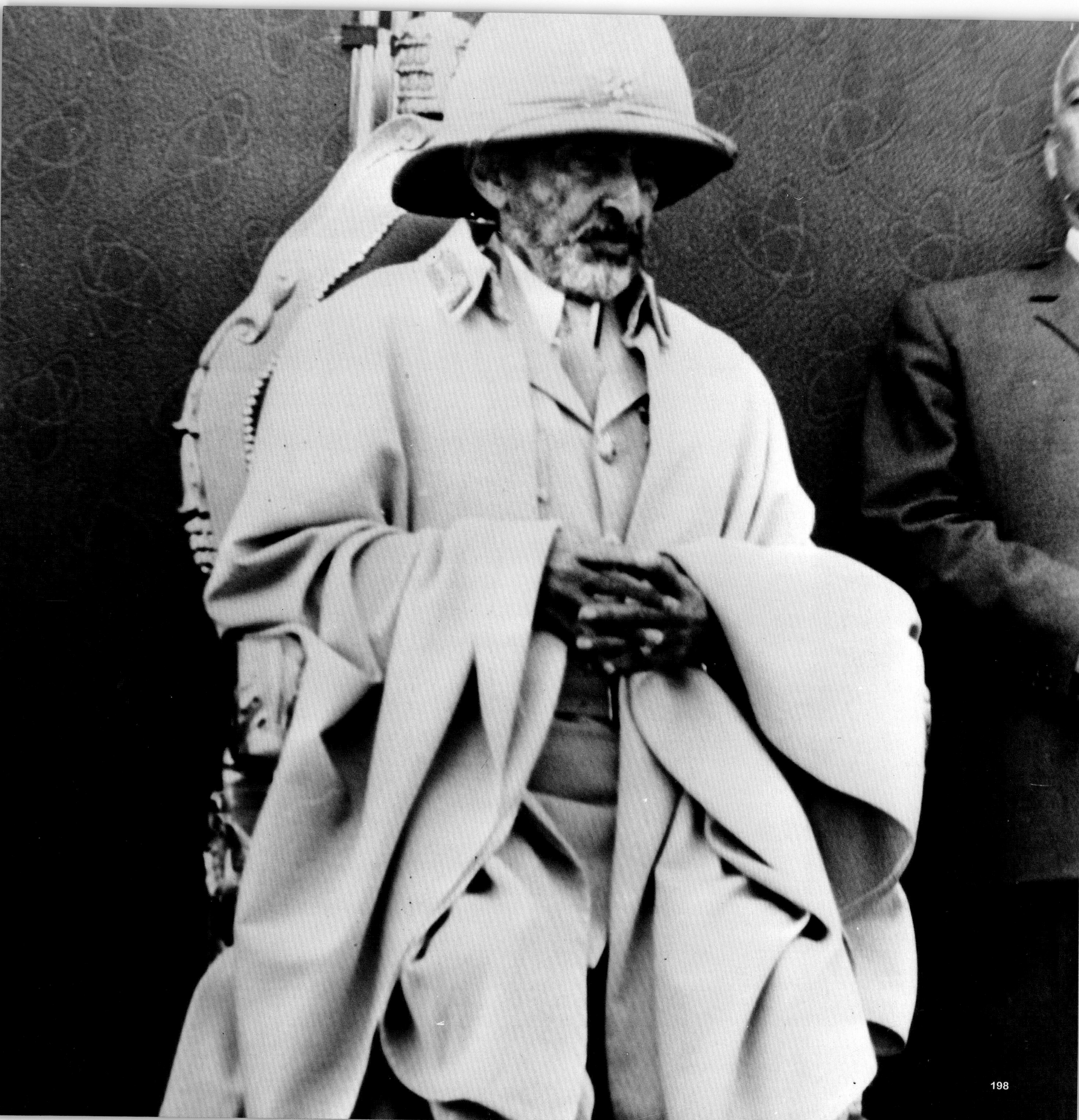

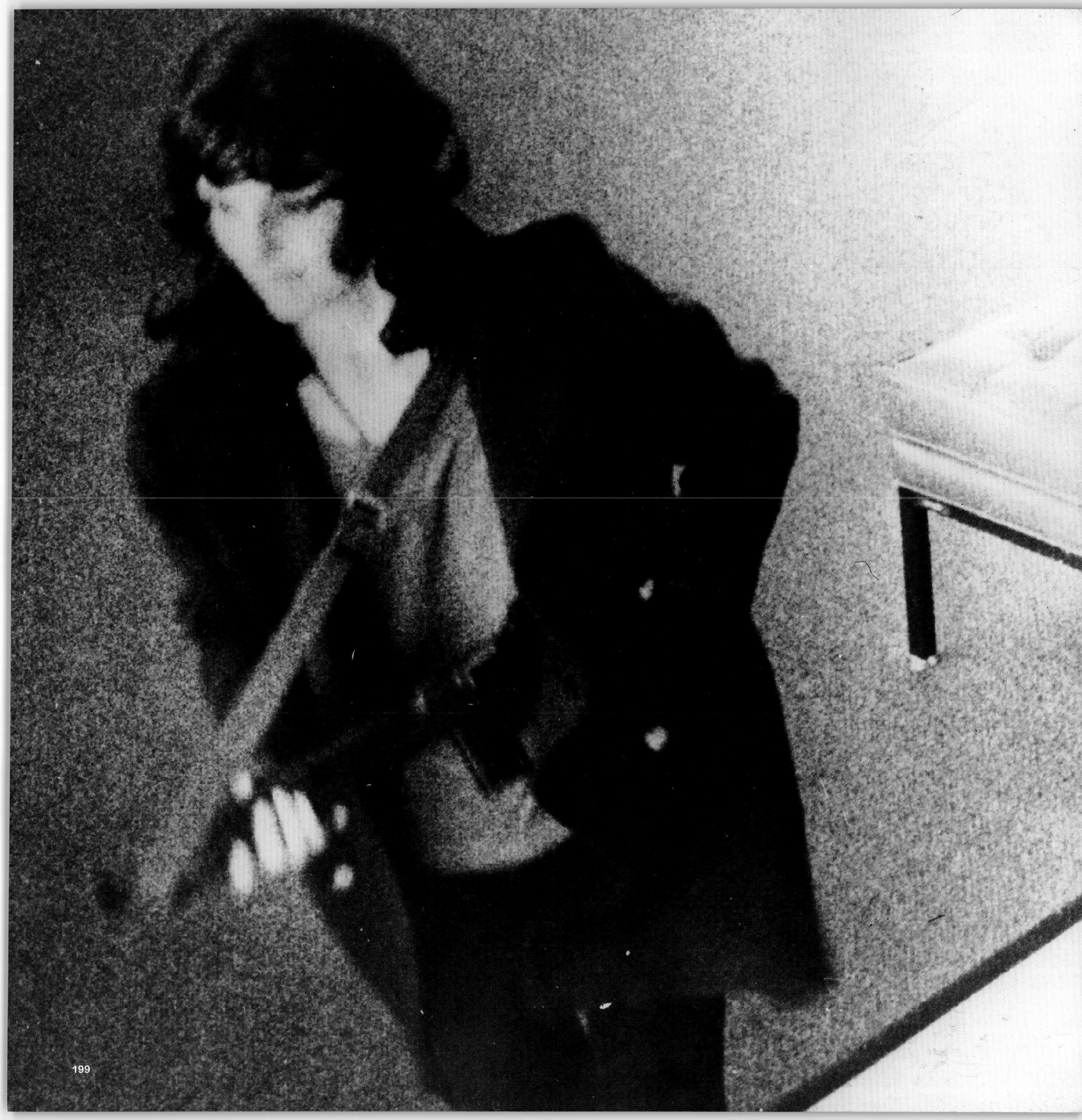

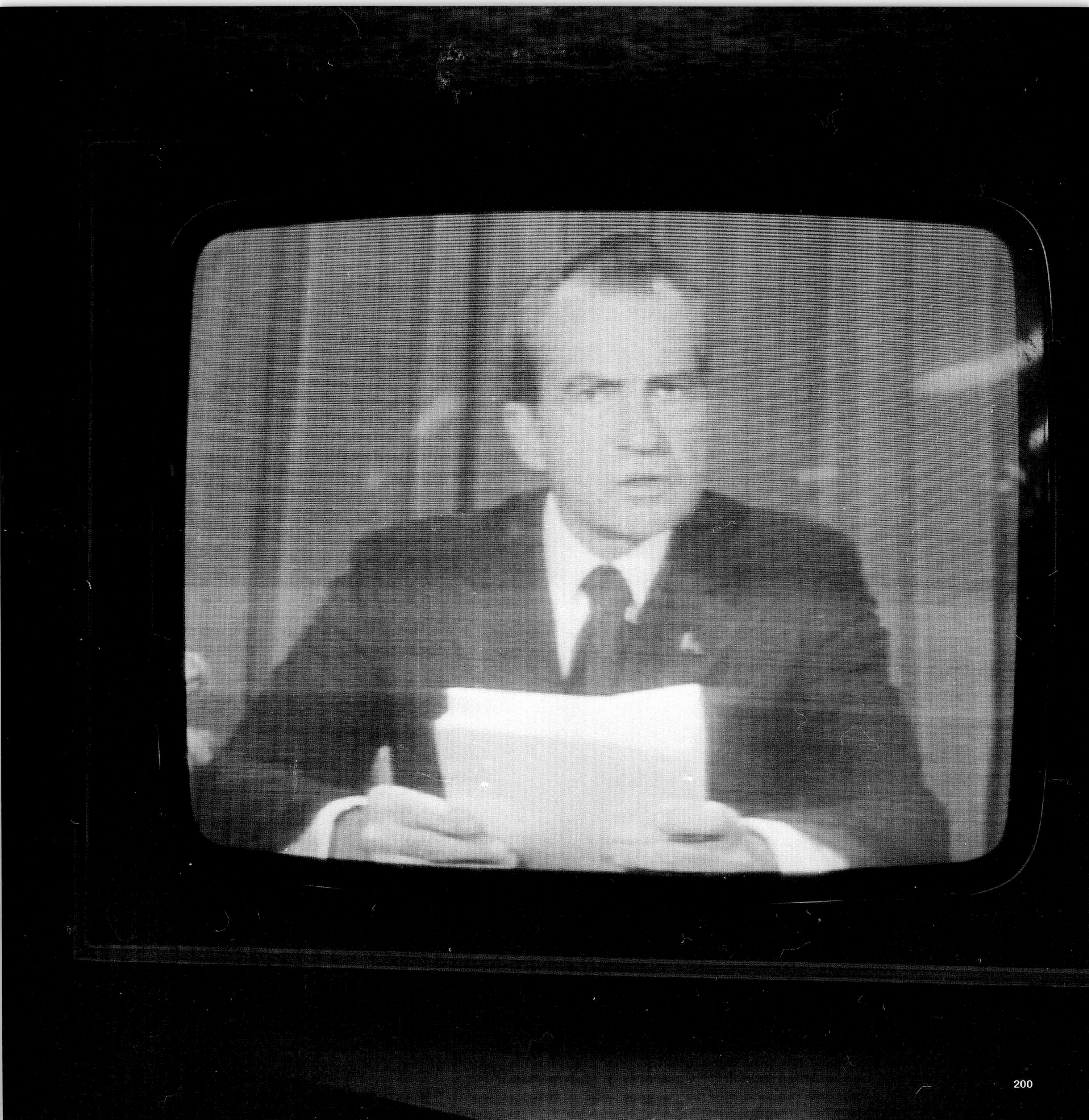

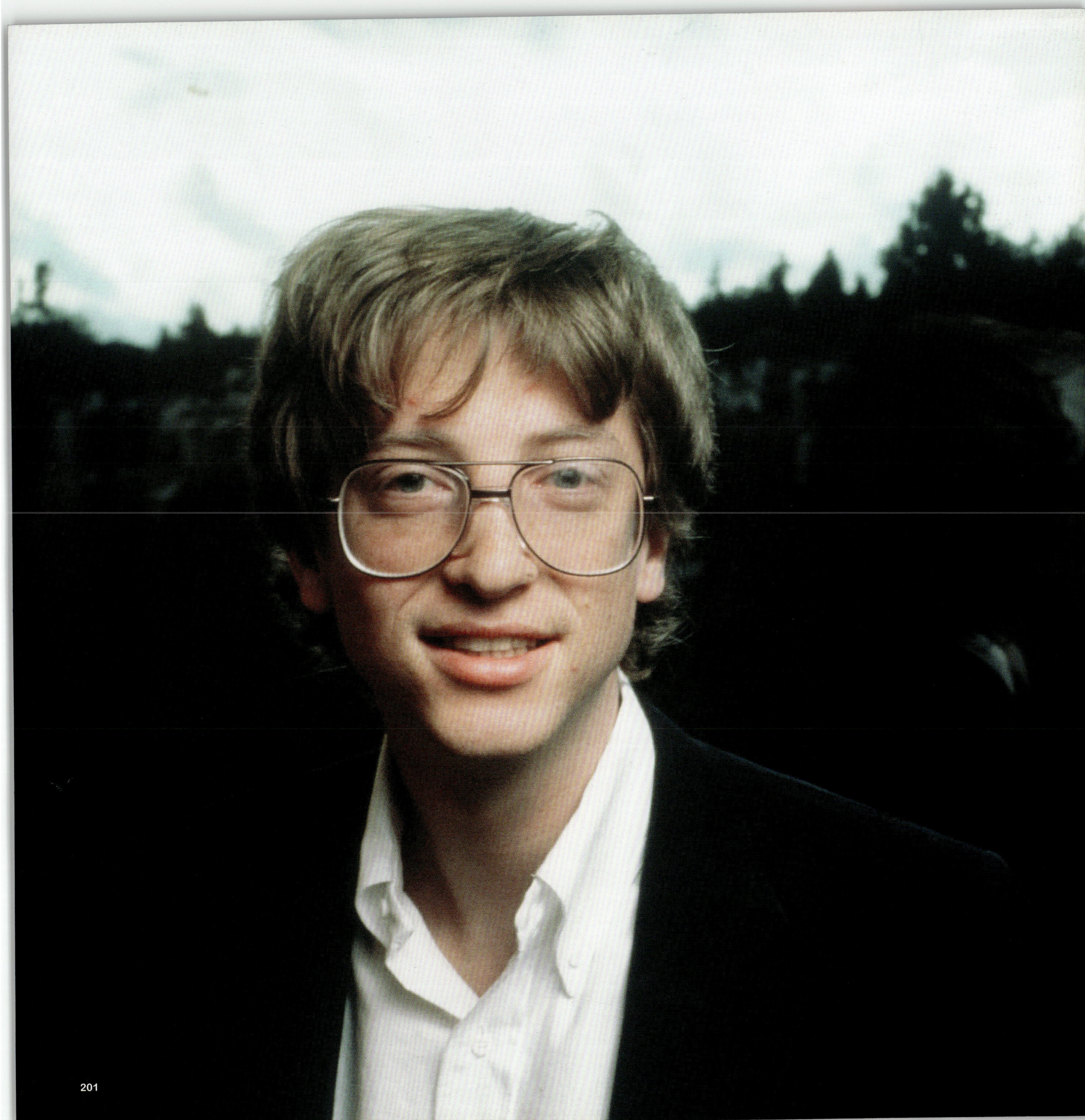

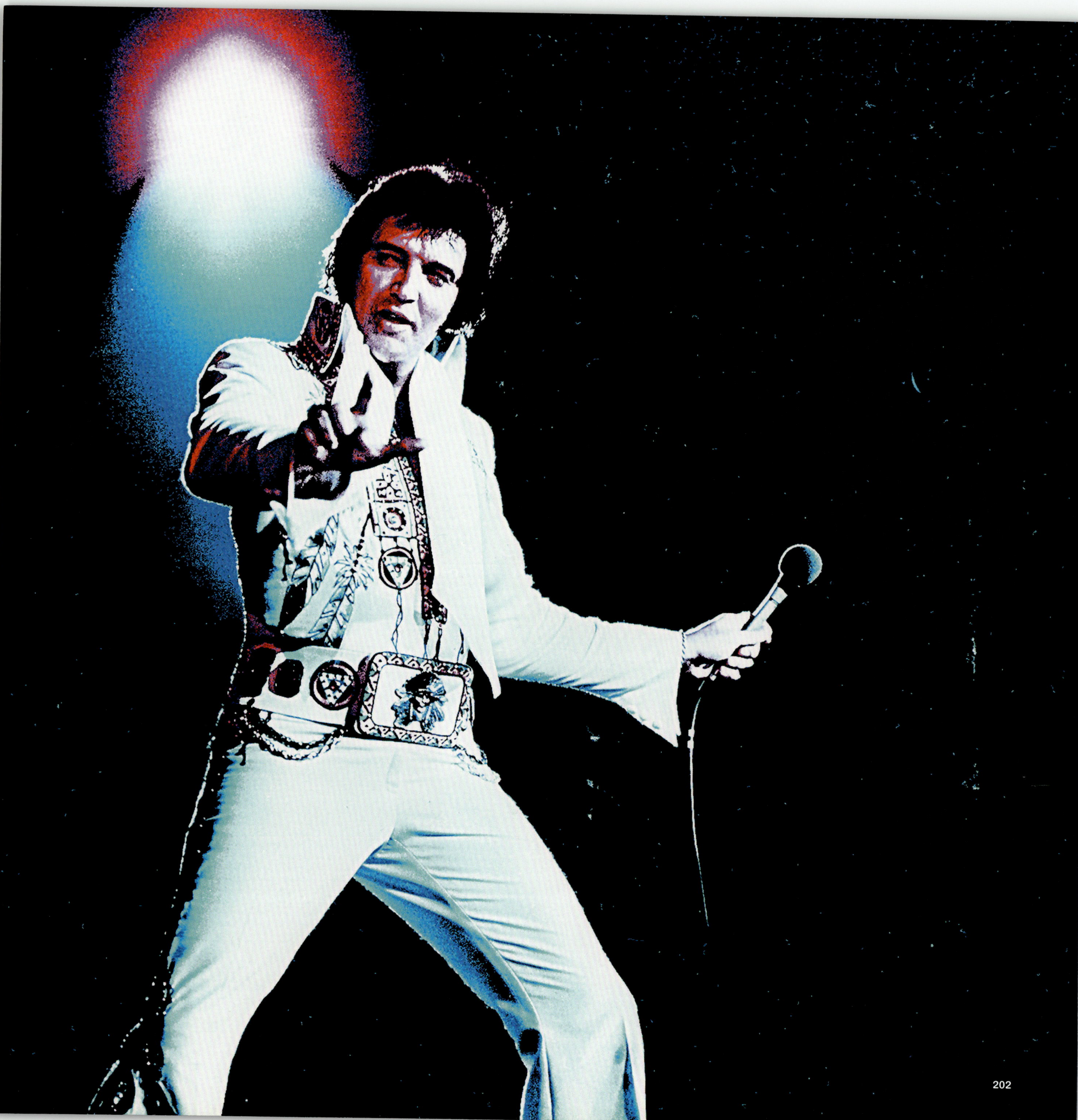

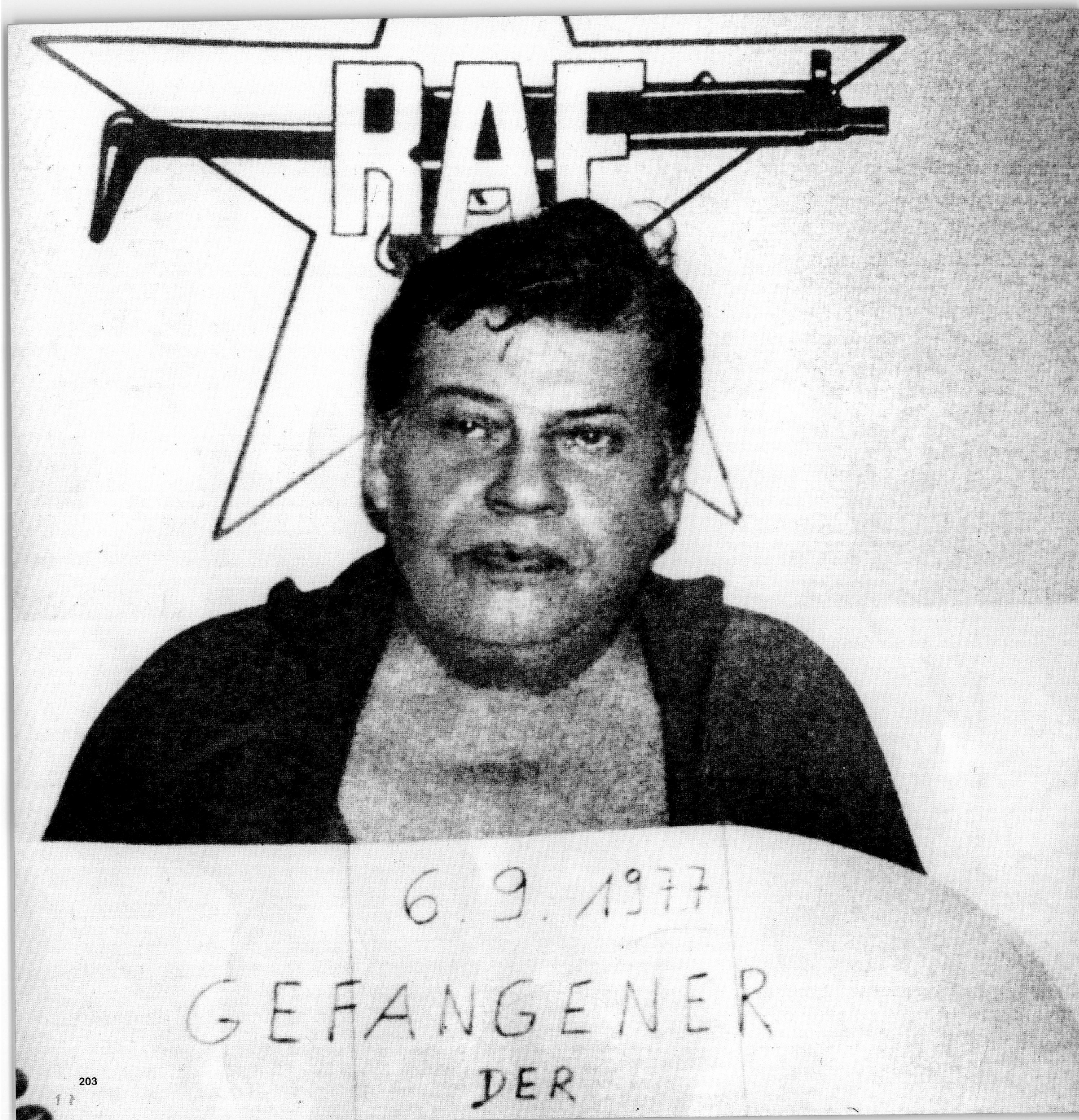
RAF
6.9.1977
GEFANGENER
DER

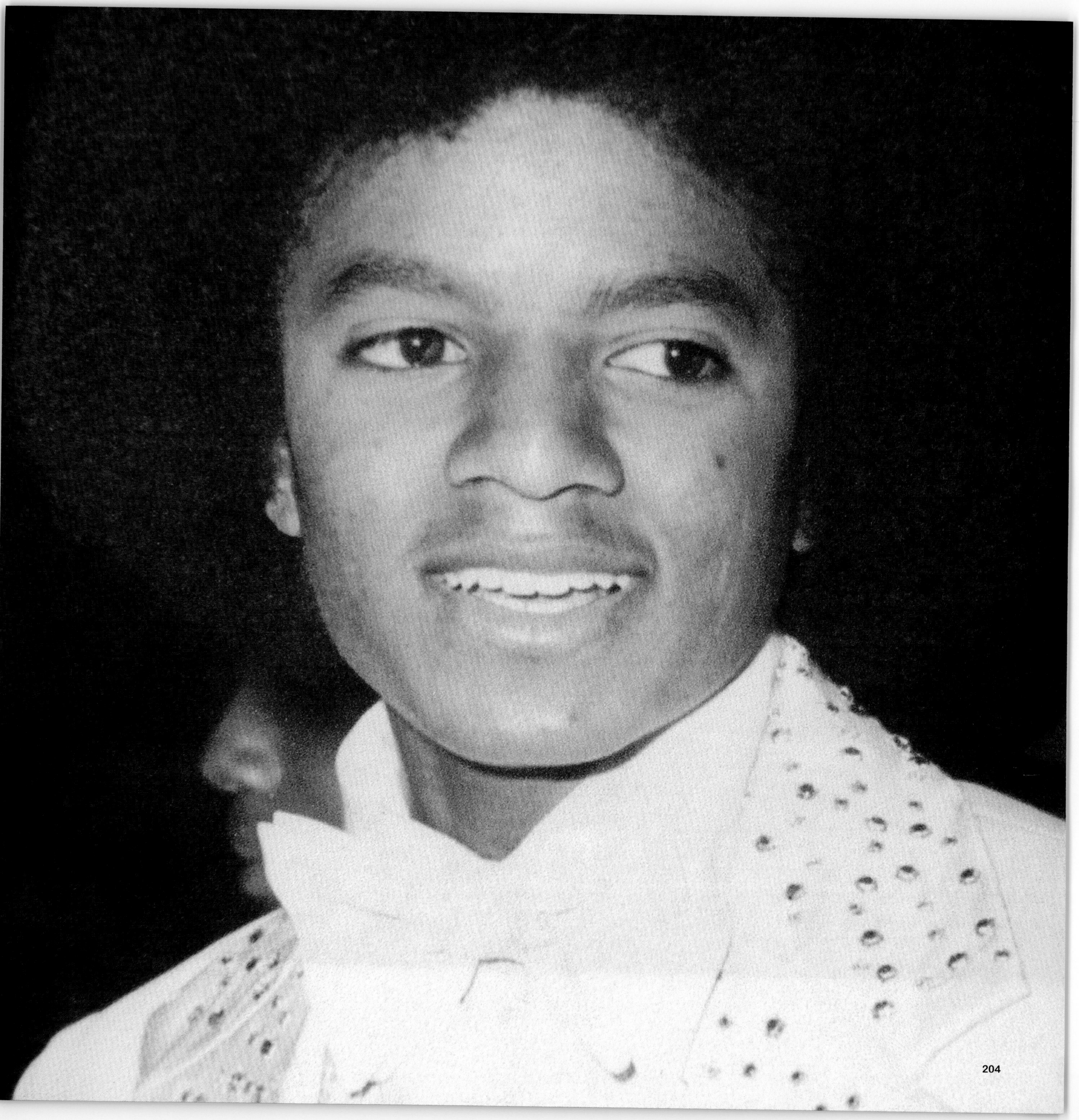

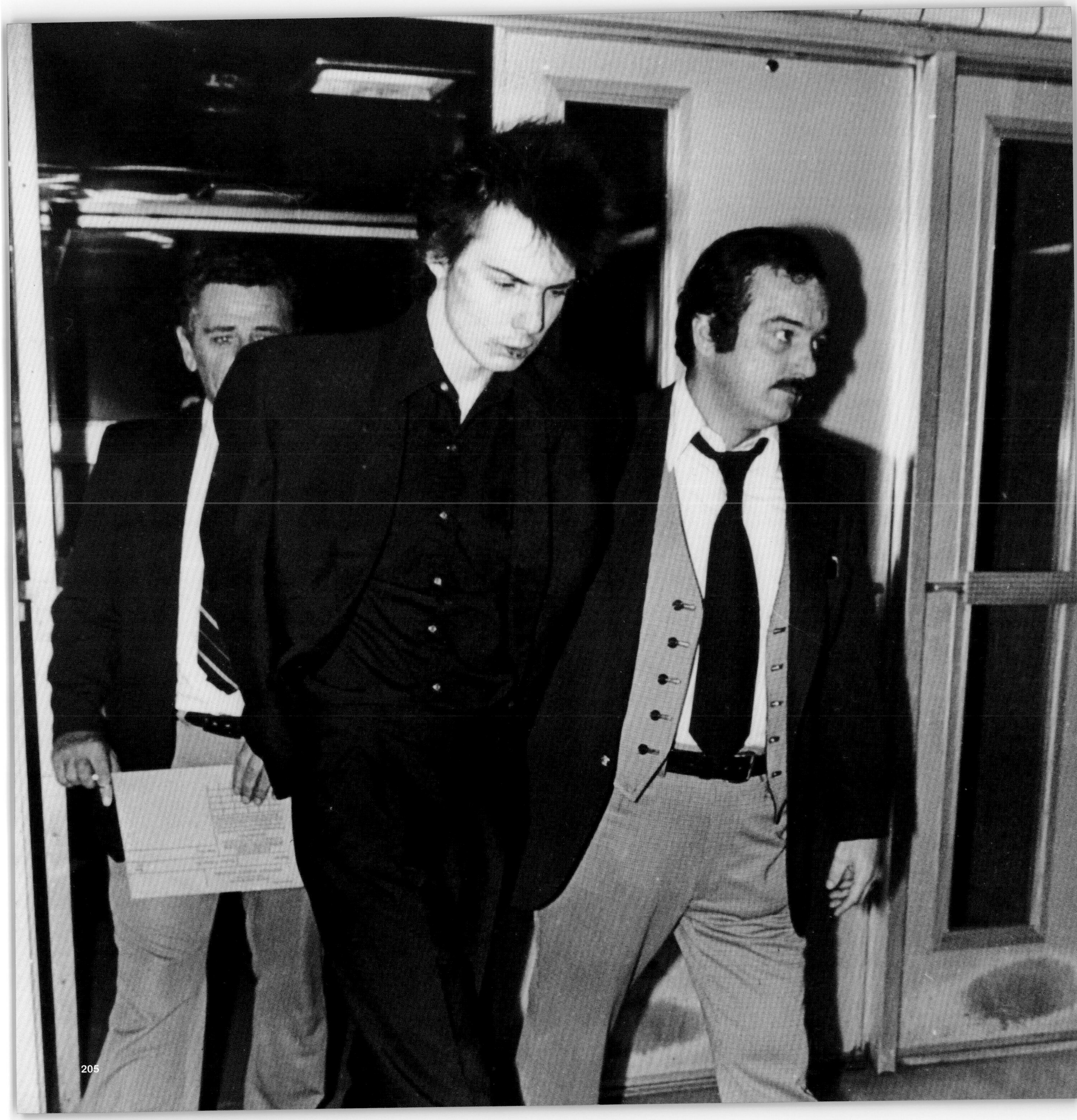

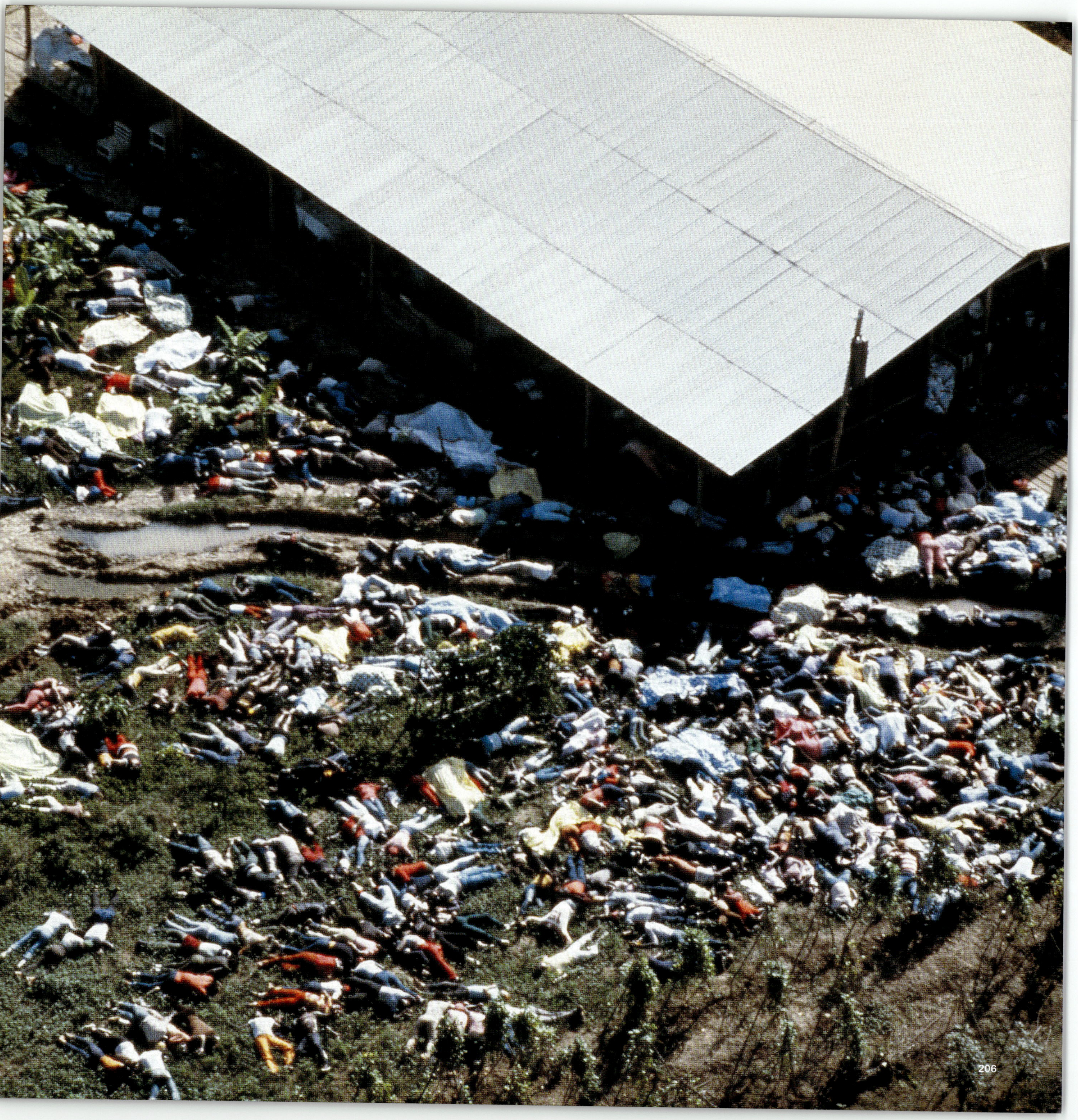

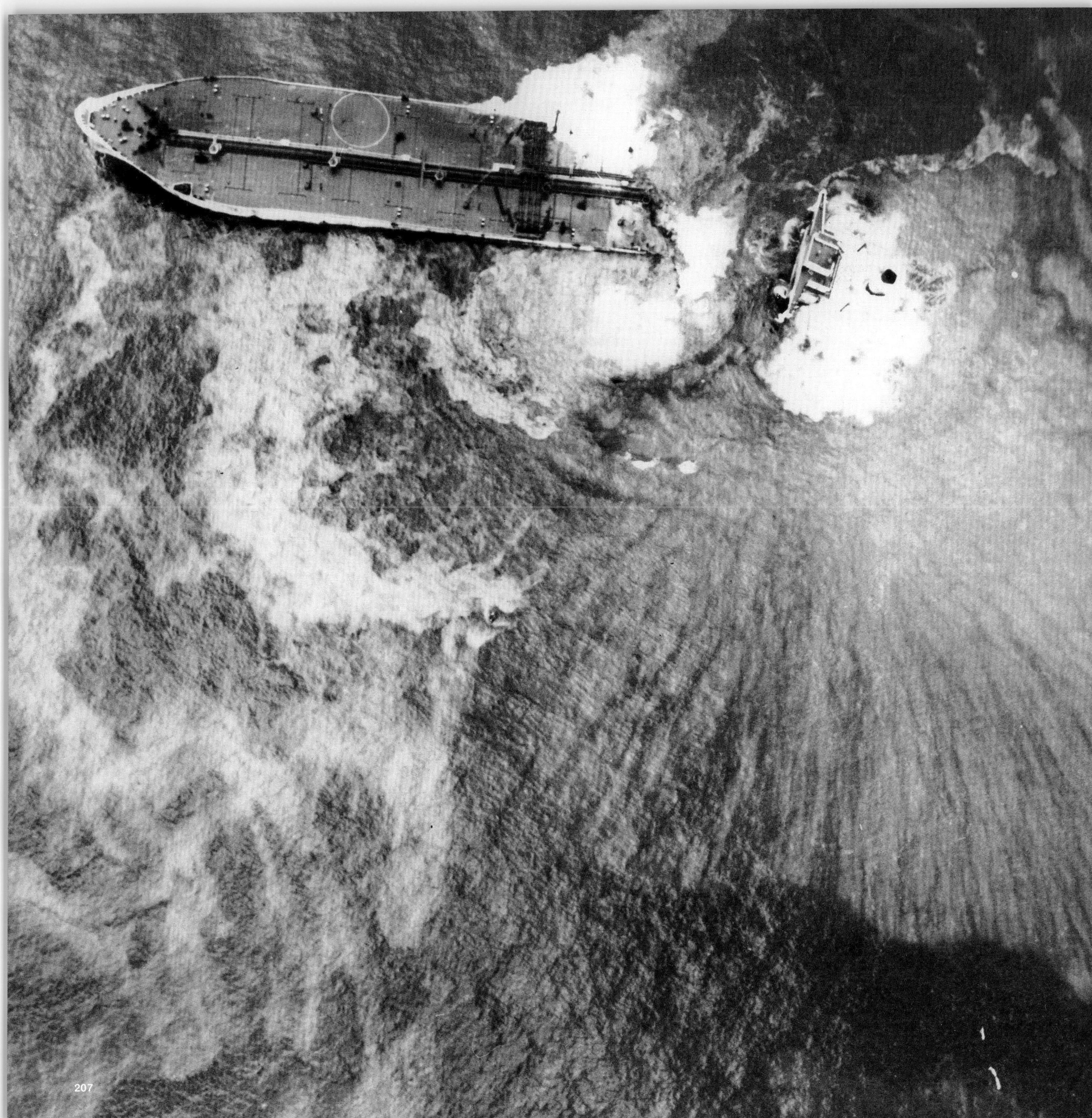

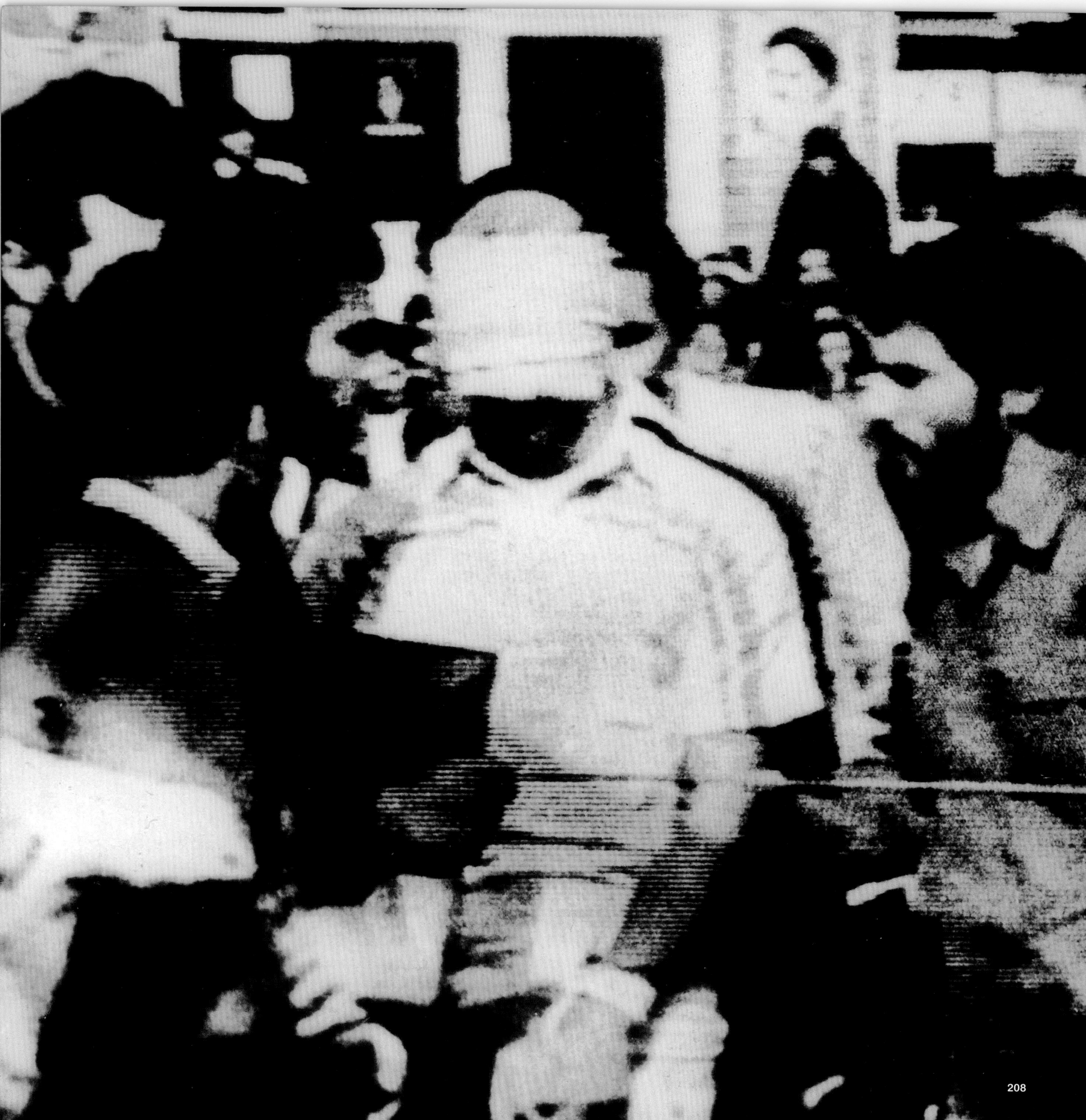

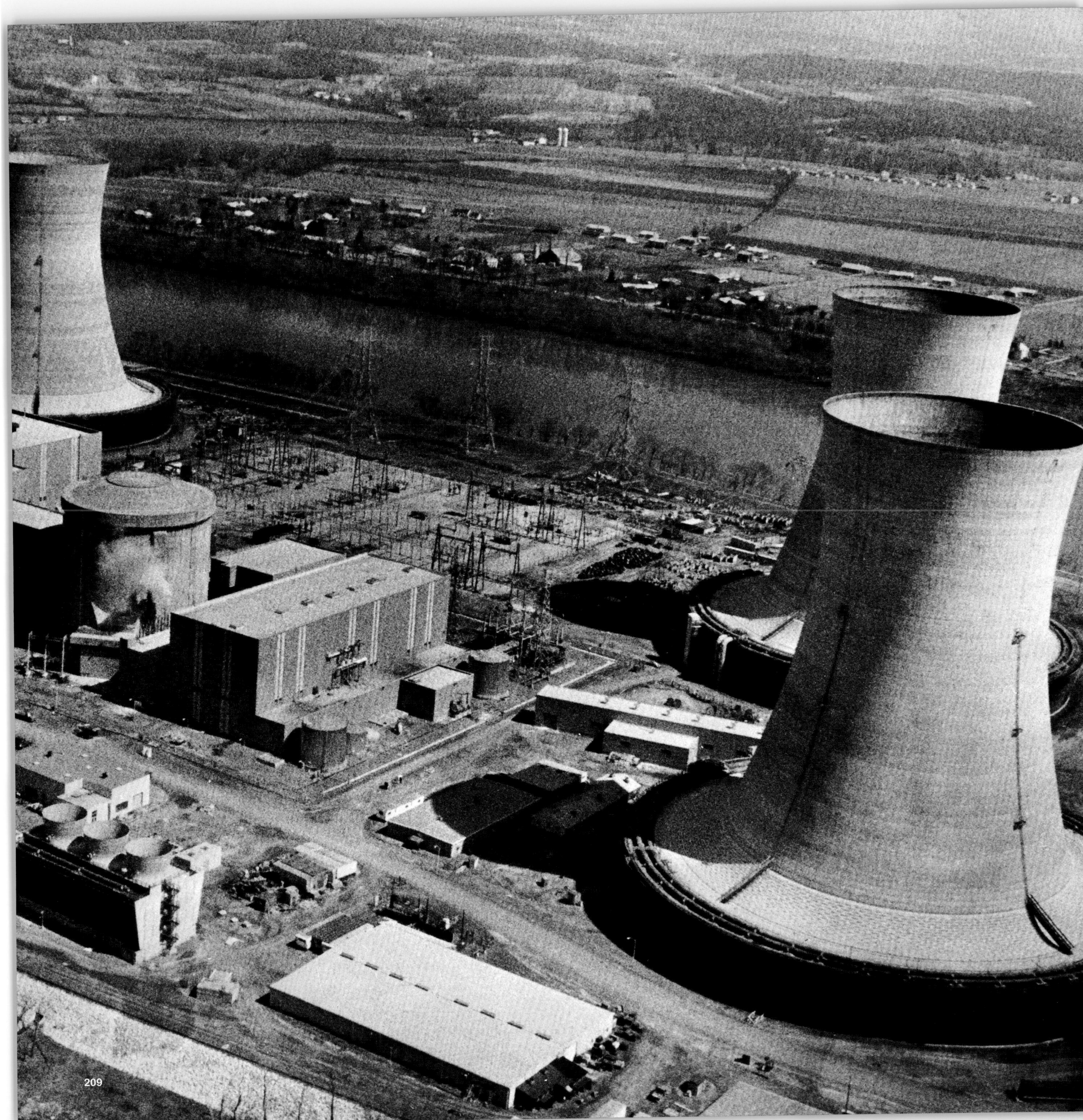

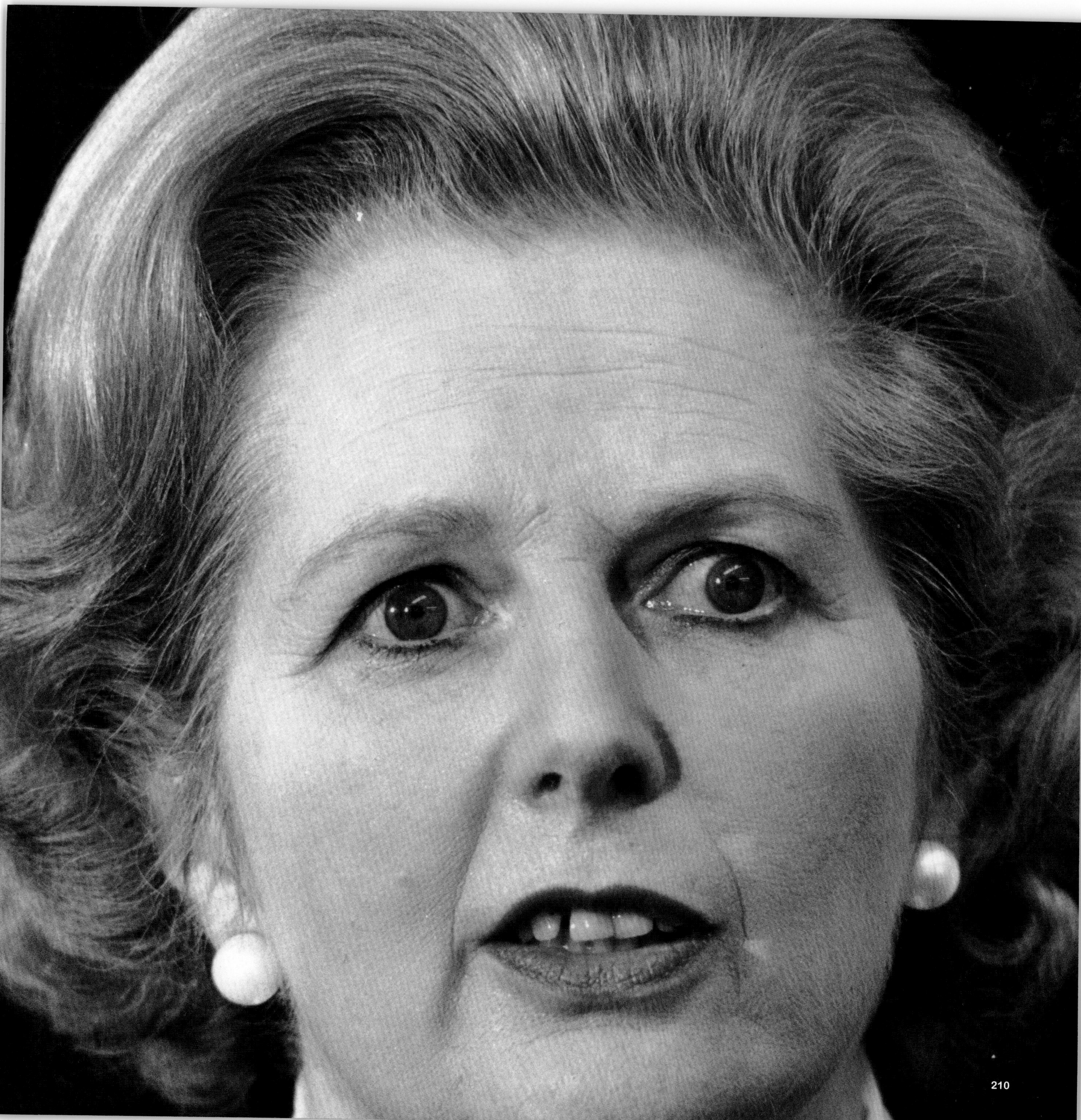

EVENING Times

SCOTLAND'S GREATEST EVENING PAPER

No. 32,848 Tuesday, December 9, 1980 12p

Ex-Beatle dies in hail of bullets

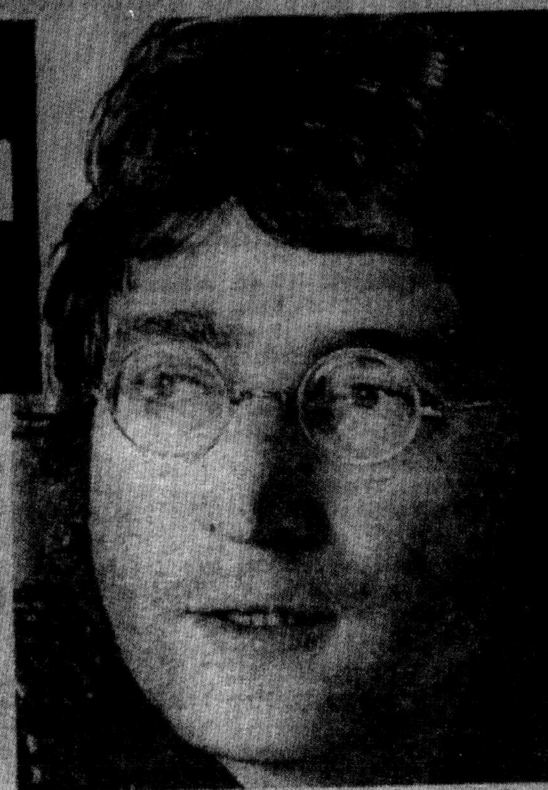

JOHN LENNON SHOT DEAD

EX-BEATLE John Lennon died in a hai bullets early today outside his lux New York home.

Police said he had been shot at le five times at point-blank range by a cra autograph hunter.

The murderer had apparently been lying in for Lennon for several hours. When the 40-yea superstar and his Japanese wife Yoko Ono arrived limousine he tackled them.

"It seems that suddenly this man pulled a gun fired at Mr Lennon," said police. "He was rushe hospital but died on the way."

Police later said that a resident of Honolulu, M David Chapman (25), had been charged with Lenn murder.

They said the murder weapon was a .38 revolver.

A passer-by said Chapman, "a pudgy kind of man," had a smirk on his face as police led him away.

A police spokesman said

By FRE WEHNE

New York.

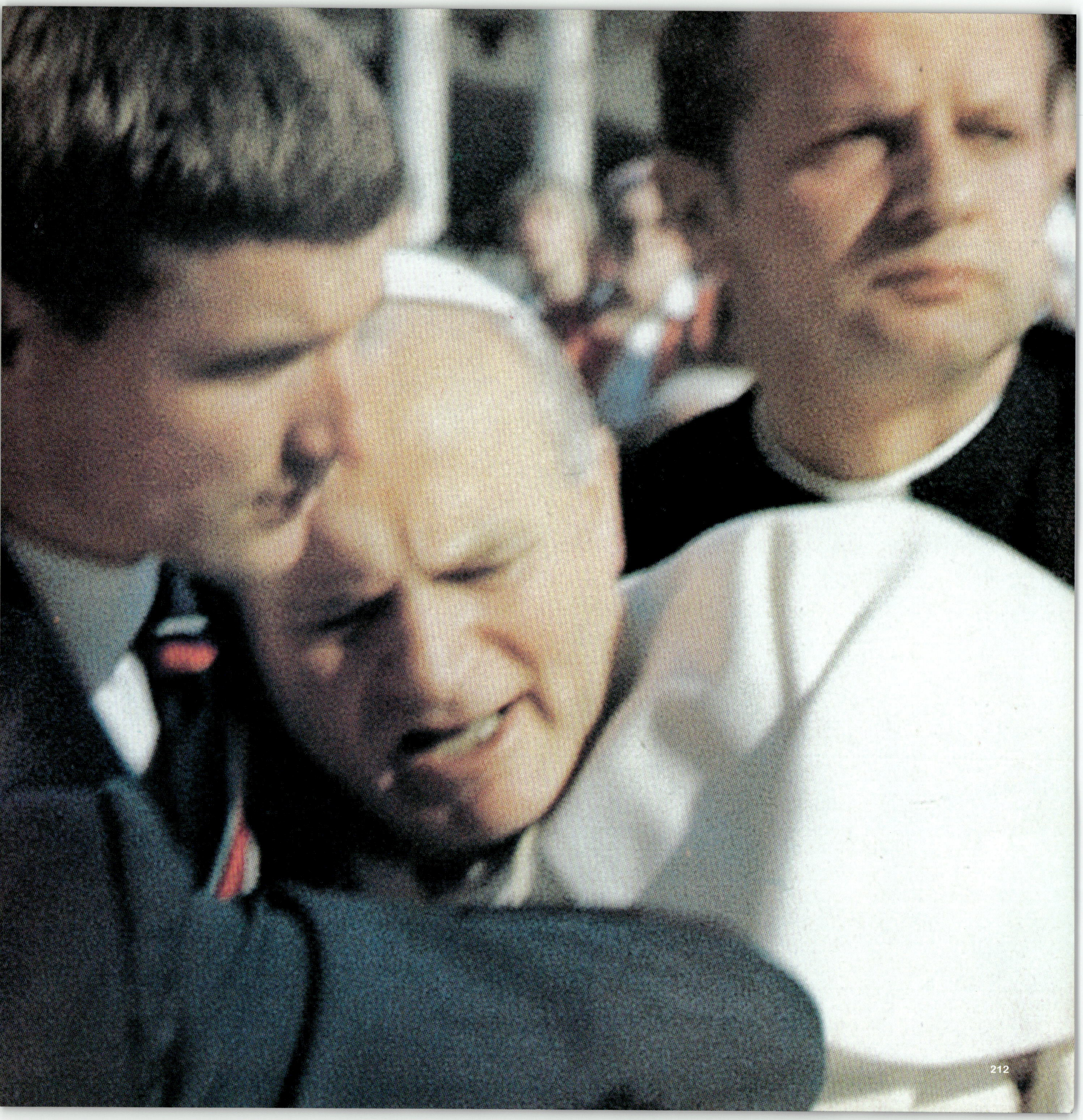

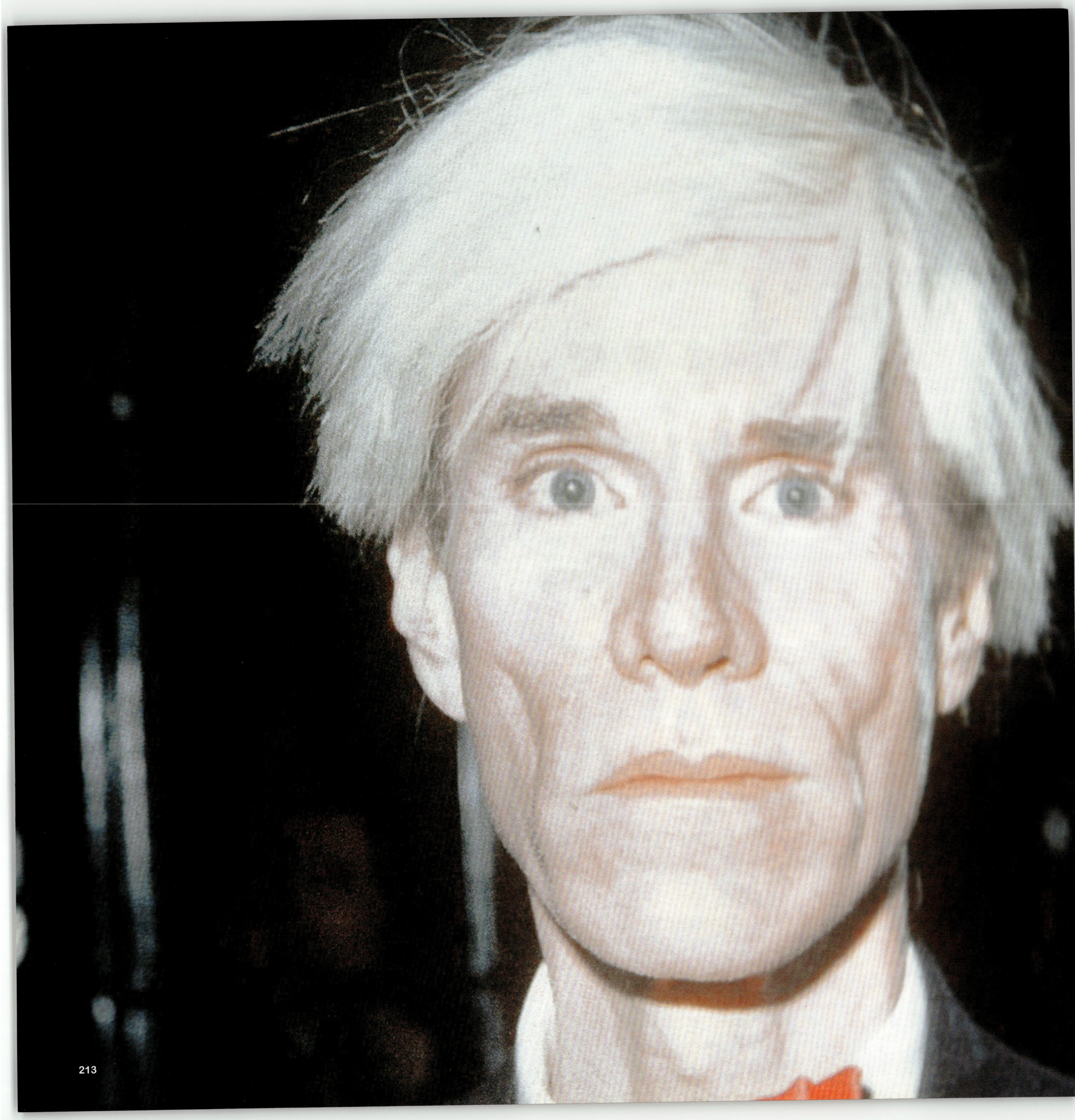

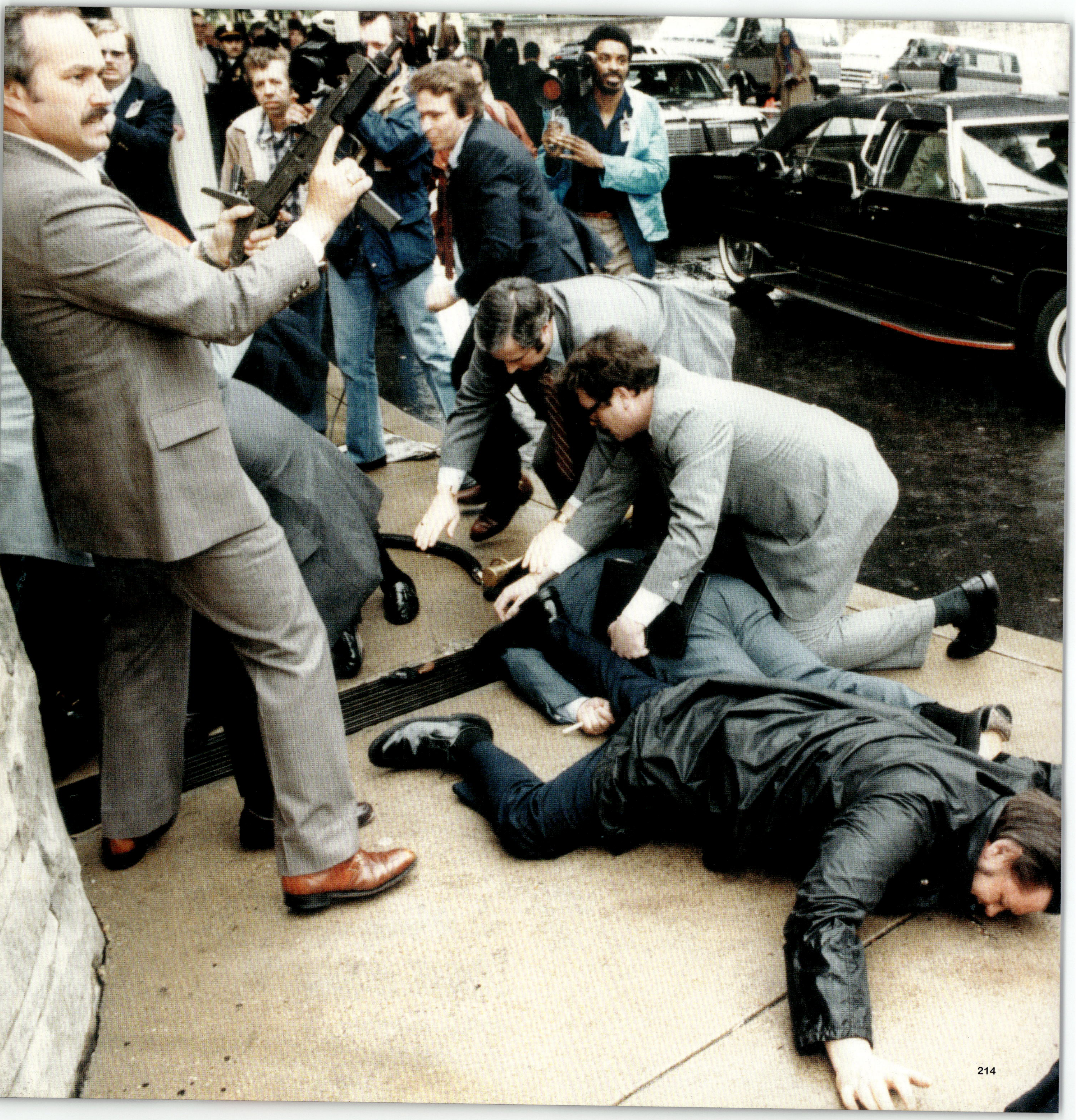

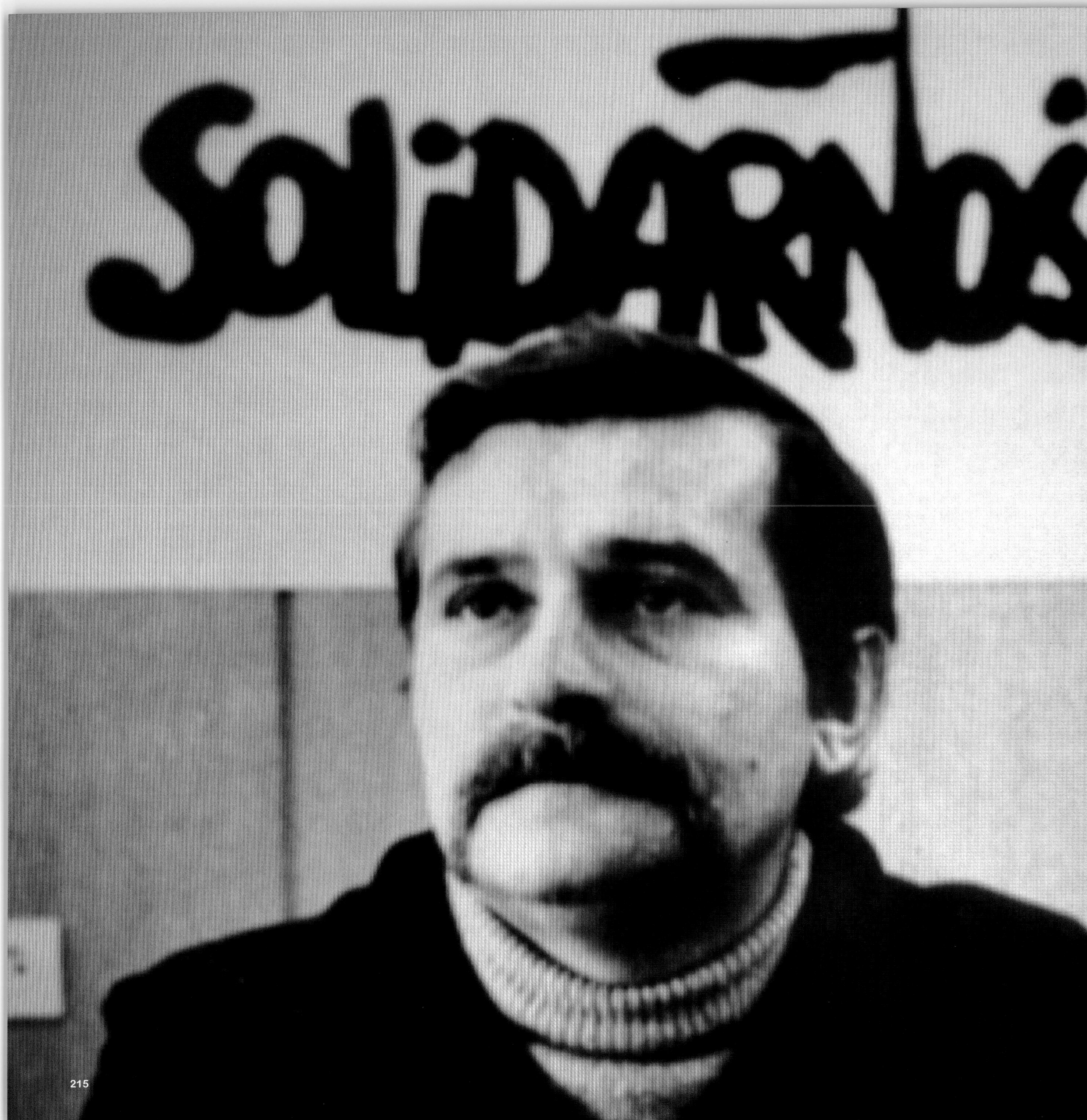

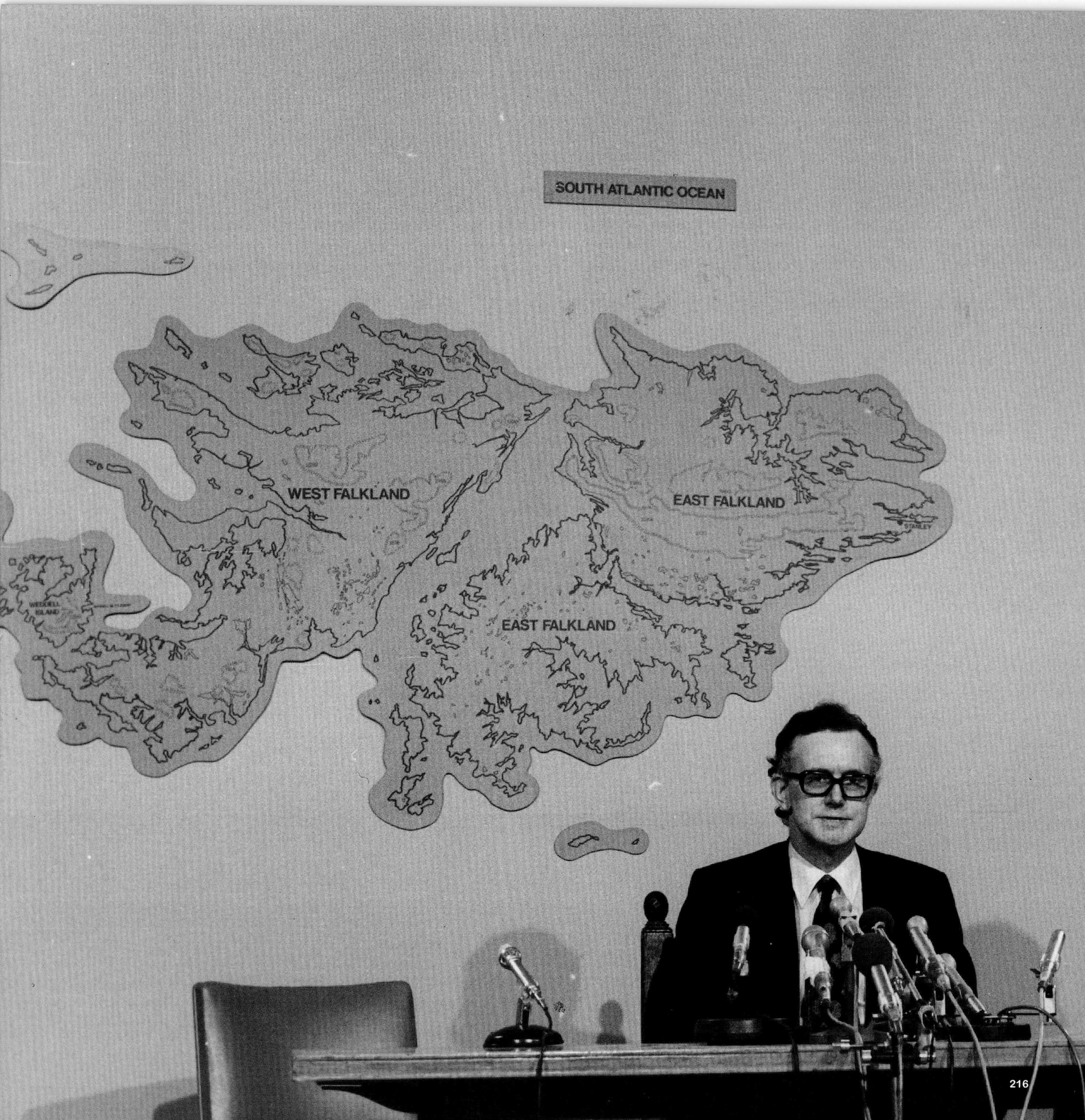
SOUTH ATLANTIC OCEAN
WEST FALKLAND
EAST FALKLAND
EAST FALKLAND

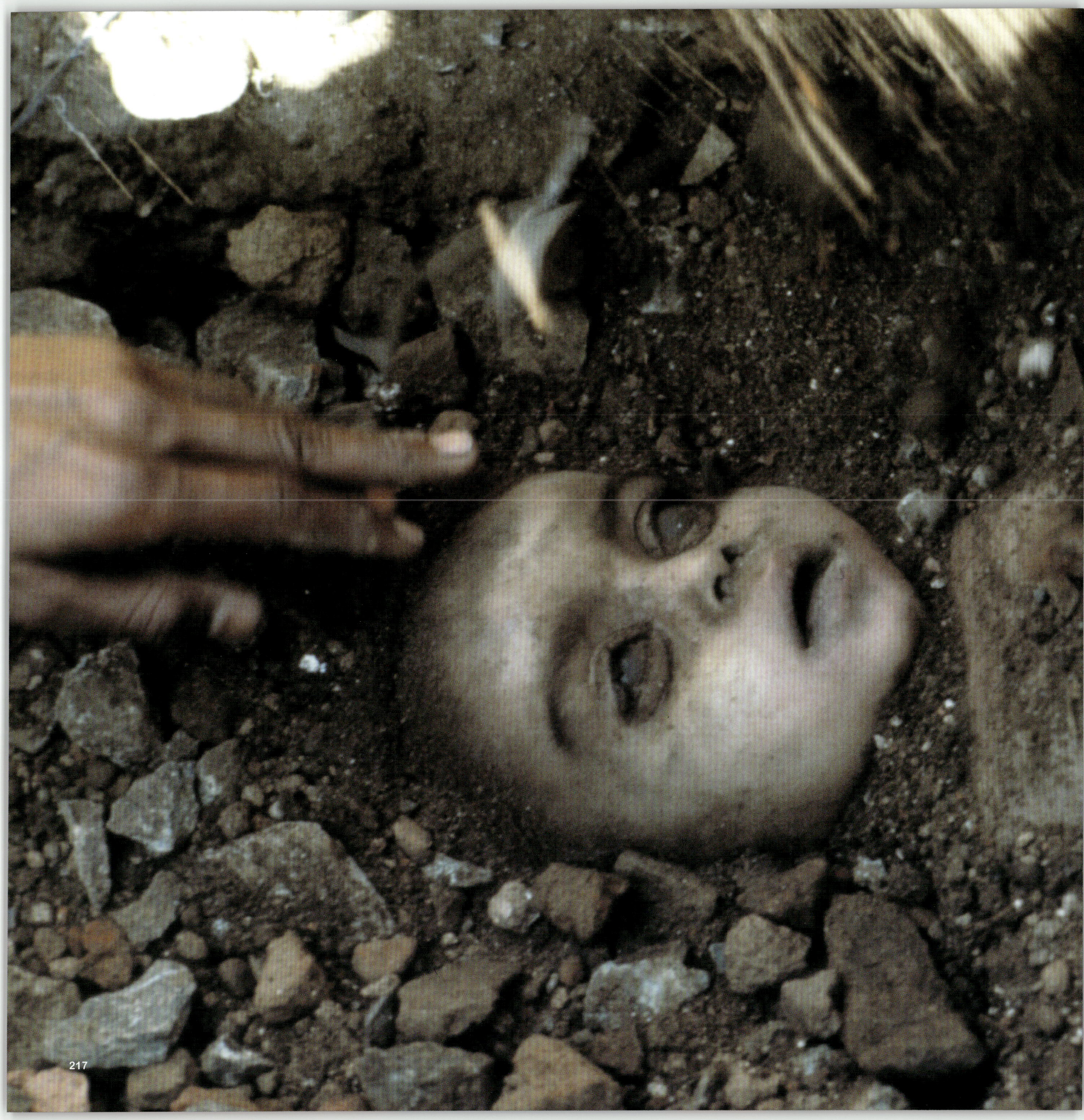

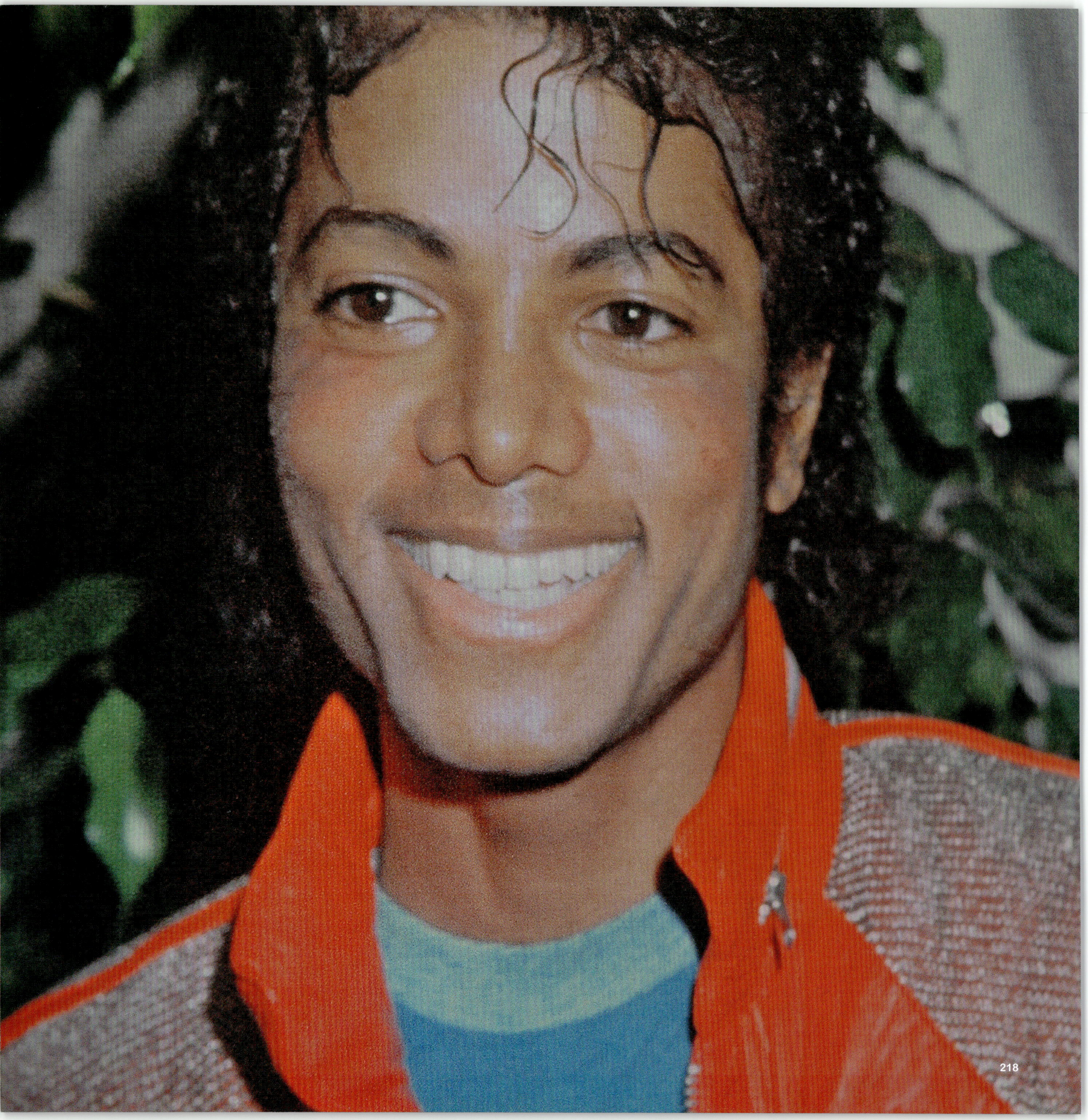

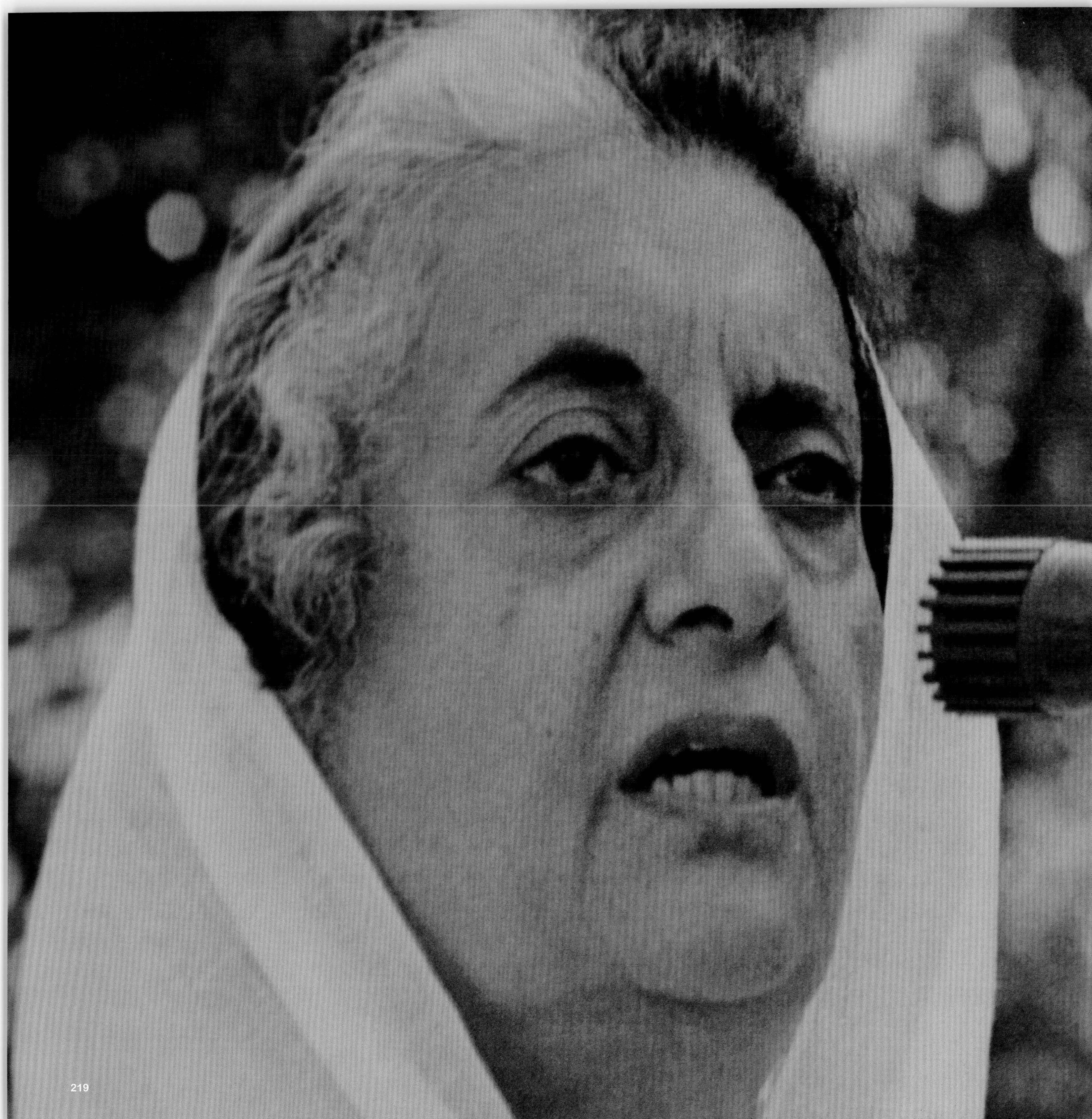

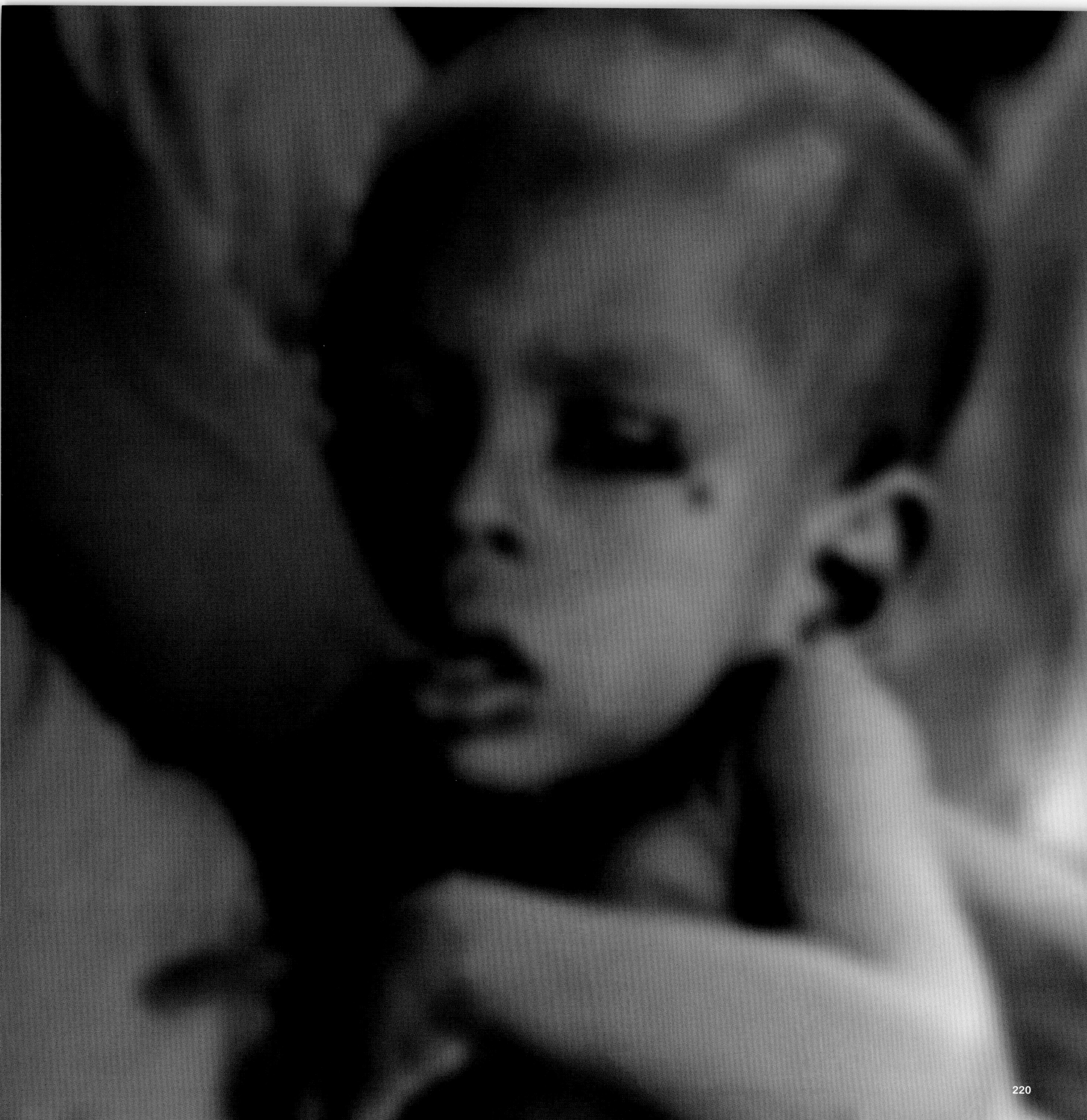

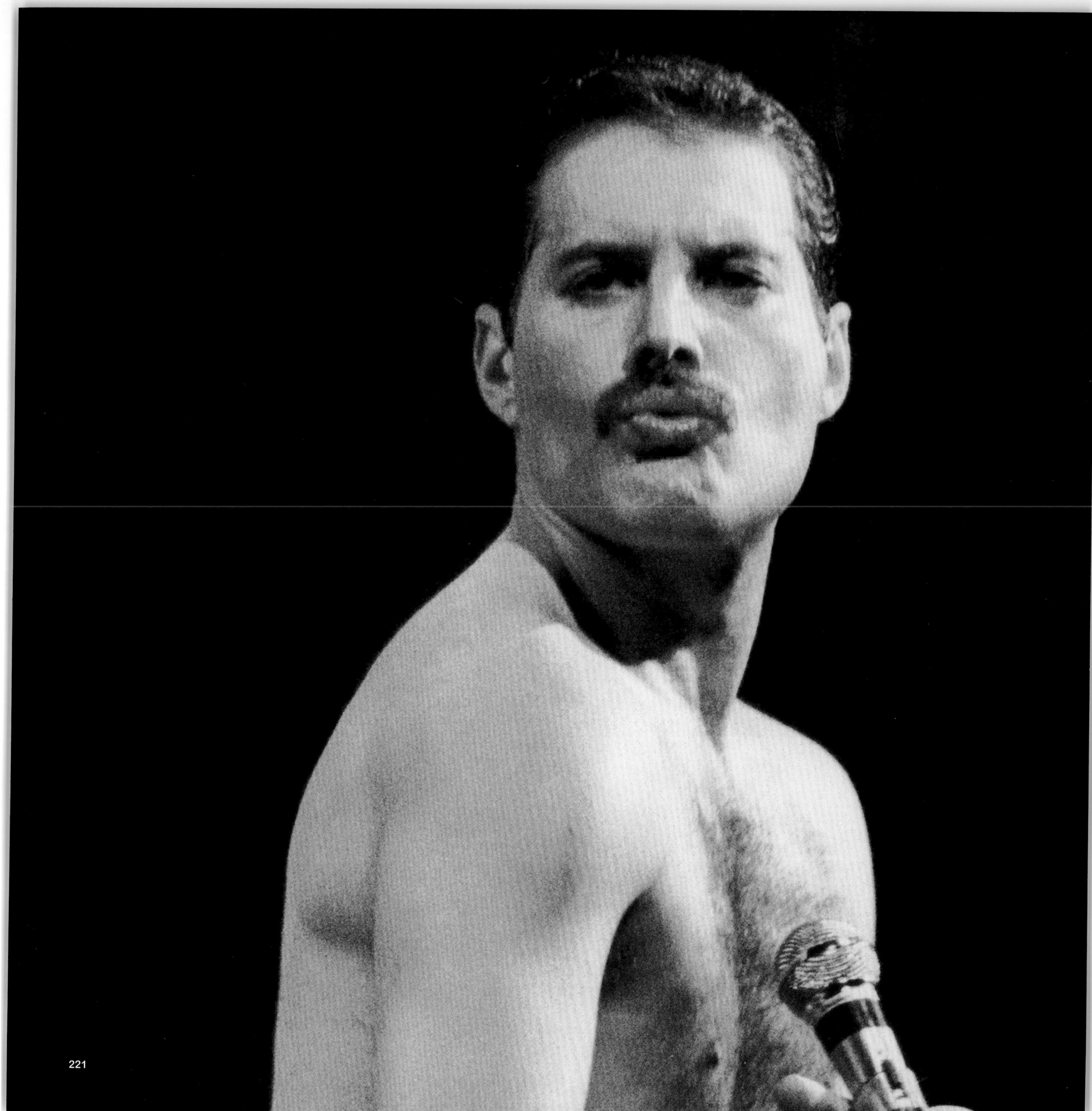

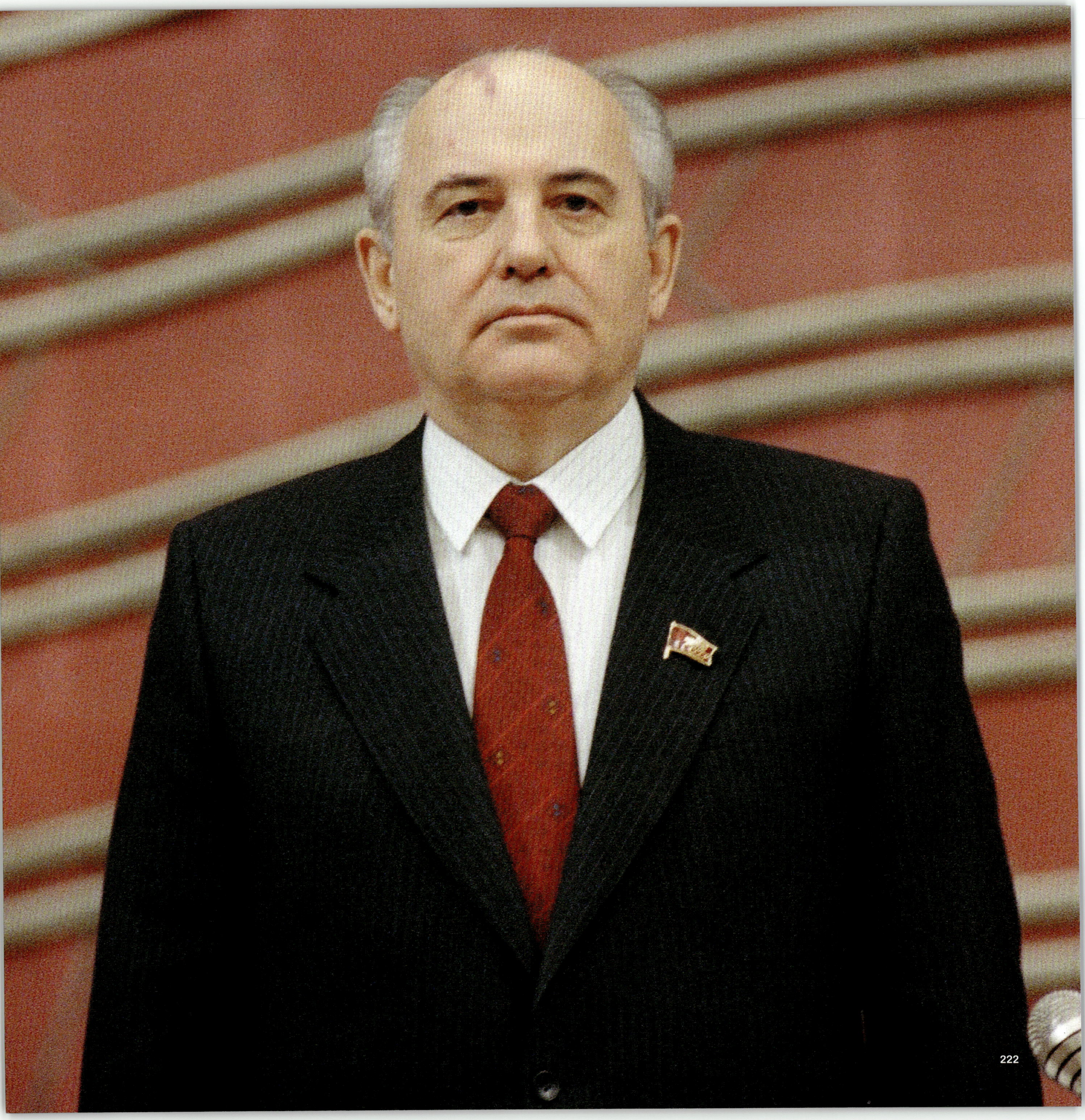

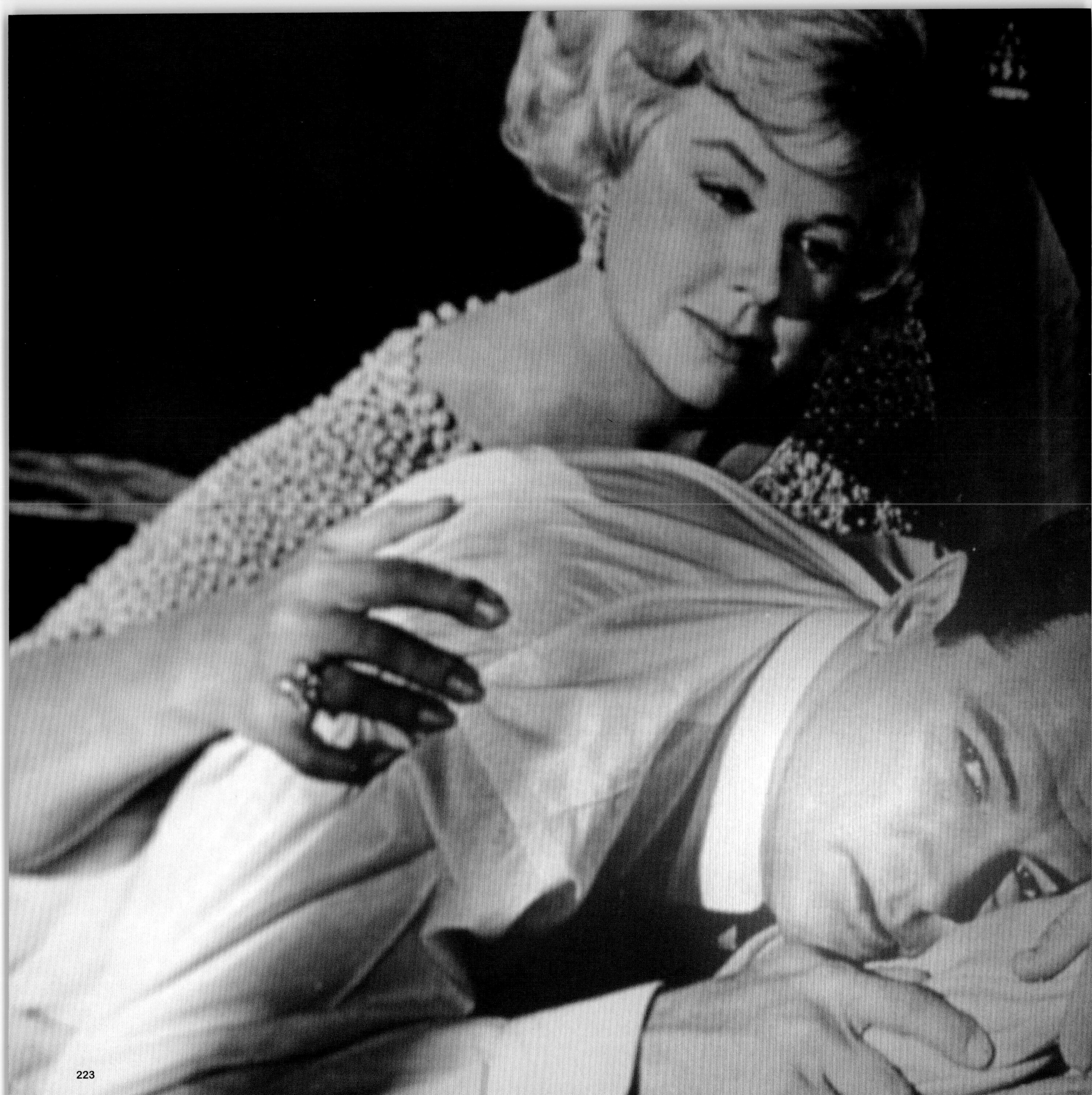

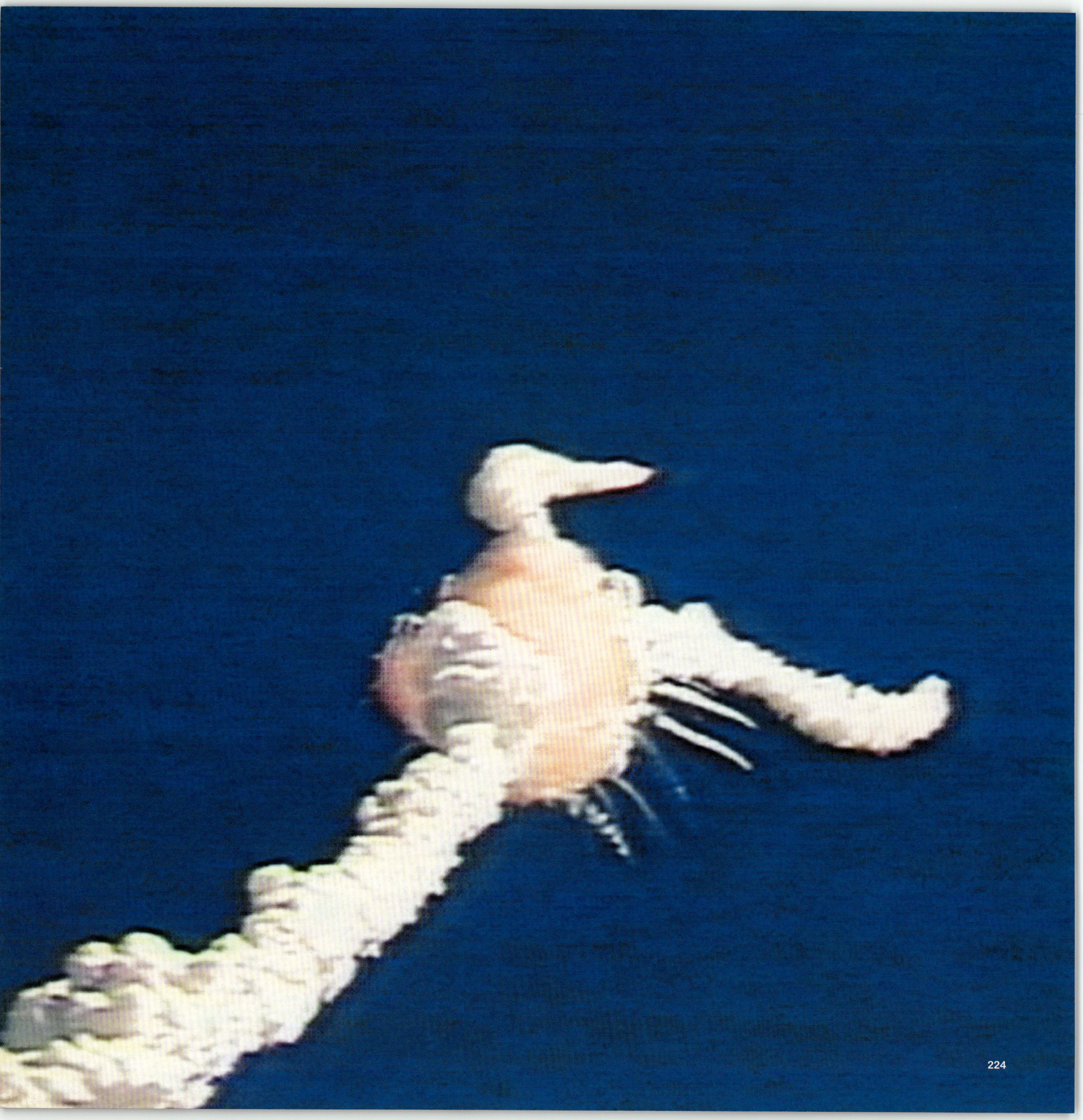

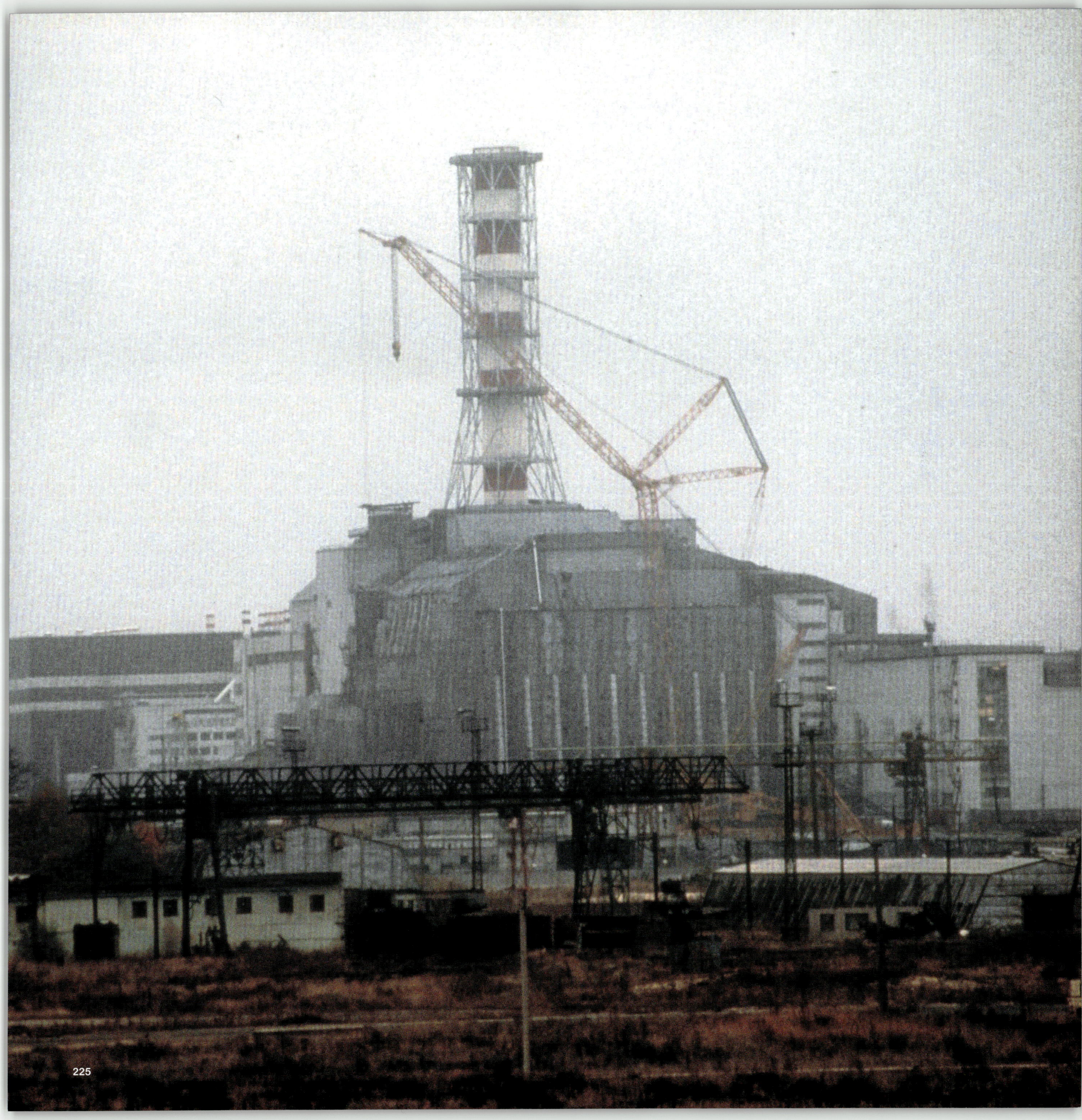

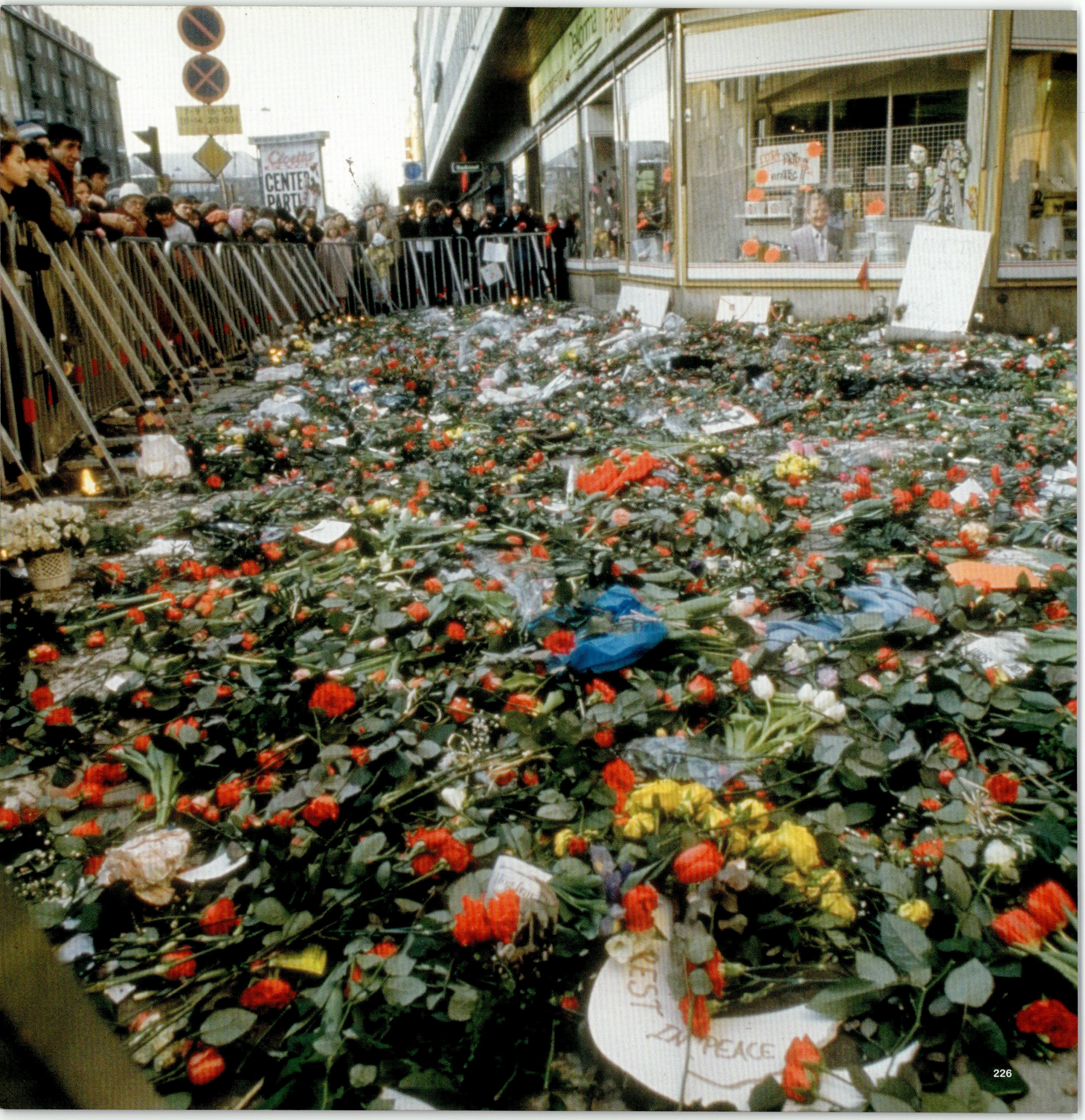
CENTER
REST IN PEACE

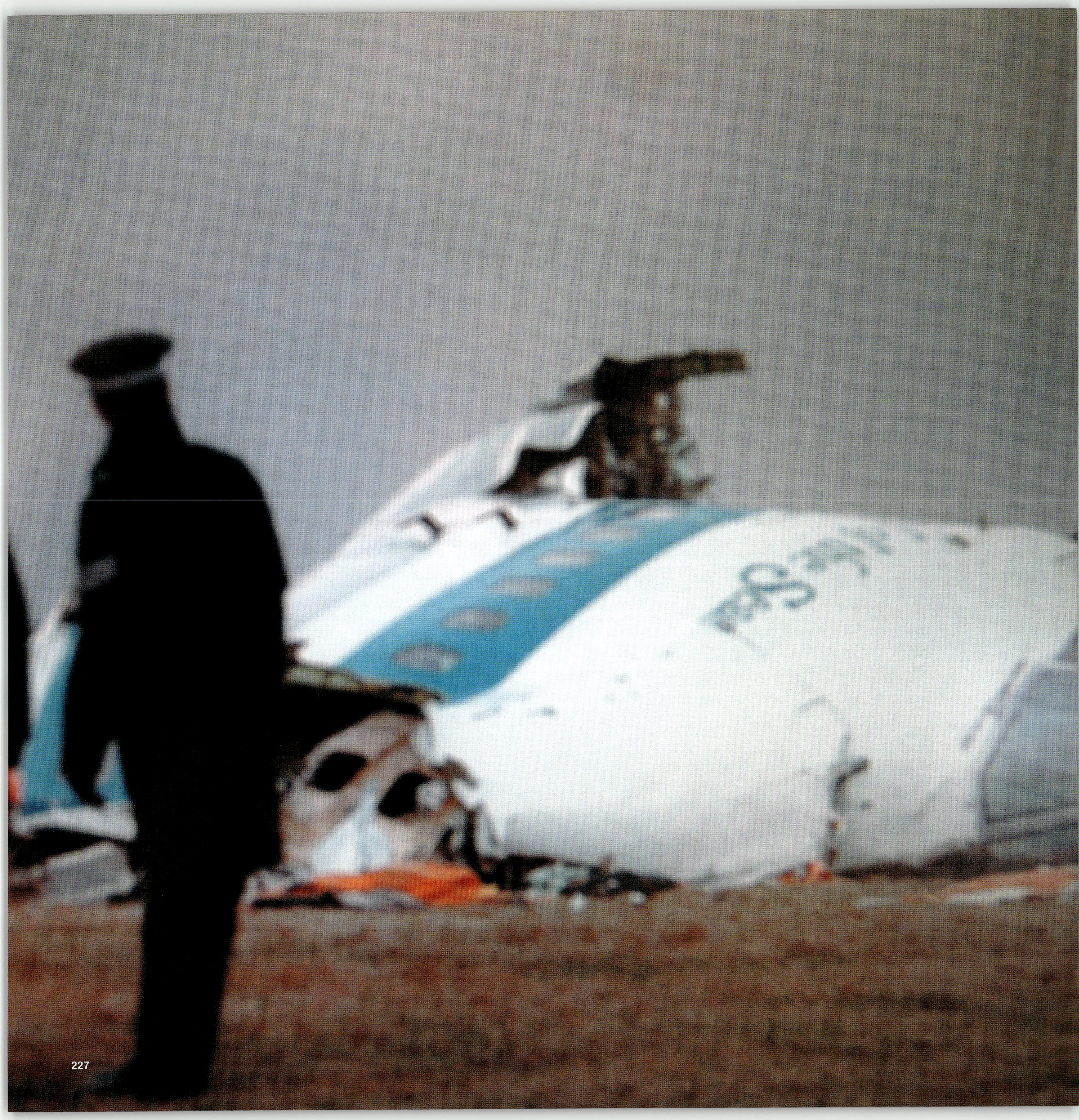

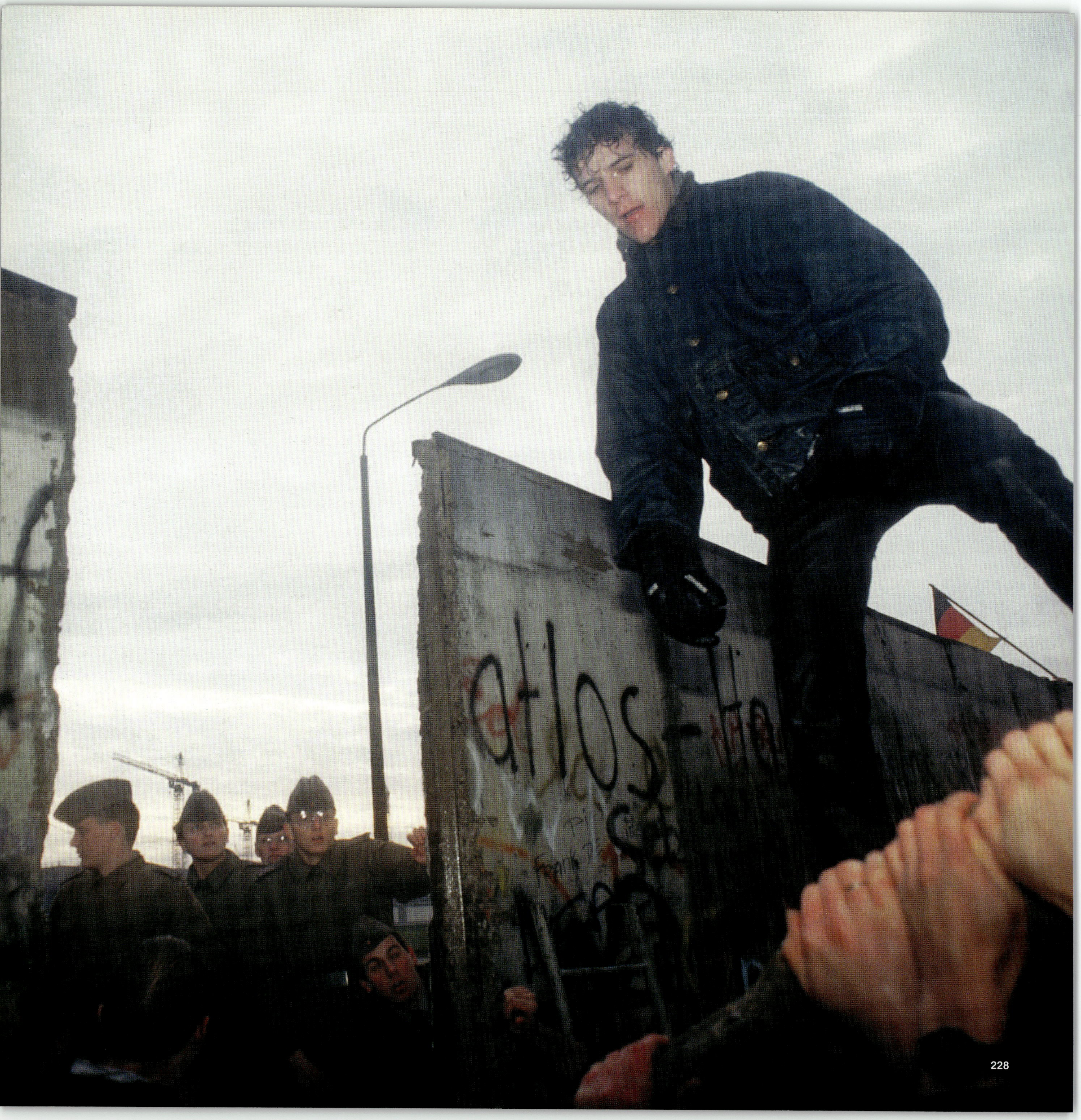
atlos

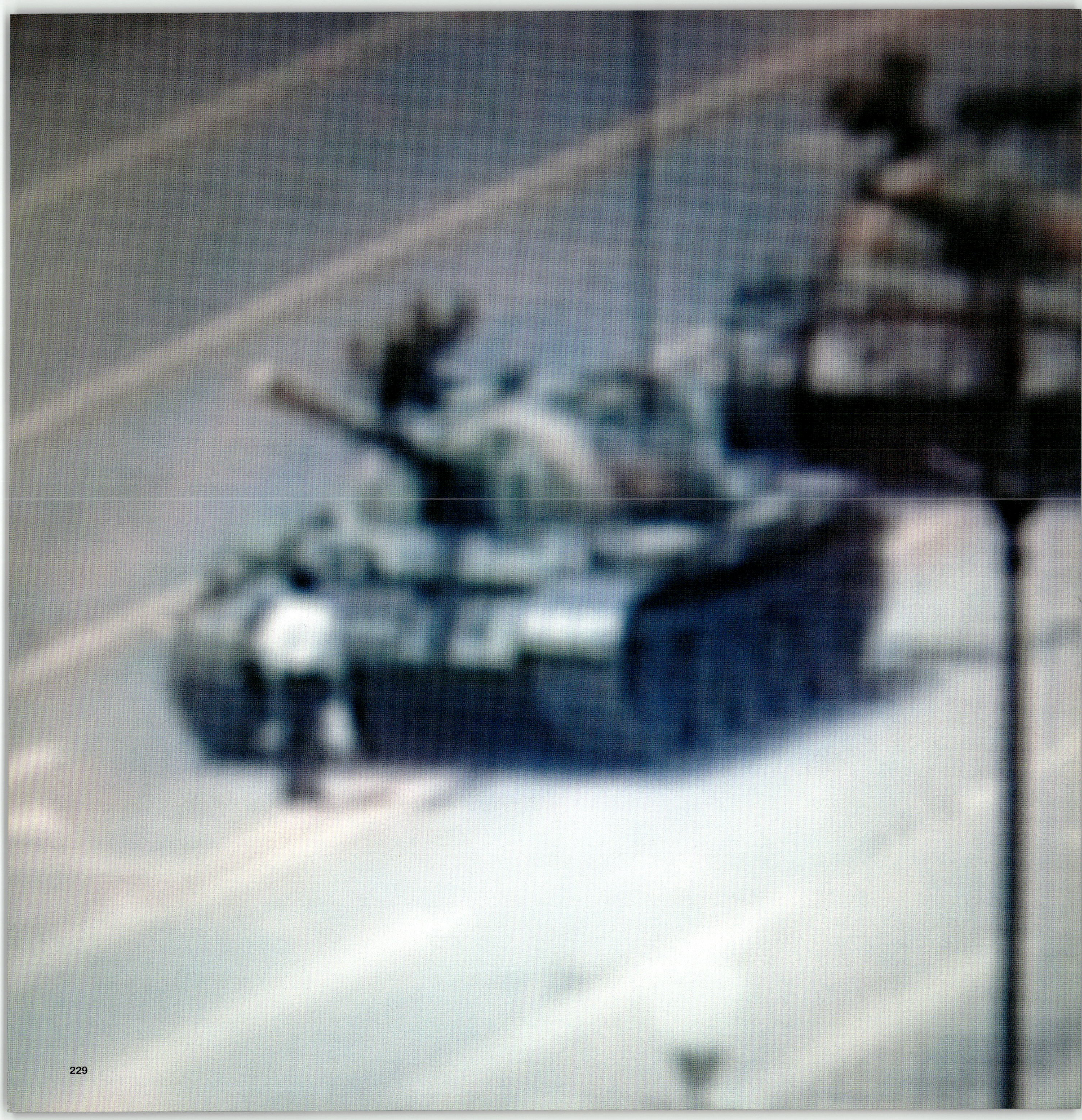

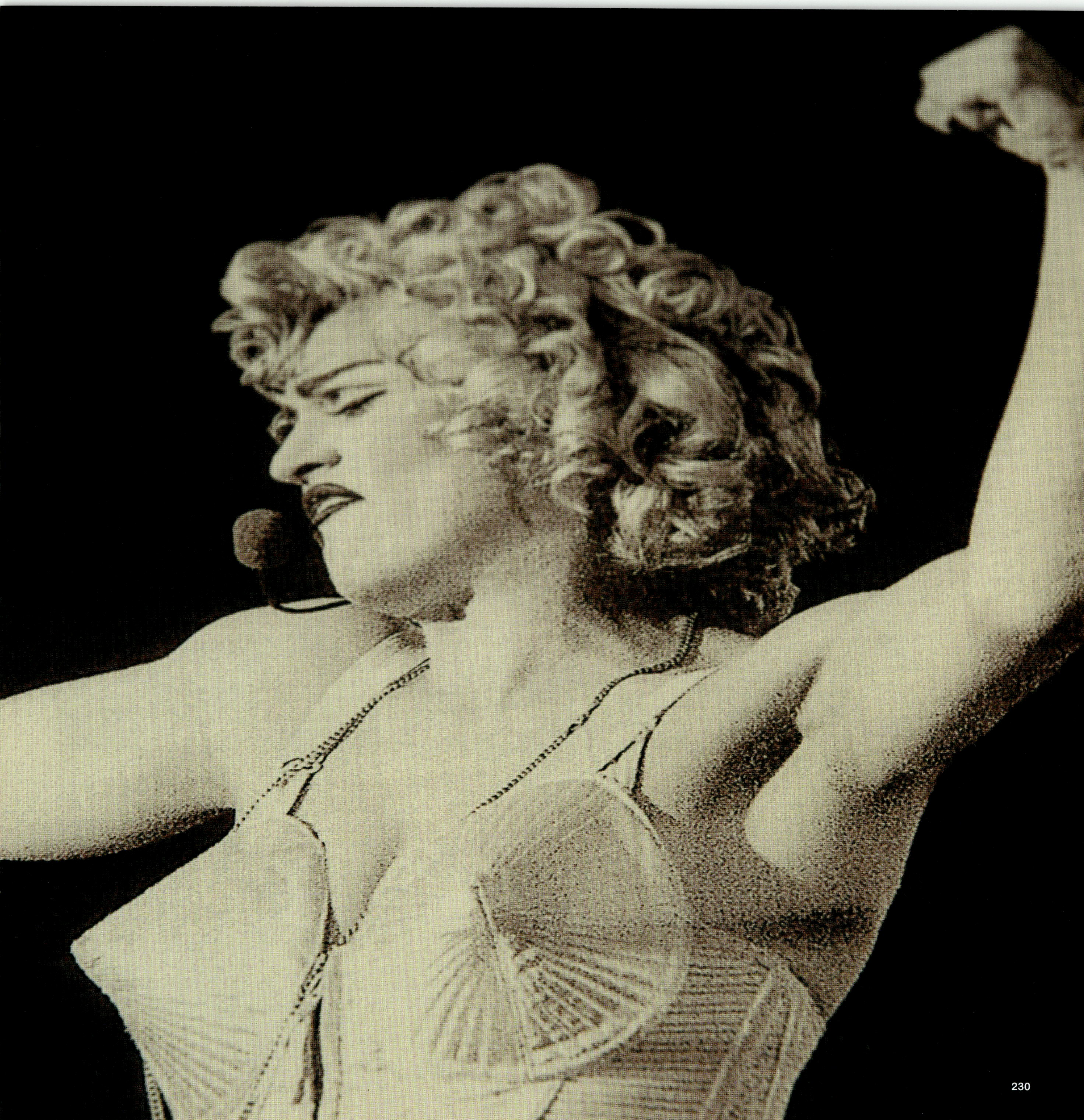

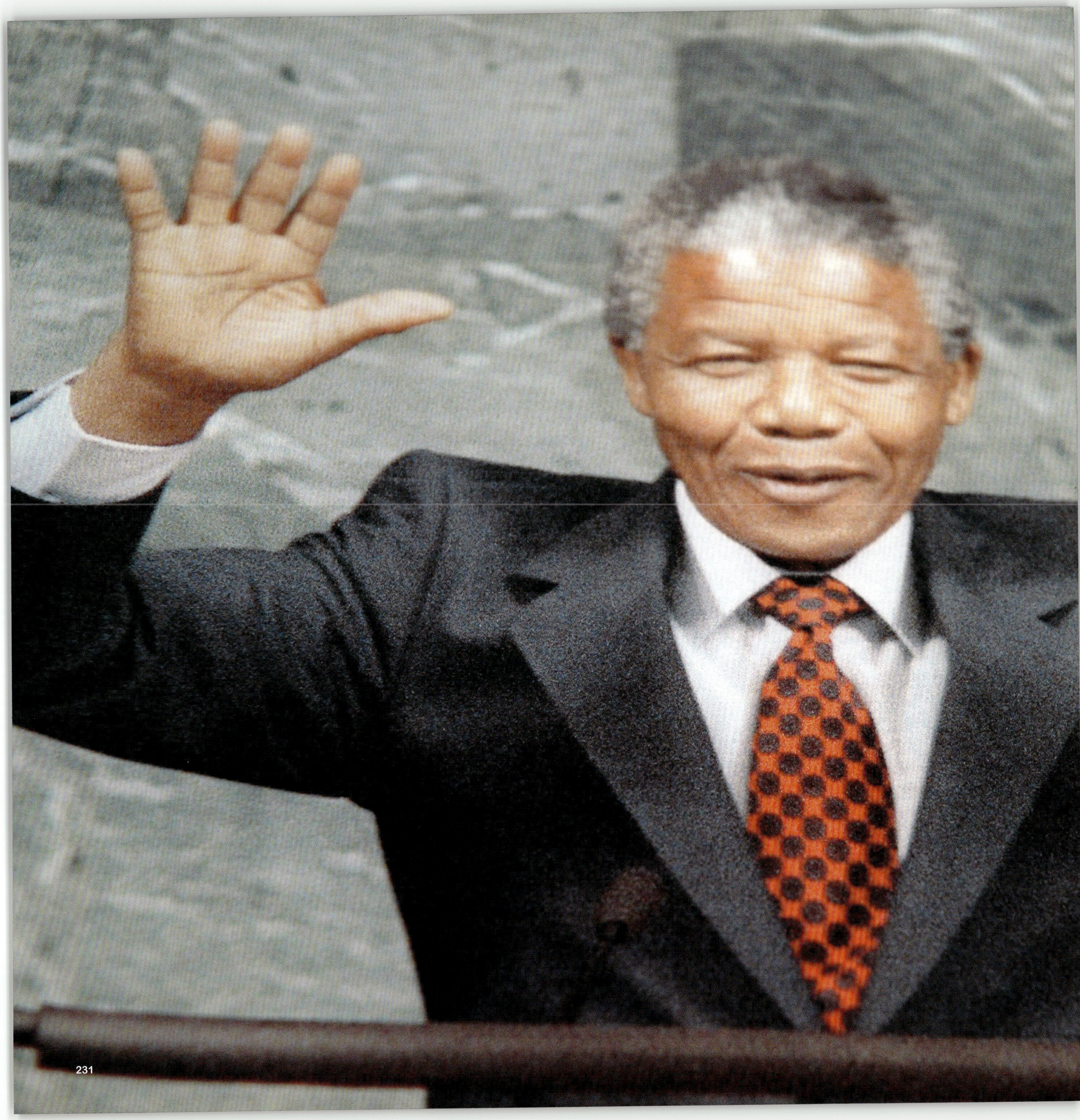

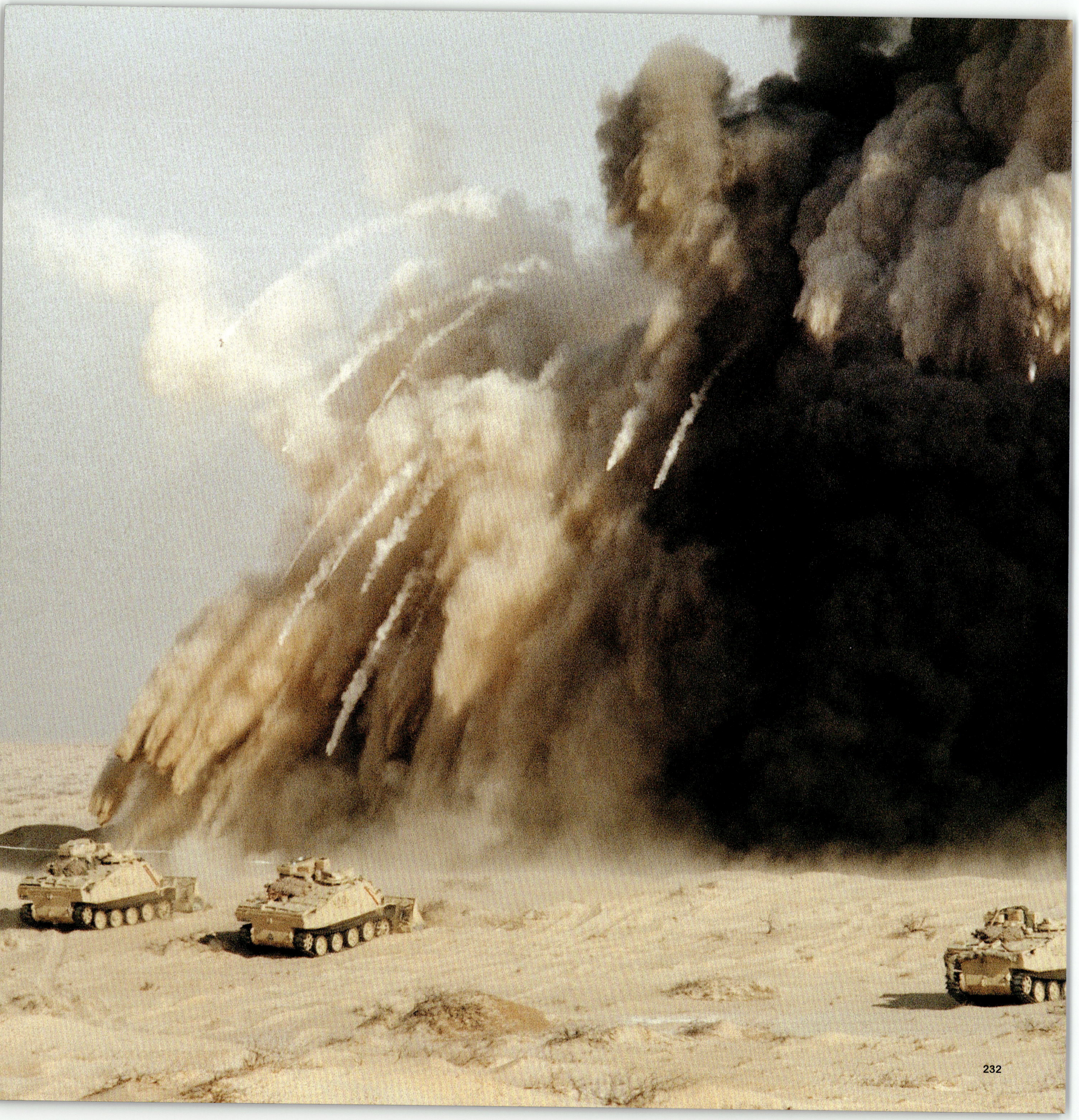

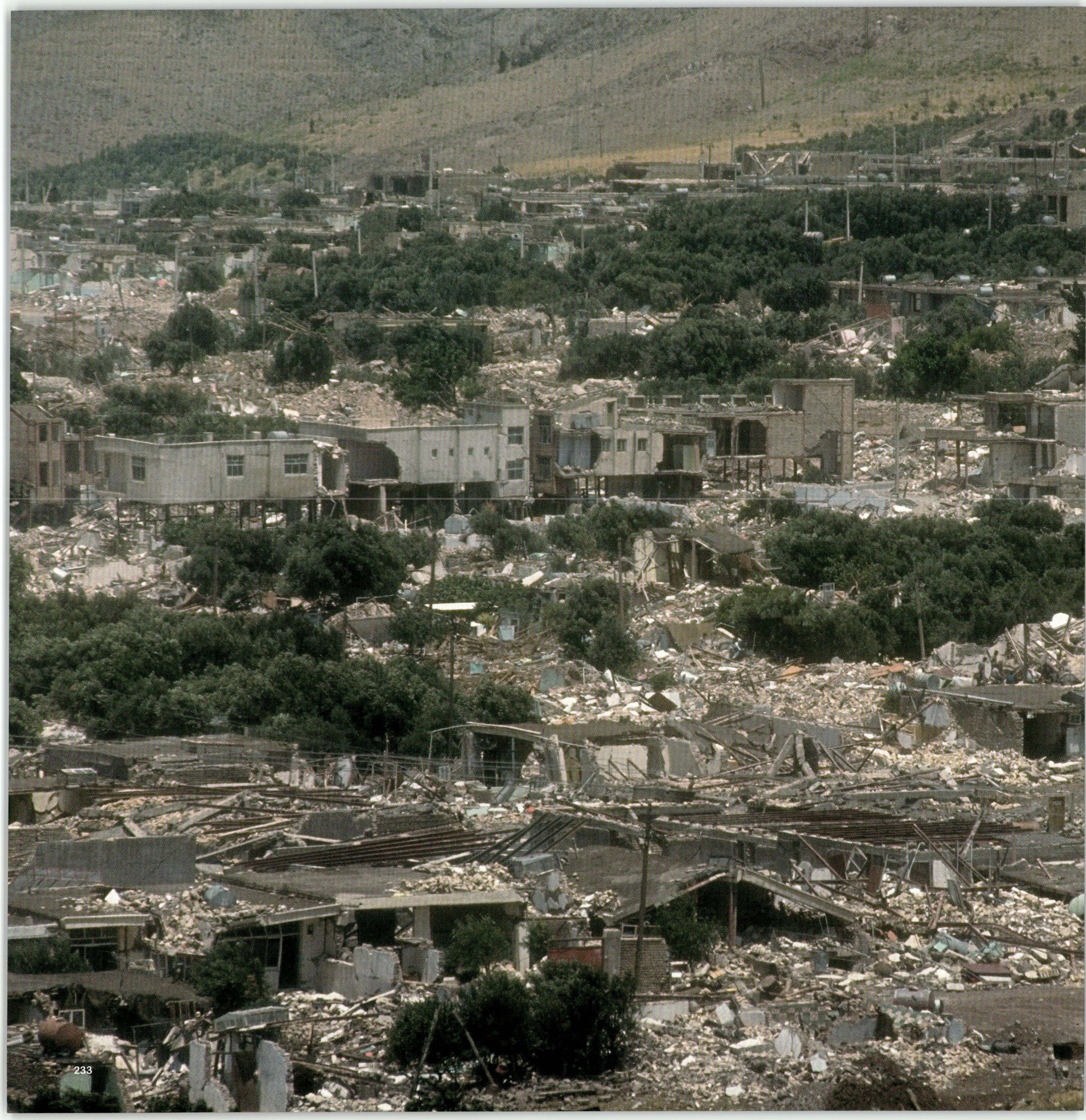

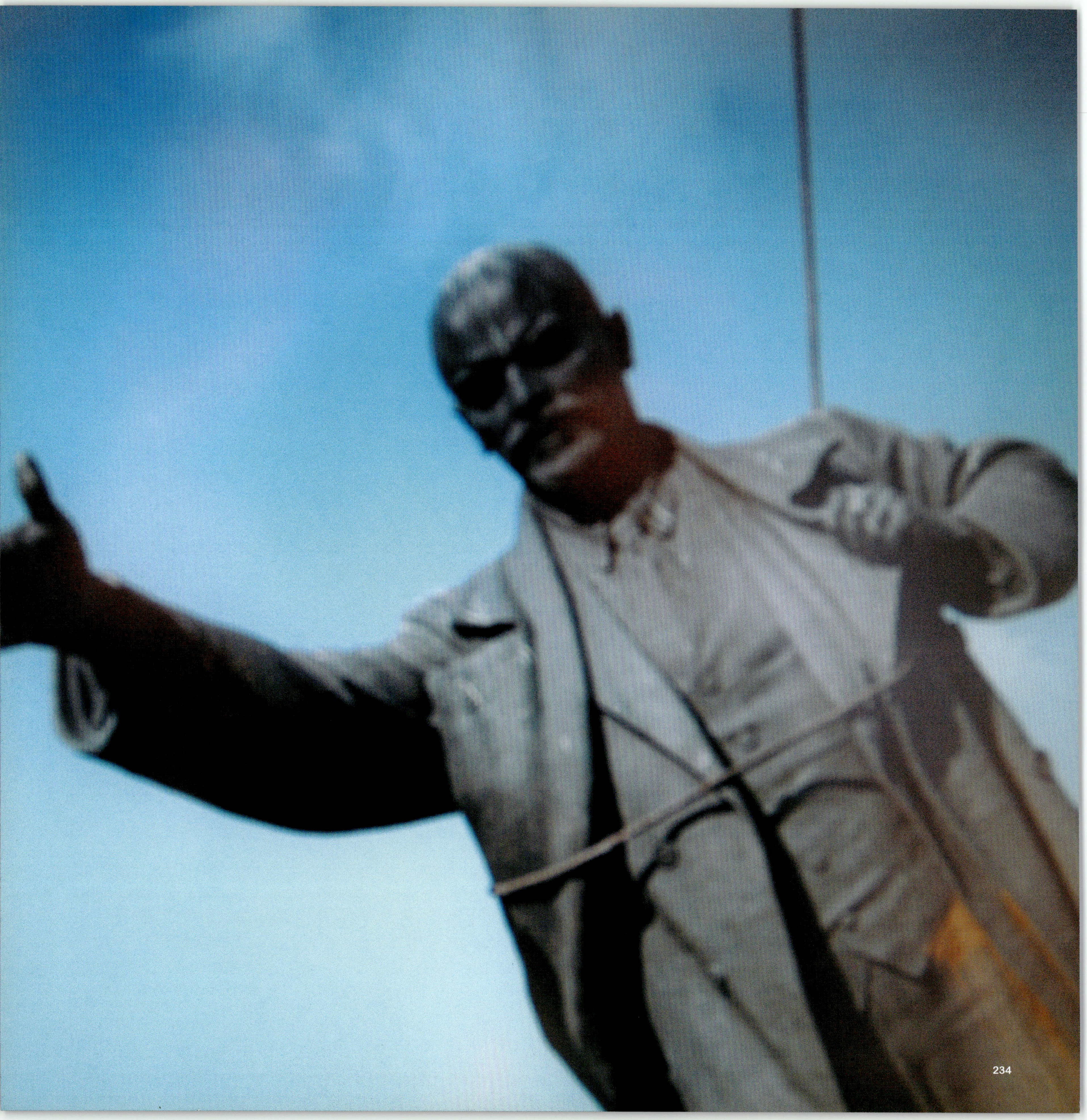

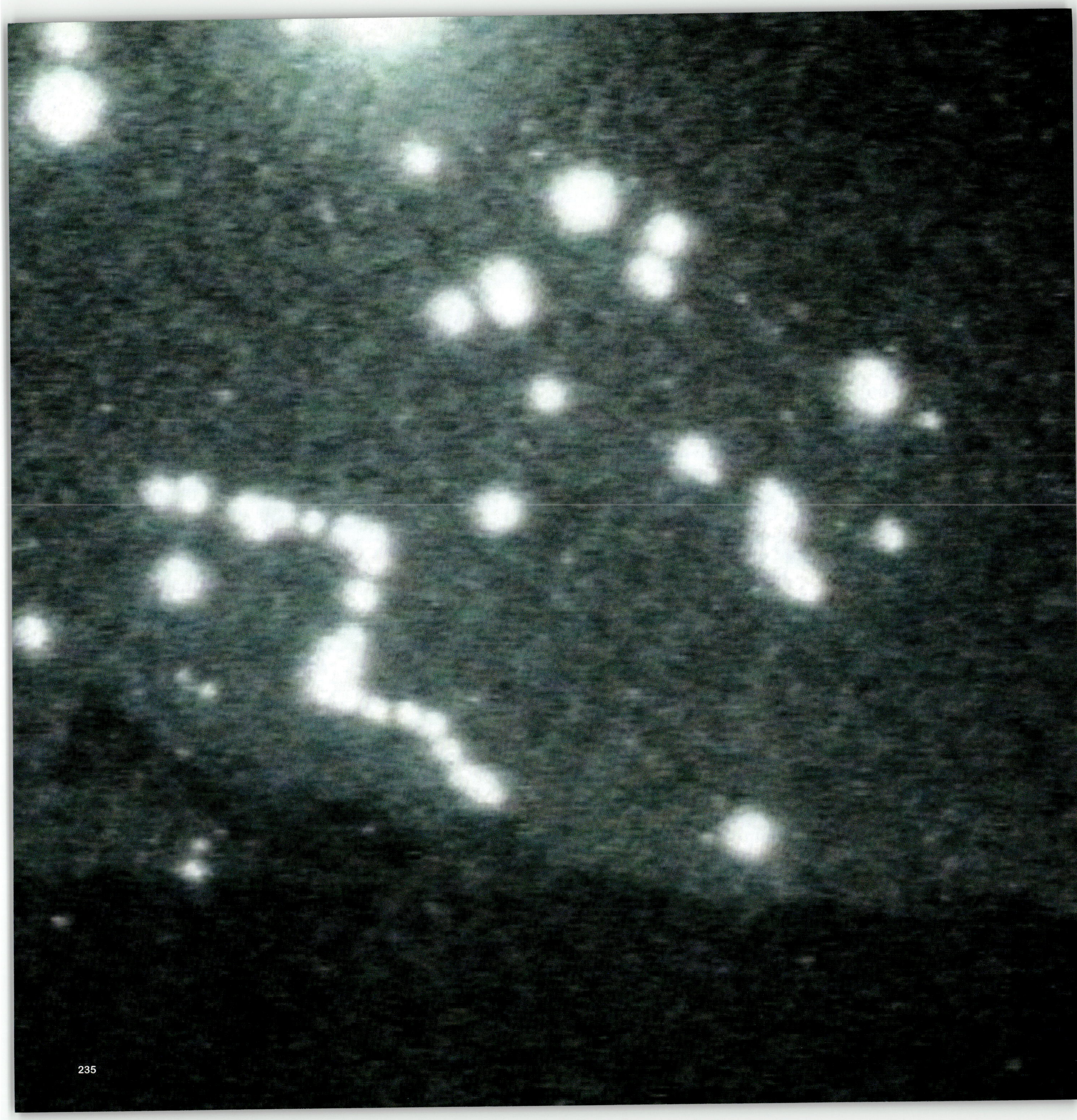

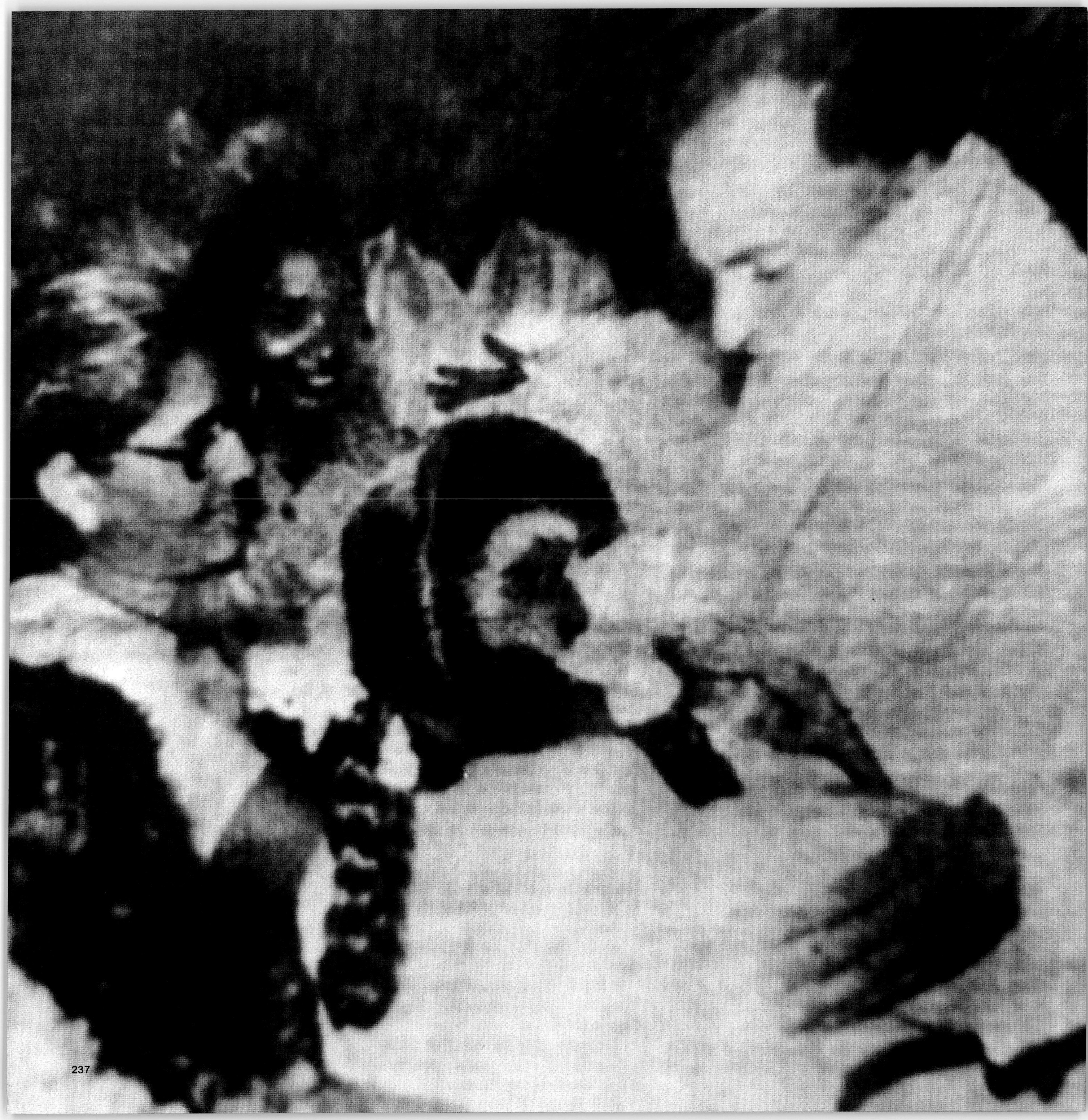

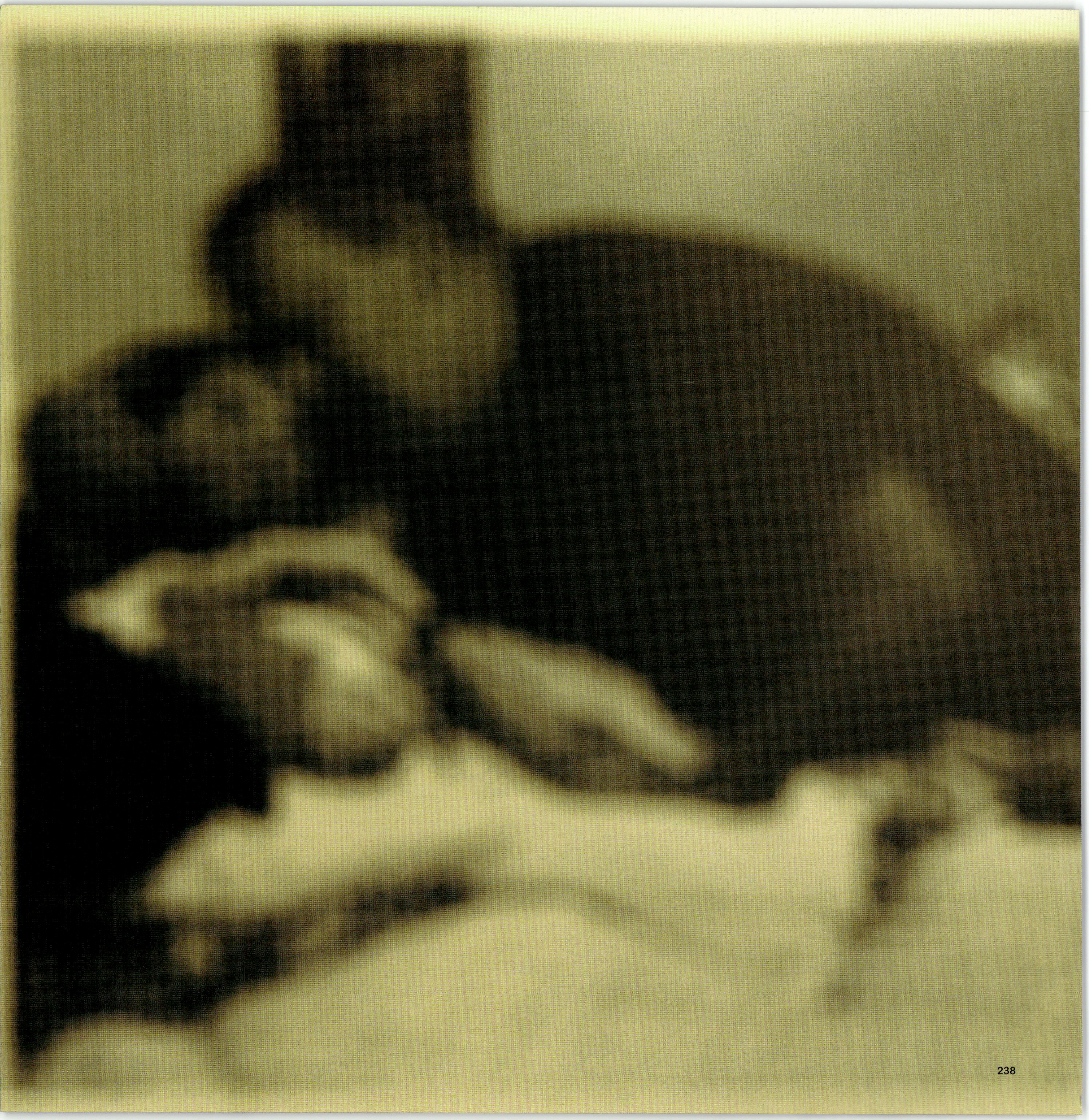

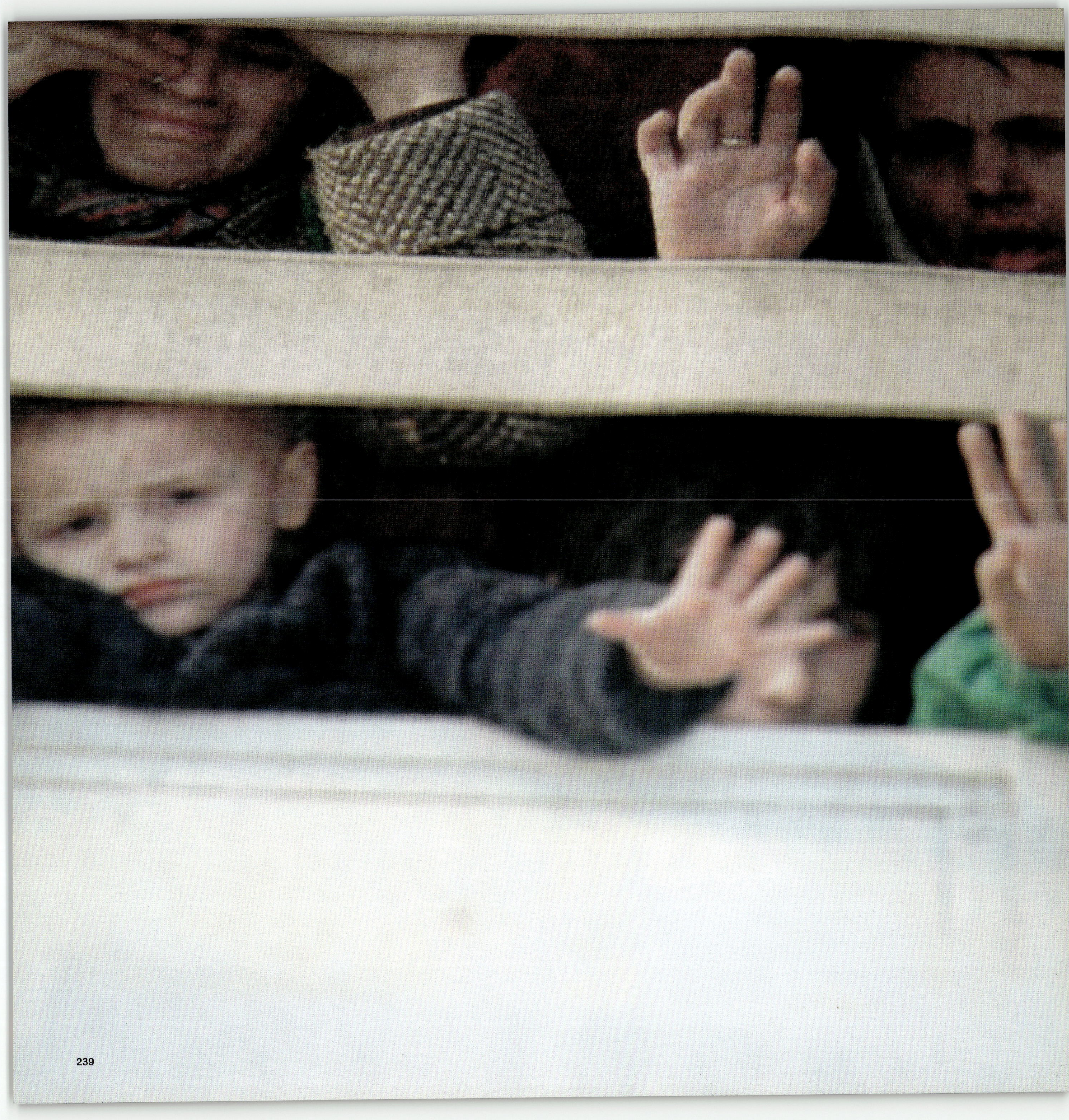

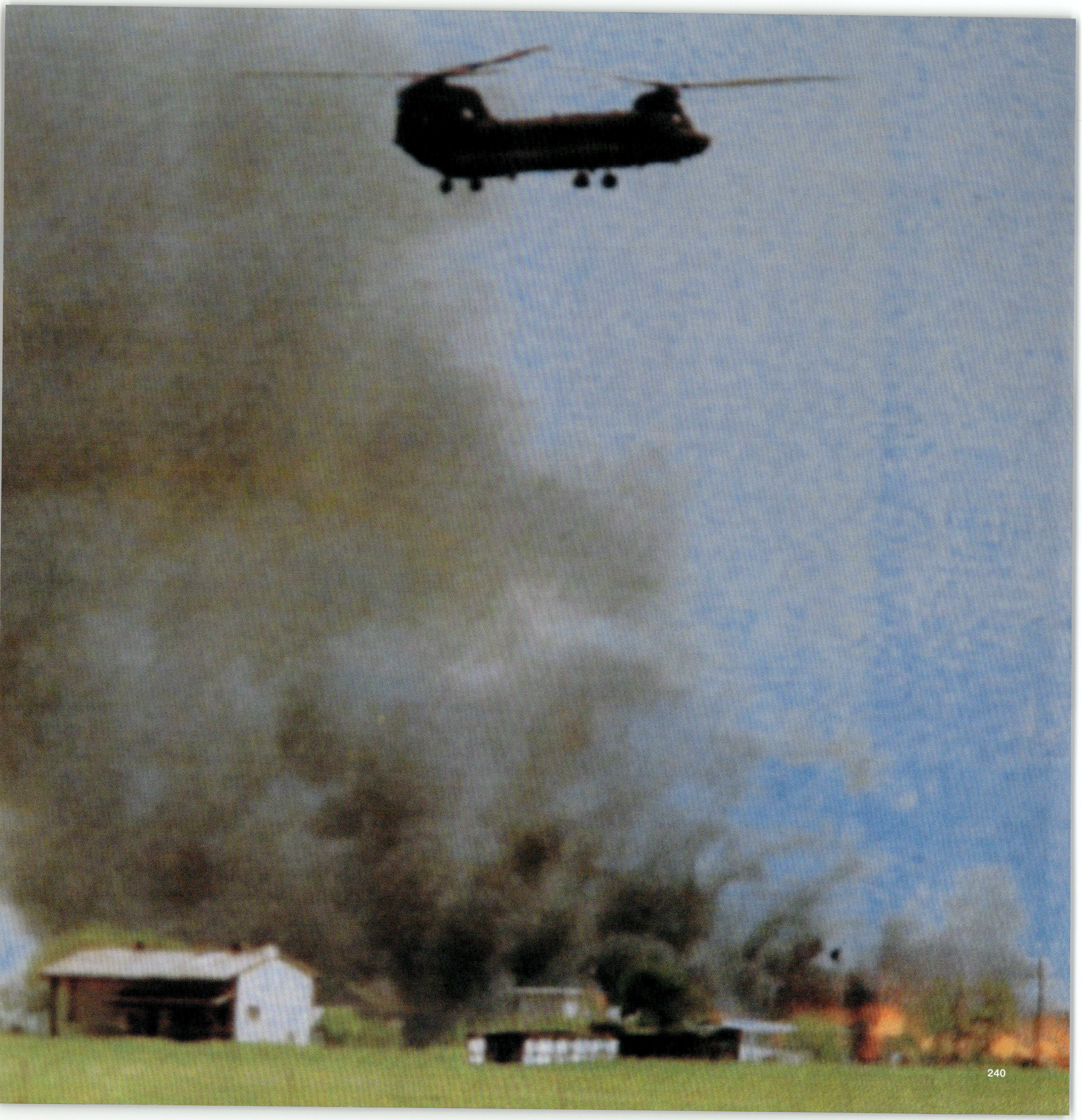

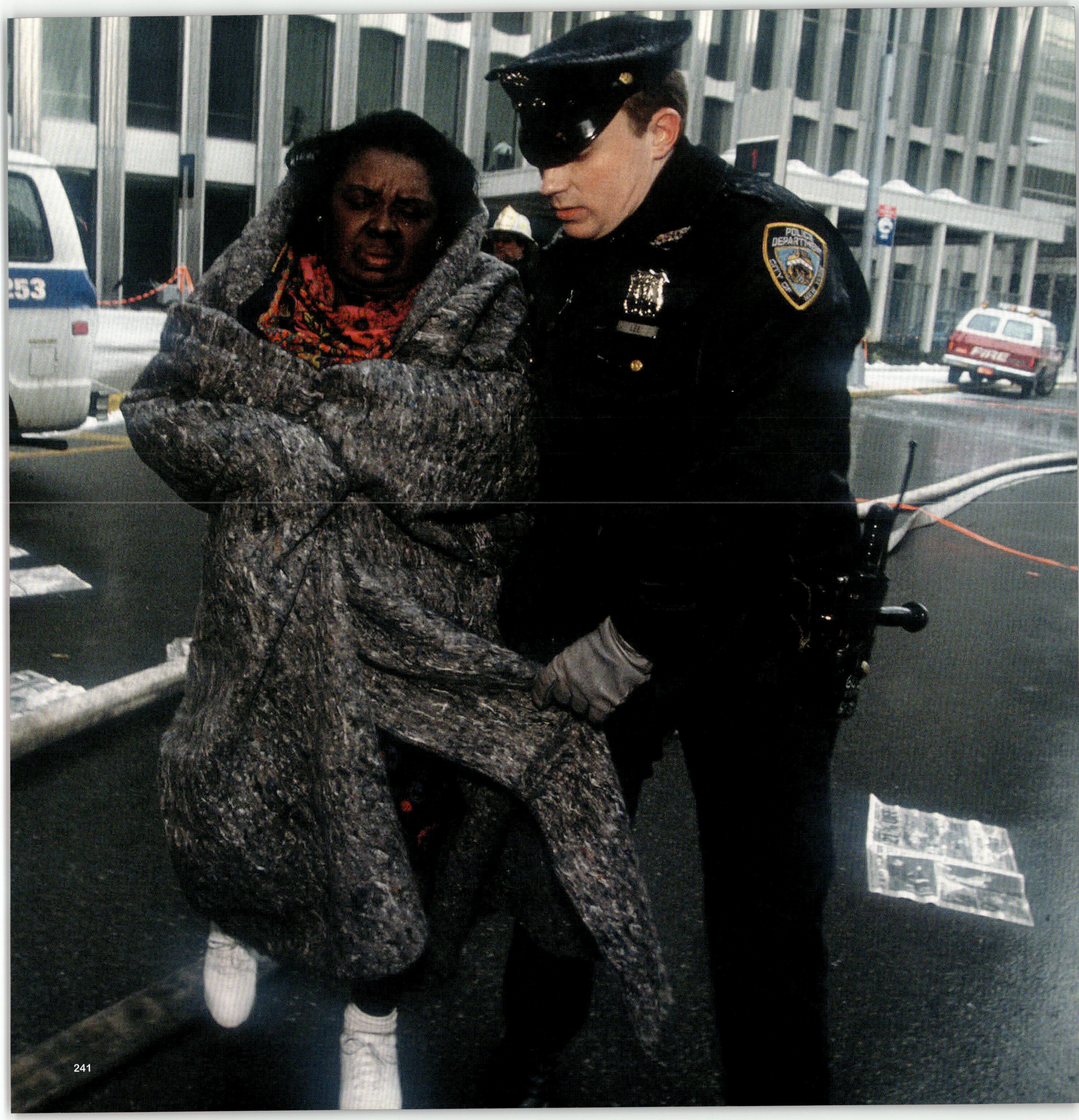
253
POLICE DEPARTMENT
FIRE

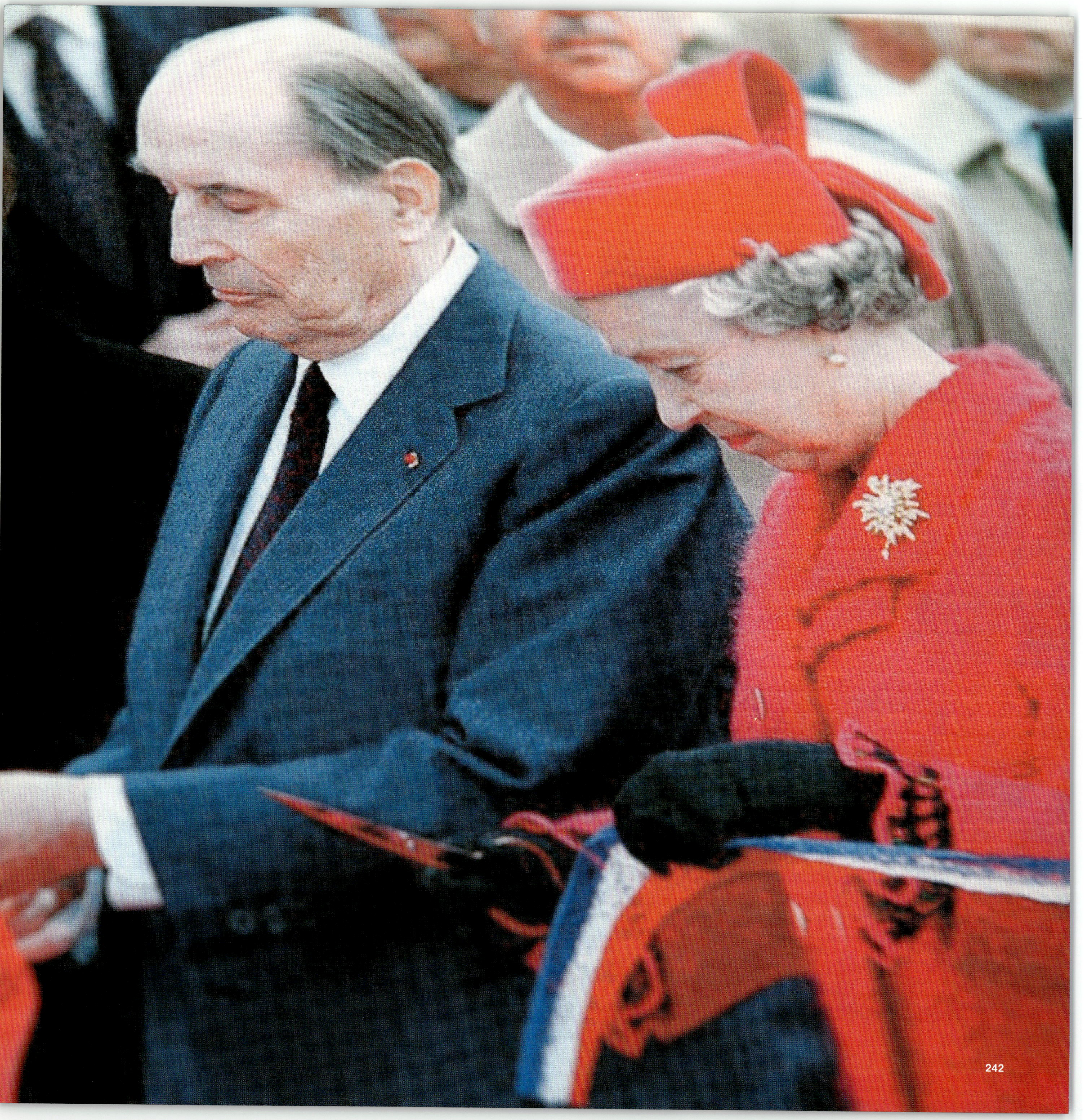

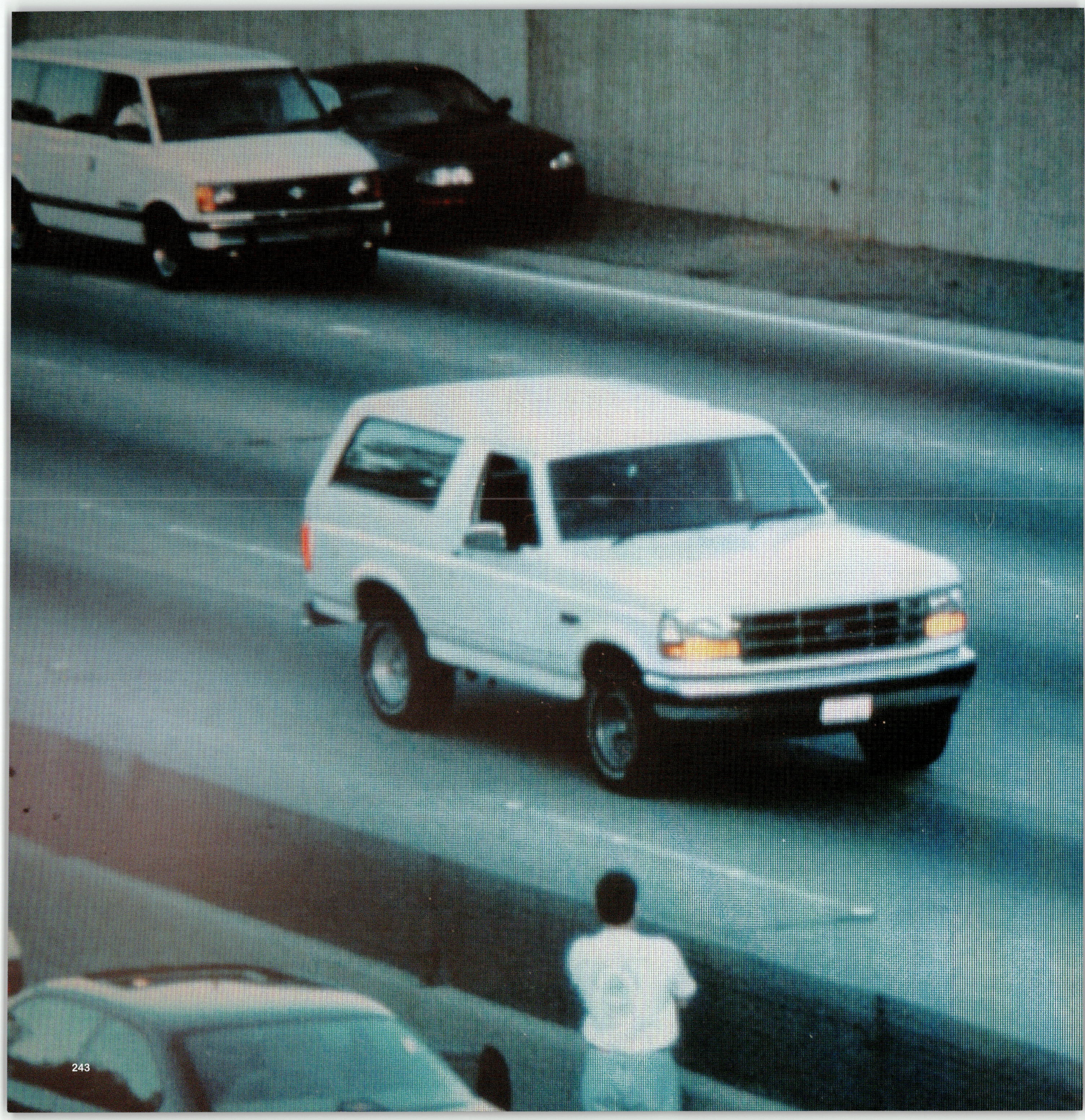

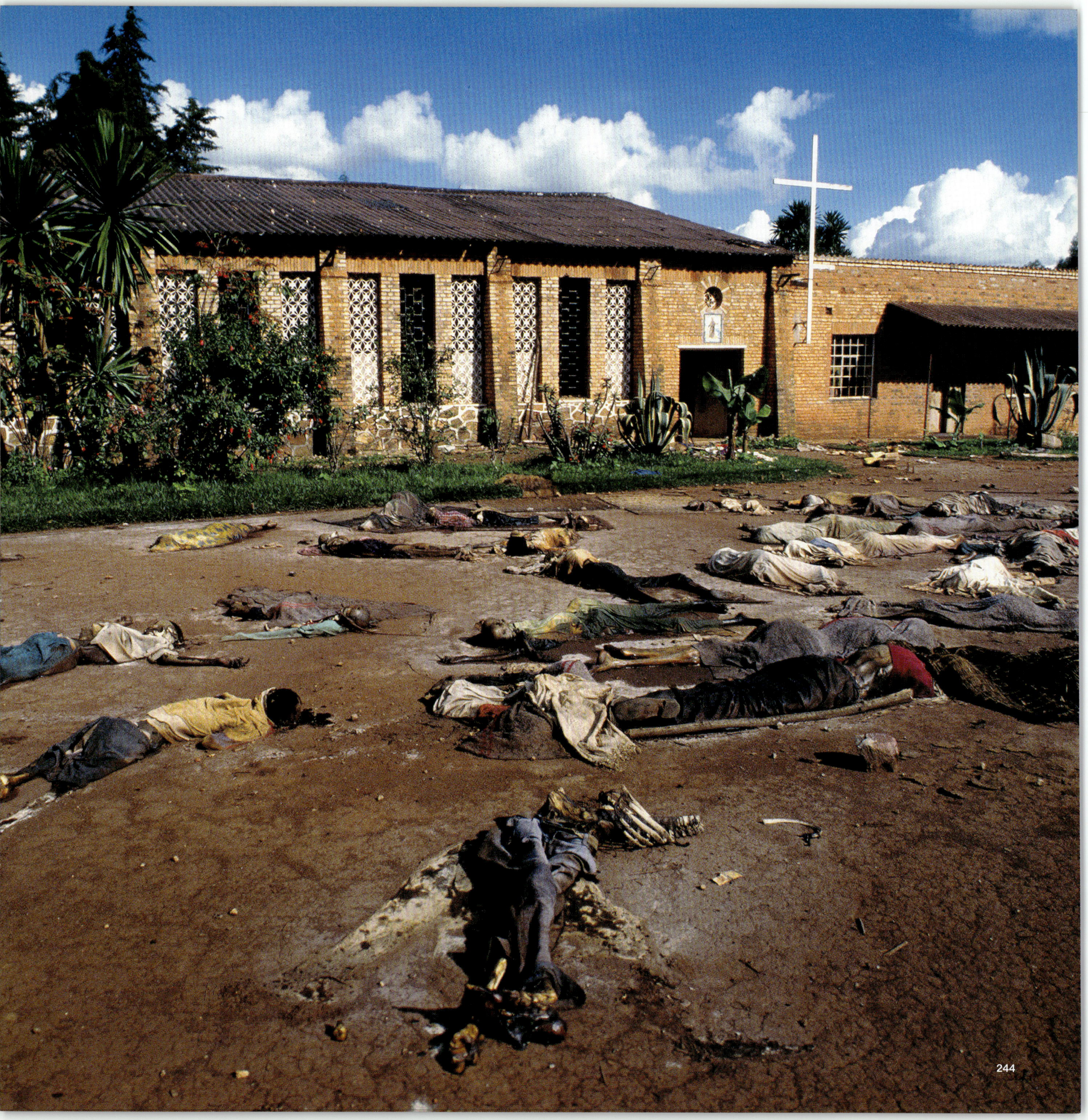

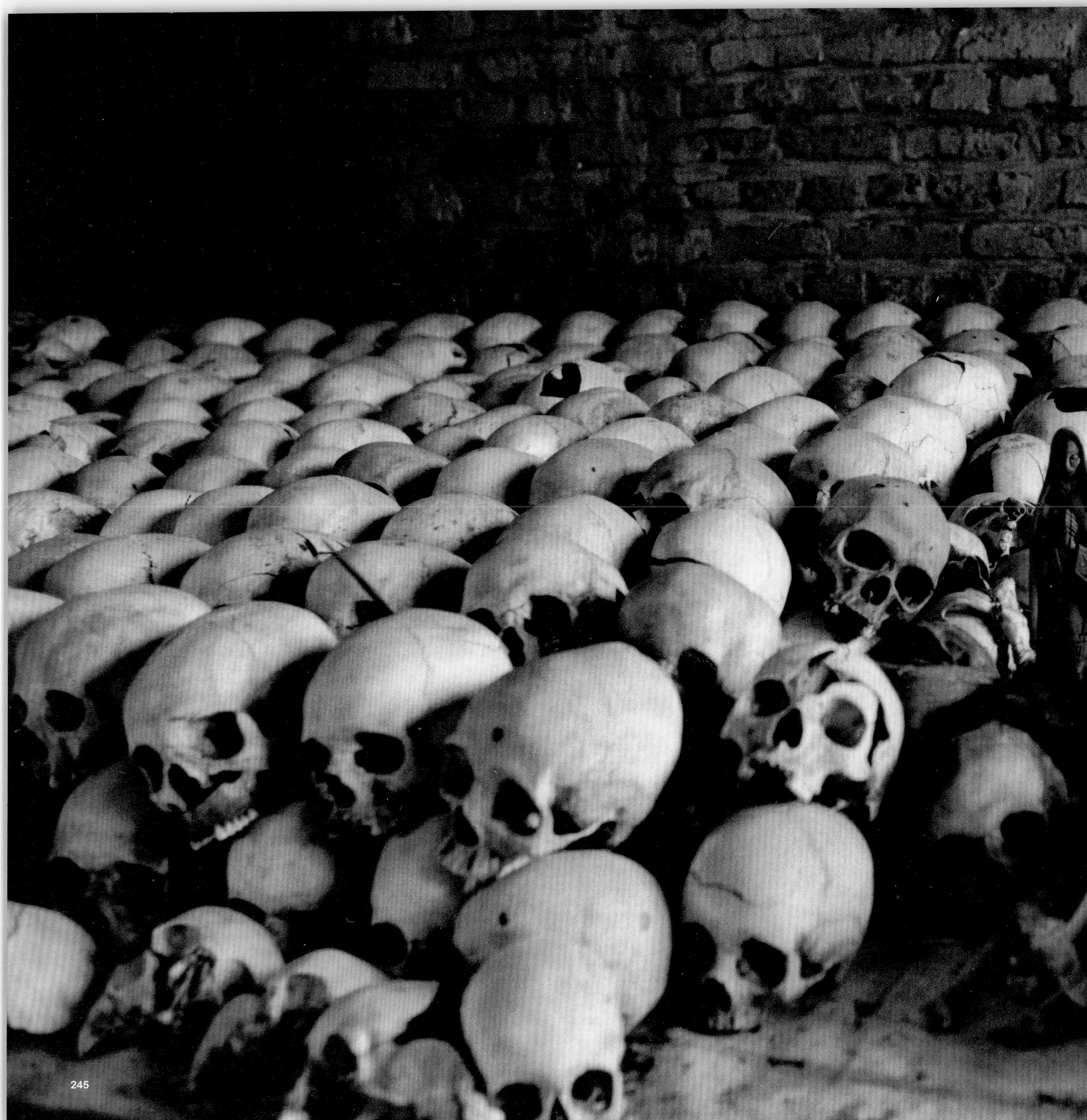

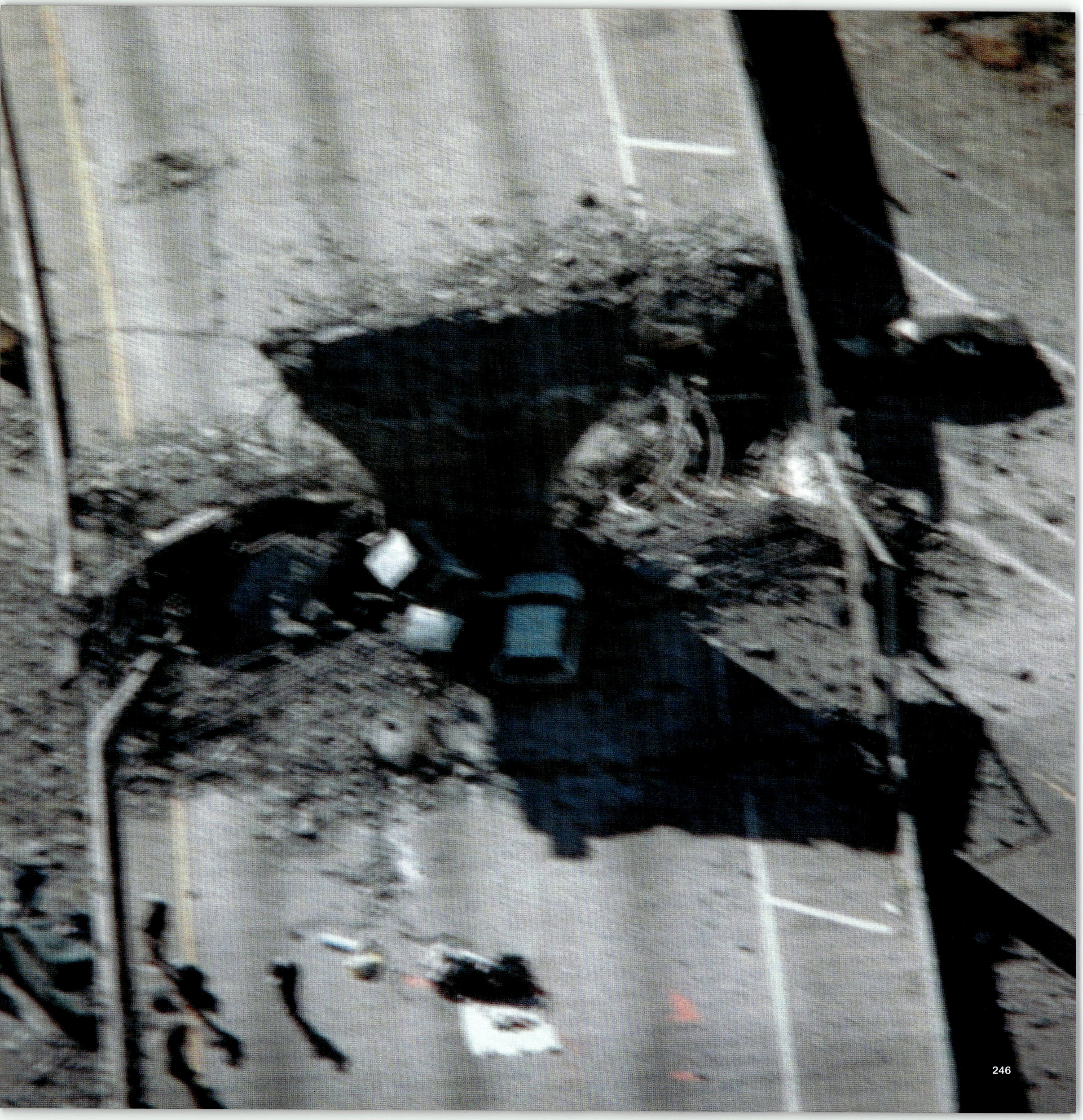

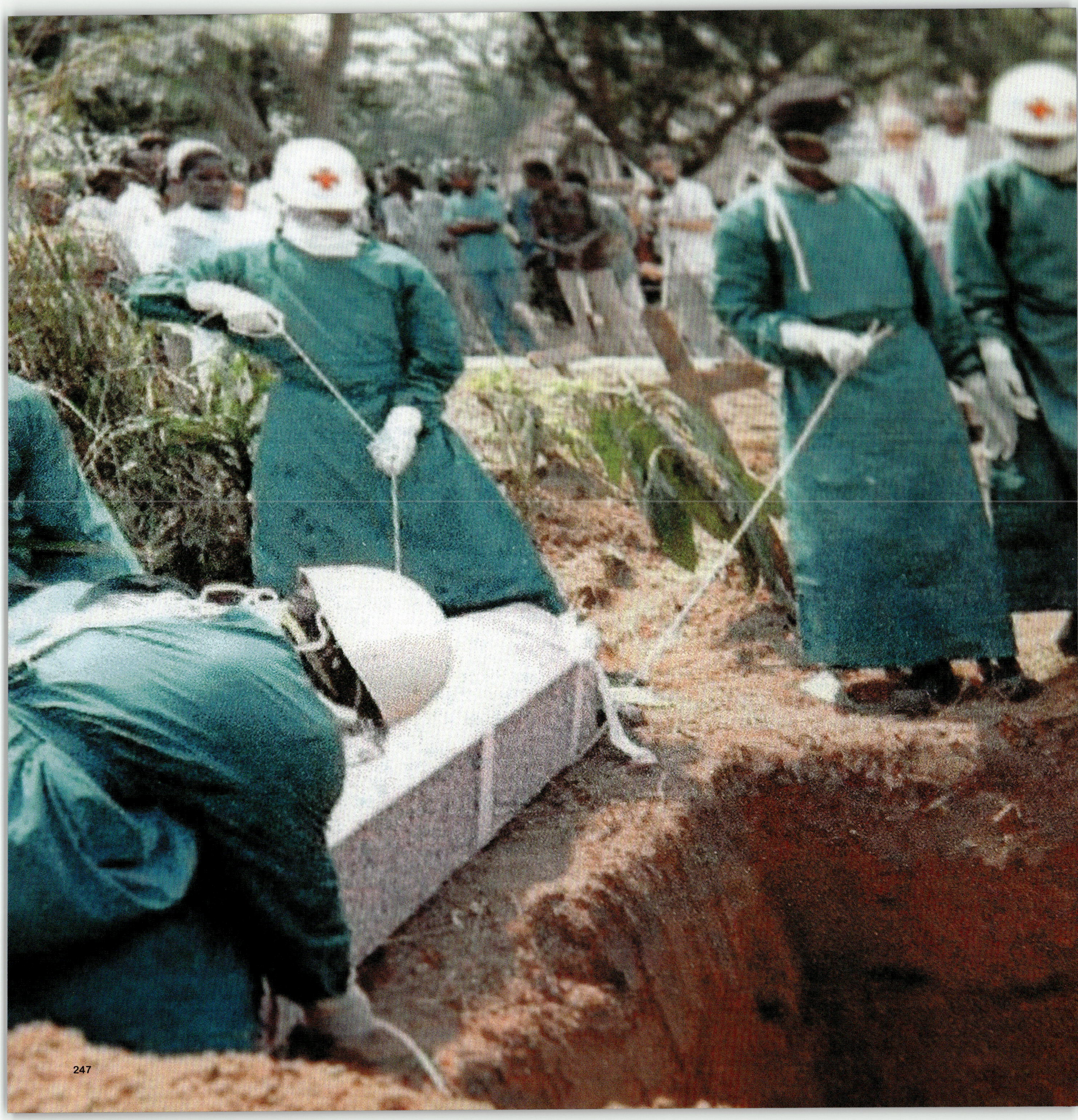

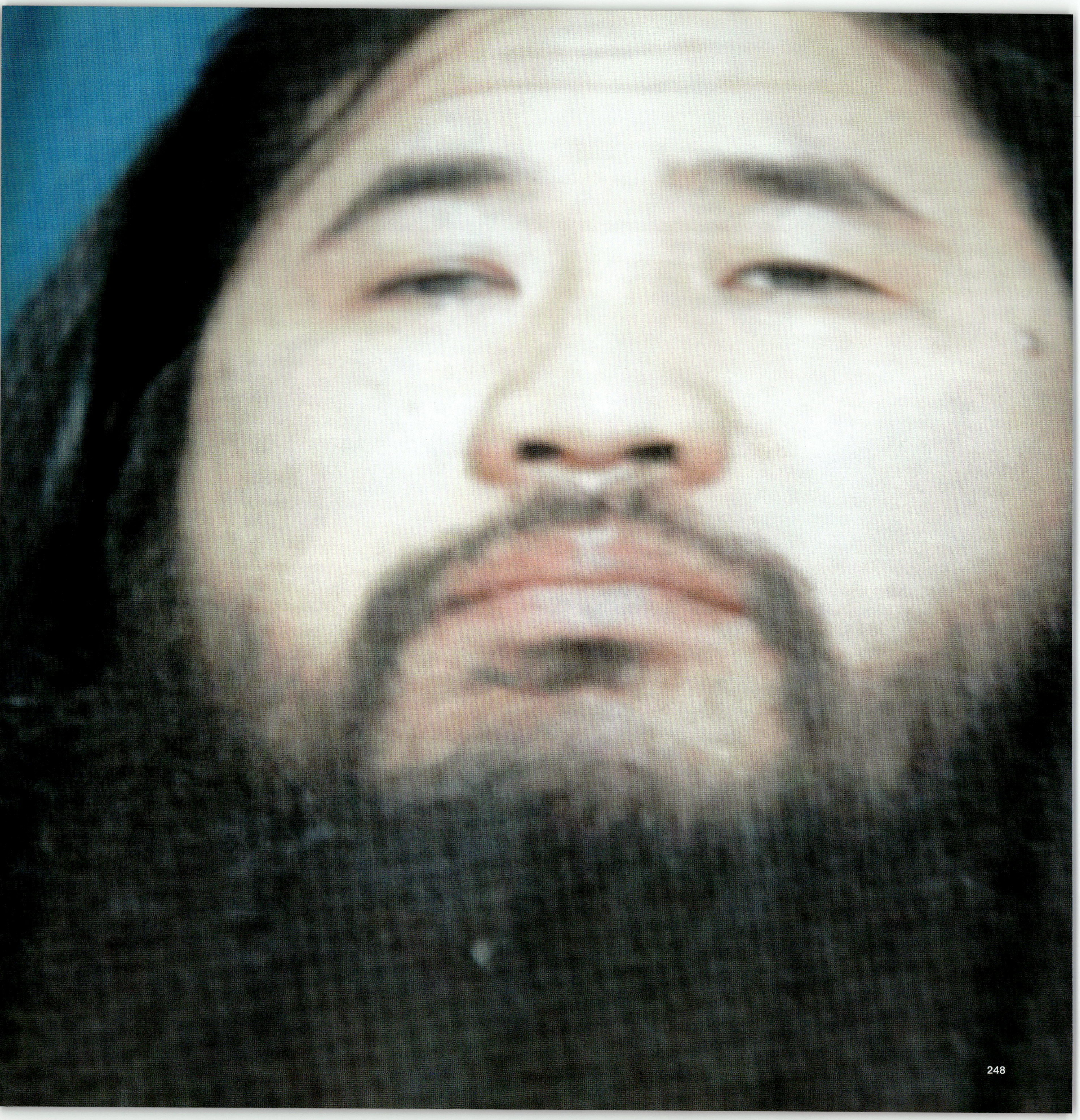

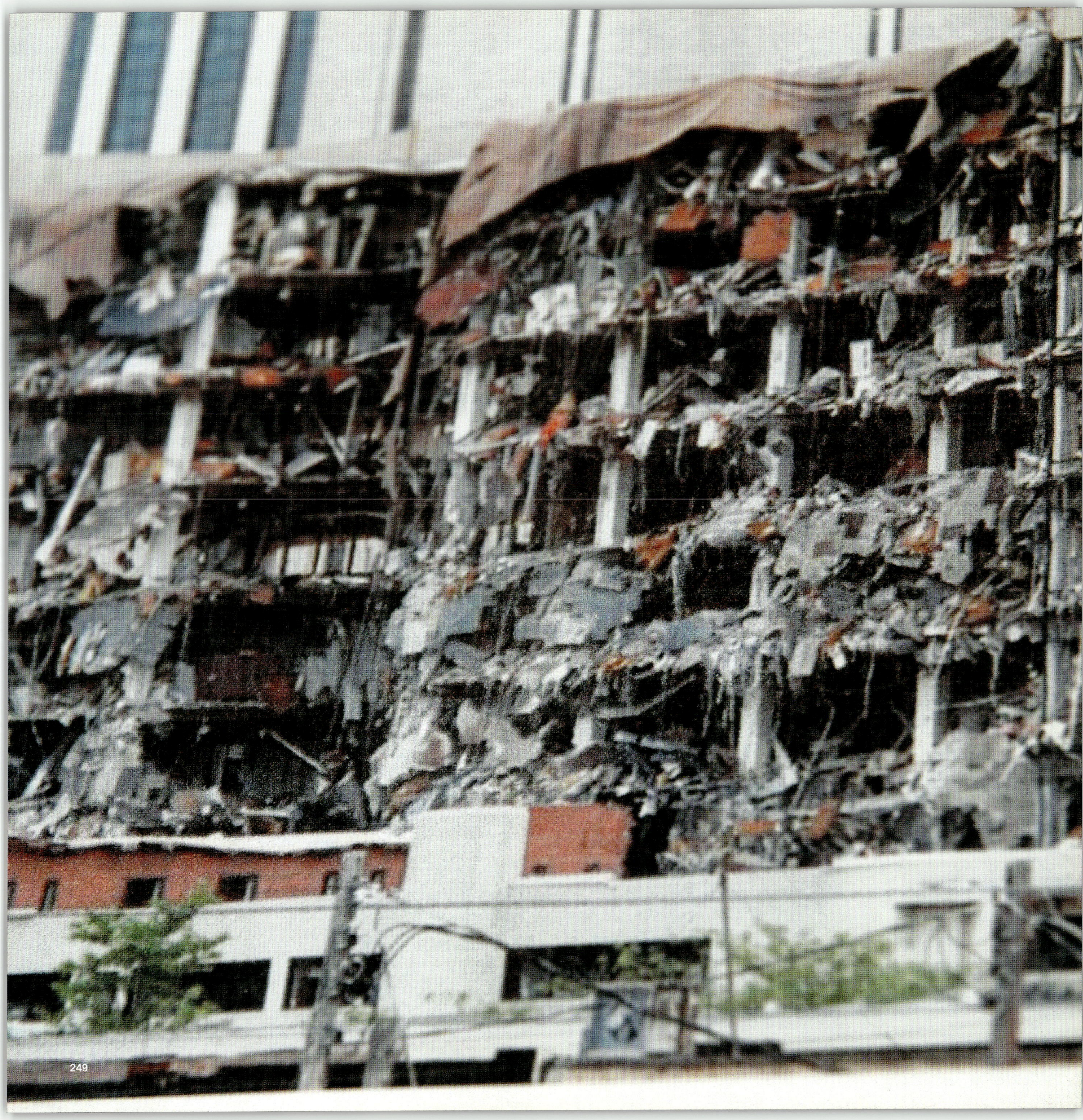

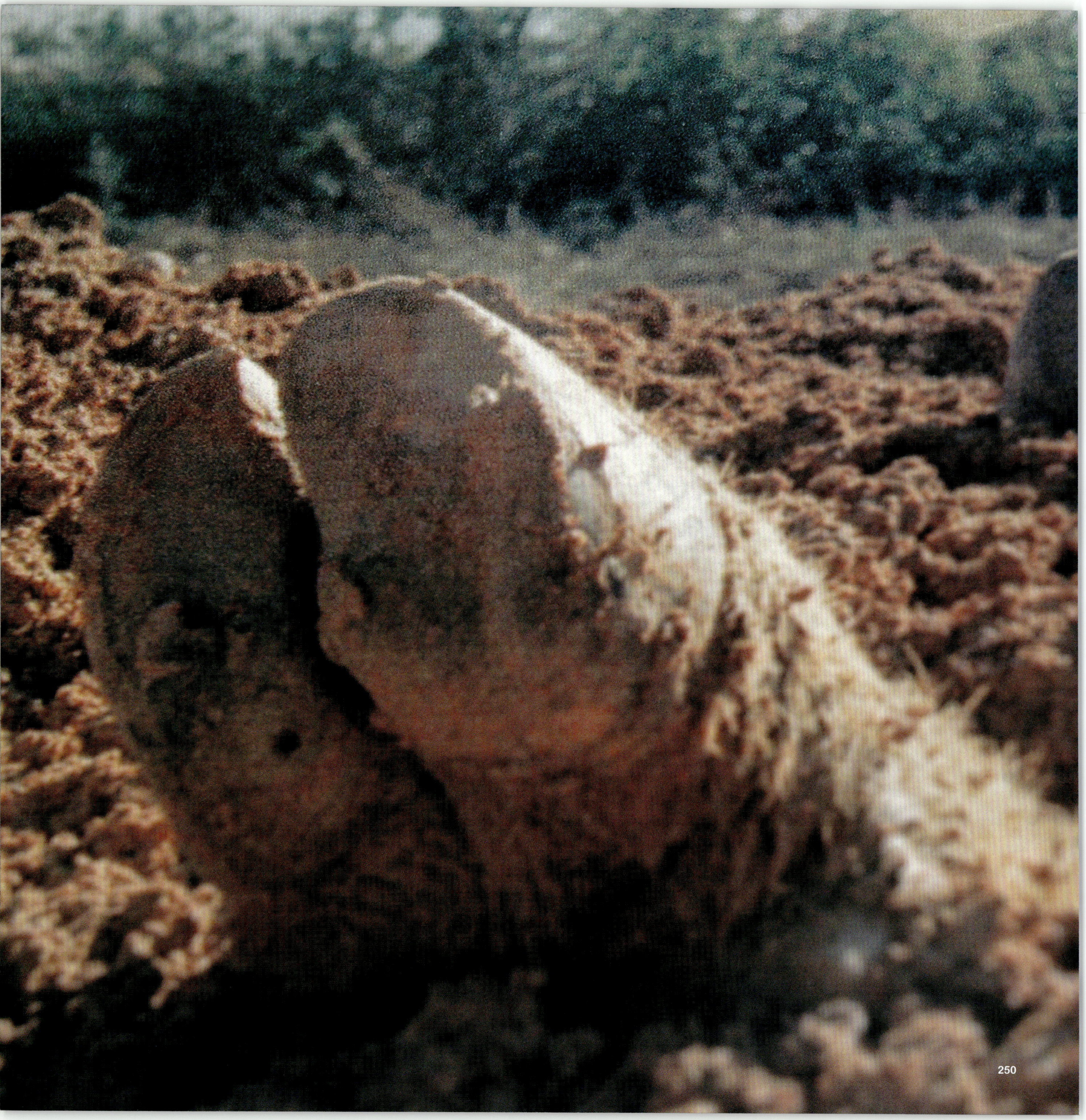

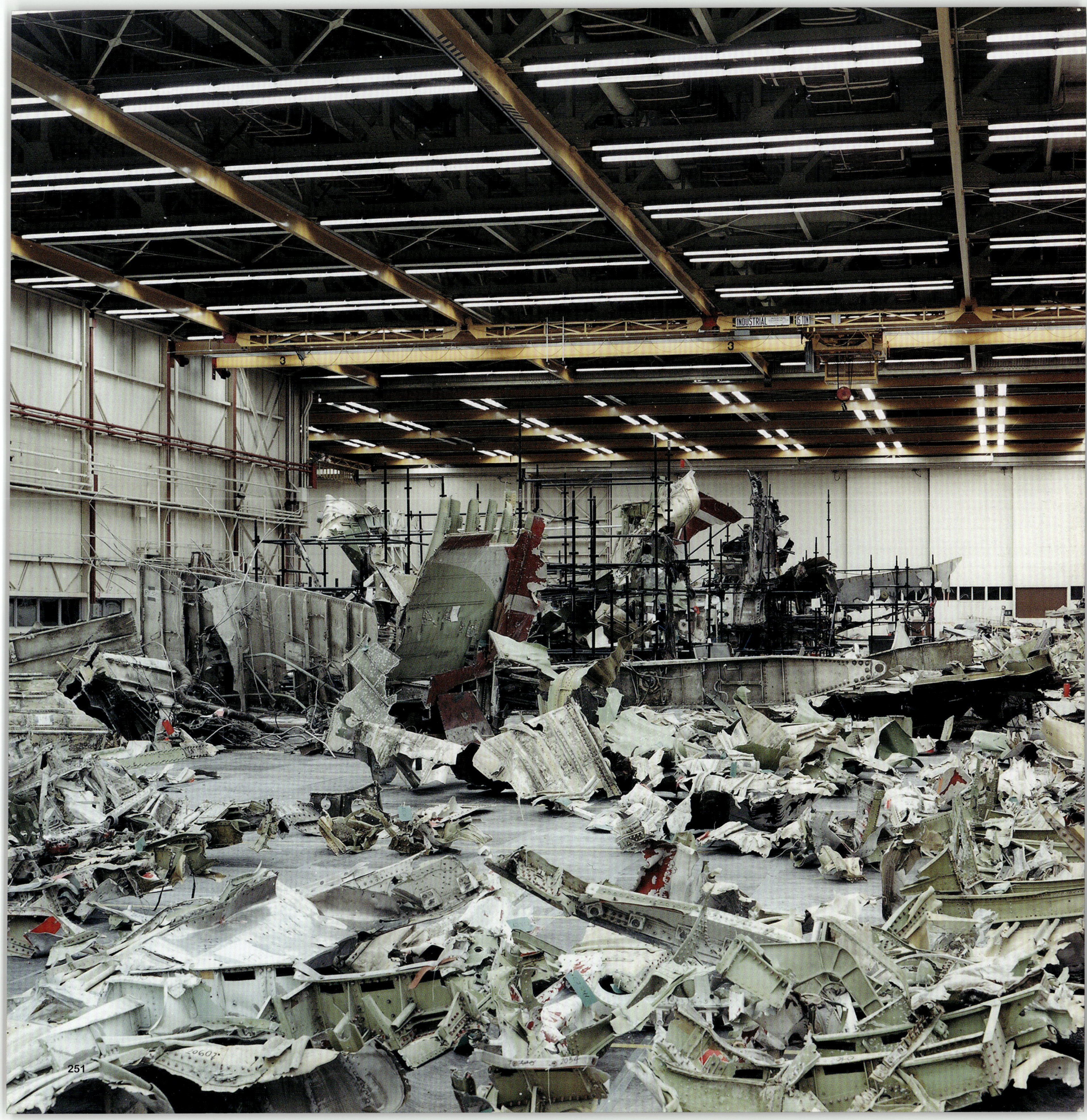
INDUSTRIAL

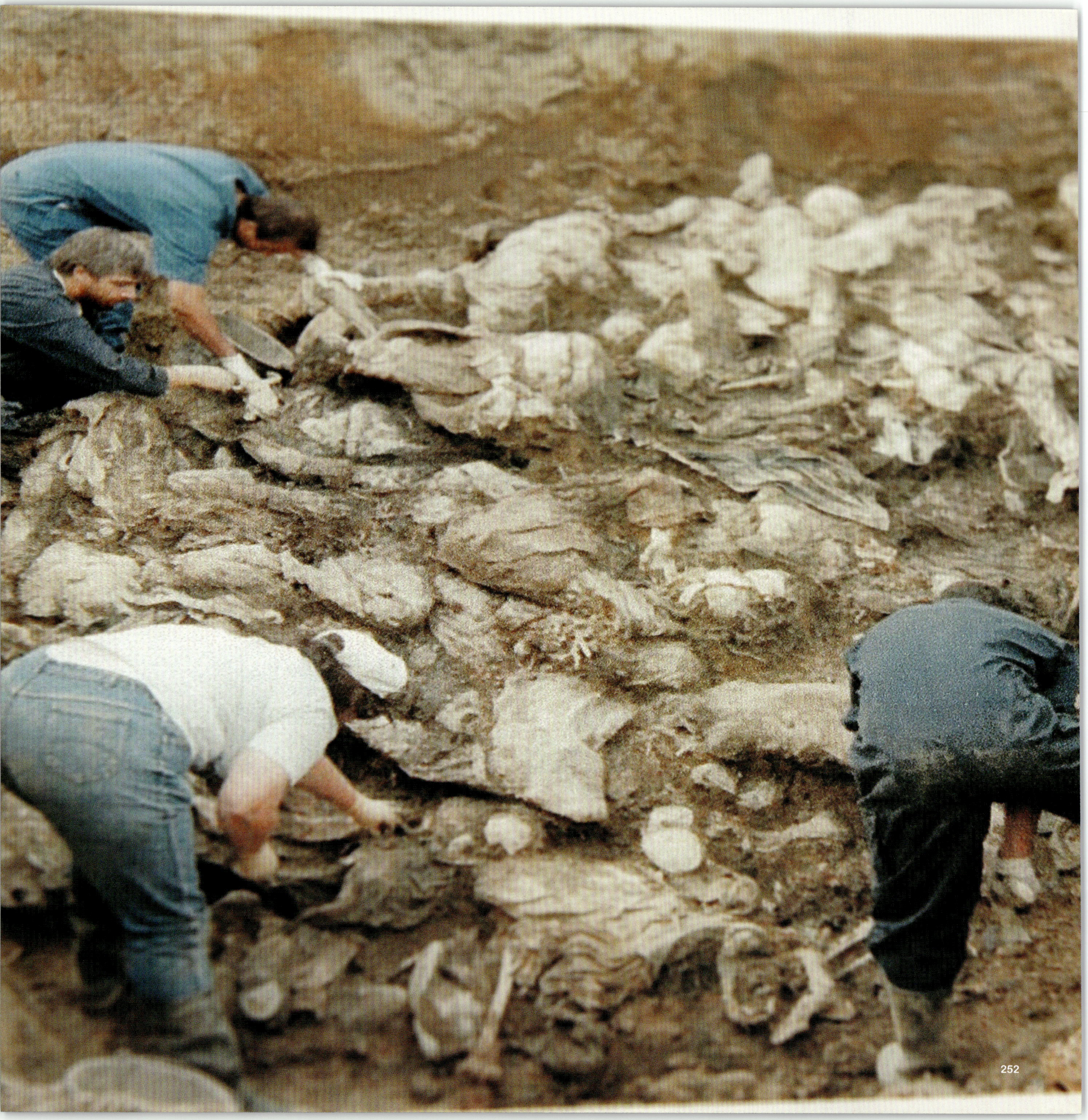

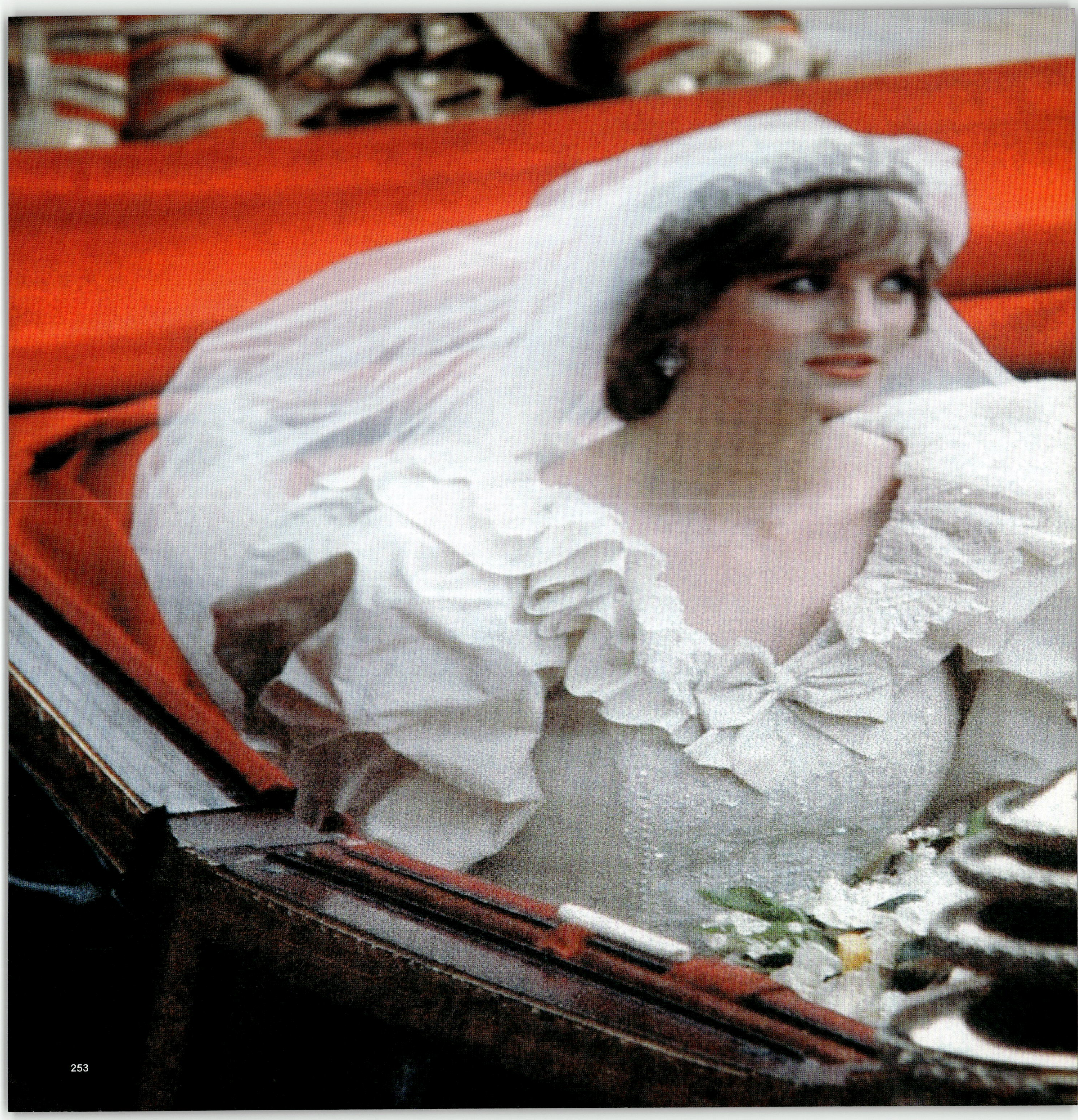

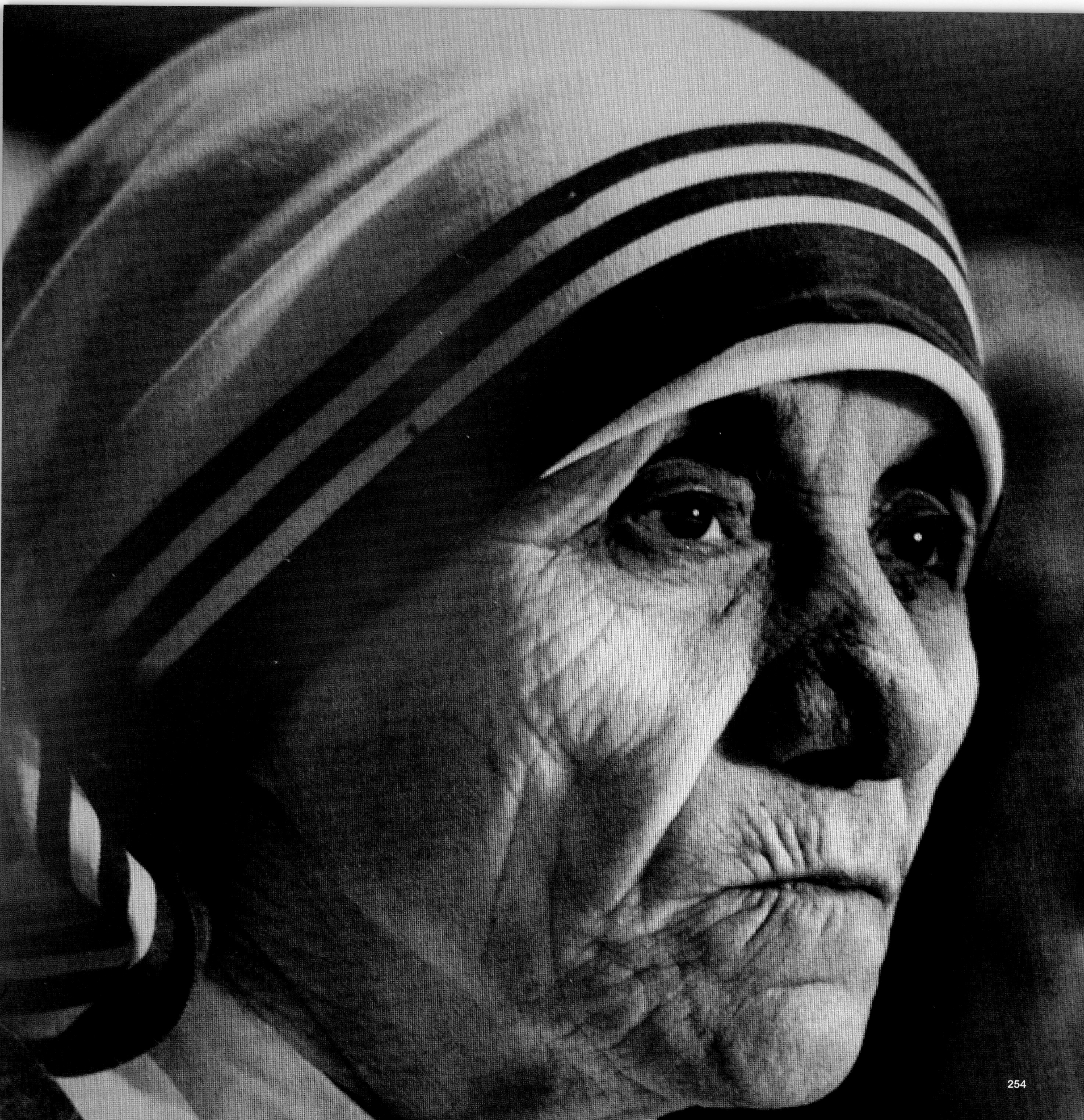

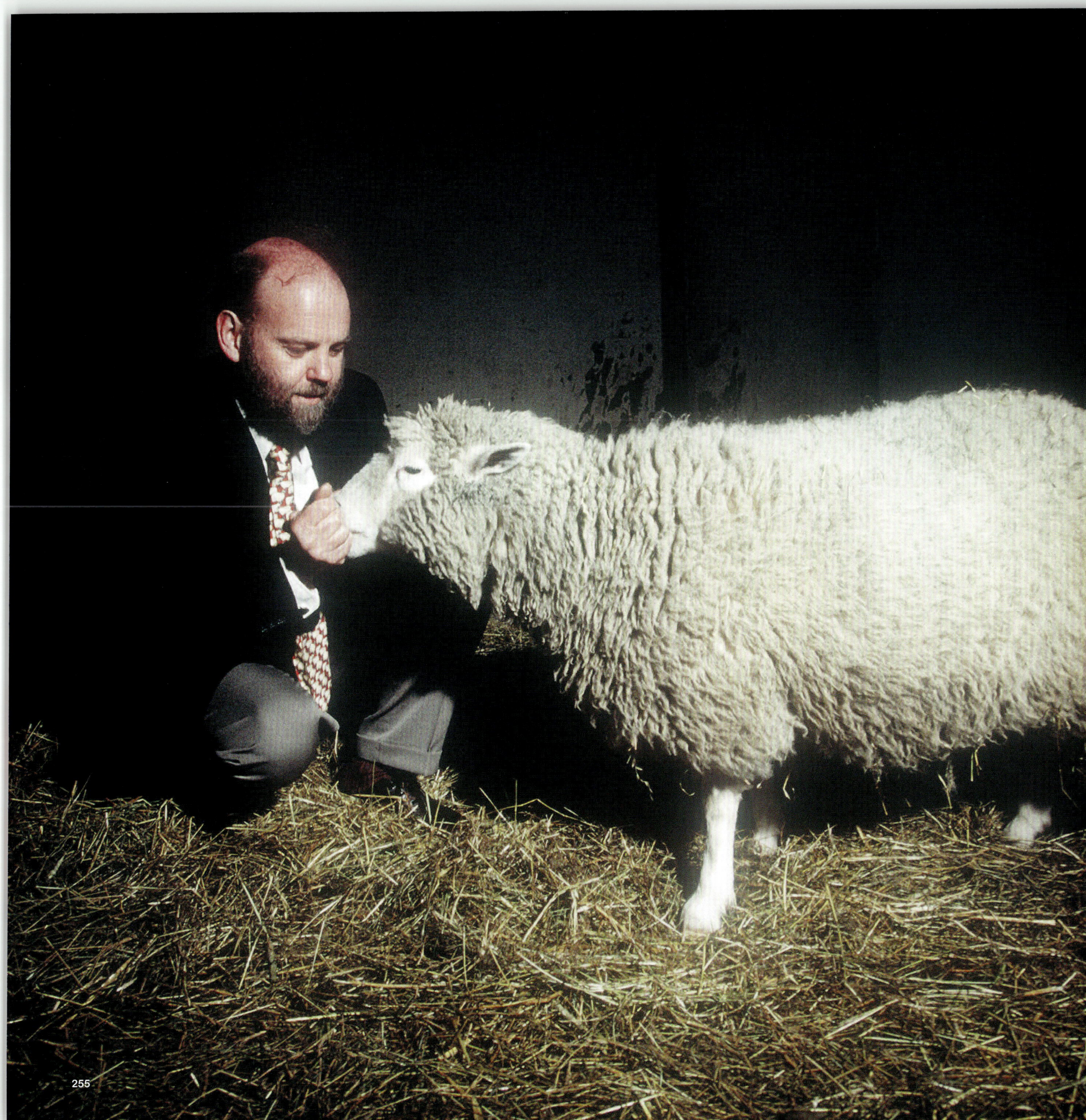

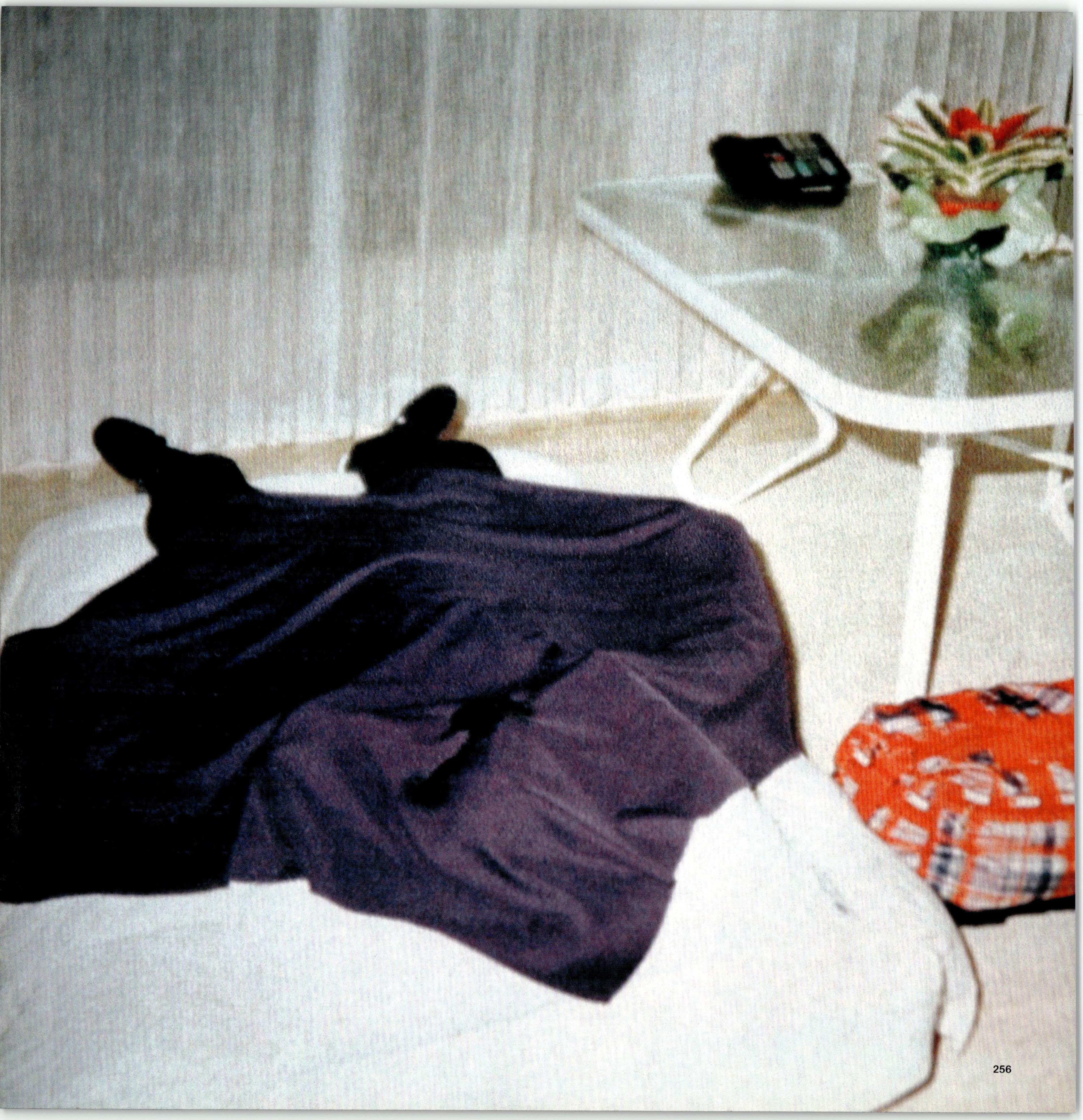

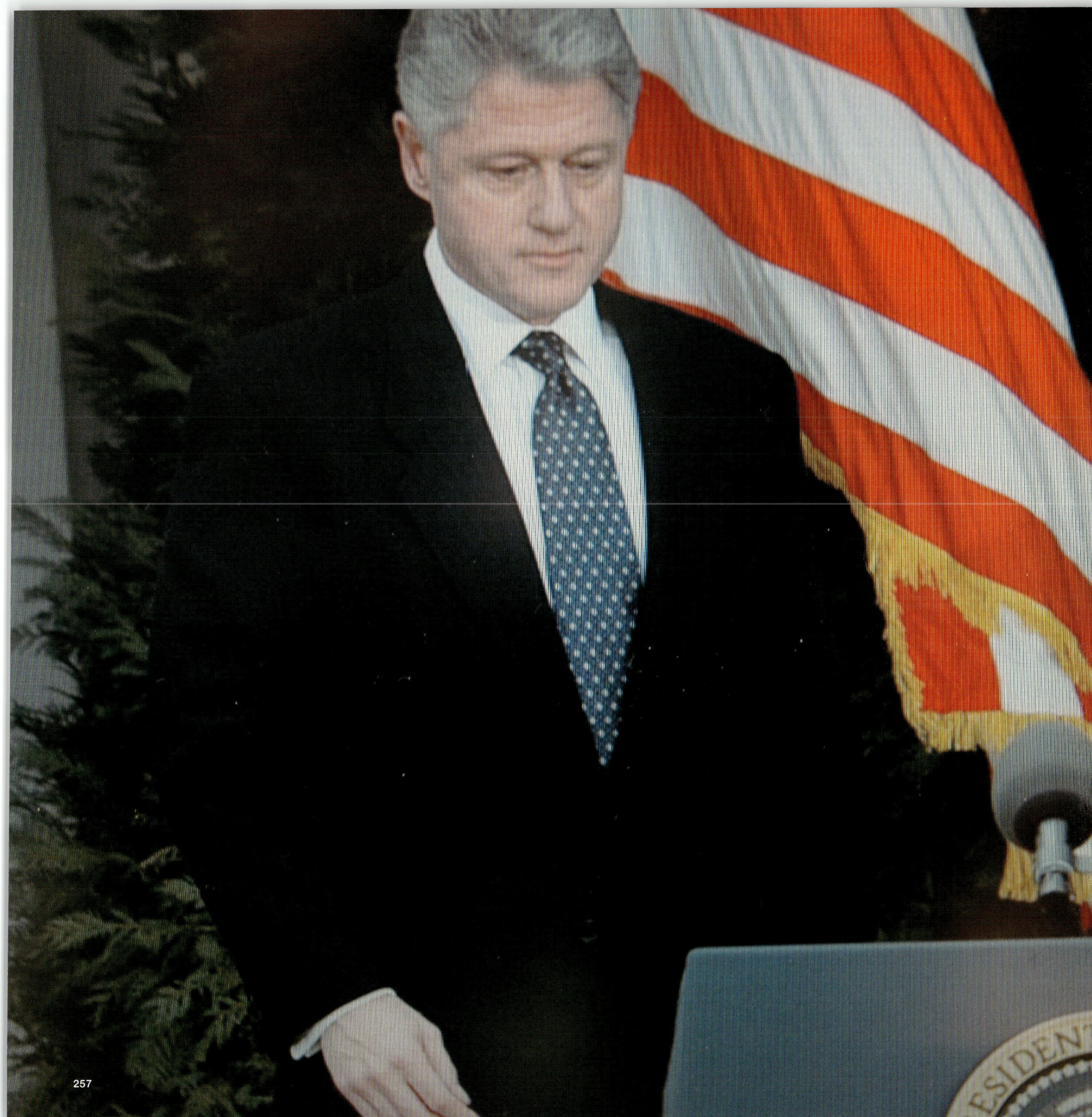

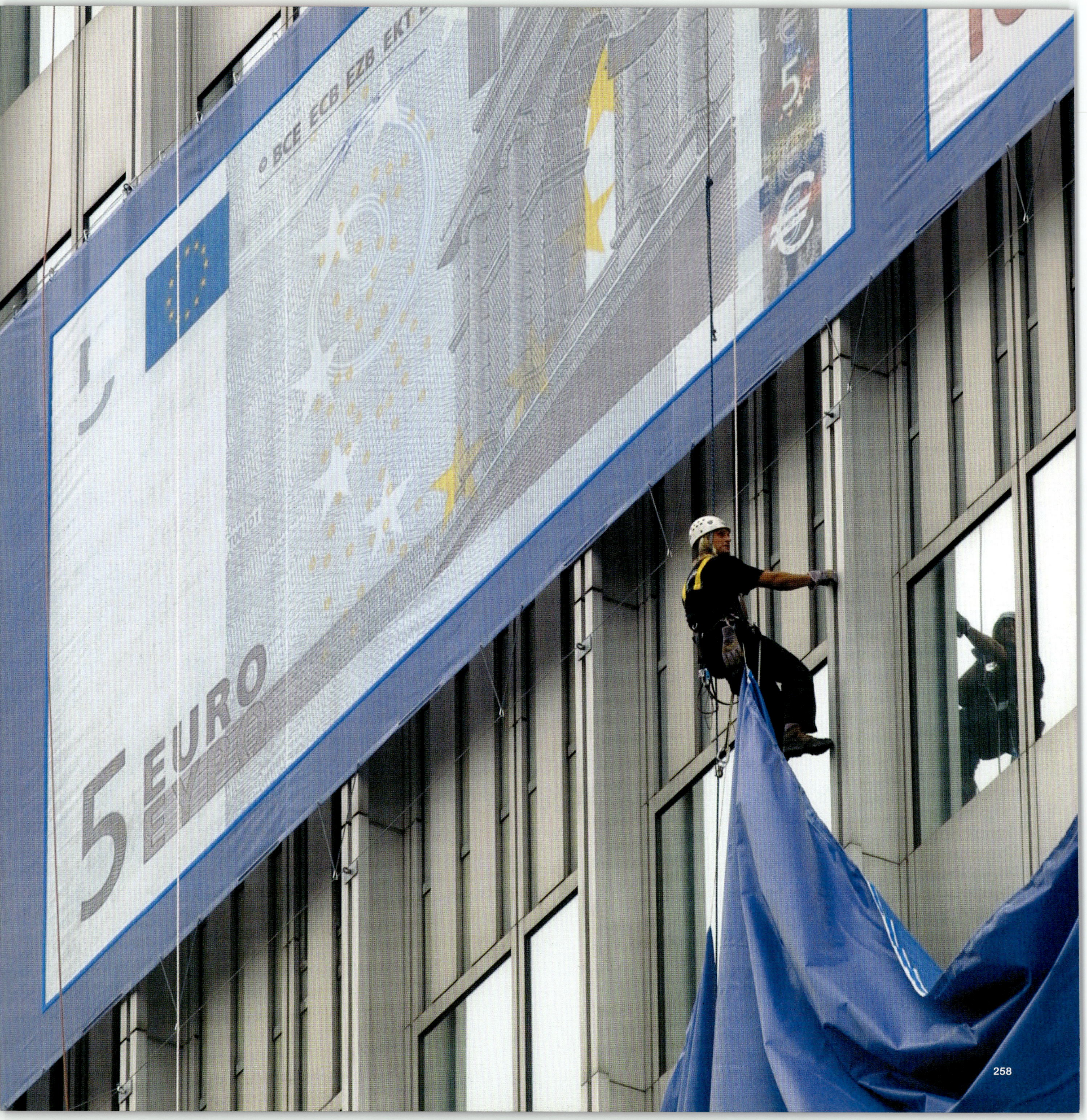
BCE ECB EZB EKT
5 EURO

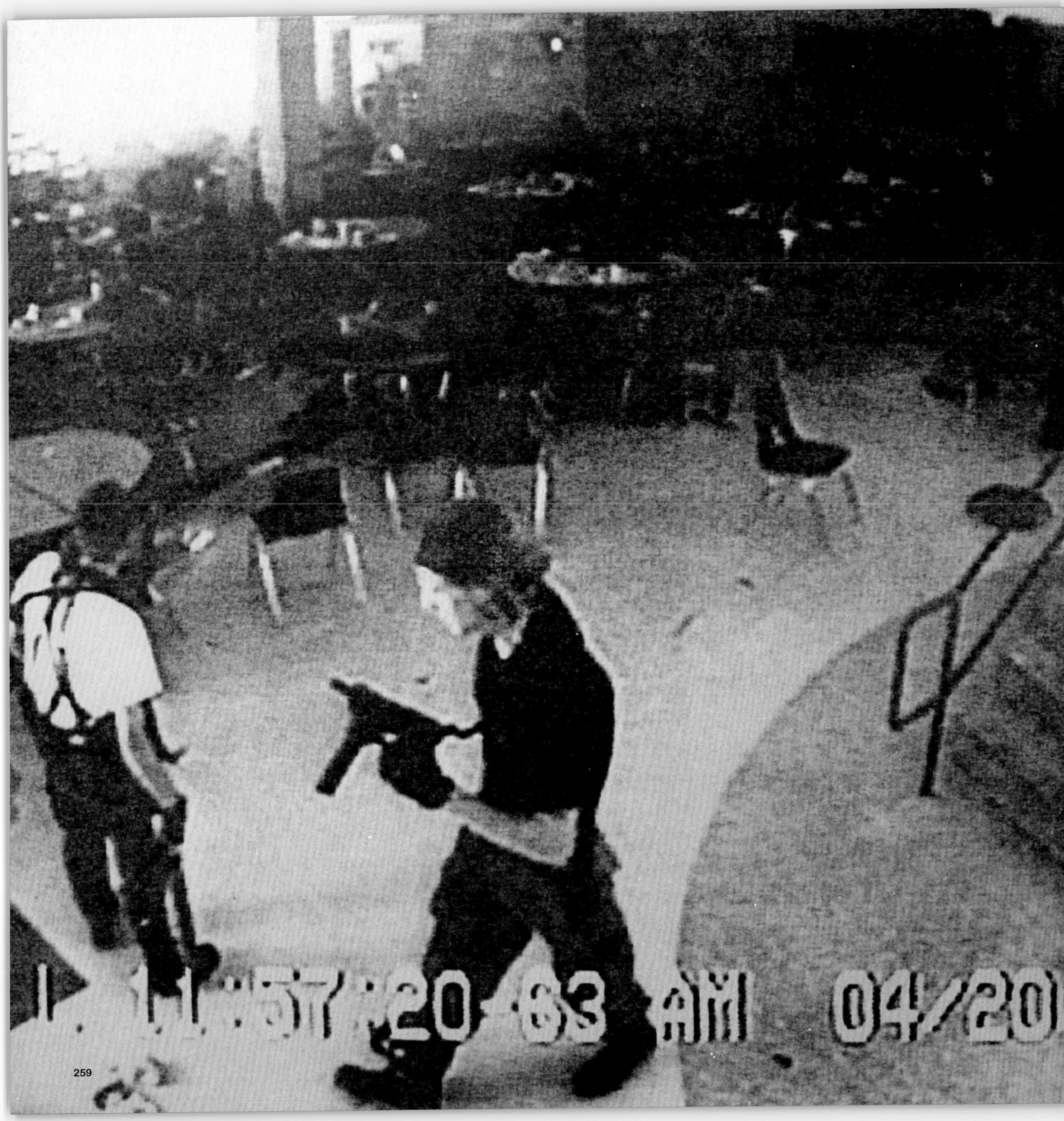

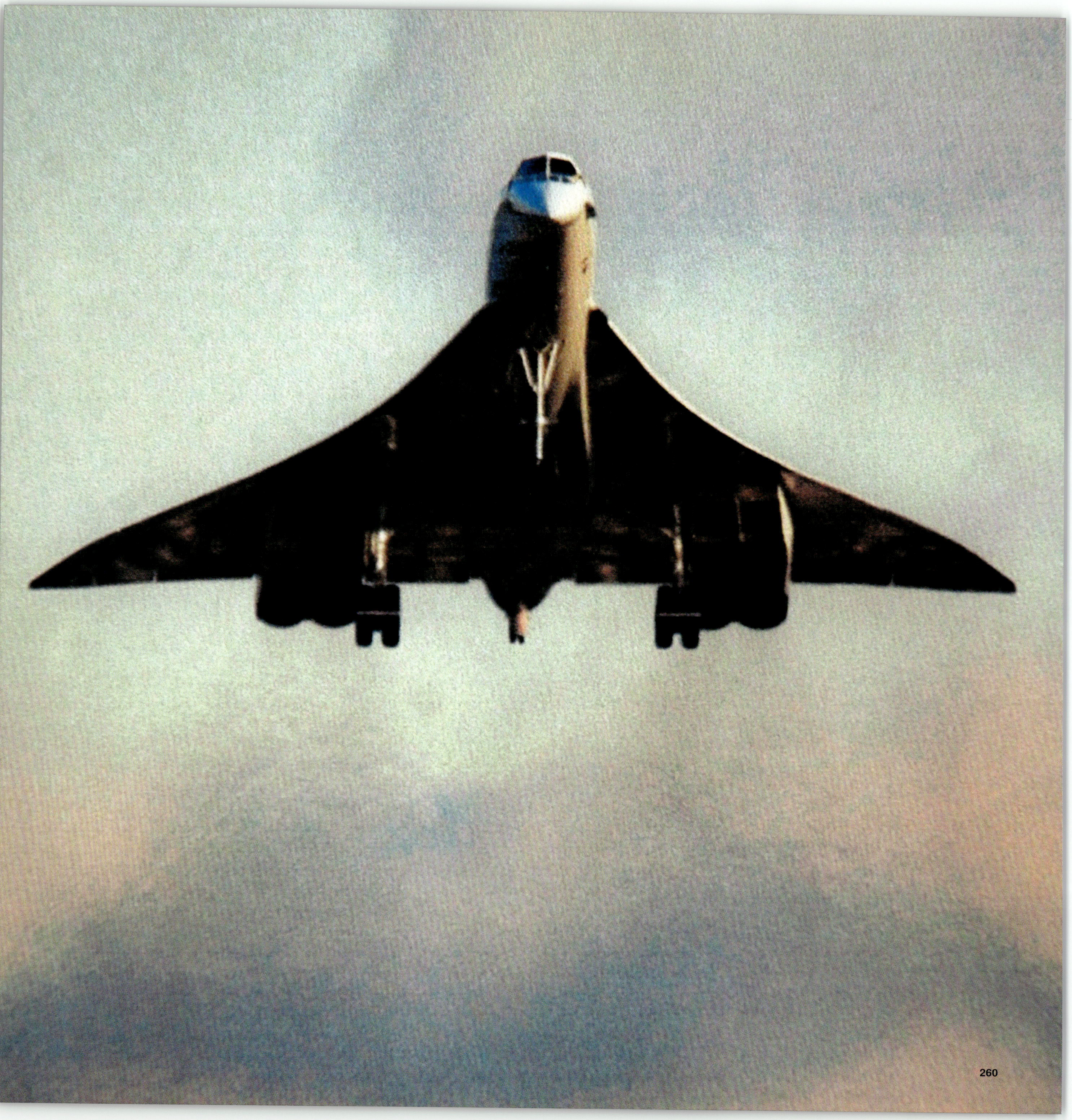

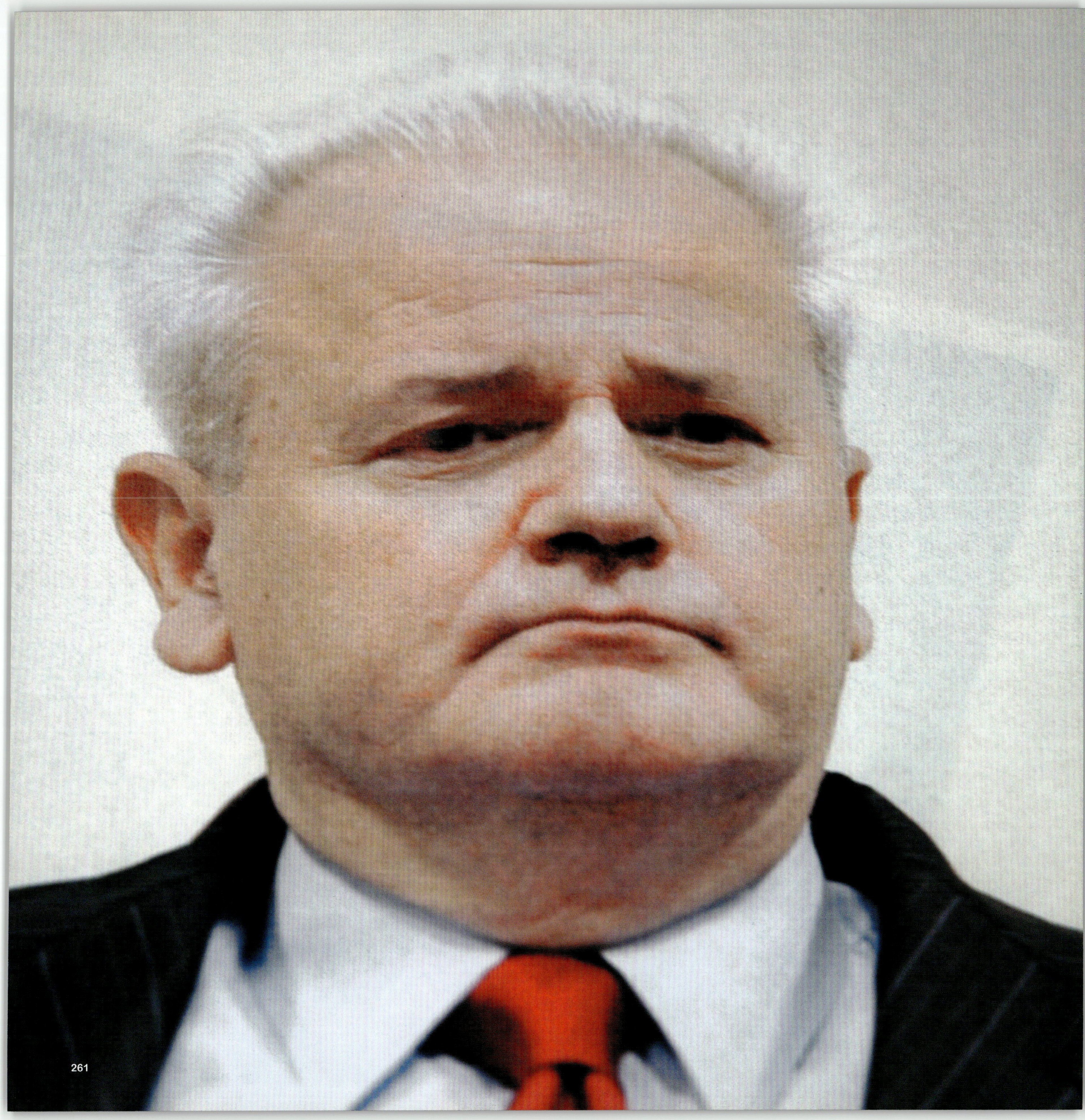

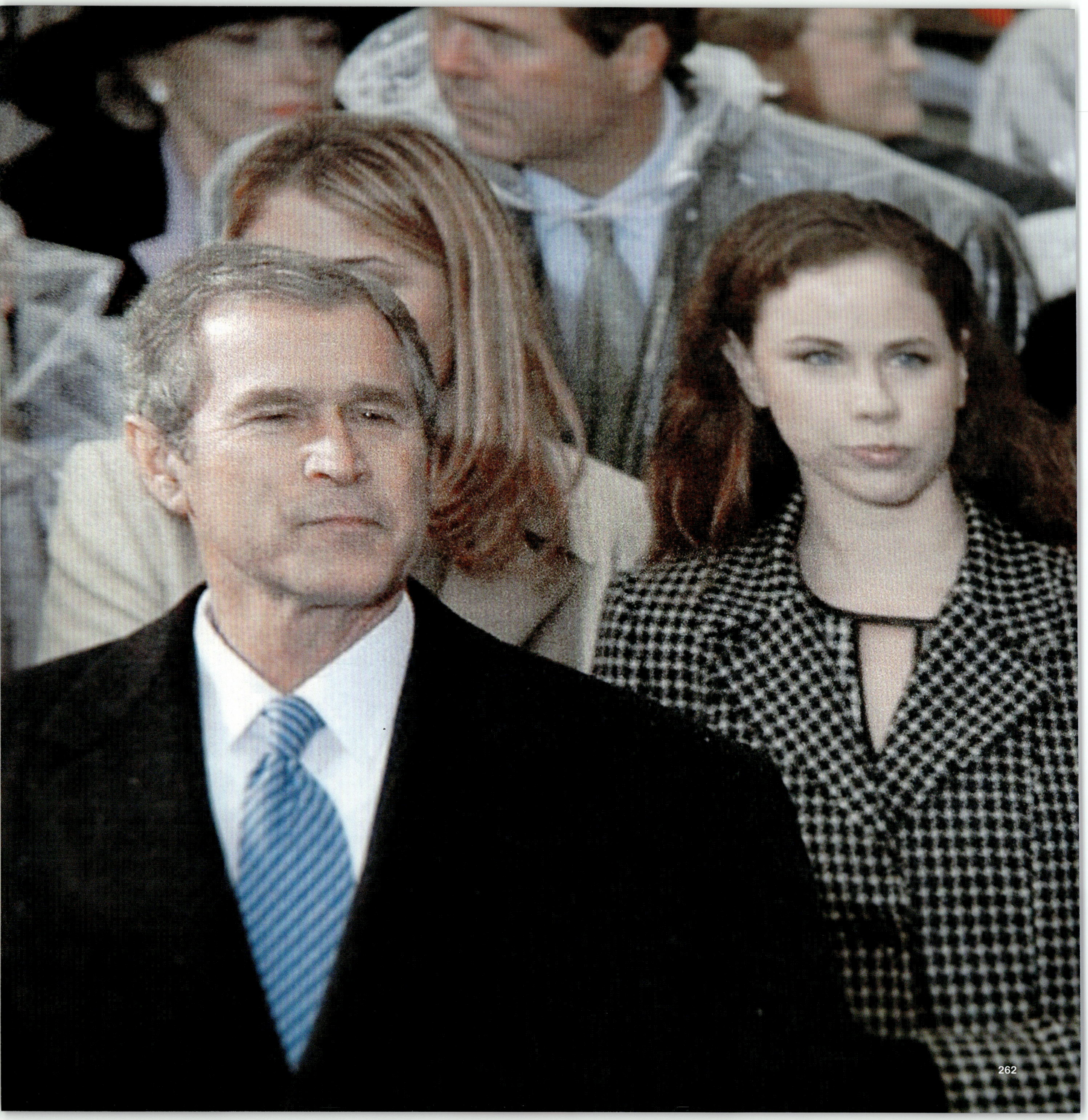

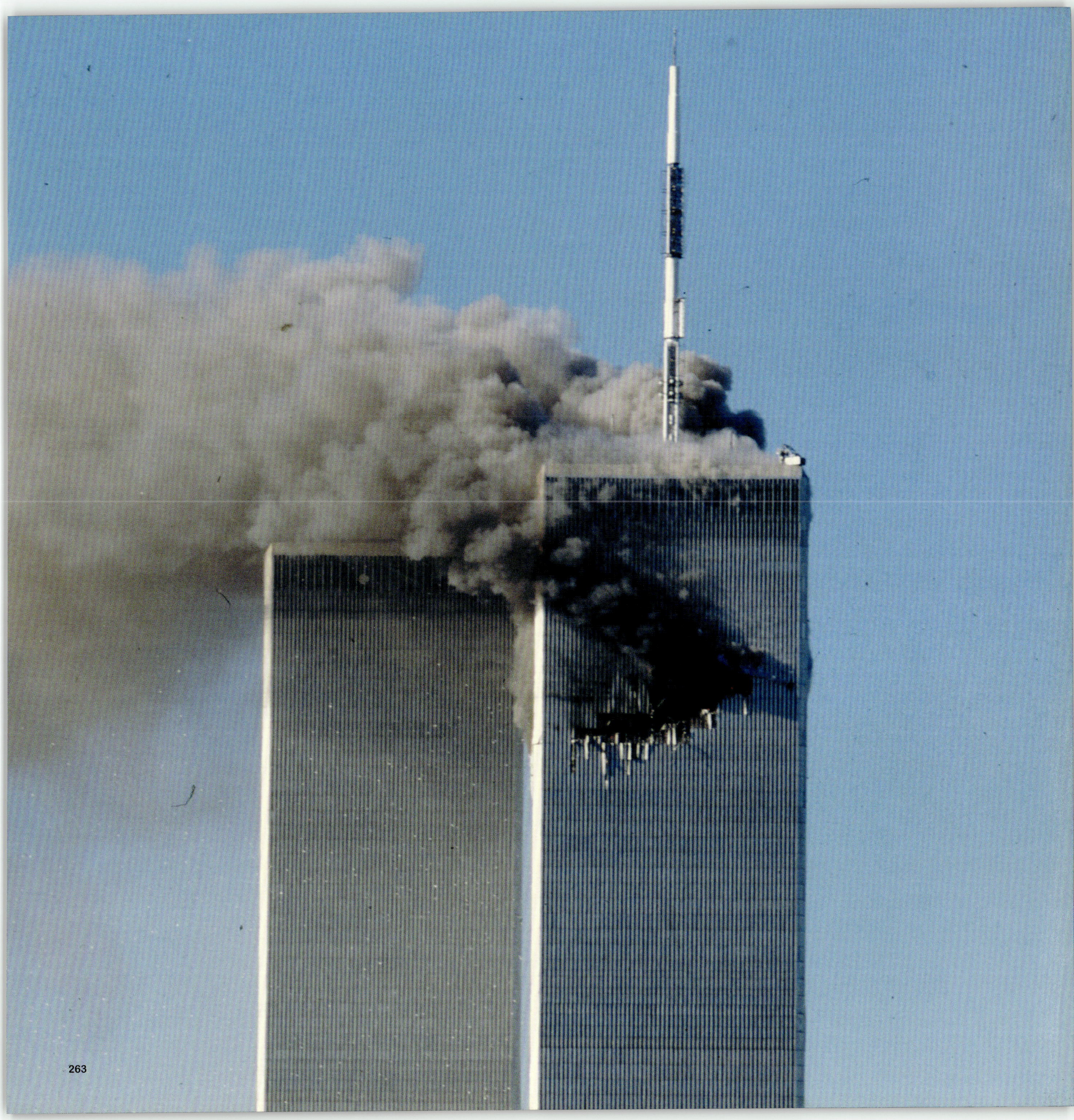

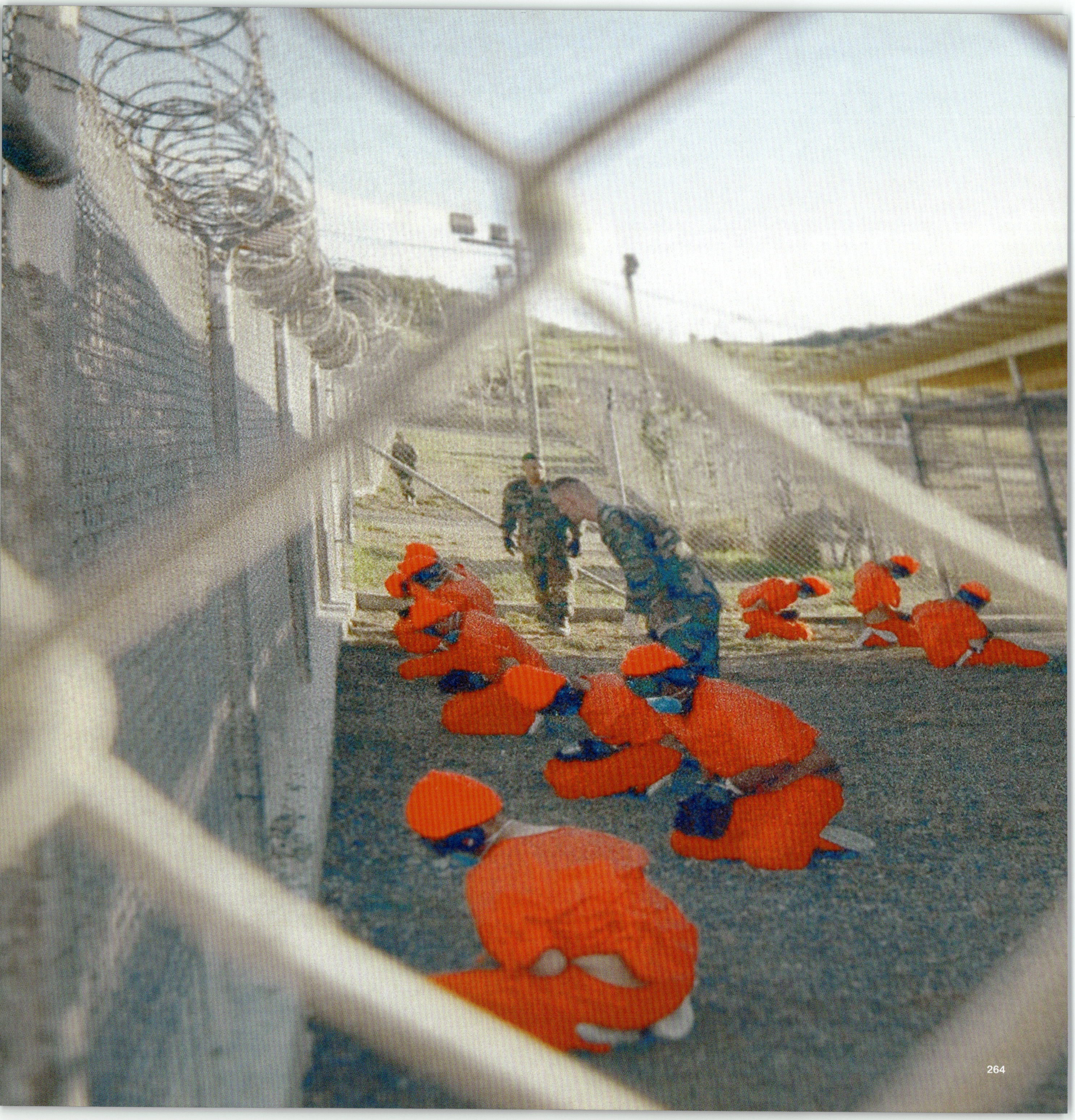

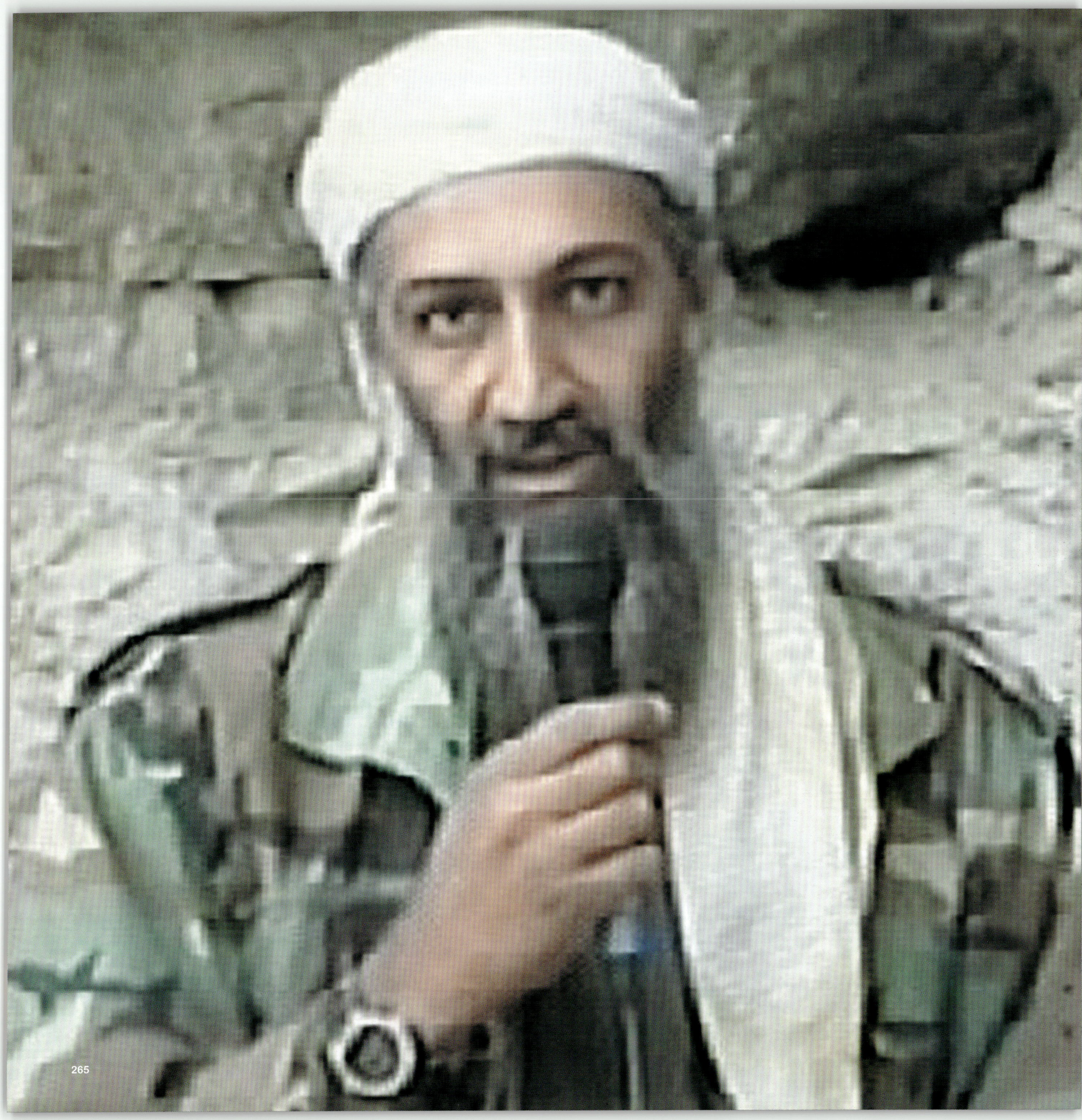

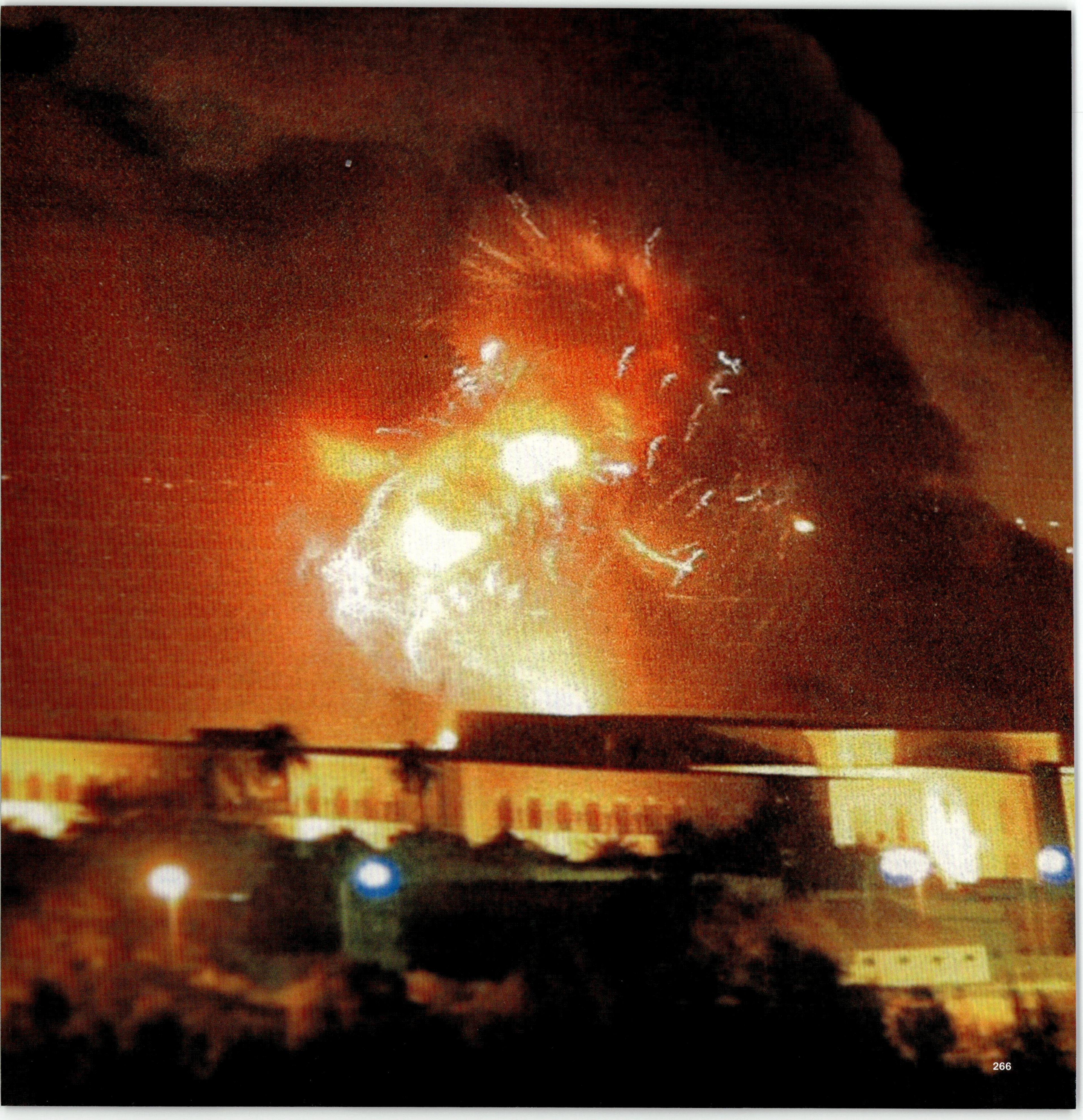

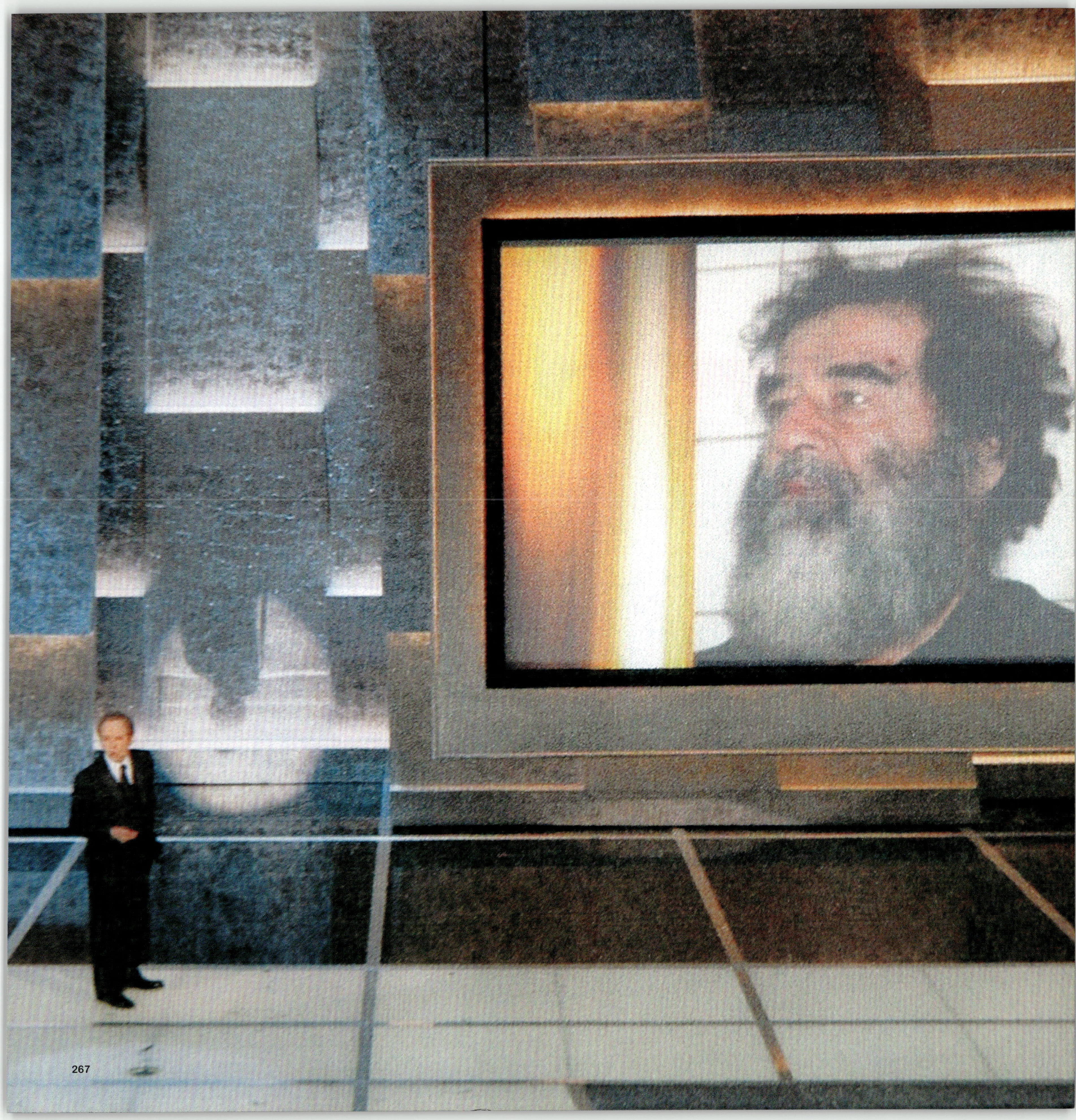

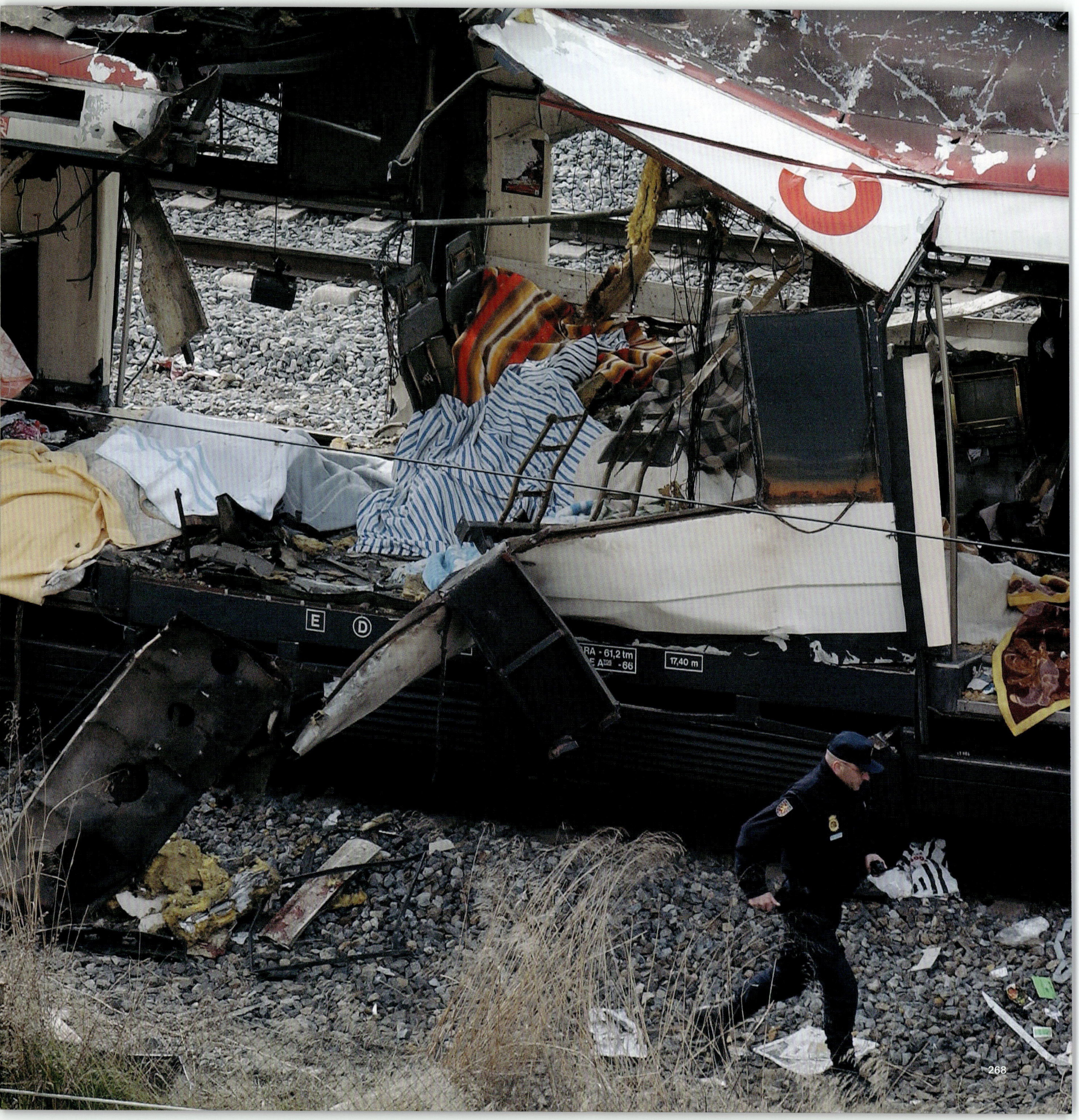
E
D
17,40 m

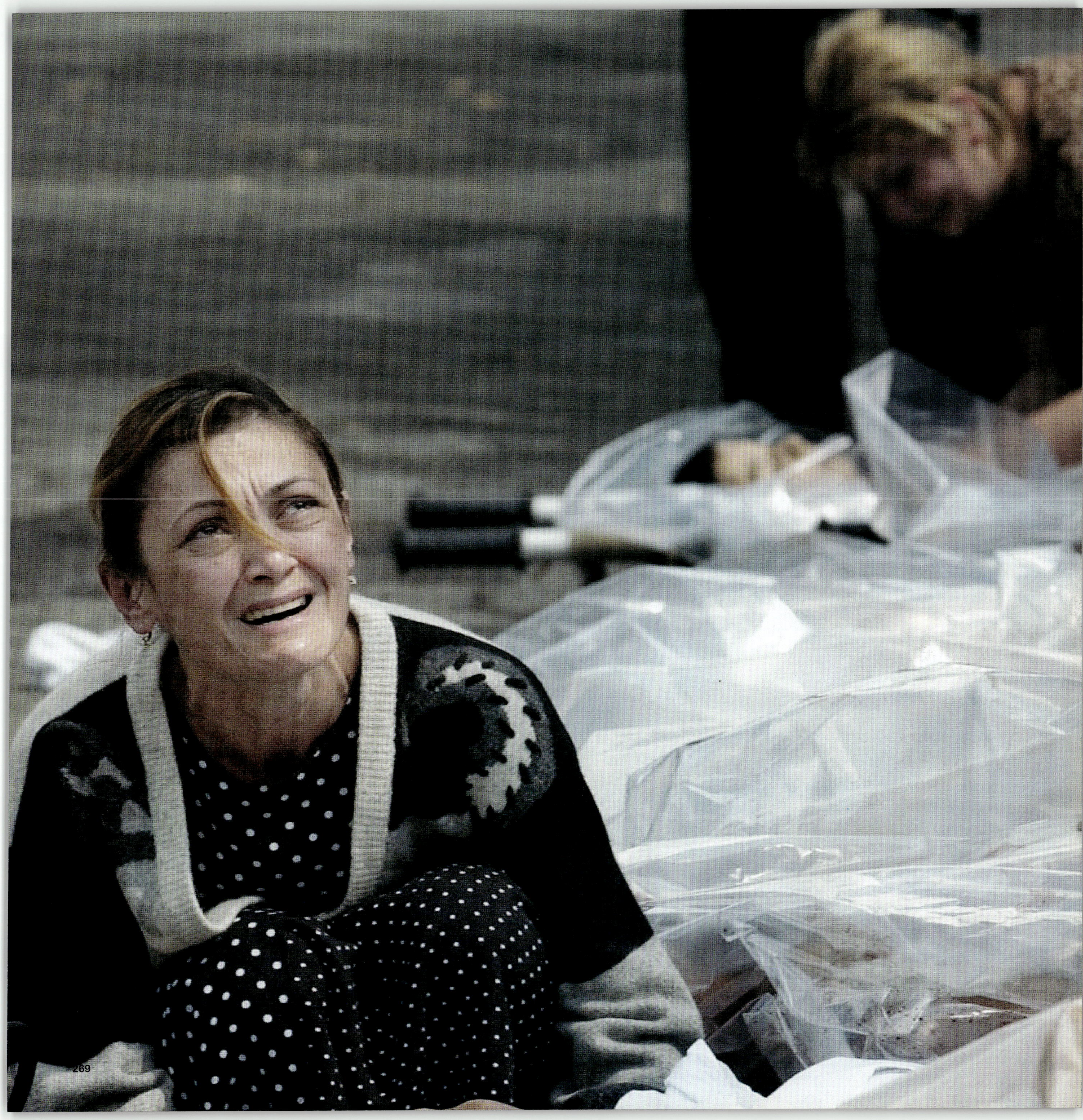

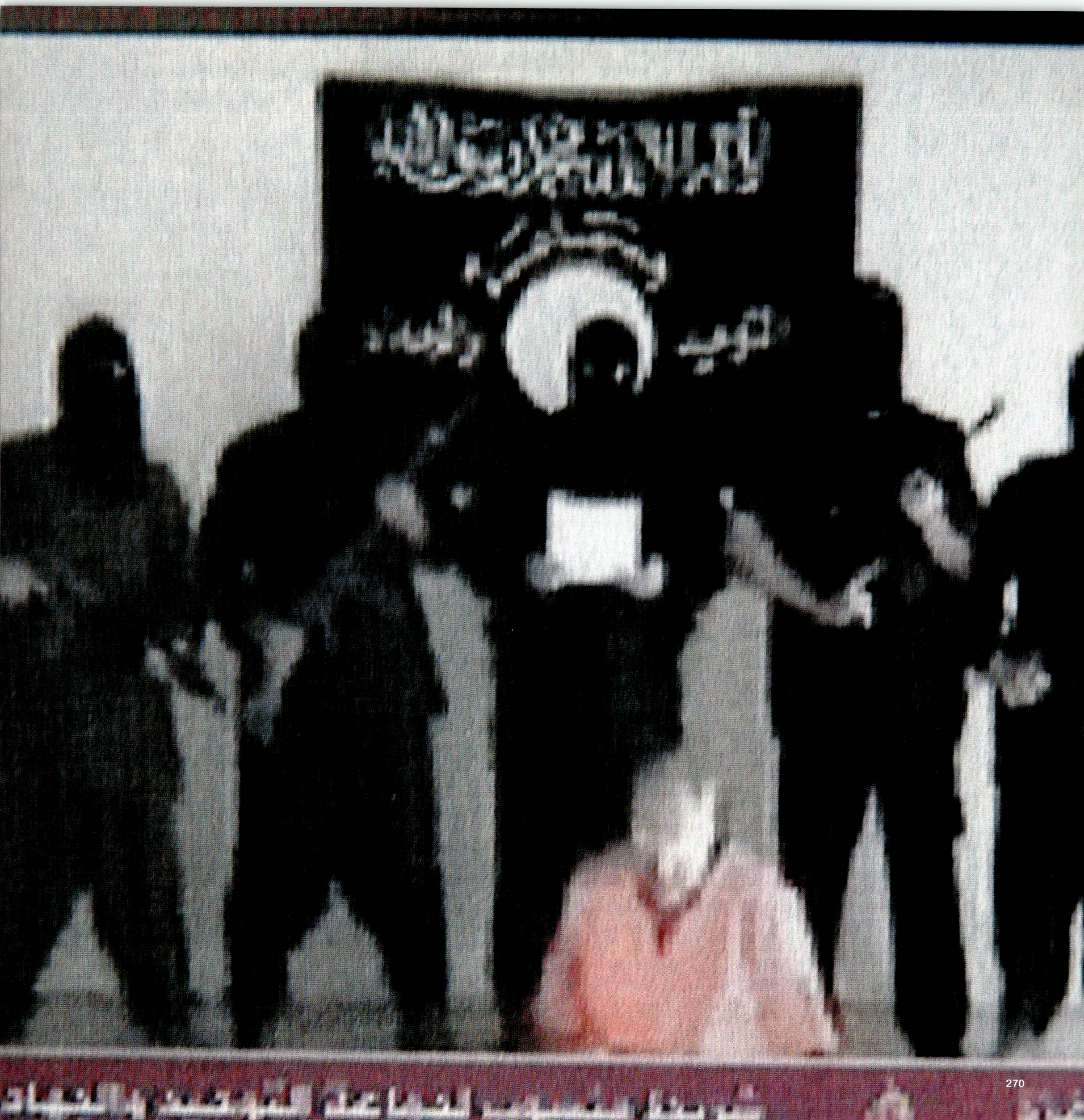

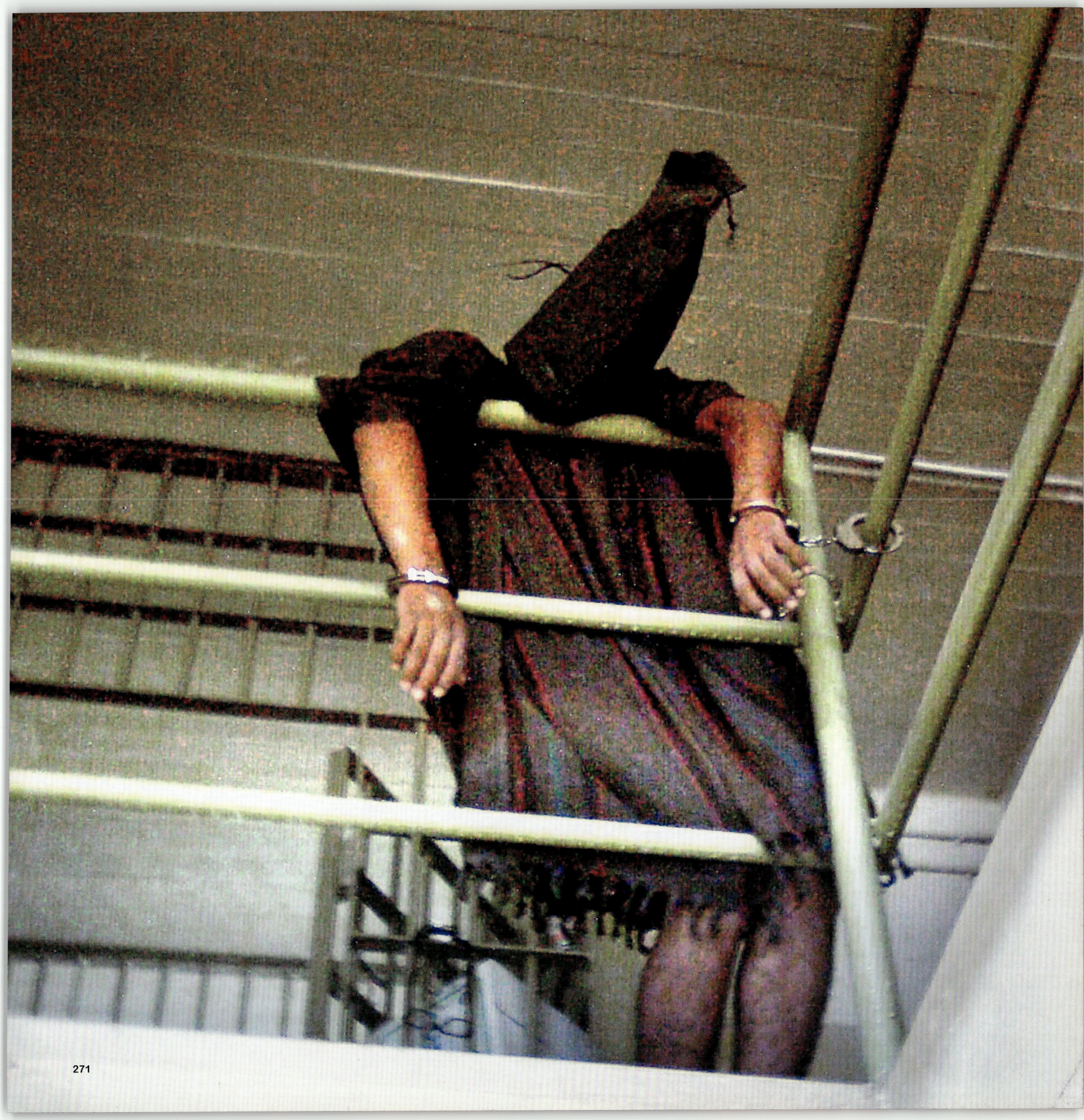

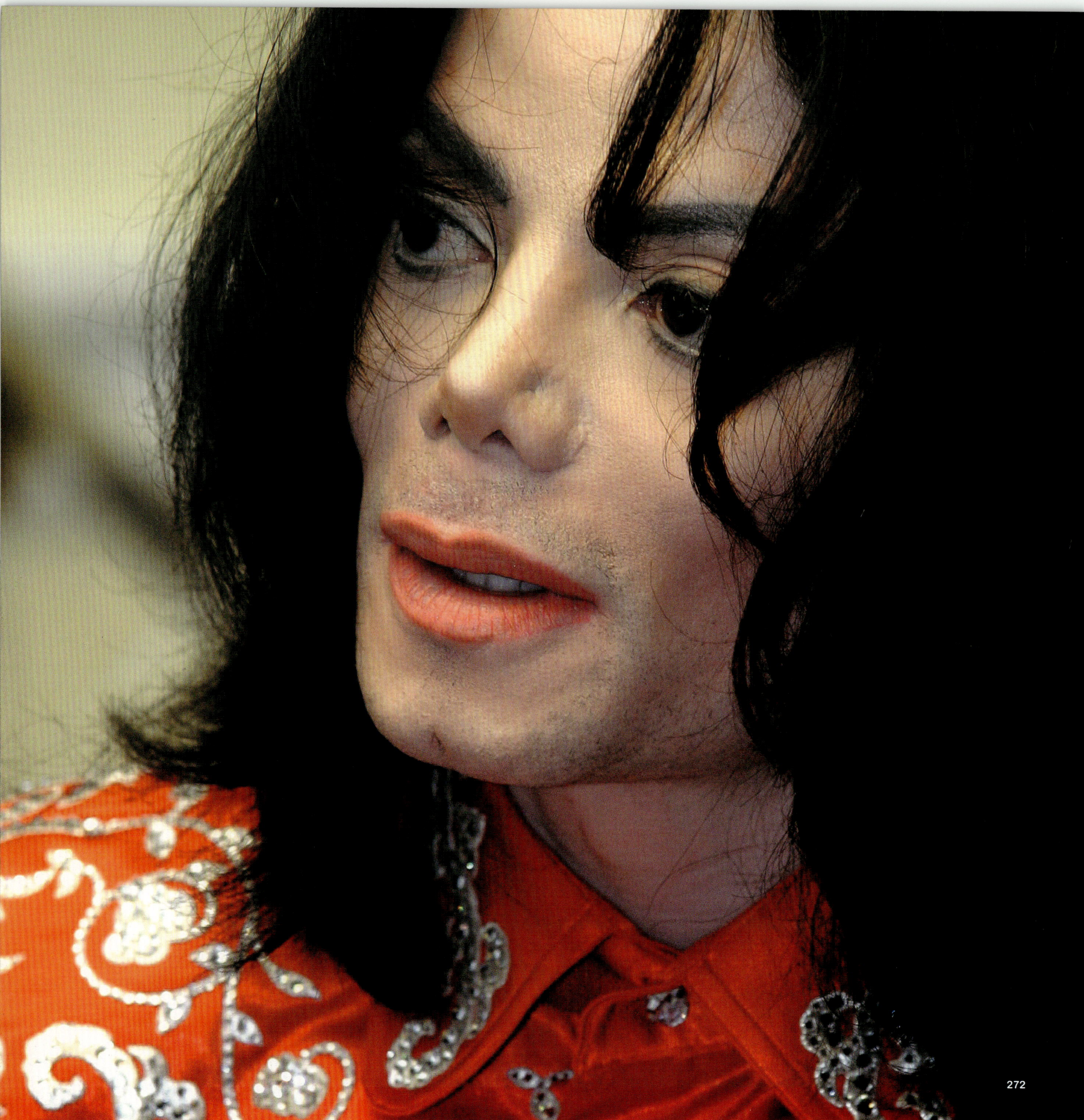

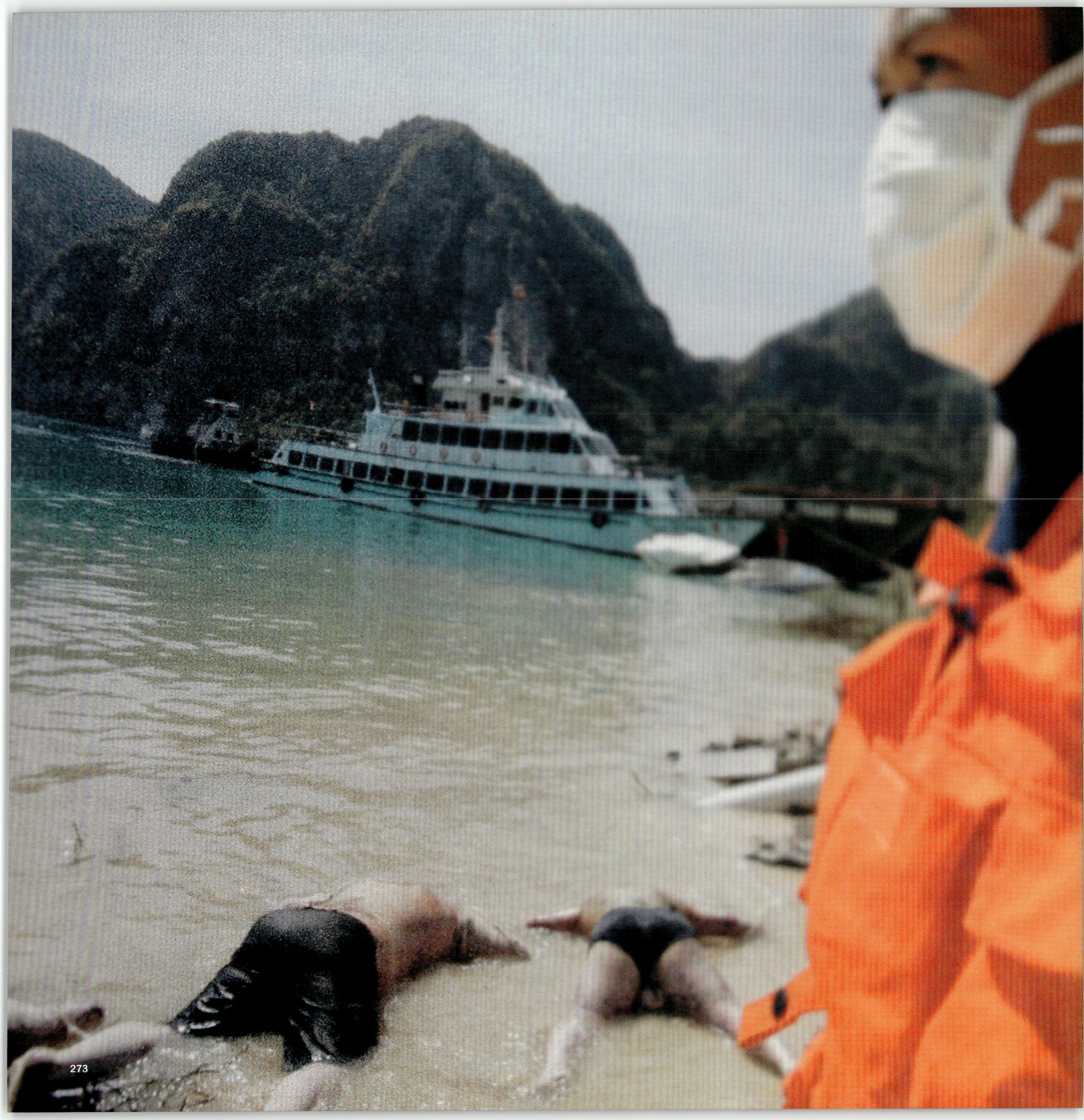

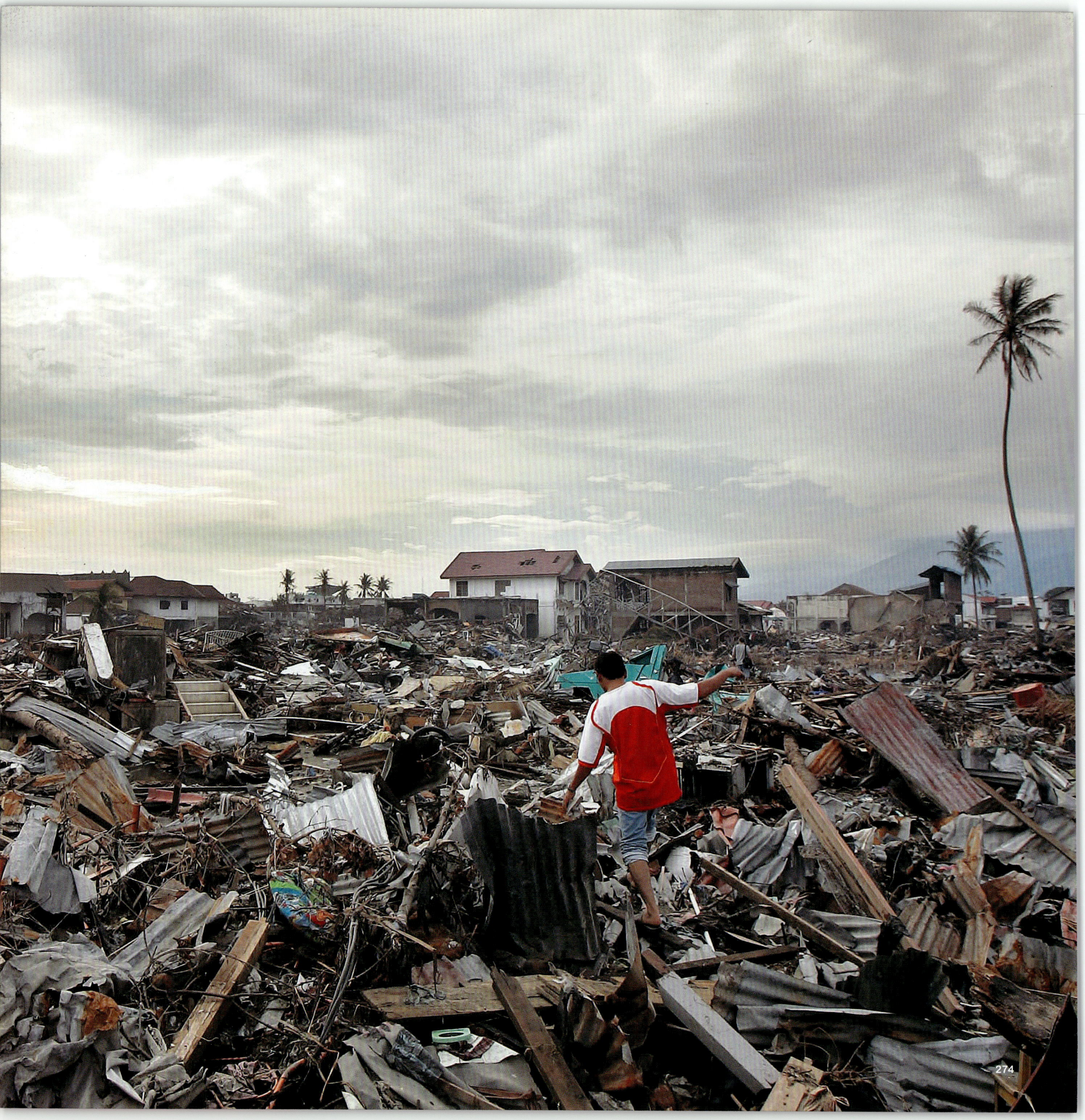

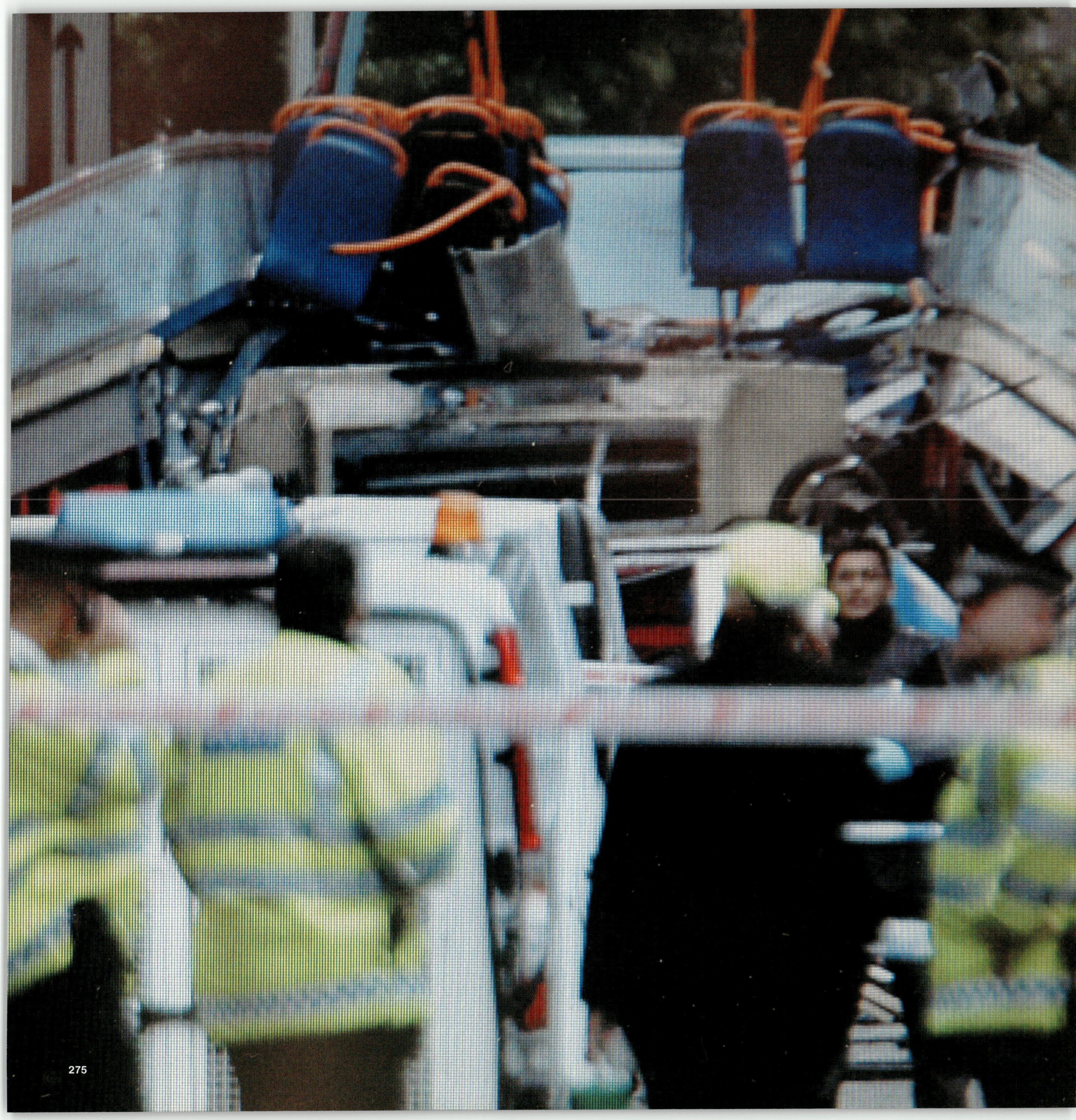

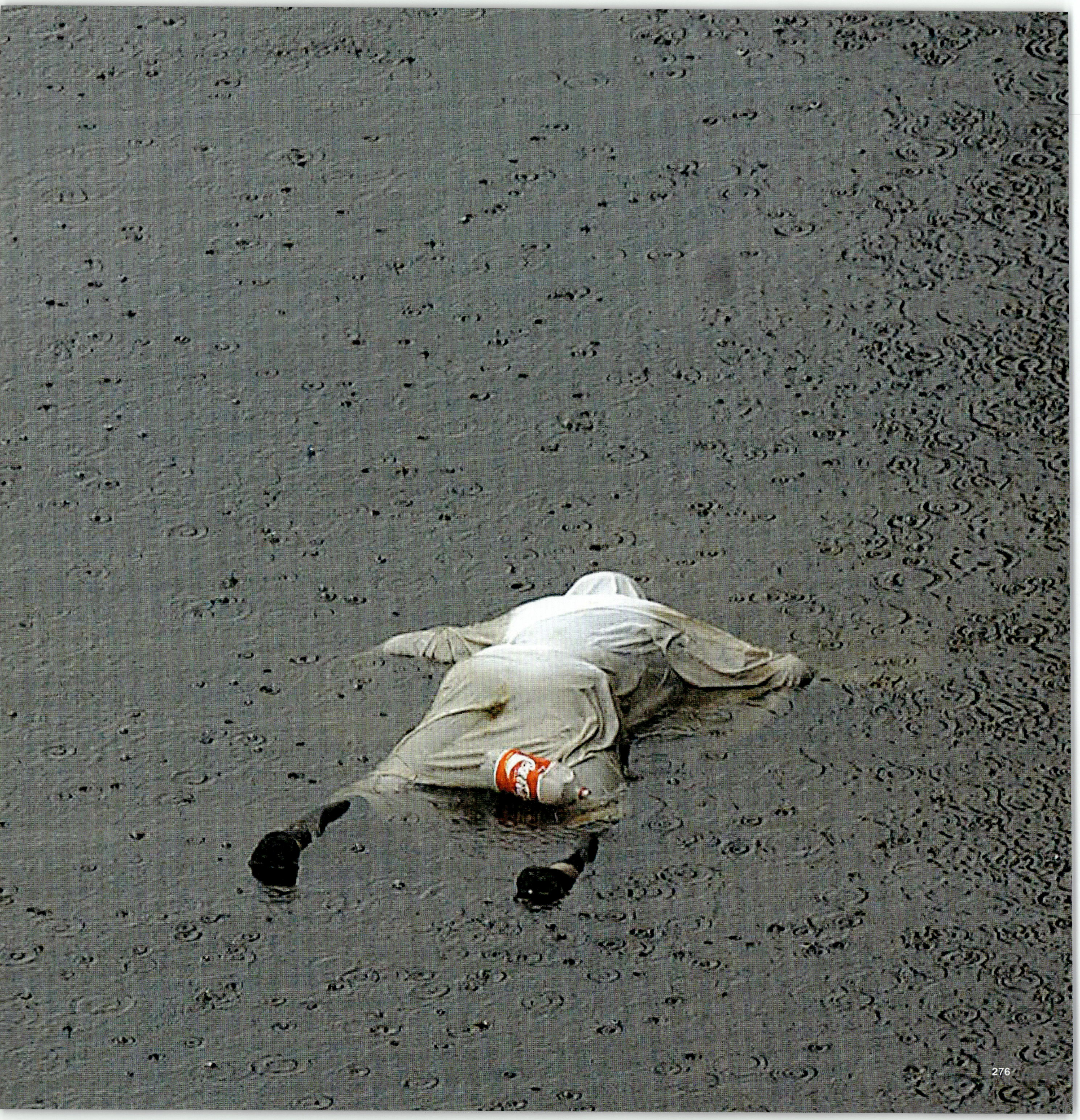

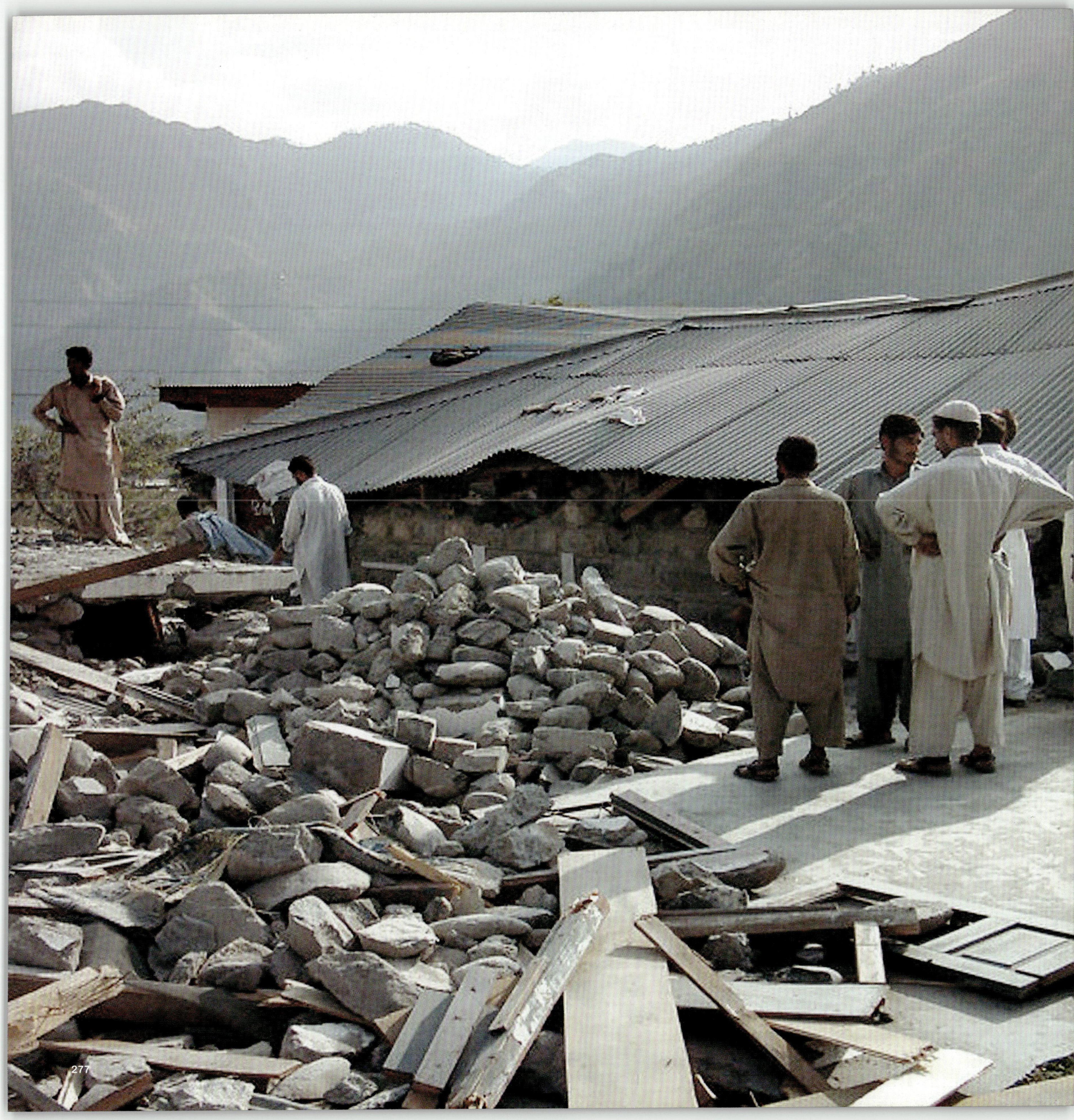

178 1966: Douglas Gordon's birth certificate. (Courtesy Douglas Gordon)

180 1966: Trial of Myra Hindley, who, with Ian Brady, committed the English serial killings known as the "moors murders." (Keystone/Getty Images)

181 1966: Moors murderer Ian Brady. (Keystone/Getty Images)

182 1966: Mao Zedong, leader of the People's Republic of China, launches the Cultural Revolution. (STF/AFP/Getty Images)

183 1967: A couple at the Festival of the Flower Children at Woburn Abbey, United Kingdom. (Pryke/Express/Getty Images)

184 1967: The body of Ernesto "Che" Guevara, executed by Bolivian forces, on public display in Vallegrande, Bolivia. (AFP/Getty Images)

185 1967: Israeli troops occupy Syrian territory during the Six-Day War. (Stan Meagher/Express/Getty Images)

186 1968: Assassination of American civil rights leader Dr. Martin Luther King Jr. (RDA/Getty Images)

187 1968: Eddie Adams's famous image of Nguyen Ngoc Loan, director of South Vietnam's national police, executing a Viet Cong officer in Saigon, in a poster for a 2000 exhibition at the Art Gallery of New South Wales in Sydney. (Greg Wood/AFP/Getty Images)

188 1968: Soviet tanks roll into Prague, ending the Prague Spring. (Bill Ray/Time & Life Pictures/Getty Images)

189 1969: The Woodstock Festival, Bethel, New York. (Hulton Archive/Getty Images)

190 1969: American rock singer Janis Joplin. (Walter Daran/Hulton Archive/Getty Images)

191 1969: Yasser Arafat becomes chairman of the Palestine Liberation Organization. (Keystone/Getty Images)

192 1969: Followers of American cult leader Charles Manson, seen here in a police mug shot, kill seven people in Los Angeles. (Hulton Archive/Getty Images)

193 1970: American pop group the Jackson 5 at the NAACP awards. (Max B. Miller/Fotos International/Getty Images)

194 1972: Break-in at the Democratic National Party headquarters in the Watergate Hotel, Washington, D.C. (Hulton Archive/Getty Images)

195 1972: Children burned by napalm in Trang Bang, South Vietnam. (AP Photo/Nick Ut)

196 1972: Members of the Palestinian paramilitary organization Black September kidnap and kill eleven members of the Israeli Olympic team in Munich. (Keystone/Getty Images)

197 1972: Members of the Women's Liberation Army demonstrate for abortion rights in New York. (Peter Keegan/Keystone/Getty Images)

198 1974: Emperor Haile Selassie of Ethiopia is deposed by a military coup. (Keystone/Getty Images)

199 1974: American heiress Patty Hearst, who was kidnapped by the revolutionary group the Symbionese Liberation Army, caught on surveillance tape taking part in a California bank robbery. (Keystone/Consolidated News Pictures/Getty Images)

200 1974: American President Richard Nixon announces his resignation. (Pierre Manevy/Express/Getty Images)

201 1975: American entrepreneur Bill Gates co-founds Microsoft Corporation. (Ed Kashi/Liaison)

202 1977: Death of American rock 'n' roll star Elvis Presley. (CBS Photo Archive/Getty Images)

203 1977: Hanns-Martin Schleyer, president of the Employer's Association and the Federal Association of German Industries, is kidnapped and killed by the Red Army Faction (aka the Baader-Meinhof Gang), which releases this photograph of him. (Keystone/Getty Images)

204 1977: American pop star Michael Jackson at the Hollywood Palladium. (Frank Edwards/Fotos International/Getty Images)

205 1978: Sid Vicious, bass player of the British punk rock group the Sex Pistols, is arrested after his girlfriend Nancy Spungen is found stabbed to death in his hotel room. (Keystone/Hulton Archive/Getty Images)

206 1978: Mass suicide of over nine hundred members of the People's Temple, led by Reverend Jim Jones, at their compound in Jonestown, Guayana. (David Hume Kennerly/Getty Images)

207 1978: The oil tanker *Amoco Cadiz* runs aground off the coast of Brittany. (Keystone/Getty Images)

208 1979: Iranian students occupy the U.S. Embassy in Tehran, taking its staff hostage. (AFP/Getty Images)

209 1979: Partial core meltdown at the nuclear power plant on Three Mile Island, near Middletown, Pennsylvania. (AFP/Getty Images)

210 1979: Margaret Thatcher becomes prime minister of England. (David Levenson/Keystone/Getty Images)

211 1980: Assassination of John Lennon, singer, songwriter, and former Beatle, in New York. (Evening Times, Glasgow, Scotland)

212 1981: Attempted assassination of Pope John Paul II in Saint Peter's Square, Rome. (Time Magazine/Time & Life Pictures/Getty Images)

213 1981: Andy Warhol at Studio 54 in New York. (Robin Platzer/Twin Images)

214 1981: Attempted assassination of American President Ronald Reagan in Washington, D.C. (Hulton Archive/Getty Images)

215 1981: Polish electrician and co-founder of *Solidarność* (Solidarity) Lech Wałęsa. (Keystone/Getty Images)

216 1982: Ian McDonald, spokesman for the United Kingdom's ministry of defense, making a statement about the Argentine invasion of the Falkland Islands. (Central Press/Getty Images)

217 1984: A child is buried in Bhopal, India, where the Union Carbide plant leaked forty tons of toxic gas, killing thousands. (Pablo Bartholomew/Liaison)

218 1984: American pop star Michael Jackson in Los Angeles. (Frank Edwards/Fotos International/Getty Images)

219 1984: Assassination of Indira Gandhi, prime minister of India, by two of her bodyguards. (Keystone/Getty Images)

220 1984: A starving child in Kambata, Ethiopia, where famine is brought on by drought and political instability. (Keystone/Getty Images)

221 1985: Singer Freddie Mercury performs with his group Queen at the inaugural Rock in Rio festival in Rio de Janeiro. (Dave Hogan/Getty Images)

222 1985: Mikhail Gorbachev, general secretary of the Soviet Union's Communist Party, introduces his policies of *glasnost* (political openness and freedom of speech) and *perestroika* (economic restructuring). (Vitaly Armand/AFP/Getty Images)

223 1985: Death of Rock Hudson, shown here with Doris Day in the 1961 film *Lover Come Back*. (Evening Standard/Getty Images)

224 1986: Explosion of the space shuttle *Challenger* minutes after its takeoff from the Kennedy Space Center at Cape Canaveral. (CNN via Getty Images)

225 1986: Steam explosion, fire, and nuclear meltdown at the Chernobyl nuclear power plant in Prypiat, Ukraine, resulting in radioactive fallout over parts of the Soviet Union, Europe, and the United States. (Arnold H. Drapkin/Time & Life Pictures/Getty Images)

226 1986: Mourners gather after the assassination of Olof Palme, prime minister of Sweden. (Francis Apesteguy/Time & Life Pictures/Getty Images)

227 1988: Plastic explosives detonate on Pan Am Flight 103, which crashes over Lockerbie, Scotland. (Letkey/AFP/Getty Images)

228 1989: The Berlin Wall falls. (Stephen Ferry/Liaison)

229 1989: A pro-democracy demonstrator faces a tank in Tiananmen Square, Beijing. (CNN via Getty Images)

230 1990: American pop star Madonna performs in Wembley, England. (Dave Hogan/Getty Images)

231 1990: South African civil rights leader Nelson Mandela released after twenty-seven years of imprisonment. (Don Emmert/AFP/Getty Images)

232 1990: Iraq invades Kuwait, leading first to economic sanctions by the U.N. and then to the Gulf War. (Patrick Baz/AFP/Getty Images)

233 1990: A town devastated by an earthquake in Iran's Gilan province. (William Foley/Time & Life Pictures/Getty Images)

234 1991: A statue of Vladimir Ilyich Lenin is dismantled in Vilnius, Lithuania, which declared its independence in 1990. (Wojtek Druszcz/AFP/Getty Images)

235 1991: An image shot from the Baghdad hotel room of CNN correspondents on the first night of the Gulf War. (CNN via Getty Images)

236 Laurence Sterne, *The Life and Opinions of Tristram Shandy, Gentleman,* 3rd ed. (London: R. and J. Dodsley, 1760), 1:73-74

237 1991: Assassination of Rajiv Gandhi, the former prime minister of India, in Sriperumbudur, Tamil Nadu. (AFP/Getty Images)

238 1992: Advertisement run by Benetton with image of David Kirby dying of AIDS. (Oliviero Toscani)

239 1993: Moslem refugees fleeing Srebrenica, under siege from Serb forces. (Pascal Guyot/AFP/Getty Images)

240 1993: The Branch Davidian compound in Waco, Texas, burns to the ground after a fifty-one day standoff between cult leader David Koresh and federal agents. (Tim Roberts/AFP/Getty Images)

241 1993: Terrorists detonate explosives in a van parked in a garage beneath the World Trade Center in New York. (Stephen Ferry/Liaison)

242 1994: French President François Mitterand and Britain's Queen Elizabeth II at the opening ceremonies for the English Channel tunnel. (Gerard Fouet/AFP/Getty Images)

243 1994: Former football star O. J. Simpson flees police cars on a Los Angeles highway after accusations that he murdered his ex-wife and her friend. (Jean-Marc Giboux/Liaison)

244 1994: Bodies of Tutsi genocide victims outside a church in Rukara, Rwanda. (Paula Bronstein/Liaison)

245 1994: The interior of a church in Ntarama, Rwanda, lined with rows of human skulls and remains. (Lane Montgomery/Getty Images)

246 1994: A magnitude 6.7 earthquake hits Southern California. (Carlos Schiebeck/AFP/Getty Images)

247 1995: Ebola virus outbreak in Zaire. (Christophe Simon/AFP/Getty Images)

248 1995: Shoko Asahara, guru of the cult Aum Shinrikyo, which is suspected of a deadly nerve-gas attack in the Tokyo subway this year. (Files, Jiji Press/AFP/Getty Images)

249 1995: Terrorist attack on the Alfred P. Murrah Federal Building in Oklahoma City. (Bob Daemmerich/AFP/Getty Images)

250 1996: Outbreak of Creutzfeldt-Jakob disease, which is transmitted by consuming the meat of animals infected with mad cow disease, in the United Kingdom. (J. Casares/AFP/Getty Images)

251 1996: TWA's Paris-bound Flight 800 explodes over the Atlantic Ocean. (Robert Sagliocca/Fbi/Time & Life Pictures/Getty Images)

252 1996: Forensic experts in The Hague with a pile of partly decomposed bodies found in a mass grave in the village of Pilica, near Srebrenica in Bosnia. (Odd Andersen/AFP/Getty Images)

253 1997: Death of Diana, princess of Wales, shown here on her wedding day in 1981. (Anwar Hussein/Getty Images)

254 1997: Death of Mother Teresa, founder of the Missionaries of Charity. (Sal Dimarco Jr./Time & Life Pictures/Getty Images)

255 1997: Announcement of the 1996 birth of Dolly, the first mammal to be successfully cloned from an adult cell. (Stephen Ferry/Liaison)

256 1997: Suicide of thirty-nine members of the religious group Heaven's Gate at their Rancho Santa Fe, California, mansion. (H/O photo supplied to Newsmakers by David McNew)

257 1998: American President Bill Clinton, who this year avoids impeachment by the Senate. (Stephen Jaffe/AFP/Getty Images)

258 1999: Introduction of the Euro, the official currency of the European Union, to world financial markets. (Sean Gallup/Getty Images)

259 1999: Shooting spree at Columbine High School committed by Eric Harris and Dylan Klebold (shown here in a video capture from a surveillance tape), who kill twelve students and one teacher before killing themselves. (Jefferson County Sheriff's Department via Getty Images)

260 2000: The Concorde crashes in Paris, killing 113 people. (Adrian Dennis/AFP/Getty Images)

261 2000: Regime of Yugoslav President Slobodan Milošević collapses. (Bas Czerwinski/AFP/Getty Images)

262 2001: Inauguration of American President George W. Bush, who takes office after the contested election against Al Gore is resolved in his favor. (Tim Clary/AFP/Getty Images)

263 2001: Two hijacked airplanes fly into and destroy the World Trade Center towers in New York. (Peter Cunningham/Mission Pictures/Getty Images)

264 2001: Taliban members in a temporary detention facility at the U.S. naval station at Guantanamo Bay, Cuba. (Shane McCoy/Mai/Time & Life Pictures/Getty Images)

265 2001: Osama bin Laden, founder of the Islamic fundamentalist organization al-Qaeda, in a video aired by the Al Jazeera television station the day that retaliatory strikes began against the terrorist forces in Afghanistan. (AFP/Getty Images)

266 2003: The presidential compound in Baghdad during a United States–led air raid. (Ramzi Haidar/AFP/Getty Images)

267 2004: Oscar host Billy Crystal jokes about captured former Iraqi President Saddam Hussein at the Academy Awards in Hollywood. (Timothy A. Clary/AFP/Getty Images)

268 2004: Commuter trains bombed in Madrid. (Getty Images)

269 2004: Terrorists take hundreds of children and adults hostages in a Beslan, Russia, school. (Sysoyev Grigory/Photas Agency/Getty Images)

270 2004: American contractor Eugene "Jack" Armstrong, in an image from a video broadcast by the Qatar Al Jazeera station, kneeling in front of members of the militant group that kidnapped and beheaded him in Iraq. (AFP/Getty Images)

271 2004: Criminal investigation into abuse of prisoners by American soldiers at the Abu Ghraib prison in Iraq. (Washington Post via Getty Images)

272 2004: American pop star Michael Jackson in Washington, D.C. (Ian Barkley/Getty Images)

273 2004: Bodies washed up on the beach on Phi Phi Island, Thailand, an area severely hit by the tsunami following the Indian Ocean earthquake. (Paula Bronstein/Getty Images)

274 2004: Buildings destroyed by the earthquake in Banda Aceh, Indonesia. (Spencer Platt/Getty Images)

275 2005: Suicide bombings on London buses and trains. (Adrian Dennis/AFP/Getty Images)

276 2005: A body caught in the floodwaters of Hurricane Katrina in New Orleans. (James Nielsen/AFP/Getty Images)

277 2005: The remains of a government girls' school, destroyed by a massive earthquake, in Gari Habibullah, Pakistan. (Syed Azhar Shah/AFP/Getty Images)

Exhibitions and Selected Bibliography

Born 1966 in Glasgow, Scotland. Lives and works in Glasgow and New York.

1984–88: Glasgow School of Art
1988–90: The Slade School of Fine Art, London

Solo Exhibitions

1987 *Experiments under Nostalgia's Umbrella* (with Craig Richardson). Third Eye Centre, Glasgow
N.R.L.A. (with Craig Richardson). Riverside Studios, London

1988 *40 years* (with Craig Richardson). Royal Scottish Academy, Edinburgh
4th Avé Festival (with Craig Richardson). Arnhem, The Netherlands
From cradle to grave (with Craig Richardson). Royal Scottish Academy, Edinburgh
The Puberty Institution (with Craig Richardson). Midland Street Car Park, Glasgow
The Puberty Institution: Refuse-consumption-decay-survival (with Craig Richardson). Third Eye Centre, Glasgow

1993 *Migrateurs.* Musée d'Art Moderne de la Ville de Paris
24 Hour Psycho. Tramway, Glasgow, and Kunst-Werke, Berlin

1994 Lisson Gallery, London

1995 *Bad Faith.* Künstlerhaus Stuttgart
Café Rooseum Espresso, Malmö
Douglas Gordon/Graham Gussin: a collaboration. The Agency, London
Entr'Acte 3. Stedelijk Van Abbemuseum, Eindhoven
Fuzzy Logic. Centre national d'art et de culture Georges Pompidou, Paris
The End. Jack Tilton Gallery, New York

1996 British Art Festival. Galleria Bonomo, Rome
Canberra Contemporary Art Space
Cinema is dead. museum in progress, Vienna
Cinéma Liberté Bar Lounge (with Rirkrit Tiravanija). FRAC Languedoc-Roussillon, Montpellier
Galerie Walcheturm, Zurich
24 Hour Psycho. Akademie der bildenden Künste Wien, Vienna
migros museum für gegenwartskunst, Zurich

1997 Bloom Gallery, Amsterdam
5 Year Drive-By. Overnight: #1. Kunstverein Hannover
Galerie Micheline Szwajcer, Antwerp
Galerie Mot & van den Boogaard, Brussels
Galerie Yvon Lambert, Paris
Galleri Nicolai Wallner, Copenhagen
Gandy Gallery, Prague
Leben nach dem Leben nach dem Leben . . . . Deutsches Museum Bonn

1998 Dvir Gallery, Tel Aviv
Empire. The Merchant City Civic Society, Glasgow (commission)
Kunstverein Hannover

1999 Centro Cultural de Belém, Lisbon
Feature Film. Atlantis Gallery, London. Traveled: Kölnischer Kunstverein, Cologne; Centre national d'art et de culture Georges Pompidou, Paris; Cinéma Max Linder, Paris; The Power Plant, Toronto; Museu Serralves, Porto
Harmony. Moderna Museet, Stockholm
Neue Nationalgalerie, Berlin
pretty much every video and film work from about 1992 until now. to be seen on monitors. some with headphones. others run silently and all simultaneously. Galeria Foksal, Warsaw
Stan Douglas and Douglas Gordon: Double Vision. Dia Center for the Arts, New York
through a looking glass. Gagosian Gallery, New York

2000 *croque-morts.* Galerie Yvon Lambert, Paris
Double Cross: The Hollywood Films of Douglas Gordon. The Power Plant, Toronto
Douglas Gordon • black spot. Tate Gallery Liverpool
Sheep and Goats. Musée d'Art Moderne de la Ville de Paris

2001 *Feature Film.* Meeting House Square, Dublin
5 Year Drive-By. Twentynine Palms, California
K21. Kunstmuseum Düsseldorf
Lisson Gallery, London
The Museum of Contemporary Art at the Geffen Contemporary, Los Angeles. Traveled: Vancouver Art Gallery; Museo de Arte Contemporáneo Internacional Rufino Tamayo, Mexico City; Hirshhorn Museum and Sculpture Garden, Smithsonian Institution, Washington, D.C.
thirteen. Gagosian Gallery, New York

2002 *Confessions of a Justified Sinner.* Kunsthaus Bregenz
Sleeper. 6 Darnaway Street, Edinburgh
what have I done. Hayward Gallery, London
What you want me to say. University of Brighton Gallery

2003 *croque-morts.* Q Gallery, Derby
Douglas Gordon: Blind Star. Andy Warhol Museum, Pittsburgh

Galerie Yvon Lambert, Paris
Play Dead; Real Time. Gagosian Gallery, New York
24 Hour Psycho. Rooseum Center for Contemporary Art, Malmö

2004 *Douglas Gordon: Fog.* Gagosian Gallery, Los Angeles

2005 *croque-morts.* Usher Gallery, Lincoln, England
Douglas Gordon's The Vanity of Allegory. Deutsche Guggenheim Museum, Berlin (as curator)

2006 Fundació Joan Miró, Barcelona

Group Exhibitions

1989 *Festival of Plagiarism.* Transmission Gallery, Glasgow
Glasgow Group. Tramway, Glasgow
Information. Paisley Museum and Art Galleries, Scotland
Live Art at the Keep. Open-Eland Studios, England
Smith Biennial. Smith Art Gallery and Museum, Stirling, Scotland
Windfall '89. Bremen

1990 Archive Room, Slade School of Fine Art, London
. . . meaning and location. Octagon Gallery, University of London
Self-Conscious State. Third Eye Centre, Glasgow
Sites/Positions. Glasgow Green, Scotland

1991 *Archive Project.* APAC Centre d'Art Contemporain, Nevers
Barclays Young Artist Award Exhibition. Serpentine Gallery, London
Bellgrove Station Billboard Project. Glasgow
London Road . . . . Orpheus Gallery, Belfast
Roderick Buchanan/Douglas Gordon. Orpheus Gallery, Belfast
Speed. Transmission Gallery, Glasgow
Walk On. Jack Tilton Gallery, New York. Traveled: The Fruitmarket Gallery, Edinburgh
Windfall '91. Seaman's Mission, Glasgow

1992 *And What Do You Represent?* Anthony Reynolds Gallery, London
Anomie. Patent House, London
Contact. Transmission Gallery, Glasgow
5 Dialogues. Naturhistoriske Samliger, Bergen, Norway
Guilt by Association. Irish Museum of Modern Art, Dublin
Instructions Received. Giò Marconi, Milan
Love at First Sight. The Showroom, London
A Modest Proposal. Milch Gallery, London
Molteplici Culture. Museo del Folklore, Rome
The Speaker Project. Institute of Contemporary Arts, London
240 Minuten. Galerie Esther Schipper, Cologne
L'u di carte. Cafe Picasso, Rome

1993 *Before the Sound of the Beep.* Paris
Chambre 763. Hotel Carlton Palace, Paris
Douglas Gordon–Simon Patterson. Gallery Gruppe Grün, Bremen
High Fidelity. Kohji Ogura Gallery, Nagoya. Traveled: Röntgen Kunst Institut, Tokyo
Left Luggage. Paris
Moving into View: Recent British Painting. Royal Festival Hall, London
Prospekt '93. Schirn Kunsthalle Frankfurt and Frankfurter Kunstverein
Purpose Built New England: Long Distance Information. Real Art Ways, Hartford, Conn.
The Return of the Cadavre Exquis. The Drawing Center, New York
Übergänge. Museum Moderner Kunst Passau
Viennese Story. Wiener Secession, Vienna
Walter Benjamin's Briefcase. Porto
Wonderful Life. Lisson Gallery, London

1994 *Conceptual Living.* Rhizome, Amsterdam
Dolphin Gallery, Oxford
Europa '94. First European Gallerist Congress, Munich
Gaze: L'impossible transparence. Carré des Art du Parc Floral de Paris
The Institute of Cultural Anxiety: Works from the Collection. Institute of Contemporary Arts, London
Minima Media. Media Biennale, Leipzig
Modern Art. Transmission Gallery, Glasgow
New Painting. Chapter, Cardiff. Traveled: Oriel Gallery, Mold, Wales
Points de vue: Images d'Europe. Centre national d'art et de culture Georges Pompidou, Paris
The Reading Room. Bookworks, London
Rue des Marins. Galerie Air de Paris, Nice
Some of my friends. Gallerie Campbells Occasionally, Copenhagen
Stain in Reality. Galerie Nicolai Wallner, Copenhagen
Wall to Wall. Southampton City Art Gallery
WATT. Witte de With, Rotterdam

1995 *Am Rande der Malerei.* Kunsthalle Bern
Aperto '95. FRAC Languedoc-Roussillon, Montpellier
Arte inglese d'oggi. Galleria Civica, Modena
The British Art Show 4. South Bank Centre, London
Chez l'un, L'AUTRE. Galerie Anton Weller, Paris
L'Effet Cinéma: Quand l'image raconte. Musée d'Art Contemporain, Montreal
Eigen + Art at the Independent Art Space, London
General Release: British Council Selection of Young British Artists. Venice Biennale
Info Art. Gwangju Biennale
installation, cinéma, vidéo, informatique. Lyon Biennale

Kopfbahnhof/Terminal. Hauptbahnhof Leipzig
On Board. Venice Biennale
Over de melancholie. Galerie Donia Cieremans, Rotterdam
Perfect Speed. MacDonald Stewart Art Centre, Guelph, Canada. Traveled: University of Southern Florida Contemporary Art Museum, Tampa
Projected Images. Venice Biennale
Pulp Fact. Photographers' Gallery, London
Scottish Autumn. Ludwig Múzeum, Kortárs Muvészti Múzeum, Budapest
Seeing Things. Galeria Antoni Estrani, Barcelona
Shift. De Appel Centrum voor Beeldende Kunst, Amsterdam
Shopping. Bordeaux, France. Traveled: New York
Take me (I'm yours). Serpentine Gallery, London. Traveled: Kunsthalle Nürnberg, Nuremberg; Castello di Rivoli, Turin
Übergänge (Transitions). National Gallery for Foreign Art, Sofia
Varje gång jag ser dig (Every Time I See You). Malmö
Wild Walls. Stedelijk Museum, Amsterdam
You Show. Knoll Galéria, Budapest

1996 *Artisti britannici a Roma.* Galleria Bonomo, Rome
Auto reverse 2. Le Magasin, Grenoble
By Night. Fondation Cartier pour l'art contemporain, Paris
Controfigura. Studio Guenzani, Milan
Entre-deux. Galerie Mot & van den Boogaard, Brussels
Found Footage: Kunst über Film. Klemens Gasser & Tanja Grünert, Cologne
Full House: Young British Art. Kunstmuseum Wolfsburg
Girls High. Glasgow School of Art. Traveled: The Fruitmarket Gallery, Edinburgh
Hall of Mirrors: Art and Film. Museum of Contemporary Art, Los Angeles. Traveled: Wexner Center for the Arts, The Ohio State University, Columbus; Palazzo delle Espozioni, Rome; Museum of Contemporary Art, Chicago
Host. OB Projects, Amsterdam
ID. Stedelijk Van Abbemuseum, Eindhoven
Institut d'art contemporain de Villeurbanne, Lyon
Itinerant Texts. Camden Arts Centre, London
Jurassic Technologies Revenant. Sydney Biennale
life/live. Musée d'Art Moderne de la Ville de Paris. Traveled: Centro Cultural de Belém, Lisbon
Looking Awry. Brazilian Embassy, Paris
Manifesta 1. Rotterdam
Nach Weimar. Kunstsammlungen zu Weimar
Out of Space. Cole and Cole, Oxford
Perfect. Galerie Mot & van den Boogaard, Brussels
Propositions. Musée départemental d'art contemporain de Rochechouart
Sawn-Off. Uppsala Konstmuseum
Scream and Scream Again. Museum of Modern Art, Oxford. Traveled: Irish Museum of Modern Art, Dublin; Museum of Contemporary Art, Helsinki
Spellbound. Hayward Gallery, London
33 ⅓. Canberra Contemporary Art Space
Travaux Publics (Public Works). Eindhoven
Traffic. CAPC Musée d'art contemporain Bordeaux
The Turner Prize Exhibition. Tate Gallery, London
21 Days of Darkness. Transmission Gallery, Glasgow

1997 *Auf dem Pluto ist es noch kälter als vermutet: Über Leben in der Peripherie.* Wacker Fabrik, Darmstadt, Germany
l'autre. Lyon Biennale
Art from the UK. Goetz Sammlung, Munich
Connexions Implicites. École Nationale des Beaux-Arts, Paris
Douglas Gordon, Hlynur Hallsson, Petra Kaltenmorgen, Silke Schatz. Villa Minimo, Hannover
Flexible. migros museum für gegenwartskunst, Zurich
Follow Me: Britische Kunst an der Unterelbe. Buxtehude and Cuxhaven, Germany
Gothic. The Institute of Contemporary Art, Boston
Hiroshima Art Document '97: Urban Mirage. Old Factory of Army Clothes, Hiroshima
Identité. Le Nouveau Musée and FRAC Rhône Alpes, Villeurbanne
Infra-slim Spaces. Soros Center for Contemporary Arts Gallery, Kiev
Kunst, Energie. Schloß Ottenstein, Austria
KünstlerInnen: 50 Positionen. Kunsthaus Bregenz
Letter and Event. apexart, New York
The Lost Ark: Animal. Centre for Contemporary Arts, Glasgow
The Magic of Numbers, Staatsgalerie Stuttgart
Material Culture: The Object in British Art in the '80s and '90s. Hayward Gallery, London
Münster Skulptur Projekte. Münster
1 Minute Scenario. Festival de Cahors, France
Past, Present, Future. Venice Biennale
Pictura Britannia. Museum of Contemporary Art, Sydney. Traveled: Art Gallery of South Australia, Adelaide; City Gallery, Wellington, New Zealand
Private Face/Urban Space: A new generation of artists from Britain. Hellenic Art Galleries Association, Athens
P.S.1 Contemporary Art Center, Long Island City, New York
Quelques motifs de déclaration Amours. Fondation Cartier pour l'art contemporain, Paris
Southampton City Art Gallery
Treasure Island. Fundaçao Calouste Gulbenkian, Lisbon
Wish You Were Here Too. Glasgow

1998 Berlin Biennale
Close Echoes. City Gallery, Prague. Traveled: Kunsthalle Krems
Crossings. Kunsthalle Wien, Vienna
Dall'interno (From Within). Galleria Juliet, Trieste
Eight People from Europe. Museum of Modern Art, Gunma, Japan

Emotion: Young British and American Art from the Sammlung Goetz. Deichtorhallen Hamburg
Everything of Value. Slot Loevestein, Gorinchem, The Netherlands
Happy Hours. Galerie Yvon Lambert, Paris
h:min:sec. Kölnischer Kunstverein, Cologne. Traveled: Kunstraum Innsbruck
Hugo Boss Prize Exhibition. Guggenheim Museum SoHo, New York
London Calling. The British School at Rome
New Works. Galerie Mot & van den Boogaard, Brussels
On the Edge: New Art from Private Collections in France. Tel Aviv Museum
Projected Allegories. Contemporary Arts Museum, Houston
Real/Life: New British Art. Tochigi Prefecture Museum of Fine Arts, Japan. Traveled: Fukuoka City Art Museum; Hiroshima City Museum of Contemporary Art; Tokyo Museum of Contemporary Art; Ashiya City Museum of Art and History
Secret Victorians: Contemporary Artists and a Nineteenth-Century Vision. The Minories Art Gallery, Colchester. Traveled: Arnolfini, Bristol; Ikon Gallery, Birmingham; Middlesborough Art Gallery; UCLA at the Armand Hammer Museum of Art and Cultural Center, Los Angeles; The Fabric Workshop and Museum, Philadelphia; Paul Kasmin Gallery, New York
Then and Now. Lisson Gallery, London
This Island Earth. An Tuireann Arts Centre and Cafe, Portree, Isle of Skye
Tuning up # 5. Kunstmuseum Wolfsburg
Wounds: Between Democracy and Redemption in Contemporary Art. Moderna Museet, Stockholm

1999 *Art in Living Room.* Contemporary Art Factory, Tokyo
Cinema, Cinema. Stedlijk Van Abbemuseum, Eindhoven
Common People: Arte inglese tra fenomeno e realtà. Fondazione Sandretto Re Rebaudengo, Turin
Contemporary Artists at Sir John Soane's Museum. Sir John Soane's Museum, London
dAPERTutto. Venice Biennale
Dimensions Variable: New Works from the British Council Collection. Ludwig Múzeum, Kortárs Muvészti Múzeum, Budapest. Traveled: Slovak National Gallery, Bratislava; Exhibition Hall, Bucharest
Documents et mensonges. Optica, Montreal
Filmic Images. Galerie Ferdinand van Dieten-d'Eendt, Amsterdam
Gesammelte Werke I: Zeitgenössische Kunst seit 1968. Kunstmuseum Wolfsburg
Geschichten des Augenblicks (Moments in Time). Kunstbau Lenbachhaus, Munich
Le Grand Praemiere Opening Show. Galleri Nicolai Wallner, Copenhagen
The History of the Turner Prize. ArtSway, Hampshire
Larmes Blanches. FRAC Haute-Normandie, Sotteville-lès-Rouen
Locally Interested. National Gallery for Foreign Art, Sofia
MEC, Glasgow
Moving Images: Film-Reflexion in der Kunst. Galerie für Zeitgenössische Kunst, Leipzig
New Art from Scotland. Museet for samtidskunst, Oslo
Notorious: Alfred Hitchcock and Contemporary Art. Museum of Modern Art, Oxford. Traveled: Museum of Contemporary Art, Sydney; Art Gallery of Western Australia, Perth; Tokyo Opera City Art Gallery; Provinciaal Museum voor Beeldende Kunsten, Hasselt, Belgium; Museum of Contemporary Art, Hiroshima City
Ragtime. Galeria Estrany-de la Mota, Barcelona
Regarding Beauty: A View of the Late-Twentieth Century. Hirshhorn Museum and Sculpture Garden, Smithsonian Institution, Washington, D.C. Traveled: Haus der Kunst, Munich
Searchlight: Consciousness at the Millennium. California College of Arts and Crafts, San Francisco
So Far Away, So Close. Encore, Brussels
Sogni (Dreams). Fondazione Sandretto Re Rebaudengo, Turin
video cult/ures. Museum für Neue Kunst/ZKM, Zentrum für Kunst und Medientechnologie, Karlsruhe
View II. Mary Boone Gallery, New York
Word enough to save a life, word enough to take a life. Clare College Mission Church, London
Xn 99: Janviers en Bourgogne. Espace des Arts, Châlon sur Saône

2000 *Au-delà du spectacle.* Centre national d'art et de culture Georges Pompidou, Paris
Between Cinema and a Hard Place. Tate Modern, London
Dream Machines. Dundee Contemporary Arts. Traveled: Mappin Art Gallery, Sheffield; Camden Arts Centre, London
5 ANS. Collection Lambert en Avignon, France
Intelligence: New British Art 2000. Tate Britain, London
Interventions: New Art in Unconventional Spaces. Milwaukee Art Museum
Let's Entertain. Walker Art Center, Minneapolis. Traveled: Portland Art Museum, Oregon; Centre national d'art et de culture Georges Pompidou, Paris; Museo Rufino Tamayo, Mexico City; Miami Art Museum
Lisson at Covent Garden. Covent Garden, London
Living with the Dutch. London
Media City Seoul 2000. Contemporary Art and Technology Biennial, Seoul
Mixing Memory and Desire. New Museum of Art, Lucerne
Museu de Serralves, Porto
On Language. Sean Kelly Gallery, New York
Out to Rock. Galerie der Stadt Schwaz, Austria
Sentimental. Galerie Yvon Lambert, Paris
Sincerely Yours. Astrup Fearnley Museet for Moderne Kunst, Oslo
There is something you should know: Die EVN Sammlung im Belvedere. Österreichische Galerie Belvedere, Vienna
Die verletzte Diva (The Wounded Diva). Kunstbau Lenbachhaus, Munich
Voilà: le monde dans la tête. Musée d'Art Moderne de la Ville de Paris

2001 *Au-delà du réel.* Musée départemental d'art contemporain de Rochechouart

The Beauty of Intimacy: Lens and Paper. Staatliche Kunsthalle Baden-Baden
Begijnhof IV: A Kiss Is Just a Kiss. Galeria Estrany-de la Mota, Barcelona
Black Box: The Dark Room in Art. Kunstmuseum Bern
Black Box Recorder: The Young Video Art from Great Britain. Bunkier Sztuki, Krakow
Circles no. 4: One for one, Museum für Neue Kunst/ZKM, Zentrum für Kunst und Medientechnologie, Karlsruhe
Le Collège/FRAC Champagne-Ardennes, Reims
The Dark: Update #4. Kunstmuseum Wolfsburg
Dévoler. Institut d'art contemporain de Villeurbanne, Lyon
Dia Center for the Arts, New York
Double Vision. Galerie für Zeitgenossische Kunst, Leipzig
Douglas Gordon, Joseph Grigely, J. Louro. Fundació Joan Miró, Barcelona
endtroducing. Villa Arson, Nice
Field Day: Sculpture from Britain. Taipei Fine Art Museum
G3NY13. Casey Kaplan Gallery, New York
Here + Now: Scottish Art 1990–2001. Dundee Contemporary Arts and Generator Projects, Dundee
Hypermental. Hamburger Kunsthalle, Hamburg
I Love Melancholy: Emotional States in British Art. Southampton City Art Gallery
Inaugural exhibition. Fundación Jumex, Mexico City
Loop. P.S.1 Contemporary Art Center, Long Island City, New York. Traveled: The Contemporary Arts Center, Cincinnati; Kunsthalle der Hypo-Kulturstiftung, Munich
Making Time. UCLA at the Armand Hammer Museum of Art and Cultural Center, Los Angeles
Monitor: Volume I. Gagosian Gallery, New York
Moving Pictures: Photography and Film in Contemporary Art. Villa Merkel/Bahnwärterhaus, Galerien der Stadt Esslingen, and Galerie im Heppächer
Open Country: Artistes écossais contemporains. Musée cantonal des Beaux-Arts de Lausanne
Project: Film and Video. Pitville Pump Room, Cheltenham
Relocation: On Moving. Sean Kelly Gallery, New York
Room 137. Hotel du Commerce, Basel
Switch. Musée départemental d'art contemporain de Rochechouart
You'll get a bang out of this. Galleri Nicolai Wallner, Copenhagen

2002 *Air Guitar: Art Reconsidering Rock Music.* Milton Keynes Gallery, England. Traveled: Cornerhouse, Manchester; Angel Row, Nottingham; Tullie House, Carlisle
Center for Contemporary Art, Vilnius
Chapter V. Art Resources Transfer, New York
Conversation? Recent Acquisitions of the Van Abbemuseum. Athens School of Fine Art
Hautnah: Die Sammlung Goetz. Museum Villa Stuck, Munich
Hollywood Is a Verb. Gagosian Gallery, London
Hollywood Revisited. Aarhus Kunstmuseum, Denmark
In dreams. Presença Galeria, Porto
Invitation. Museum für Moderne Kunst, Frankfurt am Main
Monitor: Volume 2. Gagosian Gallery, New York
Multiple Personalities. Haines Gallery, San Francisco
The Music in Me: Chapter I: Concerting an Exhibition. Gesellschaft für Aktuelle Kunst, Bremen
My Marilyn. Liljevalchs Konsthall, Stockholm
Narcissus: Twentieth-Century Self-Portraits. Scottish National Portrait Gallery, Edinburgh
New: Recent Acquisitions of Contemporary British Art. Scottish National Gallery of Modern Art, Edinburgh
Passenger: The Viewer as Participant. Astrup Fearnley Museet for Moderne Kunst, Oslo
Penetration. Friedrich Petzel Gallery and Marianne Boesky Gallery, New York
Recent Acquisitions. Scottish National Portrait Gallery, Edinburgh
Same Difference. Ydessa Hendeles Art Foundation, Toronto
Sans commune mesur: Image et texte dans l'art actuel. Musée d'art moderne Lille Métropole, Villeneuve d'Asq, France
Silence. Crestet Centre d'Art, France
Summer Reading. Gagosian Gallery, Los Angeles
Superstudio. Galerie Yvon Lambert, Paris
Tempo. The Museum of Modern Art, New York
To Whom It May Concern. CCAC Wattis Institute for Contemporary Art, San Francisco

2003 *The Air Is Blue.* Casa-Museo Luis Barragan, Mexico City
A Bigger Splash: British Art from Tate, 1960–2003. Pavilhão Lucas Nogueira Garcez-Oca and Instituto Tomie Ohtake, São Paulo
Breathing the Water. Galerie Hauser & Wirth & Presenhuber, Zurich
Brightness. Museum of Modern Art, Dubrovnik
False Innocence. Fundació Joan Miró, Barcelona
Imperfect Innocence: The Debra and Dennis Scholl Collection. Contemporary Museum, Baltimore. Traveled: Palm Beach Institute of Contemporary Art, Lake Worth
Micro/Macro: British Art, 1996–2002. Budapest Mucsarnok
Northern Grammar. Sølvberget Stavanger Kulturhus, Norway
Plunder. Dundee Contemporary Arts
Rooseum Universal Studios. Rooseum Center for Contemporary Art, Malmö
Same Time This Year. Gagosian Gallery, New York
Ten year anniversary exhibition. Galleri Nicolai Wallner, Copenhagen
Upon Reflection. Sean Kelly Gallery, New York
videoMIX. Arario Gallery, Cheonan, Korea

2004 *About Face: Photography and the Death of the Portrait.* Hayward Gallery, London
Accrochage. Galerie Jan Mot, Brussels
D'une image qui ne serait pas du semblant: La photographie écrite, 1950–2005. Passage de Retz, Paris

Disparities and Deformations: Our Grotesque. SITE Santa Fe Biennal
Encontros com o Modernismo. Museu de Arte Moderna, Rio de Janeiro
Establishing Shot. Artists Space, New York
Faces in the Crowd: Picturing Modern Life from Manet to Today. Whitechapel Art Gallery, London. Traveled: Castello di Rivoli, Turin
Figures de l'acteur. Jeu de Paume, Site Sully, Paris
Future Face. Medicine in Context Gallery at the Science Museum, London
Hypermedia. Orange County Museum of Art, Newport Beach
I feel mysterious today. Palm Beach Institute of Contemporary Art, Lake Worth
isonethingbetterthananother. Galerie Aurel Scheibler, Cologne
Making Faces: The Death of the Portrait. Musée d'Elysée, Lausanne
Marilyn: From Anastasi to Weegee. Sean Kelly Gallery, New York
Material Witness. Museum of Contemporary Art, Cleveland
Monument to Now: The Dakis Joannou Collection. Deste Foundation, Athens
Multiple Räume (1): Seele—Konstruktionen des Innerlichen in der Kunst. Staatliche Kunsthalle Baden-Baden
Noah's Ark. La Cité de l'énergie, Shawinigan, Quebec
La Nuit Américaine. Galerie Yvon Lambert, New York
The Past of the Present: Encounters with Modernism. Shanghai Art Museum. Traveled: Singapore Art Museum
Piss Off! Museum of New Art, Pontiac, Michigan
Point of View: A Contemporary Anthology of the Moving Image. The New Museum of Contemporary Art, New York. Traveled: Miami Art Central; UCLA at the Armand Hammer Museum of Art and Cultural Center, Los Angeles; Herbert F. Johnson Museum of Art, Cornell University, Ithaca
Realm of the Senses. James Cohan Gallery, New York
Remakes. CASA, Centro de Arte de Salamanca
Somewhere, Everywhere, Nowhere. Dundee Contemporary Arts and The Fruitmarket Gallery, Edinburgh
Stedelijk Museum Amsterdam at Usce, Museum of Contemporary Art Belgrade
Time Clash. Museu de Serralves, Porto
Treasure Island: 10 Jahre Sammlung Kunstmuseum Wolfsburg. Kunstmuseum Wolfsburg
Ulysses: Die unausweichliche Modalität des Sichtbaren. Atelier Augarten, Zentrum für zeitgenössische Kunst der Österreichischen Galerie Belvedere, Vienna
Uses of the Image: Photography, Film, and Video in the Jumex Collection. Espacio Fundación Telefónica, Buenos Aires
What did you expect? Galerie Jan Mot, Brussels

2005 *Baby Shower.* Galleri Nicolai Wallner, Copenhagen
La Beauté de l'Enfer (Works on Paper). Galerie Rodolphe Janssen, Brussels
Bidibidobidiboo. Fondazione Sandretto Re Rebaudengo, Turin
Body: New Art from the UK. Vancouver Art Gallery. Traveled: The Ottawa Art Gallery; Oakville Galleries, Ontario; Edmonton Art Gallery; Art Gallery Nova Scotia
Celebrate: 22 Years. Jack Tilton Gallery, New York
Changes of Mind: Belief and Transformation. Haunch of Venison, London
Evergreen. Inverleith House, Royal Botanic Garden, Edinburgh
Glasgow International
God Is Great. Venice Biennale
Irreducible: Contemporary Short Form Video. CCA Wattis Institute for Contemporary Arts, San Francisco
Reflection Part 2 (Self-Reflection). Sutton Lane, London
Skyggen (The Shadow). Vestsjællands Kunstmuseum, Sorø, Denmark
What's New Pussycat? Museum für Moderne Kunst, Frankfurt am Main

Exhibition Catalogues, Books, and Artist Publications

1989 *Windfall '89.* Bremen: 1989.

1990 *Self-Conscious State.* Glasgow: Third Eye Centre, 1990.

1991 Dunn, Alan, Francis McKee, and Nigel Rolfe. *Bellgrove Station Billboard Project.* Glasgow: 1991.
Gooding, Mel, and Andrea Schlieker. *Barclays Young Artist Award 1991.* London: Serpentine Gallery Trust, 1991.
Lewandowska, Marysia, ed. *Sight Works, Volume 2: The Missing Text.* London: Chance Books, 1991.
MacDonald, Murdo, et al. *Walk On: Six Artists from Scotland.* New York: Jack Tilton Gallery, 1991.
Sinclair, Ross. *Windfall.* Glasgow: 1991.

1992 Gillick, Liam. *Il Mistero dei 100 Dollari Scomparsi.* Milan: Giò Marconi, 1992.
Gordon, Douglas, and Simon Patterson. "Colours for Identification . . . " in *Frieze*, no 2 (1992).
Lawson, Thomas. *Guilt by Association.* Dublin: Irish Museum of Modern Art, 1992.

1993 Gordon, Douglas. "A Bad Trip," in *Prospect '93: Ein internationale Ausstellung aktueller Kunst*, eds. Beate Ermacora and Peter Weiermair. Frankfurt am Main: Frankfurter Kunstverein and Kunsthalle Schirn, 1993.
———. "In Love in Vienna," in *Viennese Story*, edited by Jérôme Sans. Vienna: Vereinigung bildender KünstlerInnen Wiener Secession, 1993.
———. "Paris Memories," on the cassette *Before the Sound of the Beep.* Paris: Galerie Gilles Peyroulet, 1993.
Gordon, Douglas. "Telephone Conversation," on the cassette *The Speaker Project.* London: Institute of Contemporary Arts, 1993.
Migrateurs. Paris: Amis du Musée d'Art Moderne de la Ville de Paris, 1993.
Roberts, James. *High Fidelity.* Nagoya: Kohji Ogura Gallery, 1993.
Sinclair, Ross. *It doesn't matter who I am. I just want to talk to you: The Sociable Art of Douglas Gordon.* Glasgow: Tramway, 1993.

1994 Goldenberg, David, Michael Corris, and John Roberts. *Flexible Response.* London: Museum of Installation, 1994.

Gordon, Douglas. "Lost, then found, then lost again: a true story, after Samuel Beckett," in *Cahier 2.* Rotterdam and Dusseldorf: Witte de With and Richter Verlag, 1994.

———. "Wall Drawing," in *Wall to Wall*, edited by Maureen Paley and Liam Gillick. London: National Touring Exhibitions and Hayward Gallery, 1994.

Sheikh, Simon. *Stan Douglas, Douglas Gordon, Joachim Koester.* Copenhagen: Galleri Nicolai Wallner, 1994.

Stain in Reality. Copenhagen: Galleri Nicolai Wallner, 1994.

Van Assche, Christine, Stéphanie Moisdon, and Dirk De Wit. *Points de vue: Images d'Europe.* Paris: Centre national d'art et de culture Georges Pompidou, 1994.

1995 *Am Rande der Malerei.* Bern: Kunsthalle Bern, 1995.

Chez l'un, L'AUTRE. Paris: Éditions Anton Weller, 1995.

Cochrane, Gail, and Flaminio Gualdoni. *Arte inglese d'oggi nella raccolta Re Rebaudengo Sandretto.* Milan: Mazzotta, 1995.

Coelewij, Leontine, and Martijn van Nieuwenhuyzen, eds. *Wild Walls.* Amsterdam: Stedelijk Museum, 1995.

Gallagher, Ann, and James Roberts, eds. *General Release: Young British Artists at Scuola di San Pasquale.* London: British Council, 1995.

Gordon, Douglas. "Berlin Visit," in *Kopfbahnhof/Terminal*, edited by Gerti Fietzek. Leipzig: Förderkreis der Leipziger Galerie für Zeitgenössische Kunst, 1995.

———. "2 days in spring," in *On Board*, edited by Jérôme Sans and Karin Schorm. Klagenfurt: Ritter Verlag, 1995.

———. "Project," in *Index* 3–4 (1995): 54–63.

Gordon, Douglas, and Liam Gillick. "Les Infos du Paradis," in *Parkett*, no. 44 (July 1995): 197–210.

Lewis, Vicky. *The British Art Show 4.* London: South Bank Centre, 1995.

shift. Amsterdam: De Appel Foundation, 1995.

1996 Biesenbach, Klaus, Rolf Bothe, and Nicolas Schafhausen, eds. *Nach Weimar.* Ostfildern: Hatje Cantz Verlag, 1996.

Bourriaud, Nicolas. *Traffic.* Bordeaux: CAPC Musée d'art contemporain, 1996.

Brougher, Kerry, and Russell Ferguson, eds. *Hall of Mirrors: Art and Film Since 1945.* Los Angeles and New York: The Museum of Contemporary Art/Monacelli Press, 1996.

Button, Virginia. *The Turner Prize 1996.* London: Tate Publishing, 1996.

By Night. Paris: Fondation Cartier pour l'art contemporain.

Codognato, Mario. *Artisti britannici a Roma.* Turin: Umberto Allemandi, 1996.

Controfigura. Milan: Studio Guenzani, 1996.

Dodd, Philip, and Ian Christie, eds. *Spellbound: Art and Film in Britain.* London: BFI Publishing and Hayward Gallery, 1996.

Iles, Chrissie. *Scream and Scream Again: Film in Art.* Oxford: Museum of Modern Art, 1996.

Lind, Maria. *Sawn-Off.* Stockholm: 1996.

Martínez, Rosa, et al. *Manifesta 1.* Rotterdam: Manifesta, 1996.

McKee, Francis, and Rein Wolfs. *Close your eyes, open your mouth.* Zurich: Museum für Gegenwartskunst.

Royoux, Jean-Christophe, and Jean-Marc Prévost. *Propositions.* Rochechouart: Musée départemental d'art contemporain, 1996.

Sandbach, Emma. *Out of Space.* Oxford: Cole and Cole, 1996.

Smith, Trevor. *33 ⅓.* Canberra: Canberra Contemporary Art Space, 1996.

1997 *Amours.* Paris and Arles: Fondation Cartier pour l'art contemporain and Actes Sud, 1997.

Gordon, Douglas. *Point d'Ironie* 3 (November 1977).

———. "Signature, 1997," edition for *Parkett*, no. 49 (May 1997): 82–83.

Gordon, Douglas, and Liam Gillick. "Sailing Alone around the World: A Correspondence between Douglas Gordon and Liam Gillick," in *Parkett*, no. 49 (May 1997): 73–76.

1998 Bloemheuvel, Marente, ed. *Douglas Gordon: Kidnapping.* Eindhoven: Stedelijk Van Abbemuseum, 1998.

Fitzgerald, Carol, ed. *The Hugo Boss Prize 1998.* New York: Solomon R. Guggenheim Foundation, 1998.

Schneider, Eckhard, ed. *Douglas Gordon: Words.* Hannover: Hannover Kunstverein, 1998.

1999 Bellour, Raymond, and Royal S. Brown. *Feature Film: A Book by Douglas Gordon.* London: Artangel Afterlives, 1999.

Benezra, Neal, Arthur C. Danto, and Olga Viso. *Regarding Beauty: A View of the Late Twentieth Century.* Ostfildern: Hatje Cantz Verlag, 1999.

Taubin, Amy, and Hal Hartley. *through a looking glass.* New York: Gagosian Gallery, 1999.

Van Assche, Christine, et al. *Douglas Gordon.* Lisbon: Centro Cultural de Belém, 1999.

2000 Francis, Mark, ed. *Douglas Gordon • black spot.* London: Tate Publishing, 2000.

Gordon, Douglas. *Déjà-vu: questions & answers: Volumes 1–3.* Paris: Musée d'Art Moderne de la Ville de Paris, 2000.

2001 Ferguson, Russell, et al. *Douglas Gordon.* Cambridge, Mass.: The MIT Press, 2001.

2002 Gordon, Douglas, and Francis McKee. *Douglas Gordon: what have I done.* London: Hayward Gallery, 2002.

2003 Obrist, Hans Ulrich. *Hans Ulrich Obrist: Interviews, Volume 1*, edited by Thomas Boutoux, 317–26. Milan: Edizioni Charta, 2003.

2004 Blazwick, Iwona, et al. *Faces in the Crowd: Picturing Modern Life from Manet to Today.* Milan: Skira editore, 2004.

Brown, Katrina M. *DG: Douglas Gordon.* London: Tate Publishing, 2004.

Monk, Philip. *Double-Cross: The Hollywood Films of Douglas Gordon.* Toronto: Art Gallery of York University and The Power Plant, 2004.
Obrist, Hans Ulrich, ed. *Do It*, 122–23. New York and Frankfurt am Main: e-flux and Revolver, 2004.

2005 Grenville, Bruce, et al. *Body: New Art from the UK.* London and Vancouver: Vancouver Art Gallery and The British Council, 2005.
Spector, Nancy, Francis McKee, and Alison Gingeras. *Douglas Gordon's The Vanity of Allegory.* Berlin: Solomon R. Guggenheim Foundation, 2005.

Articles and Reviews:

1989 "Future Dread." *The List*, December 22, 1989.

1990 McArthur, Euan. "Sites/Positions." *Artscribe* (summer 1990): 77–78.

1991 Gillick, Liam. "The Placebo Effect: Some Art in Britain." *Arts Magazine* (May 1991): 56–59.
McArthur, Euan. "Windfall." *Variant*, no. 9 (1991): 36
Slotover, Matthew. "Northern Lights: Windfall 91." *Frieze*, no. 1 (1991).

1992 Archer, Michael. "Anomie." *Art Monthly*, no. 157 (1992): 11–13.
Gillick, Liam. "Windfall." *Artscribe* (January 1992).
Troncy, Eric. "London Calling." *Flash Art* 25, no. 165 (summer 1992): 86–89.
Hunt, Ian Connolly. "Guilt by Association." *Frieze*, no. 7 (November–December 1992).

1993 Buchan, Ian. "Day of the Psycho." *Evening Times*, March 11, 1993.
Colin, Beatrice. "Speed Freak." *The List* (April 1993).
Fricke, Harald. "August Rezension." *Texte zur Kunst* 3, no. 12 (November 1993).
Lawson, Thomas. "Hello, It's Me." *Frieze*, no. 9 (March–April 1993): 14–17.
Mellor, David. "Wonderful Life." *Untitled*, no. 3 (winter 1993–94): 8.
Renton, Andrew, "Douglas Gordon: Tramway." *Flash Art* 26, no. 172.
Wilson, Andrew. "Walter Benjamin's Briefcase." *Art Monthly*, no. 172 (1993): 30–31.

1994 Archer, Michael. "Collaborators." *Art Monthly*, no. 178 (July–August 1994): 3–5.
van den Boogerd, Dominic. "It's Real but Very Fucked Up." *Metropolis M*, no. 2 (1994).
Cork, Richard. "Douglas Gordon." *The Times* (London), December 31, 1994.
Dahlqvist, Dennis. "Plankat I Köpenhamm." *Expression*, no. 7 (April 1994).
Drake, Nicholas. "Douglas Gordon." *The Standard*, December 16, 1994.
Roberts, James. "Douglas Gordon." *Paletten*, no. 219 (1994): 22–25.

1995 Benjamin, Marina. "Trigger Happy." *British Journal of Photography*, May 17, 1995.
Blazwick, Iwona. "Douglas Gordon." *Art Monthly*, no.183 (February 1995): 35–36.
Cork, Richard. "The Naked and the Undying." *The Times*, January 3, 1995.
Di Raddo, Elena. "General Release." *Tema Celeste*, nos. 53–54 (autumn 1995): 88.
Feaver William. "A Strange Ghetto of Allusions." *The Observer*, January 8, 1995.
———. "Douglas Gordon." *Art News* 94, no. 3 (March 1995): 144.
Gerber, Elisabeth. "Bern: Am Rande der Malerei in der Kunsthalle Bern." *Das Kunst-Bulletin*, no. 11 (November 1995): 33–34.
Gibbs, Michael. "Wild Walls, Stedelijk Museum." *Art Monthly*, no. 191 (November 1995): 30–32.
Hanru, Hou. "Une élégante menace." *Omnibus*, no. 8 (February 1995).
Henry, Clare. "One Man's Bubble Vision." *The Herald* (Glasgow), January 23, 1995.
Higgins, Ria. "Gun Shots." *The Face* (May 1995): 164–165.
Kingston, Angela. "Douglas Gordon." *Frieze*, no. 21 (March–April): 60–61.
Maloney, Martin. "Douglas Gordon." *Flash Art* 28, no. 182 (May–June 1995): 114–15.
Muir, Gregor. "Douglas Gordon: Lisson Gallery, Londres." *Blocnotes*, no. 8 (winter 1995): 107.
Newman, Michael. "Beyond the Lost Object: From Sculpture to Film and Video." *Art Press*, no. 202 (May 1995): 45–50.
O'Reilly, John. "Dark Deeds from the Darkroom," *The Guardian*, May 19, 1995.
Sandbach, Emma. "London: *Take me (I'm yours)* in der Serpentine Gallery." *Das Kunst-Bulletin*, no. 4 (April 1995): 48.
Wulffen, Thomas. "*Take me (I'm yours)*." *Kunstforum International*, no.131 (August–October 1995): 362–63.

1996 Affentranger-Kirchrath, Angelika. "Strategien der Verunsicherung." *Neue Zurcher Zeitung*, October 1, 1996.
Alberge, Dalya, and Russell Jenkins. "Modern Art's Jekyll and Hyde Rewarded with Monster Prize." *The Times* (London), November 29, 1996.
Beil, Ralf. "From the Moment You Hear These Words, Until You Kiss Someone with Blue Eyes." *Das Kunst-Bulletin* (December 1996).
Birnbaum, Daniel. "Sweet Nothings." *Frieze*, no. 36 (September–October 1996): 80.
Bruce, Keith. "Turner Prize Goes to Glasgow Artist." *The Herald* (Glasgow), November 29, 1996.
Cecchetto, Paolo. "Douglas Gordon." *Juliet*, no. 77 (April–May 1996): 34–35.
Cork, Richard. "Playing to the Gallery." *The Times Magazine*, October 19, 1996, pp. 38–42.
von Däniken, Hans-Peter. "Wenn sich Körper und Bewusstsein trennen." *Tages-Anzeiger*, October 15, 1996.
Fargier, Jean-Paul. "L'immobilité hypnotique de Douglas Gordon." *Le Monde* (Paris), January 6, 1996.
Gayford, Martin. "When Up Is Down and In Is Out." *The Spectator*, November 30, 1996, pp. 59–61.
Gennari, Flaminia. "Oltre manica alla moda." *Il manifesto*, May 30, 1996.
Gillick, Liam. "The Corruption of Time." *Flash Art* 29, no. 188 (May–June

Gennari, Flaminia. "Oltre manica alla moda." *Il manifesto*, May 30, 1996.
Gillick, Liam. "The Corruption of Time." *Flash Art* 29, no. 188 (May–June 1996): 69–70.
Jones, Jonathan. "Douglas Gordon: Confessions of a Justified Sinner." *Untitled*, no. 12 (winter 1996): 10–11.
Moisdon-Trembley, Stéphanie. "Biennale de Lyon." *Blocnotes,* no. 11, (January–February 1996): 80.
Morgan, Stuart. "Manifesta." *Frieze*, no. 30 (September–October): 50–51.
Morrissey, Simon. "Art & Film." *Untitled*, no. 10 (spring 1996): 3.
Quinn, Paul. "The Art of the Reel." *Tate Magazine*, no. 8 (spring 1996): 40–47.
Sans, Jérôme. "Douglas Gordon, Centre Georges Pompidou." *Artforum* 34, no. 8 (April 1996): 109–10.
Searle, Adrian. "Winning Game of Good and Evil." *The Guardian*, November 29, 1996.
Spinelli, Claudia. "Zwischen Kinoraum und Leseraum." *Basler Zeitung*, December 14–15, 1996.
Van Assche, Christine. "Six Questions to Douglas Gordon." *Parachute*, no. 84 (October–December 1996).

1997 Bevan, Roger. "Babes in Arms." *Art Newspaper*, no. 67 (February 1997): 23–26.
Bezzola, Tobia. "De Spectaculis or Who Is Kim Novak Really Playing?" *Parkett*, no. 49 (1997): 52–57.
Blom, Ina. "Slow Motion: Douglas Gordon Finds Emotional Solace." *Siksi*, no. 1 (spring 1997).
Ferguson, Russell. "Divided Self." *Parkett*, no. 49 (May 1997): 59–63.
Flood, Richard. "24 Hour Psycho." *Parkett*, no. 49 (May 1997): 47–49.
Kyriacou, Sotiris. "The Rise and Rise of British Video." *Contemporary Visual Arts*, no. 14.
Sheikh, Simon. "Kunst er blot et påskudd for en sarntale: Et interview med billedkunstneren Douglas Gordon." *Øjeblikkett*, no. 31 (spring 1997): 17.
Volkart, Yvonne. "Douglas Gordon, Museum für Gegenwartskunst, Galerie Walcheturm." *Flash Art* 30, no. 195 (summer 1997): 145–46.
Worsdale, Godfrey. "Morality Bites." *an magazine* (February 1997): 14–16.

1998 Drobnick, Jim. "Reveries, Assaults, and Evaporating Presences." *Parachute*, no. 89 (January–March 1998): 10–19.
Greenberg, Sarah. "Bouncing around Town." *Art Newspaper*, no. 86 (November 1998).
Kipphoff, Petra. "Zeit plus/minus Ewigkeit." *Die Zeit*, October 1, 1998.
Sanders, Mark. "Next Stop Barbados." *Dazed & Confused* 38 (January 1998): 54–60.

1999 Bishop, Claire. "Douglas Gordon: Are You Looking At Him?" *Flash Art* 32, no. 208 (summer 1999): 103–5.
Damianovic, Maia. "Douglas Gordon e Stan Douglas a Dia Center for the Arts, New York." *Tema Celeste* (May–June 1999).
Groys, Boris. "Douglas Gordon at Kunstverein Hannover." *Artforum* 37, no. 6 (February 1999).
Henry, Clare. "Boy Wonder to Wonder Boy." *The Herald*, May 24, 1999.
Higgie, Jennifer. "Douglas Gordon at Atlantis, London." *Frieze,* no. 48 (September–October 1999).
Homes, A.M. "Film Threat," *Vanity Fair*, no. 463 (March 1999).
Johnson, Ken. "*Douglas Gordon: Through a Looking Glass* at Gagosian Gallery." *New York Times*, April 2, 1999.
McEvilley, Thomas. "Seeing Double: Video Artists Douglas Gordon and Stan Douglas." *Interview* 29, no. 4 (April 1999).
Saltz, Jerry. "Up and Down." *Village Voice*, March 30, 1999.
Schjeldahl, Peter. "Eurosplash." *New Yorker*, May 10, 1999.
Searle, Adrian. "Hitchcock's Finest Hour." *The Guardian*, April 3, 1999.
Smith, Roberta. "Uncharacteristic Adventures in Comparative Viewing." *New York Times*, December 17, 1999.
Stoeber, Michael. "Douglas Gordon TRAILER." *Neue Bildende Kunst* (January–February 1999).

2000 Schambelan, Elizabeth. "Douglas Gordon at Gagosian." *Art in America* (May 2000), no. 5.

2001 Cheng, Scarlet. "Slo-Mo *Psycho*" and "He Tweaks the Language of Hollywood." *Los Angeles Times*, September 16, 2001.
Jamieson, Teddy. "Interview with Douglas Gordon." *Herald Magazine*, October 19, 2001, pp. 20–23.
Kantor, Jordan. "Loop at P.S.1." *Artforum* 39, no. 8 (April 2001): 137–38.
Knight, Christopher. "Skewed by the Light." *Los Angeles Times*, September 20, 2001.
Wong, Sherry. "Televisions." *Artnet Magazine*, July 22, 2001, http://www.artnet.com/Magazine/reviews/wong/wong7-22-02.asp.

2002 Allan, Vicky. "Devil in the Detail." *Sunday Herald*, October 20, 2002.
Gayford, Martin. "On the Edge of Otherness." *The Daily Telegraph*, October 31, 2002.
Godfrey, Tony. "Epic and Intimate." *Royal Academy Magazine*, no. 76 (autumn 2002).
Greenstreet, Rosanna. "Q&A: Douglas Gordon." *The Guardian*, November 2, 2002.
Güner, Fisun. "Opposites Don't Attract." *Metro*, November 5, 2002.
Hemming, Sarah. "Douglas Gordon: *What Have I Done*, Hayward Gallery." *Daily Express*, November 1, 2002.
Irving, Mark. "Escape Artist." *The Independent on Sunday*, October 27, 2002, pp. 30–33.
Lubbock, Tom. "The Dark Side." *Independent Review*, November 5, 2002.
Mullins, Charlotte. "Virtual Reality." *Southbank Magazine* (November 2002): 16–17.
Renton, Andrew. "Trust Me, I'm an Artist." *Evening Standard*, October 29, 2002, p. 43.
Saurisse, Pierre. "Douglas Gordon: Le Cinéma des Ombres." *Beaux Arts Magazine*, no. 223 (December 2002).
Searle, Adrian. "Monsters Inc." *The Guardian*, November 5, 2002, pp. 12–13.

Taylor, John Russell. "Endurance Test." *The Times* (London), November 6, 2002.

2003 Dunn, Melissa. "Douglas Gordon at Gagosian, New York." *Flash Art* 36, no. 230 (May–June 2003): 147.

Henry, Clare. "We'll Take Manhattan." *The Scotsman*, March 18, 2003.

Menin, Samuele, and Valentina Sansone. "Focus Video and Film." *Flash Art* 36, no. 228 (January–February 2003): 88–93.

Saltz, Jerry. "Elephant Man." *Village Voice*, March 24, 2003.

Smith, Roberta. "Douglas Gordon/Franz West at Gagosian Gallery." *New York Times*, March 7, 2003.

Sundell, Margaret. "Douglas Gordon at Gagosian Gallery." *Artforum* 41, no. 9 (May 2003): 167.

Yablonsky, Linda. "Douglas Gordon at Gagosian Gallery." *Art News* 102, no. 6 (June 2003): 115.

2004 Filipovic, Elena. "What Did You Expect?" *Frieze*, no. 86 (October 2004): 170.

Gleadell, Colin. "How Video Art Keeps on Moving." *The Daily Telegraph*, September 18, 2004, pp. 8–9.

Gopnik, Blake. "Drawing out the Suspense: Douglas Gordon's Slo-Mo Psycho Cuts to the Quick." *Washington Post*, February 22, 2004.

Gurewitsch, Matthew. "Douglas Gordon: A Modern-Art Case of Jekyll and Hype." *Wall Street Journal*, March 31, 2004.

Jana, Reena. "La Nuit Américaine" *Art News* 103, no. 5 (May 2004): 147–48.

Jenkins, Mark. "A Flicker of Truth in Every Frame." *Washington Post*, February 27, 2004, p. T61.

Malasauskas, Raimundas. "An Extended Family." *Tema Celeste*, no. 101 (January–February 2004).

Smith, Roberta. "Good, Evil, and Life, Head-on." *New York Times*, February 20, 2004.

Stone, Susan. "Museum Hosts *24 Hour Psycho*—Literally." National Public Radio, March 3, 2004, http://www.npr.org/templates/story/story.php?storyId=1724372.

2005 Clewing, Ulrich. "The Opposite of Dorian Gray," (interview). *db artmag* 29 (July 2005), http://www.deutsche-bank-kunst.com/art/2005/5/e/5/359.php.

Cornwell, Tim. "City Will Explore Art of Darkness with Exhibition." *The Scotsman*, February 25, 2005, p. 12.

Gleeson, David. "Self-Importance of Being Earnest: Douglas Gordon: *The Vanity of Allegory*." *The Independent*, September 13, 2005, p. 54.

Jeffrey, Moira. "Out from the Ashes of Hell." *The Herald* (Glasgow), April 22, 2005, p. 21.

Martín, Patricia. "Coleccíon Jumex: Una experiencia para aprender." *ARCO* 34 (winter 2005): 44–49.

McAulay, Robert. "Zidane's 'Portrait' on Film." *Daily Mirror*, June 13, 2005, p. 25.

Mills, Michael. "Scratch-Your-Head Mysterious." *New Times Broward–Palm Beach*, January 6, 2005.

Schlaegel, Andreas. "The Vanity of Allegory." *Flash Art* 38, no. 245 (November–December 2005): 53.

Schumacher, Mary Louise. "Video Art Exhibit Shows What's Possible, Even Good." *Milwaukee Journal Sentinel*, July 10, 2005, p. E4.

Sharp, Jasper. "The Vanity of Allegory." *ArtReview* (October 2005): 127.

"The Vanity of Allegory." *Tema Celeste*, no. 111 (September–October 2005): 109.

Index of the Plates

Instruction (Number 4). 1993
Telephone call and wall text in Bembo typeface, dimensions variable
Private collection

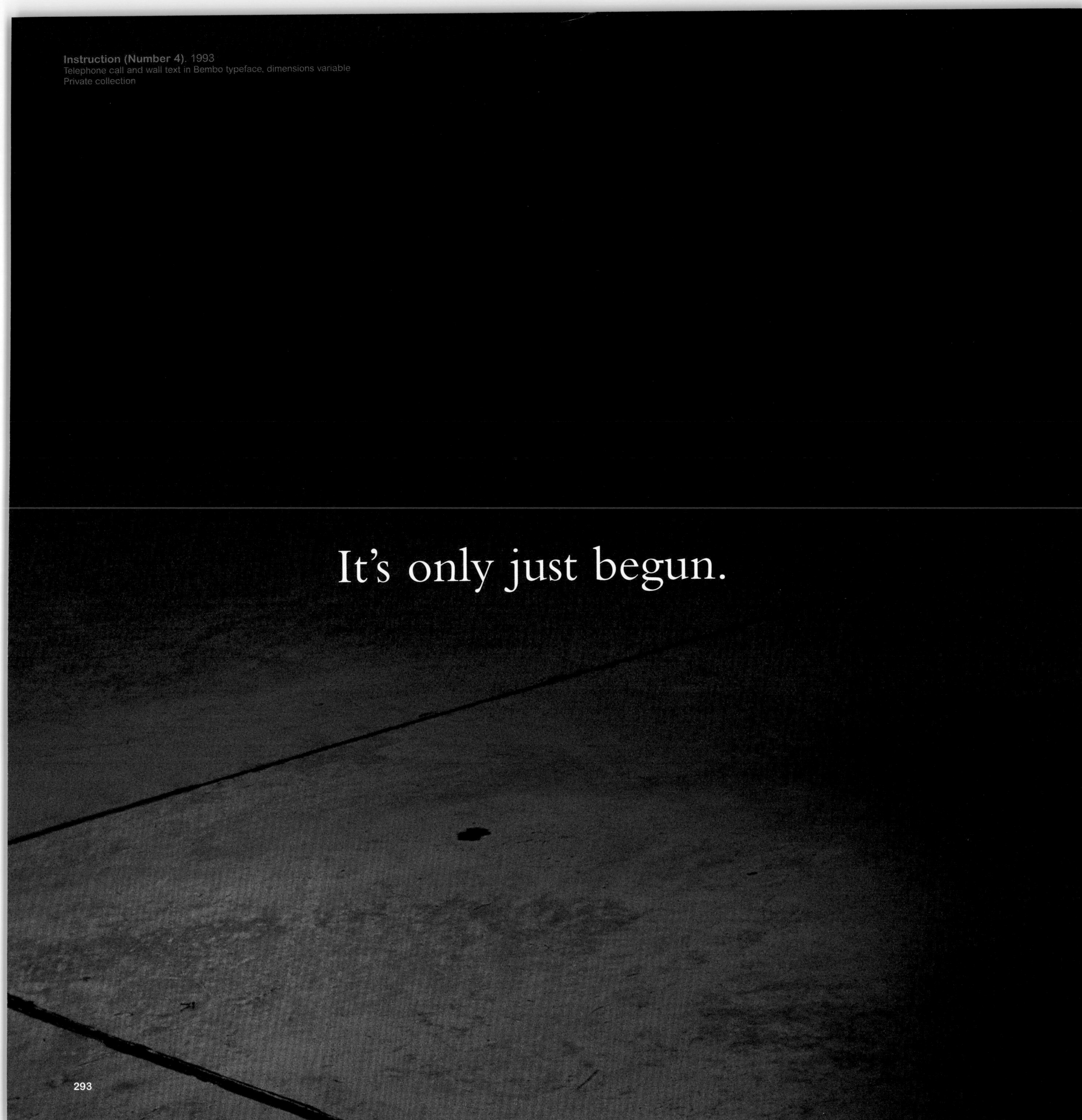

Photograph Credits

Individual images appearing in this book may be protected by copyright in the United States of America or elsewhere, and may not be reproduced in any form without the permission of the copyright holders. The following copyright and/or other credits appear at the request of the artists or their heirs or representatives. For certain images, we have been unable to trace the copyright holders. We would appreciate notification of such information for acknowledgement in future editions.

Photograph credits for the timeline images appear on pages 278–81.

- Fondazione Pasolini, Rome: 31

- Courtesy Gagosian Gallery: covers, 6–7, 90, 110, 160, 161, 164, 165, 172, 173
  from *The Searchers*. 1956. USA. Directed by John Ford. Produced by Merian C. Cooper, Patrick Ford, and C. V. Whitney. Distributed by Warner Bros. © Time Warner Entertainment Company, L.P.: 98–99
  from *Taxi Driver*. 1976. USA. Directed by Martin Scorsese. Produced by Julia Phillips, Michael Phillips, and Phillip M. Goldfarb. Distributed by Columbia Pictures © Columbia Pictures Industries, Inc. Photo by Cheryl O'Brien: 152–53
  photo by Kevin Low: 84
  photo by Robert McKeever: 115, 117, 166–67
  photo by Steven White, London: 136

- Courtesy Douglas Gordon: 3, 85, 87, 96–97, 102–3, 104–5, 106–7, 111, 112, 113, 137, 138, 139, 154, 155, 158, 159, 162, 163, 168–71, 174, 178–79
  © Douglas Gordon: 88–89
  from *D.O.A.* 1950. USA. Directed by Rudolph Maté. Produced by Joseph H. Nadel, Harry M. Popkin, and Leo C. Popkin. Distributed by United Artists. © Cardinal Pictures. Photo by Brian Forrest: 156–57
  from *Dr. Jekyll and Mr. Hyde*. 1931. USA. Directed by Rouben Mamoulian. Produced by Adolph Zukor and Mamoulian. Distributed by Paramount Pictures © Paramount Publix Corporation: 100–1
  from *Psycho*. 1960. USA. Directed and produced by Alfred Hitchcock. Distributed by Paramount Pictures © Universal City Studios, Inc.: 36–83
  from *The Song of Bernadette*. 1943. USA. Directed by Henry King. Produced by William Perlberg. Distributed by Twentieth Century Fox Film Corporation © Criterion Pictures and *The Exorcist*. 1973. USA. Directed by William Friedkin. Produced by William Peter Blatty, Noel Marshall, and David Salven. Distributed by Warner Brothers © Time Warner Entertainment Company, L.P.: 120–33
  from *Vertigo*. 1958. USA. Directed by Alfred Hitchcock. Produced by Herbert Coleman and Hitchcock. Distributed by Paramount Pictures © Alfred J. Hitchcock Productions, Inc.: 142–47
  from *Whirlpool*. 1949. USA. Directed and produced by Otto Preminger. Distributed by Twentieth Century Fox Film Corporation © Criterion Pictures. Photo by Stuart Tyson: 148–51
  photo by Boris Becker: 140–41
  photo by Peter Cox, Eindhoven: 118–19
  photo by Kevin Low: 84; photo by John Riddy, London: 86, 94, 95
  photo by Georges Meguerditchian: 108–9

- Courtesy Galerie Yvon Lambert: 134, 135, 154, 155, 158, 159

- Courtesy Lisson Gallery, London: 91, 112, 113, 116
  © Douglas Gordon: 88–89
  from *Psycho*. 1960. USA. Directed and produced by Alfred Hitchcock. Distributed by Paramount Pictures © Universal City Studios, Inc. Photo by Cheryl O'Brien: 32–33, 92–93, 114
  photo by John Riddy, London: 94, 95
  photo by Steven White, London: 136

- Courtesy The Power Plant, Toronto
  from *Taxi Driver*. 1976. USA. Directed by Martin Scorsese. Produced by Julia Phillips, Michael Phillips, and Phillip M. Goldfarb. Distributed by Columbia Pictures © Columbia Pictures Industries, Inc. Photo by Cheryl O'Brien: 152–53
  from *Psycho*. 1960. USA. Directed and produced by Alfred Hitchcock. Distributed by Paramount Pictures © Universal City Studios, Inc. Photo by Cheryl O'Brien: 32–33, 92–93, 114

- Courtesy of The Andy Warhol Foundation, Inc. / Art Resource, NY. © 2006 Andy Warhol Foundation for the Visual Arts / Artists Rights Society (ARS), New York: 29.

- From "The Man Behind the Body," by John D. Weaver, published in *Holiday* (September 1964). Photo by Maxwell Coplan: 21.

Colophon

Published in conjunction with the exhibition *Douglas Gordon: Timeline*, organized by Klaus Biesenbach, Curator in the Department of Film and Media at The Museum of Modern Art, New York, June 11–September 4, 2006

This exhibition will travel to Malba-Colección Costantini/Museo de Arte Latinoamericano de Buenos Aires, Argentina.

This publication is made possible by The Contemporary Arts Council of The Museum of Modern Art.

Produced by the Department of Publications
The Museum of Modern Art, New York

Edited by Emily Hall
Designed by Pascale Willi
Production by Marc Sapir
Printed and bound by Oceanic Graphic Printing, Inc., China

This book is typeset in Arial Rounded.
The paper is 128gsm Goldeast Matt Artpaper.

© 2006 The Museum of Modern Art, New York

All works of art by Douglas Gordon are © Douglas Gordon

Published by The Museum of Modern Art,
11 West 53 Street, New York, New York 10019-5497
www.moma.org

Library of Congress Control Number: 2006921486
ISBN: 0-87070-390-0

Distributed in the United States and Canada
by D.A.P./Distributed Art Publishers, Inc., New York
Distributed outside the United States and Canada
by Thames & Hudson Ltd., London

Front and back covers:
Hand with spot (detail). 2001
Chromogenic color print, 57 ¾ x 48" (146.7 x 121.9 cm)
Courtesy Gagosian Gallery, New York

Title page:
Mary Gordon at the Empire State Building, New York 1965.

Endpapers, front:
24 Hour Psycho. 1993
Video installation, with screen and black-and-white video, 24 hr. loop, dimensions variable
Installation view at The Power Plant, Toronto, 2000
Private collection, London

Endpapers, back:
List of Names. 1990–ongoing
Vinyl wall text in Helvetica typeface, dimensions variable
Collection Fondazione Davide Halevim, Milan

Printed in China

Trustees of The Museum of Modern Art

David Rockefeller*
Honorary Chairman

Ronald S. Lauder
Chairman Emeritus

Agnes Gund
President Emerita

Robert B. Menschel
Chairman

Marie-Josée Kravis
President

Sid R. Bass
Kathleen Fuld
Mimi Haas
Donald B. Marron
Richard E. Salomon
Jerry I. Speyer
Vice Chairmen

Glenn D. Lowry
Director

James Gara
Assistant Treasurer

Patty Lipshutz
Secretary

Celeste Bartos*
H.R.H. Duke Franz of Bavaria**
Mrs. Patti Cadby Birch**
Leon D. Black
Eli Broad
Edward R. Broida
Clarissa Alcock Bronfman
Donald L. Bryant, Jr.
Thomas S. Carroll*
David M. Childs
Patricia Phelps de Cisneros
Mrs. Jan Cowles**
Douglas S. Cramer
Lewis B. Cullman**
Gianluigi Gabetti*
Howard Gardner
Maurice R. Greenberg**
Vartan Gregorian
Kitty Carlisle Hart**
Alexandra A. Herzan
Marlene Hess
Barbara Jakobson
Werner H. Kramarsky*
June Noble Larkin*
Thomas H. Lee
Michael Lynne
Wynton Marsalis**
Harvey S. Shipley Miller
Daniel M. Neidich

Philip S. Niarchos
James G. Niven
Peter Norton
Maja Oeri
Richard E. Oldenburg**
Michael S. Ovitz
Richard D. Parsons
Peter G. Peterson*
Mrs. Milton Petrie**
Gifford Phillips*
Emily Rauh Pulitzer
David Rockefeller, Jr.
Sharon Percy Rockefeller
Lord Rogers of Riverside**
Anna Marie Shapiro
Anna Deavere Smith
Ileana Sonnabend**
Emily Spiegel**
Joanne M. Stern*
Mrs. Donald B. Straus*
Yoshio Taniguchi**
David Teiger**
Eugene V. Thaw**
Jeanne C. Thayer*
Joan Tisch*
Edgar Wachenheim III
Thomas W. Weisel
Gary Winnick
Richard S. Zeisler*

Ex-Officio

Peter Norton
Chairman of the Board of P.S.1

Michael R. Bloomberg
Mayor of the City of New York

William C. Thompson, Jr.
Comptroller of the City of New York

Jo Carole Lauder
President of The International Council

Richard Anderman and Anne Coffin
Co-Chairmen of The Contemporary Arts Council

*Life Trustee
**Honorary Trustee

ABIGAIL SIMMONS
ACHIM BERTENBURG
ADA PACITTI
ADAM BARKER-MILL
ADAM BOYD
ADAM CHODZKO
ADAM DALLAS
ADAM DONALDSON
ADAM GEARY
ADAM HIGGINS
ADAM KUCYZWSKI
ADAM McEWAN
ADAM PRIDEAUX
ADAM SQUIRES
ADAM SZYMCZYK
ADAM WARWICK
ADELE MORROW
ADELE PATRICK
ADELINE GUILLER
ADELINE PUTTMAN
ADIB FRICK
ADINE BARAK
ADOLFO MORALES
ADRIAN CRAWFORD
ADRIAN DANNAT
ADRIAN FOGARTY
ADRIAN GOUGH
ADRIAN O'DONNELL
ADRIAN SEARLE
AGNES AGNEW
AGNES BORLAND SINCLAIR
AGNES BURNSIDE
AGNES DEANS
AGNES HIGGINS
AGNES TROUBLÉ
AGOSTINO REREBAUDENGO
AGUSTIN MELLO
AIDEEN CUSACK
AILEEN McLAUGHLIN
AILEEN RODGERS
AL MASSINO
ALAN BARBOUR
ALAN CALDWELL
ALAN CAMPBELL
ALAN CARMICHAEL
ALAN CLEMENTS
ALAN CURRAL
ALAN DUNN
ALAN GALLACHER
ALAN HERMAN
ALAN HIGGINS
ALAN HUGGINS
ALAN JERMIESTON
ALAN JOHNSTON
ALAN KANE
ALAN LEITCH
ALAN McDONALD
ALAN McLEAN
ALAN MEECHAN
ALAN MICHAEL
ALAN POWER
ALAN RANKINE
ALAN ROBERTSON
ALAN RUSSELL
ALAN SMITH
ALAN TAYLOR
ALAN TAYLOR
ALAN TURNER
ALAN WOODS
ALBERTO ARIAS
ALESANDRA BONOMO
ALESSANDRO CORRIAS
ALEX CRUICKSHANKS
ALEX DEMPSTER
ALEX FERGUSON
ALEX FROST
ALEX GARDNER
ALEX GORDON
ALEX HARTLEY
ALEX HEMPSTEAD
ALEX KILLIN
ALEX LECKIE
ALEX NEW
ALEX PAPADOPOLOU
ALEX RENNIE
ALEX RIGG
ALEXANDER JOHNSTON
ALEXANDER MARIS
ALEXANDER McQUEEN
ALEXANDER MOFFAT
ALEXANDRA BÜCHLER
ALEXANDRE DAVID
ALEXANDRE MELO
ALEXIA HOLT
ALEXIS LITTLE
ALFREDO DI STEFANO
ALI MROIVILI
ALI SUBOTNICK
ALIA SYED
ALICE ANGUS
ALICE CROMBIE
ALICE MAHER
ALICE O'CONNOR
ALICE SMITS
ALICE WEINER
ALICIA FRAMIS
ALISON CURRIE
ALISON GASKELL
ALISON JENKINS
ALISON KENNEDY
ALISON MARCHANT
ALISON MATE
ALISON McDOUGALL
ALISON McLEOD
ALISON McLEOD
ALISON WATT
ALISON WILDING
ALISON WRIGHT
ALISTAIR DICKSON
ALISTAIR GARDNER
ALISTAIR GOWRIE
ALISTAIR KEDDIE
ALISTAIR McAULEY
ALISTAIR McDONALD
ALISTAIR McDONALD
ALISTAIR McLENNAN
ALISTAIR MILNE
ALISTAIR NICOL
ALISTAIR PEEBLES
ALISTAIR RUSSELL
ALISTAIR SMITH
ALISTAIR STEER
ALISTAIR WARMAN
ALISTAIR WILSON
ALISTER HIGGINS
ALLEN RUPPERSBERG
ALLESANDRA BONOMO
ALLISON SMITH
ALMA CAIRA
ALVARO CORROCHANO
ALYSON BAKER
AMANDA BROWN
AMANDA McKITTERICK
AMANDA SEBRIS
AMANDA SHARP
AMI BARAK
AMIKAM TOREN
AMOR MISTIAEN
AMY HOLMES
AMY KETTLES
ANAHITA ARDESCHIRPUR
ANDA PATERSON
ANDRÉ BALAZS
ANDRE CHEMETOFF
ANDRÉ MAGALHAES
ANDREA FISHER
ANDREA McINDEWAR
ANDREA NASHER
ANDREA ROSE
ANDREA ROSEN
ANDREA SAMUELS
ANDREA SCHLIEKER
ANDREAS BALZE
ANDREAS GEDIN
ANDREAS KOCH
ANDREAS SCHWARTZ
ANDREAS SLOMINSKI
ANDREAS VOWINCKEL
ANDRES GARZAS
ANDREW ADAIR
ANDREW BRITTON
ANDREW BROWN
ANDREW CHRISTIE
ANDREW CLARKE
ANDREW CROSS
ANDREW DAVIES
ANDREW FENN
ANDREW GILCHRIST
ANDREW GOODEARL
ANDREW GORDON
ANDREW GUEST
ANDREW HUSTON
ANDREW JAMES
ANDREW KERR
ANDREW KNOX
ANDREW LOCKHART
ANDREW McCARROLL
ANDREW McCAULEY
ANDREW McDONALD
ANDREW McGREGOR
ANDREW McINTYRE
ANDREW McKECHNIE
ANDREW McKENZIE
ANDREW McLEAN
ANDREW McLEISH
ANDREW McMILLAN
ANDREW MOSCHINSKY
ANDREW NAIRNE
ANDREW O'HAGEN
ANDREW PATRIZIO
ANDREW RENTON
ANDREW SCOTT
ANDREW SNEDDON
ANDREW TAYLOR
ANDREW WHITMORE
ANDREW WILSON
ANDRZEJ PRZYWARA
ANDY AVINI
ANDY COLLISHAW
ANDY DUNLOP
ANDY GOODEARL
ANDY LOWE
ANDY McDONALD
ANDY MILLER
ANGEL DE LA MOTTA
ANGEL ESTEBAN
ANGELA BROWN
ANGELA BULLOCH
ANGELA CHOON
ANGELA DE SOUZA
ANGELA KINGSTON
ANGELA LOCKYEAR
ANGELA REID
ANGELIKA NOLLERT
ANGELINE SCHERF
ANGELINE TACCINI
ANGUS COOKE
ANGUS FAIRHURST
ANGUS FARQUHAR
ANGUS HOOD
ANGUS McDONALD
ANGUS MILLER
ANGUS RUSSEL
ANISH KAPOOR
ANITA DRACHMAN
ANN DONALD
ANN HAMILTON
ANN LAW
ANN LEE
ANN LEWIS
ANN McGINN
ANN WISHART
ANN WRIGHT
ANNA BEST
ANNA BJERGE HANSEN
ANNA CAMPBELL
ANNA COPPOLA
ANNA GASKELL
ANNA GRIM
ANNA LAND
ANNA LENA VANEY
ANNA LIVION
ANNA MIELE
ANNA MILSOM
ANNA PANK
ANNABEL HENDERSON
ANNABEL HOWLAND
ANNABELLA JOHNSON
ANNE BARCLAY MORGAN
ANNE BEAN
ANNE CHARRANCE
ANNE COLEY
ANNE CONNOLLY
ANNE COX
ANNE CURRIE
ANNE DE VILLEPOIX
ANNE DECOCK
ANNE DUNCAN
ANNE ELLIOT
ANNE EUNSON
ANNE GALLAGHER
ANNE GEORGE
ANNE GOLDSTEIN
ANNE HOWIE
ANNE LISLEGAARD
ANNE LOUISE KIERNAN
ANNE-MARIE COPESTAKE
ANNE McDONALD
ANNE McKENZIE
ANNE McKINNON
ANNE MORRISON
ANNE OOMS
ANNE PEARSON
ANNE QUINN
ANNE ROACH
ANNE RUSSELL
ANNE SEAGRAVE
ANNE SEYMOUR
ANN TALLENTIRE
ANNE THOMPSON
ANNE VANCE
ANNE-MARIE COX
ANNE-MARIE WATKINS
ANNET GELINK
ANNETTE GORDON
ANNETTE HEYER
ANNETTE MESSAGER
ANNETTE ZIß
ANNIE FLETCHER
ANNIE GRIFFIN
ANNIE TOOP
ANNIKA STRÖM
ANNUSCHKA SHANI
ANTHONY BOURDAIN
ANTHONY FAWCETT
ANTHONY McKENNA
ANTHONY REYNOLDS
ANTOINE AUDIAU
ANTOINETTE TIRAVANIJA
ANTONI ESTRANY
ANTONIO BLASQUEZ
ANTONIO VASQUEZ
ANYA GALLACCIO
APRIL CRICHTON
ARCHIE BRECKENRIDGE
ARCHIE BUCHANAN
ARCHIE FORREST
ARCHIEBALD BLACKADDER
ARI ZOLBERG
ARLENE BRANSON
ARLETTE BROUWERS
ARLETTE GEORGE
ART COPPOLA
ARTUR MIRANDA
ÅSA NACKING
ASHER FRANKEL
ASHLEY McCORMACK
ASIA JARZYNA
ASTRID JOHNSTON
ASTRID REINHARDT
ATLE GERHARDSON
AUDREY BRANSON
AUDREY McDERMOTT
AUDREY MORRISON
AUDREY SMILLIE
AURELIE VOLTZ
AXEL BOSE
AXEL WOLKENHAUER
AYSE ERKMEN
BANKS VIOLETTE
BARBARA BOOMSMA
BARBARA BREITENFELLNER
BARBARA CLAUSEN
BARBARA ENGLEBACH
BARBARA FLYNN
BARBARA GLADSTONE
BARBARA KNOX
BARBARA STAVINI
BARBARA STEINER
BARBARA VANDERLINDEN
BARBARA VISSER
BARBARA WOODFORD
BARBARA-ANNE RUSSELL
BARR GILMOUR
BARRY ATHERTON
BARRY BARKER
BARRY BURNS
BARRY CALLAGHAN
BARRY MAGUIRE
BART DEBAERE
BARTOMEU MARI
BEA DE SOUZA
BEA VESZELY
BEAT STREULI
BEAT ZGRAGGEN
BEATRICE COLIN
BEATRICE PARENT
BEATRIX RUF
BECKY GORDON
BELINDA GUIDI
BELINDA HARLEY
BELLA McCALLUM
BELLATRIX HUBERT
BELLE CAMERON
BEN ALLEN
BEN CORSO
BEN HILLWOOD-HARRIS
BEN LANGLANDS
BEN SCHNEIDER
BEN SMART
BENEDICT HARDING
BERNADETTE MEEHAN
BERNADETTE OVENS
BERNARD COHEN
BERNARD HELZEL
BERND KLÜSER
BERNHARD PRINZ
BERNHARD STARKMANN
BERNICE MURPHY
BERT ROSS
BERTHA PETERS
BERTHOLD BELL
BERTO LECLUYSE
BERTRAND LAVIER
BETHAN HUWS
BETSY KAUFMAN
BETTINA BUSSE
BETTINA FUNCKE
BETTINA GRUBER
BETTY ANDERSON
BETTY McCORMACK
BETTY McDOUGALL
BETTY STEWART
BHAJAN HUNJAN
BICE CURIGER
BILL ALEXANDER
BILL BRECKENRIDGE
BILL BUCHANAN
BILL ENGLISH
BILL FERGUSON
BILL FURLONG
BILL HARE
BILL POTTS
BILL SCOTT
BILL WALTERS
BILL WOODROW
BILL WORTH
BILL WRIGHT
BILL WRIGHT
BILL WRIGHT
BILLEE SELLMAN
BILLY BOYD
BILLY COYLE
BILLY DONNELLY
BILLY MARSHALL
BILLY McCALL
BILLY McISAAC
BILLY MULRANEY
BLAIR CUNNINGHAM
BLAIR TAYLOR
BLAIR THURMAN
BLAKE RAYNE
BLAN RYAN
BOB MONK
BOB PALMER
BOB SAUNDERS
BOB SPEIRS
BOBBY AIRD
BOBBY BLUEBELL
BOBBY CHARLTON
BOBBY GILLESPIE
BOBBY HASS
BOBBY PATERSON
BOBBY ROUGH
BOGDANOFF HOFFMAN
BORIS ACHOUR
BOYD WEBB
BRADLEY HIRST
BRENDA CANAVAN
BRENDA HIGGINS
BRETT LITTMAN
BRIAN ARNOTT
BRIAN BOYCE
BRIAN CONNOLLY
BRIAN ELLIOT
BRIAN FALLON
BRIAN GIBB
BRIAN HUNTLY
BRIAN JENKINS
BRIAN KEENAN
BRIAN KELLY
BRIAN KENNEDY
BRIAN McEWAN
BRIAN McMAHON
BRIAN PETTIT
BRIAN PRINCE
BRIAN SMILLIE
BRIAN STEWART
BRIDGET CURTAIN
BRIDGET McGRATH
BRIGID LOWE
BRIGID TEEHAN
BRIGITTE CORNAND
BRIGITTE RAABE
BRUCE MALCOLM
BRUCE MAU
BRUCE McLEAN
BRUCE NAUMAN
BRUNO BRUNNET
BRYAN FERRY
BRYAN GEE
BRYNDÍS SNÆBJÖRNSDÓTTIR
BURKHARD RIEMSCHNEIDER
BYRON WARWICK
CALLUM INNES
CALLUM McCALLMAN
CAMERON BLACK
CAMERON KERR
CAMERON RAWLE
CAMILLA WAKEFIELD
CAOIMHÍN MAC GIOLLA LÉITH
CARA STARKE
CAREY PHILPOTT
CARL FREEDMAN
CARL MICHAEL VON HAUSSWOLFF
CARL-JOHANN VALGREN
CARMEN GIMÉNEZ
CARMEN RUIZ DE HUIDOBRO
CARMEN ZITA
CAROL CAMERON
CAROL HOGEL
CAROLE HILL
CAROLE RAMAGE
CAROL RHODES
CAROLINA BILBAO
CAROLINE ANGUS
CAROLINE BOURGEOIS
CAROLINE BROGDEN
CAROLINE BURCHILL
CAROLINE CANNING
CAROLINE DYER
CAROLINE HANCOCK
CAROLINE KIRSOP
CAROLINE MONTAGUE
CAROLINE RUSSELL
CAROLINE SCHNEIDER
CAROLINE SCOTT
CAROLINE TISDALL
CAROLINE WOODLEY
CAROLYN BARKER-MILL
CARRIE PILTO
CARSTEN HÖLLER
CARSTEN NICOLAI
CARY LEIBOWITZ
CASEY KAPLAN
CASPER DAVIES
CATH ROBERTS
CATHERINE DAVID
CATHERINE DAVIDSON
CATHERINE HOLLY-HASTED
CATHERINE McARTHUR
CATHERINE McDOUGALL
CATHERINE OPIE
CATHERINE PHILPOTT
CATHERINE ROSENFIELD
CATHERINE YASS
CATHY CHAMBERS
CATHY DE MONCHEAUX
CATHY LE BIHAN
CATHY MACLAY
CATHY PEARSON
CATHY THOMPSON
CATHY WHIPPEY
CATHY WILKES
CATHY WILLIAMSON
CATRIONA FULLERTON
CATRIONA McDONALD
CATSOU ROBERTS
CEAL FLOYER
CECIL ROACH
CÉCILE BOURNE
CÉCILE PANZIERI
CECILE PARIS
CECILY BROWN
CECILY MURRAY
CEDRIC WILLIAMS
CELIA EDELFALK
CELIA NEUBAUER
CELINE LAWSON
CENDRINE DEDISE
CERITH WYN EVANS
CHARLES ASPREY
CHARLES DE MAUX
CHARLES DUDDERIDGE
CHARLES DUNN
CHARLES ESCHE
CHARLES GILLIBERT
CHARLES JACKSON
CHARLES LeDRAY
CHARLES McKENZIE
CHARLES ROBERTSON
CHARLES SAATCHI
CHARLES SANDISON
CHARLIE AGNEW
CHARLIE BRAGG
CHARLIE CARTWRIGHT
CHARLIE HOOKER
CHARLIE LEADER
CHARLIE McDONALD
CHARLIE PHILLIPS
CHARLOTTE ELIAS
CHARLOTTE MOERKER
CHARLOTTE MULLIN
CHARLY SCZWAJCER
CHAS BAIN
CHAZ SMASH
CHEN ZHEN
CHERIE BLAIR
CHIARA BERSI SERLINI
CHIARA GABBELINI
CHRIS ALLEN
CHRIS BURDEN
CHRIS CARRELL
CHRIS COPPOCK
CHRIS CORKSEY
CHRIS CUNNINGHAM
CHRIS DERCON
CHRIS DURRANCE
CHRIS EVANS
CHRIS GILLIES
CHRIS LORD
CHRIS McGLOAN
CHRIS MULLER
CHRIS OFILI
CHRIS TAYLOR
CHRIS WALLACE
CHRIS WELSBY
CHRIS WILSON
CHRISSIE ILES
CHRISTA MAAR
CHRISTIAN BOLTANSKI
CHRISTIAN COPPOLA
CHRISTIAN HAYES
CHRISTIAN HUBERT DELISLE
CHRISTIAN MARCLAY
CHRISTIAN PHILIP MÜLLER
CHRISTIANE BERNDES
CHRISTIANE MEYER STOLL
CHRISTINA BORLAND
CHRISTINA IGLESIAS
CHRISTINA MACKIE
CHRISTINA McBRIDE
CHRISTINA RICUPERO
CHRISTINA RODRIGUEZ
CHRISTINA SEIDEL
CHRISTINE BERRY
CHRISTINE BORLAND
CHRISTINE BURGIN
CHRISTINE CAMPBELL
CHRISTINE CAMPBELL
CHRISTINE DOLBEAU
CHRISTINE FREW
CHRISTINE GORDON
CHRISTINE HILL
CHRISTINE HOHENBÜCHLER
CHRISTINE KIM
CHRISTINE MATTEO
CHRISTINE McDOUGALL
CHRISTINE QUINN
CHRISTINE VAN ASSCHE
CHRISTINE WILKINSON
CHRISTOPH GIRARDET
CHRISTOPH SCHLINGENSIEF
CHRISTOPHER BUCKLOW
CHRISTOPHER DZIADOSZ
CHRISTOPHER HUDSON
CHRISTOPHER SHANKIE
CHRISTOPHER SPERANDIO
CINDY BERNHARD
CINDY BUCHANAN
CINDY PALMANO
CINDY SUGHRUE
CLAIRE BARCLAY
CLAIRE BAXTER
CLAIRE EADIE
CLAIRE SCULLION
CLARA URSITTI
CLARE BRETT
CLARE HENRY
CLARK FINDLAY
CLARRIE RUDRUM
CLAUDE CLOSKY
CLAUDIA BÜTTNER
CLAUDIA DI GALLO
CLAUDIO GUENZANI
CLAY CULBERT
CLIFF BOWEN
CLIFF HAYNES
CLIO LLOYD-JACOB
CLIVE KELLNER
CLYDE HOPKINS
COCO KAY
COLETTE MATTEO
COLIN CARRUTHERS
COLIN DELAND
COLIN DUFF
COLIN FLANNIGAN
COLIN GORDON
COLIN GORDON
COLIN GRIFFITHS
COLIN McFARLANE
COLIN McFIE
COLIN McLEAR
COLIN PETTIGREW
COLIN PIRIE
COLIN SCOFIELD
COLIN SMITH
COLIN STEVENSON
COLLETTE HARKINS
COLLIER SCHORR
CONNIE TILTON
CONRAD ATKINSON
CONSTANTIN JAXY
CORDELIA OLIVER
COREY McCORKLE
CORINNE CASTEL
CORINNE DISERENS
CORINNE GAMBI
CORINNE GROOT
CORNELIA GRASSI
CORNELIA PARKER
CORNELIA SCHMIDT-BLEEK
CORNELIA WOLF
COSIMO PRIDEAUX
CRAIG COOPER
CRAIG GOOS
CRAIG RICHARDS
CRAIG RICHARDSON
CRAIG WILSON
CRAIG WOODS
CRAIGIE HORSFIELD
CRISTINA COLOMAR
CRISTINA ECIJA
CURRO FERREIRA
CY O'NEIL
CYNTHIA FITZGERALD
CYNTHIA WEBER
CYRIL ANDERSON
CYRILLE THOMAS
DAISY AIRD
DALE SCOTT
DAMIEN DUFFY
DAMIEN HARDING
DAMIEN HIRST
DAMIEN SMITH
DAN GRAHAM
DAN MIKHAILHATU
DAN PETERMAN
DANIEL BARBINEL
DANIEL BUREN
DANIEL DALRYMPLE
DANIEL FAUST
DANIEL McLEAN
DANIEL OLSON
DANIEL PFLUMM
DANNY CONNOLLY
DANNY FERGUSON
DANNY TURNBULL
DANNY UTRERA
DANNY UTRERA
DAPHNE WYLLIE
DARIUS KHONDJI
DARREN ALMOND
DAVE CLARK
DAVE CLARKE
DAVE COLLISHAW
DAVE DIAMOND
DAVE HAZEL
DAVE SINGH
DAVE SINGH
DAVE STOKES
DAVEY SCOTT
DAVID ALLEN
DAVID ALLEN
DAVID ARCHIBOLD
DAVID ARMSTRONG
DAVID ARMSTRONG
DAVID ASHCROFT
DAVID ASHMAN
DAVID BADGER
DAVID BARBINEL
DAVID BARRY
DAVID BURNS
DAVID CAMERON
DAVID CARSON
DAVID CLEMENTS
DAVID COHEN
DAVID CORKER
DAVID CURRAN
DAVID CURRY
DAVID CURRY
DAVID DUNLAP
DAVID DYE
DAVID DYER
DAVID EADIE
DAVID ELLIOT
DAVID FOY
DAVID FRANKEL
DAVID GORDON
DAVID GRAY
DAVID HAMMONS
DAVID HARDING
DAVID HUBBARD
DAVID HYSLOP
DAVID JOSELIT
DAVID KELLY
DAVID LAING
DAVID LAMELAS
DAVID MACH
DAVID MATTHEW WEBSTER
DAVID MAXWELL
DAVID McKENZIE
DAVID McMILLAN
DAVID MEDALLA
DAVID MEECHAN
DAVID MILLS
DAVID MITCHELL
DAVID MURRAY
DAVID PETERS
DAVID POWELL
DAVID PRATT
DAVID PROUD
DAVID RANKIN
DAVID REASON
DAVID RICHARDSON
DAVID SCOTT
DAVID SHELTON
DAVID SHERRY
DAVID SHRIGLEY
DAVID SMITH
DAVID STEVENSON
DAVID STOKES
DAVID SWAN
DAVID THORPE
DAVID TREMLETT
DAVID WARD
DAVID WATSON
DAVID WATT
DAVID WEBSTER
DAVID WEISS
DAVID WILKINSON
DAVID ZWIRNER
DAVIE CURRIE
DAVIE MILLER
DAWSON MURRAY
DEAN HAPPEL
DEAN ROSS
DEANNA PETHERBRIDGE
DEBBIE McCABE
DEBBIE THOMPSON
DEBORAH ABOUCAYA
DEBORAH COX
DEBORAH GONET
DEBORAH HAASE
DEBORAH HOLLAND
DEBORAH McINTYRE
DECLAN McGONAGLE
DEIRDRE DOUGLAS
DEIRDRE O'CONNELL
DELFIM SARDO
DENIS ANGUS DANDURAND
DENIS DALQVIST
DENIS DANDURAND
DENIS LAW
DENIS LENS
DENISE EVANS
DENISE HAWRISHIO
DENISE LEONARD
DENISE O'DELL
DENISE SPAMPINATO
DENNIS DAHLQUIST
DENNIS HOPPER
DENNIS VERMEULEN
DEREK ALEXANDER
DEREK BARNES
DEREK HAMILTON
DEREK HOPKINS
DEREK MARTIN
DEREK OGBOURNE
DEREK SCANLAN
DERMOT SEYMOUR
DES WHELAN
DESSISLAVA DESIMOVA
DETLEF LINKE
DEYAN SUDJIC
DEZ LAWRENCE
DIANA STIGTER
DIANA SYKES
DIANA THATER
DIANE MAIN
DIANNE WILLIAMSON
DIANNE WOODCOCK
DICK DELLINGPOLE
DIDIER DESCHAMPS
DIEGO MASSEY
DIETER DANIELS
DIETLAND HOFFMANN
DIETMAR ELGER
DINOS CHAPMAN
DIRK DE WITT
DIRK SNAUWAERT
DOMENIQUE CHENIVESSE
DOMIEN COPPELMANS
DOMINIC AITCHISON
DOMINIC BERLIN
DOMINIC HISLOP
DOMINIC MOLON
DOMINIC VAN DEN BOOGERD
DOMINIQUE GONZALEZ-FOERSTER
DOMINIQUE LEVY
DOMINIQUE SCLATER
DON BROWN
DON PRINCE
DON WILLIAMS
DONALD CAMERON
DONALD EACUPS
DONALD HARDING
DONALD MARX
DONALD McDONALD
DONALD McGHIE
DONALD MORRISON
DONNA JAMIESON
DONNA LYNAM
DORE STAAL
DOREEN GARDNER
DORIS LOCKHART SAATCHI
DORIS VOLL
DOROTHÉE CHARLES
DOROTHEE FISCHER
DOROTHY ALEXANDER
DOROTHY ANNE DALY
DOROTHY McISAAC
DOROTHY WHITMORE
DOUG AUBREY
DOUGAL MUNDELL
DOUGIE VIPOND
DOUGLAS BLAU
DOUGLAS BUCHANAN
DOUGLAS DUNN
DOUGLAS FOGLE
DOUGLAS GIBB
DOUGLAS GILLESPIE
DOUGLAS JACKSON
DOUGLAS LAMB
DOUGLAS McINDOE
DOUGLAS McINTYRE
DOUGLAS MORRISON
DOUGLAS PAYNE
DOUGLAS STEWART
DOUGLAS THOMPSON
DREW COWNIE
DREW DYER
DREW McALLISTER
DREW PERRY
DREW PLUNKETT
DUARD SARMENTO
DUGALD CAMERON
DUNCAN BARTON
DUNCAN CAMPBELL
DUNCAN McFARLANE
DYLAN CONNELL
DYMPNA SAVAGE
EALAN WINGATE
ECK FINLAY
ECKHARDT SCHNEIDER
ED COPPOLA
ED HUBBARD
EDDA KÖNIG
EDDIE BERG
EDDIE COYLE
EDDIE McKEE
EDDIE McKINTOSH
EDDIE PREVOST
EDMUND SPENCER
EDNA LISLE
EDNA VAN DUYN
EDOARDO GNEMMI
EDOUARD MERRINO
EDUARDO PAOLOZZI
EDUARDO PINILLOS
EDWARD ALLINGTON
EDWARD COPPOLA
EDWARD CURRIE
EDWARD DORRIAN
EDWARD HARLEY
EDWARD KRASINSKI
EDWARD LAVERTY
EDWARD McCULLOUGH
EDWARD McINDEWAR
EDWARD STEWART
EDWARD STEWART
EDWIN DAVID
EDWIN HAMBSCH
EDWIN JANSSEN
EGLANTINA ROBERTSON
EIJA-LIISA AHTILA
EILEEN COHEN
EILEEN FERGUSON
EILEEN GORDON
EILEEN LAWRENCE
EILEEN ROGERS
EILIDH SINGH
ELA STRICKERT
ELAINE BUCHANAN
ELAINE DANNHEISER
ELAINE DAVIDSON
ELAINE DERRICK
ELAINE FENN
ELAINE GORDON
ELAINE GORDON
ELAINE GOURLEY
ELAINE McGINLAY
ELAINE McKAY
ELAINE McLEOD
ELAINE NEALE
ELAINE PORCHE
ELAINE REICHEK
ELAINE THOMAS
ELENA FERNANDES
ELIJAH MOIR
ELIN JAKOBSSEN
ELIN WIKSTROM
ELISE PARRÉ
ELIZABETH BEATON
ELIZABETH BROOKS
ELIZABETH ENGLISH
ELIZABETH GORDON
ELIZABETH KING
ELIZABETH LANG
ELIZABETH LEBOVICI
ELIZABETH MAHONEY
ELIZABETH MARKEVITZ
ELIZABETH McCRAE
ELIZABETH McGILL
ELIZABETH PEYTON
ELIZABETH PLUMB
ELIZABETH ROUGH
ELIZABETH SMITH
ELIZABETH WRIGHT
ELLA KLASCHKA
ELLIE KETSEA
ÉLODIE CAZES
ELS VAN DEN BERG
ELSA GABRIEL
ELSIE MITCHELL
ELSPETH GARDNER
ELSPETH McINNES
ELWYN ELLIS
EMILIANO LLAMOSAS
EMILIO BEUTRAGUENO
EMILY BATES
EMILY KING
EMILY TSINGOU
EMMA McMULLAN
EMMA PEARL
EMMA RENNIE
EMMA SANDSBACH
EMMA WARWICK
EMMA WEBSTER
EMMANUEL PERROTIN
ENZO ENZELL
EPONCE
ERIC BAINBRIDGE
ERIC BIALAS
ERIC DUYCKAERTS
ERIC GONGRICH
ERIC MAILLET
ERIC MEZIL
ERIC NIEBERT
ERIC PALLISTER
ERIC SAMAKH
ERIC TRONCY
ERIC WATSON
ERLAND WILLIAMSON
ERNST CARAMELLE
ERNST POPPEL
ERROL FORBES
ERWIN WURM
ESTELLE SCHWARTZ
ESTHER SCHIPPER
EUAN EUGLOW
EUAN HUNTER
EUAN McARTHUR
EUAN SUTHERLAND
EUART CORRIGAN
EUGENE KELLY
EUGENIO DITTBORN
EULÀLIA VALLDOSERA
EVA ARRIGHI
EVA GRUBINGER
EVA KOHLER
EVA MARISALDI
EVA PRESENHUBER
EVA ROTHSCHILD
EVA SCHMIDT
EVE McSWEENEY
EVELEEN WRIGHT
EVELYN EACUPS
EVELYN JARDINE
EVELYN VAN HUYZEN
EVELYN WOODFORD
EVELYNE JOUANNO
EWAN BREMNER
EWAN McGREGOR
EWAN MORRISON
FABRICE HYBERT
FARQUHAR McLAY
FELICITY PENDRED
FELIM EGAN
FENELLA McKENZIE
FERGUS CALLAN
FERGUS HENDERSON
FERNANDO MEANA GREEN
FIONA ANNAN
FIONA BALLOCH
FIONA BANNER
FIONA BEVERIDGE
FIONA BRADLEY
FIONA BYRNE-SUTTON
FIONA DURDEY
FIONA FERGUSON
FIONA GILMOUR
FIONA GOURLAY
FIONA GRIFFITH
FIONA HAMILTON
FIONA LEITCH
FIONA LOGUE
FIONA McLEOD
FIONA MOIR
FIONA RAE
FIONA RUSSELL
FIONA WRIGHT
FIORENZA MENINI
FITZ O'NEIL
FLOELLA BENJAMIN
FLORENCE KANE
FLORENTINO PEREZ
FLORIAN CRAMER
FLORIAN MATZNER
FLORIAN WALDVOGEL
FRAN HEALY
FRANC MAZAURIC
FRANCES CORRIAS
FRANCESCA FIDANZA
FRANCESCO BONAMI
FRANCESCO BONOMO
FRANCESCO COLOMBO
FRANCESCO CORRIAS
FRANCESCO SIMETI
FRANCIS ALLEN
FRANCIS HARDING
FRANCIS McKEE
FRANCIS MERRINO
FRANÇOIS QUINTIN
FRANK FIETZEK
FRANK HYDE-ANTWI
FRANK LUBBERS
FRANK McAVEETY
FRANK MOORE
FRANK MORAN
FRANK RIJKAARD
FRANK STRÖPKEN
FRANZ ACKERMAN
FRANZ GRAF
FRANZ WEST
FRAUCKE KOSSACK-HUBSCHMANN
FRED BROCK
FRED HERMEL
FRED HOPKINS
FRED MARTIAL WETTER
FRED PEDERSEN
FRED ST. ELMO WHITE
FREDDY ANDERSON
FREDERIC PEREZ
FRÉDÉRIQUE ZURCHER
FREDI VON ESCHER
FREENY YIANNI
FRIEDRICH KNUFFER
FRIEDRICH MESCHEDE
FRIEDRICH PETZEL
FRITZ SCHWEGLER
FUMIO NANJO
GABRIEL JENNINGS
GABRIEL OROZCO
GABRIELLA SAND
GABY RETS
GAËL GIBSON
GAEL McDOUGALL
GAIL COCHRANE
GAIL MOFFAT
GAIL WANLESS
GARETH EVANS
GARETH FISHER
GARETH JAMES
GARNET WINTON
GARY BANDY
GARY GIBSON
GARY HUME
GARY LESTER
GARY MOUAT
GARY ROUGH
GARY SCOFIELD
GARY SPRATLING
GARY TONDA
GARY WATERSTON
GARY WEIR
GASPARD NOË
GAVIN BROWN
GAVIN COLEY
GAVIN HASTINGS
GAVIN RENWICK
GAVIN TURK
GEERT SCHRIEVER
GEOFF MARMETT
GEOFF WHITMORE
GEOFF WINGATE
GEOFFREY CARRUTH

GEORG HEROLD
GEORGE ALLEN
GEORGE ANDERSON
GEORGE BORLAND
GEORGE CULLEN
GEORGE CURRIE
GEORGE DUFF
GEORGE GARSON
GEORGE GETTINS
GEORGE GORDON
GEORGE GORDON
GEORGE GORDON
GEORGE GORDON
GEORGE HAMILTON
GEORGE HIGGINS
GEORGE HUTTON
GEORGE LYNCH
GEORGE McKINTOSH
GEORGE OLIVER
GEORGE PAVIA
GEORGE POTTER
GEORGE SMITH
GEORGE SPENCE
GEORGE WYLIE
GEORGES REY
GEORGIE HOPTON
GEORGINA STARR
GÉRALDINE BREULEUX
GERARD BYRNE
GERARD CHIRON
GERARD HOULIER
GERRIE VAN NOORD
GERRY GLEASON
GERRY LOVE
GERRY QUINN
GERRY SPEIRS
GERTI FIETZEK
GERTRUDE SANDQVUIST
GHISLAINE GERMAIN
GHISLAINE HUSSENOT
GIANNI PIACENTINI
GIJS STORK
GIJS VAN TUYL
GILANE TAWADROS
GILBERT & GEORGE
GILBERT BROWNSTONE
GILLES KAZAZIAN
GILLES PEYROULET
GILLIAN CARSON
GILLIAN CURRAN
GILLIAN DICKIE
GILLIAN DYSON
GILLIAN FARMER
GILLIAN NIXON
GILLIAN STEELE
GILLIAN TAYLOR
GILLIAN WEARING
GIÒ MARCONI
GIORGIO SADOTTI
GIORGIO VERZOTTI
GISELA SEITZ
GIULIANA GABELLINI
GITTE VILLESEN
GLEN BUCHANAN
GLEN KEAN
GLEN ONWIN
GLEN SEATOR
GLENN LIGON
GLENN LOWRY
GLENN SCOTT WRIGHT
GLYN BANKS
GOLDA MAAS
GORDON ADIE
GORDON BENNET
GORDON CALLANDER
GORDON HIGGINS
GORDON MANNING
GORDON McKECHNIE
GORDON McWATT
GORDON MOIR
GORDON MORELAND
GORDON MUIR
GORDON PIRIE
GORDON SHEARER
GORDON SMALL
GORDON TELFER
GORDON THAKERAY
GORDON THOMPSON
GORDON WEINSTEIN
GOSSE OOSTERHOF
GOTSCHO
GRAÇA MENDES PINTO
GRACE BORLAND
GRACE BORLAND SINCLAIR
GRACE LAMB
GRAEME PATERSON
GRAEME ROUGH
GRAEME TODD
GRAHAM BROWN
GRAHAM BUCHANAN
GRAHAM COWAN
GRAHAM DURWARD
GRAHAM FAGEN
GRAHAM GORDON
GRAHAM GORDON
GRAHAM GORDON
GRAHAM GOUGH
GRAHAM GUSSIN
GRAHAM HILL
GRAHAM HILL
GRAHAM HILL
GRAHAM JOHNSTONE
GRAHAM McGIVERN
GRAHAM MURRAY
GRAHAM PHELPS
GRAHAM RAMSAY
GRAHAM STALKER
GRAHAM STEWART
GRAHAM SUTHERLAND
GRAHAM WOOLISTON
GRAHAM WRIGHT
GRANT GILLESPIE
GRANT McTAVISH
GRANT QUINN
GRANYA MURRAY
GRAZIA QUARONI
GREG HILTY
GREG PATERSON
GREG WHITE
GREGOR CONNOLLY
GREGOR MUIR
GREGOR SCHNEIDER
GREGORIO MAGNANI
GREGORY GREEN

GRENVILLE DAVEY
GRETA GIANGRANDE
GUIDO PORCIANI
GUILLAUME SULTANA
GULIO PAULO PIETMARCCI
GUNTHER BECKER
GUY BRETT
GUY FROST
GUY LIMONE
GUY WILLESDEN
GWEN BENNET
H. CASPAR
H. CZECH
HAMAD BUTT
HANNAH REDLER
HANNAH VOWLES
HANS KARLSEN
HANS KNOLL
HANS RASMUS ASTRUP
HANS SITEUR
HANS ULRICH OBRIST
HANS VAN HOUWELINGEN
HARALD FETVEIT
HARALD FRICKE
HARALD SZEEMANN
HARDY OPHULS
HARMONY KORINE
HARRIET LONGRIDGE
HARRY BRENNAN
HARRY KERR
HARRY McLEAN
HARRY SCRYMGEOUR
HARRY SINGH
HARVEY JACKSON
HARVEY SHIPLEY MILLER
HAYLEY TOMPKINS
HAZEL McLAREN
HEATHA GOLDING
HEATHER ALLEN
HEATHER CANAVAN
HEATHER KILLIN
HEATHER McDONALD
HEATHER MINCHIN
HEATHER ROGERS
HEICKE HELFERT
HEIDI KOSANIUK
HEIDI TAKEOKA
HEIKE WEBER
HEIMO ZOBERNIG
HEINZ-WERNER LAWO
HELEN ARTHUR
HELEN BRADBURY
HELEN CADWALLADER
HELEN CHADWICK
HELEN DUDDERIDGE
HELEN FLOCKHART
HELEN GRIEVE
HELEN HARLEY
HELEN McCOIG
HELEN O'DONOGHUE
HELEN PATERSON
HELEN SAINSBURY
HELEN UNDERWOOD
HELEN VAN DER MEY
HELEN WINDSOR
HELEN WOODS
HELEN-MARIA NUGENT
HELGE MRUCK
HENK MAURITS
HENRIK HÅKANSSON
HENRIK PLENGE JACOBSEN
HENRY BOND
HENRY JOHNSON
HENRY MEYRIC HUGHES
HENRY SPENCE
HERBERT HAMAK
HERBIE PETERS
HERMANN STUZMANN
HERVÉ CHANDÈS
HERVÉ MIKAELOFF
HERVE SCHNEID
HESTER OERLEMANS
HESTER REEVES
HETTIE JUDAH
HIDEO SHIMADA
HILARY ROBINSON
HILARY STIRLING
HILARY TOOTH
HINRICH SACHS
HLYNUR HALLSON
HOLGER HANK
HONOR FRASER
HONORÉ D' O
HOPE GORDON
HOU HANRU
HOWARD SLATER
HUANG YONG PING
HUBERT NEUERBERG
HUBERTUS HESS
HUGH McCALLUM
HUGH MULHOLLAND
HUGH WATT
HUGHIE HOWIE
HUGO SERRA
IAIN ANDERSON
IAIN BELL
IAIN BEVERIDGE
IAIN CHRISTIE
IAIN COLLINS
IAIN DICKINSON
IAIN DONNELLY
IAIN DOW
IAIN DUNCAN
IAIN FRIEND
IAIN GALLACHER
IAIN GARDNER
IAIN GARDNER
IAIN GOODFELLOW
IAIN GOURLAY
IAIN HIGGINS
IAIN HOBERMAN
IAIN HUNTER
IAIN IRVING
IAIN MARSHALL
IAIN McCALLUM
IAIN McCOLL
IAIN McFADDEN
IAIN McGILL
IAIN McKELLAR
IAIN McKENZIE
IAIN McWILLIAMS
IAIN MONTAGUE
IAIN MUNDELL
IAIN PATON

IAIN PIERCE
IAIN RAWLE
IAIN ROBERTSON
IAIN SLACK
IAIN SPOWART
IAIN TRAVERS
IAIN TURNER
IAIN WOODFORD
IAIN WOODFORD
IAN BALCH
IAN BEADLE
IAN BROWN
IAN CONNOLLY HUNT
IAN HAMILTON FINLAY
IAN KETTLES
IAN ROUGH
IARA BOUBNOVA
IDA GIANELLI
IDA JOHANNESEN
ILDIKO ZEMENY
ILIAS PANTOS
IMOGEN STIDWORTHY
INA SOUTEC
INGEBORG ASTRUP
INGEBORG LUSCHER
INGVILD GOETZ
INIGO PEREZ
INIGO PEREZ TANERNERO
INKE ARNS
IONA PATERSON
IRENE BRANSON
IRENE HOHENBÜCHLER
IRENE McKENZIE
IRIS NEALE
ISA GENZKEN
ISAAC AHMAD
ISAAC JULIEN
ISABEL ALLEN
ISABEL HEIMERDINGER
ISABELLA HEUDORFF
ISABELLA MORA
ISABELLE CARLOS
ISABELLE LE MAÎTRE
ISABELLE SARMENTO
ISABELLE SEURET
ISOBEL BENNET
ISOBEL CARSON
ISOBEL CURRIE
ISOBEL JOHNSTONE
ISOBEL MARSHALL
ISRAEL ROSENFIELD
IVAN SMITH
IVAN UNWIN
IVOR DUDDERIDGE
IVOR WEARMOUTH
IVY KILLIN
IWAN WIRTH
IZZY METZSTEIN
JAAP GULDEMOND
JACK DONACHIE
JACK FARRELL
JACK LAMB
JACK PIERSON
JACK ROBERTSON
JACK TAYLOR
JACK TILTON
JACK WENDLER
JACK WILLIAMSON
JACK WITHERS
JACKIE BYRNE
JACKIE CUNNINGHAM
JACKIE CUSH
JACKIE FARRELL
JACKIE McALLISTER
JACKIE MEECHAN
JACKIE SACKLER
JACKIE WRATHER
JACKIE YOUNG
JACKS IRVINE
JACQUELINE BURCKHARDT
JACQUELINE CHAMBERS
JACQUELINE DONACHIE
JACQUELINE EVANS
JACQUES FOURNEL
JACQUI ABRAHAMS
JADE LINDGAARD
JAKE CHAPMAN
JAKE GASKELL
JONNY GASKELL
JAKI IRVINE
JAKKI PARRY
JAKOB FABRICIUS
JAMES BEATLEY
JAMES BUCHANAN
JAMES CANNING
JAMES CASEBERE
JAMES COLEMAN
JAMES COLERAINE
JAMES COLQUHOUN
JAMES CONLON
JAMES CORRIGAN
JAMES COSGROVE
JAMES CURRAN
JAMES CURRIE
JAMES ELPHINSTONE
JAMES GORDON
JAMES GORDON
JAMES GRAY GASKELL GORDON
JAMES HARDIE
JAMES HUGENOT
JAMES McGROARTY
JAMES McINDEWAR
JAMES PETO
JAMES ROBERTS
JAMES THORNHILL
JAMES WATSON
JAMES WATT
JAMIE BURROUGHS
JAMIE BYNG
JAMIE COHEN
JAMIE TAYLOR
JAMIL AHMAD
JAN AVGIKOS
JAN DEBBAUT
JAN DIBBETS
JAN FLORIZOONE
JAN GORDON
JAN GRAY
JAN MOT
JAN STEVENS
JAN VAN ADRICHEM
JAN VAN BROECKHOVEN
JAN-WILLEM POELS
JAN WINKELMANN

JANE ALSTON
JANE BATES
JANE BECK
JANE CONNOLLY
JANE FRITH
JANE HALLIDAY
JANE HAMLYN
JANE LEE
JANE McGREGOR
JANE MOORE
JANE RALEIGH
JANE RITCHIE
JANE ROLO
JANE WARRILOW
JANE WILSON
JANET CARDIFF
JANET EMERY
JANET GORDON
JANET ROONEY
JANICE HUNTER
JANICE KIRKPATRICK
JANICE McNAB
JANICE REDMAN
JANICE SHARP
JANIE NICOLL
JANINE CIRINCIONE
JAQUELINE McFADZEAN
JARI LAGER
JAROSLAV ANDEL
JASON BOWMAN
JASON DODGE
JASON HALLETT
JASON RHOADES
JASON SHERIDAN
JAVIER GOMEZ
JAY JOPLING
JAYNE TAYLOR
JEAN BAIRD
JEAN-BAPTISTE BRUANT
JEAN BORLAND
JEAN BORLAND SINCLAIR
JEAN CAMERON
JEAN-CHARLES BLAIS
JEAN-CHRISTOPHE ROYOUX
JEAN CLOW
JEAN DE LOISY
JEAN FISHER
JEAN-FRANÇOIS TADDEI
JEAN GAVIN
JEAN GRAHAM
JEAN-LUC PEERS
JEAN-MARC BUSTAMANTE
JEAN-MARC FERRARI
JEAN MARMETT
JEAN-MAX COLLARD
JEAN McCABE
JEAN McDOUGALL
JEAN ROBERTSON
JEAN SPENCER
JEANETTE BLACKWOOD
JEANETTE CHRISTIANSEN
JEANETTE McCALLUM
JEANETTE SANDERS
JEANETTE USTVEDT
JEAN-JACQUES RULLIER
JEAN-MARC PREVOST
JEANNE DUNNING
JEFF MONGRAINE
JEFF WIZNIEWSKI
JEM LEIGH
JEMIMA PYNE
JEMIMA WYATT
JENNI LOMAX
JENNIFER FLAY
JENNIFER GORDON
JENNIFER GREEN
JENNIFER RUSSELL
JENNIFER WILLIAMSON
JENNY EADON
JENNY GREEP
JENNY TESTA
JENS HAANING
JENS HEISE
JENS HOFFMANN
JENS VOLZ
JEPPE HEIN
JEREMY DELLER
JEREMY DICKINSON
JEREMY MILLAR
JEREMY SHALLCROSS
JEREMY STEVENSON
JEREMY VALENTINE
JEREMY VANEY
JÉRÔME SANS
JERRY NEUNER
JES BRINCH
JESSICA SAND
JESSIE WASHBURNE-HARRIS
JILL HAIG
JILL HAMMOND
JILL RITBLAT
JILL SILVERMAN
JIM BERRY
JIM BIRREL
JIM BUCHANAN
JIM BUCKLEY
JIM BURNS
JIM COCHRANE
JIM CONNELL
JIM COWNIE
JIM GALLACHER
JIM GILBERT
JIM GORDON
JIM HAMLYN
JIM HAROLD
JIM JONES
JIM KELMAN
JIM LAMBERT
JIM LAMBIE
JIM LUSK
JIM McDONALD
JIM McLUSKEY
JIM McNAUGHT
JIM PATTISON
JIM QUIG
JIM SHAND
JIM SHEDDEN
JIM SPENCE
JIM STEWART
JIM UNSWORTH
JIM WALKER
JIM WATT
JIM WEBB
JIMENA BLAZQUEZ

JIMMY DOS SANTOS
JIMMY KNOX
JO DEANS
JO SPARK
JO STRUYVEN
JO VOLLEY
JOACHIM KOESTER
JOAN BAKEWELL
JOAN DONALD
JOAN FAGEN
JOAN GASKELL
JOAN JONAS
JOAN McSTAY
JOAN NESBITT
JOAN YOUNG
JOANNA MYTKOWSKA
JOANNE DICK
JOANNE SCOFIELD
JOANNE TATHAM
JOÃO FERNANDES
JOAO OLIVIERA
JOÃO PENALVA
JOCHEN GERZ
JOCK BRECKENRIDGE
JOCK McINNES
JOE CONNOLLY
JOE HALL
JOE KEOGH
JOE KUM JIM
JOE LAY
JOE MATUNIS
JOE McGINN
JOE NEVIN
JOE STRUMMER
JOEL ABBOT
JOEL BARTOLOMEU
JOEL WACHS
JOELLE PIJAUDIER
JOEP VAN LIESHOUT
JOEY KOTTING
JOHAN GRIMONPREZ
JOHANNE DEBAS
JOHANNE KÖNIG
JOHANNES KAHRS
JOHN AIKEN
JOHN ALLEN
JOHN BALDESSARI
JOHN BEAGLES
JOHN BEAVER
JOHN BLAIR
JOHN BORLAND
JOHN BRAZENALL
JOHN BUTLER
JOHN BYRNE
JOHN CALCUTT
JOHN CANAVAN
JOHN CARSON
JOHN CLARK
JOHN CLARK
JOHN COLIN
JOHN CRADDOCK
JOHN CRAIG
JOHN CREED
JOHN CRUICKSHANKS
JOHN CUMMINGS
JOHN CUNNINGHAM
JOHN DAVIDSON
JOHN DODDS
JOHN DOUGLAS
JOHN FARQUHAR-SMITH
JOHN FORRESTER
JOHN FREEL
JOHN GILMOUR
JOHN GOOD
JOHN GORDON
JOHN GORDON
JOHN GORDON
JOHN GORDON,
JOHN GORTON
JOHN HAMILTON
JOHN HAZARD
JOHN HIGGINS
JOHN HILLIARD
JOHN ISAACS
JOHN JORDAN
JOHN KELLY
JOHN KINDNESS
JOHN LATHAM
JOHN LILLEY
JOHN MAGUIRE
JOHN MALLEY
JOHN MALLEY
JOHN MASSEY
JOHN McCARTNEY
JOHN McCLENAHAN
JOHN McCORMACK
JOHN McCROSSAN
JOHN McDONALD
JOHN McDOUGALL
JOHN McDOUGALL
JOHN McDOUGALL
JOHN McGROARTY
JOHN McINDEWAR
JOHN McINNES
JOHN McISAAC
JOHN McKECHNIE
JOHN McMAHON
JOHN MILLAR
JOHN MILLAR
JOHN MORTIMER
JOHN MUNDELL
JOHN NICOL
JOHN NICOL
JOHN O'DONNELL
JOHN OLIVER
JOHN ORMEROD
JOHN PAUL LATHAM
JOHN PETER
JOHN PRIME
JOHN QUINN
JOHN RIDDY
JOHN ROACH
JOHN RUSSELL
JOHN SAYERS
JOHN SHANKIE
JOHN SHAW
JOHN SILVERMAN
JOHN SIMMONS
JOHN SPENCE
JOHN STANTON
JOHN STEVENSON
JOHN TAYLOR
JOHN THAKERAY
JOHN TORIE
JOHN URQUHART

JOHN WEBER
JOHN WELDON
JOHN WHITEMAN
JOHN WILLIAMS
JOHN WILLIAMSON
JOHN WOODCOCK
JOHNNY MILLER
JOHNNY McKEE
JOHNNY SPENCER
JOHNNY WALKER
JOHNNY WILKES
JON BEWLEY
JON ELICEGUI
JON KESSLER
JONAS ECKBERG
JONAS MEKAS
JONATHAN BLACKWOOD
JONATHAN BRENTNALL
JONATHAN CALLAN
JONATHAN EACUPS
JONATHAN JONES
JONATHAN MONK
JONATHAN UTRERA
JONATHAN WALLER
JONATHAN WATKINS
JONATHON CASSELLS
JONI SIGHVATSON
JONNA KITARUTH
JONTY TARBUCK
JORDAN BASEMAN
JORDI JUNCOSA
JORG HEROLD
JORG MULDER
JORGE DEL VALLE
JORGE PARDO
JORGE SIMONET
JOS VAN DER HEYDEN
JOSE TOUREE
JOSEF ORTNER
JOSEP DANANA
JOSEPH CAMPBELL
JOSEPH DAVIE
JOSEPH KOSUTH
JOSEPH McMENEMY
JOSEPHINE WILSON
JOSH COLE
JOSH LEVINE
JOSIE WALKER
JOYCE PATERSON
JOYCE RYAN
JUAN MUÑOZ
JUDE BURKHAUSER
JUDITH BARAK
JUDITH BARRY
JUDITH FINLAY
JUDITH HEGGIE
JUDITH McDERMOTT
JUDITH NESBITT
JUDITH SPARK
JUDITH SPENCE
JUDITH WEIK
JUDITH WINTER
JUDY ADAM
JUDY LUBKE
JUDY SCHULICH
JÜRG JUDIN
JULIA BOLZ
JULIA HOLBERRY
JULIA LANGLEY
JULIA LITTLE
JULIA PEYTON-JONES
JULIA RADCLIFFE
JULIA SULLIVAN
JULIAN EMENS
JULIAN OPIE
JULIAN SPALDING
JULIÃO SARMENTO
JULIE BECKER
JULIE CRAWFORD
JULIE GOUGH
JULIE HANNAH
JULIE JACKSON
JULIE LAW
JULIE ROBERTS
JULIE ROBERTS
JULIE RUSSELL
JULIE WILDE
JULIEN VANEY
JULIET DEAN
JULIETTE WALSH
JULIUS WARWICK
JUNE HOPKINS
JUNE MOFFAT
JUNE TAYLOR
JUNIPER TEDHAMS
JUNKO YAMAMOTO
JÜRGEN BOCK
JÜRGEN BORCHERS
JÜRGEN KNUDSEN
JÜRGEN PARTENHEIMER
JUSTIN CARTER
JUSTIN HENDERSON
JUSTINE KURLAND
JUTTA EBERHARD
KAI KARLSEN
KARA VANDER WEG
KAREL SCHAMPERS
KAREN BAULD
KAREN DAY
KAREN ESLEA
KAREN FORBES
KAREN KELLY
KAREN KILIMNIK
KAREN McQUEEN
KAREN MULLET
KAREN MURPHY
KAREN MURRAY
KAREN RUBINSTEIN
KAREN SHAW
KAREN STRANG
KAREN VAUGHAN
KAREN WILSON
KAREN WOODLEY
KARIN FERGUSON
KARIN SANDER
KARIN SCHORM
KARL PITTON
KAROLE VAIL
KARSTEN SCHUBERT
KASPER KÖNIG
KATALIN NERAY
KATARINA KNUDSEN
KATE BURVILLE
KATE DAW

KATE GREY
KATE HENDERSON
KATE MITCHELL
KATE MOODY
KATE MOONEY
KATE MORRISON
KATE ROBINSON
KATE SOWERBY
KATHARINA SIEVERDING
KATHERINA GUNJERSSON
KATHERINE WOOD
KATHLEEN DONACHIE
KATHLEEN KARLSON
KATHRYN MESSNER
KATHRYN VON MALTZAHN
KATHRYN WITTNEVAN
KATHY TEMIN
KATIE NICOLL
KATRINA BROWN
KATRINA McCABE
KATY BROWN
KATY SENDER
KATYA MAAS
KAY McLEAN
KAY PALLISTER
KAY ROBERTS
KAYA WOODLEY
KEIKO SHIMADA
KEITH ARNATT
KEITH BATES
KEITH COVENTRY
KEITH FARQUHAR
KEITH HARTLEY
KEITH INGHAM
KEITH MALCOLM
KEITH MILLAR
KEITH MILLER
KEITH PIPER
KEITH RODRIGUEZ
KEITH ROWBOTTON
KEITH WILSON
KEKO MORALES
KELLIE FELTMAN
KELLY GORDON
KELLY McDONALD
KEN GILL
KEN GILMARTIN
KEN GORDON
KEN HAY
KEN HOLMES
KEN MITCHELL
KEN NEIL
KEN ROBB
KEN SIMONS
KENJI YANOBE
KENNETH HAMILTON
KENNETH HOLMES
KENNETH HUNTER
KENNETH McKAY
KENNY MEECHO
KENNY SNEDDON
KENT BENCH
KERRY BERCHEM
KERRY BROUGHER
KETIL NERGAARD
KEVIN GASKELL
KEVIN GRIM
KEVIN HENDERSON
KEVIN KELLY
KEVIN LOW
KEVIN MCMONAGLE
KEVIN MURPHY
KIKA GATTOLINI
KIKI SMITH
KIM ADAMS
KIM GORDON
KIM NICOL
KIM SEUNG DUK
KIM SWEET
KIMBERLEY GUNDLE
KIRSTEN MOSHER
KIRSTY BARTON
KIRSTY BELL
KIRSTY COHEN
KIRSTY McCASKILL
KIRSTY McGHIE
KIRSTY OGG
KIRSTY WARK
KIT HOBERMAN
KITTY SCOTT
KLAUS BIESENBACH
KLAUS BUßMANN
KLAUS WERNER
KOBE MATTHYS
KOHJI OGURA
KONRAD FISCHER
KONRAD KLAPHECK
KOO JEONG-A
KOOS VAN DER MEER
KRISTA BLAKE
KRISTA VAN KOLTSCHOTTEN
KRISTINA TIEKE
KUMI YAMASHITA
KURT JOHANNESEN
KWABENA OWUSU
LANI RUBIN
LARRY GAGOSIAN
LATIF MIRZA
LAURA HUDSON
LAURA LORCA
LAURA McINNES
LAURA McLEAN
LAURA MICHAEL
LAURA SARMENTO
LAURE GENILLARD
LAUREN KELLY
LAUREN McCAFFREY
LAURENCE BOSSÉ
LAURENCE HARVEY
LAURENCE MALLEY
LAURIE ANDERSON
LAWREN MABEN
LAWRENCE WEINER
LEAH CORKER
LEE BLACK
LEE BUL
LEE DICKSON
LEE HIGGINS
LEIGH COX
LEIGH FRENCH
LEIGH MARTIN
LEILA GALLOWAY
LEO HORSEFIELD
LEO KÖNIG

LEONARD RIGGIO
LEONTINE COELEWEIJ
LESLEY ANGUS
LESLEY MACH
LESLEY MILLAR
LESLEY PUNTON
LESLEY SHAW
LESLEY SMITH
LESLIE BELL
LESLIE CAMHI
LESLIE McFIE
LESLIE STEPHENS
LESTER WARWICK
LEWIS BIGGS
LEWIS BRIGHTON
LIAM GALLAGHER
LIAM GILLICK
LIAM KELLY
LIAM McKENZIE
LIESBETH ABBENES
LIESBETH BEK
LIISA ROBERTS
LILI KIM RI-HYE
LILLIAN LESTER
LINDA GRAHAM
LINDA GREEN
LINDA KEENAN
LINDA KILLIN
LINDA KNOX
LINDA MORROW
LINDA ROBERTSON
LINDA TAYLOR
LINDA TONDA
LINDA WHITMORE
LINDA WILLIAMS
LINDA ZUCK
LINDSAY DUMAS
LINDSAY GORDON
LINDSEY ORR
LISA BELLEN
LISA BILLARD
LISA DARLING
LISA KIM
LISA MAY POST
LISA ROSENDAHL
LISBETH McCARROLL
LIVIA MONTE
LIZ ADAMSON
LIZ ADES
LIZ BROOKS
LIZ CAMERON-MURPHY
LIZ HALSTEAD
LIZ JACKSON
LIZ McLEAN
LIZ RHODES
LLOYD BERTENBURG
LLOYD DUNN
LOCH ADAMSON
LOCKY MORRIS
LOIS NESBITT
LORENZO RODRIGUEZ
LORIN DAVIES
LORNA ALLEN
LORNA BATES
LORNA McGREGOR
LORNA MORRISON
LORNA RODRIGUEZ
LORNA SIMPSON
LORNA WAITE
LORRAINE DAVIN
LORRAINE DERRICK
LORRAINE HUGHES
LORRAINE LOVE
LORRAINE McINTYRE
LORRAINE RUSSELL
LORRAINE TURLEY
LOTHAR BAUMGARTEN
LOTHAR HEMPEL
LOTTA ANTONSSON
LOU REED
LOUIS JAMME
LOUISE BRADLEY
LOUISE FLESHING
LOUISE GORDON
LOUISE HOPKINS
LOUISE McSTAY
LOUISE NERI
LOUISE SCULLION
LOUISE SHAMBROOK
LOUISE TAYLOR
LOUISE WILSON
LUC STEELS
LUCIA NOGUEIRA
LUCY BACON
LUCY BROWN
LUCY BYATT
LUDWIG PELTZER
LUIS DE MIRANDA
LUIS MATA
LUISA METZEL
LUK LAMBRECHT
LUKAS EINSELE
LUKE BENNET
LUNA MERRINO
LUTZ DRIEVER
SYLVIE BUSCHMANN
LYN EVANS
LYN GARDNER
LYNDAL JONES
LYNDSAY TAYLOR
LYNN GIRDWOOD
LYNNE COOKE
LYS HANSEN
MAARTEN BERTHEUX
MAARTEN OLDENHOF
MACHA ROESINK
MADELINE PAK
MAGDALENA JETELOVA
MAGGIE BOLT
MAGGIE McKAY
MAGGIE MOIR
MAGGIE WYLLIE
MALCOLM DICKSON
MALCOLM THWAITE
MALVINA PUSEK
MAMIE McDOUGALL
MANDY CRUIKSHANKS
MANDY NANNY
MANEL CLOT
MANFRED PERNICE
MANFRED STUMPF
MANON DE BOER
MANUEL WAROZ
MARC CURRIE

MARC GUILLER
MARC OVERMARS
MARC SANCHEZ
MARC SAPIR
MARCEL BAETTIG
MARCEL BIEFER
MARCEL MATTEO
MARCO BELLEN
MARCO BRAMBILLA
MARCO SPINELLI
MARCUS BASTEL
MARCUS COLE
MARCUS GEIGER
MARCUS TAYLOR
MARCUS WATERLOO
MARENTE BLOEMHEUVEL
MARGARET AHMAD
MARGARET ARCHBOLD
MARGARET BARRON
MARGARET BRIGHTON
MARGARET BROWN
MARGARET DOBBIE
MARGARET HAMILTON
MARGARET HEWITT
MARGARET HUTTON
MARGARET McHARG
MARGARET MILLER
MARGARET NELSON
MARGARET PETTIGREW
MARGARET PHELPS
MARGARET RICHARDSON
MARGARET ROGERS
MARGARIDA VEGA
MARIA BLUME
MARIA BREER
MARIA DOYLE
MARIA EICHHORN
MARIA LIND
MARIA LINDBERG
MARIAN GOODMAN
MARIANNA AMATULLO
MARIANNE WALTHER
MARIE-ANGE GUILLEMINOT
MARIE-CLAUDE BEAUD
MARIE DEBRUGEROLLE
MARIE MEEHAN
MARIE-SOPHIE CARRON DE LA CARRIÈRE
MARIE STARKMANN
MARIE THERESE TONER
MARIE WOODS
MARIE-ANN McCULLOUGH
MARIEVI GREEN
MARIJKE ROEF
MARIJKE VAN WARMEDAM
MARIN SADOWSKI
MARINA ABRAMOVIC
MARINA BASSANO
MARIO CODOGNATO
MARIO FAZZI
MARION FRIEL
MARION GORDON
MARION KENNEDY
MARION McDOUGALL
MARION McLEOD
MARION MOIR
MARION MOIR
MARISSA PALLISCO
MARIUS BABBIAS
MARJORIE ALLTHORPE-GUYTON
MARK ALBELA
MARK BAILEY
MARK BEAVER
MARK BEEVER
MARK BLOCH
MARK CONNOLLY
MARK CURRAH
MARK DEY
MARK DION
MARK DONNADIEU
MARK FIRTH
MARK FRANCIS
MARK GALLACHER
MARK GATTI
MARK GREER
MARK LATIMER
MARK LEE
MARK LEWIS
MARK MALLEY
MARK McCAULEY
MARK McCROSSAN
MARK McLEISH
MARK O'NEIL
MARK PAWSON
MARK PIMLOTT
MARK ROSE
MARK SANDERS
MARK STEVENSON
MARK STEWART
MARK TAYLOR
MARK TODD
MARK VERNON
MARK WALLINGER
MARK WHITMORE
MARKUS MULLER
MARLENE BOYLE
MARLENE DUMAS
MARLEEN WOLFS
MARSHA GORDON
MARTA NANNY
MARTHA McCULLOUGH
MARTHA NANNY
MARTIJN SANDERS
MARTIJN VAN NIEUWENHUYZEN
MARTIN BOYCE
MARTIN BULLOCH
MARTIN CREED
MARTIN DOWDS
MARTIN GIBB
MARTIN GOSTNER
MARTIN HOPKINS
MARTIN HOPKINSON
MARTIN JARVIS
MARTIN McGEOWN
MARTIN PEERS
MARTIN SMART
MARTIN TIERNEY
MARTIN YOUNG
MARTINE ABOUCAYA
MARTINE BEUGNET
MARTINE BOHNE
MARTINE GOLDMAN
MARTINE ORMEROD
MARY BLACK
MARY BOONE